Categorical Propositions

The Four Standard Forms

A: All *S* are *P*   **E**: No *S* is *P*

I: Some *S* are *P*   **O**: Some *S* are not *P*

The Traditional Square of Opposition

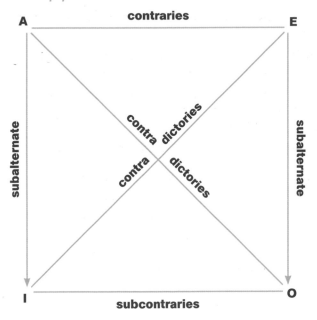

Immediate Inferences

Each statement in the left column is logically equivalent to the statement directly across from it in the right column.

CONVERSION

E: No *S* is *P*   No *P* is *S*

I: Some *S* are *P*   Some *P* are *S*

OBVERSION

A: All *S* are *P*   No *S* is non-*P*

E: No *S* is *P*   All *S* are non-*P*

I: Some *S* are *P*   Some *S* are not non-*P*

O: Some *S* are not *P*   Some *S* are non-*P*

CONTRAPOSITION

A: All *S* are *P*   All non-*P* are non-*S*

O: Some *S* are not *P*   Some non-*P* are not non-*S*

FIFTH EDITION

The Art of Reasoning

An Introduction to Logic

DAVID KELLEY

AND

DEBBY HUTCHINS

W. W. NORTON & COMPANY

Independent Publishers Since 1923

Norton & Company has been independent since its founding in 1923, when William Warder Norton and Herter Norton first published lectures delivered at the People's Institute, the adult education division of York City's Cooper Union. The firm soon expanded its program beyond the Institute, publishing books by celebrated academics from America and abroad. By midcentury, the two major pillars of Norton's publishing program—trade books and college texts—were firmly established. In the 1950s, the Norton family transferred control of the company to its employees, and today—with a staff of five hundred and hundreds of trade, college, and professional titles published each year—W. W. Norton & Company stands as the largest and oldest publishing house owned wholly by its employees.

Editor: Ken Barton
Associate Editor: Katie Pak
Project Editor: Taylere Peterson
Managing Editor, College: Marian Johnson
Production Manager: Eric Pier-Hocking
Media Editor: Sarah Rose Aquilina
Media Editorial Assistant: Jessica Awad
Managing Editor, College Digital Media: Kim Yi
Media Project Editor: Cooper Wilhelm
Ebook Production Manager: Sophia Purut
Marketing Managers: Michael Moss and Kim Bowers
Design Director: Rubina Yeh
Designer: Lisa Buckley, Lissi Sigillo
Director of College Permissions: Megan Schindel
Composition: Achorn International
Manufacturing: LSC Crawfordsville

Library of Congress Cataloging-in-Publication Data

Names: Kelley, David, 1949- author. | Hutchins, Debby, author.
Title: The art of reasoning : an introduction to logic / David Kelley and Debby Hutchins.
Description: Fifth edition. | New York : W.W. Norton & Company, [2021] | Includes bibliographical references and index.
Identifiers: LCCN 2020032371 | ISBN 9780393664690 (paperback) | ISBN 9780393421774 (epub)
Subjects: LCSH: Reasoning. | Logic.
Classification: LCC BC177 .K38 2021 | DDC 160—dc23
LC record available at https://lccn.loc.gov/2020032371

ISBN: 978-0-393-66469-0 (pbk.)

W. W. Norton & Company, Inc., 500 Fifth Avenue, New York, NY 10110
wwnorton.com

W. W. Norton & Company Ltd., 15 Carlisle Street, London W1D 3BS

2 3 4 5 6 7 8 9 0

About the Authors

David Kelley earned his PhD in philosophy from Princeton University. He has taught at Vassar College and Brandeis University, and written extensively in epistemology and other fields.

Debby Hutchins earned her PhD in philosophy from Boston College and has taught at Texas A&M University, Boston College, Fitchburg State University, Gonzaga University, and South Texas College. She has received numerous awards for teaching logic, and her research focuses on the application of cognitive science to logic pedagogy.

In a republican nation whose citizens are to be led by reason and persuasion and not by force, the art of reasoning becomes of first importance.

—Thomas Jefferson

Contents in Brief

Contents

CHAPTER 6 Categorical Syllogisms

CHAPTER 7 Reasoning with Syllogisms

CHAPTER 8 Propositional Logic

CHAPTER 9 Natural Deduction in Propositional Logic

Preface

The Art of Reasoning is a textbook designed for courses in introductory logic or critical thinking. From the very beginning, through many editions, The Art of Reasoning has had a practical focus, reflected in its title. Logic is an art as well as a science. The art of reasoning is of vital importance for all the issues we confront and all the decisions we make, in every domain of life. The organization of the text, the exercises, and the learning tools are designed to interest and motivate students by showing the difference good reasoning can make in their studies—and in their lives.

Our goal is to make this book a valuable resource for the classroom instructor. As experienced teachers, we believe the most important means to that end is to write in a way that will hold the interest of students, so that they come to class prepared to move beyond the basics. We have therefore tried to explain the standards of good thinking in a clear, engaging, conversational style. On each topic, we follow an arc of learning: beginning with a clear, straightforward, relevant example; then extracting the core concept or principle; and then moving on to further applications, implications, and additional examples. And we keep theoretical discussion to a minimum, including only those points necessary to make the standards and techniques intelligible.

New in the Fifth Edition

Informed by years of teaching experience and research on how students best learn logic, the Fifth Edition makes The Art of Reasoning an even more effective teaching tool for introductory logic. Debby Hutchins, an expert logic teacher and learning researcher, joins the Fifth Edition as coauthor.

New features:

- InQuizitive, Norton's award-winning, easy-to-use adaptive learning tool, personalizes the learning experience for students and helps them master—and retain—key learning objectives.
- Review, Solve, and Apply features give students a consistent framework for working and understanding the problems.
- Exercises are designed in incremental fashion, now in three tiers of increasing integration. This improved scaffolding reinforces mastery and builds confidence as students work through each chapter.
- A new chapter on cognitive biases, persuasion, and false or slanted news highlights how we can fool ourselves and be fooled by information sources.
- Chapters on induction have new sections on legal and moral reasoning, Bayes' theorem in probability, and pseudoscience.

A Consistent Learning Framework

Every chapter includes three kinds of learning tools to help students assimilate the material:

- Review features provide a quick reference for important definitions, principles, and rules.
- Solve features place learning tools in students' hands by showing them how to implement the techniques found in the book including diagramming, backward reasoning, and using colors and shapes to improve their own ability to see patterns.
- Apply features show how logic can be applied in real-world contexts. Some of these units show students how they can put logic to work right now, to use it in other courses or to improve their scores on the LSAT, GRE, or other standardized tests. Some highlight the ways logic is used in other fields such as computer science, medicine, law, even fiction and film. Still others point to the ways logic is shaping the

cutting-edge technology of the future. We think students will find these features to be useful, informative, and fun.

For example, an Apply box in Chapter 6 uses a Venn diagram to show which actors have appeared in the Marvel Cinematic Universe (shown here).

APPLY Diagraming the Avengers

In this book, we've used two- and three-circle Venn diagrams; that's all we need for logic. But Venn diagrams are not limited to logic. Variations of Venn diagrams are also used in the theoretical sciences as well as in applied fields such as information technology and medicine. In fact, Venn diagrams can be adapted to analyze relationships between almost any type of set. Are you a fan of the Avengers series? The Marvel Cinematic Universe is incredibly complex with many reoccurring characters and interesting plotlines. The four-circle Venn below depicts the sole and overlapping appearances of MCU actors Robert Downey Jr., Chris Evans, Chris Hemsworth, and Mark Ruffalo. With a more complex Venn, we could have added other MCU actors—say, Scarlett Johansson and Jeremy Renner, for example. The other diagram is a five-oval Venn. See if you can find sets of information that map onto it. But no Marvel—that's our thing!

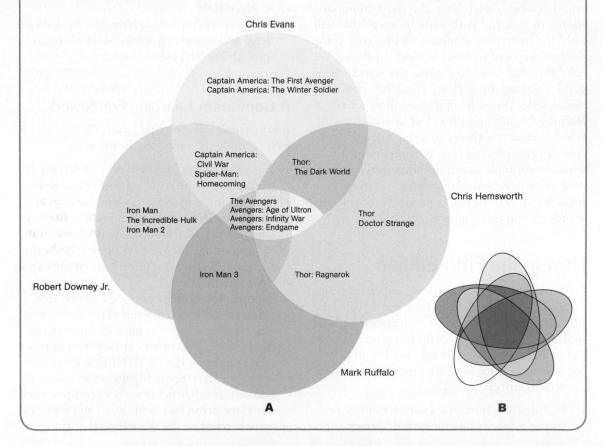

A Focus on Incremental Learning and Problem Solving

Each chapter contains abundant exercises of different types and levels of difficulty. The text includes nearly 3,000 exercise items, with thousands of additional exercises in the test bank and InQuizitive, Norton's easy-to-use, online adaptive learning tool described in more detail below. For this edition, we have built a tripartite pedagogical structure to enhance student learning.

- Following most sections are exercises that are skill specific, reinforcing new concepts and techniques introduced in that section. This allows students to focus on the new material without being overwhelmed by too much information at once.
- Integrative exercises, indicated by this green flag, provide a crucial second layer of pedagogy. [Integrative Exercise] They help students integrate new skills with those from one or more previous sections, in order to build out their logical repertoires.
- Each chapter also includes a set of exercises called Putting It All Together. These exercises are not merely a supplement or "extra practice," but a distinct third level of pedagogy allowing students to develop a higher level of reasoning by applying their skills in many different combinations on different sorts of tasks. Some of these exercises are more challenging versions of the in-chapter exercises. But many are creative, requiring students to come up with their own definitions, arguments, and explanations. Some chapters feature writing assignments designed to promote both good reasoning and good writing.

In response to requests from reviewers, exercise examples vary in length and complexity and are drawn from works in many disciplines—politics, science, literature, and history—so that all students will encounter at least some material from fields they are familiar with. In the text and exercises, we choose real-world examples to help students see how the standards of thinking apply to the sorts of issues they actually encounter in their everyday experience, in political debate, and in the other courses they take across the curriculum.

Distinctive Themes in *The Art of Reasoning*

In keeping with our practical focus and our assessment of student needs, we want to highlight two themes that underlie the pedagogy of *The Art of Reasoning*. They recur throughout the book as part of its DNA and distinguish it from other texts.

The first is the concept of *objectivity*. We think it is important for students to understand objectivity as the ultimate goal and standard of good reasoning, as explained in the Introduction, and instructors have told us that it helps students understand what logic is all about. We return to the theme often in other chapters, especially in Chapter 4: Cognitive Biases. Every logic teacher and textbook, of course, promotes objectivity by explaining the forms of reasoning and associated standards of validity and cogency, by discussing fallacies, etc. But we think it is also important for students to have an explicit grasp of objectivity as the overarching goal of understanding the world by rational means, especially at a time when they are surrounded by so much irrationality—false or arbitrary claims by leaders, "fake news," conspiracy theories, dogmatic partisanship, and the like.

A second pedagogical theme is our emphasis on *concepts and conceptual organization*. The ability to form new concepts, apply them accurately, and relate them to other concepts is essential to every field. This ability is an active topic of research in cognitive science and education, and both the research and anecdotal reports from instructors indicate that many students are weak in this regard. The material on classification in Chapter 1 (Sections 1.1–1.3) is rarely covered in other texts, but we find that a clear understanding of genus-species hierarchies makes it much easier for students to master other topics, such as categorical syllogisms (Chapters 5–7) and inductive generalization (Chapter 11). Greater facility with concepts will also help students master the many logical terms they will be asked to learn.

Organization

Part One, Language and Reasoning, covers the basic linguistic tools required for thinking clearly and the basic elements of argument analysis and evaluation. Chapter 1: Concepts and Propositions begins with concepts, classification, and definitions, providing the foundation for all reasoning; and goes on to cover propositions as assertions, giving students the preparation they need to identify the premises and conclusions of arguments. Chapter 2: Argument Analysis begins the treatment of arguments and introduces key logical concepts—premise and conclusion; deduction and induction; and validity, soundness, strength, and cogency—along with a simple diagramming technique. Chapter 3: Fallacies focuses on the fallacies most often encountered in everyday thought and speech and indicates the contexts in which each fallacy is most likely to be committed. The chapter is reorganized in a way that will be more familiar to most instructors.

Chapter 4: Cognitive Biases, new to the Fifth Edition, complements the chapter on fallacies. Whereas fallacies are logical errors, cognitive biases are systematic psychological tendencies to make errors in seeking and interpreting information. Chapter 4 addresses the most common biases, drawing on psychological research by Amos Tversky and Daniel Kahneman, among others. Along the way, the chapter discusses vulnerability to biased sources, including "fake news," and persuasive techniques that exploit those vulnerabilities. It also provides strategies for countering bias.

Part Two, Deductive Logic, covers both traditional and modern deductive logic. Chapters 5 and 6 introduce categorical propositions and categorical syllogisms, respectively. We have increased both the number and types of exercises in these chapters. Chapter 7: Reasoning with Syllogisms begins with the traditional versions of disjunctive and hypothetical syllogisms. It then provides a unique method for analyzing deductive arguments as they typically occur in ordinary language, including complex arguments that involve combinations of categorical, hypothetical, and disjunctive syllogisms. The chapter will be useful for instructors who do not plan to cover modern formal logic, or who would like a transition between traditional and modern logic.

For instructors who *do* cover modern symbolic logic, the next three chapters deal with propositional (Chapters 8 and 9) and predicate (Chapter 10) logic. For the Fifth Edition, we have added material to address two of the most common challenges to student success: pattern recognition and proof strategy (see here an example from Chapter 9: Natural Deduction in Propositional Logic):

For statement forms, as we saw, the instances of the variables p, q, r, etc., need not be simple component statements. The same is true for argument forms. Each of the following arguments, for example, has the form *modus ponens*:

$A \supset (B \lor C)$

A

$\overline{(B \lor C)}$

$(G \bullet H) \supset (J \bullet K)$

$G \bullet H$

$\overline{J \bullet K}$

$(N \bullet O) \supset [(P \lor (Q \supset R)]$

$(N \bullet O)$

$\overline{[(P \lor (Q \supset R)]}$

$[(S \supset (T \lor \sim U)] \supset \sim \lor$

$S \supset (T \lor \sim U)$

$\overline{\sim \lor}$

- Research in neuroscience confirms that pattern recognition can be improved by associating the new patterns with more familiar ones; we provide visual cues within the chapter and teach students simple techniques they can use as needed.
- Research—and our own teaching experience—shows that novices can better identify proof strategies by reasoning backward from the conclusion. Consequently, we greatly expand our explanation of this technique and use innovative exercises to guide students through the process.

These chapters are reorganized to reflect the way most instructors tell us they teach this material. All propositional translations and truth tables are presented together in Chapter 8: Propositional Logic.

Chapter 10: Predicate Logic is expanded to include new sections on proving invalidity and on identity. These chapters have an increased number and variety of exercises, including many with applications of the logic to examples in natural language—everything from arguments in science, religion, and law to Robert Frost's poetry. Exercises are balanced to test the items students need to master, with roughly equal representations of each method, inference rule, etc.

Part Three, Inductive Logic, begins with Chapter 11: Generalization and Causality, which introduces inductive generalization with basic rules to avoid hasty generalization and goes on to discuss Mill's methods for causal inference. Chapter 12: Analogical, Legal and Moral Reasoning is substantially revised to offer a more streamlined system for analyzing arguments by analogy. It includes a new section on analogies in moral and legal reasoning, with classic and contemporary examples in each area, such as Peter Singer's argument about the moral responsibility to relieve suffering in poor countries. Chapter 13: Statistical Reasoning covers the basic concepts and standards for evaluating the kinds of statistical arguments students will frequently encounter in the media. Chapter 14: Probability is an introduction to probability judgments and the probability calculus, with a new section on Bayes' theorem, emphasizing its meaning and applications. Finally, Chapter 15: Explanation and Science deals with the analysis and evaluation of explanations. It provides standards for evaluating the adequacy of explanations and the truth of hypotheses. We use these standards in a new section on pseudo-explanations, showing how they apply to pseudo-history (e.g., alien astronauts build the pyramids) and pseudoscience (e.g., vaccines cause autism).

Course Options

There is more material in the book than can be covered in a one-semester course, even at the brisk pace of a chapter a week, and many different selections of chapters are possible. For most chapters, it is also possible to use particular sections. Here are our recommendations for common types of courses:

- A course in *introductory logic*, including traditional syllogistic and some modern logic, might begin with selected portions of Chapter 1 (Sections 1.1–1.3 on concepts and classification and Sections 1.4–1.6 on definitions), Chapter 2 (Sections 2.1–2.5 on argument analysis), Chapter 3 (fallacies), and Chapter 4 (Section 4.1 on confirmation bias); and then move on to Chapters 5 and 6 (traditional syllogism). For instructors who want to cover some modern formal logic, we recommend Chapter 8 (Section 8.1 on connectives), Chapter 9 (Sections 9.1 and 9.2 on constructing propositional proofs), and Chapter 11 (generalization and causality).
- A course in *informal logic and critical thinking*, emphasizing basic skills in analyzing language and reasoning, might cover the four chapters in Part One (language and reasoning), Chapters 5–7 (traditional categorical logic), and selected material on induction—Chapters 11, 12, and 15.
- A course in *modern formal logic* might include Chapter 2 (Sections 2.1–2.4 on argument analysis) as an introduction, then Chapters 8 and 9 (propositional logic), and Chapter 10 (predicate logic). Time permitting, a course might include selections from Part Three (inductive logic), such as Chapter 11, 13, or 14.

This table lays out each recommended course option, with relevant chapters for each option indicated by color hue. Optional chapters are shaded lighter, and for chapters that are only partly applicable, the relevant sections are also listed.

Chapter	Topic	Introductory Logic	Informal Logic and Critical Thinking	Modern Formal Logic
PART ONE Language and Reasoning				
1	Language: Concepts and Propositions	Sections 1.1–1.6		
2	Argument Analysis	Sections 2.1–2.5		Sections 2.1–2.4
3	Fallacies			
4	Cognitive Biases	Section 4.1		
PART TWO Deductive Logic				
5	Categorical Propositions			
6	Categorical Syllogisms			
7	Reasoning with Syllogisms			
8	Propositional Logic	Section 8.1		
9	Natural Deduction in Propositional Logic	Sections 9.1–9.2		
10	Predicate Logic			
PART THREE Inductive Logic				
11	Generalization and Causality			
12	Analogical, Legal and Moral Reasoning			
13	Statistical Reasoning			
14	Probability			
15	Explanation and Science			

Extensive and Adaptive Assessment Resources

Access the digital resources and ebook at digital.wwnorton.com/artofreasoning5.

InQuizitive

This Fifth Edition is accompanied by InQuizitive, Norton's award-winning formative, adaptive online learning tool. InQuizitive activities personalize the learning experience for students, helping them master—and retain—key learning objectives from the text, which have been revised with InQuizitive in mind. Available for each chapter, the activities help students grasp foundational course concepts, including propositions, argument analysis, fallacies, cognitive biases, Venn diagrams, truth tables, proofs, and induction, in a system that's proved to help students learn.

Through answer-specific feedback, a variety of question types, and game-like elements such as the ability to wager points, students are motivated to keep working until they've mastered the concepts. As a result, students arrive better prepared for class, giving more time for targeted discussion and practice. Because InQuizitive motivates students to keep practicing and builds their confidence with the most important course concepts, assigning it consistently can help improve test grades. A robust activity report makes it easy to identify challenging concepts and intervene with at-risk students, and the convenience of learning management system (LMS) integration saves instructors time by allowing InQuizitive scores to report directly to the LMS gradebook.

Ebook

Norton Ebooks give students and instructors an enhanced reading experience at a fraction of the cost of a print textbook. Students are able to have an active reading experience and can take notes, bookmark, search, highlight, and read offline. As an instructor, you can even add your own notes for students to see as they read the text. Norton Ebooks can be viewed on—and synced among—all computers and mobile devices.

Instructor Resources

The text is also supported by a full test bank—approximately 2,750 questions keyed and categorized according to learning objectives, section, and difficulty level—and available for import into instructors' campus LMS. The Solutions Manual, for instructors only, has full answers to every set of exercises in the text—nearly 3,000 individual problems—over and above the Selected Answers available to students. An additional resource is a set of lecture PowerPoint slides that outline the major takeaways of each section.

Acknowledgments

We are indebted to many friends and colleagues, past and present, who have offered advice and encouragement, sent us examples, and otherwise contributed to *The Art of Reasoning*.

For the Fifth Edition, we are grateful to those who provided expert advice and creative ideas. We are especially grateful to Mason Cole, VISTA Academies, who suggested our Marvel Universe Apply box, among other ideas; Andrew Hill, The Catholic University of America, whose comments and ideas improved every chapter; Jason Walker, an ethicist and philosopher of law whose expertise made possible our new section on moral and legal reasoning in Chapter 12; and Jeffrey Zents, South Texas College, who offered valuable advice for our section on Bayes' theorem.

Special thanks also to:
Lee Basham, South Texas College

Nick Braune, Professor Emeritus, South Texas College
Shane Drefcinski, University of Wisconsin, Platteville
Daniel Montez, Sr., South Texas College
Daniel Montez, Jr., South Texas College
David Palacios, student assistant, South Texas College
Ray Peace, Valdosta State University
James Pearson, Bridgewater State University
Linda Reardan, California State Polytechnic University, Pomona
David Shaenfield, Sacred Heart University
Bryan H. Smith, South Texas College
Seth Vannatta, Morgan State University
Deborah Villalon, Valley Nature Center
Cole Williams, General Mills
Members of a Flat Earth Society (who wish to remain anonymous)

We have also had the benefit of comments from numerous instructors who reviewed earlier drafts of the text, its problem sets, or its digital resources:

Gabriel R. Camacho, El Paso Community College
Louis Colombo, Bethune-Cookman University
Simon Cushing, University of Michigan, Flint
Lauren Dickey, University of Kentucky
Craig Fox, California University of Pennsylvania
Michael Futch, University of Tulsa
Thomas Gilovich, Cornell University
Mara Harrell, Carnegie Mellon University
S. B. Jamil, Miami Dade College
Scott Lilienfeld, Emory University
Cecelia Mun, University of Nevada, Las Vegas
Nathaniel Nicol, Washington State University
Elizabeth Oljar, University of Detroit, Mercy
Matthew Olsen, Millikin University
Joe Pettit, Morgan State University
Jeffrey Wells Roland, Louisiana State University
Mark D. Sadler, Northeast Lakeview College
Melvin Sanchez, Long Beach City College
Donald W. Schaffner, Rutgers University
E. Stackle, Loyola Marymount University
Michael Thompson, University of North Texas
Ann Voelkel, Blinn College

Over the years, many instructors have provided comments and reviews on earlier editions of *The Art of Reasoning* Rod Adams (Front Range Community College), Mahesh Ananth (Indiana University, South Bend), Nathan Anderson (Eckerd College), Janet Andrews (Vassar College), Benjamin Arah (Bowie State University), Monica Aufrecht (Linfield College), Justine Baker (Pierce College), Robert Barnard (University of Mississippi), Ronald Barnette (Valdosta State University), Thora Bayer (Xavier University of Louisiana), James Beebe (University of Buffalo), Dave Beisecker (University of Nevada, Las Vegas), Bruce Bethell (University of Illinois, Urbana–Champaign), Peter Boltuc (University of Illinois at Springfield), Charles Bolyard (James Madison University), Vanda Bozicevic (Bergen Community College), Marshell Bradley (Sam Houston State University), Jurgis Brakas (Marist College), Patrick Brissey (University of South Carolina), Tom Buford (Furman University), Robert Burch (Texas A&M University), Michael Burke (St. Joseph's College, New York), Charles Byrne (University of Illinois, Urbana–Champaign), Michael Byron (Kent State University), Lloyd Carr (Rivier College), Jennifer Caseldine-Bracht (Indiana University–Purdue University, Fort Wayne), Gladys Childs (Texas Wesleyan University), Drew Christie (University of New Hampshire), Daniel Cohen (Colby College), Jay Conway (California State University, Los Angeles), Brett Coppenger (University of Iowa), Victor Cosculluela (Polk State College), Michael Coste (Front Range Community College), Steve Cowan (Louisiana College), Helen Daly (Colorado College), Raymond Darr (Southern Illinois University, Edwardsville), Julian Davies (Siena College), Peter Dendle (Pennsylvania State University), Gianluca Di Muzio (Indiana University Northwest), Jill Dieterle (Eastern Michigan University), Sarah Donovan (Wagner College), Gregory Doolan (Catholic University of America), Keith Dromm (Northwestern State University of Louisiana), Dennis Earl (Coastal Carolina University), C. E. Emmer (Emporia State University), Jonathan Evans (University of Indianapolis), Frank Fair (Sam Houston State University), Joel Feldman (Rider University), Edward Feser (Pasadena City College), Richard Findler (Slippery Rock University), Peter Fosl (Transylvania University), Martin Fowler (Elon College), Steven Gamboa (California State University, Bakersfield), John Gibson (University of Louisville), Mark Gilbertson (Texas Lutheran University), John Gist (Western New Mexico University), Ben Gorman (York College of Pennsylvania), Frank Grabowski (Rogers State University), Roger Hall (West Valley College), Liam Harte (Westfield State College), Amanda Hicks (State University of New York at Buffalo), James Hill (Valdosta State University), Judith Hill (Saginaw Valley State University), Charles Hornbeck (Keene State University), Charles Hughes (Chapman University), John Humphrey (Minnesota State University, Mankato), Elaine Hurst (St. Francis College), Peter Hutcheson (Texas State University), Jeffrey Irwin (Carnegie Mellon University), Christine James (Valdosta State University), Michael Jordan (Iona College), Rebecca Kajs (Anne Arundel Community College), Holly Kantin (University of Wisconsin, Madison), Jerry Kapus (University of Wisconsin, Stout), Catherine Kemp (John Jay College), Ethan Kosmider (Stony Brook University), Adam Kovach (Marymount University), Sunita Lanka (Hartnell College), Sanford Levy (Montana State University), Kenneth Livingston (Vassar College), James Loftis (Loraine County Community College), Joseph Lombardo (St. Joseph's College of New York), Zhaolu Lu (Tiffin University), Amy MacArthur (High Point University), Jennifer McErlean (Siena College), Timothy McGrew (Western Michigan University), Audrey McKinney (Texas State University), Vicente Medina (Seton Hall University), Andrew Mills (Otterbein College), Michael Monge (Long Beach City College), Daniel Murphy (St. Peter's College), Erica Neely (Ohio Northern University), John Olson (Normandale Community College), Michael Papazian (Berry College), Michael Patton (University of Montevallo), Thomas Pearson (University of Wisconsin, Parkside), Mark Pestana (Grand Valley State University), Daniel Petersen (Hartnell College), Alan Rhoda (University of Notre Dame), David Richards (Cayuga Community College), Michael Rombeiro (St. Joseph's College of Maine), Michael Rooney (Pasadena City College), Glenn Sanford (Sam Houston State University), Fred Seddon (Pennsylvania State University, Altoona), David Seltzer (Pennsylvania

State University), Patrick Shade (Rhodes College), Richard Shedenhelm (University of Georgia), Aeon Skoble (Bridgewater State College), Arnold Smith (Kent State University), James Smith (Calvin College), Renee Smith (Coastal Carolina University), Harvey Solganik (Southwestern Baptist Theological Seminary), James South (Marquette University), George Spangler (California State University, Long Beach), Andrew Spear (Grand Valley State University), Gordon Steinhoff (Utah State University), Alfred Stewart (Midwestern State University), Peter Suber (Earlham College), Chris Surprenant (Tulane University), Mate Szabo (Carnegie Mellon University), Edward Trudeau (Catholic University of America), Matthew Turner (Francis Marion University), Russell Wahl (Idaho State University), Susan Dawn Wake (Rochester Institute of Technology), Sara Waller (Montana State University), Ronald Weed (University of New Brunswick), John Wingard (Covenant College), Mia Wood (Pierce College), Elaine Yoshikawa (Arizona

State University), and Steven Zusman (Illinois State University). Thank you all.

Needless to say, none of the people we have mentioned is responsible for the use we have made (or failed to make) of their comments, which in many cases were highly critical.

Any book is a collaboration between author and publisher, and we have been particularly fortunate in that regard. During the years we have worked on *The Art of Reasoning*, we have come to rely on the enthusiasm and professionalism of the staff at W. W. Norton & Company. For the Fifth Edition, we are particularly indebted to Ken Barton, Katie Pak, and Sarah Rose Aquilina for the extraordinary thought, care, and patience they devoted to this project. The team that worked with them to publish and promote this edition—Taylere Peterson, Connie Parks, Jessica Awad, Eric Pier-Hocking, Michael Moss, Kim Bowers, Lissi Sigillo, and Megan Schindel—was stellar. Thank you all.

Introduction

This is a book about thinking. It's a book about *how* to think.

In a broad sense, the word "thinking" refers to anything that goes on in our minds. When we say, "A penny for your thoughts," we want to know what's on your mind—whether it's a feeling, a memory, a question, an anxiety, a problem you're trying to solve, or a daydream. As long as you are conscious, there is always something going on up there. In *this* sense, you can't help thinking. You don't need this book. You just have to stay awake. In a narrower sense, however, thinking is a particular *kind* of mental activity, the kind involved in solving a problem, planning an action, studying for a test, or defending your position on a controversial issue. This is still a pretty broad concept, but we have excluded some things.

In the first place, we can distinguish thinking from feeling. Thinking is a cognitive process we use in the attempt to gain knowledge or to understand something, as distinct from our emotional responses to things. This distinction does not mean, as people too often assume, that someone with strong emotions is necessarily illogical or that a logical person must be unemotional. On the contrary, there is no reason we cannot have both: clear, logical minds and passionate feelings. But thinking and feeling do have different roles to play, different jobs to do, in our mental lives.

Second, thinking is purposive. It differs from activities such as daydreaming and fantasizing in which we simply let our minds wander where they will. Thinking is something we have to *do*, usually with some degree of effort. And because it aims at a goal, it is something that can be done with varying degrees of success. You may or may not succeed in solving a problem, forming a plan, grasping something you read, or proving your case. In this way, too, it differs from daydreaming, where the concepts of success and failure don't really apply. Thinking is a skill. It's a skill that everyone has in some degree, but it is also a skill that everyone can improve.

Logic is both a science or an art. By "science" we the mean a body of knowledge to be learned, like physics or history. By "art" we mean a skill or craft to be mastered, like carpentry or playing the piano. We are going to approach logic primarily as an art. Of course, we can't separate the art from the science completely. A carpenter must know something about the properties of wood, a piano player something about musical theory. In the same way, we'll have to learn some of the principles that make up the science of logic. But not all of them—only those necessary for developing the skill of thinking. From time to time we will point out some of the theoretical questions that arise in the course of our discussions, for those who may wish to pursue them, but this is not primarily a text in logical theory. It is a text on the art—the skill—of reasoning.

How can we improve this skill? Let's consider an analogy with the game of tennis. If we want to improve our skill at tennis, we need to do two things. We need to learn more about the rules and strategies of the game. And we need to practice the moves that implement those rules and strategies—to practice serving, volleying, rushing the net, and so forth. The same is true for the activity of thinking. There are certain rules and strategies of thinking, certain standards that tell us when we have achieved a clear understanding of some subject or succeeded in proving a case. Our first task is to learn what these standards are and to understand why they are correct. Our second task is to practice applying these standards to a variety of examples drawn from everyday life, from politics, and from the different subjects one studies in school. The more practice we get, the more effectively we can incorporate the standards of logic into our habits of thought. That's why this book has a lot of exercises.

Before we begin, let's get an overview of the range of standards and techniques that we're going to be learning about.

Reasoning

When we engage in thought, our goal is normally to find out something. We are trying to answer a question, solve a problem, prove a conclusion, or learn a body of material. We want to know why the car will not start, or which candidate to vote for, or what is the cheapest way to get home for the holidays, or what the man or woman of our dreams really feels about us. In all these cases, we can't acquire this knowledge by direct observation. We have to do some reasoning. Reasoning is a process of thought in which we make inferences: Starting with information we already have, an inference draws some further conclusion based on that information. For example, if your car will not start but the lights still work, you can infer that the problem is not a dead battery.

Logic is the study of the methods and standards of inference. Throughout this book, we will be talking about different kinds of inferences and about which ones to use in which sorts of situations. We will study rules for evaluating inferences and learn to distinguish good inferences from bad ones. As a preview, let's look at a particular case.

Every state (except one) has passed laws requiring that seat belts be used in cars, at least for people in the front seat. Supporters of the law say that those who wear seat belts have a better chance, statistically, of surviving an accident than those who don't. Opponents often point to particular cases in which someone survived because he was *not* wearing a seat belt. Which is the better sort of evidence? Are the opponents making too much of the exceptions? Are the supporters making proper use of the statistics? Let's assume for the sake of discussion that wearing seat belts really is safer. Is that enough to justify the law? No—not by itself. The greater safety of seat belts would justify the law only if we take the position that the government should require us to do what is safe. Some people defend that position. Others say we should be free to decide these things for ourselves. So there are really two issues here: the safety of seat belts and the proper role of government. Can the second one be settled by statistical evidence? If not, then what sort of evidence *is* relevant?

The purpose of logic is to answer the sort of questions we raised in the last paragraph. Logic alone won't tell you whether to support mandatory seat belt laws. It *will* give you a method to follow in making that decision and backing it up. It will show you how to break an issue down into subissues, so that you can be sure to consider all the relevant points. It will give you standards for deciding what sort of evidence is appropriate to a particular issue. And it will give you standards for determining how much weight to give a piece of evidence.

The value of these logical standards is not limited to political arguments. In many college courses, students are presented with competing ideas or theories and asked to discuss them critically. In a philosophy class, the issue might be the existence of free will; in literature, it might be different interpretations of *Hamlet*. Whatever the subject, discussing ideas critically means presenting reasons for or against them. In our personal lives we all have choices to make, major ones or minor, and here too we need to weigh the reasons on each side and try to consider all the relevant issues.

Logic can also help us develop other, more subtle skills. Most of us have been in discussions that were frustrating because they kept going around in circles. That often happens when people "talk past each other"—when they are not really addressing the same issue. Suppose someone argues that it's wrong to treat abortion merely as a medical procedure, like removing an appendix, because the fetus is a potential person. Someone else argues that a woman should have the right to make decisions concerning her own body. These two people are both dealing with the topic of abortion, but they may not be addressing quite the same issue. The first person may be trying to show that abortion is morally wrong, while the second is denying that it should be made illegal. Whether abortion is right or wrong in moral terms and whether it should be legal or illegal are different issues. They are related (which is why they are easily confused), but not identical.

If the two people could identify the difference, they might find that they don't disagree after all. The one who says that abortion should be legal might be willing to agree that abortion is nevertheless a serious action that would be wrong to take without an equally serious reason. And the one who says that abortion is morally wrong might be willing to agree that it's still a decision that a woman should be legally free to make on her own. Of course, the argument might not work out so neatly. But we'll never know until we try, and we can't try until we know how to distinguish one issue from another. That's a skill that logic can help us develop.

In this particular case, the problem of talking past each other would be fairly easy to fix because the two different issues are signaled by two different words: "immoral" versus "illegal." A more difficult problem occurs when two people are using the same word but with two different meanings. Suppose there is an argument over whether student work should be graded. If one person is referring specifically to letter grades, while the other is referring to *any* form of evaluation, they are probably going to talk past each other. If we take the different meanings of the word into account, we would have to say that here again the people are not debating the same issue. But the problem is harder to fix because the difference in meaning lies below the surface of the language. And "grade" is a fairly concrete word. Think of the possibilities for miscommunication in words like "democracy," "freedom," "love," or "art."

This brings us to another area of logic: concepts and definitions. People often talk past each other when they use words with different meanings. Even when that is not a problem, it is always valuable to make the meaning of our words as clear and explicit as possible. Some concepts, such as "democracy," are extremely hard to define, and great minds have spent lifetimes in the effort. Logic won't guarantee success, but it can give us a method to follow, and the method will pay immediate dividends in the clarity and precision of our thinking. It will also make it easier to master new concepts and words that are introduced in most courses at school.

So far we have talked about skills involved in taking ideas apart: breaking an issue down into its components, distinguishing between closely related ideas, and analyzing the meaning of a word. But we also need to put our ideas together again. Thinking involves synthesis as well as analysis, integration as well as differentiation. To understand a line of reasoning, we need to break it down into its parts, but we also need to put it in its wider context. In working on a problem, the most creative solutions often come when we notice similarities to problems in other areas. In a college course, it's important to understand each component of the material, but it's equally important to organize the material as a whole into a logically coherent framework.

Indeed, we can often integrate ideas from different courses. In a religion or ethics class, for example, you might discuss the idea that love of money is the root of all evil. How does that relate to the economist's description of money as a medium of exchange? In a political science class on democracy, you might discuss the idea that people are capable of governing themselves. Is that supported or contradicted by what you've learned in psychology, history, and philosophy? As these examples illustrate, integration means the awareness of logical relations on a larger scale. An idea in one area may provide evidence for an idea in another, quite different area. Or the two ideas may contradict each other—in which case they cannot both be right. An understanding of logic will help you spot these relationships.

Objectivity

As you can see from our discussion so far, thinking is a complex skill. It has many component activities, each with its own methods and standards. But these methods and standards have a common purpose: to help us be *objective*. As a mental orientation and practice, objectivity has two essential elements. (1) It means, first of all, a commitment to finding the *truth*. It means recognizing that reality is what it is, independent of what we think or feel about it. Facts are facts. (2) But facts do not reveal themselves to us automatically. Knowledge of reality has to be acquired by a complex process of thought that is self-directed and subject to error. So the second element of objectivity is the commitment to using the *methods of reason*, including the methods and forms of reasoning you will explore in this book.

To some extent, objectivity is a matter of choice: the choice not to indulge in wishful thinking, not to let bias or prejudice distort our judgment, and so forth. But there's more to it than that. Objectivity also involves a skill. Even with the best will in the world, we can't really be objective unless we know how to use our cognitive equipment: how to follow and evaluate the arguments we hear, how to isolate the relevant issues clearly, how to avoid ambiguity and vagueness in the words we use.

The essence of objectivity is the ability to step back from our train of thought and examine it critically. This is a virtue because it is the only way to avoid jumping to conclusions, the only way to check the results of our thinking, the only way to make sure that we are in touch with the facts. The results of our thinking cannot be any better than the processes by which we arrive at them. There is no "Book of Life" with answers in the back where we can see whether we got it right. Good thinking is a self-directed, self-correcting process, and you are the only one who can take responsibility for steering your own mind in the right direction. The methods and standards we discuss in this book will give you a compass.

Objectivity also has a social aspect. It means not only presenting your own ideas logically but also listening to what others say. Objectivity does not require that you be neutral, nonpartisan, or indifferent to the issue. It does require that you try to look at the matter from the other person's perspective. Even if your view is right, it is rare that any single perspective reveals the *whole* truth. Objectivity requires that you give a fair hearing to the evidence and arguments for the other side. Even if you reject them in the end, knowing *why* you reject them will give you a better understanding of your own position.

Another aspect of objectivity is especially important in communicating with others. To get our ideas across successfully, we have to take account of the other person's context. A point so obvious to us that it hardly seems worth mentioning may not be obvious to someone else, and if we fail to mention it, he may not understand what we are saying. Objectivity is the ability to step back from our own thinking so that we can see it critically, through the eyes of someone who does not share our outlook, our context of knowledge, our preferences, or our idiosyncrasies. All that we can reasonably ask of our audience is the ability to follow logical connections. In this respect, logic, like language, is a shared framework without which we could not communicate.

This sort of objectivity is especially important in writing, where readers are not present to ask questions if the message isn't getting through. If we fail to make clear what issue we are addressing, or if we use terms in new or ill-defined ways, readers can't interrupt to ask what we are talking about. They are stuck with what we've put down on paper. If our presentation is vague, or fails to consider a relevant alternative, or makes a questionable assumption, they can't stop us to ask for an elaboration. In writing, therefore, we have to be on our best behavior, logically speaking. Many writing problems are really problems in logical thinking. Conversely, writing exercises are one of the best ways to practice the techniques of logic, and you will find many such exercises in this book.

Speaking of exercises, we want to offer a final word of advice and encouragement. There are three kinds of exercises in each chapter. At the ends of most sections within a chapter, you will find skill building exercises designed to help you master the. material in a given section You will also see exercises with a special icon indicating an integrative exercise. These exercises will help you combine your new skills with those learned in previous sections. A final and very important set of exercises at the end of each chapter is Putting It All Together. These exercises call on all the skills you have learned in the chapter and ask you to use those skills in different combinations. They often involve real-life examples; and they are a bit more challenging than the in-chapter exercises. Answers for exercises with stars next to them can be found at the back of the book.

It's going to take a certain amount of effort to improve your thinking skills and to build the muscles of your mind. As the ads for health clubs often say, "No pain, no gain." But the process can also be fun. The exercises in this book are designed to make the effort enjoyable. And you can expect to take pleasure and pride in the results of your efforts: the sense of mental clarity and mastery you will get from the ability to organize your thoughts, to make logical connections, to understand the world around you, to see past the blinders of little minds and enjoy the company of great ones.

Language & Reasoning

Part 1 is concerned with the basic elements and standards of reasoning. Later sections will deal with the details of specific forms of reasoning, but here we will cover the elements and standards that pertain to reasoning in general and that will be of value in all your studies as well as everyday life.

Language is the medium in which we think, communicate, and reason. Words expand the range of our senses, bring order to our experiences, allow us to learn from the experiences of others, and preserve the thoughts of preceding generations. In learning to speak, each of us has acquired an amazingly powerful and versatile set of tools. But the tools will not do what we want unless we know how to use them properly. So before we turn to reasoning per se, we need to master these tools. We need to know how to define the concepts our words express and how they combine into statements, which we analyze in terms of the propositions they assert. That will be the focus of Chapter 1, Language: Concepts and Propositions.

Chapter 2 will introduce the basic unit of reasoning, which in logic is called an argument. We'll learn how to identify the premises and the conclusion of an argument and begin our study of how to analyze and then evaluate its logical structure. Chapter 3 is concerned with fallacies—spurious arguments in which the premises may appear to support the conclusion but do not really support it. We are going to review some of the more common fallacies and learn how to spot them in everyday thought and speech. In Chapter 4, we will add to our understanding of potential pitfalls in reasoning by reviewing some of the psychological factors that give rise to errors.

1 Language: Concepts and Propositions

LEARNING OBJECTIVES

On successful completion of the chapter, you will be able to:

✓ Understand differences in levels of abstraction among concepts. (1.1–1.2)

✓ Learn rules for organizing concepts in classification hierarchies. (1.3)

✓ Learn to evaluate and construct definitions of concepts. (1.4–1.6)

✓ Understand how words and grammatical structure determine what a statement does and does not assert. (1.7–1.8)

One of the major functions of language is to divide the world up into categories. Except for proper names, most words stand for groups of things—tigers, tables, tests, and so forth; or common features of things—their characteristics, actions, etc. Organizing a set of things into groups is called classification, and a word that stands for such a group expresses a concept.

In the first three sections of this chapter, we will learn the rules for classifying things in the most effective way, and we'll see how concepts can be arranged in hierarchies of species and genus.

To use concepts with precision and to understand the relationships among different concepts, we need to define them. In Sections 1.4 through 1.6, we will learn how to evaluate and construct definitions.

In the final two sections, we'll see how to identify propositions and how to tell whether two statements assert the same or different propositions.

1.1 Concepts and Referents

Suppose that we ask you to classify the courses you've taken in college. You might classify them by subject matter: art, biology, history, etc. Or you might classify them by level: introductory, intermediate, advanced. Whichever way you choose, you are grouping together courses that have something in common and distinguishing them from other courses. In effect, you are creating a set of file folders in your mind and then putting each course into the proper folder.

Classifying things together into groups is something we do all the time, and it isn't hard to see why. Imagine trying to shop in a supermarket where the food was arranged in random order on the shelves: tomato soup next to the white bread in one aisle, chicken soup in the back next to the AA batteries, one brand of cream cheese in front and another in aisle 8 near the Oreos. The task of finding what you want would be time-consuming and extremely difficult, if not impossible.

In the case of a supermarket, someone had to design the system of classification. But there is also a ready-made system of classification embodied in our language. The word "dog," for example, groups together a certain class of animals and distinguishes them from other animals. Such a grouping may seem too obvious to be called a classification, but this is only because you have already mastered the word. As a child learning to speak, you had to work hard to learn the system of classification your parents were trying to teach you. Before you got the hang of it, you probably made mistakes, like calling the cat a dog. If you hadn't learned to speak, the whole world would seem like the unorganized supermarket; you would be in the position of an infant, for whom every object is new and unfamiliar. In learning the principles of classification, therefore, we'll be learning about the structure that lies at the core of our language.

Whenever we classify, we make use of concepts—ideas that represent classes of things we have grouped together. In classifying your courses, you used concepts such as ART, HISTORY, and INTRODUCTORY. (We will use capital letters to indicate a concept.) To learn the word "dog," you had to acquire the concept DOG. A scientist who discovers a new phenomenon forms a concept for that class of thing and expresses the concept in a new word (e.g., "quark"). As these examples illustrate, concepts and words are intimately related. A concept is an idea; a word is the linguistic vehicle we use to express the idea. And the things that a concept stands for are called the **referents** of the concept. The referents of DOG, for example, are all the individual dogs in the world. We can diagram the relation between a concept and its referents as follows:

```
          ┌─ DOG ─┐
  ●  ●  ┆ ●  ●  ●  ┆ ●  ●
```

The black dots stand for individual objects. The bracketing lines indicate that certain objects (Marley, the next-door neighbor's dog, etc.) are included within the concept—they are the referents of DOG—while other things are excluded (my cat, the Taj Mahal, and everything else in the world that is not a dog).

Now consider the concept ANIMAL. We could diagram this separately, and the diagram would look like the one we just did for DOG. But these concepts are obviously related: dogs are a type of animal. That means we can represent both concepts in the same diagram:

Notice that all the referents included in DOG are also included in ANIMAL, but ANIMAL includes many other things as well—cats (as the diagram indicates), squirrels, fish, and all the other types of animals. ANIMAL is a broader concept because it includes more than the narrower concept DOG. Whenever we encounter this relationship, we use the term **genus** for the broader concept and the term **species** for the narrower one. A genus is a class of things regarded as having various subcategories (its species). Thus DOG and CAT are both species within the genus ANIMAL. If a species is a file folder, a genus is a file drawer containing many folders.

You may be familiar with the idea of genus and species from biology, where they are part of an elaborate system of classification with many levels: species, genus, family, etc. In logic, however, the terms "genus" and "species" have a more flexible meaning. Here, a genus can be any group to which a species belongs. That's why we said ANIMAL is a genus; in biology, it is a kingdom. And a species can be any subcategory within a given genus. "Genus" and "species" are relative terms, like "mother" and "daughter." Your mother is also a daughter—in relation to *her* parents. In the same way, a given concept can be either a genus or a species, depending on our perspective. DOG is a species in relation to ANIMAL, but it is a genus in relation to the narrower concept BEAGLE.

By using the genus–species relationship, we can create very complex systems of classification. For instance, the items in your house can be classified as TABLES, CHAIRS, etc.; these are species of the genus FURNITURE, which in turn is a species of the genus MAN-MADE OBJECTS or ARTIFACTS. If you classified your courses by subject matter—ART, HISTORY, ECONOMICS, PHYSICS—you might go on to classify these disciplines into wider groups, such as HUMANITIES, SOCIAL SCIENCES, and PHYSICAL SCIENCES. Indeed, *every* concept can be placed within some hierarchy of genus and species (and, as we will see, most concepts can be placed within many different hierarchies).

The referents of our concepts are *concrete*; each is a single, individual object. If we had separate names for each referent (as we do in the case of people or cities), the names would also be concrete. But a concept (such as PEOPLE or CITY) is *abstract*. The word "abstract" here means two things. It means first that a concept refers to a group of objects, not just to a single thing (as a name does). The concept PEOPLE includes all human beings; CITY includes all cities. Second, a concept is abstract because it groups together things that differ from one another. There are many differences among people, among cities, among the referents of any concept. We group them together, not because they are identical, but because they are *similar*.

Abstractness is a relative property. Any concept is abstract to some degree. But a species is less abstract than the genus to which it belongs. The genus is a larger and broader group; it has more referents than the species does. And the referents of the genus are less similar to each other than are the referents of the species. There are many more differences among animals, taken as a group, than there are among dogs. Thus, as we move up a species–genus hierarchy, we are moving in the direction of greater abstractness. As we move down the hierarchy, we are moving in the direction of greater concreteness.

It's important to stress that the term "concrete" is not limited to physical, tangible things, nor does the term "abstract" mean "intangible." The feelings we have at a given moment, for example, are not tangible, but they are concrete: each is an individual, particular occurrence. And the concepts we use to classify feelings are measured in the same way as other concepts. The concept LOVE is more abstract than its species, such as ROMANTIC LOVE or MATERNAL LOVE, but less abstract than its genus, EMOTION.

The distinction between abstract and concrete allows us to extend our notion of classification. So far, we have been classifying objects: animals, furniture, cities, etc. But we also have concepts for qualities (like colors), for actions (like running), and for relationships (like marriage). These concepts can also be placed in species–genus hierarchies according to their degree of abstractness. RED, BLUE, and GREEN are species of the genus COLOR, which might in turn be classified as a species of the genus PHYSICAL QUALITY (as distinct from nonphysical qualities such as intelligence). RUNNING, WALKING, and SWIMMING are species of the genus LOCOMOTION. MARRIAGE and FRIENDSHIP are species of the genus PERSONAL RELATIONSHIP. (In our society, marriage is also a legal relationship; this is an example of the way hierarchies of classification can overlap.)

You can see that in all these cases, the genus is the more abstract concept, the species the more concrete. *Every* concept, not just those for objects or entities, has some particular degree of abstractness, and every concept fits into some species–genus relationship. This fact is the basis for the technique of defining concepts, which we will study later in the chapter.

EXERCISE 1.1

I. For each of the following pairs of concepts, first determine which is the genus, which the species; and then try to name two other species of the same genus.

∗1. MAN, ANIMAL

2. GARMENT, COAT

3. VEHICLE, CAR

∗4. BASEBALL, SPORT

5. AUTOBIOGRAPHY, NONFICTION BOOK

6. BAKE, COOK

∗7. COUNTRIES, EUROPEAN

8. ANGER, EMOTION

9. COURAGE, VIRTUE

∗10. BURRITO, TORTILLA DISHES

11. SCALDING, HOT

12. ARISTOCRAT, DUKE

∗13. STATES OF MATERIAL SUBSTANCES, SOLID

14. RUNNING, JOGGING

15. TOOTH, BICUSPID

∗16. MAUSOLEUM, BURIAL PLACE

17. TIMEPIECE, WATCH

18. PERCEIVE, SMELL

∗19. SQUARE, RECTANGULAR

20. ORGANISM, PLANT

II. Arrange the following lists in terms of order of increasing abstractness.

∗1. Performer, Lady Gaga, singer

2. Cattle, organism, mammal, steer, animal

3. Quadrilateral, square, figure, rectangle

∗4. Alloy, steel, mineral, metal

5. Google, corporation, multinational company, institution

6. U.S. president, Thomas Jefferson, national leader

∗7. Telephone, iPhone, mobile telephone, communication device

8. Durable good, manufactured object, refrigerator, appliance

9. *Moby Dick*, literature, novel

∗10. Brother, family member, sibling, kin

11. Tart, pie, pastry

12. Jump, leap, move

∗13. Cardigan, garment, top, sweater

14. Psychological disorder, schizophrenia, psychosis

15. Islam, Sufism, worldview, religion

1.2 Rules of Classification

Classification is the process of sorting things into categories. The set of things to be classified—animals, college courses, or whatever—constitutes a genus, and the task is to subdivide the genus into species so that each item can be assigned its place. There is usually more than one way to do this, as we noticed earlier in regard to college courses, depending on our needs, our purposes, and the kind of information we have available. But even if there is no single best way of subdividing a genus, some ways are better than others, and there are guidelines for selecting the better ones.

1.2A Consistent Principle

Suppose you tried to classify your courses into the following categories: ART, BIOL-OGY, HISTORY, ECONOMICS, and INTRODUCTORY. Where would you put "Intro-duction to Art"? Because your categories overlap, we don't know whether to classify this as an introductory course or an art course. The first rule of classification is that differ-ent species must not overlap. We express this in logic by saying that different species must be **mutually exclusive**: Each species must exclude all the members of every other species. At the same time, a good classification divides up the genus completely, allow-ing us to assign every member of the genus to one or another of the species. We express this in logic by saying that the classification must be **jointly exhaustive**: All the species taken together (jointly) must cover (exhaust) all the objects that fall under the genus. If you had also taken a philosophy course, for example, then the classification of courses we gave earlier would not be jointly exhaustive.

A good classification should divide the genus into species that are mutually exclu-sive and jointly exhaustive. How do we go about creating such a classification? Let's consider first an example of how *not* to do it. In one of his stories, Jorge Luis Borges describes a mythical book called *The Chinese Emporium of Benevolent Knowledge*:

> On those remote pages it is written that animals are divided into (a) those that belong to the Emperor, (b) embalmed ones, (c) those that are trained, (d) suckling pigs, (e) mermaids, (f) fabulous ones, (g) stray dogs, (h) those that are included in this classification, (i) those that tremble as if they were mad, (j) innumerable ones, (k) those drawn with a very fine camel's hair brush, (l) others, (m) those that have just broken a flower vase, (n) those that resemble flies from a distance. [Jorge Luis Borges, Other Inquisitions 1937–1952]

These categories are obviously not mutually exclusive. A stray dog (g) might well resemble a fly from a distance (n); an animal belonging to the Emperor (a) might also be drawn with a very fine camel's hair brush (k). The categories overlap in numerous ways. Strictly speaking, the classification *is* jointly exhaustive because of "others" (l). But that's cheating: "Others" is a "miscellaneous" category. Without it, the classification would leave out many animals.

It's not hard to see why the classification is inadequate. It does not follow any *con-sistent principle* for dividing up the genus. It jumps from the question of ownership (a), to condition after death (b), to training (c), and so on. Since there is no necessary rela-tionship among these various principles, the classification is bound to be chaotic. In classifying, we should try to follow a consistent principle. If we classify college courses by subject matter, we should stick to that principle throughout and not include species like INTRODUCTORY that involve a different principle. Similarly, there are various ways to classify furniture: by function (tables, chairs, etc.), by style of design (Danish, Colonial, Mission, etc.), by material (wood, plastic, chrome, etc.). But whichever principle we choose, we should follow it consistently.

When we diagram a classification, we can represent the principle we're following by enclosing it within brackets under the name of the genus. For example:

As the diagram illustrates, the principle is an attribute that all members of the genus possess, and the species are defined by the way they differ in regard to that attribute. Thus, in the diagram on the left, the concept TABLE groups together things that have the same *function* and distinguishes them from chairs and couches, which have different functions. In the diagram on the right, the concept DANISH groups together articles of furniture that have the same *style* and distinguishes them from furniture designed in other styles. We can find this same structure in any system of classification, though it may not always be so easy to name the principle explicitly.

The need for a consistent principle does not require a *single* principle. Animal species, for example, differ from each other in many ways: shape, color, and other external properties; internal anatomy and physiology; behavior; method of bearing young; and so on. Biologists use all these properties in classifying animals. It is appropriate to use multiple principles of classification whenever we are dealing with complex phenomena; in such cases, a single principle would often be artificial and not very useful. When we use more than one principle, however, we should take extra care to make sure that the resulting categories are mutually exclusive.

The first rule for classifying, then, is to use a single principle or set of principles consistently so that the resulting categories are mutually exclusive and jointly exhaustive. In many cases, however, this will leave more than one possible way to divide the genus. A second rule will help us select among those alternatives.

1.2B Essential Attributes

The second rule is to use a principle based on the *essential* attributes of the things we are classifying. An essential attribute is a fundamental one, an attribute that makes a thing what it is. If we divide a genus according to an essential attribute, we are grouping together things that are fundamentally similar and separating things that are fundamentally different. And because a fundamental attribute underlies and explains many of a thing's superficial attributes, things that are fundamentally similar will probably have many attributes in common; things that share a superficial, nonessential attribute may well have nothing else in common.

Let's consider the animal kingdom once again. Biologists classify animals into the categories MAMMAL, REPTILE, AMPHIBIAN, BIRD, INSECT, etc. The principles they use include mode of reproduction (does the animal lay eggs or bear its young alive?), internal physiology (vertebrate vs. invertebrate, warm-blooded vs. cold-blooded), and means of locomotion (swimming, flying, crawling). These principles are aspects of two attributes fundamental to all forms of life: An organism must maintain itself by acting on the environment, and it must reproduce itself. This classification of animals, then, is based on essential principles, and the advantages of the classification are obvious. Animals that survive and reproduce in similar ways are likely to have a great deal in common and can naturally be studied as a group.

By contrast, suppose that we classify animals according to a nonessential attribute such as color:

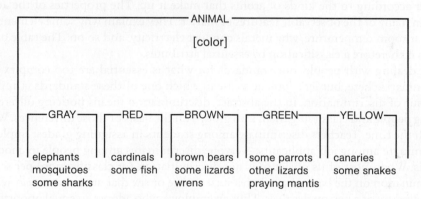

Of course this is not a complete classification of animals, but it does indicate what's wrong with classifying them according to this attribute. The items that are grouped together in each category have nothing else in common. The differences among elephants, mosquitoes, and gray sharks are much more fundamental than the superficial similarity in color. And the similarities between green and brown lizards are much more fundamental than the superficial differences in color. As a result, this classification is useless. Knowing that a certain animal belongs to one of these categories tells you almost nothing about it. Imagine having to act on the information that a gray animal was approaching, without knowing anything else about it!

How does the distinction between essential and nonessential attributes apply to other areas? Let's look at a few examples. The essential attribute of a man-made object is usually its function. Such objects are created to serve a purpose, and the purpose explains why they are designed the way they are. If you came across an unfamiliar tool in a museum, your first question would probably be: What's it for? If you knew the answer to that question, then you would understand why the tool has a certain shape and internal structure, why it is made of the material it is, and so on. The same is true for human institutions. Thus, if you were studying corporations, it would be natural to classify each according to its function: Does the corporation produce goods or services? Is it a nonprofit or for-profit organization?

In the physical sciences, essential attributes are those that underlie and explain the surface properties we can observe directly, and scientists have pushed deeper and deeper

---

REVIEW Two Rules of Classification

1. A single principle or set of principles should be used consistently so that the categories (species) are mutually exclusive and jointly exhaustive.

2. The principle or principles used should identify essential attributes.

---

into the structure of matter in the search for these underlying causes. Ancient Greek philosophers, for example, divided matter into four elements: earth, air, water, and fire. Modern chemists have replaced that early system with the table of elements, classifying matter according to the kinds of atoms that make it up. The properties of the atoms explain many of the observable features of matter: They explain why some elements are gases at room temperature, why metals conduct electricity, and so on. The table of elements is therefore a classification by essential attributes.

In dealing with people, our standards for what is essential are too complex even to summarize here, but let's look at a case in which one of these standards is applied: the issue of discrimination. In the abstract, discrimination means noticing differences among people and classifying them into groups on the basis of those differences. We do this all the time. Teachers discriminate among students in assigning grades; employers discriminate among job applicants; everyone discriminates among people in choosing friends. What most of us object to is not discrimination (or classification) per se, but discrimination on the basis of attributes such as race or sex that are not *essentially* related to the treatment a person deserves. Thus an employer who adopts an equal opportunity policy is choosing to classify job applicants by ability, training, and character rather than by race or sex—on the ground that ability, training, and character are essentially related to job performance, whereas race and sex are not.

The word "essential" always has the sense of "fundamental" or "important." But as the preceding examples illustrate, standards for what is fundamental or important vary from case to case. Identifying essential attributes may take years of research (as in science), and it always takes a good deal of thought. Unfortunately, there is no simple, mechanical rule we can follow in distinguishing essential from nonessential principles of classification. You will have to use your judgment, and you will have to accept the possibility that reasonable people may disagree. Nevertheless, the examples also indicate the value of looking for essential attributes: They bring clarity and coherence to the organization of our knowledge.

In addition, we need to remember that classification serves a purpose, and our purpose affects what we take to be essential. So far, we have taken for granted that our purpose is to understand the nature of the things being classified, on the basis of the similarities and differences among them. That is, we are considering the things as they are in themselves. In and of itself, for example, the essential attribute of a piece of furniture is clearly its function. But an interior designer, who is concerned primarily with aesthetic issues, may need to classify furniture by style. In relation to that specialized practical purpose, it is legitimate to regard style as essential.

APPLY Classifying Courses

Colleges that have a distribution requirement must divide the curriculum into various categories. Here is one actual example. Do you see any problems with it? Do you think there might be some practical reasons why the college used this system of classification?

Arts	Foreign Languages and Literatures	Social Sciences	Natural Sciences
Art	Arabic	Anthropology	Astronomy
Dance	Chinese	Economics	Biology
Drama	French and Francophone Studies	Education	Chemistry
English	German Studies	Geography	Cognitive Science
Film	Greek and Roman Studies	History	Computer Science
Music	Hebrew	Philosophy	Earth Science
Physical Education	Hispanic Studies	Political Science	Mathematics
	Italian	Religion	Physics
	Japanese	Sociology	Psychology
	Russian Studies		

EXERCISE 1.2

Evaluate each of the following classifications. First determine whether it uses a consistent principle and is mutually exclusive and jointly exhaustive. If it passes that test, then determine whether the principle used is essential. If it is not, try to think of a specialized purpose for which the principle might be essential.

＊1. Books: paperbacks, hardbacks, first editions

2. Medicines: antibiotics, laxatives, pills, antihistamines

3. Foods: meats, vegetables, junk food, fruits, breads

＊4. Movies: thrillers, Westerns, pornographic, foreign

5. Students: under 5 feet tall, 5 to 6 feet tall, over 6 feet tall

6. Wine: Chardonnay, red, Merlot, French, sparkling

＊7. Sports: team, aquatic, individual, noncompetitive

8. Trees: leaf-shedding, evergreen, shade

9. Cars: economy, oversize, intermediate, compact, standard, full-size

＊10. Shoes: walking, athletic, leather, dress

11. Colors: blue, orange, warm, red, primary

12. People: those who would rather be hosts, those who would rather be guests

✳13. Jobs: clerical, sales, managerial, service, manual

14. Countries: developed, underdeveloped

15. Countries: free, unfree, partially free

1.3 Levels of Organization

So far we have treated classification as if it were always a matter of sorting things into categories or dividing a genus into species (two ways of describing the same operation). And this is indeed the task we face when we start from scratch. But we do not always start from scratch. We often deal with concepts that reflect preexisting classifications, and the task we face is to locate the concepts at the right level of a species–genus hierarchy.

Suppose you were studying religious affiliations. People describe themselves as Baptists, Methodists, Catholics, Jews, Muslims, and so forth. These are indeed different religious groups, but they do not all belong on the same level of classification; they are not all species of a single genus. Jews, for example, should not be compared directly to Methodists. They should be compared to Christians—a category that we did not include in the list. And Catholics should be compared to Protestants, another term missing from the list. Thus the classification might look like this:

This diagram illustrates several points. First, concepts on the same level of organization should have roughly the same degree of abstractness. It is clear in this case that CATHOLIC and PROTESTANT belong on the same level and that BAPTIST and METHODIST are narrower (less abstract) subdivisions within the category PROTES-

TANT. Second, when it is necessary to separate levels in this way, we must often add concepts that were not given to us originally. The new concepts in this case are PROTESTANT and CHRISTIAN, and we indicate that they were not on the original list by putting them in parentheses. Finally, the diagram gives us ideas about ways in which we might want to flesh out the classification: Are there other religions besides Christianity, Judaism, and Islam? Are there other branches of Protestantism? Are there categories within the major religions?

This sort of analysis is often required when you are learning a new subject and have to learn a new set of concepts. Separating the different levels of organization will help you understand the concepts much more clearly than if you try to master each concept as an isolated unit. In a course in legal theory, for example, you might encounter concepts like FELONY, TRESPASS, MISDEMEANOR, HOMICIDE, and TORT (see the diagram that follows). In order to grasp these concepts, you would need to understand that felonies and misdemeanors are the two species of *crimes* regarded as offenses against public order and prosecuted by the state; and that a tort (such as trespass) is considered a *civil wrong*, an offense for which a private individual must bring suit.

In addition to clarifying the new concepts, this diagram would provide a skeleton or outline for organizing all the other crimes and offenses you learn about.

Notice that one of the concepts we had to fill in here was the genus, OFFENSES. This is the first case we've seen in which the genus was not given at the outset, but it is not an uncommon case. When you are learning a new set of concepts or organizing an old set, you will often have to find an overarching concept for the entire domain. Such generic concepts will of course be more abstract than concepts for the corresponding species, and it may help to be familiar with some of the highest-level abstractions we use to organize our knowledge of the world. One fundamental distinction is between living and nonliving (animate vs. inanimate) objects. Another distinction is between natural objects (living or nonliving) and man-made ones. Yet another basic division is between physical and mental phenomena: the external world of material things versus the internal world of thoughts and feelings. (Mental phenomena in turn are often divided into

SOLVE Organizing Concepts

To organize related concepts into a classification diagram:

1. Find the highest-level (most abstract) genus.

2. Identify concepts that are species of that genus; they should all have the same degree of abstractness.

3. Identify the principle of division that applies to the concepts in step 2; put the principle in brackets.

4. For each concept in step 2, identify any other concepts that are its species, and identify the principle of division (the single principle by which the concept has been divided into species).

5. Repeat step 4 for as many levels as necessary.

cognitive and affective states—thinking vs. feeling.) Perhaps the most abstract set of generic concepts is one devised by the ancient Greek philosopher Aristotle. He divided the world into things (in the sense of whole objects), actions, relations, quantities, times, and places. When you are looking for a genus, it may help to remember these fundamental concepts. You may not need anything so abstract, but if you are stuck, they may help you get oriented.

One final word of warning: Classification is the process of dividing a genus into its species. This is not the same as breaking an object down into its parts or elements. Engines and driveshafts are parts of cars, but they are not themselves types or species of cars. In this case, the point is pretty obvious, but it's easy to get confused when we are learning new concepts. Suppose you have just learned in biology that an enzyme is a type of protein, and that a protein is a large organic molecule made up of a sequence of amino acids. Because enzymes are a species of protein, you could use the diagram on the left to capture the relationship:

But the diagram on the right is fundamentally incorrect. An amino acid is *not* a species of protein. It is a component of a protein. Both the species–genus and the part–whole relations are important for our understanding of the world, but they should not be confused.

EXERCISE 1.3

I.   Integrative Exercise   For each series of items below, first identify a genus to which all the items belong, and then turn that genus into a species by thinking of a higher-level genus.

✳1. Glider, helicopter, jet

  2. Knife, fork, and spoon

  3. Tragedy, comedy, melodrama, farce

✳4. FBI, IRS, State Department

  5. Granite, marble, slate

II.   Integrative Exercise   Fill in the blanks indicated by XXX in the classification diagrams below.

✳1.

2.

III.   Integrative Exercise   Arrange the following concepts in a classification diagram, making sure that each concept is on the appropriate level of abstractness and adding concepts where necessary to complete the diagram.

✳1. BEER, WHISKEY, ALE, CHARDON-NAY, ALCOHOLIC BEVERAGES, BOURBON

  2. HUMANITIES, ECONOMICS, PHILOSOPHY, SOCIAL SCIENCES, PHYSICS

  3. LEAF-SHEDDING TREES, LET-TUCE, CARROT, DANDELION, PINE, OAK

✳4. SPRINTS, HURDLES, PARALLEL BARS, GYMNASTIC EVENTS, 100-METER BREASTSTROKE, DIVING

5. MUSIC, LITERATURE, PAINTING, POETRY, VISUAL ARTS, STILL LIFE

6. FRIEND, CLIENT, RELATIVE, COLLEAGUE, AUNT, HUMAN RELATIONSHIPS

*7. HORIZONTAL, RECTANGULAR, LARGE, ROUND, INFINITESIMAL, VERTICAL

8. HONESTY, VICE, LAZINESS, INTEGRITY

9. MARXISM, LIBERALISM, CONSERVATISM, SOCIALISM, LIBERTARIANISM

*10. ANGER, WISH, MEMORY, LOVE, COGNITION

*IV. Integrative Exercise The classification diagram below violates several of the principles discussed in this section. Identify the errors and fix the diagram.

1.4 Definitions: Their Nature and Function

Concepts serve as mental file folders that help us organize our knowledge about classes of similar things. **Definitions** tell us what is in the folders. In the case of simple, relatively concrete concepts—such as TABLE or RUNNING—we can get along pretty well without definitions. We can tell just by sight whether something is a table, whether someone is running. But most concepts are more abstract and more complex. By telling us what they stand for, and how they relate to other concepts, definitions are an important tool of knowledge. To see more clearly *why* definitions are so valuable, let's look at some of the problems they help us to solve.

First, a definition can clarify the boundaries of a concept. A child who has just learned the concept PLANT can point to some obvious and clear-cut examples, such as houseplants or outdoor shrubs. Such cases are called "paradigm" or "prototypical" examples. But it will take a while before the child understands the full range of the concept PLANT, which includes trees, moss, and so on. At a more advanced level, a person might understand that the category of social sciences includes such prototypical examples as economics, but not be sure whether geography fits. One major function of definitions is to tell us what is and is not included in a concept by giving us a test or rule for membership.

Some people argue that a concept can never have completely sharp borders. On the color spectrum, for example, orange lies on the border between red and yellow, and it isn't clear which way to classify it. Nor can we solve the problem by treating orange as a separate category between red and yellow, because then there would be colors on the borderline between red and orange. In biology, the one-celled organism *Euglena* sits on the border between plants and animals: It has chlorophyll and engages in photosynthesis, like a plant, but it also has flagella for swimming, like an animal. Fortunately, we do not have to settle the theoretical issue of whether concepts can—or should—have completely sharp borders. The important point is that there are *degrees* of precision in understanding a concept's boundaries, and definitions help us to become *more* precise.

A second function of a definition is to clarify the relationships among concepts. Concepts are not isolated, self-contained units; they form networks of interrelated ideas. We have already seen that they fit together into genus–species hierarchies. But there is more to it than that. A concept groups things together into classes on the basis of similarities. In some cases, like TABLE, the objects and their similarities are perceptible. You can literally see the similarity among tables. In such cases, we can employ what is sometimes called an *ostensive definition*: pointing and saying, "Things like *that*." More often, however, the referents of a concept and the attributes they have in common are not directly observable, and we have to learn about them by means of other concepts that we already understand.

Consider the concept GOVERNMENT. If you were trying to explain this concept to someone, what concrete objects could you point to? A police officer? The flag? The White House? These are merely symbols or instruments of government and would convey only a child's understanding of the concept. Actual examples, such as the U.S. government, are not things you can literally point to. You would have to explain in abstract language that the concept GOVERNMENT refers to an *institution*, with the *authority* to make *laws* for a *society*, to *enforce* those laws, and to protect its *citizens* against *foreign* threats. Each of the italicized words expresses a concept necessary for understanding what governments have in common; each is a link in a long chain that connects the concept GOVERNMENT to its referents in reality. If the chain is weak—if the person doesn't understand the intervening concepts—then he won't really understand the concept GOVERNMENT either.

Our ability to acquire new concepts on the basis of old ones is enormously valuable. It allows us to expand our knowledge and to profit from discoveries made by other people. But it poses the danger that we will acquire a concept only as a vague idea, without any clear understanding of the class of things it actually stands for. It also poses the danger that different people using the concept will have radically different ideas of what the concept includes. Definitions help us ward off these dangers. They keep a concept tied to its referents by relating it clearly to other concepts that serve as links in the chain.

A third function of a definition is to provide a summary statement about the referents of our concepts. If we think of a concept as a file folder where we put all the information we have about a certain class of things, then we have to realize that these folders may contain enormous amounts of information. In one way or another, for example, virtually all knowledge in the humanities and social sciences is relevant to the concept HUMAN. Definitions help us keep our filing system in order by giving us summary statements about what is in each folder. A good definition *condenses* the knowledge we have about the referents of a concept, giving us just the highlights, the key points, the

---

REVIEW **The Main Functions of Definitions**

Definitions:

1. State the criteria for membership in the class of referents.

2. Indicate the relationship between a concept and other concepts.

3. Condense the knowledge we have about the referents of a concept.

---

essence. Because it performs this service, a definition is valuable even in cases, such as HUMAN, where we already know what class of things the concept stands for.

Within the broad framework of the functions we have discussed so far, definitions can serve a variety of more specific purposes. We're going to be concerned primarily with definitions of concepts that we employ frequently in everyday thought and language. But for specialized purposes in science, law, and other technical fields, we may also need to introduce a new word or give a new meaning to an old word. We may need to give more precise boundaries to a concept. Or we may need to clarify the role that a concept plays in a complex theory. As we will see, however, the type of definition that works well for ordinary concepts can also be adapted to these other contexts.

This type is called a definition by genus and differentia. To understand what this means, consider a classic example: "Humans are rational animals." Notice that the definition has two parts. The term "animals" names the wider class to which humans belong; it classifies us as a species of the genus ANIMAL. A genus is a class of things regarded as having various subcategories (its species). The term "rational" specifies an attribute that distinguishes us from other species of the same genus. This part of the definition is called the **differentia**—it differentiates humans from other animals. In effect, we are assuming a classification of animals in terms of the principle "mode of cognition," and then defining our species by our rational mode of cognition. A differentia can rarely be expressed in a single word, like "rational," but it always serves the same function of differentiating a concept from other species within the same genus. Thus the genus is like your last name, which indicates the family you belong to; the differentia is like your first name, which distinguishes you from other members of your family.

In light of what we have said about the functions of a definition and about its genus–differentia structure, we can now define the very concept of DEFINITION itself:

A definition is a statement that identifies the referents of a concept by specifying the genus they belong to and the differentia (the set of essential characteristics) that distinguishes those referents from other species in the genus, along one or more principles of division.

1.5 Rules for Definitions

If we're looking for a definition, why not just use the dictionary? Isn't that what dictionaries are for? Well, yes and no. A dictionary is a good place to begin our search for a definition. But dictionaries are concerned with *words*. They often give nothing more than synonyms and rarely provide the full context we need to understand the *concept* that a word expresses. To define a concept, we usually have to go beyond the dictionary. Logicians have identified six rules for constructing a type of definition that is suitable for general purposes:

1. A definition should include a genus and a differentia.
2. A definition should be neither too broad nor too narrow.
3. A definition should state the essential attributes of the concept's referents.
4. A definition should not be circular.
5. A definition should not use negative terms unnecessarily.
6. A definition should not use vague, obscure, or metaphorical language.

1.5A Genus and Differentia

1. A definition should include a genus and a differentia.

The most common way to violate this rule is to leave out the genus. And the usual sign of this omission is the use of the word "when," as in "fear is when you think you're in danger." What's missing in this definition is the genus: Fear is the *emotion* one feels in response to the awareness of danger. The word "where" is sometimes used in the same way, as in "a denouement in a story is where the conflict is resolved and the story ends." Here again, the genus is missing. This definition does not tell us what *kind* of thing a denouement is—namely, an element or a stage in the plot of a literary work.

Like the differentia, the genus need not be specified by a single word. If we define an automobile as a motor vehicle intended for personal transportation, the genus is contained in the phrase "motor vehicle." A definition of USER SESSION might be: "A user session at a website occurs when a unique user is present on a site for a specified length of time," which distinguishes it from a hit, which occurs each time a user views a different page at a site. This definition includes a genus even though it uses the word "when," because it describes the user session as a unit of measure for usage of a website, in contrast with another measure, a hit. From a logical standpoint, user sessions and hits are two species of the genus "unit of measure for website usage." The definition makes this clear. When we define a concept that designates an action, we often use a verb phrase, as in "to practice is to perform an activity for the sake of improving one's skill." The genus here can be restated as "an activity one performs." The English language gives us many ways to specify a genus. To identify the genus, we need to look for the element in a defining statement that refers to a wider class.

A definition by genus and differentia builds on what we have learned about classification. The genus not only helps us identify the referents of a concept, but also conveys a great deal of information about them. If you don't know what a *peso* is, for example, the most useful thing I can tell you is that it's a unit of Mexican currency. In the same way, the statement that humans are animals locates our species within the biological order and conveys a vast amount of information in summary form—that we are living beings, that we are mortal, that we have specific needs for survival and reproduction, and so on.

EXERCISE 1.5A

For each proposed definition, identify the genus (if it has one) and the differentia.

∗1. Snow is precipitation consisting of flakes or clumps of ice crystals.

2. A tree is a plant with thick roots.

3. A landfill is where you take refuse.

∗4. A bargain is an opportunity to buy something at an unusually low price.

5. A pen is a handheld writing implement that uses ink.

6. To diet is to select the food one consumes for purposes of health or appearance.

∗7. A touchdown is when one team completes a run or pass across the other team's goal line.

8. Government is an institution with the authority to make laws for a society, to enforce those laws, and to protect its citizens against foreign powers.

9. Charisma is when someone can charm or influence others.

∗10. To feel alienated is to feel wrongfully detached from certain people or things.

11. Popular music is music with wide appeal that is typically distributed to large audiences through the music industry.

12. Envy is a feeling of resentment toward someone else's possessions or advantages.

1.5B Co-Extensive and Essential Attributes

2. A definition should be neither too broad nor too narrow.

A definition is too broad if it includes things that are not referents of the concept. For example, the definition "Humans are two-legged animals" is too broad because the defining phrase "two-legged animal" includes birds as well as humans. We can represent this problem in a diagram:

A definition is too narrow if it fails to include things that *are* referents of the concept. An example would be "Humans are religious animals." This definition is too narrow because, no matter how widespread religious belief may be, some people are atheists. We can see this by drawing a diagram:

Being too narrow and being too broad are opposite flaws in a definition. But both involve the relation between the concept and its referents. One purpose of a definition is to identify the referents of a concept. A definition that does not pick out the right referents—one that includes too much or too little—is not doing its job. It is like an incompetent doorkeeper at a party, letting in people who weren't invited or turning away people who were.

We can tell whether a definition is too broad or too narrow by looking for **counterexamples**. A counterexample is a particular instance that proves a definition wrong. If a definition is too narrow, a counterexample is something that belongs in the concept but is excluded by the definition. Atheists are counterexamples to the definition of humans as religious animals. If a definition is too broad, a counterexample is something that does *not* belong in the concept but is included in the definition. Birds are counterexamples to the definition of humans as two-legged animals. Let's look at a few other cases. "A college is a degree-granting educational institution." A counterexample would be a law school. Law schools are degree-granting educational institutions, but they are not colleges. So this definition includes too much; it's too broad. "A cigarette is a sheaf of chopped tobacco rolled in white paper." What about the brands that are rolled in brown paper? They are counterexamples proving that the definition does not include enough; it's too narrow.

We should notice, finally, that a definition can be simultaneously too broad *and* too narrow. Suppose, for example, that we define murder as the act of killing another person outside a military context. By this definition, killing someone in self-defense would be an act of murder, but it isn't. So this definition is too broad. But it is also too narrow. Suppose a soldier kills another member of his own regiment in cold blood. This would be murder, but the definition would exclude it because it occurred in a military context. So the same definition can violate the rule in both ways: It can be both too broad and too narrow.

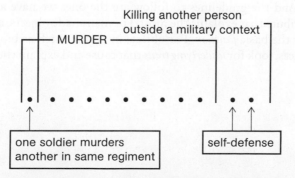

3. A definition should state the essential attributes of the concept's referents.

The referents of a concept often have many attributes in common. Some are relatively superficial, some are essential. As we saw in discussing classification, "essential" means *fundamental*: an essential attribute causes or explains the existence of other attributes. For example, the heart makes a certain thumping noise, so we might try to define it as "the organ that goes lub-dub, lub-dub." But the "lub-dub" sound is a superficial trait; it is merely a by-product of the heart's essential function, which is to circulate the blood. This essential function explains many of the heart's other properties: the way it beats, the way it is hooked up to the veins and arteries, even the sound it makes. But explanation is a one-way street. The "lub-dub" sound does *not* explain the heart's function. Remember that one purpose of a definition is to condense the knowledge we have about the referents of a concept. Defining by essential attributes is the best way to achieve this purpose, because then you convey not only the particular attributes named in the definition, but also the ones they underlie and explain.

The rule of essentiality applies to the genus as well as the differentia. Dogs, for example, belong to various wider groups: they are animals, they are playmates, they are a means of self-defense. But ANIMAL would be the best genus to use for general purposes in defining DOG, because a dog's animal nature is more fundamental and explains more about it than does the fact that it can play with human beings or defend them.

In regard to the differentia, the rule of essentiality will help us choose among attributes when there is more than one that would differentiate a concept from other species of the same genus. Consider the concept HUMAN. Many attributes, in addition to the faculty of reason, are common and distinctive to humans: language, social institutions, the accumulation of knowledge from one generation to the next, laws, moral codes, certain complex emotions such as reverence, a sense of humor, a brain of a certain size and complexity, a certain physical shape and posture. But reason is the common element, the underlying cause, for many of these attributes. Not for all of them—reason doesn't seem to have much connection with our physical shape and posture. But it is reason that allowed us to develop abstract language and technology, to create social institutions based on general rules and laws, to pass along knowledge to the next generation, and so forth. Reason gives us a differentia that condenses the greatest amount of knowledge about the concept HUMAN.

As with choosing an essential principle in classification, there is no hard and fast rule for determining which attributes are essential. Our view of what is essential to a class of objects may change as we acquire more knowledge about them, and it may involve controversial issues on which people disagree. The rule of essentiality means this: Pick the most essential attribute you can, given everything you know, using your best judgment. And the guidelines to follow are the ones we have already discussed: Look for the attribute that explains the most. For man-made objects, actions, and institutions, look for the basic *function*. For objects in nature, such as biological species or physical substances, look for *underlying traits* that cause and explain the more superficial attributes.

EXERCISE 1.5B

Identify the rule violated by each of these definitions. If the definition is too broad or too narrow, find a counterexample.

✳1. A *blizzard* is when it snows sideways.

2. A *salad* is a food dish containing lettuce.

3. *Blood* is a bodily fluid that is red.

✳4. A *file folder* is an item of stationery designed to organize one's papers.

5. A *pleat* is a fold in the fabric of a skirt.

6. An *advertisement* is what's disseminated in the media to encourage people to buy or use a product or service.

✳7. A *telephone* is an electronic device that uses audio transmitting to communicate between two or more people.

8. A *watch* is a device used for telling time and worn on the wrist.

9. *Cosmetics* are substances applied to the face to alter appearance.

✳10. An *antidote* is a substance that counteracts snakebite.

11. A *pen* is a writing implement that can be clipped to a pocket.

12. *Nodding* is when you move your head forward and down, indicating assent.

✳13. A *calculator* is an electronic instrument that has replaced the slide rule.

14. A *book* is a nonperiodical text.

15. A *test* is an activity in which someone demonstrates ability or knowledge according to specified standards.

1.5C Other Rules

4. A definition should not be circular.

Suppose we define *ownership* as the legal relation between people and the things they own. Because this definition uses the word "own," it defines the concept OWNERSHIP in terms of itself. Instead of explaining what it means to own something, it assumes that we know this already. It tells us how the concept relates to itself, but not how it relates to other concepts or to reality. This definition doesn't go anywhere; it just moves in a circle.

The same problem arises if we use synonyms in a definition. Suppose we define ownership as the legal relation between people and things they *possess.* "Own" and "possess" are synonyms, different words that express the same concept. In terms of concepts, therefore, the definition is still circular: The concept OWNERSHIP is still being used to define itself. The same objection would apply if we define *man* as the *human* animal, *large* as the attribute possessed by something that is *big*, or *folly* as a *foolish* act. In each case, the italicized words are synonyms. To avoid such circularity, it is useful to ask: What contrast is the concept intended to draw? For example, what is the difference between owning a dress and borrowing it or trying it on in the store? How are humans different from other animals? What makes an action a folly as opposed to a wise action?

Circularity can take an even subtler form when two different concepts are used to define each other. Suppose that we define a doctor as a professional who offers medical services to patients. So far, so good: DOCTOR and PATIENT are distinct concepts. But if we now define a patient as a person who receives the services of a doctor, then we have a circular *pair* of definitions. A better approach would be to define the doctor–patient relationship first; then we could define both DOCTOR and PATIENT in terms of that relationship.

5. A definition should not use negative terms unnecessarily.

At the beginning of the 20th century, the automobile was described as a "horseless carriage." That phrase certainly does describe the automobile, but it would not be a good definition. The differentia "horseless" tells us about one source of power that automobiles do *not* use. But there are many sources of power automobiles do not use; what we want to know is the source they *do* use. As another example, suppose that when we introduced the term "differentia," we defined it as the part of the definition that is not the genus. That would not have been much help to you in understanding what a differentia is. In general, negative definitions should be avoided because knowing what a thing is *not* doesn't tell us much about what it *is*. For that reason, a negative definition usually violates the rule of essentiality as well.

Some concepts, however, are inherently negative and thus require negative terms in their definitions. A *bachelor* is a man who is not married; *failing* means not succeeding; an *empty* space is one with nothing in it. How do we know whether a concept is negative? In some cases, a suffix or prefix gives us a linguistic clue: *im*mortal, worth*less*, *a*symmetric. In the absence of such clues, you will have to use your judgment. There are no hard and fast rules, but it's a good idea to look first for a positive attribute, then fall back on a negative one only if the search fails.

6. A definition should not use vague, obscure, or metaphorical language.

We might think of this as the "clarity" rule. The purpose of a definition is to clarify our understanding of a concept. At the very least, therefore, the language we use in a definition should not be *less* clear than the concept being defined. Unfortunately, there are too many ways of being unclear to list them all here, but vagueness, obscurity, and metaphor are the three most common.

A *vague* definition is unclear because it does not give any precise criterion for membership in the concept. Suppose we define *maturity* as the stage of psychological development in which a person becomes well-adjusted. How do we tell whether a person is well-adjusted? Does adjustment mean passive acceptance of the social environment, or can it include a critical outlook? Is it primarily a set of cognitive skills, an emotional state, or both? As these questions indicate, the term "well-adjusted" is vague. It's unclear who belongs in the class of well-adjusted people and who doesn't; the class has highly indefinite boundaries. Of course, the concept MATURITY itself has indefinite boundaries, but a definition shouldn't make the problem worse.

An *obscure* definition is unclear because it uses abstract or technical language that is more difficult to understand than the concept itself. An example would be a definition of *death* as the cessation of one's participation in finitude. The problem here is not necessarily one of vagueness. In the appropriate context of a philosophical theory about human life and afterlife, this definition might have a perfectly clear and definite meaning. But that's the problem: it has a clear meaning only in a specialized context.

For general purposes, the defining terms are too obscure to be useful. The same is true of many technical definitions in law, science, or other specialized areas. Such definitions may be perfectly clear to specialists, but if the concept is employed outside the specialty, then we also need a general-purpose definition that is intelligible to laymen.

A *metaphorical* definition is unclear because it doesn't convey the literal meaning of the concept, but only an analogy that we have to interpret. A famous Broadway musical maintained that "Life is a cabaret." Like any good metaphor, this one uses a simple image to convey a complex thought that would take many paragraphs to explain in literal terms. But for a definition, we need the literal terms. A metaphor leaves too many questions unanswered. In exactly what ways is life like a cabaret? How far does the analogy extend? Is this the essential truth about life or just one perspective? Metaphors are valuable tools of thought and communication, but they can't do the work of definitions.

Altogether, then, there are six rules of definition. These rules give us standards for evaluating definitions proposed by other people and guidelines for creating definitions—as we will see in the next section.

REVIEW Rules for Definitions

1. A definition should include a genus and a differentia.
2. A definition should not be too broad or too narrow.
3. A definition should state the essential attributes of the concept's referents.
4. A definition should not be circular.
5. A definition should not use negative terms unnecessarily.
6. A definition should not use vague, obscure, or metaphorical language.

EXERCISE 1.5C

I. **Integrative Exercise** For each of the following definitions, identify the genus (if it has one) and the differentia. Then identify which rule (or rules) it violates.

✳1. A *necklace* is a jewel worn on a pendant around the neck.

2. A *tree* is a plant with thick roots.

3. *Art* is any object or action created by an artist.

✳4. A *squirrel* is a rat in a fur coat.

5. *Garbage* is what's left when you finish eating.

6. A *conspiracy* is a collusion in machination.

✳7. A person has *integrity* when he or she plays by the rules.

8. A *bar* is a wooden counter where alcoholic beverages are served.

9. *Seeing* is visually perceiving.

✳10. A *drunk* is a person who is not sober.

11. *Education* is when someone learns something.

12. *Eloquence* is the ability to arouse emotions by means of words.

*13. *Disappointment* is not getting what you want.

14. *Running* is an aerobic activity useful for quick weight loss.

15. An *orphan* is a person who does not have a living parent.

*16. A *debate* is an exercise in obscuring the weakness in one's own position by browbeating one's opponent.

17. A *conservative* is a person who opposes legalized abortion.

18. A *stranger* is a friend one has yet to meet.

*19. A *jacket* is an outer garment designed to protect the wearer from cold, wind, and rain.

20. *Liberty* is a political condition in which people are free.

II. **Integrative Exercise** The verbal form of a definition is often used for jokes, witty observations, or insights. Ten examples are given below. If these were intended as serious definitions, what rules would they violate?

*1. "A gentleman is a person who never insults another person unintentionally." [Anonymous]

2. "Happiness is having a large, loving, caring, close-knit family in another city." [George Burns]

3. "Propaganda is the art of persuading others of what you don't believe yourself." [Abba Eban]

*4. "Hypocrisy is the tribute that vice pays to virtue." [La Rochefoucauld]

5. "Old age is when the liver spots show through your gloves." [Phyllis Diller]

6. "Home is the place where, when you have to go there, they have to take you in." [Robert Frost]

*7. "Conservative, n. A statesman who is enamored of existing evils, as distinguished from the Liberal, who wants to replace them with others." [Ambrose Bierce]

8. "What is a cynic? A man who knows the price of everything, and the value of nothing." [Oscar Wilde]

9. "A definition is the enclosing a wilderness of ideas within a wall of words." [Samuel Butler]

*10. "Love means never having to say you're sorry." [Erich Segal]

1.6 Constructing Definitions

Definitions do not appear out of thin air. It's up to us to construct our own. To come up with definitions that satisfy the rules we've learned, we need a procedure we can follow—a technique for constructing definitions.

Of the six rules of definition, the first three are the most important. If you can find a genus and differentia that, together, are neither too broad nor too narrow, and that state the essential attributes of the referents of the concept, you can be pretty sure that your definition will satisfy the remaining three rules. We can think of those other rules as backup tests. To define a concept, therefore, the first step is to find the genus. Then look for a differentia that states the essential attributes of the referents and distinguishes them from other species of the same genus. Finally, double-check your definition by looking for counterexamples and by making sure that your definition is not circular, negative, or unclear. Let's look a little more closely at each step. Then we'll apply our techniques to a particular case.

If we start by finding the genus, it will make the rest of the job easier. Suppose we want to define CUP. We would use what we know about classification to locate the concept in a genus–species hierarchy:

Now we know that our definition will have the form, "A cup is a drinking vessel that ___." And we're in a good position to fill in the blank—to find the differentia. We know we have to distinguish cups from mugs and glasses, so we'll look for properties such as shape or function that will best do the job.

In defining a term, we are concerned only with its literal meaning, not with any metaphorical use. A metaphor typically applies a concept from one genus to things in some other genus. An army, for example, is a military organization, but the term "army" is used metaphorically to describe nonmilitary groups that are similar in one way or another, such as an army of ants. If we tried to define ARMY in such a way as to include these metaphors, we couldn't use MILITARY ORGANIZATION as the genus. Indeed, there is no genus we could use, because we could not possibly anticipate every metaphorical use of the term. But we don't need to include the metaphorical uses. The purpose of a definition is to give the *literal* meaning of a concept.

When we choose a genus, we need to consider the appropriate level of abstraction. As noted, the genus of CUP would be DRINKING VESSEL. But a drinking vessel is a kind of *utensil*, which is a kind of *tool*, which is a kind of *man-made object*. Each of these terms is more abstract than the one before and covers a wider range of things. Any of them could serve as the genus. Why choose the narrowest one, DRINKING VESSEL? The answer lies in the rule that a definition should state essential attributes. If we choose UTENSIL as the genus for CUP, then our differentia would still have to include the information that a cup is a utensil used for drinking. That's the function of a cup, and the function explains why a cup has a certain size and shape. The function is an essential attribute, so we might as well include it in the genus.

In contrast, we used ANIMAL as the genus in defining HUMAN, but this is *not* the narrowest genus. Humans are also *vertebrates*, *mammals*, and *primates*. Each of these terms is narrower, less abstract, than the one before. Again, any of them could serve as the genus. Why choose the wider genus, ANIMAL? Once again, we consider which features of humans are essential. The feature we share with other vertebrates, for example, is a spinal column. However important that feature of our anatomy may be, it is not as fundamental as the biological attributes we share with all animals: being alive, having needs for sustenance, reproducing, etc. Our similarities to other primates, mammals, or vertebrates are not as essential as our similarity to all animals. So unless we have a specialized purpose, as biologists do, there is no need to mention these other similarities. Remember that a definition is selective. Its purpose is to condense the information we have about a concept by stating only the fundamental facts.

The main thing to keep in mind when you look for a differentia is that it should distinguish the referents of the concept from the referents of other species in the same genus. It should name an attribute possessed by all the referents of the concept and not possessed by members of the other species; this will ensure that the definition is neither too broad nor too narrow (rule 2). You may be able to find many attributes shared by all the referents, but you should not include them all unless they are all necessary to distinguish the concept from other species in the genus. Once again, a definition should be selective, so look for the essential attribute (rule 3).

When we apply rule 2, we should keep in mind the possibility of borderline cases. Suppose we're defining CITY. Cities are distinguished from other municipalities mainly on the basis of population. Our definition should thus include any place large enough to be considered a city and exclude any place too small. A place with 1,000 residents is obviously a village or town, while a metropolis of 2 million is clearly a city. But there is no sharp line between a large town and a small city. So how would we define CITY?

We have two choices. If we do not have any specialized need for precision, then we should define a city simply as a *large* metropolis. The term "large" clearly includes the metropolis of 2 million, it clearly excludes the village of 1,000, and it leaves the borderline area unclear. Thus it matches the content of the ordinary concept, including the indefinite areas around the borders. In general, we can expect a definition to help clarify boundaries, but we cannot expect it to set more definite boundaries than the concept itself has. However, if we do need a concept with a precise borderline, as we may if we are taking a census or doing economic research, then we will have to specify a precise criterion of population size and turn the concept into a technical one. A definition of this type is sometimes called a "precising definition."

A precising definition is a special case of a more general type: the **stipulative definition**. A stipulative definition introduces a new word by specifying that it shall mean such and such. We may need to do this in the case of new technological products (e.g., blockchain software), new scientific discoveries (e.g., quarks), new professions (e.g., programming), and so forth. We may also need to give a new meaning to an old word; in physics, for example, "work" is defined as the product of the force applied to an object and its displacement in the direction of that force. Stipulative definitions are not subject to rule 2. Because the term being defined has no antecedent meaning, the definition cannot be too narrow or too broad. But this does not mean that such definitions are arbitrary. They are appropriate only when the referents of the new term are important enough, and distinctive enough, to require their own concept. And once we have created the new concept, its definition is still subject to rule 3: It should state the essential attributes of those referents.

When we apply rule 3 to a definition (whether stipulative or ordinary), there's another qualification to keep in mind. As we have seen, an essential attribute is one that underlies and explains other attributes of the referents. One of the goals of science is to identify such attributes. But it is not always appropriate to incorporate scientific theories when we define a concept for ordinary use. We can define water as the substance with the chemical structure H_2O, because that chemical structure, which explains many of the other properties of water, is so well established that it has become common knowledge. But it would *not* be appropriate to define man as the animal with the most complex brain—even though that complexity is likely to be what gives us our capacity for reason. The problem here is that the relationships between the brain and reason are

---

SOLVE　Constructing Definitions

To construct a definition for a concept *C*:

1. Find the genus of the concept—the broader concept that includes *C* and other, related concepts from which one needs to distinguish *C*.

2. Choose a differentia that distinguishes *C* from other concepts in the same genus.

If there is more than one distinguishing attribute, choose the most essential one.

3. Check to make sure that the resulting definition is not circular, unnecessarily negative, or unclear.

4. Look for counterexamples to your definition.

---

not very well known yet; the available theories are speculative and incomplete, and it wouldn't serve our purpose to incorporate them into a definition. So the rule of essentiality must be qualified: The differentia should name the most essential attributes that are fairly well understood.

For the same reason, it is not a good idea to include controversial information in a definition. Our concepts, and the definitions we give them, provide the framework for thought and discussion. Ideally, the framework should be a neutral one, so that people on opposite sides of an issue can rely on a common understanding of the relevant concepts in presenting their arguments and thus understand each other. I may be convinced, for example, that psychological depression results from repressed anxiety, but this theory about the unconscious cause of depression is controversial. If I'm going to discuss the matter with a psychologist who rejects that theory, we should define depression in terms of properties we can agree on, such as the conscious feelings involved.

Once we have established the genus and differentia, the final step is to test our definition. We should make sure that it is not circular, that it is not negative (unless the concept itself is a negative one), and that it does not use vague, obscure, or metaphorical language. And we should make an effort to find counterexamples. That is, we should look for things that are included in the concept but would be excluded by the definition: They would prove that the definition is too narrow. And we should look for things that are *not* included in the concept, but *would* be included by the definition; in that case, our definition is too broad. If we have looked for counterexamples and haven't found any, then we can be more confident that our definition is correct.

Let's see how the general procedure works in practice by trying to define the concept GAME. This is a fairly abstract concept, covering indoor games played with cards, boards, or dice; outdoor games played with balls; races of all kinds; and even simple things like throwing a ball against a wall and catching it before it hits the ground. Let's see whether we can come up with a definition that covers all of these diverse activities.

As usual, we should start by looking for the genus. A game is a kind of human activity, so we need to contrast it with other human activities. The first thing that should occur to us is that games can be contrasted with jobs. There's a basic difference between working and playing; games belong in the second category. Of course, people sometimes describe their jobs as games, as in "I'm in the real-estate game." But this is clearly a metaphor: It's intended to startle the listener precisely because a job is *not* literally a game. So games belong in the genus we've described as "play." To make it clear that we are talking about the leisure activities of adults as well as children, let's use the term *recreation*. What else does this genus include? In addition to games, RECREATION includes activities such as hobbies and pastimes, vacation traveling, and dancing. Our classification now looks like this:

This is not an exhaustive list of recreational activities. (Can you think of any others?) And of course recreation and work are not the only activities that human beings engage in. Among other things, we have left out family and social life. But this classification is enough for our purposes.

Before we turn to the differentia, let's pause to consider the nature of the genus we have isolated. Recreation is an activity and so is work. The difference clearly has something to do with goals and rewards. It will help us to understand games if we explore this difference a little further. What goal does one pursue in work? Take a doctor as an example. In one respect, a doctor's goal is restoring people to health: That is the function of medicine. In another respect, a doctor's goal may be to make money, or to help people, or to use his mind in solving problems. Notice that the first goal is common to all doctors: Restoring health is a goal intrinsic to medicine; it is the *function* of medicine. However, the personal goals that doctors have are not intrinsic to medicine as a profession. They vary from one doctor to another; they're a matter of the individual's *motivation*. We could draw this same distinction between function and motivation in any line of work.

Now let's consider recreation. Here, too, personal motivation differs from one individual to another. Some people play to relax, while others play to prove themselves; professional athletes and gamblers play for money. The common element in any given type of recreation, therefore, will have to be a goal intrinsic to the activity itself—a goal analogous to the function of a given line of work. This is where the essential difference lies between work and recreation. In any type of work, the function is producing a good or service that has value in its own right, apart from the activity of producing it. In recreation, the intrinsic goal is not productive in that sense. The activity is an end in itself, something we do merely for the sake of doing it. This would be true even for a professional athlete, who is being paid to play the game, to create an exciting spectacle that other people want to see. In that sense the athlete is working, not playing. But the game itself (football, golf, or whatever) is still a form of recreation because the goals internal to the game (getting a touchdown, sinking the putt) are not valuable in and of themselves. They have value only as elements in an activity that people value for its own sake.

Keeping all this in mind, let's try to find a differentia that will distinguish games from other types of recreation. Some games are played with cards, others with balls, others with boards; some are physical, some are mental; some involve mostly skill, others mostly luck. So none of these properties can serve as our differentia, which has to be a property common to all the referents. What about competition between players? Most games do have a competitive element, but this definition would still be too narrow, because some games do not involve competition. Solitaire and sudoku are counterexamples. Couldn't we say, though, that in these cases we are competing against ourselves? We often do describe solitary games this way. The problem is that this description is metaphorical. If we took it literally, it would mean that you are your own opponent. If you are competing against yourself, and you win, who loses?

But let's not give up yet. When you play solitaire, you may not literally be competing, but it's still true that you can win or lose. That's because the rules of the game set a certain goal, such as turning up all the cards; if you achieve the goal, you win. Here we have something that looks like a universal property, and an essential one. What would a game be without *rules*? In every game, there is a set of rules that says what the goal is (the object of the game) and also says what means you can use to achieve the goal. This is what creates the challenge of a game and leads us to use the metaphor of competing with ourselves. Even in competitive games, the existence of rules is a more essential attribute than competition, because the rules create the competition: They specify the number of players and the terms on which they will compete.

Our definition, then, might be stated as follows:

> A game is a form of recreation constituted by a set of rules that specify an object to be attained and the permissible means of attaining it.

Notice the word "constituted" here. It was carefully chosen to convey the idea that the very structure of the game depends on the rules. Notice also that the differentia fits in well with our analysis of the genus. We saw that recreation should not be distinguished from work in terms of personal goals. Either activity can be done for fun or profit. They should be distinguished rather in terms of the goals intrinsic to the activities. And our differentia tells us where a game's internal goal comes from.

Let's test the definition by looking for counterexamples. Is it too broad? Would it include anything that is not a game? It's certainly true that other recreational activities are governed by rules. In skiing, there are traffic rules—you shouldn't bump into other people. In stamp collecting, stealing the stamps you want would violate the law. But each of these rules is superimposed on an activity that could be done without them. They do not give the activity its goal; they merely impose external constraints on the means one can use. So these activities are not constituted by rules in the way our definition requires.

Is the definition too narrow? Would it exclude any games? What about throwing a ball against a wall and catching it? Well, in a sense, there is a rule here that specifies a goal and the permissible means: "Throw the ball against the wall and catch it before it bounces." That isn't much of a rule. But then this isn't much of a game. It is not clear whether this activity satisfies our definition, but it's equally unclear whether the activity should be considered a game. What we have here is a borderline case, and, as we have seen, we cannot demand that a definition have sharper boundaries than the concept it defines (unless we need to turn the concept into a technical one). All we can ask is that the definition include everything that is clearly a member of the concept, exclude everything that is clearly not a member, and leave the same set of borderline cases uncertain.

So far as we can see, therefore, our definition is a good one. You'll have to decide for yourself whether you agree—perhaps there is something we have overlooked. But regardless of whether we agree on the outcome, the process of reasoning behind it illustrates the technique to follow in defining a concept.

EXERCISE 1.6

I. **Integrative Exercise** Complete each of the following definitions of the italicized concepts, using the procedures described in this section.

*1. A *newspaper* is a periodical that is _____, containing _____.

2. *Flattery* is _____ that is excessive and _____.

3. An *apartment* is _____.

*II. **Integrative Exercise** Arrange the following concepts in a classification diagram, showing the species–genus relationships. Then define each concept.

TABLE, BED, FURNITURE, DESK, CHAIR

1.7 Propositions and Word Meaning

Consider the following statements:

Most cars have four wheels.

The Empire State Building is over 1,000 feet tall.

Jack is a Baptist.

The theory of relativity in physics has been well confirmed by experiments.

Each of these statements has a linguistic form as an English sentence. And each of the sentences has a meaning; it expresses a thought. The meaning or thought is a **proposition**.

When we engage in reasoning, the units of thought are propositions. Understanding propositions is a vital skill in reasoning. When we take a position on an issue, we are asserting that a certain proposition is true. If we can't distinguish between propositions that are similar but not identical, then we don't really know what we believe, and we can't tell whether someone else's position contradicts our own. When we weigh the evidence for and against some conclusion, we need to use the principles of logic that we are going to cover in later chapters, and those principles identify certain relations among propositions. In this section, we will study propositions—what they are and how to tell them apart.

A proposition is a complete thought, normally expressed in a complete sentence, making a statement that it is either true or false. The first proposition, for example, uses the concept CAR, which designates a category of things, but the sentence also *says* something about cars, something that is either true or false. In the same way, the phrase "the Empire State Building" names a certain structure in New York City but does not say anything about it, whereas the second proposition does make a definite statement. And even if you don't happen to know whether the statement is true or false, you know that it must be one or the other.

Propositions, and the sentences that express them, must have a subject and a predicate:

Subject	Predicate
Most cars	have four wheels.
The Empire State Building	is over 1,000 feet tall.
Jack	is a Baptist.
The theory of relativity in physics	has been well confirmed by experiments.

The subject term refers to some thing or class of things, and the predicate says what the subject is or does. A proposition must have this basic structure—subject and predicate—in order to be complete. A subject without a predicate, or a predicate without a subject, is not a complete thought that is either true or false. For example:

Game 1 in the playoffs

The Pillsbury Dough Boy

ran too fast for me to catch him

was two blocks south of the library

The first two examples might serve as subjects, the second two as predicates, but none of them by itself is a proposition.

A proposition, to summarize, is the thought that a sentence expresses—or, more precisely, the content of that thought—while a sentence is the linguistic vehicle we use to express it, just as an individual word is the linguistic vehicle we use to express a concept. The term "statement," finally, is usually understood to mean a proposition as expressed linguistically. When we are not focused on the difference between thought and expression, we will use "statement" interchangeably with "proposition." But it is important here at the outset that you understand the difference. Two different sentences may express the same proposition, just as two different words may express the same concept. And a single sentence may express more than one proposition. In this section, we will see how individual words contribute to the meaning of a sentence and how variations in the words it uses can affect the proposition it asserts. Then we'll turn to the grammatical structure of the sentence and see how the rules of grammar allow us to formulate more and more complex sorts of thoughts.

Suppose we have two sentences that differ only in one word: "Jack is an X" and "Jack is a Y." If "X" and "Y" express the same concept, then these two sentences assert the same proposition; if the words express different concepts, then the sentences assert different propositions. That's the general rule, and it's often easy to apply. If the two words are synonyms, the resulting sentences make the same statement:

Jack is a *lawyer*.

Jack is an *attorney*.

"Lawyer" and "attorney" are different words, but they express the same concept, so both sentences express the same proposition despite the different words.

If the words are unrelated, the sentences make different statements:

Jack is *tall*.

Jack is *married*.

"Tall" and "married" obviously express different concepts, so these sentences express different propositions.

The tricky cases are those in which the words are related but not identical in meaning:

Jack is a *Baptist*.

Jack is a *Christian*.

Baptists are one denomination of Christians, so the propositions are related. If the first is true, then the second must also be true. But "Christian" is a more abstract term; it is a genus that includes other denominations besides Baptists. So here again the sentences express different prepositions.

There is no single rule for determining whether two words express the same concept. We need to use our understanding of word meanings—including what we've learned about classification and definitions—to ask whether the words pick out the same class of things; and, if so, whether they isolate those things on the basis of the same distinguishing properties. But it will help to consider two specific issues: word connotations and metaphors.

1.7A Connotations

Two words that express the same concept are usually considered to be synonyms: "couch" and "sofa," "car" and "automobile," "own" and "possess," and so on. But sometimes words that express the same concept have different *connotations*. They convey different images or feelings; they elicit different associations in our minds; they express different attitudes. For example, in a letter of recommendation for a student, I could make the same point with either of two sentences:

Felicia has *firm command* of the subject matter.

Felicia has a *thorough understanding* of the subject matter.

These sentences assert the same proposition, because the italicized phrases express the same concept. But the first conveys the image of power and control over the material, whereas the second is more bland; it doesn't really convey any image at all. A good writer makes use of such differences in connotation to achieve a desired effect. But we shouldn't be misled by different connotations into thinking that different propositions have been asserted. This is especially important when the connotations involve strong positive or negative attitudes.

On the negative side, we have derogatory slang terms for racial and ethnic groups and for professions. To pick two of the less offensive ones: "cop" used to be a derogatory term for a policeman; "shrink" is an impolite term for a psychotherapist. In each case, the slang term stands for exactly the same class of people as the more polite term and expresses the same concept. The *only* difference is in connotation. On the positive side, the clearest examples are euphemisms. "Sanitary engineer" describes the same occupation as "garbage collector," but has a more dignified sound. In an earlier age, when people were more delicate in discussing bodily functions, it used to be said that animals *sweat*, men *perspire*, ladies *glisten*.

We need to be careful, though. Words that differ in connotation may also differ in literal meaning; they may not express the same concept. An unmarried couple who share the same address are sometimes described as *living together*, sometimes as *living in sin.* There's an obvious difference in meaning here: one phrase implies a moral judgment by classifying the couple with sinners; the other does not.

Before we decide that two words differ merely in connotation, therefore, we should make sure that they do not also differ in literal meaning. We should ask whether they attribute different properties to their referents or classify them in different ways.

EXERCISE 1.7A

For each pair of sentences that follows, determine whether the sentences express the same proposition.

✻1. a. You have a lovely view from your window.
    b. You have a beautiful view from your window.

2. a. Stealing is a sin.
    b. Stealing is a crime.

3. a. It's a pleasure to meet you.
    b. It's an honor to meet you.

✻4. a. Wendy is a journalist.
    b. Wendy works for a newspaper.

5. a. It was a tense moment.
    b. It was an anxious moment.

6. a. Henry proposed to her.
    b. Henry asked her to marry him.

✻7. a. The elderly person ahead of me was doing about 25 miles per hour.
    b. The geezer ahead of me was doing about 25 miles per hour.

8. a. George is a mellow individual.
    b. George is an unmotivated slob.

9. a. Paul broke up with Diane.
    b. Paul dumped Diane.

✻10. a. The activist was zealous about her cause.
    b. The activist was fanatical about her cause.

11. a. The lovers were preoccupied with each other.
    b. The lovers were obsessed with each other.

12. a. The smile she gave him when he left was insincere.
    b. The smile she gave him when he left was forced.

✻13. a. The enemy's intelligence operative was terminated with extreme prejudice.
    b. The enemy spy was deliberately killed.

14. a. That remark was offensive.
    b. That remark was insulting.

15. a. Pat had a good time at the party.
    b. Pat didn't have a bad time at the party.

1.7B Metaphors

A special problem arises in the case of metaphors. Strictly speaking, a metaphor is a particular figure of speech in which one thing is equated to another in order to bring out some point of similarity, as in the example we discussed earlier: "Life is a cabaret." In this strict sense, metaphors are distinguished from other figures of speech such as similes ("Life is like a box of chocolates"). But we will use the term "metaphor" more broadly here to include *any* nonliteral use of language.

We have seen that metaphors are not appropriate in definitions, but they are extremely valuable in other contexts, and we use them all the time. They allow us to make our language more colorful and interesting; they convey similarities and shades of meaning that would otherwise be difficult to express. For that very reason, however, it is often difficult to interpret a metaphorical sentence, to formulate in literal terms the proposition it asserts.

For example, when the poet Robert Burns said "My love is like a red, red rose," he was making a comparison. But in what respects? He wasn't making a biological comparison: he didn't mean that he was dating a form of plant life. Presumably he meant his love was beautiful—that is the literal meaning of the metaphor. Yet the two statements

My love is like a red, red rose

and

My love is beautiful

do not express quite the same proposition. "Beautiful" is a very abstract word. The point of this metaphor is to convey the particular *kind* of beauty she has: the dark and delicate, regal beauty of a red rose, not the more exotic beauty of an orchid, or the sturdier, sunnier beauty of a daffodil. And roses have thorns. So perhaps the poet also means to say that his love is prickly and temperamental. You can see that it would be extremely hard to find a literal statement that asserts exactly the same proposition.

Why do we have to find a literal translation? Why can't we just say that the poet is expressing the proposition: My love is like a red rose? Well, sometimes we *can* let it go at that. We can savor the metaphor without analyzing it. In the context of reasoning, however, where we are concerned with the logical relationships among propositions, a literal translation is usually necessary. To know how a given proposition is logically related to others, we have to know exactly what the proposition does and doesn't say. If two people are using metaphorical terms in an argument, we won't know whether they are really talking about the same issue until we formulate their positions in literal terms. For example:

She: You always keep your feelings bottled up inside.

He: You want me to let everything just hang out there?

In these situations, we have to interpret metaphors, and the only rule we have is a fairly vague one: we should give as full, sensitive, and reasonable an interpretation as we can. Usually it is not difficult to find a reasonable interpretation. In our example, the literal meaning behind the metaphors of "bottled up" and "hang out there" is being less or more emotionally expressive and responsive.

Few of the metaphors we encounter are as rich in meaning as the ones we find in poetry. For example, to describe something as a "Band-Aid solution" is to say that it doesn't solve the underlying problem, but is only a short-term or superficial treatment. This is a one-dimensional metaphor and is easily put into literal terms.

Our language is also filled with "dead" metaphors: words so often used to express an idea metaphorically that they now contain the idea as part of their literal meaning. Thus we often speak of *grasping* a fact: "Grasp" is a physical metaphor for the mental act of understanding, but it has been used so often that *understanding* is now considered one of the literal meanings of the word. In the same way, we often describe pains as *sharp*, people as *dense*, spicy food as *hot*, relationships as *stormy*, and so on. If you think about it, you can see that each of the italicized terms is based on a metaphor that is now incorporated into its literal meaning. In such cases, there is no need for interpretation at all.

SOLVE Words in Propositions

To determine whether two sentences assert the same proposition:

1. Use techniques of classification and definition to identify the concepts the words express.

2. Ignore differences in connotation.

3. Find a literal interpretation of all metaphors.

EXERCISE 1.7B

I. For each of the metaphorical statements below, formulate a literal equivalent.

✲1. The teacher's announcement was electrifying.

2. Kim is not dealing from a full deck.

3. Jamal's boss ripped his head off at a staff meeting.

✲4. The budget that the president submitted to Congress was dead on arrival.

5. They never clean their attic; it's like the bottom of a bird cage up there.

6. He had a nagging feeling that she was lying.

✲7. The article glossed over the controversy.

8. Jerry was a loose cannon.

9. Fannie Mae and Freddie Mac would have gone under if not for a government bailout.

✲10. Roger was such a good salesman; he could talk a possum out of a tree.

II. **Integrative Exercise** For each word below, find two other words that express the same concept, one with a more positive connotation, the other with a more negative connotation. If you were given "elderly person," for example, you might complete the series as follows:

Positive	Neutral	Negative
senior citizen	elderly person	geezer

You may use metaphors as well as literal terms.

✲1. Government official

2. Physically disabled

3. Deceased person

✲4. Overeating

5. Dirty

6. Prostitute

✲7. Elated

8. Businessman

9. Married

✲10. Mentally disabled

1.8 Propositions and Grammar

1.8A Propositions and Sentence Structure

Some people seem to think grammar is an arbitrary, conventional set of rules—a kind of verbal etiquette, with no more objective basis than the convention that the fork goes on the left side of the plate. Nothing could be further from the truth. Most grammatical rules and structures serve the purpose of maintaining clarity in thought and speech. A sentence is made up of words, but if it is to have any meaning, the words cannot be put together randomly. They must be structured in a certain way, just as building materials—bricks, beams, pipes, and shingles—must be put together in a certain way to make a house. The rules of grammar tell us how to put words together, just as a blueprint tells us how to assemble a building. A mastery of grammar allows us to formulate a thought clearly, no matter how complex or subtle it is, and to express the thought in a way that allows other people to share and appreciate it.

There is much that could be said about the cognitive role of grammar, but our concern in this chapter is specifically with the way the grammatical structure of a sentence affects the propositions it expresses. There are three basic points we need to be aware of in this regard:

1. Two different grammatical structures can be equivalent, just as two words can be synonymous.
2. A single sentence can assert more than a single proposition.
3. A sentence does not always assert every proposition that it expresses.

1. Two different grammatical structures can be equivalent, just as two words can be synonymous.

We've seen that it is possible to replace a word in a sentence with a synonym for the word without changing the proposition the sentence asserts. We can also change the word order without changing the proposition. For example:

The Mets beat the Red Sox.

The Red Sox were beaten by the Mets.

"The Mets" is the subject of the first sentence, "the Red Sox" is the subject of the second; the first is in the active voice, the second in the passive; but they describe the same action and express the same proposition. The same is true for:

Jane did better than Tom on the test.

Tom did worse than Jane on the test.

In this case we reversed the order of "Jane" and "Tom" and replaced "better" with "worse," but the two sentences describe the same relationship between their test scores. Logically, they are equivalent; they assert the same proposition.

2. A single sentence can assert more than a single proposition.

This is true even of the simplest type of sentence, which contains a single subject and predicate, because we can use adjectives and other modifiers to incorporate additional information. Suppose someone says,

We live in a red house near the lake.

The statement contains the following information:

> We live in a house.
> The house is red.
> The house is near the lake.

Each of these is a proposition asserted by the sentence, and the speaker is saying that each proposition is true.

Here is an example of a somewhat more complex sentence, along with a breakdown into its constituent propositions:

> Samuel Morse, who invented the telegraph and made a fortune from it, was also a painter whose work is highly regarded and often exhibited.

> > Samuel Morse invented the telegraph.
> > Samuel Morse made a fortune from the telegraph.
> > Samuel Morse was a painter.
> > Samuel Morse's work is highly regarded.
> > Samuel Morse's work is often exhibited.

Once again, the sentence asserts each of these propositions. If it is true, then the five propositions must be true as well, and vice versa. The original sentence is a much more economical way of presenting the information, but it is logically equivalent to the constituent propositions, taken as a set.

When we encounter a complex sentence like this one, how do we identify the constituent propositions? The best approach is to imagine that we are the ones making the statement and to ask: What has to be true for the statement as a whole to be true? How many distinct facts are involved? Or we can imagine that someone else has made the statement and think of all the possible ways of challenging it. Think of all the propositions that, if they were false, would undercut the statement as a whole.

3. A sentence does not always assert every proposition that it expresses.

So far in this chapter, we have been talking about the distinction between propositions and sentences and the relationship between them—the ways in which a sentence expresses one or more propositions. Now we need to consider another distinction and another relationship. When we use a sentence to make a definite statement, we are *asserting* the proposition: We are saying that it is true. But we can also think about possibilities that may or may not be real. In such cases, the content of the thought is a proposition, but you are not committing yourself to its truth. When you put the thought into words, you express the proposition without asserting it.

The grammar of English gives us many ways of expressing propositions without asserting them. Here's a typical example:

> The reelection of the president depends on whether [the economy will improve by November].

The proposition in brackets—that the economy will improve by November—is contained in the statement as a whole, but the speaker is not asserting that this component proposition is true. He's only asserting that the president's reelection depends on whether or not it turns out to be true. Suppose you are the speaker, and someone walks into the room halfway through the statement; all he hears is ". . . the economy will improve by November." If he assumes that you are making a prediction and chides you later, when the prediction turns out false, you would object that you weren't actually committing yourself to the truth of the proposition. We indicate this fact by saying that the statement *expresses* the component proposition, but does not *assert* it.

In the remainder of this section, we will look at some of the specific grammatical structures that determine what propositions a sentence asserts and which of them are unasserted. The more you are able to see past the surface complexities of language to its propositional content, the easier you will find it to understand and apply the rules of logical inference we will cover in the rest of the book.

REVIEW Propositions and Sentence Structure

1. Two different grammatical structures can be equivalent, just as two words can be synonymous.

2. A single sentence can assert more than a single proposition.

3. A sentence does not always assert every proposition that it expresses.

EXERCISE 1.8A

I. Determine whether the following pairs of sentences assert the same proposition.

*1. a. The couch is in front of the window.
   b. The window is behind the couch.

2. a. The salmon struggled to swim upstream.
   b. The salmon fought their way upstream.

3. a. I spilled the coffee.
   b. The coffee was spilled.

*4. a. The paintings were interspersed with the drawings.
   b. The drawings were among the paintings.

5. a. The man who painted my house is the brother of my best friend.
   b. My best friend's brother painted my house.

II. Integrative Exercise   List the component propositions in each example below.

*1. She arrived in time but out of breath.

2. The ice on the river is thick enough to hold our weight.

3. A bald man wearing pajamas chased the tax collector down the street.

*4. Beavers, which are a type of rodent, build dams that can flood a whole valley.

5. The most annoying thing about Jenny, my ex-girlfriend, was that she chewed her nails.

III. **Integrative Exercise** Determine whether the italicized proposition in each of the sentences below is asserted or unasserted.

✳1. I don't care whether *it rains*.

2. I could fly if *I had wings*.

3. The prosecution said the butler committed the murder, but in fact *the butler was out playing Bingo that night*.

✳4. The photos were disqualified because the judges found that *they had been altered*.

5. The abandoned wooden church, gray and dusty, looked as if *it was built a hundred years ago*.

1.8B Connectives

As we saw, a single sentence can assert more than a single proposition. Now let's consider a specific way we can do this. In the sentence "Jack *and* Jill went up the hill," "and" joins two subjects to make two statements: that Jack went up the hill and that Jill went up the hill. We can do the same thing with predicates, as in "Jack fell down *and* broke his crown," or with two complete sentences where the square brackets indicate the component propositions:

[Jack fell down and broke his crown] and [Jill came tumbling after].

When we join two complete sentences in this way, the result is a compound sentence. There are many other words that perform the same function as "and," such as:

[Nothing works any more] *but* [nobody cares].

[I went to the kitchen] *because* [I was hungry].

[He ran from the scene], *for* [he was afraid].

After [the storm passed], [the temperature dropped].

In grammar, these connecting words are called conjunctions. In logic, however, we use the term "conjunction" in a narrower sense, to refer specifically to "and." We refer to the whole class of words used to make compound sentences as **connectives**. Connectives always join two or more components, like the ones indicated in brackets above, which we can represent symbolically as p, q, etc. The result is a new compound sentence that expresses a compound proposition—p and q; p but q; p because q; p, for q; after p, q; etc.—that is treated as a distinct proposition, above and beyond p and q. The reason is that compound propositions normally say something more than just the sum of their parts.

In the second sentence above, for example, the statement asserts that I went to the kitchen, it asserts that I was hungry, and it asserts that there is a certain relationship between these facts: My hunger was the cause or reason for going to the kitchen. That relationship is additional information we get through the connective. Many other connectives are like "because" in asserting a relationship of dependence, including "since," "whenever," "therefore," and "so that." Connectives like "after," "before," "when," "while," and "where" assert a relationship of time or place. Connectives like "but," "although," and "even though" assert a relationship of contrast or seeming opposition.

In all these cases, the conjunction combines component propositions into a statement in which *all* components are being asserted as true. Thus in a statement with the form *after p, q*, such as "After I do the dishes, I'll go out for a walk," we are asserting *p* ("I'll do the dishes"), we are asserting *q* ("I'll go out for a walk"), and we are asserting a connection between *p* and *q*: Doing the dishes will occur before going for a walk.

This is not the case, however, with certain other connectives. Consider the following statements:

If [my cat could talk], [I'd be ruined].

Either [my cat is talking], *or* [I am hearing things].

Unless [it rains today], [the Yankees will play the Red Sox].

A statement using one of these connectives asserts that a certain relation exists between the component propositions, but does not assert the components themselves. The first sentence does not assert that my cat can talk, nor does it assert that I am ruined; all it says is that *if* the first were true, the second would be true as well. In the same way, the second sentence does not assert that my cat is talking, nor does it assert that I am hearing things; all it says is that one or the other of these propositions must be true. And the last one does not actually assert that the Yankees will play the Red Sox, since it leaves open the possibility that rain will cancel the game. In all of these examples, therefore, only one proposition, the compound one, is actually being asserted. The components themselves are being expressed but are *unasserted*.

A statement may include more than one connective, joining more than two components. We have seen an example already: [Jack fell down] *and* [broke his crown] *and* [Jill came tumbling after]. In this case, each of the three components is asserted. That will not always be the case, as in these statements:

If [a student lacks the prerequisite for Psychology 234] *but* [gets the permission], [he may enroll].

UNASSERTED   UNASSERTED   UNASSERTED

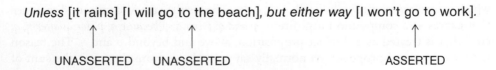

Unless [it rains] [I will go to the beach], *but either way* [I won't go to work].

UNASSERTED   UNASSERTED   ASSERTED

EXERCISE 1.8B

In each example below, identify the connective(s) and the component propositions. Then determine whether those component propositions are asserted (a) or unasserted (u).

∗1. His mind was racing, but his body was in the lead.

2. I'm okay, and you are a cockroach.

3. Either the clinic will be open over the holidays, or a doctor will be on call.

∗4. After the ice storm ended, the trees glittered in the sun.

5. If Dick and Mindy get married in Anchorage, none of their friends will come to the wedding.

6. While the bride lowered her veil, the bridesmaid fluffed her train.

∗7. If Sparky hears the car in the driveway, he runs to the back door.

8. The Becketts will move to Arizona unless Mr. Beckett is not offered the promotion.

9. Either Congress will pass legislation allowing children of undocumented immigrants to remain in the United States or Neya will be deported to El Salvador.

∗10. If Vladimir Putin wants to generate domestic support in Russia, he needs to expand control over neighboring countries and portray the United States as an enemy.

1.8C Restrictive and Nonrestrictive Clauses

A clause is a grammatical unit containing a subject and a predicate. Every sentence, therefore, contains at least one clause. But it may contain more. We have just seen how connectives serve to combine two or more clauses. The connective relates one clause, taken as a whole, to another clause, taken as a whole. A different type of structure can be seen in the following example:

Japanese people, who eat lots of fish, have fewer heart attacks.

The main clause in this sentence asserts the proposition that Japanese people have fewer heart attacks. But the sentence also contains a subordinate clause—"who eat lots of fish"—that modifies a particular phrase in the main clause: the subject, "Japanese people." As a result, the statement also asserts the proposition that the Japanese eat lots of fish.

This structure is known as a *relative clause*, because it relates one clause to a particular word in another clause. A relative clause normally begins with a *relative pronoun*: "who" or "whom," "which," or "that." And a relative clause normally asserts a proposition in addition to the one asserted by the main clause, as in the example above. But this is not always the case, as we can see by comparing it with:

Japanese people who eat lots of fish have fewer heart attacks.

What is the difference between these sentences? Well, in the second one, the relative clause restricts the reference of the term "Japanese people" to a certain subclass of

Japanese people: those who eat lots of fish. As a result, we are making a single statement about that subclass, and we are not making any statement about the Japanese people as a whole. We could diagram the statement as follows:

In our first example, by contrast, the commas tell us that the clause introduces a separate point and does *not* restrict the reference of the subject term. So the first example makes two statements: that the Japanese (as a whole) have fewer heart attacks and that the Japanese (as a whole, again) eat lots of fish. Thus:

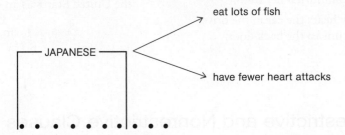

It's clear that the presence or absence of the commas makes a big difference to the meaning of these sentences, even though all the words are the same. A clause like the one in the second example is called a *restrictive* clause, because it restricts the reference of the term it modifies; a clause like the one in the first example is called a *nonrestrictive* clause, because it does *not* restrict that term's reference. To be clear about what proposition is being asserted, we need to know what class of things we are talking about. When a relative clause is involved, therefore, we must consider whether it is restrictive or nonrestrictive.

If we want to identify all the propositions asserted in these statements, the analysis would be as follows:

Sentence	Relative Clause	Asserted Propositions
Japanese people who eat lots of fish have fewer heart attacks.	Restrictive	The Japanese who eat lots of fish have fewer heart attacks.
Japanese people, who eat lots of fish, have fewer heart attacks.	Nonrestrictive	1. The Japanese have fewer heart attacks. 2. The Japanese eat lots of fish. 3. The Japanese eat lots of fish and the Japanese have fewer heart attacks.

Notice that in the third proposition of the nonrestrictive clause we have replaced the relative pronoun with "and" to make it clear that two distinct component propositions are being asserted.

The relative clauses in these sentences modify the subject term "Japanese people." Relative clauses can also modify a term in the predicate, and the same distinction between restrictive and nonrestrictive applies. For example:

Sentence	Relative Clause	Asserted Propositions
Kira hit the boy who was insulting her.	Restrictive	Kira hit the boy who was insulting her.
Kira hit the boy, who was insulting her.	Nonrestrictive	1. Kira hit the boy. 2. The boy was insulting her. 3. Kira hit the boy and the boy was insulting her.

In the first sentence, the relative clause beginning with "who" is restrictive. It isolates the particular boy whom Kira hit from any other boys present in the situation. So the sentence asserts only one proposition: that Kira hit the boy who was insulting her. In the second sentence, the relative clause is nonrestrictive. Presumably there is only one boy in the situation, or a particular boy has been identified by some earlier statement, so that we know to whom "the boy" refers. Then the relative clause makes an additional statement about him. In this case, the component propositions are that Kira hit the boy, and that the boy insulted her. And the statement as a whole makes the conjunctive assertion number 3: "Kira hit the boy and the boy was insulting her." Once again we have replaced the relative pronoun with "and" to make it clear that two distinct component propositions are being asserted.

EXERCISE 1.8C

Identify the relative clause in each sentence below, and determine whether it is restrictive or nonrestrictive.

✳1. People who live in glass houses shouldn't throw stones.

2. I love jewels that are expensive.

3. I love diamonds, which are expensive.

✳4. Wars that are waged in self-defense are justified.

5. The driver behind me, who has his headlights on bright, is a pain in the neck.

6. I prefer true/false tests, which give you a 50% chance of getting the answer.

✳7. We are looking for a person who was last seen wearing a Minnesota Twins baseball cap.

8. My accountant, who is very good, does not do his own taxes.

9. The wars that America wages against insurgencies rather than nation-states have had limited success.

✳10. Last semester I took a course in multivariable calculus, which is really hard.

1.8D Noun Clauses

Suppose you are discussing a candidate for public office, and someone mentions the candidate's unusual religious affiliation. You might find yourself saying:

[That Johnson is a Druid] is irrelevant.

The phrase within the brackets is called a noun clause because the whole clause functions as a noun. Like any clause, it contains a subject ("Johnson") and a predicate ("is a Druid"). Unlike the relative clauses we considered earlier, however, it doesn't modify anything, neither the subject nor the predicate, in the main clause. Rather, it *is* the subject. The noun clause turns the sentence "Johnson is a Druid" into the subject of a longer, more complex sentence. As a result, you have asserted two propositions. You have asserted that Johnson is a Druid. And you have asserted that this fact is irrelevant. In contrast, suppose you had said:

It is irrelevant [whether Johnson is a Druid].

Once again, the bracketed words are a noun clause and the subject of the sentence. You are still expressing two propositions here and still asserting that Johnson's religion is irrelevant. But this time you are *not* asserting that Johnson is a Druid. The word "whether" implies that you are leaving this as an open question.

A noun clause can also occur in the predicate of a sentence. It will still express a proposition, but once again the proposition may or may not be asserted. Compare these two sentences:

The president knows that war is imminent.

The president believes that war is imminent.

In both cases we are making an assertion about the president. In both cases we use a noun clause, "that war is imminent," to convey what it is that the president knows or believes. And in both cases the noun clause expresses a proposition. The difference is that the first sentence asserts the proposition, while the second does not.

If we say the president *knows* that war is imminent, we imply that the imminence of war is a fact. You can't know what isn't so. In the first sentence, therefore, we are not only attributing a certain view to the president, we are also endorsing his view as correct. So we are making two assertions: one about the president, the other about war. In the second, however, we are *not* endorsing the president's view. The word "believes" does not carry this implication. Even if we happen to agree with him, we are not committing ourselves. So in this case we are not asserting the proposition expressed by the noun clause. The only thing we're asserting is the proposition that the president does have this belief.

Notice that the difference between these two sentences results from the verbs we used: "knows" versus "believes." The English language contains a large class of verbs that we use to describe what people say and think. We can classify these verbs on the basis of whether or not they imply the endorsement of what is said or thought. Thus:

In the column on the left, we are making an assertion about *X*, but we are not asserting *p*. We mention *p* only to describe *X*'s thought or statement. In the column on the right, however, we *are* asserting *p*. In addition to the statement about *X*, we are committing ourselves to the truth of *p*. In the study of argument, it is crucial to know whether a speaker is endorsing a given proposition as one of his own premises or merely reporting that someone else accepts that proposition. (This distinction is less clear when a speaker makes this sort of statement about himself or herself. If Christiane Amanpour says, "I believe that war is imminent," she might well intend it as an assertion that war is imminent, not merely as an assertion about her own state of mind. In that case, there is no difference between "I believe . . ." and "I know. . . ." In such first-person statements of belief or conviction, you will have to judge from the context what the speaker intends to be asserting.)

SOLVE Asserted and Unasserted Propositions

A single sentence may express more than one proposition. To identify the component propositions:

1. Ask what facts are being asserted, i.e., what claims would have to be true for the sentence as a whole to be true.
2. Distinguish nonrestrictive clauses, which introduce a distinct proposition, from restrictive clauses, which do not.

A component proposition may be either asserted or merely expressed. To determine whether a proposition is asserted, ask whether the speaker is committing himself to its truth. Remember that:

1. In sentences of the form *p or q* and *if p then q*, the component propositions *p* and *q* are not asserted.
2. In sentences with a noun clause following a verb like "believes," "says," etc., the proposition expressed by the clause is not asserted.

EXERCISE 1.8D

Integrative Exercise For each of the following sentences, identify the propositions it asserts (a) and those it does not assert (u).

✳1. The little girl thinks that animals can talk.

2. John acknowledged that he had made a mistake.

3. I would like diamonds for Christmas, but I haven't been good this year.

✳4. He is convinced that two plus two equals four.

5. The dog, who loves his master, defended him against attack.

6. Gena, a dance student, decided that yoga would be a beneficial complement to her ballet training.

✻7. Samantha suspected that Zack was planning a surprise birthday party for her.

8. Many insects communicate by means of chemical substances, known as pheromones.

9. I met a man who had only one shoe.

✻10. If you buy two pairs of jeans, the third pair is free; and if your purchase is over $50, you get 30% off.

11. Graphic novels are becoming popular again, but as an art form rather than as commercial entertainment.

12. If Deborah takes the new job, she will make more money.

✻13. David was driving well above the speed limit, although he knew better.

14. People who believe in ghosts stay away from graveyards and deserted houses.

15. The Greek philosopher Democritus believed that all objects are made of atoms.

✻16. Professional baseball players, who make a lot of money, should not complain that the season is too long.

17. Samuel Taylor Coleridge, an English Romantic poet, would have finished "Kubla Khan" if he had not been interrupted.

18. The airline pilot was ready to take off, so he radioed the tower and signaled to the traffic controller.

✻19. The city planner called the zone developer because she wanted to find out whether the area had been marked and the architect had been chosen.

20. Although Miss Devon, the district attorney, did not have enough evidence to convict the thief, she knew that he was guilty.

21. After a harsh editorial appeared in the student newspaper, the president of the college said that students should be seen but not heard.

✻22. Because he is a living organism, man is mortal; because he is rational, he is aware of his mortality.

23. The politician realized that if he modified his stance on the smoking ban, he would have a better chance of winning the election.

24. The sweat glistened on the cowboy's brow as he decided whether the approaching man, who was dressed in black, was going to start a fight or leave him alone.

✻25. When we found our seats at the racetrack, we could hear the announcer reporting that Pardon My Dust was already ahead of Try Me, but he thought Try Me still had a chance at winning the handicap.

CHAPTER REVIEW

Summary

- Classification is the process of putting things together into groups on the basis of similarities. A concept is an idea that represents such a group. The concepts involved in a system of classification are organized into hierarchies of species and genuses. Every concept is abstract to some degree; a genus is more abstract than its species.
- When we subdivide a genus into species, we should use a consistent principle, so that the species are mutually exclusive and jointly exhaustive. We should also use essential attributes, so that the members of each species are fundamentally similar to each other and fundamentally different from members of other species.
- When we learn a new set of concepts, we need to identify genus–species relationships among the concepts. Concepts at the same level of abstractness should be placed at the same level in the hierarchy.
- The function of a definition is to identify the referents of the concept, condense the knowledge we have about the referents, and relate the concept to other concepts.
- A definition should mention the genus to which the concept belongs and the differentia (the set of essential characteristics) that distinguishes those referents from other species in the same genus. A definition should be neither too broad nor too narrow. It should not be circular, or use negative terms unnecessarily, or use language that is unclear.
- In constructing a definition, we should find the genus first, then look for a differentia that isolates the right class of referents and names their essential attributes, and finally double-check the result by looking for counterexamples and checking against the other rules.
- A proposition is a statement that is either true or false, normally expressed in a declarative sentence containing a subject and a predicate.
- To identify the proposition or propositions asserted by a sentence, we must consider the meanings of the words composing the sentence. In this context, two words are considered to have the same meaning if they express the same concept, even if they differ in connotation. When a word or phrase is being used metaphorically, we must find a literal interpretation if we are to determine what proposition is being asserted.
- It is possible to vary the grammatical structure of a sentence without changing the proposition it asserts. Grammatical devices such as connectives, restrictive and nonrestrictive clauses, and noun clauses allow us to combine more than one proposition into a single complex sentence. So to identify the components of a complex proposition, we must break that sentence down into its components, and differentiate between those propositions the sentence asserts and those it merely expresses.

Key Terms

classify (p. 2)

referent (p. 3)

genus (p. 4)

species (p. 4)

mutually exclusive (p. 7)

jointly exhaustive (p. 7)

definition (p. 16)

differentia (p. 18)

counterexample (p. 21)

stipulative definition (p. 28)

proposition (p. 32)

connective (p. 41)

Putting It All Together

I. In each of the following sentences, replace any **boldfaced** words with more abstract ones and any *italicized* words with more concrete ones.

∗1. Joan *walked* across the room.

2. The tall stranger **whirled** around and dashed his *drinking implement* against the fireplace.

3. Our daughter is going out with a *nice* young man.

∗4. My **kingdom** for a **horse**!

5. Mary expressed herself *with feeling*.

6. Life is but a *nonobjective sensory experience*.

∗7. A **government** cannot exist without popular support.

8. The only problem with Jeff is that he has this *thing* about math.

9. Around the bend lay a set of *dangerous* rapids.

∗10. In the years ahead, our country will face *many* problems.

II. For each of the following genuses, one species has been listed. List as many more as you can. If you are not familiar with the classification of terms within any of the genuses, use a dictionary or an encyclopedia.

∗1. Publications: magazine, . . .

2. Seasonings: herbs, . . .

3. Parts of speech: noun, . . .

∗4. Causes of death: accidents, . . .

5. Dishonest ways of manipulating people: flattery, . . .

III. | Integrative Exercise | Each of the following passages proposes a system of classification for some domain. Identify the concepts the author is using, diagram the genus–species relationships among them, and note any points at which the passages fail to make these relationships clear.

∗1. "The human species, according to the best theory I can form of it, is composed of two distinct races, the men who borrow, and the men who lend." [Charles Lamb, *Essays of Elia*]

2. "Digital computers operate by carrying out a number of discrete steps, each of which involves the change of one or more basic engineering components from one physical state to another. (Usually, only two states are possible.) Analog computers are not like this, because the physical parameters used to represent information are continuously variable—like voltage levels, for instance." [Margaret Boden, *Artificial Intelligence and Natural Man*]

3. Lakes and ponds are standing bodies of water. A pond is a body of standing water that occupies a depression in the earth's surface. A lake is generally larger than a pond. A stream is any body of moving water that

flows to progressively lower elevations, in a relatively narrow but clearly defined channel on the surface of the ground. Rivers and brooks are types of streams, and rivers are larger than brooks. [Adapted from *Glossary of Geology*, R. L. Bates and J. A. Jackson (Eds.), 3rd ed., American Geological Institute]

∗4. "We can distinguish altogether three kinds of 'monopoly': those achieved through legal means; those achieved through means that are illegal only because of antitrust and other laws intended to make monopoly difficult; and monopolies achieved through means that are criminal by any standards—means that would be criminal whether or not they were aimed at monopolizing business." [Thomas C. Schelling, *Choice and Consequence*]

5. The term "myth" is sometimes used broadly to refer to any traditional story about the past. But anthropologists sometimes use the

term in a narrower sense to mean one specific type of story. Myths in this sense are stories about gods, including creation myths about how the world came to be, and narratives about the interactions of the gods with each other and with human beings. Legends, by contrast, are stories about humans, including real people in the past, such as the Greek hero Odysseus and his struggle to return home after the Trojan War or the story of George Washington telling the truth after chopping down the cherry tree. Myths are also distinguished from folklore, such as fairy tales, Aesop's fables, etc.

6. "Carbohydrates, proteins (which are made up of amino acids), fats, minerals, vitamins, and water are all nutrients—absorbable components of foods—and necessary for good health. Nutrients are necessary for energy, organ function, food utilization, and cell growth. . . .

   "Micronutrients, like vitamins and minerals, do not themselves provide energy. The macronutrients—carbohydrates, fat, and protein—do that, but only when there are sufficient micronutrients to release them." [Earl Mindell, *Vitamin Bible*]

∗7. "The sources of the Shariah are of two types: revealed and non-revealed. There are only two revealed sources—first, the Quran; second, the teaching and exemplary conduct (Sunna) of the Prophet Muhammad, including his sayings, acts, and tacit approval (or lack of condemnation) of the conduct of his Companions and some of the customs of Arabian society. . . .
   "Another source of Shariah is ijtihad, which literally means 'striving.' It is defined as exertion by a qualified scholar to the best of his or her ability to deduce the ruling of a particular issue from the evidence found in the sources. Unlike the revelation of the Quran and the Sunna, which ended with the Prophet's death, juristic reasoning continues to be the principal source and instrument that keeps the law consistent with the realities of social change." [Mohammad Hashim Kamali, "Law and Society: The Interplay of Revelation and Reason in the Shariah." In John L. Esposito (Ed.), *Oxford History of Islam*, Oxford University Press]

8. "From the standpoint of the individual all contributions to government are either gratuitous, contractual or compulsory. Every governmental revenue must fall within one of these three great classes. Individuals may make the government a free gift, they may agree or contract to pay, or they may be compelled to pay. . . .
   "The taxing power may manifest itself in three different forms, known respectively as special assessments, fees and taxes. These three forms are all species of taxation in the wider sense, so far as they differ on the one hand from contractual revenue, . . . and on the other hand from the remaining divisions of compulsory revenue, like expropriation and fines. What is common to all three is that they are compulsory contributions levied for the support of government or to defray the expenses incurred for public purposes. That is the essence of the taxing power. But, although they are all forms of taxation in this wider sense, the differences between fees and special assessments on the one hand, and taxes in the narrower sense on the other, are so marked that they must be put into separate categories." [Edwin R. A. Seligman, *Essays in Taxation*, 10th ed.]

IV. **Integrative Exercise**   First, state which rule (or rules) is violated by each of the following definitions; then reformulate it so that it is a good definition of the italicized term.

∗1. An *army* is the branch of a country's military that uses tanks.

2. A *lamp* is a movable light source that is intended for indoor use and that rests on the floor.

3. A *handshake* is when two people clasp each other's right hand.

∗4. A *genus* is the generic class to which the referents of a given concept belong.

5. A *disease* is a condition of an organism requiring medical attention.

6. A *veterinarian* is a doctor specializing in the care of cats and dogs.

*7. A *craftsman* is someone who makes what he does look easy.

8. A *gullible* person is a person who can be fooled. (Note: This is not circular merely because "person" is repeated; we are trying to define GULLIBLE, not PERSON.)

9. *Thinking* is purposeful mental activity the goal of which is to avoid error.

*10. *Psychology* is the science that studies human behavior.

11. A *condominium* is a nonrented unit in a multi-unit residential building.

12. An *iron* is what you use to press clothing.

*13. To *reform* is to improve an organization by changing its policy.

14. An *executive* is a person responsible for executing a policy.

15. A *capital offense* is a crime for which the accused is not likely to receive bail.

V. Integrative Exercise   Evaluate each of the following definitions. If you think it is faulty—in some cases, this will be a difficult and controversial decision—state what rule or rules you think it violates.

*1. "History may be defined as the discovery and description of past events." [Michael Shermer, "History at the Crossroads," *Skeptic*]

2. "Poverty can be defined objectively and applied consistently only in terms of the concept of relative deprivation. . . . Individuals, families and groups in the population can be said to be in poverty when they lack the resources to obtain the types of diet, participate in the activities and have the living conditions and amenities which are customary, or are at least widely encouraged or approved, in the societies to which they belong." [Peter Townsend, *Poverty in the United Kingdom*]

3. "PROPEL: means 'apply a force to'; its object must be under a certain size and weight, but for our purposes we will say that any object is acceptable." [Roger Schank, "Representation and Understanding of Text," in *Machine Intelligence* 8]

*4. "A crime is an act committed in violation of a law that prohibits it and authorizes punishment for its commission." [James Q. Wilson and Richard Herrnstein, *Crime and Human Nature*]

5. "Frankness is saying whatever is in our minds." [Richard C. Cabot, *The Meaning of Right and Good*]

6. "I define a free press as one that protects and, if need be, strengthens government of the people, by the people, and for the people." [Walter Karp, "Forum: Can the Press Tell the Truth?" *Harpers Magazine*]

*7. "Democracy is the recurrent suspicion that more than half of the people are right more than half of the time. It is the feeling of privacy in the voting booth, the feeling of communion in the libraries, the feeling of vitality everywhere. Democracy is a letter to the editor. Democracy is the score at the beginning of the ninth. It is an idea which hasn't been disproved yet, a song the words of which have not gone bad. . . ." [E. B. White, "Democracy"]

8. "A democratic government has always meant one in which the citizens, or a sufficient number of them to represent more or less effectively the common will, freely act from time to time, and according to established forms, to appoint or recall the magistrates and to enact or revoke the laws by which the community is governed." [Carl Becker, *Modern Democracy*]

9. "A memory is anything that happens and does not completely unhappen." [Edward de Bono, *Lateral Thinking*]

*10. "Literature is the effort of man to indemnify himself for the wrongs of his condition."

[Ralph Waldo Emerson, "Walter Savage Landor"]

11. "Thinking is a momentary dismissal of irrelevancies." [Buckminster Fuller, *Utopia or Oblivion*]

12. "What is a symbol? A symbol is often defined as 'something that stands for something else.'" [Erich Fromm, "The Nature of Symbolic Language"]

∗13. "[An experiment is] an operation carried out under controlled conditions in order to discover an unknown effect or law, to test or establish a hypothesis, or to illustrate a known law." [*Webster's New Collegiate Dictionary*, 9th ed.]

14. "First, what is meant by anguish? The existentialists say at once that man is anguish. What that means is this: the man who involves himself and who realizes that he is not only the person he chooses to be, but also a lawmaker who is, at the same time, choosing all mankind as well as himself, cannot help escape the feeling of his total and deep responsibility." [Jean-Paul Sartre, "Existentialism"]

15. "Robbery is forcible stealing. A person forcibly steals property and commits robbery when, in the course of committing a larceny, he uses or threatens the immediate use of physical force upon another person for the purpose of 1) preventing or overcoming resistance to the taking of the property or to the retention thereof immediately after the taking; or 2) compelling the owner of such property or another person to deliver up the property or to engage in other conduct which aids in the commission of the larceny." [New York State, *Penal Law*]

∗16. "A tax is a compulsory contribution from the person to the government to defray the expenses incurred in the common interest of all, without reference to special benefits conferred." [Edwin R. A. Seligman, *Essays in Taxation*]

17. "There are two sorts of avarice: the one is but of a bastard kind, and that is, the rapacious appetite of gain; not for its own sake, but for the pleasure of refunding it immediately through all the channels of pride and luxury: the other is the true kind, and properly so called; which is a restless and insatiable desire of riches, not for any farther end or use, but only to hoard, and preserve, and perpetually increase them." [Abraham Cowley, "Of Avarice"]

18. "Mr. Prouty then pressed the questions that are central to the case and to the verdict [in the obscenity trial of a museum showing explicit photographs]: Who determines art? And how does one know if something is art?

"Mr. Sobieszek said that 'if it's in an art museum, it is intended to be art and that's why it's there.'" ["Clashes at Obscenity Trial on What an Eye Really Sees," *New York Times*]

∗19. "All of this suggests that we define a living thing as any semiclosed physical system that exploits the order it already possesses, and the energy flux through it, in such a way as to maintain and/or increase its internal order." [Paul Churchland, *Matter and Consciousness*]

20. "Unlawful harassment is a form of discrimination that may be defined as unwelcome conduct that has the purpose or effect of creating a hostile or intimidating environment where the conduct is sufficiently severe or pervasive to alter the working, learning or living conditions of a reasonable person." [Brown University Discrimination and Harassment Policy]

VI. One italicized word is used in each set of sentences below. Consider the use of that word: Does it express the same concept in each of the sentences in the set? Does it express two different concepts? Or does what it expresses in one sentence involve a metaphorical extension of the concept it expresses in the other(s)?

∗1. a. Cotton clothes will *shrink* if put in the dryer.
b. My *shrink* says I worry too much about being perfect.

2. a. It's my *party*, and I'll cry if I want to.
b. Will the Wilson *party* please come forward—your table is ready.

3. a. I think I failed the trigonometry *test* today.
b. I took my car in to have the battery *tested*.
c. At a certain age, children misbehave to *test* their parents.

∗4. a. My history teachers always *stress* the importance of using primary sources.
b. Between her job and her marital problems, Beth is subject to a lot of *stress*.
c. Cast iron will break under *stress*, while wrought iron will bend.

5. a. The earth completes one *revolution* around the sun in 365 days.
b. The philosophy of natural rights played an important role in the *revolution* of the American colonies.
c. "Glisten" is a *revolutionary* new hair care product.

VII. Define each of the following concepts.

∗1. BACHELOR

2. DIFFERENTIA

3. BORROW

∗4. COMPUTER

5. OBEY

6. JOURNALISM

∗7. NOVICE

8. JEALOUSY

9. BILL (in the sense of a telephone bill)

∗10. FAMILY

VIII. For each of the following sets of words, use what you know about definitions to explain the relationships among them. Decide which members of each set are synonymous, and explain the difference in meaning between nonsynonymous words.

∗1. Game, sport

2. Brave, bold, courageous

3. Hurt, offend, insult

∗4. Sincere, honest, frank

5. Educate, instruct, train

6. Idealist, crusader, zealot

∗7. Adorn, decorate, garnish

8. Seductive, tempting, attractive

9. Weary, tired, exhausted

∗10. Memo, note, letter

IX. Integrative Exercise For each of the following sentences, find another sentence that will express the same proposition (or propositions). You may change the words, or the grammatical structure, or both, so long as the meaning is preserved.

∗1. Joanne and Bob met for lunch.

2. The dog fell asleep on the couch.

3. It probably won't rain today.

∗4. It is raining heavily.

5. The police officer apprehended the alleged perpetrator at the crime scene, a commercial eating establishment.

6. Shakespeare was both a poet and a playwright.

✳7. Since Wednesday is a holiday, the mail will not be delivered.

8. All men are created equal.

9. If I move to Chicago, where my family lives, I will be able to see them more often.

✳10. John Calvin said that people are innately evil, but I don't believe him.

X. **Integrative Exercise** The following statements are from accident reports that people have filed with insurance companies. Identify the propositions they assert (a) and those they do not assert (u).

✳1. "A pedestrian hit me and went under my car."

2. "I collided with a stationary truck coming the other way."

3. "I pulled away from the side of the road, glanced at my mother-in-law, and headed over the embankment."

✳4. "The pedestrian had no idea which direction to go, so I ran over him."

5. "As I approached the intersection, a stop sign suddenly appeared in a place where no stop sign had ever appeared before."

6. "I told the police that I was not injured but on removing my hat, I found that I had a fractured skull."

✳7. "An invisible car came out of nowhere, struck my vehicle, and vanished."

8. "Coming home, I drove into the wrong house and collided with a tree I don't have."

9. "The indirect cause of this accident was a little guy in a small car with a big mouth."

✳10. "The accident happened when the right front door of a car came around the corner without giving a signal."

XI. **Integrative Exercise** For each of the following sets of propositions, write a single sentence in which all the propositions are asserted. You may reword them so long as you do not change their meaning.

✳1. John ran 7 miles yesterday. John has been practicing for the marathon. John did not find the run very strenuous.

2. Opposites are usually not attracted to each other. Lauren loves opera. George hates opera. Lauren and George have been happily married for 10 years.

3. Freedom of speech is a necessary component of a democracy. Ruritania censors newspapers. If freedom of speech is a necessary component of a democracy, then a country that censors newspapers is not a democracy.

✳4. The law generally holds a manufacturer responsible for harm caused by its product. If the manufacturer warns a buyer that a product is dangerous, the law will not hold the manufacturer responsible for harm. If a buyer is harmed by a product through the buyer's own negligence, the law will not hold the manufacturer responsible for the harm.

XII. **Integrative Exercise** The following passages are very repetitive. Determine how many distinct component propositions each one asserts; then rewrite it so that each proposition is asserted only once.

✳1. The problem with Hamlet is that he is very indecisive. He can't seem to make up his mind about anything. He's always thinking about what he should do, but he never does it. He seems unwilling to make a decision, to take a stand. He wanders around pulling his hair out, and nothing ever comes of it.

2. The soul is immortal. It does not die, but lives forever. It existed before birth, and will continue to exist after death. It is completely indestructible. There is nothing that can make it go out of existence. The soul exists forever, and cannot be destroyed. It is therefore separate from the body. The soul is one

thing, the body another. The body dies; the soul lives forever. They are utterly distinct.

3. "Could you imagine your mailbox jammed with parcels every day? Free parcels of every size coming to you from all over the world direct to your doorstep. . . . All of this could be yours and more with this amazing system that jams gifts in your mailbox almost every day of the week.

"These free parcels are yours just for the asking. I absolutely guarantee that you will get parcels delivered to you almost every day of the week. . . .

"Imagine coming home to free gifts almost every day of the week. . . . Direct to your doorstep the mailman will deliver your free parcels. This is an absolute reality and can be yours with this amazing system that loads your home with different parcels from all over the world just for the asking." [Magazine advertisement]

XIII. [Integrative Exercise] For each of the following passages, list all the propositions it expresses; then indicate which are asserted and which are merely expressed.

*1. "Man is born free, and everywhere he is in chains." [Jean-Jacques Rousseau, *The Social Contract*]

2. "Last night I dreamt I went to Manderley again." [Daphne du Maurier, *Rebecca*]

3. "Happy families are all alike; every unhappy family is unhappy in its own way." [Leo Tolstoy, *Anna Karenina*]

*4. "Blessed are the poor in spirit: for theirs is the kingdom of heaven.
Blessed are they that mourn: for they shall be comforted.
Blessed are the meek: for they shall inherit the earth." [*Gospel According to St. Matthew*]

5. "It is a truth universally acknowledged, that a single man in possession of a good fortune, must be in want of a wife." [Jane Austen, *Pride and Prejudice*]

6. "I come to bury Caesar, not to praise him.
. . . The noble Brutus
Hath told you Caesar was ambitious;
If it were so, it was a grievous fault,
And grievously hath Caesar answer'd it."
[William Shakespeare, *Julius Caesar*]

*7. "But not only has the bourgeoisie forged the weapons that bring death to itself; it has also called into existence the men who are to wield those weapons—the modern working class—the proletarians." [Karl Marx and Friedrich Engels, *Manifesto of the Communist Party*]

8. "Men fear Death, as children fear to go in the dark; and as that natural fear in children is increased with tales, so is the other." [Francis Bacon, "Of Death," *Essays*]

9. "I went to the woods because I wished to live deliberately, to front only the essential facts of life, and see if I could not learn what it had to teach. . . ." [Henry Thoreau, *Walden*]

*10. "We hold these truths to be self-evident, that all men are created equal, that they are endowed by their Creator with certain unalienable Rights, that among these are Life, Liberty, and the pursuit of Happiness. That to secure these rights, Governments are instituted among Men, deriving their just powers from the consent of the governed. . . ." [Declaration of Independence]

*XIV. [Integrative Exercise] Suppose that you are an attorney representing a plaintiff (X) who is suing a defendant (Y) for fraud, and suppose that the legal definition of fraud is as follows:

Fraud consists of a misrepresentation of existing fact upon which the defendant intends that the plaintiff will rely and upon which the plaintiff justifiably relies to his detriment.

How many distinct propositions would you have to prove in order to win your case?

Argument Analysis 2

There are some things we can know simply by observation. You can tell whether it is raining simply by looking outside. You can tell whether the bath water is warm by putting your hand in it. Your own experience, including the memory of things you perceived in the past, is your basic window on the world. But no matter how much you've seen and done, only a small portion of the world has passed before your window. For every fact you have observed directly, you know a great many things that you haven't observed.

For example, how do you know what year you were born? Obviously you did not witness your own birth. You were told about it by your parents, who did experience the event, and you trust what they told you. In the same way, you know that George Washington was the first president of the United States because you learned it from a history teacher or textbook. In this case, neither the teacher nor the writer of the textbook witnessed Washington's presidency, any more than you did. But they learned about it from other people, who learned it from still others, extending back in a chain to people who were alive in 1788 and kept records of events at that time. A great deal of our knowledge comes from other people in this way. Because we can communicate what we experience, human beings can merge their separate windows into one giant window.

Still, much of the world lies beyond even that window. We have knowledge that transcends the collective experience of human beings in general. We know things about the origins of our planet, the reaches of outer space, the inner life of atoms—none of which has been directly observed by anyone. We make judgments about right and wrong, about character, about the rights of citizens—none of which is a matter of simple observation. In such cases, we proceed by means of reasoning. When we reason, we use relationships among propositions to push our knowledge beyond the limits of what we can experience directly. In this chapter, we will begin our study of the reasoning process.

LEARNING OBJECTIVES

On successful completion of the chapter, you will be able to:

- Distinguish arguments from non-arguments and identify the premises and conclusion. (2.1)

- Diagram arguments, showing the relationship between premises and conclusion and use diagrams to assess the logical strength of arguments. (2.2–2.3)

- Explain the differences between deductive and inductive arguments. (2.4)

- Identify implicit premises in arguments and distill the core arguments in longer works. (2.5–2.6)

2.1 Elements of Reasoning

Consider the proposition:

Rivers in Taiwan flow downhill.

We know that this proposition is true. But how do we know? Few of us have actually been to Taiwan to observe the rivers there or have even talked to people who have seen them. But we can establish the truth of sentence 1 by reasoning. We know from experience that the fluid nature of water makes it flow in the direction of the forces acting on it, and we know that the primary force is gravity, which pulls water downhill. These are general principles that apply everywhere, and they imply that rivers in Taiwan must behave like rivers in our own environment.

Here is another statement that calls for reasoning:

The government should restrict ownership of handguns.

This is one side of a controversial political issue. In this case, unlike the previous one, people tend to have strong opinions for or against the proposition, and they often argue about it. For that very reason, questions of truth and falsity may seem inappropriate here. But they are appropriate. When people argue about gun control, they are not merely voicing personal preferences, as if they were talking about flavors of ice cream. They are trying to show that their position is true—and they will offer reasons. An *advocate* of gun control might argue that government should pursue the goal of reducing crime, and that restricting ownership of handguns would reduce crime. An *opponent* of gun control might argue that restricting ownership of handguns would violate the right of self-defense.

2.1A Premise, Conclusion, and Argument

These examples involve different types of reasoning, but they also illustrate a common pattern. In each case we are concerned with evidence for the truth of some proposition. In logic, this proposition is called a **conclusion**. The evidence in support of the conclusions consists of other propositions called **premises**. Thus each of our examples involves the use of premises to support a conclusion:

Rivers in Taiwan

Premise 1: Water flows in the direction of the forces acting on it.
Premise 2: The primary force acting on rivers in Taiwan is gravity.
Premise 3: Gravity pulls downward.
Conclusion: Rivers in Taiwan flow downhill.

Gun control—for

Premise 1: Restricting ownership of handguns would reduce crime.
Premise 2: Government should pursue the goal of reducing crime.
Conclusion: The government should restrict ownership of handguns.

Gun control—against

Premise 1: Restricting ownership of handguns would violate the right of self-defense.
Conclusion: The government should not restrict ownership of handguns.

For each conclusion, we have identified the premises that provide the evidence for that conclusion, and we have formulated those premises as distinct propositions.

A set of premises together with a conclusion is called an **argument**. In everyday speech, this term is often used to mean a quarrel between two people. But it is also used to mean an appeal to evidence in support of a conclusion. In logic, we use the term *argument* in the latter sense. It means a set of propositions in which some propositions (the premises) are asserted as support or evidence for another (the conclusion). Another way to put this is to say that the conclusion is *inferred* from the premises. Thus an argument can also be described as an inference, and we will use those terms interchangeably.

Each of the examples above is an argument. By contrast, consider the following exchange:

John: The government ought to ban handguns.
Mary: That's not a good idea.
John: Why not? I think it's a good idea.
Mary: Well, I don't.

In everyday speech, we might say that John and Mary are arguing about gun control. But neither of them is offering an argument in the logical sense; they are just expressing their views without giving reasons.

In this chapter, we will study the basic techniques for analyzing and evaluating arguments. Before we turn to this topic, however, let's consider how we can *recognize* an argument.

2.1B Recognizing Arguments

When we listen to someone speak, or read a written text, we expect there to be some relationship among the statements, some organizing principle or structure. There are various structures, not all of them arguments. In a *narrative*, for example, there is usually no argument; instead, the author simply describes a sequence of events, and the organizing principle is the order of their occurrence, as in the following passage from George Orwell's *1984*:

Winston Smith, his chin nuzzled into his breast in an effort to escape the vile wind, slipped quickly through the glass doors of Victory Mansions, though not quickly enough to prevent a swirl of gritty dust from entering along with him.

A *descriptive* passage states a series of facts about something; the series may be organized in various ways, but again there is usually no argument, as in another passage from *1984*:

The Ministry of Truth was startlingly different from any other object in sight. It was an enormous pyramidal structure of glittering white concrete, soaring up, terrace after terrace, 300 metres into the air.

Descriptive passages appear in many nonfiction fields as well. Indeed, much of what we read and hear is description rather than argument: news reports about events, or statements of fact in history, science, and other fields. If evidence for the fact is provided, backing up the description, then we have an argument. If not, then we don't. The same is true for *opinions*:

That movie was terrible!

My grade on the English exam is unfair.

Serena Williams is the best player in professional tennis.

The minimum wage should be raised.

Each of these statements expresses the speaker's opinion. All of them invite the question, "Why? Why do you believe that?" If the speaker provides a reason, then again we have an argument; if not, not.

We also need to distinguish arguments from *explanations*. In an argument, we are trying to show that some proposition—the conclusion—is true. In an explanation, we are trying to show *why* it is true. To see the difference, compare the following two statements:

It will probably rain tomorrow, because a cold front is moving in.

It rained yesterday because a cold front moved in.

In both cases, the word "because" indicates a relationship between the cold front and rain. But the relationship is not the same in both cases. In sentence 1, we are using the presence of a cold front as evidence that it will rain; we are offering an argument. In sentence 2, we already know that it rained. We don't have to offer an argument for that proposition; we know it is true because we observed the rain directly. What we are doing instead is stating the *cause* for the rain; we are offering an explanation. In an argument, we reason forward from the premises to the conclusion; in an explanation, we reason backward from a fact to the cause or reason for that fact.

	Argument		**Explanation**	
Premise	A cold front is moving in		Cause	A cold front moved in
	↓			↑
Conclusion	It will probably rain tomorrow		Effect	It rained yesterday

These various types of nonargument patterns often occur in combinations. Consider this item from the *Washington Post*:

President Trump on Tuesday said he is pulling the United States out of the international nuclear deal with Iran. . . .

Trump's decision, announced at the White House, makes good on a campaign pledge to undo an accord he has criticized as weak, poorly negotiated and "insane." . . .

The move amounts to Trump's most significant foreign policy decision to date. While he cast the U.S. action as essential for national security and a warning to Iran . . . it could also increase tensions with key U.S. allies.

The tradition in journalism was to separate reporting the facts—about a hurricane, a crime, an election result—from interpreting and expressing opinions, which is the function of editorials. The *Post* story illustrates how that line has been blurred today. The first paragraph states a fact about Trump's action; it's a description. The second is an interpretation of his motives, a kind of explanation. The third expresses an opinion and a warning. But there is no argument here. The assertions of facts, interpretation, and opinion are just that—assertions, without offering reasons to accept them as true.

Here's another example: In his book *1491*, Charles C. Mann describes the devastating impact on native Americans of diseases brought by Europeans, especially smallpox:

> The smallpox virus is thought to have evolved from a cattle virus that causes cowpox; a now-extinct virus responsible for horsepox; or, perhaps most likely, the camelpox virus. . . . People who survive the disease become immune to it. In Europe, the disease was such a constant presence that most adults were immune. Because the Western Hemisphere had no cows, horses, or camels, smallpox had no chance to evolve there. Indians had never been exposed to it—they were "virgin soil" in epidemiological jargon.

In the first sentence, we have a statement of scientific theory but without the evidence to support that theory. The rest of the passage offers an *explanation* for why Native Americans were so vulnerable to smallpox, a fact that the author has already established. So this is not an argument either.

What distinguishes an argument from these other patterns is the effort to support a statement logically. The author doesn't just tell us something that he takes to be true; he also presents *reasons* intended to convince us that it *is* true. This intention is usually signaled by certain verbal clues. For example, the word "therefore" indicates that a statement is intended as a conclusion. The word "because" usually indicates a premise. There are many such indicator words and phrases in English. The more common ones are listed in the Solve box on the next page.

When you encounter such words, it is a good sign that you are in the presence of an argument and you can use the indicators to distinguish the premises from the conclusion.

But you cannot use them mechanically. Some of the words are used in contexts other than argument. In the statement "Since I arrived in Dry Gulch, I haven't seen a single green thing," the word "since" indicates a temporal relation, not a logical one. However, the absence of indicator words does not necessarily mean the absence of an argument. If I say "Dry Gulch is an arid place—I haven't seen a single green thing," I am offering evidence in support of a conclusion, even though I used no indicator words. And, as we saw, "because" can indicate an explanation rather than an argument.

To recognize an argument, the most important technique is to read carefully, asking what point the author is trying to make, isolating the propositions asserted, and identifying the relationships among them.

Let's look at an example from a speech by President Ronald Reagan in 1984:

> "The truth is," Mr. Reagan said, "politics and morality are inseparable, and as morality's foundation is religion, religion and politics are necessarily related. We need religion as a guide." [*New York Times*]

There are three propositions here: (1) politics and morality are inseparable; (2) morality's foundation is religion; and (3) religion and politics are necessarily related. The final

SOLVE Indicator Words

To identify premises and conclusions, look for the following indicator words:

Premise indicators	Conclusion indicators
Since	Therefore
Because	Thus
As	So
For	Consequently
Given that	As a result
Assuming that	It follows that
Inasmuch as	Hence
The reason is that	Which means that
In view of the fact that	Which implies that
	Necessarily

sentence—"We need religion as a guide"—is essentially a restatement of 3. Do we have an argument? Well, the word "as" indicates that 2 is intended as a premise. The word "necessarily" suggests that 3 is a conclusion. It means: If you accept 1 and 2, you should accept 3 as well. So in essence Mr. Reagan was saying: Politics depends on morality, morality depends on religion, therefore politics depends on religion. That's an argument.

Let's consider one more example.

> The rule of law means that people should be punished only for a breach of a law, not by the arbitrary discretion of government. It means that laws should be clearly stated and made known to the public. And it means that laws should be applied uniformly to everyone—everyone is equal before the law.
>
> The rule of law is a worthy ideal. To the extent that it can be achieved, it allows people to know which actions will and will not get them in trouble with the law. It is also fair in treating all people without discrimination.

The first paragraph is a description of the rule of law. Though it describes an ideal, and is cast in positive terms, it does not actually make a case for the ideal. It is not an argument. The second paragraph does provide an argument. No indicator words are used, but the paragraph clearly makes a case for the conclusion that the rule of law is a worthy ideal by offering two premises in support of it.

So far we have asked you to distinguish arguments from nonarguments in a basically intuitive way, with some help from indicator words. The distinction will become easier to draw as you learn more about the inner workings of arguments—a topic we will turn to next.

EXERCISE 2.1

For each of the following paragraphs, determine whether it contains an argument. If so, identify the premises and the conclusion. If the paragraph does not contain an argument, identify whether it is a narrative, a description, an opinion, or an explanation.

∗1. We parked at the trailhead and began our hike up Mt. Washington, walking through a dense forest. After 2 hours we reached the halfway point and stopped to eat lunch.

2. It's important to have sturdy boots for this hike, because the trail is very rocky.

3. There are streams to cross and some muddy places, so it is good to have waterproof boots.

∗4. From the top of the mountain, we could see other mountains to the north and the south. None were as high as Washington. A cold wind blew across the entire chain.

5. Since these peaks are above the tree line, hikers are totally exposed to the weather.

6. The Greek island of Lesbos was the home of the ancient poet Sappho. The philosopher Aristotle also spent two years on the island doing biological research. Since ancient times, the main product of Lesbos has been olives, since the climate is ideally suited to the olive tree.

∗7. In biology, Aristotle argued, we can't explain the birth of an animal, including a human being, solely in terms of the material elements of procreation. For a new animal is a complex organism, with its material elements organized into complex forms, with a specific arrangement of organs, limbs, and other parts. After all, it cannot be an accident that humans produce new humans, not fish or birds, and likewise with every species.

8. Demographers, who study population trends, predict that Africa will exceed every other continent in population growth over the next century, since birth rates will be highest there and life expectancies growing rapidly.

9. Budapest is the capital of Hungary. Its two parts, Buda and Pest, are divided by the Danube River. They were originally separate cities but were united in 1873, when the country was part of the Austro-Hungarian Empire.

∗10. In 2018, Hungary's prime minister, Victor Orban, was becoming increasingly autocratic, as evidenced by the facts that he curtailed freedom of speech, increased his power over the legislature, limited the role of the independent judiciary, and imposed financial costs on organizations that opposed his policies.

11. Should colleges and universities impose limits on freedom of speech? No. To understand an issue, it's necessary to examine arguments from all sides, and that is best done through the freedom of all positions to make their case.

12. In his defense of freedom of speech, Supreme Court Justice Oliver Wendell Holmes said, "The principle of free thought is not free thought for those who agree with us but freedom for the thought we hate."

∗13. There have to be campus rules governing speech. Insults, slurs, and other verbal attacks can be an assault on people, causing pain and loss of dignity. And they do not contribute anything to education.

14. Depression is a condition characterized by changes in appetite, sleep patterns, and energy levels. Depressed individuals often have trouble concentrating and finding pleasure in activities they used to enjoy.

15. In an experiment involving twins raised in different families, psychologists found that the children had significantly similar rates of depression. This indicates that depression is more strongly affected by one's genetics than by one's environment.

＊16. Treating depression with medication is the same as treating any illness with medication. Therefore, the patient should not stop taking the medication just because his symptoms have gone.

17. Although depression is an undesirable experience, it can sometimes serve a useful function. Some researchers believe that depression, like pain, signals damaging behavior and thought patterns. So, people with depression can potentially improve their condition by becoming more aware of their emotions and habitual attitudes.

2.2 Diagramming Arguments

We can think of the premises as the raw materials for an argument and the conclusion as the final product. To understand an argument, we need to know what happens in between—on the factory floor, so to speak. We need to analyze the inner workings of the argument, the individual steps that lead from premises to conclusion. Once we have *analyzed* the argument, we can go on to *evaluate* it: Is it a good argument? Does it provide a good reason to accept the conclusion? Analysis and evaluation are the two basic tasks we are going to discuss in this chapter. We will begin with analysis in this section and move on to evaluation in later sections.

To analyze an argument, we can use a diagramming method that employs just two symbols but is flexible enough to handle arguments of any complexity. One symbol is an arrow pointing from premise to conclusion. This arrow represents a single step in reasoning—the relationship between a premise and the conclusion. Suppose you argued against gun control on the ground that it would violate the right of self-defense. Then your reasoning could be diagrammed as follows:

Restricting handgun ownership violates the right of self-defense.

↓

The government should not restrict handgun ownership.

This is an extremely simple argument. It has a single premise, and there is a single step in the reasoning. So the structure of the argument is fully represented by a single arrow.

But what if there is more than one premise? Then we have a decision to make. In some cases, the premises are dependent on one another: Two or more premises work together to make a single argument for a conclusion. In other cases, the premises are independent: They do not work together; each one offers a separate line of support for the conclusion. These two patterns are diagrammed in different ways, so we have to decide which pattern is present in a given argument. To illustrate the distinction, let's reexamine two arguments that we have already discussed.

The first is Ronald Reagan's argument about politics and religion. In essence, he said: (1) politics depends on morality, and (2) morality depends on religion, therefore (3) politics depends on religion. This argument illustrates the first pattern—an argument with dependent premises. Premises 1 and 2 must be combined in order to have an argument for 3. The premise that politics depends on morality, taken by itself, does not tell us anything about religion, so it doesn't give us any reason to think that politics depends on religion. In the same way, the premise that morality depends on religion, taken by itself, does not tell us anything about politics, so again we would have no reason to think politics depends on religion. It is only when we put the premises together that we have an argument. We represent this fact by using a second symbol, the plus (+) sign, to join the premises. Using the numbers to stand for the individual propositions, we would diagram the argument like this:

We use a single arrow, drawn from the line joining the premises, to represent the fact that the premises together make up a single argument.

By contrast, consider the argument about the rule of law. In this case, the conclusion is stated first, so we give it the number 1. In diagramming arguments, it does not matter how we number the premises and conclusion, as long as we give each proposition its own number. So it is easiest to number them in the order they are stated.

(1) The rule of law is a worthy ideal. To the extent that it can be achieved, (2) it allows people to know which actions will and will not get them in trouble with the law. (3) It is also fair in treating all people without discrimination.

This argument illustrates the second pattern: premises 2 and 3 *independently* support the conclusion. If the rule of law allows people to know the legal consequences of their actions, as stated in 2, that gives us some reason to think the rule of law is a worthy ideal, regardless of whether it is also fair. And the fairness of the rule of law, as stated in 3, provides a reason for considering it a worthy ideal, regardless of premise 2. So in diagramming this argument, we don't use the plus sign. We use two arrows to join each premise to the conclusion separately:

To tell whether a set of premises is dependent or independent, we look at each premise separately and ask whether the kind of support it offers to the conclusion depends on the other premises. A good way to pose the question is to suppose that the other premises are unknown or even false. If that would significantly affect the logical impact of the premise in question, then the relationship among the premises is one of mutual dependence, and a plus sign should be used in the diagram. In contrast, if the premise in question would still give us a reason for accepting the conclusion, then it is independent of the other premises and should be diagrammed with a separate arrow. The goal is to put together those premises that form a single line of thought and separate them from premises that represent distinct lines of thought. But this is not always easy. If the relationship between premises is unclear, it is a good idea to treat them as dependent. As we learn more about specific types of argument, we'll learn more about what sorts of premises must be combined to support a conclusion.

In an argument with independent premises, two (or more) arrows will converge on the conclusion. Can we have the opposite situation? Can we have arrows diverging from a single premise to two or more different conclusions? That is, can a single fact serve as evidence for more than one conclusion? Certainly—as we noticed earlier, the law of gravity implies that water flows downhill, but the law of gravity has many other implications: that the roof of a building needs to be supported, that a rocket needs a certain velocity to go into orbit around the earth, and so on. These would be distinct arguments, but because they rely on the same premise, we can combine them in a single diagram. If we numbered all these different propositions, starting with the law of gravity itself as 1, the diagram would look like this:

In all the arguments we have examined so far, a given proposition served as either a premise or a conclusion, but not as both. But that's only because we have been dealing with very simple arguments. In everyday thinking, as well as in science and other academic subjects, we often find chains of inferences: A premise gives us evidence for a certain conclusion, which in turn supports a further conclusion, and so on. Or conversely, we look for a premise to back up our position, and then look for a further premise to back up the first premise, and so on. For example, if someone opposes gun control on the ground that it violates the right of self-defense, we might ask: Why assume that people have such a right? The person might answer: Because people have a right to life, and therefore have a right to defend themselves. So we have four propositions to deal with:

1. People have a right to life.
2. People have a right to defend their lives.
3. Gun control violates the right of self-defense.
4. The government should not restrict gun ownership.

And the argument would be diagrammed:

This argument has two steps, and proposition 2 serves both as the conclusion of the first step and as a premise of the second. An argument can have any number of premises, any number of steps.

Point 1 in the following page's Review box is true of all arguments; indeed, it is true by the very definition of an argument. Points 2 through 4 describe the various ways in which arguments can differ in structure, and for each one we have a way of representing it in a diagram. So no matter how complex an argument is—no matter how many steps it has, or how many conclusions each premise supports, or how many premises support each conclusion—we should now be able to represent it in a diagram.

Now let's use the diagramming method to construct an argument of our own. Consider the proposition that extremely sarcastic people feel inadequate. Let's see whether we can find an argument to support the claim. We might notice that chronic sarcasm, especially when it is not provoked, seems to express hostility. And why would someone express unprovoked hostility all the time? Isn't it usually because the person feels inadequate in some way? Let's write these ideas down in a list. And since the order in which we number the propositions in an argument is arbitrary, we'll start with the conclusion this time:

1. Extremely sarcastic people feel inadequate.
2. Extreme sarcasm is a form of unprovoked hostility.
3. Unprovoked hostility results from feelings of inadequacy.

Sentences 2 and 3 are clearly dependent premises; neither one alone supports the conclusion. So when we diagram the argument, we get:

Now suppose someone challenges us on premise 2—or suppose we ourselves wonder why it strikes us as true. Can we offer any further argument for it? After all, sarcasm can be playful and witty. It can be an indirect way of expressing fondness or any number of other feelings. Yes, we might answer, that's true in small doses. But chronic and extreme sarcasm always seems to have the goal of undercutting or belittling another person. And the desire to undercut someone, when it isn't provoked, is a kind of hostility. So now we have two further premises:

4. Extreme sarcasm is an effort to undercut someone.
5. The desire to undercut someone is a kind of hostility.

REVIEW Diagramming Arguments

1. An argument must have at least one premise and one conclusion; use an arrow to represent the link between them.

2. A single conclusion may be supported by more than one premise; use a plus sign and a single arrow for dependent premises, convergent arrows for independent ones.

3. A single premise may support more than one conclusion; draw divergent arrows.

4. An argument may have more than one step, so that a given proposition can be both a conclusion (of one step) and a premise (of another step); use separate arrows to represent each step, with the final conclusion on the bottom line.

Like 2 and 3, these are dependent premises, so we can expand the diagram thus:

Now we have an argument in two steps. If we were to discuss the issue thoroughly, we would have to look for reasons to support premise 3, and we would want to consider other lines of evidence as well. The diagram would get more and more complex. But we would proceed in the same fashion, listing premises and adding them to the diagram as we go.

EXERCISE 2.2

I.   For each of the following arguments, you are given the structure of the diagram; fill in the numbers at the appropriate places.

✱1. (1) I shouldn't go home this weekend not only because (2) I have too much studying to do, but also because (3) I can't afford the trip.

2. (1) Cheating on schoolwork is wrong because (2) it is dishonest.

3. (1) Cheating on schoolwork is wrong because (2) it means relying on someone else's knowledge, whereas (3) the purpose of education is to learn how to rely on your own knowledge.

*4. (1) Regular exercise strengthens muscles, (2) strengthens the cardiovascular system, and (3) lowers cholesterol. For all those reasons, (4) one should exercise regularly.

5. Since (1) my car won't start, (2) I will have to take the bus, so (3) I need to take exact change for the fare.

II. In each of the following arguments, identify the conclusion. Then determine whether the premises are dependent or independent.

*1. (1) To be a lawyer, you need to be good at keeping track of details, and (2) Lenny is terrible at that, so (3) he shouldn't go into law.

2. (1) Molly is a very bright child. (2) She began speaking on her first birthday, whereas (3) most children do not begin to speak until later.

3. (1) At the trial, Harris said he was in Milwaukee that night, but (2) he later told me that he was in Chicago. One way or another, then, (3) he is a liar.

*4. (1) Edward prefers Frigidaire to Amana. (2) Edward always buys Frigidaire appliances, even though (3) the Amana store is cheaper and (4) closer to his home.

5. (1) Thomas Jefferson had a profound effect on America, inasmuch as (2) he drafted the Declaration of Independence, (3) served as ambassador to France during a crucial period in the young country's history, and (4) negotiated the Louisiana purchase.

6. (1) We cleaned out all the water that flooded the basement before and (2) all the windows were shut the last time it rained. (3) Now there's water in the basement again, so (4) there must be a leak somewhere.

*7. (1) Governor Baldacci originally told the press that he opposed raising the state income tax. (2) He has since signed a bill to increase the tax, which means that (3) he changed his mind.

8. (1) When a pencil is put into water, it remains straight. (2) But our eyes perceive it as bent. Therefore, (3) our senses are flawed.

9. (1) The military must invade the city. (2) It needs supplies, and (3) if it moves ahead without taking the city, there will be enemies both behind and in front of it.

*10. (1) He sat next to me in class today, and (2) the other day he smiled when I ran into him at the library. (3) I think he is interested in me.

III. [Integrative Exercise] Diagram each of the following arguments. (For further practice, diagram the examples in Exercise 2.1 on pages [63–64] that you have determined are arguments.)

*1. Annette must be wealthy. Last week she bought a diamond choker for her ocelot.

2. That movie was terrible. The plot was incoherent, the theme was trite, and the acting was not very good.

3. Johnson finished his last project in only 4 days. Because he's such an efficient worker, he deserves a promotion.

*4. I don't think it would be a good idea to take the American Revolution course this term, because it conflicts with a course I need for my major, and my schedule would have more balance if I took a science course instead.

5. Everyone needs to understand how the structure of language can affect the way we think. But since this is difficult to appreciate in the case of our native language, it is valuable to study a foreign language.

6. Key West, the southernmost city in the continental United States, is located at the tip of the Florida peninsula. This means not only that it enjoys year-round warm weather, but also that it is vulnerable to Caribbean hurricanes.

*7. Business conditions will improve over the next year, and when they do so, corporate profits will increase. Increasing profit levels will drive up stock prices. So I am confident that investing in the stock market is a good idea.

8. Government regulation tends to delay the introduction of new drugs. If a drug is harmful, regulators get blamed for approving it; but if it is beneficial, they get no reward for approving it. So regulators have an incentive to be excessively cautious.

9. China's program of building military bases in the South China Sea is dangerous. It violates the rights of other countries to territorial waters, it threatens freedom of seaborne commerce, and it could lead to military conflict with the United States and its allies in the region.

*10. Raising the age of retirement would both decrease an expenditure and generate revenue for the government. It would reduce the number of years that citizens drew money from Social Security, and people would continue to pay income and social security taxes during their additional years of employment.

2.3 Evaluating Arguments

A diagram is a valuable tool of analysis. It is like an X-ray picture of an argument, revealing its internal structure. Once we understand that structure, the next step is to *evaluate* the argument, to determine how good an argument it is. How do we measure that value? What standards shall we use? The basic standard is that an argument is good to the extent that it provides evidence for the truth of its conclusion. That, after all, is the goal of reasoning: to determine the truth or falsity of propositions that we are not in a position to verify directly by sense perception.

To provide evidence for a conclusion, an argument must have two essential attributes. First, its premises must be true. An argument is an attempt to establish the truth of a proposition by relating it to facts we already know. So we have to start from facts; false premises don't prove anything. Second, the premises must be logically related to the conclusion in such a way that if the premises *are* true, the conclusion is likely to be true as well. In other words, it is not enough that the premises be true; they must also support the conclusion. They must provide evidence that the conclusion is true.

These two standards of evaluation are largely independent. On the one hand, we can have premises that are true but provide no support for an unrelated conclusion. It is certainly true that dogs bark and that dogs are animals, but those propositions do not support the conclusion that cats make nice pets. On the other hand, we can have premises that are false but that are still logically related to a conclusion in such a way that, if they *were* true, they *would* support that conclusion. Consider the argument:

> (1) All fish breathe through gills, and (2) whales are fish. Therefore (3) whales breathe through gills.

Premise 2 is false. Nevertheless, the conclusion follows from the premises; if both premises were true, the conclusion would have to be true as well.

For any given conclusion, different arguments can provide different degrees of support. Suppose, for example, that Lenny Lightfinger is accused of stealing Mary Mobil's car. Compare the following two bodies of evidence:

> Lenny Lightfinger was once convicted of auto theft; therefore he stole Mary Mobil's car.

> Lenny Lightfinger was seen by several witnesses entering Mary's car and driving it away; the car was later found one block from his home, and his fingerprints were on the steering wheel; therefore he stole her car.

Let's assume that the premises in both arguments are all true. Nevertheless, it is clear that the premise in the first argument provides very little evidence for the conclusion; it might justify a slight suspicion of Lenny, but nothing more. In the second argument, however, we have solid evidence of Lenny's guilt. The conclusion that he was the thief is the only conclusion that seems consistent with the premises.

One of the most important goals of logic is to provide standards for measuring the degree to which a given set of premises supports a conclusion. These standards are extremely valuable, even when we aren't sure whether the premises are true. When we encounter an argument that strikes us as wrong, the standards will help us locate the problem and state our objections precisely. When we encounter an argument whose conclusion we agree with, the standards will help us resist the temptation to put more weight on the argument than it deserves. And if we're not sure whether a proposition is true or false, the standards will tell us what sort of evidence would be relevant.

To illustrate the different degrees of support, consider the types of evidence we might use to support the conclusion that someone named Harry is a lousy driver. At the bottom end of the continuum is the argument that he got a parking ticket. This premise gives no support whatever to the conclusion. Now suppose we learned that Harry once dinged his door in a parking lot. That is not much evidence, but it's something. It's enough to raise a question in our minds. If we acquired the additional information that he failed Drivers' Ed three times and was involved in a major accident, we would have much better support for the conclusion; this evidence makes it probable that he is not a good driver. Finally, if we knew that his vision was 20/200 and that he had trouble telling the brake pedal from the accelerator, our premises would make the conclusion virtually certain.

The general principle illustrated by the preceding example is that we assess the degree of support by seeing how much free play there is between premises and conclusion. The technique is to assume that the premises are true and then ask whether there could still be reasonable doubt as to whether the conclusion is true. Assuming that the premises are true, are there rival conclusions that would be equally consistent with the premises? In the case of Harry the driver, the argument that he once dinged his door provides very little support for the conclusion that he is a lousy driver. That is because even a good driver can have such a minor accident if, for example, he was in a hurry to make an appointment, or was trying to park in a tight spot. The argument does not rule out these rival conclusions.

This method of assessing degree of support relies on your general ability to assess how much free play there is between the premises and the conclusion of an argument. As we proceed in the study of logic—starting with the next section of this chapter—we will discuss further techniques for evaluating specific kinds of arguments. These techniques will help sharpen your ability to distinguish degrees of support.

EXERCISE 2.3

Each pair of arguments that follow has the same conclusion. Determine which one has the greater logical strength. Remember that your assessment should depend not on whether you agree with the premises or the conclusion but on whether the relationship between the premises and the conclusion is strong.

✳1. a. It's probably going to rain tonight; my trick knee is aching.
   b. There's a cold front moving in from the west, and the barometer is falling, so it's probably going to rain tonight.

2. a. Cross-country skiing is one of the best forms of exercise: My sister is a cross-country skier, and she's in great shape.
   b. Cross-country skiing uses all the major muscle groups and gives

the cardiovascular system a good workout, so it is an ideal form of exercise.

3. a. Business conditions will improve over the next year, and when they do so, corporate profits will increase. Increasing profit levels will drive up stock prices. So I am confident that investing in the stock market is a good idea.

 b. Investing in stocks is a good idea. My cousin Vinny, who's a broker, says the market is going up.

*4. a. Gelato is a better product than ice cream because it's popular with young, progressive people who are concerned about politics and the arts.

 b. Gelato is a better product than ice cream because it has fewer calories, less fat, and a richer taste.

5. a. The fact that average wages of manufacturing workers increased by a factor of 5 since 1900 indicates that the standard of living has improved a great deal since then.

 b. In 1900 there were no laptop computers, no Papa John's pizza, no Disneyland. Our standard of living has certainly improved since then.

6. a. Marriage is a good institution because it creates jobs for people in the bridal industry.

 b. Marriage is a good institution because all married people are happy.

*7. a. John must have been lying when he said he was home Saturday night, because in the past he has never stayed home on a Saturday night.

 b. I saw John at McGinty's Bar Saturday night, so he was lying when he said he stayed home.

8. a. Weaver is guilty of the murder of Taylor. The evidence: The murder weapon was found in Weaver's possession, and a witness testified that he was at the scene of the crime.

 b. Weaver is guilty of the murder of Taylor. The evidence: The murder weapon was found in his possession.

9. a. Affirmative action programs increase the amount of record-keeping and red tape that a school or business has to deal with, which makes these programs very expensive. They should be abolished.

 b. People should be treated the same regardless of race and sex, but affirmative action programs require that people be treated differently depending on their race and sex. Such programs should therefore be abolished.

*10. a. The government's banning Muslim women from wearing a burqa in public spaces is detrimental to individual liberty. Wearing the burqa is an instance of religious expression, and freedom of religion is crucial to individual liberty.

 b. The government's banning Muslim women from wearing a burqa in public spaces is detrimental to individual liberty. The ban is xenophobic in motivation, it causes tension within the Muslim community, and it makes Muslim women feel uncomfortable.

2.4 Deduction and Induction

So far we have treated all arguments as a single class, defined by the use of premises to support a conclusion. But there are many different types of argument, different patterns of reasoning. These narrower classes have distinctive structures, and in later chapters we will learn specific methods for analyzing and evaluating them. It is important now, however, to understand the broad distinction between two basic types of argument: deduction and induction.

The following arguments illustrate the difference:

> A detective investigating a murder notices that nothing was taken from the victim's wallet. He might reason as follows: (1) If robbery were the motive, the money would have been taken, but (2) the money was not taken, so (3) robbery was not the motive.

> A scientist investigating an outbreak of disease examines a random sample of the victims. She discovers (1) that all of them had recently eaten strawberries from California, and, as far as she can tell, (2) that the people in the sample had nothing else in common. The scientist concludes (3) that something in the strawberries was causing the disease in all the victims.

The first argument is an example of a **deductive argument**. The conclusion (3) follows necessarily from premises 1 and 2. If those premises are true, they guarantee the truth of the conclusion: It would be impossible for the conclusion to be false. The second argument is an **inductive argument**. The conclusion is certainly supported by the premises, but it would be possible for the conclusion to be false even if the premises are true. The conclusion applies not just to the particular victims in the sample, but to all cases of the disease: The scientist is inferring that the strawberries (or food containing the same chemical elements) causes the disease in people she has not examined. Logicians sometimes describe this feature of induction by saying that it is *ampliative*: The conclusion amplifies—it goes beyond—what the premises state. As a result, the truth of the premises does *not* guarantee the truth of the conclusion; there is some possibility, however small, that the conclusion is false.

Both deductive and inductive arguments have certain common forms. We will explore these forms in detail in Part 2 (Deductive Logic) and Part 3 (Inductive Logic). To get a better sense of the differences between deduction and induction, however, let's consider a few of the more common forms.

2.4A Deductive Arguments

The simplest forms of deduction are *syllogisms*, deductive arguments with two premises and a conclusion. One type of syllogism is illustrated by the detective's argument (A). The first premise of that argument is a statement of the form *if p, then q*: if robbery were the motive, then the victim's money would have been taken. Statements of this form are called *hypothetical* statements, and the argument is a *hypothetical syllogism*. The premise is a compound statement which, as we saw in Chapter 1, does not assert that either of the component propositions *p* and *q* is true, nor that either of them is false; what it asserts is a relationship between *p* and *q*. But premise 2 does assert that *q* is false—the money was not taken. So it follows necessarily that *p* must be false as well—robbery was not the motive.

If robbery were the motive, then the victim's money would have been taken.	If p, then q
The victim's money was not taken.	Not-q
Therefore, robbery was not the motive.	Not-p

You can see that the conclusion simply draws out the implication of the premises. If both premises are true, the conclusion must be true as well. Accepting the premises and denying the conclusion would be a contradiction.

Another hypothetical syllogism is the mirror image of the first. Instead of denying q in the hypothetical premise, it affirms p: *if p, then q; p, therefore q.* Suppose the detective notices that the victim died of a gunshot to the back. He reasons,

If the victim died of a gunshot to the back, he was murdered.	If p, then q
The victim died of a gunshot to the back.	p
Therefore, the victim was murdered.	q

You can also see that in both inferences, the conclusion follows because of the repetition of the component propositions, as indicated by the abstract form on the right. The implication is that the conclusion will follow in *any* argument with the same form. For example,

If I'm out of gas, then my car won't run.	If Fatima has the flu, she has a fever.
My car is running.	She has the flu.
I'm not out of gas.	She has a fever.

The same is true for all deductive arguments. The abstract form of such arguments reveals the pattern of repetition among the premises and conclusion, and it is the pattern that determines whether or not the conclusion follows.

Another form of hypothetical syllogism has two hypothetical premises and a hypothetical conclusion. For example,

If robbery were the motive, then the victim's money would have been taken.	If p, then q
If the victim's money were taken, then the bills would have the perpetrator's fingerprints.	If q, then r
If robbery were the motive, then the bills would have the perpetrator's fingerprints.	If p, then r

There are also syllogisms that have *disjunctive* premises of the form *either p or q.* As with hypothetical statements, disjunctive statements do not assert either of the components as true (or false); they assert only that one or the other is true. But if we also know that one of them is not true, we can draw the obvious conclusion in a disjunctive syllogism:

Either the motive for the murder was robbery or it was vengeance.	Either p or q
The motive was not robbery.	Not-q
The motive was vengeance.	p

Once again, you can see that the conclusion of the syllogism follows necessarily from the premises because of the relations between the components, and that the conclusion will follow in any argument of the same form.

Another type of deductive argument involves noncompound statements, and the conclusion follows because of the repetition of subject and predicate *terms* in the statements. These are called *categorical syllogisms* because the premises and conclusion assert something as categorically true. Here are a few examples of this type, beginning with an inference we discussed previously.

All water flows downhill.	All S are P
All rivers in Taiwan are water.	All R are S
Therefore, all rivers in Taiwan flow downhill.	All R are P
No U.S. Senator is under the age of 30.	No S is P
Chuck Schumer is a U.S. Senator.	Schumer is S
Therefore, Chuck Schumer is not under the age of 30.	Schumer is not P

Notice that both arguments involve a relationship between a general concept and a narrower subdivision or instance of that concept. In the first, water is a wider concept (a genus) of which rivers are one type (a species), so anything true of water in general must be true of rivers. In the second, the concept is U.S. Senators, of whom Schumer is an instance. So what is true of all Senators—including the constitutional qualification regarding age—must be true of him.

In each of these deductive arguments, there is no gap between premises and conclusion. If the premises are true, the conclusion *must* be true as well. If you accept the premises but deny the conclusion, you contradict yourself. This property is known as **validity**. A deductive argument is valid when it is impossible for the premises to be true and the conclusion false. If an argument is intended as deductive but does not meet this criterion, it is invalid. Suppose, for example, that our detective found that money *was* taken from the victim's wallet and then reasoned as follows:

If robbery was the motive, then the victim's money would have been taken.
The victim's money was taken.
Therefore, robbery was the motive.

This argument is somewhat similar in form to argument A, so we would classify it as deductive, but it is invalid because the premises could be true and the conclusion false. For example, the murderer might have killed for revenge but taken the money to cover his tracks. The following deductive arguments are likewise invalid:

The woman just appointed CEO at Megacorp is either very smart or very ambitious.
She is very ambitious.
Therefore she is not very smart.

All voters are citizens.
Some citizens are not taxpayers.
Therefore, some taxpayers are not voters.

A deductive argument is either valid or invalid. Validity does not come in degrees. It is either possible or impossible for the premises to be true and the conclusion false. In the first case the argument is invalid, period; in the second it is valid.

2.4B Inductive Arguments

Inductive arguments also have various common forms. One common form is *generalization*: drawing a general conclusion about a class of things by observing a sample of the class. A general statement has the form *All Ss are P*, where *S* is a class of things and *P* is a property of those things. To take a simple example, you know that fire generates heat, not because you have observed every case of fire, worldwide, but because you have observed enough cases to draw the general conclusion. Generalizing from a sample has the form:

Sample 1: The flame in a gas stove generates heat.	S_1 is *P*
Sample 2: A candle flame generates heat.	S_2 is *P*
Sample 3: The fire in the fireplace generates heat.	S_3 is *P*
And so on with other samples. . . .	Etc . . .
All fire generates heat.	All *Ss* are *P*

Another common form of induction is a *causal inference*, illustrated by argument B given earlier. A causal inference is an attempt to show that some factor in a situation is the cause of a given effect—in our example, that eating strawberries from California caused the people to get sick. Causal inferences look for a common factor that is present in all the cases in which the effect occurs. If there is only one common factor, we have evidence that it is the cause. To simplify, suppose that three of the people who got sick had the following items for dinner:

Person 1: strawberries, steak, potatoes, green beans	Case 1: $a, b, c, d \rightarrow E$
Person 2: strawberries, steak, potatoes, broccoli	Case 2: $a, b, c, e \rightarrow E$
Person 3: strawberries, chicken, rice, green beans	Case 3: $a, f, g, d \rightarrow E$
Strawberries cause sickness.	*a* causes *E*

The general form of a causal inference involves the various factors in the situation—*a*, *b*, *c*, etc.—and the effect *E*. If there is only one factor that is present when the effect occurs, we can infer that that factor is the cause. Notice that the conclusion is a general statement. From information about a sample of people who got sick after their meal, the scientist infers that strawberries like these will cause *any* person who eats then to get sick.

Another kind of inductive argument moves in the opposite direction, drawing a conclusion about some particular thing or event from a generalization about that type of thing or event. Such arguments are called *statistical inferences*. For example:

Most seniors at Baxter College complete the requirements for graduation on time.	Most *Ss* are *P*
Alonzo is a senior at Baxter College.	*A* is an *S*
Alonzo will complete the requirements for graduation on time.	*A* is *P*

If the first premise stated that *all* seniors will complete the requirements for graduation on time, this would be a deductive argument. But the premise says only that most seniors will do so. It is therefore possible that Alonzo will be an exception. The argument provides reasonably good support for the conclusion, depending on exactly what percentage of seniors complete the requirements for graduation. But the truth of the premises would not guarantee the truth of the conclusion.

Yet another common form of induction is called *argument by analogy*. We draw a conclusion about one thing because of its similarity to something else that we know more about. Suppose you are shopping for a new car and leaning toward a Honda Civic. A friend has the same model of Civic, from the same year, with the same features. He says his car is comfortable and handles well, so you infer that your Civic would have those properties as well.

Your friend's car and yours are the same model and year, with the same features. Your friend's car is comfortable and handles well.	A and B have properties S_1, S_2, S_3 A is P
Your car will be comfortable and handle well.	B is P

In an argument by analogy, one premise states the properties that two things are known to have in common. The other premise says that the comparison object A (your friend's car in this case) is known to have a further property P, and you infer that B (your car) will also have that property. We often use argument by analogy in thinking about people; in using history to predict future political and economic outcomes; and in problem solving, when we compare the problem at hand to other problems that we know how to solve.

These forms of arguments illustrate the ampliative nature of induction. Even in a good inductive argument, the conclusion goes beyond the information given in the premises. The distinction between valid and invalid is therefore not applicable. Instead, we evaluate such arguments in terms of their **strength**. Unlike the qualitative distinction between valid and invalid deductive arguments, inductive strength comes in degrees. When the scientist in argument B infers that the strawberries caused the disease, the argument has some strength. But the victims might have had something else in common, something that the scientist has not yet checked out. Or the victims might have reacted to the strawberries for diverse, idiosyncratic reasons that would not apply to people in general. Thus the argument could be made stronger by examining more cases, by testing other possible factors and ruling them out, and by finding the underlying mechanism by which something in the strawberries affects the body. For induction, in other words, there is a continuum from relatively weak support to very strong support. As we move along the continuum by gathering more evidence, we increase the likelihood that the conclusion is true.

It is also possible for a strong inductive argument to be *weakened* by further evidence. In the statistical inference about Alonzo, suppose that the percentage of seniors who complete the requirements for graduation is 95%. If that is all we know, the inference that Alonzo will complete the requirements is very strong. But if we then learn that he has a failing grade so far in two of his courses, we need to add that fact as another premise in the argument, which lowers the degree of support for the conclusion. The general point is that the strength of an inductive argument can be raised or lowered as we expand our context of knowledge.

2.4C Validity and Soundness, Strength and Cogency

As we noted in the previous section, we evaluate arguments by two standards:

1. Are the premises true?
2. How well do the premises—if they were true—support the conclusion?

It is very important to understand that these are two separate questions. The truth of the premises is a matter of how they relate to the facts of reality. That's a different issue

---

SOLVE Deductive vs. Inductive Arguments

To determine whether an argument is deductive or inductive:

1. *Look for indicator words*: Conclusion indicator words like "therefore" and "it follows that" are used with arguments of any type. But some indicator words, like "necessarily," tend to be used specifically for deductive arguments. Others, like "probably," indicate induction.

2. *Consider degree of support*: If the premises seem intended to guarantee the conclusion, the argument is likely to be deductive. If not, it is more likely to be inductive.

3. *Identify the pattern*: Check to see whether the argument fits one of the common forms of deductive and inductive arguments.

Deductive			Inductive	
Hypothetical syllogisms	If p, then q p ___ q	If p, then q Not-q ___ Not-p	Generalization	S_1 is P S_2 is P S_3 is P ___ All Ss are P
	If p, then q If q, then r ___ If p, then r			
Disjunctive syllogism	Either p or q Not-q ___ p		Causal inference	Case 1: $a, b, c, d \rightarrow E$ Case 2: $a, b, c, e \rightarrow E$ Case 3: $a, f, g, d \rightarrow E$ ___ a causes E
Categorical syllogism	All S are P All R are S ___ All R are P		Statistical inference	Most Ss are P A is an S ___ A is P
			Argument by analogy	A and B have properties S_1, S_2, S_3 A is P ___ B is P

from how the premises relate to the conclusion. Now that we understand the distinction between deductive and inductive arguments, and between validity and strength, we can understand standards 1 and 2 at a deeper level.

In deduction, question 2 is a question about validity. As we have seen, a valid deductive argument is one in which the conclusion follows necessarily from the premises. The validity of the argument does *not* depend on whether the premises are true. We saw an example in the previous section:

> All fish breathe through gills.
> Whales are fish.
> Therefore, whales breathe through gills.

This categorical syllogism has a false premise (whales are fish) and a false conclusion. But it's a valid syllogism: if whales *were* fish, it would follow that they *would* breathe through gills. Accepting the premises but denying the conclusion would be a contradiction.

The distinction between the truth of the premises and the validity of the argument can be confusing because we use the concept of truth in defining validity: In a valid argument, it is impossible for the premises to be true and the conclusion false. That is, *if* the premises are true, then the conclusion must be true as well. But that's a big "if." As an if–then statement, this standard of validity does *not* assert that the premises *are* true. It only asserts a relationship between the premises and the conclusion.

To clarify the distinction, let's consider all the possibilities for truth and validity in deductive arguments, using categorical syllogisms as examples:

	Valid	Invalid
True premises, true conclusion	All wines are fermented. Chardonnay is a wine. Chardonnay is fermented.	All wines are fermented. Beer is fermented. Beer is not wine.
True premises, false conclusion	No valid case	All wines are fermented. Beer is fermented. Beer is wine.
One or both premises false, true conclusion	Distilled drinks contain alcohol. Beer is a distilled drink. Beer contains alcohol.	All alcoholic drinks are distilled. Beer is a distilled drink. Beer contains alcohol.
One or both premises false, false conclusion	All wines are fermented. Bourbon is a wine. Bourbon is fermented.	All alcoholic drinks are distilled. Beer is not a distilled drink. Beer does not contain alcohol.

The table shows that, with one exception, there are valid and invalid arguments for every combination of truth or falsehood in the premises and the conclusion. The exception, of course, is the case of true premises and a false conclusion. In that case, any argument must be invalid, by the very definition of validity.

The same pattern applies to induction. Consider two inductive arguments:

Few islands are independent countries.	Few islands are independent countries.
Ellis Island is an island.	Iceland is not an island.
Ellis Island is not an independent country.	Mexico is not an independent country.

In the argument on the left, the premises are true, and the inference is strong. In the inference on the right, the second premise and the conclusion are false, but the inference is just as strong. The first premise is a generalization that is true of most islands. If we knew nothing about Iceland except that it is an island, the conclusion would follow with the same degree of strength as the first argument.

What about the case of true premises and a false conclusion? No deductive inference can be valid in that case. But the conclusion of an inductive argument does not follow necessarily from the premises. Even if the premises are true, and the argument is strong, there is still some possibility, however small, that the conclusion is false. For that very reason, we do not use validity as a standard in induction; we use strength. A strong argument is one in which the premises, if true, make it *likely* that the conclusion is true. So if an inductive argument with true premises does not make the conclusion likely, the argument cannot be strong, just as a deductive argument with true premises and a false conclusion can be valid.

We have stressed the distinction between the two standards for evaluating arguments—the truth of the premises on the one hand, validity and strength on the other—because logic is concerned primarily with the latter. Logic is concerned with the various types of argument by which we can support conclusions. The truth of the premises in those arguments is usually a matter of our personal observations, or of fields other than logic such as history or science.

But of course we do want to base our reasoning on the facts—on true premises. And so we have special terms for arguments that meet both standards.

If a deductive argument is valid and its premises are true, we say that the argument is **sound**.

> Deduction: Sound = Valid + True premises. If one or more premises are false, or if the argument is invalid, or both, it is unsound.

If an inductive argument is strong and its premises are true, we say that it is **cogent**.

> Induction: Cogent = Strong + True premises. If one or more premises are false, or if the argument is weak, or both, it is uncogent.

Finally, it is worth noting that induction and deduction normally work together. Deductive arguments typically apply general knowledge that we have already acquired to new instances. But we first had to acquire that general knowledge by inductive reasoning. Each individual step in an argument will be either inductive or deductive, but the argument as a whole—the case for believing the conclusion is true—normally requires that the premises of any deductive step be supported by induction. In argument A, for example, the detective's deductive conclusion rests on the premise that if robbery had been the motive, then something would have been taken from the victim's wallet. How does the detective know this? He learned it by observing human nature in general and the behavior of criminals in particular. On the basis of these observations, he drew the inductive generalization that people normally carry money in wallets, that thieves know this, and that robbery is a common motive for murder but not the only one.

As another example, consider an argument we diagrammed earlier: that extreme sarcasm is a form of unprovoked hostility, which results from feelings of inadequacy. This argument would best be construed as deductive. To make its deductive character clear, we might formulate it as follows:

> All extremely sarcastic people are acting from unprovoked hostility.
> <u>All people who act from unprovoked hostility feel inadequate.</u>
> Therefore, all extremely sarcastic people feel inadequate.

In this argument as stated, the conclusion necessarily follows from the premises. Now suppose that we want to provide evidence for the second premise. We might consider the people we know who tend to act from hostility. If they all tend to feel inadequate, then we have some inductive evidence for the generalization about human psychology. We could strengthen the evidence by doing psychological experiments that use larger samples of people and objective measures for hostility and inadequacy. But the evidence would still be inductive because it involves a generalization from the sample of people in the experiment to the class of all humans.

Conversely, inductive arguments often involve deductive steps, at least implicitly. In argument B given earlier, the scientist looking for a common factor among the victims of the disease probably did not ask whether they all rooted for the same baseball team. Why not? Because she knows that only biochemical processes in the body cause disease; being a Yankees fan is not a biochemical process, so it could not cause the disease.

> Only biochemical processes can cause disease.
> <u>Being a Yankees fan is not a biochemical process.</u>
> Being a Yankees fan cannot cause disease.

That's a deductive inference.

REVIEW Deduction and Induction

1. A deductive argument attempts to show that its conclusion follows necessarily from the premises, so that the conclusion must be true if the premises are.

2. A deductive argument is either valid or invalid. If it is valid, then it is impossible for all of its premises to be true and its conclusion to be false. Otherwise it is invalid. If it is valid and all of its premises are true, the argument is sound.

3. An inductive argument attempts to show that the conclusion is supported by the premises even though the conclusion amplifies—it goes beyond—what the premises state.

4. Inductive arguments have degrees of strength, and a given argument can be strengthened or weakened through additional evidence. If the argument is strong and all of its premises are true, it is cogent.

Deduction: Sound = Valid + True premises

Induction: Cogent = Strong + True premises

EXERCISE 2.4

I. Determine whether each of the following arguments is deductive or inductive. If it is deductive, is it valid or invalid?

✳1. No Greek philosopher taught in a university, but some Greek philosophers were great thinkers. Therefore, some great thinkers have not taught in a university.

2. Barbara is a liberal. She's a strong advocate of environmentalism, and most environmentalists are liberals.

3. All Romans are Italians; all Italians are Europeans; so Romans are Europeans.

✳4. Two flowers of the same cultivar were planted in adjacent plots. The first was fertilized with Miracle-Gro and it flourished; the second was not and it didn't. Therefore, Miracle-Gro stimulates plant growth.

5. If a triangle has angles of 30° and 60°, then its third angle is 90°. If an angle in a triangle is 90°, then it is a right triangle. So if a triangle has angles of 30° and 60°, then it is a right triangle.

6. Thanks to St. Patrick, no snake lives in Ireland. Since snakes are reptiles, that means no reptiles live in Ireland.

✳7. Lady Gaga is like Madonna in a lot of ways. She's edgy and iconoclastic, she keeps reinventing her persona, she's a talented performer and has huge talent for self promotion. Madonna has had a long and successful career, so Lady Gaga probably will too.

8. No machine is capable of perpetual motion, because every machine is subject to friction, and nothing that is subject to friction is capable of perpetual motion.

9. Either Jesus was telling the truth when he said he was the son of God or he was insane. But he wasn't insane, so he was actually the son of God.

✳10. The plan to build a new factory does not have a provision for construction delays, so its cost estimates are likely to be too low. Experienced contractors know that most building projects on this scale do have delays, which add to the expense of the project.

11. If the tectonic plates under the Atlantic Ocean are moving apart, there will be volcanic activity in Iceland—and there is volcanic activity there. So the tectonic plates are separating.

12. Everything we know about was created at a certain point in time, as a result of causes that existed before. So the universe itself must have been created by a being that existed before the universe.

✳13. The fossil record shows that certain dinosaurs, like birds, were capable of winged flight. Although the birds that exist today are different in many ways, they do share a number of anatomical features with that class of dinosaurs, including scales, hollow bones, expanded pneumatic sinuses in the skull, 3-fingered opposable hands, and 4-toed feet. We can conclude that birds evolved from those dinosaurs.

14. Either health care is a right or it is something that individuals have to

earn. Since health care is something that has to be earned, it isn't a right.

15. The economic crisis of 2008–2009 is like the panic of 1873 in that it was caused by a bubble in real estate, after which banks severely tightened their lending practices, and both consumers and businesses were hobbled by the inability to get loans. The recession of the 1870s lasted more than 3 years, so the recession following the 2008–2009 crisis could not have ended in less time.

∗16. Everything that has a beginning must also come to an end. Thus, because the universe had a beginning, it must eventually come to an end as well.

17. When someone has a physical illness, that person is not judged for being ill and feels no shame. In the same way, a person with a mental ill-

ness should not be judged for being ill and should not feel ashamed.

18. Many European and West Asian languages are strikingly similar in their vocabulary and syntax. Consequently, these languages probably descended from a single ancestral language, which is often called Proto-Indo-European.

∗19. It is commonly held that telling lies is immoral, and that thievery is immoral as well. Therefore it follows that lying, properly understood, is a sort of thievery.

20. It is often said that death is like falling into a deep, dreamless sleep. But since we observe that it is always possible to return to wakefulness, even from the deepest of sleep, we should also think that it is possible to return from death to life.

II. Review the table on page 80 that shows examples of valid and invalid deductive arguments for combinations of true and false premises and conclusions.

1. Determine whether each of the eight cells in the table is sound or unsound.

2. Create a parallel table for induction, with examples of strong and weak

arguments, using this template; and indicate whether each argument is cogent or uncogent.

	Strong	Weak
True premises, conclusion true	Few islands are independent countries. <u>Ellis Island is an island.</u> Ellis Island is not an independent country.	
True premises, conclusion false		
One or both premises false, conclusion true		
One or both premises false, conclusion false	Few islands are independent countries. <u>Mexico is an island.</u> Mexico is not an independent country.	

2.5 Implicit Premises

People rarely express in words *all* the premises they are using in an argument. Most arguments contain some premises that are assumed but not stated. We refer to these as **implicit premises** to distinguish them from the explicit premises that are actually stated. Suppose we are planning a hiking trip, and I tell you that Sally can't come because she has a broken leg. My argument clearly assumes that people with broken legs can't go hiking, but I didn't state that premise, because it was too obvious. Everyday speech would be horribly stilted and tedious if we stated all our premises explicitly. It makes sense to state only the new, the substantive, or the controversial premises of an argument.

But sometimes it is the substantive and controversial premise that goes unspoken, making an argument seem more plausible than it really is. Suppose I argue that since bungee-jumping is dangerous, there ought to be a law against it. This argument relies on the implicit premise that the government should ban things that are dangerous. This is not an assumption that everyone would accept; it relies on a particular view about the proper role of government, and really should be supported logically before one uses it to derive a further conclusion.

So when we analyze an argument, it is important to identify the implicit premises. They can then be labeled—using letters instead of numbers to distinguish them from explicit premises—and included in the diagram. The argument about Sally, for example, would be diagrammed as follows:

1. Sally has a broken leg.
a. No person with a broken leg can go hiking.
2. Sally can't go hiking.

Notice that 1 and *a* are dependent premises. This will always be the case when we fill in implicit premises. Our justification for reading an implicit premise into an argument is that the assumption is necessary in order to link a stated premise with the conclusion. By the very nature of the case, the implicit premise has to work together with some explicit premise. If we supply a new *independent* premise, we are adding a new line of argument and not merely analyzing the argument at hand. Notice, too, that the argument is now a deductive one. If premises 1 and *a* are both true, then the conclusion must be true as well. This will not always be the case when we fill in implicit premises, however, for reasons that we will discuss in a moment.

In the argument above, it was easy to identify the implicit premise. It is not always so easy, and it will be helpful to have certain rules to follow. To understand these rules, we have to keep in mind what our goal is. Identifying implicit premises is a means to the goal of analyzing an argument. The point of argument analysis is to understand what the premises of an argument are and how they relate to the conclusion. In the case of implicit premises, however, we also need to consider what assumption would be necessary for the argument to provide good support for the conclusion. Identifying implicit premises is also a means, therefore, to the goal of evaluating an argument. In light of these goals, there are two basic rules we should follow:

1. The premise we supply should narrow the logical gap between the stated premise and the conclusion.
2. The premise we supply should not commit us to more than is necessary.

Let's see how these rules apply to a specific case. Suppose you are taking French, and you learn that some of your classmates are failing; you infer they do not enjoy the subject. In diagram form:

1. Some students are failing French.

↓

2. Those students are not enjoying French.

What is the implicit premise in your argument? Consider the following candidates:

French is a Romance language.

Paris is beautiful in the springtime.

People never enjoy something that they find difficult.

Students never enjoy subjects in which they are failing.

Using rule 1, we can eliminate the first two candidates, both of which are irrelevant to the conclusion. Neither of them will help close the gap in the argument as stated. Rule 2 will help us choose between the remaining candidates. Both of the latter two would close the gap in the argument. Indeed, each of them would eliminate the gap entirely by making the argument deductive. But notice that the third premise is a much more sweeping generalization than the fourth; it applies to all people and all activities, whereas the last premise applies only to students and the subjects they are studying. Since the last premise serves our purpose without committing us to as much as the third one would, it is the one we should choose.

Sometimes we have to supply more than one premise in order to make sense of an argument. Consider the earlier example about gun control:

1. Restricting ownership of handguns will reduce crime.

↓

2. The government should restrict ownership of handguns.

To connect the premise with the conclusion, we need to say something about the government's responsibility for reducing crime. Is the assumption that the government should take every means possible to reduce crime? No. That assumption would commit us to far more than is necessary. It would imply that the government should put troops in armored cars on every street corner, force people to ask permission before they leave their homes, and engage in all manner of other police-state tactics. For the argument to have any plausibility, the real assumption must be that the government should take any measures that will reduce crime without unduly sacrificing other values (such as

> ### REVIEW Finding Implicit Premises
>
> To identify the implicit premise in an argument, look for a premise that:
>
> 1. Closes the logical gap between the stated premises and the conclusion.
>
> 2. Does not commit the speaker to more than is necessary.

liberty). But now we must introduce an additional implicit premise to the effect that restricting handgun ownership will not unduly sacrifice other values. The complete argument now goes like this:

   1. Restricting handgun ownership will reduce crime.
   a. The government should take any measures that will reduce crime without unduly sacrificing other values.
   b. Restricting handgun ownership will not unduly sacrifice other values.
   2. The government should restrict handgun ownership.

In diagram form, it looks like this:

In all the examples we have discussed so far, we supplied an implicit premise that made the argument deductive. Doing so has the advantage of eliminating any gap between premises and conclusion, so that we can then focus our attention exclusively on whether the premises are true. In some cases, however, it is more reasonable to supply a premise that makes the argument inductive. Consider an example from the previous section: *It will probably rain tomorrow, because a cold front is moving in and cold fronts usually bring rain.* Suppose that second premise had been left unstated. In that case, we would need to choose between two possible implicit premises:

   Cold fronts usually bring rain.

   Cold fronts always bring rain.

The first premise is true, and it gives us an inductive argument that is pretty strong. The second premise gives us a deductive argument, but only at the cost of a premise that is false. The trade-off isn't worth it.

EXERCISE 2.5

Integrative Exercise Identify the implicit premise(s) in each of the following arguments.

*1. Tom is a very successful salesman, so he must be an outgoing person.

2. The doorbell just rang. Someone must be at the door.

3. Cheating is dishonest and therefore wrong.

*4. This sample of copper melted at 1063°C in the laboratory. Therefore, all copper has a melting point of 1063°C.

5. Politicians who are convicted of crimes should not be returned to office, so Congressman Jones should not be re-elected.

6. The arresting officer had not read Johnson his Miranda rights, so the judge had to let him go, even though he confessed to the Pine Street burglary.

*7. The traditional vinyl record, played on top-of-the-line equipment, can reproduce the spatial features of music such as the positions of the instruments in an orchestra. So in that respect it is superior to most mp3 recordings.

8. The government should continue to deregulate the telecommunications industry, because we need an industry that can act quickly and flexibly to exploit the new communications technology.

9. The plays attributed to Shakespeare exhibit a profound intelligence, but Shakespeare himself never went to college, and therefore could not have been very intelligent. So someone else wrote his plays.

*10. When testing the effects of a new drug, it's important to isolate the physical effects of the drug from the psychosomatic effects of taking it. Therefore, one must use a placebo.

11. The washing machines and dryers at the laundromat only accept quarters. So I will need to get change before I take my laundry there.

12. The Australian tiger snake is one of the most venomous snakes in the world and is responsible, on average, for 12 deaths each year. Bites can be properly treated only with antivenom. Therefore if you are bitten by this snake, it is extremely important to seek out a hospital immediately.

*13 Since the subway train didn't stop at this platform, it must have been an express train.

14. Because magnets aren't attracted to this can, I know it's not made of steel. Thus it must have been made from pure aluminum.

15. Even though Nigel is very talented, and has sold a few of his sculptures, he will never be a great artist. Being a great artist requires more than talent. All great artists must be willing to devote themselves entirely to their art.

2.6 Distilling Arguments

In order to analyze the structure of an argument, we have to identify its premises and conclusion. So far, we have done this simply by going through the statement of the argument and numbering the propositions. But this technique works only for short arguments and only when the argument is presented in a fairly condensed and straightforward way. It works well for newspaper editorials and letters to the editor, and for paragraphs in which an author summarizes his argument. But some arguments are presented over the course of an entire essay or book. Such arguments are normally more complex than the ones we have considered up to this point, and they may not contain a summary statement. The reader may be left to extract the main argument from a mass of illustrations, historical background, explanatory material, dramatic narratives, digressions, and so on. In these cases, it would be tedious at best to number every statement in the essay or book, since we would have to ignore most of them. At the same time, an important premise or conclusion might not be stated explicitly—it might be present only as the central point or drift of a passage—and the numbering system would fail to include it.

Before we can analyze or evaluate such an argument, therefore, we have to *distill* it from the work as a whole. In effect, we have to write our own summary statement of the argument. (It is often a good idea to do this literally: Write out a paragraph summarizing the argument concisely, and then use the paragraph as the basis for diagramming.) This requires that we step back from the text of the argument and ask ourselves some questions. What is the author's basic purpose? What conclusion does he want us to accept? What evidence does he offer for that conclusion? Why does he think this evidence proves his case? As we answer these questions, we can write down the propositions—the premises and the conclusion—as we identify them and put them into a diagram of the argument.

When we restate an argument in our own words, the distinction between explicit and implicit premises becomes blurred. Instead of a clear distinction, we have a continuum, from propositions that the author clearly endorses, to those that are suggested but not stated in so many words, to those that are entirely implicit and unspoken. As a result, it may be very difficult to tell which propositions should be given numbers (as explicit statements) and which should be given letters (as implicit ones). The safest approach in this context is to number all of them, and then to apply to all of them the rules for identifying implicit premises. Because we are putting the argument in our own words, we have to be especially careful not to commit the author to more than is necessary for him to make his case.

Arguments of the kind that we need to distill are usually complex. They often have multiple steps from premises to intermediate conclusions to the final conclusion. And they often have multiple lines of argument converging on a single conclusion. The diagramming method gives us a way to analyze arguments of any degree of complexity. To *evaluate* arguments of this kind, we need to qualify a distinction we drew in discussing deduction and induction. A deductive argument is either valid or invalid; the premises either do or do not guarantee the truth of the conclusion. We evaluate inductive arguments, however, in terms of strength: the degree to which the premises support the conclusion. But now we are dealing with complex arguments that may include both deductive and inductive components, and the strength of the argument as a whole is a function of the strength of all its components. To evaluate such an argument as a whole, we will use the term "strength" in a broader sense, even if the argument includes deductive components.

Let's look at several examples that will illustrate the process of distillation. The first is an argument for population control, based on the idea that material resources, like a pie, have to be divided among people:

> There is only so much pie. We may be able to expand the pie, but at any point in time, the pie is finite. How big a piece each person gets depends in part on how many people there are. At least for the foreseeable future, the fewer of us there are, the more there will be for each. [Johnson C. Montgomery, "The Island of Plenty"]

This is a brief argument, formulated rather clearly. It might seem we could analyze it by the technique set forth earlier in this chapter, numbering the propositions as stated and diagramming the structure. But there is a problem. The core of the argument is presented in the form of a metaphor, and we have to extract its literal meaning.

At one level, the metaphor is easy to interpret. The pie represents a society's material wealth: the sum total of goods and resources. And each person's share of that wealth is a piece of the pie. So we could go through the passage, translating into literal terms, and the result would be:

1. The world is finite.
2. At any point in time, there is a fixed amount of wealth.
3. At any point in time, the fewer people there are, the larger each person's share of the wealth will be.
4. For the foreseeable future, reducing the number of people will increase each person's share of wealth.

But our analysis is not yet complete. Notice that proposition 3 pertains to a given moment in time, whereas 4 refers to the foreseeable future. This creates a gap in the argument. If we have a fixed amount of wealth being divided up at a certain moment, it's a mathematical certainty that fewer people would mean larger shares for each. But if we are talking about the foreseeable future, we have to consider how wealth is produced. In particular, we have to consider whether reducing the number of people might reduce the total amount of wealth and, conversely, whether more people might produce more wealth. If each new person produces as much as he consumes, a 10% rise in population might bring a 10% rise in wealth; a 10% fall in population would bring an equivalent decline in wealth. Either way, each person's share would remain the same.

The metaphor of a pie serves to exclude this possibility. We picture the pie already baked, and of course its size does not depend on the number of people waiting at the table. For a full analysis of the argument, then, we must translate this dimension of the metaphor into literal terms. We must extract from it proposition 5: For the foreseeable future, the amount of wealth does not depend on the number of people. And 5 must be combined with 3 in order to bridge the gap between the present and the foreseeable future:

We have now distilled the author's argument. Our analysis identifies the premises implicit in the metaphor and their logical relationships. To evaluate the argument, we assess the strength of each step, on the principle that an argument with more than one step can be no stronger than its *weakest* step. As we saw in analyzing the argument, the steps from 1 to 2 and from 2 to 3 are very strong. Indeed, we could cast those steps in mathematical terms, which would make them deductive. In the initial diagram, however, the step from 3 to 4 is weak. That's why we supplemented it with premise 5 as an implicit premise. As we have seen, analysis and evaluation work hand in hand when we are dealing with implicit premises. With 5 in place, we now have a fairly strong argument overall. Notice, though, that the gain in strength does not come free. We paid for it by adding a premise whose truth is far from obvious. To back it up, the author would need to add a lot of inductive evidence and deal with the objections of economists who reject it.

Let's turn now to a second example. This is a longer passage from the British writer G. K. Chesterton, and it will bring out other aspects of distilling an argument.

> It is not fashionable to say much nowadays of the advantages of the small community. . . . There is one advantage, however, in the small state, the city, or the village, which only the wilfully blind can overlook. The man who lives in a small community lives in a much larger world. He knows much more of the fierce varieties and uncompromising divergences of men. The reason is obvious. In a large community we can choose our companions. In a small community our companions are chosen for us. Thus in all extensive and highly civilized societies groups come into existence founded upon what is called sympathy, and shut out the real world more sharply than the gates of a monastery. There is nothing really narrow about the clan; the thing which is really narrow is the clique. The men of the clan live together because they all wear the same tartan or are all descended from the same sacred cow; but in their souls, by the divine luck of things, there will always be more colours than in any tartan. But the men of the clique live together because they have the same kind of soul, and their narrowness is a narrowness of spiritual coherence and contentment. . . . A big society exists in order to form cliques. A big society is a society for the promotion of narrowness. It is a machinery for the purpose of guarding the solitary and sensitive

individual from all experience of the bitter and bracing human compromises.
[G. K. Chesterton, *Heretics*]

This is an arresting argument because it is paradoxical. Chesterton is saying that life in a small village is, in a sense, more cosmopolitan than life in a large city. And he flaunts the paradox by restating it in a variety of ways. This makes the passage colorful as a piece of writing, but somewhat redundant in logical terms, and we need to boil the argument down to its essence.

As usual, our first step is to identify the conclusion. Chesterton is defending the small community by describing a trait that he considers advantageous, and the passage is an effort to persuade us that small communities do have this trait. The point is put most concisely in the sentences: "The man who lives in a small community lives in a much larger world. He knows much more of the fierce varieties and uncompromising divergences of men." What are these "varieties" and "divergences"? Chesterton does not give us any detailed analysis, but it is clear that he is talking about psychological differences among people—differences in character, opinion, values, personality. If we use the term "personality" to include all these factors, we can formulate his conclusion as:

1. A person who lives in a small community acquires a deeper knowledge of the variety in human personality than does a person who lives in a large community.

The essential argument for this conclusion is presented in the next few sentences. In a large community we can select our companions—the people we interact with. And we tend to choose people who are similar to ourselves, so that our companions are likely to represent a single type of personality. In a small community, however, we have to interact with the people who happen to be our neighbors. Since we do not choose them, the laws of probability ("the divine luck of things") make it likely that they will represent a wider range of human personalities. We can formulate this argument as follows:

2. A person in a large community can select his companions.
3. People tend to select companions who are similar to themselves in personality.
4. A person in a large community will be exposed primarily to a single type of personality.
5. A person in a small community cannot select his companions.
6. Unchosen companions are likely to be diverse in personality.
7. A person in a small community will be exposed to many types of personality.

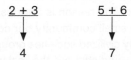

Propositions 4 and 7 will have to be combined to support the conclusion, because the conclusion makes a comparison between large and small communities. But notice that those propositions refer to the types of personalities with which we have actual experience, whereas the conclusion is a statement about our knowledge of human variety. There is a gap here, and it is bridged by an assumption that is implicit in the passage, though very close to the surface. This assumption is:

8. Knowledge of personalities depends on actual experience with them.

So the second step of the argument can be diagrammed:

$$4 + 7 + 8$$

$$1$$

Now that we have distilled the argument, drawing chiefly on the first half of the paragraph, we can see that the rest of the paragraph is repetition and embellishment. Chesterton restates the general argument in terms of the particular case of the clan, which allows him to contrast the clan with the clique, which allows him to talk about the narrowness of a big society. All of this adds color and drama, but it does not add anything substantive to the logical structure of the argument. To evaluate the strength of the argument, we would examine each of the component arguments and ask whether there is a significant gap between its premises and conclusion. In the inference from 2 and 3 to 4, for example, we assume that the premises are true: People in a large community can select their companions, and tend to select other people like themselves. But the conclusion, 4, is about the range of personalities people are *exposed to*, and that is a larger class. People who live in a city interact not only with their friends but with shopkeepers, co-workers, people attending the same concert or sports event, etc. Is it reasonable to think that these groups will be as homogeneous as one's friends? That is the kind of question we need to raise about each step in Chesterton's argument in order to arrive at an overall assessment of its strength.

As a final example of distilling an argument, let's consider a passage from Alexis de Tocqueville's *Democracy in America,* a classic work you may have encountered in history or political science courses. Tocqueville was a French thinker who visited America in the 1830s and later published his observations. The United States was then a very young country, and its democratic system of government was still a novelty by comparison with European nations that retained many trappings of aristocracy. In this excerpt, Tocqueville is concerned with the difference between democracy and aristocracy in terms of political rights: individual rights to freedom and property, and the rights to participate in government decisions by voting and other forms of civic engagement. In an aristocracy, such rights depend on one's place in the class hierarchy; in a democracy, the rights are extended to all citizens (though citizenship at the time was not universal). Which system, he asks, is more stable and likely to endure? With that context in mind, here is the passage:

> The government of democracy brings the notion of political rights to the level of the humblest citizens, just as the dissemination of wealth brings the notion of property within the reach of all the members of the community; and I confess that, to my mind, this is one of its greatest advantages. I do not assert that it is easy to teach men to exercise political rights; but I maintain that, when it is possible, the effects which result from it are highly important; and I add that, if there ever was a time at which such an attempt ought to be made, that time is our own. It is clear that the influence of religious belief is shaken, and that the notion of divine rights is declining; it is evident that public morality is vitiated, and the notion of moral rights is also disappearing: these are general symptoms of the substitution of argument for faith, and of calculation for the impulses of sentiment. If, in the midst of this general disruption,

APPLY Diagrams in Law

Argument diagrams can become highly complex. In the early 20th century, legal theorist John H. Wigmore developed a method for diagramming the extensive body of evidence involved in a trial, using different symbols to distinguish evidence and counterevidence, circumstantial evidence and testimony, etc. Here is a portion of his diagram for a criminal case.

you do not succeed in connecting the notion of rights with that of personal interest, which is the only immutable point in the human heart, what means will you have of governing the world except by fear? [*Democracy in America*, Volume 1, Chap. XIV]

This is a more difficult passage to analyze than the previous examples. We will have to distill the issue Tocqueville is concerned with, and delve below the smooth surface of his prose to uncover his argument.

Tocqueville states his conclusion in the first sentence:

1. Extending political rights to all citizens is a great advantage of democracy (over aristocracy).

He doesn't say what the advantage is—not in this statement nor elsewhere in the passage, not in so many words. But it is clear from the context that he is concerned with the stability of a political system, its ability to endure over time by engaging the loyalty of the people.

What then is the argument? To begin our analysis, notice that he is drawing a broad distinction between aristocracy and democracy, so we might expect that his argument will have two basic strands: the distribution of political rights in aristocracy is unstable, whereas the distribution in democracy is stable. In logical terms, we should expect independent arguments, one against aristocracy and the other in favor of democracy. And that is indeed what we find.

The argument against aristocracy turns on the premise that aristocracy limits political rights by class. People born into higher classes have more rights, due to their status, than do people in lower classes. This is an implicit premise; it's inherent in an aristocratic system and Tocqueville can take it for granted. And this inequality, he says, is no longer sustainable.

2. Aristocracy limits political rights by class.
3. Aristocracy is not stable.

2

3

Tocqueville explains this inference in the middle of the paragraph, where he talks about religion, divine right, and public morality. His point is that the acceptance of the unequal rights of people in an aristocratic system depends on a belief in the justice of the hierarchy. But this belief depends on accepting the divine right of rulers, appointed or at least endorsed by God; and on the emotional (sentimental) acceptance of a common morality. But times are changing, and these beliefs are eroding. (He is thinking of the Enlightenment emphasis on reason and the capitalist system of individual enterprise.) Religion is being undermined as reason ("argument") replaces faith; public morality based on sentiment is being undermined by means–end reasoning in pursuit of individual goals ("calculation"). So we can flesh out the argument against the stability of aristocracy by stating these points as premises and intermediate conclusions:

4. The acceptance of unequal political rights depends on a belief in the justice of the hierarchy.
5. Belief in the justice of the hierarchy depends on accepting divine rights and accepting public morality by sentiment.
6. The acceptance of divine rights and public morality is declining.
7. Religious belief is shaken.
8. Public morality is disappearing.

9. Argument is replacing faith.
10. Calculation is replacing sentiment.

And we can diagram the argument:

The other, independent strand of his argument provides the case for the stability of a democratic system. It is stated in the final sentence. Tocqueville's argument is that democratic political rights give every citizen a personal stake in the system, tied to self-interest; and because self-interest is an immutable part of human nature, it will be more stable. We can analyze the argument as follows:

11. Democracy extends political rights to all citizens.
12. The equal possession of political rights gives each citizen a stake in the system.
13. Personal interest is the only immutable aspect of human nature.
14. Democracy is stable.

We have now completed the analysis of the component arguments Tocqueville gives to support his conclusion that democracy has an advantage over aristocracy:

His argument is plausible, and it would be easy to accept the gist of it from a casual reading. But in fact it depends on a number of assumptions about rights, human nature, and political systems, and on Tocqueville's observations about intellectual and cultural changes in his time—some of them relevant to our time as well. By distilling his argument, we can make those assumptions explicit and examine whether they are true.

These examples illustrate the process of distilling an argument from a text in which it is not laid out for us step by step. The interpretation of such arguments is inherently more difficult, more subject to uncertainty and alternative readings, than was the case for the arguments treated earlier in this chapter. But once we have distilled an argument, the basic tools of analysis and evaluation are the same.

SOLVE Distilling Arguments

1. Separate the argument from illustrations, digressions, and other material not relevant to the argument. Write your own summary statement of the argument.

2. Identify the conclusion. What point is the author's "bottom line"? What is he trying to establish?

3. Work back from the conclusion to isolate separate lines of inference, each with its intermediate conclusion.

4. Identify the premises in each line of inference.
   a. Rephrase stated premises as needed.
   b. Identify unstated (implicit) premises.
   c. In both cases, apply the standards for attributing implicit premises: They should close a logical gap in the argument and not commit the author to more than is necessary.

5. Diagram the argument from initial premises to intermediate conclusions to final conclusion.

EXERCISE 2.6

Integrative Exercise   Distill and diagram the following arguments—a scene from "The 'Gloria Scott'" by Arthur Conan Doyle, and an argument against online classroom courses adapted from *The Chronicle of Higher Education*.

*1. "Come now, Mr. Holmes," said he, laughing good-humoredly. "I'm an excellent subject, if you can deduce anything from me."

"I fear there is not very much," I answered; "I might suggest that you have gone about in fear of some personal attack within the last twelve month."

The laugh faded from his lips, and he stared at me in great surprise. "Well, that's true enough," said he, . . . "though I have no idea how you know it."

"You have a very handsome stick," I answered. "By the inscription I observed that you had not had it more than a year. But you have taken some pains to bore the head of it and pour melted lead into the hole so as to make it a formidable weapon. I argued that you would not take such precautions unless you had some danger to fear."

2. Students are more likely to cheat in online courses than in classroom courses. When students take an exam in an online course, there is no one to monitor them. With the Internet at their fingertips, students can look up answers online. Also, students might ask more advanced students to answer a particular question or take their exams for them—taking an introductory biology exam would be no trouble for someone 3 years into a biochemistry major. There are simply more ways to cheat in online courses, without being caught, than there are in classroom courses. And although they might not admit it, many students will cheat or help others cheat if they can do so without being caught.

CHAPTER REVIEW

Summary

- Reasoning is the process of providing evidence for the truth or falsity of a proposition by relating it logically to other propositions.
- An argument is a set of propositions in which some—the premises—are asserted as support or evidence for another—the conclusion. Arguments are usually, though not always, signaled verbally by indicator words.
- To analyze an argument is to identify its logical structure: the logical relationships between premises and conclusion.
  - The various possible relationships can be diagrammed using arrows and plus signs.
  - Diagrams distinguish between dependent and independent premises and they identify the individual steps in an argument.
- To evaluate an argument, (1) we determine whether the premises are true, and (2) we assess the degree to which the premises, if true, support the conclusion. Logic is primarily concerned with 2: assessing the degree of support that the premises *would* provide the conclusion *if* the premises are true.
  - The primary method is to estimate the size of the gap between premises and conclusion.
  - Another method is to find the assumed premise that would close the gap and to estimate the plausibility of that premise.
  - In either case, the strength of an argument containing more than one component is a function of the strength of the components. An argument with more than one step is only as strong as its weakest step.

- Arguments can be divided into two broad categories: deductive and inductive.
- A deductive argument attempts to show that its conclusion follows necessarily from the premises.
  - A deductive argument is valid if the conclusion does follow necessarily. In that case, it would be impossible for the premises to be true and the conclusion false. Otherwise the argument is invalid. There are no degrees of validity.
  - A deductive argument is sound if it is valid and its premises are true.
- An inductive argument, attempts to show that the conclusion is supported by the premises even though the conclusion amplifies—it goes beyond—what the premises state.
  - Inductive arguments have degrees of strength in how well the premises support the conclusion; and a given argument can be strengthened or weakened through additional evidence.
  - An inductive argument is cogent if it is strong and its premises are true.
- Many arguments are not stated in brief, concise form, but are presented over the course of longer works such as an entire essay or book. In these cases we need to distill the core argument and put it in our own words, by identifying what conclusion the author is trying to prove and what premises are used to support it.

Key Terms

conclusion (p. 58)

premise (p. 58)

argument (p. 59)

deductive argument (p. 74)

inductive argument (p. 74)

validity (p. 76)

strength (p. 78)

sound (p. 81)

cogent (p. 81)

implicit premise (p. 85)

Putting It All Together

I. **Integrative Exercise** Diagram each of the following arguments.

∗1. You have to be very quiet to see deer in the woods. Deer tend to run when they hear noise.

2. Consciousness cannot be explained by the laws of physics and chemistry, so it is not a physical phenomenon.

3. I'm sure now that Richard and Lisa are in love. They both have that dreamy look, and besides, I just saw them talking together.

∗4. You shouldn't ask a friend to keep a secret from his or her spouse. Marriage is a more intimate relationship than friendship, and one should not ask someone to compromise a more intimate relationship for the sake of a less intimate one.

5. It is extremely dangerous to carry a can of gasoline in the trunk of your car. Gasoline is highly flammable, and it has tremendous explosive power. After all, when it is burned in your engine, a gallon of gas is capable of propelling 2 tons of metal for 20 miles or more.

6. We shouldn't give in to the demands of terrorists when they take hostages. That will only convince them that their tactic works and thus encourage them to use it again.

∗7. Without welfare, some poor people would have no means of support, so we must not eliminate welfare. The government has a duty to provide everyone with at least the essentials of life.

8. Welfare is a form of expropriation: It takes money out of one person's pocket and puts it into someone else's. Since the function of government is to protect individual rights, including property rights, it should not be running welfare programs.

9. Welfare programs are intended to help poor people. But such programs create a sense of inadequacy and a loss of self-esteem in recipients, consequences that do not help poor people. A better solution to poverty is a universal guranteed income, which puts all people on the same footing.

∗10. People are allowed to vote when they are 18, and males have to register for the draft then. Since 18-year-olds are considered old enough to have these responsibilities, surely they are old enough to decide whether to have a drink. The drinking age should not be 21.

11. Religious cults typically demand that followers regard the leader's life as more valuable, and his judgment more reliable, than their own. A person with high self-esteem would not find either demand acceptable, so you won't find many people with high self-esteem as members of cults.

12. The case against playing baseball on artificial turf is unassailable. Fake turf makes the ball bounce unnaturally and intensifies high temperatures, often by as much as 20 or 30°F during summer day games. Players tend to injure their legs more often and more seriously on artificial turf. And it has contributed to the decay of many traditional baseball skills, such as bunting and the positioning of fielders.

∗II. **Integrative Exercise** Evaluate each of the arguments in Exercise I. Consider whether alternative conclusions would be consistent with the premises as stated, and identify implicit premises in the arguments.

III.   Integrative Exercise   Determine whether each of the following passages contains an argument. If it does, diagram the argument.

✱1. "For some years the suspicion had existed among the more inspired geneticists that viruses were a form of naked genes. If so, the best way to find out what a gene was and how it duplicated was to study the properties of viruses." [James Watson, *The Double Helix*]

2. "The more complicated the forms assumed by civilization, the more restricted the freedom of the individual must become." [Benito Mussolini, Grand Fascist Council Report]

3. "The balance of nature is preserved through the deaths of countless individual organisms which come into conflict with others. The lion lives at the expense of the antelope, zebra, and giraffe, whom it kills in order to sustain its own life. The snake lives at the expense of rodents, and if the snakes were eliminated the rodent population would explode until most of them died of starvation." [John Hospers, "Humanity vs. Nature," *Liberty*]

✱4. "There's something inherently repugnant about judging people by their skin color. Partly it's because it seems wrong to punish or reward people for something over which they have no control. Partly it's because race is almost never relevant to a person's suitability for anything. Partly it's that the very ethic of individualism demands that we treat people as individuals, not as members of a group." [Alex Kozinski, "Color and Caution," *New Republic*]

5. "We should frankly recognize that there is no side of a man's life which is unimportant to society, for whatever he is, does, or thinks may affect his own well-being, which is and ought to be a matter of common concern, and may also directly or indirectly affect the thought, action, and character of those with whom he comes in contact." [L. T. Hobhouse, *Liberalism*]

6. "There are three possible parts to a date, at least two of which must be offered: entertainment, food, and affection. It is customary to begin a series of dates with a great deal of entertainment, a moderate amount of food, and the merest suggestion of affection. As the amount of affection increases, the entertainment can be reduced proportionately. When the affection is the entertainment, we no longer call it dating. Under no circumstances can the food be omitted." [Judith Martin, *Miss Manners' Guide to Excruciatingly Correct Behavior*]

✱7. "The 2010 oil spill from the Deepwater Horizon well in the Gulf of Mexico released some 200,000 tons of methane into the waters of the Gulf. Within a few months, the methane had disappeared. A team of oceanographers concluded that it was consumed by methanotrophs, bacteria that ingest methane. The waters surrounding the drill head were depleted of oxygen, which the bacteria burn when they consume methane. 'If the methane had just traveled someplace else and was hiding, we wouldn't see any reductions in dissolved oxygen,' [oceanographer John] Kessler said. 'But if it were consumed by microbes, we should see some reductions in dissolved oxygen, which we did.'" [Brian Vastag, "Methane-gobbling Bacteria Were Hard at Work in Gulf Oil Spill, Scientists Say," *Washington Post*]

8. "The existence of biological predispositions [toward crime] means that circumstances that activate criminal behavior in one person will not do so in another, that social forces cannot deter criminal behavior in 100 percent of a population, and that the distributions of crime within and across societies may, to some extent, reflect underlying distributions of constitutional factors." [James Q. Wilson and Richard Herrnstein, *Crime and Human Nature*]

9. "Neither parole nor probation are justifiable. . . . They are a demonstrable failure in reducing inmate recidivism. They undermine

the deterrent impact of the law on criminals, while demoralizing crime victims with their outrageous leniency. Most important, they jeopardize public safety." [Robert James Bidinotto, *Criminal Justice: The Legal System vs. Individual Responsibility*, 86]

＊10. "I'm a sick man . . . a mean man. There's nothing attractive about me. I think there's something wrong with my liver. . . . "I've been living like this for a long time, twenty years or so. I'm forty now. I used to be in government service, but I'm not any more. I was a nasty official. I was rude and enjoyed being rude. . . . "When petitioners came up to my desk for information, I snarled at them and felt indescribably happy whenever I managed to make one of them feel miserable." [Fyodor Dostoyevsky, *Notes from Underground*]

11. "To a plant, breathing involves a built-in cost–benefit analysis. The wider the gas-exchanging pores on the leaf surface are open, the greater the supply of carbon dioxide for photosynthesis. But wide-open pores also allow evaporation of water, so the plant must balance the benefits of increased carbon dioxide against the cost of water loss." [J. A. Miller, "Plant 'Sight' from Pores and Pumps," *Science News*]

12. "A foolish consistency is the hobgoblin of little minds, adored by little statesmen and philosophers and divines. With consistency a great soul has simply nothing to do. He may as well concern himself with his shadow on the wall. Speak what you think now in hard words and to-morrow speak what to-morrow thinks in hard words again, though it contradict everything you said to-day." [Ralph Waldo Emerson, "Self-Reliance"]

＊13. "This month is the 600th anniversary of the famous Boar's Head Dinner at Queen's College, Oxford. "It was around this time of year in 1395 that a student wandering in Shotover Forest was attacked by a wild boar. "He managed to strangle the beast with the volume of Aristotle he had been reading, and it was brought back to the college with the book still in its mouth. "In commemoration, Queen's College has held a Boar's Head dinner in November ever since. "By tradition, the boar is always served with something in its mouth, like a lemon or an apple (but not a book)." [Associated Press]

14. "There are good reasons to believe that polyphony existed in Europe long before it was first unmistakably described. It was probably used chiefly in nonliturgical sacred music; it may have been employed also in folk music, and probably consisted of melodic doubling at the third, fourth, or fifth." [Donald Jay Grout, *A History of Western Music*]

15. "Most of the basic elements of structure and function of all organisms, from bacteria to humans, are remarkably similar—in some cases, identical. We all use the same sorts of proteins made up of an identical set of twenty amino acids; we all use the same nucleic acids made up of the same four bases as genetic material. We all have similar machinery for oxidizing our food and producing our energy and for doing our cellular work, including the building of ourselves. We store, replicate, and use genetic information in the same way. The genetic code, the cipher for translating inherited information into living substance, is the same in all of us. These truths are pillars of support for evolution's first premise—that we all had a common origin." [Mahlon Hoagland, *Toward the Habit of Truth: A Life in Science*]

＊16. "A tree trunk does not grow from the bottom up, as some people think, lifting its branches as it grows. A tree develops vertically only at the top while increasing its girth below to support the weight of its growing crown; the points at which the branches spring from the trunk stay at the same levels. You can see this fact demonstrated if you drive along a country road where pastures are fenced with barbed wire nailed to trees. The fencing may have been nailed up so long ago that the trunks now envelop the wire, but it is still at the height at which it was originally placed, as you can verify from the height of wires on nearby fence posts." [James Underwood Crockett, *Trees*]

17. "Let me now re-emphasize . . . the extreme looseness of the structure of all objects. . . . [T]here is no perceptible object that does not consist of a mixture of matter and vacuity. In the first place, we find that in caves the rocky roofs exude moisture and drip with trickling drops. Similarly in our own bodies sweat oozes from every surface; hairs grow on the chin and on every limb and member; food is suffused through every vein, building and sustaining the most outlying parts even to the nails. . . . The stone partitions of houses are pervious to voices and to scent and cold and heat of fire, which penetrates also through hard iron." [Lucretius, *The Nature of the Universe*, translated by Ronald Latham]

18. The title of Master Bladesmith is awarded by the American Bladesmith Society. To earn the title, according to an article in the *New Yorker* (2008), a knife-maker must create a knife that can "accomplish four tasks, in this order: cut through an inch-thick piece of Manila rope in a single swipe; chop through a two-by-four, twice; place the blade on his forearm and shave a swath of arm hair; and finally, lock the knife in a vise and permanently bend it ninety degrees." [Todd Oppenheimer, "Sharper," *New Yorker*]

*19. "A struggle for existence inevitably follows from the high rate at which all organic beings tend to increase. Every being, which during its natural lifetime produces several eggs or seeds, must suffer destruction during some period of its life, and during some season or occasional year, otherwise, on the principle of geometrical increase, its numbers would quickly become so inordinately great that no country could support the product. Hence, as more individuals are produced than can possibly survive, there must in every case be a struggle for existence, either one individual with another of the same species, or with the individuals of distinct species, or with the physical conditions of life." [Charles Darwin, *The Origin of Species*]

20. The highest-flying bird so far observed "is a Rüppell's griffon, a kind of vulture native to a large swath of Africa. In November 1973, one was sucked into a commercial aircraft engine at 37,000 feet over Ivory Coast. (The plane landed safely.) Bar-headed geese have been observed at 29,500 feet as they migrate over the Himalayas, and demoiselle cranes can reach about 26,000. These birds can fly so high, says Gil Myers, assistant curator at Smithsonian's National Zoo, in part because a special type of hemoglobin in their blood makes oxygen intake more efficient." [*Smithsonian Magazine*]

IV. Determine whether each of the following arguments is inductive or deductive. If it is deductive, is it valid or invalid? If it is inductive, evaluate its strength.

*1. Either our house is haunted or there are a number of squirrels living in our attic. Since we know that there are at least three squirrels living in the attic, our house must not be haunted. Whew! What a relief!

2. American football and rugby have many similarities, so they probably carry approximately the same risk of injury for players.

3. We're already four weeks into the summer and it has rained on every Sunday so far. So I'm avoiding making any outdoor Sunday plans for the rest of the summer, because I know they would all be rained out.

*4. All of the recipes in this book require salt. And a few of my favorite lamb dishes are in this book. So at least some lamb recipes need salt.

5. The director promised that if our 4:00 play rehearsal runs past 6:30, she'll buy pizza for the whole cast and crew. And she also said that when we first arrive, we're going to spend an hour being fitted for costumes before we

do a complete run-through of the 2 hour play. So I'm expecting pizza!

6. Neveah said that she's going to buy a new cell phone next month. And more than 75% of cell phones sold worldwide use the Android operating system. So Neveah's new phone will be an Android.

*7. Nothing in my closet has any real monetary value. But everything that reminds me of my childhood is in there. Therefore nothing that reminds me of my childhood has any monetary value.

8. Halley's Comet is named after Edmund Halley, who observed it in 1682. It has been observed again every 75 to 76 years since then. Therefore, Halley's Comet will continue to be observed every 75 to 76 years.

9. If any *Saturday Night Live* cast member has a longer run than Kenan Thompson (the recordholder as of 2019), that person will have to be very talented. And Cecily Strong is very talented. So she will have a longer run than Kenan Thompson.

*10. I want to buy my wife a diamond ring for our anniversary. And the jeweler carries white, black, and yellow diamonds. While I think black diamonds are beautiful, my wife doesn't like them. And I refuse to spend money on yellow diamonds. So I suppose her ring will have to be a white diamond.

11. If this treasure map is a fake, then following it won't lead to a real treasure chest. And the map has already been exposed as a hoax. So if we follow it, the only treasure we should expect is the adventure of a wild goose chase.

12. The insurance company's inspector said that our deck doesn't look safe, so the company didn't want to sell us a policy until we fixed it. But we've added some safety railing and reinforced the floors. With these improvements, we should now be able to buy a policy from the company.

*13. The triceratops looked a lot like a modern rhinoceros. Since the rhinoceros lives in Africa and Asia, the triceratops must have lived in Africa and Asia as well.

14. Everyone in my geology class is collecting rocks for a project. And I noticed that Skyler is making a rock collection for a project. So Skyler must be in my geology class.

15. The characters in the show were either puppets or marionettes. But there were no strings above them, and too little space above the stage for anyone to control them from there. So they must have been puppets.

V. For each of the following propositions, construct (a) an inductive argument and (b) a deductive argument to support it. Diagram your arguments, and make them as strong as possible (even if that means using premises you don't actually agree with).

1. The athletes at a college or university should have to meet the same academic standards as other students.

2. The government should pay tuition for anyone who wants a college education.

3. Anyone caught cheating on a final exam should be expelled from school.

4. Public high-school officials should not have the right to search students' lockers for drugs.

5. Before the age of 21, everyone should have to spend a year in mandatory national service, working in the military or in domestic government programs.

VI. Integrative Exercise   Identify the implicit premises in the arguments below.

∗1. "Robbery had not been the object of the murder, for nothing was taken." [Arthur Conan Doyle, *A Study in Scarlet*]

2. "A cat knows how to anticipate. If they didn't, they could never hunt birds or mice or other sportingly fleet prey." [Roger A. Caras, *A Cat Is Watching*]

3. "You see, we don't believe that any of the investment information you can get in financial newsletters, magazines and newspapers will ever make you rich. That's because mass publications, by definition, are written for the masses. They've got to be somewhat trite and conventional." [Promotional letter, Royal Society of Lichtenstein]

∗4. "No man is allowed to be a judge in his own cause, because his interest would certainly bias his judgment. . . ." [James Madison, *Federalist Papers*, No. 10]

5. "All languages are the product of the same instrument, namely, the human brain. It follows, then, that all languages are essentially the same in their deep structure, regardless of how varied the surface structure might be." [National Council of Teachers of English, "Students' Right to Their Own Language"]

6. "How often have I said to you that when you have eliminated the impossible, whatever remains, however improbable, must be the truth? We know that he did not come through the door, the window, or the chimney. We also know that he could not have been concealed in the room, as there is no concealment possible. Whence, then, did he come?" "He came through the hole in the roof!" "Of course he did. He must have done so." [Arthur Conan Doyle, *The Sign of Four*]

∗7. "Since everyone has some understanding [of what life is all about]—some world view, no matter how limited or primitive or inaccurate—everyone has a religion." [M. Scott Peck, *The Road Less Traveled*]

VII. Integrative Exercise   Use each of the following propositions as a premise in an argument. You may look for a conclusion that will follow from the proposition directly, or you may combine the proposition with other premises to support some conclusion (the latter approach is recommended). Make your argument as strong as possible, and diagram it as you go. When you are finished, write a paragraph expressing the argument as clearly and persuasively as you can.

1. Los Angeles is located near a fault line.

2. It's a warm and sunny day.

3. Fraud is a form of theft.

4. People with radically different standards of personal hygiene rarely find each other attractive.

5. Rock stars make much more money than philosophy professors.

6. Adults are responsible for their actions.

7. Men and women have the same basic capacities for productive work in every field.

8. No one is going to live forever.

9. War is the most destructive of human activities.

10. Freedom is worth risking one's life for.

Fallacies 3

In the broadest sense of the term, a **fallacy** is any error in reasoning. But the term is normally restricted to certain patterns of errors that occur with some frequency, usually because the reasoning involved has a certain surface plausibility. To the unwary, the premises of a fallacious argument seem relevant to the conclusion, even though they are not; or the argument seems to have more strength than it actually does. This is why fallacies are committed with some frequency.

We are going to study fallacies now for two reasons. The first is to help you avoid them in your own thinking and identify them when they are used against you in debate. The second reason is that understanding why these patterns of argument are fallacious will help us understand the nature of good reasoning. Just as doctors increase their understanding of health by studying diseases, we can gain clarity about good arguments by seeing what is wrong with bad ones.

The fallacies discussed in this chapter should not be regarded as a complete list. The varieties of bad reasoning are too numerous to catalog here. For one thing, as we saw in the previous chapter, there are invalid forms of deductive argument. For example:

LEARNING OBJECTIVES

On successful completion of the chapter, you will be able to:

- ✅ Identify fallacies of relevance: subjectivism, appeal to majority, appeal to emotion, appeal to force, or *ad hominem*. (3.1)
- ✅ Identify inductive fallacies: appeal to authority, false dichotomy, *post hoc*, hasty generalization, accident, slippery slope, composition, or division. (3.2)
- ✅ Identity fallacies of presumption and diversion: begging the question, equivocation, appeal to ignorance, or diversion. (3.3)

If robbery were the motive, then the victim's money would have been taken.	If *p* then *q*
The victim's money was taken.	*q*
Therefore, robbery was the motive.	Therefore, *p*

The argument is invalid because the premises could be true and the conclusion false. For example, the murderer might have killed for revenge but taken the money to cover his tracks. The abstract form of this argument is indicated on the right, and, as we saw in the previous chapter, any argument with the same form is invalid. Such errors are called formal fallacies, and we will examine them when we study deduction. This chapter is concerned with informal fallacies, in which the error is not simply a matter of the argument's form. Even so, we have included only those informal fallacies that are most common in everyday discussion and that illustrate something about the nature of good reasoning. Many of these fallacies were identified and labeled by medieval logicians and thus have Latin names, but we will use the English names for most of them.

We have grouped the fallacies into three categories based on their similarities to and differences from each other.

You should be aware, however, that this is not a standard, widely accepted classification. In fact, there is no standard classification. Logicians debate about the best way to classify these errors, and each textbook has its own system. This may seem surprising. Of all people, you might think, logicians would have worked out a proper system of classification by now. The explanation is partly that bad reasoning is often bad in more than one way, and even experts can disagree about which specific errors are the most important. In addition, fallacies differ along two essential dimensions: They involve an error of reasoning and they have the capacity to deceive us. While the first dimension is a matter of logic, the second is a matter of psychology. Just as optical illusions occur because of the way our visual system works, psychologists have found that we are more vulnerable to certain errors than to others because of the way our minds work. But the logical and psychological dimensions do not always match up exactly. We will explore the psychological dimension in the next chapter.

Our classification of fallacies is the one that we have found most natural and most useful for students in learning about fallacies. In the end, though, the important thing is to understand the fallacies themselves.

3.1 Fallacies of Relevance

In the previous chapter we discussed the various ways in which the premises of an argument can support a conclusion and the degree of support they provide. A minimum condition for such support is that the premises are *relevant* to the conclusion. Fallacies of relevance are attempts to support a conclusion with premises that may appear to be relevant but in fact are not.

3.1A Subjectivism

The fallacy of **subjectivism** is committed whenever we hold that something is true merely because we *believe* or *want* it to be true. Thus, if *p* is the proposition in question, subjectivism has the form:

In an argument of this sort, a subjective state—the mere fact that we have a belief or desire—is being used as evidence for the truth of a proposition. But the thoughts and feelings that pass through our minds may or may not correspond to reality. That's why we need a logical method of *discovering* whether they are true; that's why objectivity is a virtue in the first place.

The fact that someone prefaces a statement with the words "I think" or "I feel" does not necessarily imply subjectivism. This is a conventional way of expressing a view, and the person may go on to offer a perfectly objective argument. Nor are statements *about* our thoughts and feelings necessarily subjective. Suppose I am trying to tell whether the emotion I am feeling is resentment or justifiable anger. My thought process may be either objective or subjective: objective if I am open to the evidence, subjective if I decide that it is justifiable anger merely because I can't bear to think of myself as resentful. In other words, subjectivism is not an issue of what a statement or conclusion is about; it's an issue of the kind of evidence one uses to support a conclusion. The fallacy is committed only when someone uses the mere fact that he believes or feels something as a reason for thinking it to be true.

It is unlikely that you will ever hear someone commit the fallacy of subjectivism in the pure form diagrammed earlier. As with most fallacies, the pure, textbook cases are too obviously fallacious for anyone to fall for them. In real life, the fallacies take more subtle and disguised forms. Here are some examples:

I'll think about that tomorrow.

This is Scarlett O'Hara's line from *Gone with the Wind*. It is her way of dealing with unpleasant facts. The point, of course, is that tomorrow never comes: She is simply putting the facts out of mind, on the implicit assumption that they will then cease to exist. Subjectivism is not only a way of *adopting* conclusions on subjective grounds, but also—and probably more often—a way of *evading* them. Some people have perfected the skill of ignoring what they don't want to see, and most of us indulge this habit occasionally. If the habit were put into words, it would take the form "I don't want to accept *p*, therefore *p* isn't true." That's subjectivism.

I was just brought up to believe in X.

This statement typically occurs when people encounter challenges to their basic convictions. In a discussion of premarital sex, for example, someone might respond to arguments condoning this practice by saying "Well, I was just taught to believe it's wrong." The fact that one was brought up to believe something may explain how one came to have that belief, but it doesn't explain why one *ought* to believe it; it does not provide any reason for thinking that the belief is true. It simply reinforces the claim that one has that belief. This is not to say that you are irrational if you refuse to abandon a long-held belief just because you've heard an argument against it that you can't answer on the spot. Many of our beliefs—especially on fundamental issues of religion, ethics, and politics—are rooted in a lifetime of experience and reflection. We can't always put that experience and reflection into words right away, and we shouldn't throw out a well-rooted belief on the basis of a single counterargument. But we shouldn't ignore the counterargument, either. To dismiss it on the grounds that it's easier and less threatening not to reexamine our convictions is a type of subjectivism.

That may be true for you, but it isn't true for me.

Suppose two people are discussing man's biological origins. Pat argues that our species arose by evolution; Mike, a creationist, says, "Well, that may be true for you, but it's not for me." What does Mike mean when he says that something is (or is not) true for him? Perhaps he means simply that he does (or does not) believe it. In that case, the statement means: You may believe in evolution, but I don't. There's no fallacy here, just the recognition that a disagreement exists, without any claim as to which side is right. But if this is what he means, he should say so directly and not introduce the concept of truth. The point of introducing the concept of truth is usually to give an objective gloss to a belief without having to provide evidence for it; or to paper over a disagreement by suggesting that both sides are legitimate, even though they contradict each other and cannot both be true. In either case, the concept of something as "true for me" contains an element of subjectivism: It attributes objective status to a proposition merely because one happens to believe it. At the very least, the phrase ought to be a warning flag to keep an eye out for the fallacy.

3.1B Appeal to Majority

People have criticized the Roman Catholic Church for opposing birth-control measures even though many Catholics do not believe birth control is wrong. This criticism is an appeal to majority belief, which is a fallacy for essentially the same reason that subjectivism is. The argument has the form:

The majority (of people, nations, etc.) believe *p*

↓

p is true

In this case, the subjective state of large numbers of people, not just a single person, is being used as evidence for the truth of a proposition. But the argument is still subjectivistic—and still fallacious. At various times and places, majorities have believed that the earth is flat, that bathing is unsanitary, and that certain women should be burned as witches.

The fallacy of **appeal to majority** is committed whenever someone takes a proposition to be true merely because large numbers of people believe it (regardless of whether those people actually constitute a majority). This fallacy probably occurs more often in political debate than in any other area. One version is the argument from tradition—as in "I oppose socialized medicine because it is inconsistent with our tradition of private medical practice." To say that a principle or policy is traditional is merely to say that it was widely accepted by our predecessors. The mere fact that they accepted it does not prove it correct. Another version of the fallacy might be called the "wave of the future" argument—as in "Every other progressive nation has already adopted a program of government-provided health care; the United States likewise should abandon its outmoded system of private medicine." To say that some principle or policy is the wave of the future—or to argue that we should get "on the right side of history"—is merely to say that many people or countries have already accepted it. An appeal to their preferences in support of that principle or policy is, once again, an appeal to majority. The only difference between these opposing arguments is that they appeal to *different* majorities.

The fact that such an appeal is fallacious doesn't mean we should ignore majority opinion. Objectivity requires a willingness to consider the views of others. If large numbers of people have accepted a principle or policy, it may well be because the principle is true, the policy a good one. The possibility is certainly worth exploring. When we explore it, however, we should look for objective evidence; mere popularity doesn't count.

3.1C Appeal to Emotion

This fallacy is the attempt to persuade someone of a conclusion by an **appeal to emotion** instead of evidence. A person who commits this fallacy is hoping that his listeners will adopt a belief on the basis of a feeling he has instilled in them. In effect, he is hoping that *they* will commit the fallacy of subjectivism.

The appeal may be intended to arouse various emotions: outrage, hostility, fear, pity, guilt, or whatever. It may take the form of rhetorical language that is heavily laden with emotive connotations, as in propaganda and other sorts of incendiary political speech. A politician who seeks to cut back immigration, for example, might appeal to hostility toward foreigners. Advocates of welfare programs often appeal to pity for the poor, disabled, or elderly (appeal to pity has its own Latin name, *argumentum ad misericordiam*). The fallacy may also take the form of visual images that have a strong emotional impact. On television, for example, you can find examples of the fallacy not only in advertising but also in news and documentary programs that use images to sway the viewer.

Rhetoric and other emotive devices are not fallacious per se. If you have a logical argument to back up a conclusion, there is nothing wrong with stating it in such a way that your audience will endorse it with their feelings as well as their intellects. Good writers and speakers combine logic and rhetoric to produce exactly that effect. Even in advertising, the emotional pitch may be accompanied by a bona fide reason to buy the product. The fallacy occurs only when rhetoric *replaces* logic, only when the intent is to make an audience act on emotion *instead* of rational judgment.

How can we tell when this intent is present? A good test is to translate the argument into neutral language. If the translation leaves a large gap between premises and conclusion, then there is reason to suspect that the emotive language (or visual image, as the case may be) was intended to make a nonrational appeal to the audience. Let's apply this test to some examples.

In a famous speech, Martin Luther King Jr., said:

> I have a dream that one day this nation will rise up and live out the true meaning of its creed: "We hold these truths to be self-evident—that all men are created equal." . . . I have a dream that one day even the state of Mississippi, a desert state sweltering with the heat of injustice and oppression, will be transformed into an oasis of freedom and justice. I have a dream that my four little children will one day live in a nation where they will not be judged by the color of their skin but by the content of their character. [Quoted from *Let the Trumpet Sound*, by Stephen B. Oates]

This passage certainly makes an appeal to the emotions. But it is not fallacious because we can distill a logical argument implicit in what King says. The argument starts by invoking the principle that all men are created equal. As stated in the Declaration of Independence, it is the political principle that all people have equal rights and should be equal before the law. But King is using the principle in a broader moral sense to mean that people should be judged by morally relevant traits, not by accidents of birth that have no moral relevance. Since skin color is not a morally relevant trait, but character is, King has a strong argument for his conclusion. In diagram form:

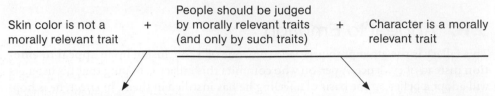

| Skin color is not a morally relevant trait | + | People should be judged by morally relevant traits (and only by such traits) | + | Character is a morally relevant trait |

People should not be judged by skin color   People should be judged by their character

The emotional devices in King's speech—the repetition of "I have a dream," the description of Mississippi as a "desert state," the reference to his children—do not compete with or replace his argument. They simply make the meaning of the abstract principles more concrete and vivid.

By way of contrast, let's look at an argument that does commit the fallacy. The following example is taken from a political advertisement by a state employees' union:

> THE RETURN OF THE PRIVATEERS
> A long time ago, politicians hired private companies to do government work.
> They were mercenary ships, called privateers.
> *We know them as pirates.*
> Today, right here in New York State, politicians are trying to hoist the same old idea. This time around, calling it privatization.
> Let them get away with it, and privateers will be loose again.

Privatization is a policy adopted by some state governments of hiring private companies to collect garbage, maintain parks, and so forth, rather than having these jobs performed by state employees. Some people argue that private companies do the job more efficiently and thus save the government money. Some people argue the opposite—that it's more efficient for government to do these jobs. But the passage quoted above can hardly be considered an argument at all. It relies solely on the negative emotions associated with the privateers, who were private sea-captains authorized by their governments to attack and loot the merchant ships of their enemies. In neutral language, the argument would be:

Governments once contracted with private
interests to loot the ships of other nations.

New York State should not contract with private
companies to collect garbage, maintain parks, and so forth.

This is an extremely weak argument, as we can see by noting the implicit premise required to link the stated premise with the conclusion. The implicit premise is that what was wrong with the privateers was that they were private. But surely what was

SOLVE *Argumentum ad Populum*

Because of its frequent use in politics, appeal to emotion is sometimes associated with appeal to majority. And the two fallacies often do occur together, when an argument appeals to the desire to go with the crowd, to jump on the bandwagon. Some theorists treat appeal to emotion and appeal to majority as the same fallacy, called "appeal to the people" (*argumentum ad populum*). But the fallacies are different:

1. Appeal to majority aims to convince you that a statement is true because many people believe it.
2. Appeal to emotion aims to convince you by swaying your emotions, regardless of whether those emotions have anything to do with the opinions of others.

wrong was that they engaged in looting. And looting would have been wrong even if done by the governments with their own ships and sailors. The authors of the advertisement are obviously hoping that the emotionally laden image of pirates will keep us from raising such objections.

3.1D Appeal to Force (*Argumentum ad Baculum*)

The 18th-century essayist Joseph Addison once wrote (with tongue in cheek):

> There is a way of managing an Argument . . . which is made use of by States and Communities, when they draw up a hundred thousand Disputants on each side, and convince one another by dint of sword. A certain grand Monarch was so sensible of his strength in this way of Reasoning, that he writ upon his great Guns—Ratio Ultima Regum, The Logick of Kings. [*The Spectator*, No. 239]

Addison's remark is sarcastic: The use of force is *not* a type of reasoning, but is actually its antithesis. A threat is not an argument; a club (in Latin, *baculum*) is not a reason. If I "persuade" you of something by means of threats, I have not given you a reason for thinking the proposition is true; I have simply *scared* you into thinking, or at least into saying, it is true. In this respect, the appeal to force might be regarded as a form of the appeal to emotion.

An **appeal to force** may well involve direct coercion. When a government engages in censorship, for example, it uses force to prohibit the expression of certain ideas and to compel agreement with other ideas. The point of this control over verbal expression is to influence what people believe. But the fallacy need not involve actual *physical* force or violence. It is committed whenever *any* sort of threat is used, and nonphysical threats are probably more common than physical ones. When parents threaten to withdraw their support unless a child adopts their religious beliefs, when a teacher threatens a dissenting student with a lower grade, when someone "persuades" a friend by threatening the loss of affection—they are committing forms of this fallacy. As the examples illustrate, the fallacy is usually committed in the effort to breed conformity in belief, and society has many nonphysical means of intimidating people into accepting the conventional views. Dissenters may be held up to ridicule, threatened with moral disapproval ("Only a pig would believe *that*"), told they aren't "cool," and so on. Whenever intimidation of this sort replaces logic in an effort to persuade, it is no less fallacious than the use of actual force.

3.1E *Ad Hominem*

Ad hominem ("at the person") is the Latin name for an argument that rejects or dismisses another person's statement by attacking the person rather than the statement itself. As we will see, there are different forms of this fallacy, but all of them involve some attempt to avoid dealing with a statement logically, and in each case the method is to attempt to discredit the speaker by citing some negative trait. An *ad hominem* argument has the form:

X says p + X has some negative trait

p is false

This is a fallacy because the truth or falsity of the statement has nothing to do with the character, motives, or any other trait of the person who makes the statement. And if someone offers an argument for his position, then his character and motives do not matter for the strength of the argument. We have to evaluate the argument on its merits.

ABUSIVE *AD HOMINEM*   In its crudest form, the *ad hominem* fallacy involves nothing more than insults—calling one's opponent an idiot, slob, lowlife, airhead, fascist, bleeding heart, Neanderthal, and so on through the rich vocabulary of abuse our language offers. Unlike the other fallacies, moreover, this one is committed fairly often in its crude form. In personal disputes, disagreement often breeds anger, and angry people hit below the belt. In politics, *ad hominem* arguments are a common technique of propaganda and a common device of politicians who try to enlist support by attacking their enemies or undermining their rivals. In the Republican Party primary debates during the 2016 election, for example, Donald Trump responded to some of his opponents by disparaging their looks, which of course have no relevance to the positions and policies they advocated.

In **abusive *ad hominem*** arguments, there is rarely any connection between the abusive allegation and the speaker's statement; the allegations are simply insults. A *circumstantial ad hominem*, by contrast, attempts to discredit a person's statement by citing some trait that *appears* to have some relevance to the statement, though it actually doesn't.

TU QUOQUE   One common form of circumstantial *ad hominem* is called **tu quoque** ("you're another"). It's the claim that the person's statement is inconsistent with the person's behavior or prior statements. The classic example is the patient who says to his doctor: "How can you tell me I should stop smoking when you still smoke yourself?" The fact that a doctor doesn't take his own advice hardly means that it isn't good advice. The doctor could very well reply, "Smoking isn't good for me, either. But do as I say, not as I do." Or suppose someone criticizes you for telling a white lie. If your critic is himself a notorious liar, you would probably be tempted to say, "Look who's talking!" This response is certainly understandable, but it is fallacious. The fact that someone else is guilty of an accusation doesn't prove that you are innocent. It may be unseemly for the pot to call the kettle black, but the kettle is black nonetheless. A hypocrite may still say something true or make a valid argument.

In politics, *tu quoque* arguments often cite an inconsistency between a speaker's position and positions he has taken previously. Both Democrats and Republicans have expressed concern about the power of the President and executive branch—usually when the President is from the other party. So a frequent response is, "Well, you weren't worried about executive power when your guy was President." These statements by politicians may well be inconsistent, but the inconsistency is not a good argument against any viewpoint about the proper scope of executive power. That issue is to be settled by the criteria for good government, such as the U.S. Constitution and other factors. A speaker's position on this issue can (and should) be based on those factors. The fact that he took a different position in the past is not a refutation of the position.

POISONING THE WELL Another form of circumstantial *ad hominem* attempts to impugn someone's objectivity by alleging a vested interest, emotional commitment, or political agenda. The name comes from the ancient tactic in war of depriving an enemy of its water supply by poisoning its wells. By analogy, this fallacy seeks to deprive an opponent's statement or argument of credibility by impugning his possible motives for the statement or argument. Here's an academic example:

> In the constitutional struggles of the seventeenth century, the modern theory of natural law—the theory of individual rights—was eventually perfected. Stripped of the trappings which each particular theorist hung upon it, the bare theory was a simple pattern of . . . assumptions which, in the opinion of the men whose interests they served, were as obviously true as the axioms of Euclid. [Richard Schlatter, *Private Property*]

The natural law theory in politics said that individuals had certain inalienable rights that government could not violate, including the right to acquire and dispose of private property. This passage describes one aspect of the theory: that such rights were held to be self-evident, like axioms of geometry. The author clearly does not agree with this view. But instead of presenting a reasoned argument against it, he takes a shortcut: He implies that the principle of property rights seemed self-evident only because it served the political interests of those who were wealthy. This tactic is is obviously fallacious. The fact that someone might have a nonrational motive for supporting a position does not mean the position is false, and it certainly does not mean we can decide ahead of time that all his arguments for the position can be dismissed.

In campus debates, **poisoning the well** is all-too-often used in rejecting someone's position with the claim that he or she is racist, sexist, privileged, homophobic, or motivated by other assumed prejudices. Sometimes these claims are simply abusive

APPLY *Ad Hominem* and the LSAT

Preparing to take the Law School Admissions Test? Practice using your knowledge of informal fallacies. In the LSAT's logical reasoning section, the most common question-type is the flaw question, which presents a brief argument, then asks you to identify the flaw (fallacy) in the argument's reasoning. One of the most common flaws in logical reasoning is the *ad hominem*, particularly examples that accuse someone who makes a claim of either hypocrisy or a conflict of interest (circumstantial *ad hominem—tu quoque* or poisoning the well). Many test-takers are fooled because the language can sound somewhat legalistic. As we

have seen, however, hypocrisy and conflict of interest are not evidence against the claim. In both cases, the argument dismisses a proposal because of some characteristic of the *source* rather than the *substance* of the proposal.

Fallacies will not be identified by name in the answer choices so it helps to know how the LSAT describes them. Common wording for *ad hominem* includes descriptions such as: "The author rejects a claim because of its source rather than its content," or "The argument attempts to discredit a theory by discrediting those who espouse that theory."

ad hominem fallacies. But they usually seem to involve an effort to poison the well of anyone who questions or does not agree with the arguer's view on issues of equality. For example:

> X is white, so X's view about affirmative action can be dismissed.
>
> Y is Hispanic, so of course he will support more open immigration.
>
> Z has argued for lowering taxes. Big surprise—his family is wealthy.

As arguments against the ideas of X, Y, and Z, these are all fallacious attempts to poison the well.

In face-to-face disputes, poisoning the well often takes the form of the statement, "You're just saying that because. . . ." For example: "You're only supporting Julie for class president because she's your friend," or "You're just against distribution requirements because you don't want to take any science." If you have given an argument for distribution requirements, or in favor of Julie's candidacy, the strength of your argument is unaffected by the existence of other motivations you may have for your position. Such statements are insulting. They say, in effect, "I won't even listen to what you have to say because I know ahead of time that you can't be objective; your reasoning is nothing more than a mouthpiece for your emotions and your vested interests." This is a particularly insidious form of the *ad hominem* fallacy because it can undercut your confidence in your ability to think objectively; it breeds self-doubt and timidity. It's true that we have to be careful not to let our judgment be biased by subjective factors. But we should not accept undeserved accusations that we are guilty of this (or any other) logical sin.

REVIEW **Fallacies of Relevance**

---

1. **Subjectivism**: using the fact that one believes or wants a proposition to be true as evidence of its truth.

2. **Appeal to majority**: using the fact that large numbers of people believe a proposition to be true as evidence of its truth.

3. **Appeal to emotion**: trying to get someone to accept a proposition on the basis of an emotion one elicits.

4. **Appeal to force** (*argumentum ad baculum*): trying to get someone to accept a proposition on the basis of a threat.

5. *Ad hominem*: using a negative trait of a speaker as evidence that his statement is false or his argument weak.

EXERCISE 3.1

Identify which of the fallacies discussed in this section—subjectivism, appeal to majority, appeal to emotion, appeal to force, or *ad hominem*—is committed in the statements below.

✳1. Of course Jane is going to be successful. Everyone says so.

2. "Hank is a really sharp dresser." "What about the purple plaid pants he wore last night?" "I don't want to think about that."

3. Boy: "It's my milk money. Stealing is wrong, you shouldn't take it." Bully: "Well I'm bigger and stronger, and I think that I should take it."

✳4. How can you say that animals have rights and should not be killed, when you eat meat?

5. "Fine. Go ahead and marry him. Why should you care about breaking your mother's heart? I guess you love him more than me—but why should I care? Who am I to complain? I'm only your mother. I only spent twenty years trying to make a good match for you, a nice boy, and now you run off. . . ."

6. You can argue all you want that democracy gives us only the illusion of control over the government, but I don't buy it. I was brought up to believe in the democratic system.

✳7. Our video series "The Key to Life" will vastly improve your career, your relationship, and your emotional well-being—just ask the thousands of people who have made it work for them!

8. Why should Congress consult the Joint Chiefs of Staff about military funding? They are military men, so obviously they will want as much money as they can get.

9. I think you will find that this merger is the best idea for our company, especially because disagreement may indicate that this company is not the right place for you.

*10. Teacher to student: "And finally, in reconsidering your position, you might remember who gives the grades in this course."

11. After the accident I was in, I was so upset I couldn't sleep for weeks; I'd wake up with my heart pounding, hearing the sound of the other car crushing the metal of my car door. Cars should be built more solidly than they are.

12. Television commentators are always attacking big business for making "obscene profits," but the media companies they work for have higher profits than almost any other industry.

*13. "He's clearly not qualified for the job—I get a bad feeling just talking to him."

14. How can you believe that John is innocent? I don't see how we can go on being friends if you believe that.

15. Mayor McPherson says that homelessness is a social problem, but that's always the mantra of a bleeding-heart liberal.

*16. People in favor of leaving health care to the private sector have suggested that those with preexisting conditions get loans to cover their costs, instead of insurance. But this idea is completely ridiculous! Are you telling me that we're going to take a young man, suffering from chronic diabetes or muscular dystrophy, struggling every day with his disease, and make him spend his life as an indentured servant to a bank?

17. The most effective way to increase government revenues would be to raise the corporate income tax, since opinion polls show widespread support for this approach.

18. John Stuart Mill says that happiness is the oscillation between tranquillity and excitement. But he spent years dealing with terrible depression, so he can't really know what happiness is.

*19. Nicole advised me that it was best to be totally honest in a relationship, but her love advice can't be very good: She's been divorced twice.

20. Foreign imports are wrecking our economy and savaging our workers, the backbone of this country. Buy American! Before you spend your money on that Honda, think of the guy in Detroit whose kids may not eat tomorrow. Before you buy those Italian pumps, ask yourself whether a little glamour is worth the job of the shoemaker in Boston who's worked all his life to make an honest living.

21. The Golden Rule is a sound moral principle, for it is basic to every system of ethics in every culture.

*22. Mike Tepp tried to convince the board that it would be most profitable to invest in the advertising department. That seems like a convenient position for someone who's up to take over the advertising department next month.

23. Sure, on paper, Florenski looks like the better fighter. He's more experienced, he's won more matches, and he even has a better trainer. But my gut tells me that McMasters will beat him in tonight's fight.

24. Imagine that it's election night. Your young daughter sits nervously next to you, perched on the edge of

the couch, an "Elect Selena Young" sticker proudly displayed on her jacket, excitedly watching the election results pouring in, hoping that she'll finally see a woman in the governor's mansion, hoping to be given hope. And then she hears the announcement that Young has lost by one vote, the vote *you* didn't cast.

How will you answer when your daughter looks sadly into your eyes and asks, "Why?" For your state, for your daughter, for yourself, vote Young!

∗25. Montpelier, Vermont, needs to open a McDonald's franchise as soon as possible, given that it's the only U.S. state capital without one.

3.2 Inductive Fallacies

Fallacies in the category of inductive fallacies include arguments that "jump to conclusions." What makes them fallacious is a weak inductive component. As we saw in the previous chapter (Section 2.4), the logical strength of an inductive argument is a matter of degree, depending on how thoroughly we have taken account of the factors relevant to the conclusion. The fallacies in this section all involve a significant logical gap because they fail to consider a wide enough context of relevant information. The problem is not the premises per se. Unlike the premises in fallacies of relevance, the premises of these arguments could provide genuine evidence. But the evidence is inadequate or incomplete in ways that the argument overlooks. We could just treat such arguments as inductively weak. But the patterns of argument we're going to study in this section have features that make them appear to be stronger than they actually are. As with other kinds of fallacy, learning to see past the appearance will help us avoid poor reasoning.

3.2A Appeal to Authority (*Argumentum ad Verecundiam*)

An authority is someone whose word carries special weight, someone who can speak *with* authority because of expertise in some area of knowledge such as law, science, or medicine. Most of us lack firsthand knowledge of the evidence for the theory of relativity, the DNA model of genes, the effects of carbon dioxide on climate, the procedure for an appendectomy. On these and countless other issues, we accept the authority of experts in the various fields. When we do so, our reasoning can be diagrammed as follows:

X says p

↓

p is true

If such an argument is to have any strength, *X* must be credible, and credibility depends on two factors. First, *X* must be *competent* to speak on the subject; he must have genuine expertise in the relevant field. Second, *X* must be *objective*, stating what he knows without distortion or deceit. In other words, *X* must be someone who not only *knows* the truth, but who also *tells* the truth. Both conditions are essential for credibility. Ideally, we should have a positive reason to think that *X* is competent and objective. At the very least, we must not have any evidence that *X* is *in*competent or *non*objective.

It is perfectly appropriate to rely on authorities if the conditions of credibility are satisfied. If they are not satisfied, however, the **appeal to authority** is fallacious.

The first condition is often violated when people speak outside their fields of expertise. For example, advertisers often use celebrity endorsements—a basketball star praises his favorite brand of orange juice, a famous actor extols the virtues of a luxury car. If the role of the celebrity is merely to add glamour, there's no fallacy involved, because there's no attempt at logical argument. But the advertiser's point is usually to persuade you that the product is good because someone you respect says so. That's a fallacy. Skill on the basketball court does not imply a discriminating taste in orange juice, nor does acting ability give one expertise in judging cars. When people of talent or expertise speak on matters outside their fields, their opinions carry no more weight than that of any layman.

How can we tell whether someone is an expert in a given field? In the next chapter, we will consider in more depth how to tell whether an appeal to experts in the media and other sources is credible. For now, a few criteria are pretty obvious:

- *Education*: Degrees and other credentials indicate that someone has completed a systematic course of education and training in the field—academic degrees such as a Ph.D. in a scientific field; professional degrees in medicine, law, and other fields; and certificates from training programs in software, automobile maintenance, plumbing, etc. Credentials aren't everything, but it is no accident that the word "credential" has the same Latin root as "credibility."
- *Position*: The fact that someone is hired for a position indicates that he inspired confidence in those who hired him. The fact that someone has kept a position over time is evidence that he is performing competently and gaining more and more experience.
- *Achievement*: Significant achievement in a field—such as a scientific discovery, a successful business start-up, or the invention of a new medical procedure—is obviously a sign of expertise. But a record of achievement on any scale reflects a proportionate degree of expertise.

None of these factors is decisive. But each of them can provide inductive evidence for a person's expertise, and the strength of the evidence depends on the particular case.

It often happens, though, that experts disagree. A criminal defendant is said to be insane by one psychiatrist, sane by another. One economist says that a change in the tax code will eliminate jobs, another says that it will create jobs. Across a wide array of issues, specialists disagree. What should we do when we encounter such disagreements? The first thing to do, of course, is to make sure that we are dealing with a genuine dispute among experts and not simply an effort by some non-expert to challenge well-established principles or theories. If the dispute is a genuine one, then we have to take both sides into account. An argument that appeals only to one group of experts is fallacious.

The second condition for credibility is that the alleged authority be objective. Obviously, we cannot peer into a person's mind to see whether he is thinking objectively. But there are certain red flags that should at least raise a question about objectivity. Vested interests are an obvious example. When people stand to gain money or other personal benefit from making an assertion, it is reasonable to consider whether that benefit is biasing their judgment. Since celebrities are paid to appear in advertisements, for example, they have an obvious motive for praising the product regardless of what they really think about it. Emotional commitments are another red flag. Doctors do not operate on members of their own family, and lawyers say that an attorney who represents himself in court has a fool for a client.

Political agendas are yet another kind of red flag. Government policies, and debates about those policies, depend on a wide range of specialized knowledge, from physics to medicine to economics to military strategy. Like the rest of us, experts in these fields can have political views that sometimes bias their judgment about the facts. A climate scientist who strongly favors government environmental regulation may overstate the evidence for global warming; a scientist who opposes such policies may be too quick to dismiss the evidence. In addition, much of the research we find in the media is conducted by advocacy groups or industry trade groups who have an interest in a political cause. Good reporters are careful to acknowledge the orientation of such groups.

We should be careful, however, to weigh these factors fairly. A red flag is merely a warning sign; it raises a question but does not answer it. With enough imagination, and enough cynicism, we can find a reason to impugn anyone's objectivity. If we go to that extreme, however, then we ourselves are not being objective: We are ignoring the fact that a genuine commitment to the truth can override the incentives for distortion or deceit. We would also lose the advantages of having specialists in different fields; we lose the advantages of cooperation in the pursuit of knowledge. The cognitive division of labor, like any other social arrangement, depends to some extent on mutual trust. So it seems more reasonable to presume an expert innocent until proven guilty—that is, to presume he is objective unless we have good reason to doubt it. In any case, we should be even-handed. On economic issues, for example, government and industry experts should be judged by the same standard, regardless of whether we favor more or less government regulation.

In weighing the objectivity of authorities, finally, we should be careful not to commit the fallacy of *ad hominem*. A circumstantial *ad hominem*, as we saw in the previous section, claims that someone's statement is *false* because he has a vested interest or other motive for making the statement. An appeal to authority claims that some statement is *true* because an expert has said so, assuming that he is competent and objective.

Ad hominem	**Appeal to authority**
X says p + X has a vested interest in p	X says p + X is a competent and objective expert
↓	↓
p is false	p is true

Evidence that the authority is not competent or not objective may eliminate any reason for thinking that what he says is true, but it doesn't show that what he says is actually false. We are left with no evidence one way or the other.

3.2B False Dichotomy

Suppose you tell me that Diane is not rich, and I infer that she is poor. I have obviously failed to take account of other alternatives. Rich and poor are the extremes on a scale that contains many intermediate degrees of wealth. Again, suppose you say that you do not identify with political conservatives and I infer that you are a liberal. I am ignoring the other political positions that you might hold, along with the possibility that you have not adopted *any* position. Such inferences have the general form:

That is a deductively valid form of argument. But the soundness of any such inference depends on whether the premises take account of *all* the relevant alternatives. The fallacy of **false dichotomy** occurs when we fail to do so, when we exclude relevant alternatives without justification.

Another name for this fallacy is "false alternative," because the premises of such arguments often posit two alternatives, as in the examples above and in premises such as the following:

Either you are with us or you are against us.

Either we reduce Social Security benefits or government spending will wreck the economy.

Either we increase Social Security benefits or elderly people will starve in the streets.

The essence of the fallacy, however, is not the number of alternatives but the fact that they do not exhaust the possibilities. That can occur whether an argument posits two, three, or any number of alternatives. If the list is incomplete—if it excludes a further alternative that is relevant to the issue—the argument is fallacious. For example, a man in an unsatisfying marriage might try to justify cheating on his wife by appealing to the premise:

I can (1) stay with her and be unfulfilled, or (2) leave and be lonely, or (3) stay but have affairs on the side.

This assumption ignores other possibilities, such as discussing the problem with his wife or seeking therapy. If the man chooses (3) on the grounds that (1) and (2) are unacceptable, he has committed the same fallacy as in arguments based on the first three premises.

As these examples illustrate, considering a range of alternatives plays a major role in reasoning. When we reason about the truth or falsity of a conclusion, we rarely consider the conclusion in a vacuum. Instead, we have in mind a range of other possible conclusions. When we think about whether to take a certain action, we weigh it against other options. When we consider a hypothesis to explain why something happened, we test it against other hypotheses. In short, thinking often involves a choice among alternatives. For that reason, it is important to be alert to the fallacy of false dichotomy.

The best safeguards against this fallacy are an open mind and a good imagination. No matter how certain we are of our conclusions and our arguments, it is always worthwhile to stop and ask: Is there anything I've overlooked? Could there be some other explanation for these facts? Is there some other perspective one might take? When we can't find the solution to a problem, it is often because we are making an assumption that excludes alternative approaches.

If we are not satisfied with any of the standard positions on a given issue, it may be because they all make some assumption that should be called into question, thus opening up other possible positions. In U.S. elections, for example, there are usually just two candidates for any office that have a real chance of winning, a Democrat and a Republican. In deciding how to vote, you may find both of them have too many negatives—in their policy positions, their character, etc.—for you to support either one. But are those are the only alternatives? Only if you assume that you have to vote for one of the major party candidates. So you might question that assumption. If there's a third-party candidate, you could vote for him or her; even if that person has no chance of winning, you are still expressing your political views. Or you could choose not to vote. Some people argue citizens have an obligation to vote; it's a civic duty. Others argue that by lowering voter turnout, you are sending a signal to the major parties to field better candidates. Whatever side you might take on that issue, you first need to see that voting Democrat and voting Republican are not the only alternatives.

3.2C *Post Hoc*

The Latin name of this fallacy is short for *post hoc ergo propter hoc*: "after this, therefore because of this." The fallacy has to do with causality, and it has the structure:

A occurred before *B*

A caused *B*

Such reasoning is fallacious because many events that precede a given event have nothing to do with it, as in the old joke: "Why are you whistling?" "To keep the elephants away." "But there aren't any elephants around here." "See? It works."

The **post hoc** fallacy is probably the source of many superstitions. Someone, somewhere, had a run of bad luck and attributed it to breaking a mirror, walking under a ladder, stepping on a crack, or some other previous action. A student does well on an exam and thereafter always wears the same "lucky" sweater on exam days. More serious examples of the fallacy occur in situations where causal relationships are extremely complex and difficult to identify. Stock market advisers, for instance, sometimes make predictions on the basis of a few indicators that happened to precede a previous rise or fall in prices. *Post hoc* reasoning can also occur in speculation about the causes of historical events such as the Civil War, the causes of economic phenomena such as the Great Depression, or the causes of sociological trends such as crime rates.

It's certainly true that if we want to know what caused an event or phenomenon *B*, we have to *start* by identifying the factors that preceded it. But we can't stop there. To show that some particular factor *A* was the cause, we have to find evidence that there is some stronger connection between *A* and *B* than just a before-and-after relationship. When we study inductive reasoning in Part 3, we will study in detail the types of argument that provide such evidence. For now, we will have to rely on our intuitive judgment. When someone presents an argument that *A* caused *B*, ask yourself: Could it be merely a coincidence that *A* happened just before *B*? Is *A* the *kind* of thing that could have an effect on *B*? Has the person offered any explanation of *how A* affected *B*? Could *A* be only one factor among others in causing *B*?

3.2D Hasty Generalization

Each of the following is a general proposition, or generalization:

> Water always flows downhill.
>
> Large breeds of dogs have shorter life spans than smaller ones.
>
> People in France are not very friendly to tourists.
>
> Italians are quick-tempered.
>
> Stockbrokers drive BMWs.
>
> Bill never gets anywhere on time.

General propositions make a claim about a category of things (water, dogs, Italians, etc.), attributing some characteristic to all members of the category. As the last statement illustrates, however, a generalization may be about a particular individual; what makes it a generalization is that it attributes a general pattern of behavior to that individual.

General propositions play a vital role in reasoning. They allow us to reap the advantages of having concepts: We form a concept for a type of thing, and then generalize about the attributes and patterns of action shared by things of that type. This saves us the trouble of having to discover from scratch the features of every particular thing we encounter. Knowing about the life spans of large versus small dogs, for example, can help us in choosing a pet.

General propositions are normally supported by observing a sample of particular cases. But we often draw conclusions too quickly, on the basis of insufficient evidence. This fallacy, known as **hasty generalization**, can take many forms. A single bad experience while traveling can prejudice our view of an entire city or country (as in the third example above). Most of us have stereotypes about ethnic groups, professions, or people from different regions of the country, based on our exposure to a few individuals (as in the fourth and fifth). Even a judgment about the character or personality of an individual is a generalization drawn from our observation of that person on various occasions. And we can jump to conclusions about ourselves: We make a mistake, fail a test, have a problem in a relationship, and then draw a sweeping conclusion about our inadequacies.

In Part 3, we are going to study the proper methods and precautions for generalizing from particular cases. But the essence of the method is to ask ourselves whether we have considered a wide enough context. Two contextual factors are especially important if we want to avoid hasty generalization: the *number* and the *variety* of cases in the sample from which we generalize. It is rarely if ever possible to draw a legitimate generalization from a single instance, or even from a few; we should consider a larger sample. I may have met a few stockbrokers who drive BMWs, for example, but if I asked around I would quickly find some who don't. We should also look at a *variety* of instances. For example, we might observe that Bill is late for work not just on one occasion but on many. It would still be hasty to conclude that he never gets *anywhere* on time. Is he also late for parties, dates, ball games? If so, we have much stronger evidence that his problem has to do with time in general rather than with work.

Of these two factors, variety is usually the more important one. If you liked a certain novel and wanted to know whether you might like all the author's works, it would obviously be useless to read another copy of the same novel; you would want to sample other novels by that author. To take a more realistic situation, suppose you are buying a car and want to know whether a certain dealer offers good service on the cars it sells. You might ask other customers of that dealer. If you ask people who are very similar, you run the risk that they are not representative of the dealer's clientele. If those customers are all friends of the dealer, for example, or if they are all lawyers who are good at negotiating service contracts, then the generalization that this dealer offers good service might well not be true for other people—including yourself. To avoid hasty generalization, we want to base our generalization on a sample of particular cases that are representative of the wider group. Seeking variety in our sample is the best way to get a representative sample.

3.2E Accident

Hasty generalization is a fallacy that can occur in moving from particular cases to a generalization. There is also a fallacy, called **accident**, that can occur when we move in the opposite direction by applying a generalization to a particular case. This fallacy consists in applying a generalization to a special case without regard to the circumstances that make the case an exception to the general rule. Accident is the fallacy of hasty application.

For example, matches are made to light when they are struck correctly, so I can infer that the next match I strike will perform as advertised. But what if the match is wet? If I disregard that fact and expect the match to light, I am committing the fallacy. Again, consider the generalization that birds fly. What does this imply about penguins? If we infer that penguins must be able to fly because they are birds, or conversely that they can't be birds because they can't fly, we commit the fallacy of accident. Penguins are properly classified as birds for anatomical and evolutionary reasons, even though the adaptation of their wings to swimming, and the heavy layer of body fat to insulate them from the cold, prevent them from flying.

In everyday speech, "accident" refers to something that is unexpected or happens by chance. In logic, however, the word retains the older meaning: "a nonessential property or quality of an entity or circumstance" (*Merriam-Webster's Collegiate Dictionary*, 11th ed.). Generalizations typically apply to things in virtue of the things' essential properties. When a generalization has an exception, it's usually because of some accidental (i.e., nonessential) feature of that particular thing. Matches are designed to be used dry; if my matches got soaked in the rain, that's an accidental feature. Penguins evolved from birds and they adapted to finding food in the cold waters of the Antarctic; their inability to fly is a by-product, and thus in a sense is accidental.

The classic examples of accident involve the application of moral principles to particular situations. Take the principle that one should always tell the truth. What if a mugger on the street asks you where you live? Applying the principle mechanically to this situation by answering the question truthfully would be a rather dangerous case of fallacious thinking. Even if you lie but feel guilty about doing so, the feeling of guilt presumes that you *should* have told the truth to the mugger. Drawing that conclusion is fallacious whether you act on it or not. As an exercise for yourself, you might take other moral principles and imagine exceptional cases in which applying the principle would commit the fallacy. When we apply a given principle to a particular situation, we need to take account of other principles that may also apply and take account of any unusual consequences that might arise from applying the principle. It will not always be clear what the best decision is, and reasonable people may disagree. The point is not to apply the principle mechanically without considering the context.

Another common form of accident is extrapolating a generalization beyond the range in which we established its truth. For example, we have all learned that water boils at 212°F. But that measurement was made at sea level. It would be fallacious to assume that the generalization is true for all locations. That's not the case, as you have probably also learned. At higher altitudes, where the atmospheric pressure is lower, water boils at lower temperatures.

Not all generalizations have exceptions. In mathematics, there is a principle that if you have two equal quantities and subtract the same amount from both, the quantities will still be equal. That principle is true in all cases. In any area, on any topic, a strictly universal generalization has the form "All P are Q," and "all" means *all*, without exception. If even one P is not Q, then the generalization is false. But if the generalization is true, we can safely infer that any particular instance of P will be Q. (This is one of the major forms of deductive inference, and we will examine it at length in Part 2.) If a generalization does have exceptions, moreover, and if we know exactly how and why the exceptions occur, we can qualify the generalization and restore it to strict universality. For example, we can qualify the generalization "water boils at 212°F" by adding "at sea level."

For many generalizations, however, we may not know all the qualifications that would be needed to make them exception-proof. Or the exceptions may be so rare that we don't bother to add the qualification. The fact is that in wide areas of knowledge— including ethics, law, and politics and the properties and behavior of living species, to name a few—many of the generalizations we rely on have exceptions, and we need to avoid the fallacy of accident.

3.2F Slippery Slope

You have probably heard the phrase "slippery slope." It's a cliché, but it is a pretty good metaphor for the kind of situation in which, once you take the first step in a certain direction, circumstances will pull you further in that direction whether you like it or not, and you may slide too far down the slope. We have a number of other common expressions for asserting that one decision, action, or event will set off a train of causes leading on to some result beyond what we intended—usually an undesirable one.

> "If you give him an inch, he'll take a mile."

> The Marxist takeover in country *X* had "a domino effect" of inciting rebellions in neighboring countries.

> Giving in to small temptations leads you down "the primrose path" to immorality.

> Changing the grading standards had "a ripple effect" throughout the college.

> The antitrust laws were "the camel's nose in the tent" (or "the thin edge of the wedge") leading to further government regulation of business.

> The collapse of the subprime mortgage market "snowballed" into a crisis in all financial markets.

There's no question that the kind of causal sequence described by these expressions actually occurs. We can all think of slippery slopes in our past experience, and historians can provide us with many examples of how nations started down slippery slopes from the decisions of their leaders. But our concern is with arguments. A slippery slope *argument* is the attempt to show that some action or policy *will* lead on to a series of further consequences and should be avoided for that reason. Such arguments are usually directed against something that might otherwise seem desirable, or at least harmless, by trying to show that it would be the first step onto a slippery slope. People who defend free speech, for example, sometimes argue as follows:

> We should oppose any effort by government to censor obscene books, movies, or other forms of expression, no matter how offensive we may find such material. The reason is that once government has the power to ban obscenity, that precedent will open the door to further controls on speech: banning racist remarks, then speech that the majority finds offensive, then speech that opposes government policies, and so on until no one is free to say anything without government permission.

The argument assumes that such a loss of freedom would be very bad, so we should not take the first step of censoring obscenity. Thus the general form of slippery slope arguments is:

(There need not be exactly four items in the series of projected consequences; there could be any number.)

The **slippery slope** fallacy occurs when we posit a sequence of effects without good reason for thinking they will actually follow. This often happens in the heat of debate, when people exaggerate the likelihood of further consequences; or when people imagine dangers down the road, where their imagination is driven more by fear than by objective evidence. For example, suppose a teenager comes home an hour late one night, and a parent argues that that is the first step down a slippery slope:

> First it's staying out late, then it's not calling home, then it's a few drinks with friends, then wild parties, and before you know it, your life will be completely out of control. Someday you'll be glad that you had a curfew.

Unless the teenager has a history of being grossly irresponsible, the parent's argument seems exaggerated, not to say paranoid.

Slippery slope arguments can be good ones if the slope is real—that is, if there is good evidence that the consequences of the initial action are highly likely to occur. The strength of the argument depends on two factors. The first is the strength of each link in the causal chain; the argument cannot be stronger than its weakest link. The second is the number of links; the more links there are, the more likely it is that other factors could alter the consequences. The argument for free speech, for example, posits a series of steps by which government would expand its control over more and more kinds of speech, once the precedent of censoring obscenity was established. The argument assumes that government seeks to expand its power over people. Even if that is true, however, it does not mean that government can expand its power indefinitely without provoking opposition. So we can't assume that a ban on obscenity—the first step down the slope—will lead inexorably to censorship of all speech. Since each step is more intrusive than the one before, it is plausible that each step would provoke more opposition and thus become less likely. At best, therefore, this is a weak argument. Because it assumes that government power will expand inexorably, without recognizing any other factor, we would say that it is also fallacious.

Slippery slope arguments are very common in discussions of social and political issues. At the same time, such arguments are often used to persuade other people of a conclusion that the arguer has accepted for other, deeper reasons. For example, some people who use the slippery slope argument against censoring obscenity are opposed to censorship primarily because it inherently abridges individual freedom, not because it may have further consequences. That does not affect the strength of the slippery slope argument itself; people can have multiple arguments for a given conclusion, and each argument is what it is—it has whatever strength it has—regardless of how important it may be to a given person. But putting forward a slippery slope argument when it is not the main reason one accepts a conclusion *is* rather disingenuous. And, in such cases, refuting a slippery slope argument may do nothing to change the arguer's mind.

3.2G Composition and Division

The fallacy of **composition** consists in inferring that what is true of a part must be true of the whole. Of course, parts and wholes sometimes do have the same properties.

Every page in a newspaper is flammable, and so is the newspaper as a whole. But not every property is like this. We commit the fallacy of composition when we jump to a conclusion about the whole without considering whether the nature of the property in question makes it reasonable. The radio in my car was made by Motorola, but that does not imply that Motorola made my car as a whole. Every snowflake on my lawn is star-shaped and fell from the sky, but the snowball I make has neither of those properties. The fallacy of **division** is the mirror image of composition: It is the inference that what is true of the whole must be true of the parts. The fact that my car gets 25 miles to the gallon does not mean that the radio gets 25 miles to the gallon—a statement that hardly even makes sense. The fact that my car was made by General Motors does not mean that GM made every part.

Composition		**Division**	
Whole ↑ Part(s)	Inferring that the whole must have a property (merely) because one or more parts have the property	Whole ↓ Part(s)	Inferring that the parts must have a property (merely) because the whole has the property

The fallacies of composition and division can also occur in thinking about groups as well as individual things—when we are treating the group as a single whole. Suppose, for example, that every member of a college football team is a senior. We obviously

---

SOLVE   Composition and Division versus
Hasty Generalization
and Accident

Compare the diagrams above with the diagrams for hasty generalization and accident (p. 123). As you can see, composition has a certain similarity to hasty generalization. But hasty generalization applies to individual things and the *general classes* to which they belong, whereas composition applies to the parts of an individual thing and that *individual* thing as a whole. To see the difference, consider again the radio in my car. The radio is a member of the general class of audio equipment. It would be hasty to generalize that all audio equipment is made by Motorola, just because my car radio is. That is a different error from composition: inferring that Motorola made my car just because it made the radio. In the same way, the fallacy of division has a certain similarity with accident, but the latter involves a hasty application of a generalization about a class of things, whereas division is an inference from an individual thing to its parts.

cannot infer that the football team itself is a senior; that would be composition. Conversely, the team has properties as a team (e.g., a budget of $X from the college) that do not apply to individual players; inferring that the left guard Harold has a budget of $X would be a case of division. The same distinction applies to statements about general classes. Compare the statements:

> Human beings are animals.
>
> Human beings evolved 100,000 years ago.

The first is a general statement about humans. It applies to each and every one of us. If we have the additional premise that X is a human being, we can validly infer that X is an animal. But the second is a statement about the human species as a whole, as a single biological unit. It does *not* apply to individual humans as members of the species. The fact that the species evolved 100,000 years ago does not imply that you evolved—came into existence—back then.

It isn't likely that anyone would make the absurd inferences we have used so far to illustrate composition and division. So let us turn to cases in which these fallacies are more likely to be committed. One case is the use of statistics. Compare the statements:

> American steel companies are profitable.
>
> The average American steel company is profitable.

The first statement is also a generalization, about each instance of a class. You could therefore infer that any given company is profitable. But an average is a statistical fact about a class as a whole. So the second statement does not support the inference that a given company is profitable, and we would commit the fallacy of division if we made that inference.

People commit the fallacy of composition with other statistical information, too. Treatment for mental disorders is less expensive per-person than treatment for cancer. But it would be composition to infer that total spending on mental disorders is less than total spending on cancer treatment. That depends on the number of patients who seek treatment for these conditions. As it happens, there are many more people being treated for mental disorders than for cancer, so that total spending is roughly the same.

Political issues are another area in which these fallacies occur. A society is made up of individual people. What is true of individuals may or may not be true of society as a whole, and vice versa, so we have to be careful to avoid composition and division. For example, a newspaper editorial argues for government economic planning by asking, "Why is planning considered a good thing for individuals and business but a bad thing for the national economy?" The fact that individuals need to plan how they are going to earn a living and spend their income does not imply that society as a whole should plan how wealth should be produced and distributed throughout the economy. Whether national planning is a good idea depends on a host of other questions, such as whether government planners are capable of performing this task, and whether they have the right to supersede the decisions that individuals and businesses make about how to use their resources. Because the editorial ignores these issues and makes a simple inference from parts to the whole, the argument is a case of composition.

REVIEW Inductive Fallacies

Appeal to authority (*argumentum ad verecundiam*): using what an authority says as evidence for the truth of a proposition when the conditions for credibility are not satisfied.

False dichotomy: excluding relevant possibilities without justification.

Post hoc: using the fact that one event preceded another as sufficient evidence for the conclusion that the first caused the second.

Hasty generalization: inferring a general proposition from an inadequate sample of particular cases.

Accident: applying a generalization to a special case in disregard of qualities or circumstances that make it an exception to the generalization.

Slippery slope: arguing against a proposed action or policy by claiming, with insufficient evidence, that it will lead to a series of increasingly bad consequences.

Composition: inferring that a whole has a property merely because its parts have that property.

Division: inferring that a part has a property merely because the whole has that property.

EXERCISE 3.2

Identify which of the fallacies discussed in this section—appeal to authority, false dichotomy, *post hoc*, hasty generalization, accident, slippery slope, composition, or division—is committed in the statements below.

*1. Don't go down to River Road. I was down there once and got mugged. They're all thieves down there.

2. If she loved me, she would have called me back tonight. She didn't, so she must hate me.

3. I think America should be more careful about the international organizations we join and the treaties we sign. After all, wasn't it George Washington himself who warned against "foreign entanglements"?

*4. Flowers require soil, water, and sunlight to grow. Foxglove grows in the shade, so it must not be a flower.

5. Although I'm happy about the raise I got today, I'm also a little worried. The last time I got a raise my car got stolen the next morning.

6. Tell your representative that you don't want health care reform! If the health care reform is passed, private insurance companies won't be able to compete with the public option. With the private companies out of the picture, individuals will only be able to turn to the public option, and then it will be up to the government to decide whether we should live or die.

*7. I'm sure this outfit will look great. It's got leopard print, zebra print, plaid, and polka dots, and I like each of those patterns.

8. To solve our transportation problems, we have to put more money into mass transit. CBS News said so last night.

9. My son says he's ready to get married, but I don't think so. I'm his mother, and I know him best.

∗10. On the basis of the rambling speech Madeleine gave at the school assembly last week, I would say she's not a good public speaker.

11. How can you say that you washed the car? Did you wash every part—under the hood, around the muffler, under the seats?

12. One should always keep appointments. So even though José is an hour late, we should continue to wait for him.

∗13. Congressman Jones denies that he's a liberal, so he must be a conservative.

14. I will vote for whomever the Democrat Party chooses as its candidate. If these experienced politicians think that someone is fit to represent them in office, then that person must be a good leader.

15. Twenty-five years after graduation, Harvard alumni have incomes much higher than that of the average college graduate. A Harvard education must be the road to riches.

∗16. Everyone on the Dream Team is the best player in his position, so the Dream Team is the best team around.

17. If their band accepts this mainstream record deal, they'll be selling out! Next they'll get corporate sponsors for their tour, and then we'll be hearing their songs redone as commercial jingles for toothpaste.

18. A pile of stones will topple if it is not stacked vertically. So it is impossible to build a stone arch.

∗19. Either Tom was telling the truth when he said his grade average was 3.7 or he was lying. But he wasn't telling the truth, since his average is actually 3.6, so he was lying.

20. It's good to put water in your body, so it must be good to put water in your lungs.

21. I've seen my daughter's teachers underestimate her ability in math and science. This just goes to show that educators in America are sexist.

∗22. Stock prices fell dramatically 2 years ago, after Congress raised tariffs, and they just raised tariffs again, so expect another crash in the market.

23. The committee for education showed that budget cuts to the art and music departments did not diminish the academic performances of students in the past, and so argued that upcoming cuts wouldn't either. But Mrs. Jensen says the budget cuts will diminish academic performances, and I think a teacher who's in the classroom every day knows a lot more about education than a committee.

24. Dr. Kingston should not have given that choking man the Heimlich maneuver. He cracked one of his ribs, and a doctor's first principle is to "do no harm."

∗25. If pharmaceutical companies aren't monitored by the government, then individual consumers will have to be completely responsible for learning every detail about the medicines that they take. The majority of people don't have enough time or expertise to take on this responsibility, so we should leave it to the government.

26. University admissions departments should not be allowed to give preference to the children of alumni. This will lead to the perpetuation of a predominantly white upper class, which will make it increasingly difficult for minorities to achieve upward mobility.

27. The last time I stretched my arms first and my legs second, I won my race. So that stretching sequence must have increased my speed.

*28. The catalog said it was a gold figurine, but these accents are made of silver! So it is not actually a gold figurine.

29. In an important way, a choir is a living, breathing being, since it is composed of singers, who are living, breathing beings.

30. Our school's basketball team has lost every one of its first six games this season, so I know we won't win a single game all year.

3.3 Fallacies of Presumption and Diversion

In the previous sections, we examined arguments that are fallacious either because they introduce irrelevant considerations into the reasoning process (emotions, threats, personal traits) or because they fail to consider a wide enough context of information. In this section, we'll examine fallacies that involve more subtle logical errors within the argument itself.

3.3A Begging the Question (Circular Argument)

Begging the question is the use of a proposition as a premise in an argument intended to support that same proposition. The point of reasoning is to shed light on the truth or falsity of a proposition (the conclusion) by relating it to other propositions (the premises) that we already have some basis for believing to be true. If our reasoning does nothing more than relate p to itself, then it hasn't gained us anything. It has not given us a *reason* to think p is true. Circular arguments are no more productive than circular definitions.

The most obvious way to commit the fallacy would be simply to restate the conclusion as a premise, in an argument of the form:

$$p$$
$$\downarrow$$
$$p$$

This usually occurs only when the proposition is formulated in two different ways, so that it is not immediately apparent that the person is simply restating the conclusion. For example: "[1] Society has an obligation to support the needy, because [2] people who cannot provide for themselves have a right to the resources of the community." Statement 2 expresses the same proposition as 1: "society" means the same thing as "community," "the needy" are the same class of people as "those who cannot provide for themselves," and the obligation mentioned in 1 is merely another way of expressing the right mentioned in 2. Both statements, therefore, should be given the same number, and the diagram would be:

$$1$$
$$\downarrow$$
$$1$$

People typically beg the question in this way when a proposition seems so obvious to them that they aren't sure what further evidence could be given for it, so they keep restating it in the hope that some formulation will strike the listener as plausible and lead him to agree.

A more subtle form of the fallacy occurs when the circle is enlarged to include more than one step: The conclusion p is supported by premise q, which in turn is supported by p (though there could be any number of intervening steps). Suppose I am arguing with an atheist about the existence of a supreme being. He asks why I believe that God exists, and I say, "Because the Bible says so." If he then asks why he should take the Bible's word for it, and I answer that the Bible is trustworthy because it is the Word of God, I am arguing in a circle: My premise assumes the existence of God, which was precisely the question at issue. As this example illustrates, circular reasoning of this

---

APPLY BTQ Abuse

The phrase "beg the question" is often misused to mean something other than the logical fallacy. "That begs the question" does not mean "That raises the question," or "That avoids the question."

Merriam-Webster gives these examples on its website:

1. "The U.S. Postal service says that personal letter delivery is at an all-time low. . . . Which begs the question: are open letters the only kind the future will know?" *Time Magazine*

2. "It's not the first time a fan has been injured by a batted ball or broken bat flying into the stands, nor is it likely to be the last. But that begs the question: Why are teams putting fans at risk in the first place?" *The Chicago Tribune*

While such usage of the phrase is common, it is also opposed by many people who want to retain the original meaning as a name for the fallacy of circular reasoning. There is even a website, http://begthequestion.info, that offers a card you can "give to public speakers, bosses, writers, preachers, politicians, or random people on the subway and bus whom you hear getting it wrong."

type often occurs in debates when we try to answer an objection by falling back on the conclusion we are trying to establish.

COMPLEX QUESTION An indirect form of begging the question is known as the **complex question** or *loaded question*. Suppose I accuse you of having cheated on a test, and when you deny it I say, "Why are you lying to me?" Any answer you give will imply that you were indeed lying, and thus that you did cheat. The reason for this is obvious. Despite its appearance, the question is not simple but complex; it is loaded with an implicit assumption. There are really two questions here: "Are you lying?" and "If so, why?" We can't even raise the second question, much less answer it, until we have answered the first one. By not asking the first question, I have simply assumed that the answer to it is "Yes"—I have begged that question. Strictly speaking, it is not the question itself—"Why are you lying"—that is fallacious. A question is not an assertion or an argument. But such questions rest on certain assumptions. In asking the question, I am implicitly asserting that you did lie (i.e., that you did cheat). I am thus assuming the very thing I need to prove.

3.3B Equivocation

We have seen that an argument links one or more propositions used as premises with a proposition that serves as the conclusion. We have also seen that what a proposition asserts depends (in part) on the words used to express it. The fallacy of **equivocation** occurs when a word switches meaning in the middle of the argument—when it expresses one concept in one premise and another concept in another premise or in the conclusion.

Consider the following argument:

[Letter] grades are a crude and mechanical device that does
not measure the nuances of student performance

↓

Student work should not be graded [evaluated]

The conclusion is not supported by the premise because the term "grade" has shifted its meaning. The claim that letter grades are a poor evaluation device hardly implies that student work should not be evaluated at all; if anything, it implies that we should find a better means for measuring performance.

In this example, the equivocation occurred because a word was used in both a narrower sense, to designate a species (letter grades), and in a wider sense to designate a genus (evaluation as such). This illustrates a common pattern in which a word's meaning is broadened in the course of an argument.

Another way in which this happens is by the metaphorical extension of a concept. The term "censorship," for example, refers to a restriction on someone's freedom of speech by a government, using the coercive threat of fines, jail, or worse. But the term is sometimes used metaphorically for other constraints on the ability to express oneself. It would be equivocation to switch between these meanings, as in the following argument:

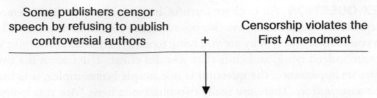

Some publishers censor speech by refusing to publish controversial authors   +   Censorship violates the First Amendment

Some publishers violate the First Amendment by refusing to publish controversial authors

In premise 1, the term "censor" is used in the metaphorical sense, since the newspapers are merely choosing not to publish certain authors rather than literally threatening them with legal sanctions. But in premise 2, the term is used in its literal meaning, so the conclusion does not follow.

As an argument employs more complex and abstract concepts, equivocation becomes more of a danger. The best way to avoid the danger is to use the techniques for clarifying and defining concepts that we studied in Chapter 1.

3.3C Appeal to Ignorance (*Argumentum ad Ignorantiam*)

Suppose I claim that politician *X* is having an affair with an aide. "Prove it," you say. "Can you prove that he's not having an affair?" I ask—and thereby commit the fallacy of **appeal to ignorance**. This fallacy consists in the argument that a proposition is true because it hasn't been proven false. To put it differently, it is the argument that a proposition is true because the *opposing* proposition hasn't been proven true. Using the symbol $-p$ to stand for the denial or negation of p, the fallacy has the structure:

$-p$ has not been proven true

p is true

This is a fallacy because a lack of evidence for $-p$ does not imply that there is evidence for p. All it means is that we do not know that $-p$ is true. I can't prove that a storm is not brewing in the atmosphere of Jupiter, but that would hardly count as evidence that a storm *is* brewing. The absence of evidence usually means that we simply don't know enough to make a judgment. Such ignorance cannot be transmuted into knowledge, any more than brass can be transmuted into gold.

In the preceding examples of the fallacy, the proposition p was a positive claim: that *X* is having an affair, that a storm is brewing on Jupiter. But the fallacy can also be committed when p is a negative claim. The absence of evidence that *X is* having an affair does not prove that he isn't; the absence of evidence that a storm *is* brewing doesn't prove that one *isn't*. In the diagram for the fallacy, *p* may be either negative or positive, and −*p* will have the opposite quality; the structure of the fallacy is the same in either case. Strictly speaking, there is a logical symmetry between positive and negative claims.

In practice, however, the fallacy is normally committed by those who assert the positive. The reason is that we rarely have occasion to assert that something is *not* the case until someone has suggested that it *is*. Suppose I suddenly announced that there is an invisible leprechaun hovering over your left shoulder. Naturally, you would be skeptical, and you would ask what reason I had for believing this (we couldn't settle the matter by looking, since I said it was invisible). I'm the one making the assertion here, so I have to provide evidence. Apart from my statement, it would never occur to you to deny that there is an invisible leprechaun over your left shoulder.

As a rule, it is the positive claim that puts the ball in play and the positive claim that carries the initial burden of proof. If someone makes an unsupported statement, therefore, the proper response is not to make an equally unsupported denial. Nor should you accept the burden of disproving the person's statement; if you do, you are cooperating in an implicit appeal to ignorance. (This is a trap that paranoid people often spring on their listeners: They make an arbitrary claim about a conspiracy against them and then take their claim to be vindicated unless others can disprove it.) The proper response is simply to point out that the claim is unsupported and ask the person to provide some evidence for it. If evidence *is* forthcoming, then the ball is in your court; if you do not find the evidence convincing, it is your responsibility to explain why.

One application of this rule is the legal principle that a person is innocent until proven guilty. To assert that someone is guilty is to make a positive claim: that the person committed a certain act. Thus in a court of law, the burden of proof rests with the party who brings the charges. But we need to be careful here. The prosecution's failure to establish guilt on the part of the defendant does not prove that the defendant didn't commit the crime. We would commit the fallacy of appealing to ignorance if we thought so. In this respect, the legal rule goes beyond the burden of proof principle. It also reflects the ethical principle that it is better to let a guilty person go free than to punish an innocent one.

3.3D Diversion

The fallacy of **diversion** occurs when there is a conclusion to be considered but someone offers an argument that diverts attention away from that conclusion.

MISSING THE POINT The paradigm case of diversion, often called **missing the point**, involves arguing for a different, but seeming related, conclusion. In effect, the argument changes the issue in the middle of the discussion. A prosecutor in a child abuse case might go on and on about the horrors of child abuse—the child's suffering and future psychological problems, statistics showing that the problem is a growing one, and so forth—when the real issue is whether the defendant is guilty of the crime. The argument would run:

1. The defendant is guilty of child abuse.
2. Child abuse is an awful crime.

3, 4, . . . , *n*. Statements concerning immediate and long-term effects on children, statistics on the extent of the problem, and other evidence.

The prosecutor's strategy is obvious. He is diverting attention from 1 to 2, because 2 is much easier to prove. Who could deny that child abuse is awful? At the same time, however, he is hoping that the jury will not notice the diversion and that the strength of the argument for conclusion 2 will carry over in their minds to 1, even though the defendant's guilt is a completely separate question.

A common form of missing the point occurs in regard to human actions and their consequences. Virtually any action has some effects that are not intended, and often not even foreseen. The fact that your action had a certain consequence, therefore, does not necessarily mean that you intended it, and I would commit the fallacy of diversion if I tried to prove your intent solely by showing that the action did have that consequence. Suppose you go to the library one evening and miss a call from your mother. There may have been no way to anticipate the call. Even if there were, you may have felt that doing work at the library was more important and that missing the call would have to be an unfortunate by-product of going there. To prove that you were deliberately trying to avoid the call, we would need some positive evidence of that intent. It would be diversion to argue that you wanted to miss the call if the only evidence is that you did go to the library. In the same way, it would be fallacious to argue that the U.S. Labor Department is controlled by labor unions just because some decision turns out to be of benefit to union members; once again, we need evidence of intent, not merely of consequence.

STRAW MAN Another form of diversion is called the **straw man** argument. This fallacy occurs in debate when someone distorts an opponent's position, usually stating it in an oversimplified or extreme form (like a scarecrow made of straw), and then refutes the distorted position, not the real one. For example, suppose you are a student in my class, and you come to me with the suggestion that I allow more class discussion. I would commit the straw man fallacy if I replied: "I don't want to give the entire class period over to an aimless bull session, because no one would learn anything." This may be an excellent argument against giving the entire class period over to an aimless bull session, but that is not what you suggested. (If you diagram this example, you will see that it fits the pattern of diversion.) Straw man arguments occur most often when issues are complex and emotions run high. Look for them especially in politics and in quarrels between friends and lovers.

As the previous example indicates, diversion can occur with negative arguments (*against* your idea that I allow more class discussion) as well as positive ones (*for* the conclusion that the defendant is guilty of child abuse). The negative version is sometimes called "*ignoratio elenchi,*" a Latin phrase for a fallacy that the ancient Greek philosopher

Aristotle identified. It means "ignorant refutation." But the logical fault is the same, whether the argument is intended to support or refute a claim.

RED HERRING Sometimes an argument distracts from the conclusion to be discussed, not by arguing for a different conclusion, as in missing the point, but by introducing irrelevant points that don't really support any conclusion but nevertheless divert attention from the issue. This version of diversion is often called a **red herring**—herring turns red when it is smoked, and a smoked fish has such a powerful smell that dragging it across the ground will throw a dog off the scent.

A common example (widely mocked on *The Simpsons* and elsewhere) is "Think of the children." It invokes the natural human care for children in arguments about everything from gun control, to pornography, to government debt, to climate change—using that distracting emotion to support or counter a position that is not really about children per se. In this respect, many red herring arguments can also be seen as appeals to emotion.

Politicians often commit the red herring fallacy when they dodge a hard question. A reporter asks a member of Congress why he or she voted to expand a certain welfare program, despite its high cost. Answer: "I have always been an advocate of fairness and community. The strength of America is the strength of its communities, and I'm proud to help make our communities better places for the people of this country." This answer does not address the economic question the reporter asked, but it isn't really an argument for any other conclusion.

NON SEQUITUR   Before we leave the subject of fallacies, a word about the term "*non sequitur*," a Latin phrase whose literal meaning is "It does not follow." In everyday discourse, the term is often used to describe a wild leap or disconnect in a conversation or narrative, sometimes for deliberate comic effect. When an argument is described as a *non sequitur*, it is often because the premises seem completely unrelated to the conclusion.

> She: Why are you wearing your shirt backward?
> He: Because there's going to be a lunar eclipse tonight.
> [Pause]
> She: That's it? That's your reason?

In logic, the term has been given various meanings. It is sometimes used broadly to mean any argument in which the conclusion does not follow from the premises. In that sense every fallacy is a *non sequitur*. It is sometimes used more narrowly as another name for diversion (and its special forms missing the point, straw man, and red herring). Because the premises in a case of diversion are used to support a conclusion that is different from the intended one, this fallacy is a particularly clear case of an argument in which the conclusion simply does not follow from the premises. In yet another sense, *non sequitur* fallacies are a miscellaneous category of bad arguments that do not fit the specific patterns of any of the named fallacies.

In light of these different meanings, we have not used the term in classifying and describing the fallacies in this chapter, nor in the exercises that ask you to identify the fallacy committed by a given argument. Nevertheless, it is a useful term to have at your disposal. When you encounter an argument whose conclusion just doesn't follow, and you aren't sure or can't remember which specific fallacy it commits, it is safe to describe it as a *non sequitur*.

REVIEW Fallacies of Presumption and Divergence

1. **Begging the question** (circular argument): trying to support a proposition with an argument in which that proposition is a premise.
2. **Equivocation**: using a word in two different meanings in the premises and/or conclusion.
3. **Appeal to ignorance** (*argumentum ad ignorantiam*): using the absence of proof for

a proposition as evidence for the truth of the opposing proposition.

4. **Diversion**: trying to support one proposition by diverting attention to another conclusion or issue.

EXERCISE 3.3

Identify which of the fallacies discussed in this section—begging the question, equivocation, appeal to ignorance, or diversion—is committed in the following statements.

∗1. No one has proved that global warming is actually occurring, so I'm sure it isn't.

2. It would be a crime to let that dessert go to waste. Since I am a law-abiding citizen, I'd better eat it.

3. Why are you so skeptical about ESP? Can you prove that it doesn't exist?

∗4. No one has shown that aliens did not create the crop circles. So the crop circles must have been made by aliens.

5. Only short poems, not long ones, can be good. Of course, many so-called poems, such as *Paradise Lost*, take up a large number of pages. But if they are any good, they must really be collections of short poems, because a long poem as such cannot be of any great value.

6. The safety inspector has suggested that American Traveler airlines delay the introduction of its new fleet for another year because of engine prob-

lems. But it has been widely shown that air travel is safe.

You are seven times more likely to get in a car accident than an airplane accident, not to mention that airport security measures have increased dramatically in the past 10 years, lowering the risk of people bringing weapons aboard a plane.

∗7. George's coaches say he has a real gift for football. So because his skill is a gift, he doesn't deserve any credit for it.

8. Abortion should be illegal because it's criminal to deliberately kill another human being.

9. There can't be a law without a lawgiver. But nature operates in accordance with laws, like the law of gravity, so there must be a Lawgiver above nature.

∗10. Maryam says she loves me. I don't know whether to believe her or not, but I guess I do, because I don't think she would lie to someone she loves about something that important.

11. Hard-core pornography is disgusting and offensive to any civilized person, so it cannot be included in the right to free speech.

12. "I don't see how you can support distribution requirements. Don't you want students to have any choice about their courses?"

*13. The federal government should save Puerto Rico from default, for Puerto Rico deserves such aid.

14. Helping someone who is in trouble is the right thing to do. So if you don't help someone who's in trouble, you're violating his rights.

15. The layoffs at Acme Corporation were obviously racist in intent, since more than 60% of the people laid off were Black or Hispanic.

*16. Scientists have never been able to demonstrate conclusively that animals are conscious like us, or that they have subjective experiences. Therefore they aren't and they don't.

17. People who trip sometimes skin their knees. And my cousin just got back from a trip to Australia, so I'm worried that we might need to bandage his knees at the airport.

18. Customer in shoe store: "I kind of like these shoes, but I don't know. . . . They're pretty expensive." Salesperson: "Well you could spend that much for dinner at a fancy restaurant. Wouldn't you like to look your best at a top-notch place?"

*19. Officials at the CIA are worried that there might be a mole in their Langley office. But Peterson's Pest Control is advertising that they can eliminate moles in less than a week for under $200. So the CIA should just hire Peterson's.

20. Our town needs to adopt a strict leash law. If we allow people to turn every sort of wild animal loose on our streets, then no one will be safe.

21. Poverty will continue to increase in the West Stratherford neighborhood, because over time, people there will have less and less money.

*22. I was a little worried about whether or not it's safe to use mothballs as bath beads. But when I Googled it, I didn't get any results saying that it's dangerous. So it must be safe.

23. The new Captain Pat Riot action figure is the perfect gift for your child's birthday. It's made of 100% nontoxic material, it has no small parts that your child might swallow, it's shatter-resistant, dishwasher safe, and has received over 10,000 hours of safety testing. Buy yours today!

24. ABBA is the greatest pop music group of all time. They won the 1974 Eurovision Song Contest, performed together for 10 years, had 14 top 40 hits, and a hit musical (*Mamma Mia!*) based on their music.

*25. Because telling the truth is a universal moral obligation, every individual has an ethical responsibility to speak truthfully.

CHAPTER REVIEW

Summary

- A fallacy is an argument in which the premises appear to support the conclusion but actually provide little or no support. This chapter covered three categories of fallacies that occur fairly often in everyday thought and speech:
  - Fallacies of relevance attempt to support a conclusion with premises not relevant to the conclusion.
  - Inductive fallacies of context jump to a conclusion without considering a large enough context of evidence.
  - Fallacies of presumption and diversion involve errors in the relation between premises and conclusion.

- The 17 common fallacies we studied are listed, along with some of their specific forms, in the Key Terms section. This is not an exhaustive list of errors in reasoning; it includes only the more common and more significant ones.
- A given argument may commit more than one fallacy. If you encounter such an argument, in the exercises at the end of this chapter or in real life, you should try to identify all the fallacies it commits.

Key Terms

fallacy (p. 105)

FALLACIES OF RELEVANCE

subjectivism (p. 106)
appeal to majority (p. 108)
appeal to emotion (p. 109)
appeal to force (*argumentum ad baculum*)
  (p. 111)
ad hominem (p. 112)
  abusive *ad hominem* (p. 112)
  tu quoque (p. 112)
  poisoning the well (p. 113)

INDUCTIVE FALLACIES

appeal to authority (*argumentum ad verecundiam*) (p. 118)
false dichotomy (p. 120)
post hoc (p. 121)

hasty generalization (p. 122)
accident (p. 123)
slippery slope (p. 126)
composition (p. 126)
division (p. 127)

FALLACIES OF PRESUMPTION AND DIVERSION

begging the question (*circular argument*)
  (p. 131)
  complex question (p. 133)
equivocation (p. 133)
appeal to ignorance (*argumentum ad ignorantiam*) (p. 134)
diversion (p. 135)
  missing the point (p. 135)
  straw man (p. 136)
  red herring (p. 137)

Putting It All Together

I. **Integrative Exercise** Identify the fallacy (or fallacies) committed by each of the following arguments.

* 1. The Beatles were the best rock group of the 1960s—they sold more records than any other group.

2. "That was a great movie."
"Why do you think so?"
"Well, I just loved it."

3. The seatbelt law should be repealed. It starts with the government making citizens do small things, like wearing seatbelts and helmets for biking, then it's curfews and policemen asking to see your papers, and then people will be afraid to do anything without seeking government approval first.

* 4. We can maintain our military strength by bringing back the draft and increasing the military budget, or we can cut spending and become a militarily weak nation. Which option do you favor?

5. How can you deny that the belief in an afterlife is universal? After all, everyone believes in it.

6. I just broke up with my boyfriend—it just goes to show I'll never make a relationship work.

* 7. If we pass a law to require that guns be registered with the government, it will be easier for the government to take the next step of confiscating guns. So we must oppose gun registration now.

8. This must be an important event. The *New York Times* gave it four columns on the front page.

9. Opinion poll question: Do you favor more money for welfare programs, or do you feel we should let people starve in the streets?

*10. The spokesman for Wild West cigarettes says that advertisements do not get people addicted to cigarettes. But in a recent poll, 45% of Americans agreed that smoking advertisements affect whether people smoke or not, and 67% think that advertisements increase the number of cigarettes that smokers have.

11. Both President Bush and President Obama have allowed their religious views to influence the government policies they support, and this is not right. Next there will be a national religion, and the government will persecute dissenters.

12. Salesman to customer: "I think you'll find that those shoes are the ones you want. Shall I wrap them up, or would you prefer to wear them?"

*13. No one can criticize the Freudian theory unless he has been psychoanalyzed, for opposition to the theory is normally caused by unconscious resistance, arising from the Oedipal complex, which distorts one's thinking.

14. My logic teacher says it's a fallacy to appeal to authority, but I noticed in class today that she cited Aristotle in answering an objection we had.

15. Six months after President Hoover took office in 1929, the stock market crashed and the Great Depression began. He is therefore responsible for this tragic episode in our nation's history.

*16. Elephants live in tropical climates where there is plenty of vegetation. So we probably won't see any at the Chicago zoo.

17. The U.S. federal government should enact polices to provide day care for families who cannot afford it. Governments in all other industrialized nations have taken steps toward national child care.

18. Because she couldn't find a position as a teacher, Jackie was forced to take a job in data entry. But no one should be forced to work, so the police should investigate Jackie's situation.

∗19. I'm shocked to hear you preaching atheism. Does your father know you believe that?

20. Eight out of ten doctors support a woman's right to have an abortion. How can you deny that this is a genuine right?

21. This dish ought to be delicious, since I love everything that goes into it.

∗22. Mr. Nakamura said there was to be no talking during the test. So it's fair that Jamie had points deducted for asking to go to the bathroom because she felt sick.

23. "C'mon, spend the night with me."
"Why should I?"
"Why shouldn't you?"

24. Interviewer: Senator, you voted for the new missile defense system. Would you explain your reasons, particularly in light of criticisms about the effectiveness of the system? Senator: I'd be glad to. America needs a strong defense. We'd all like to live in peace with the other nations of this world, but we deceive ourselves if we think we can do that without being prepared to defend ourselves and our allies, our rights and our interests. It's a dangerous world out there, and I'd be derelict in my duty to the people of this nation if I allowed us to lie down and cry "Uncle."

∗25. Wilson used abusive language toward the child who threw a stone at his car. Since child abuse is a crime, he should be reported to the authorities.

26. Studies show that most men who are married live longer, happier lives than men who do not get married. Therefore, if Troy wants a long happy life, he should marry Jennifer.

27. "The poor nations of the world will have to learn to produce their own food if they are to solve the problem of hunger in the long run."

"That's a heartless position. You wouldn't say that if you had ever really been hungry."

∗28. Democracy is the best political system. Therefore China should adopt a democratic system now.

29. Many people say that Picasso was a great artist, but are we supposed to admire a man who beat his mistresses?

30. Bill Smith has lived all his life in Maplewood. From his schoolboy days, when he was a wrestling champ, to his service as a church deacon and downtown merchant, he has always been ready with a friendly smile and a helping hand. With his wife Mary, he has raised a family here. He has deep roots in our community and wants to make it an even better place to live. Vote for him for town council.

∗31. You weren't in class today, and you weren't in your room when I called. Why are you avoiding me?

32. The percentage of whites who are on welfare is higher than the percentage of Asians who are. Whites therefore make up a larger portion of the welfare population.

33. As a determinist, I believe that none of our actions results from free choice and that all of them are determined by the strongest motive acting upon us. To be sure, it sometimes does seem that we choose to act on the weaker of two motives. But if so, it only shows that the motive that seemed weaker was really the stronger of the two, since it determined our action.

∗34. Human life depends on an environment that includes the existence of a large number of diverse species of plants and animals. Therefore we must do everything possible to prevent the extinction of any species.

35. Student to teacher: "How can you give me a C in this course? I've been getting Bs from all my other teachers. Maybe your grading standards are too high."

II. [Integrative Exercise] Taking each of the propositions that follow as a conclusion, make up an argument that commits the fallacy named in brackets. Try not to make the fallacy too blatant; instead, make it as subtle and persuasive-sounding as you can.

✱1. Mary lied when she said she saw a ghost. [False dichotomy]

2. Children should not be spanked. [Appeal to authority]

3. I'll pass this course. [Subjectivism]

✱4. The United States should adopt regulatory policies favoring entrepreneurs. [Appeal to majority]

5. Megadoses of vitamin C can cure cancer. [*Post hoc*]

6. Many crimes result from television violence. [Appeal to ignorance]

✱7. Capitalism exploits the working class. [Appeal to emotion]

8. *Moby Dick* is the greatest novel ever written. [Diversion]

9. U.S. savings bonds are a good investment. [Appeal to force]

✱10. Logic is worth studying. [Begging the question]

III. [Integrative Exercise] Identify any fallacies committed in the following passages.

✱1. "Received the Amulet at 2:00 p.m. on Friday. Went to Bingo at 6:00 p.m. and won $50.00. The next day I won $300.00! I'm very happy because I was about to give up Bingo, cause I wasn't winning." [Testimonial for Magic Square Amulet]

2. "I think in my country, in my family, I think that I believe that a marriage should be between a man and a woman. No offense to anybody out there, but that's how I was raised." [Carrie Prejean, 2009 Miss USA pageant. Fox News]

3. Sister James: I don't think Father Flynn did anything wrong.
Sister Aloysius Beauvier: You just want things to be resolved so you can have simplicity back. [*Doubt* movie]

✱4. "After deciding to sell his home in Upland, California, novelist Whitney Stine pounded a 'For Sale' sign into his front yard. But he deliberately waited to do so until 2:22 p.m. one Thursday.
"The house sold three days later for his asking price—$238,000. And Mr. Stine credits the quick sale to the advice of his astrologer, John Bradford, whom he has consulted for 12 years in the sale of five houses.

" 'He always tells me to put out the sign according to the phases of the moon, and the houses have always sold within a few months,' Mr. Stine says." [Kathleen A. Hughes, "Thinking of Buying or Selling a House? Ask Your Astrologer," *Wall Street Journal*]

5. A premed student to her sculpture professor: "My lowest grade last year was in your class. It brings down my grade point average, and then I may not get into medical school. I'm taking sculpture to expand my horizons, and it shouldn't affect my life."

6. Socrates: The guards will have all wives in common, their children will also be common, and parents will not know which children are theirs nor will children know which parents belong to them.
Glaucon: That is a larger and more powerful wave than the first one, and both its credibility and its usefulness are more doubtful.
Socrates: I don't see how anyone could dispute the utility of having wives and children in common, but the possibility of getting it accepted is another matter. [Plato, *Republic*, Book V]

*7. "Finally, in finding the $5 billion punitive award [against Exxon Corporation for the *Valdez* oil spill] justified, you are applying a different standard from the one you apply to yourself. Last year *The Times* joined in a brief that argued that a $10 million punitive damage verdict against another news medium should be set aside." [Letter to the Editor (from the chairman of Exxon), *New York Times*]

8. "Nothing is more irritating than taking a bottle of wine to someone's house and having them put it away, unopened. There are only two possible messages there: 1) This stuff is so bad, I'd never be caught dead serving it, or 2) This stuff is so good, I certainly wouldn't want to share it with *you*." [Dorothy J. Gaiter and John Brecher, "When You're Asked to Bring the Wine," *Tastings, Wall Street Journal*]

9. "Abortion is America's modern day holocaust. The taking of innocent human life has inflicted incalculable misery. The human suffering and the spiritual blindness caused by abortion are beyond comprehension. God is a compassionate and a just God, but His justice will not sleep forever. We must not—we cannot—remain silent when millions of innocent unborn children are killed every year." [Mathew Staver endorsing *40 Days For Life*]

*10. "[The classical liberals] put forward their ideas as immutable truths good at all times and places; they had no idea of historic relativity. . . . The tragedy is that although these liberals were the sworn foes of political absolutism, they were themselves absolutist in the social creed they formulated." [John Dewey, *Liberalism and Social Action*, pp. 33–34]

11. "But don't wrangle with us so long as you apply, to our intended abolition of bourgeois property, the standard of your bourgeois notions of freedom, culture, law, etc. Your very ideas are but the outgrowth of the conditions of your bourgeois production and bourgeois property . . ." [Karl Marx and Friedrich Engels, *Communist Manifesto*]

12. Father Brendan Flynn: You haven't the slightest proof of anything!
Sister Aloysius Beauvier: But I have my certainty! And armed with that, I will go to your last parish, and the one before that if necessary. I'll find a parent. [*Doubt* movie]

*13. "White House spokesman Robert Gibbs defended Obama's all-out campaign for Chicago's Olympics bid by claiming America will see a "tangible economic benefit." But as is always the case with sports corporate welfare disguised as "economic development," an elite few will benefit more than others." [Michelle Malkin, "All President's Cronies Are Going for Gold," *Investors Business Daily*]

14. "[Rev. Wieslaw Jankowski] cited the case of a woman who asked for a divorce days after renewing her wedding vows as part of a marriage counseling program. What was suspicious, he said, was how the wife suddenly developed a passionate hatred for her husband.
"'According to what I could perceive, the devil was present and acting in an obvious way,' he said. 'How else can you explain how a wife, in the space of a couple of weeks, could come to hate her own husband, a man who is a good person?'" ["Ritual of Dealing with Demons Undergoes a Revival," *Washington Post*]

15. "Tall and handsome, [Karl Marx's collaborator Friedrich] Engels had a taste not just for ideas but for the good life—wine, women, riding with the Cheshire hunt—and seems to have felt little sense of irony that all these things were paid for by the proletariat's back-breaking labor." ["A Very Special Business Angel," *Economist.com*. © 2009 The Economist Newspaper and The Economist Group.]

*16. "Sen. Rudman advanced a 'pizza theory' to resolve disputes; budget negotiators were stalled for five hours but reached agreement

20 minutes after Rep. Aspin had pizza delivered." [*Wall Street Journal*]

17. "Voting 'yes' for the new Iranian constitution will satisfy the will and wrath of God Almighty." [Ayatollah Kohmeini, quoted on ABC News]

18. Many studies have shown that men on average have greater upper-body strength than women. So Daniel is bound to win the push-up competition with Camila.

∗19. "We do not believe that any [telephone] service efficient, progressive and permanent can be given by companies not making fair profits. No community can afford to be served by unprofitable or bankrupt companies which are bound to give inefficient, unprogressive service." [Theodore M. Vail, *AT&T Annual Report*]

20. "No reason can be given why general happiness is desirable, except that each person, so far as he believes it to be attainable, desires his own happiness. This, however, being a fact, we have not only all the proof which the case admits of, but all which it is possible to require, that happiness is a good: that each person's happiness is a good to that person, and the general happiness, therefore, a good to the aggregate of all persons." [John Stuart Mill, *Utilitarianism*, IV]

21. "The insurance companies and [the Republicans] will fight the inclusion of a public option with every bit of power they can muster. They'll call it 'socialized medicine'— but by now we should all have realized that Republicans will call any health care reform Democrats propose 'socialized medicine.'" [Paul Waldman, "The Public Option and the Hope of Health Care Reform," *American Prospect*]

∗22. "For as to reason or good judgment, inasmuch as it alone makes us men and distinguishes us from the beasts, I prefer to believe that it exists whole and entire in each of us, and in this to follow the opinion commonly held by the philosophers, who say that there are differences of degree only between accidents, but not at all between forms or natures of individuals of the same species." [René Descartes, *Discourse on Method*]

23. Meg Griffin: Dad, we can't leave now. My entire life depends on getting my license. If I can't drive, I'll never have a boyfriend, never get married and then I'll have to adopt a kid. . . . [*Family Guy* episode "I Never Met the Dead Man"]

24. Argument for free markets—"A U.S. college education costs 297% more now than it did in 1979. Meanwhile, a Happy Meal costs 40% less. The first is subsidized; the second isn't." [CATO Institute's Twitter Feed]

∗25. "Dogs at TAMU Need a Merry Christmas— Let's Get Them Out of the Lab! The dogs who are used in cruel muscular dystrophy experiments at Texas A&M University don't get a holiday break from their suffering. Take action!" [People for the Ethical Treatment of Animals website]

IV. | Integrative Exercise | Diagram each of the following arguments, and assess it for logical strength. Identify any fallacies you think it commits.

∗1. "An individual obviously is created at conception, because everyone was once a zygote, but no one was ever an unfertilized ovum or a sperm." [Letter to the editor, *New York Times*]

2. It's appalling that many of our young soldiers have to spend second and third tours in Iraq and Afghanistan, fighting for our nation, while we at home fuss over sports and the affairs of celebrities. If we're going to fight this war, we ought to institute a draft. That way, there will be enough soldiers that none have to spend more than one tour in risky combat zones unless they want to. The institution of a draft is the only just way to proceed. [Adapted from a letter to the editor in *Boston Globe*]

3. "For tire consumers who can barely afford to replace a worn tire, an increase [in price due to tariffs on tires imported from China] . . . would be dramatic. This would increase the risk that some consumers will not replace worn tires when they should. It is an invitation to have more tire-related accidents on our roads." [Roy Littlefield, "Where Rubber Hits the Roadblock," *Washington Times*]

*4. "If the task of the painter were to copy for men what they see, the critic could make only a single judgment: either that the copy is right or that it is wrong. . . . No one who has read a page by a good critic . . . can ever again think that this barren choice of yes or no is all that the mind offers." [Jacob Bronowski, *Science and Human Values*]

5. "The fact that a majority of the States, reflecting after all the majority sentiment in those States, have had restrictions on abortions for at least a century seems to me as strong an indication there is that the asserted right to an abortion is not 'so rooted in the traditions and conscience of our people as to be ranked fundamental.'" [*Roe v. Wade*, J. Rehnquist, dissenting]

Cognitive Biases   4

The fallacies we discussed in the previous chapter are logical errors, mistakes about whether or to what extent certain types of arguments support their conclusions. Recognizing and avoiding these errors are important elements in the *skill* of thinking objectively. It's also important to recognize and deal with *psychological tendencies* that can interfere with objectivity. Understanding these factors involves psychology as well as logic, and psychologists have studied a number of them. Collectively they are known as **cognitive biases**. In this chapter we will examine the most common of these biases and the ones that have most distorting effects on our thinking.

Many have been known for a long time and are familiar to most people. Others have been identified by psychological research. We will discuss three categories of biases:

1. Some biases are tendencies that can affect thinking in general, whatever the topic or type of reasoning involved. In Section 4.1, we will consider the most important one, confirmation bias, along with biases in information sources. We will discuss other general biases in Section 4.2.
2. Heuristic biases are cognitive rules of thumb that are often useful but can lead us astray.
3. Finally, there are biases motivated by self-regard and defensiveness.

Some writers interpret the psychological research to mean that the biases are inescapable, that the processes that give rise to them are hard-wired into the human mind as distorting prisms. But that conclusion does not follow from the research. For one thing, the people who make that claim do not think *their* conclusion is the product of bias. The researchers are using scientific methods to study how the mind works, and present their findings as true, not as the results of their own biases. If they can overcome bias, why not the rest of us? More to the point, being aware of our vulnerability to biases gives us the opportunity to avoid and correct them. Helping you achieve that awareness is the purpose of this chapter.

LEARNING OBJECTIVES

On successful completion of the chapter, you will be able to:

- Identify cases of confirmation bias and fact-check information sources. (4.1)
- Distinguish belief bias from hindsight bias by identifying examples of each. (4.2)
- Identify the different quantitative errors in heuristic biases: representativeness, availability, and anchoring. (4.3)
- Recognize different forms of cognitive dissonance and attribution bias. (4.4)
- Apply strategies for countering cognitive biases. (4.5)

4.1 Confirmation Bias and Biased Sources

4.1A Confirmation Bias

Confirmation bias is the tendency to look for and take account of evidence supporting a conclusion, assumption, or hypothesis; while ignoring, downplaying, or failing to seek evidence against it.

Confirmation bias is the single most important bias we are going to consider, and it is widely understood. Indeed, one of the best descriptions of it was written four centuries ago by Francis Bacon, an English philosopher and statesman. The language of his description may seem archaic to modern ears, but it is worth quoting because it covers every important aspect of confirmation bias:

> The human understanding when it has once adopted an opinion . . . draws all things else to support and agree with it. And though there be a greater number and weight of instances to be found on the other side, yet these it either neglects and despises, or else by some distinction sets aside and rejects, in order that by this great and pernicious predetermination [prejudice] the authority of its former conclusions may remain inviolate. [Francis Bacon, *The New Organon*, 1620]

Confirmation bias takes many forms. The most common, perhaps, occurs in arguments between people holding different views on some issue. Each person marshals evidence for his opinion and discounts evidence the other side puts forward, in the effort to "win" the argument and maybe even persuade the other person. In some cases, to be sure, such debates can serve a useful purpose in bringing to bear a wider range of evidence than any one person can assemble. In the adversarial system of Anglo-American law, for example, attorneys on each side make the strongest case they can and try to undermine their opponent's case. That's not a bias. It's their job. And it serves the court's larger purpose of reaching an objective verdict.

What makes confirmation bias a *bias* is that it operates below the surface, as a mindset that interferes with our ability to think objectively. Consider some examples:

Traits and stereotypes: When we are angry at someone, our minds tend to multiply examples of how that person has wronged or offended us and to forget the other times when the person was fair or kind. At a more general level, we form impressions of people as having certain traits—cautious or adventurous, outgoing or shy, for example—and then pay more attention to behavior that confirms the trait than to actions not consistent with it; so our impression of the person gets solidified and becomes immune to counterevidence. On a still more general level, we form stereotypes of *kinds* of people, and those stereotypes can be reinforced by confirmation bias. A man who thinks women are bad drivers will notice a woman driving slowly in the passing lane because she confirms the stereotype ("See? What did I tell you?") and not pay attention to the many women who drive as well as or better than he does—or to the many men who are lousy drivers.

Trends and patterns: We are always looking for trends and patterns to make sense of the world around us. A great deal of research shows that human beings are avid pattern seekers, and it's good that we are. Generalizing from experience is a form of inductive inference. It allows us to expand our knowledge, develop scientific theories, and formulate principles to guide our actions, among other benefits. But we can generalize too quickly, as we saw in discussing the fallacy of hasty generalization. It has been said in jest that we identify 200% of the actual patterns that exist in reality. And one of the reasons is confirmation bias: Once we notice what might be a pattern we pay more attention to supportive examples than to counterevidence. When the economy seems to be declining, for example, we pay heightened attention to things that confirm the trend: every house with a "For Sale" sign, every drop in the stock market, etc., is a confirmation. Indications that the economy may be stable or improving, like a drop in unemployment, are ignored or explained away.

Self-confirming worries: Psychological states such as moods and phobias can become self-confirming through confirmation bias. Hypochondriacs tend to see every little pain or twinge—which most people would consider minor—as evidence of a serious illness and rush to the doctor. People with paranoia tend to see every misfortune as evidence of someone's malign intention, and maybe a conspiracy. (Depression is another example, as the Apply box describes.)

Information sources: Much of the information we use to form and support our beliefs comes from outside—from the people we know; from newspapers, TV, and radio; from

---

APPLY Depression and Confirmation Bias

Cognitive behavioral therapy or CBT has been widely used in the treatment of depression. The essence of this approach is identifying biases in the patient's thinking and helping the patient overcome them. Aaron Beck, one of the founders of CBT, discovered that depressed people tend to see events and themselves in terms of "loss, failure, and depletion," which support a "schema" of helplessness. Beck goes on to note that the fundamental problem is confirmation bias:

> The patient who views herself as helpless can identify what defines "helplessness." The patient may indicate that helplessness is characterized by the inability to accomplish anything on her own. As part of this definition, the therapist should inquire as to which behaviors would exemplify helplessness and which behaviors would exemplify the opposite

of helplessness—effectiveness. Establishing what counts as evidence—given the definition—is an important part of being in a position to disconfirm a proposition. Thus, if the patient's definition is that helplessness is "at any time, not accomplishing your goal," it is unlikely that the proposition that she is helpless can ever be disconfirmed. . . . The clinician can ask, "How could we know that you are ever effective? What would count as evidence that you are effective at times?" Given the confirmation bias underlying schematic processing, it is often the case that personality schemas are not open to disconfirmation, since "contrary evidence" is not considered relevant. . . . [Robert L. Leahy, Judith Beck, and Aaron T. Beck, "Cognitive Therapy for the Personality Disorders," in *Handbook of Personology and Psychopathology*, ed. Stephen Strack] social media; from teachers and experts. And we tend to rely on sources that share our views rather than seeking news and ideas that challenge them. (In the next part of this section, we will discuss problems with media sources in more detail.)

Since confirmation bias involves the failure to take account of evidence against a belief, the solution is obvious: Look for evidence that challenges your view and weigh that evidence objectively. But that's easier said than done because the bias operates automatically as a result of psychological factors, both emotional and cognitive.

One emotional factor is the desire for certainty. Uncertainty can be uncomfortable. It means being in doubt about something, being up in the air, and having to spend time and effort coming to a conclusion. So some people will take the shortcut of adopting a conclusion that might be true, back it up with some confirming evidence, and never really put it to the test. But this "get certain quick" approach has the same flaws as "get rich quick" schemes. Knowledge, like wealth, has to be earned by devoting time and effort to the goal.

Another emotional factor is that we can easily become invested in our beliefs, so that any challenge to them becomes a threat we don't want to deal with. There's comfort in holding on to cherished beliefs, especially convictions about religion, ethics, and politics, as well as beliefs about people we are close to in our lives. In these areas, to be sure, our convictions may be deeply rooted in prior thought and experience, and it would not be reasonable to abandon them the first time we encounter an objection. But it would not be reasonable, either, to ignore the objection, much less to isolate ourselves from challenge by surrounding ourselves exclusively with like-minded people.

Psychologists have also identified certain *cognitive* tendencies underlying confirmation bias. One of them is that it is simply easier to think of evidence that would support a conclusion than to think of evidence against it. In a famous experiment, psychologist P. C. Wason gave people the numbers [2 4 6] and told them that the series conforms to a simple rule. Their task was to discover the rule. They were to form a hypothesis about what the rule might be and test the hypothesis by giving the experimenter another set of three numbers; the experimenter then said whether that set conformed to the actual rule. Many people in the experiment guessed that the rule could be numbers increasing in intervals of 2. To test that hypothesis, they gave sets conforming to that rule, like [6 8 10], and were told that that set conformed to the experimenter's rule. They would sometimes continue giving other sets of numbers increasing by 2 and were told that those sets also met the rule.

Sequence	My Hypothesis about Rule	Does Experimenter Say It Fits His Rule?
2, 4, 6		Yes
7, 9, 11	Counting up by twos	Yes
20, 22, 24	Counting up by twos	Yes

Do you see the problem? If you think the rule is numbers increasing by 2, each additional positive case of the rule adds little if any support to your hypothesis. Instead, you should give a set *not* consistent with your hypothesis, like [3 7 12]. If that negative case does not fit the experimenter's rule, you have better support for your hypothesis. But in Wason's experiment, you would get a positive answer, and that would definitely tell you that your hypothesis is wrong. (The actual rule was simply any series of increasing numbers.) In other words, trying to *disconfirm* your hypothesis would be of more value in discovering the actual rule than would trying to *confirm* your hypothesis by positive examples. Yet most people failed to use this strategy.

Another cognitive source of confirmation bias is the limit on what we can hold in mind consciously at any time. Suppose you are thinking about what to get your mother for her birthday. There's an open-ended number of possible gifts, too many to hold in mind all at once. It's easy to fixate on the first idea that occurs to you, weigh the pros and cons of that idea, and—because all of that is a lot to hold in mind—not attend to other possibilities. Psychologists have found that information acquired early in a process of inquiry tends to carry more weight than later information, often by giving rise to a belief that is then supported by confirmation bias.

In light of these emotional and cognitive bases for confirmation bias, we need strategies for overcoming them. Here are some that have particular value:

Talk with people who have different views. As with the adversary system of justice we mentioned earlier, discussion and debate can bring up points that we haven't thought of. It's rare that any one person has all the relevant facts. And even if you do not end up changing your mind, knowing the best arguments for the opposing view strengthens your confidence in your view. As the 19th-century philosopher John Stuart Mill wrote:

> The steady habit of correcting and completing his own opinion by collating with those of others, so far from causing doubt and hesitation in carrying it into practice, is the only stable foundation for a just reliance on it. . . . Knowing that he has sought for objections and difficulties, instead of avoiding them, and has shut out no light which can be thrown upon the subject from any quarter—he has a right to think his judgment better than that of any person, or any multitude, who have not gone through a similar process. [*On Liberty*]

In considering an opposing viewpoint, it's important to do so with an honest desire to learn the reasons for that view. If we consider those reasons with the goal of refuting or discounting them, then we are indulging confirmation bias, not countering it. Indeed, some experiments have revealed a "backfire effect": People who focus on discounting the evidence for an opposing view can become even more convinced of their own view, and discussions among people with opposing views can become even more polarized.

Ask yourself, "How might I be wrong in what I believe? What would count as evidence against my belief?" Some psychological research has found that merely asking people to consider how they might be wrong and to generate alternative positions or hypotheses improves accuracy almost as much as getting an alternative judgment from someone else.

Ask yourself what's more important, being right or getting it right? It is very easy to get attached to our beliefs and then become defensive when they are challenged, as if our very self-esteem depends on being right. You probably know people who treat argument as a blood sport; they're out to win and crush the opposing side. That's not a very objective approach to reasoning. Wouldn't it be better to base your self-esteem on a commitment to finding the truth? (We will discuss this point in more depth in the final section.)

EXERCISE 4.1A

*I. Suppose you were in the Wason experiment, trying to discover the rule for sets of three numbers. You are given [2 4 6] as an example that fits the rule. Counting up by twos is one possible rule. Find four other rules and sets of numbers to test them.

II. For each statement below, name a way to check for evidence that might weigh against it. We have done the first one for you as an example.

*1. Drinking eight glasses of water per day is needed to maintain health.

   Your answer might be: drink water only when you're thirsty and monitor your health; and/or search online for the "eight glasses a day rule."

2. Two courses in anatomy are needed to become a physician's assistant.

3. All public universities require the SAT for admission.

*4. A border wall will decrease illegal immigration.

5. Raising the minimum wage by 10% will increase the income of low-wage workers.

6. Raising the minimum wage by 10% will lead employers to eliminate some low-wage jobs.

*7. High fructose corn syrup is more damaging to health than table sugar.

8. Vitamin C prevents colds.

9. The United States was the first country to ban slavery.

*10. Americans are facing an obesity epidemic.

4.1B Biased Sources

Confirmation bias is a problem that we bring to the task of acquiring information. But the sources we acquire information *from*, especially the media, have their own biases that play into ours. Confirmation bias is a way of fooling ourselves, but we can also be fooled by biased sources.

On political issues, for example, conservatives get most of their news from media with a conservative outlook, liberals from liberal media. With the sheer volume of media available today, most people are exposed to news from many different sources and points of view. But confirmation bias can still affect the degree of *trust* we place in different sources. A survey by the Pew Research Center, for example, found that conservatives and liberals put much more trust in media reflecting their point of view. The stark differences are evident in the degree of trust and distrust in the conservative-leaning Fox News and the more liberal MSNBC:

Media Source	Liberals (%)		Conservatives (%)	
	Trust	Distrust	Trust	Distrust
Fox News	6	81	88	3
MSNBC	52	9	7	75

Remember that confirmation bias includes not only the failure to seek contrary evidence but also the tendency to downplay it when we do encounter it. So even if we are exposed to news from a wide range of sources, it's easy to dismiss information at odds with our views on the grounds that the source is untrustworthy.

NEWS, OPINION, AND OBJECTIVITY To counter that bias, it's important to maintain a critical perspective on sources of information. And there is a basic standard we should employ.

A news report is a form of *testimonial evidence*, a broad category that includes any use of someone's statement as evidence for the truth of that statement. For example, I ask you what time it is; you look at your watch or phone and tell me; and I accept what you say as correct. An eyewitness in a criminal trial states under oath what he or she saw, and the jury takes that testimony as evidence about the crime. Wikipedia says that the United Nations was formed in 1945, and we take that as fact. The general form of testimonial evidence is:

$$X \text{ says } p$$
$$\downarrow$$
$$p \text{ is true}$$

Here X can be any source: a stranger giving us the time, a news report, a reference book or website, an expert who makes a statement about his field, etc. In the case of the expert, we are appealing to authority, as we discussed in Chapter 3. As we saw there, appeal to authority is not necessarily a fallacy. Expert opinion can be good evidence for a conclusion if the expert is *credible*. The same is true for any type of testimonial evidence. Credibility in turn depends on two factors, competence and objectivity. *Competence* means that the person making the statement is in a position to know that the statement is true. In the case of authorities, the expert must have genuine expertise in the relevant field; in the case of a trial, the witness must actually have been at the scene. *Objectivity* means that the person is stating what he knows without distortion or deceit. To be credible, in other words, X must be someone who knows the truth and tells the truth. So, the full diagram for the use of testimonial evidence is:

$$X \text{ says } p \quad + \quad X \text{ is competent to know } p \text{ and } X \text{ is objective}$$
$$\downarrow$$
$$p \text{ is true}$$

What do the standards of competence and objectivity mean as applied to the media? To begin with competence: Journalists need not have specialized expert knowledge about the news they cover. Suppose a reporter—let's call her Zoe—is covering a flood on the Missouri River. She does not need to be an expert in the causes of floods or the construction of levees. But she does need to find the facts about the height of the flood waters, the levees that were breached, the consequences for people living near the river, etc. In this context, competence means being in a position to know, through observation, interviews, and research. It means firsthand reporting rather than simply repeating what other reporters have said, relying on a company's press release, or using other secondhand sources.

The second standard, objectivity, is more complicated. To see why, let's begin with the root meaning of the concept. Objectivity means a commitment to seeking the truth. A person can be objective in pursuing the truth even when he hasn't found it yet, and even when he has arrived at a false conclusion. Truth and falsity are concepts that apply to the *products* of thought—conclusions, theories, etc.—depending on whether they correspond to the facts or fail to do so. But objectivity means a commitment to seeking the truth in the *process* of thinking, by using rational methods, actively seeking relevant information, remaining open to new evidence, and putting aside distorting factors such as wishful thinking, emotional resistance to unpleasant facts, or loyalty to a group.

Traditional media applied this standard in a specialized way by separating factual reporting from editorial opinion—a cognitive division of labor between providing information and interpreting it. Matters of fact are more amenable to clear confirmation, less subject to disagreement; whereas interpretive articles and editorials rely on more extensive evidence and argumentation, which bring more of the writer's own perspective into play. To be sure, the general standards of objectivity apply just as much to expressions of opinion as they do to statements of fact. Opinion writers exercise objectivity in the fundamental sense when they take account of the facts, use logical arguments, and ground their value judgments in consistent principles, as opposed, say, to venting personal animosity in a vituperative screed full of arbitrary accusations and logical non sequiturs. For our purposes, however, factual reporting is more important. It's what we should rely on primarily in acquiring information relevant to our views, pro or con.

Some media critics claim that even factual reporting cannot be objective because it involves selectivity. Journalists have to select what stories to cover and, for any story, what facts are significant enough to include. These judgments necessarily reflect the journalists' background knowledge of the world and assumptions about what is important. That is not a bias per se, but it raises the possibility of slanted coverage. Good journalism employs countermeasures like editorial oversight, the use of fact-checkers, maintaining independence from sources with an ax to grind, etc.

The traditional separation of news from opinion, however, is becoming more and more blurred, even in major newspapers like the *New York Times*, broadcast networks like ABC and Fox, and other mainstream media. They are becoming more like opinion magazines, selecting what to cover and how to cover it on the basis of a particular point of view. They have an agenda, a definite slant. Outlets with this approach can strive to verify facts, and support opinions with good evidence, but fact and opinion are more intertwined.

As consumers of news, therefore, we have a more difficult task when we look for information about events and issues we're interested in. Difficult—but not impossible. The two most important strategies to follow are (1) to distinguish clearly between fact and opinion and (2) to compare the coverage of an event or fact by different media.

Distinguish between fact and opinion: Consider the following two statements about health care.

In 2018, spending on health care programs was the largest segment of the U.S. federal budget.

European countries, which spend less on health care than the United States, have better health outcomes.

The first is a factual statement. You may not know whether it is true, but its truth or falsity can be determined by checking the federal budget numbers. Statement 2 is an opinion because of the claim that European health systems have better outcomes. That's a value judgment, and it depends on what standard we use—average life span of citizens, infant mortality, waiting times for surgery, availability of emergency care, etc. Reasonable people can disagree about the relative importance of such factors. That is not to say that opinions are necessarily subjective, but they have to be supported by argument, not by simply looking up a statistic.

In distinguishing between fact and opinion, we need to strive to avoid our own biases. Researchers have found that some people tend to classify statements they agree with as factual and statements they disagree with as opinions, regardless of what category the statements actually belong in. In one study by the Pew Research Center, participants were given a list of statements to classify, including two about immigration:

Immigrants who are in the United States illegally have some rights under the Constitution.

Immigrants who are in the United States illegally are a very big problem for the country today.

The first is a factual statement; it's a matter of law (and it's true). But over 40% of the participants called it an opinion. The second is clearly an opinion, but nearly a third said it is factual. In both cases, the answers were influenced by views about immigration.

Compare sources: As we noted earlier, a good strategy for countering confirmation bias is talking to people with opposing views. The same strategy is useful in regard to the media. If a factual statement in the news is significant for your beliefs, it's worth checking other sources. If a news channel airs a story about a confrontation at a political rally, do other sources describe the event the same way? Do the stories give you clear and consistent information about what actually happened? The internet makes it fairly easy to double-check news. Publications and broadcast channels have online sites, and there are news aggregators like Google News you can check. And you should look for sources with a different outlook. With the increasing tendency in the media to blend news and opinion, it can be difficult to separate the factual content of a news item from the writer's opinion. In addition, as we noted earlier, reporting is necessarily selective, so relevant facts may be omitted from a story due to the reporter's viewpoint. Media with similar outlooks often have similar slants on the news. If a source with a different outlook reports the same facts, you can have more confidence that you are getting accurate information.

SOCIAL MEDIA AND "FAKE NEWS"   So far we have been discussing major (or mainstream) media such as newspapers, magazines, and broadcast and cable news channels. These media all have sites on the internet, but their online versions retain the form of traditional media. Articles are edited, and editorial standards like fact-checking are still employed. The internet also has a vast array of other sites for information, often not edited, such as blogs and podcasts. On the positive side, these sources allow people to report on things that don't fit the agendas of the mainstream media. They allow experts to go deeper into their fields than the major media can, and to speak directly to readers rather than through reporters who quote them selectively. But this freedom comes with a risk: It is harder to assess the credibility of self-published news and opinion. Some sites are anonymous. Some sites peddling slanted "news" or outright misinformation are designed to look like reputable sites.

Social media have also become major sources for news. Surveys show that a majority of people get at least some news through social media, and most of them check only one source. The problem here is that platforms like Facebook, Twitter, and YouTube partly tailor news feeds to the views of users, based on the issues and links that users reveal an interest in. As a result, it is all too easy to become trapped in a self-confirming bubble. Moreover, it is often not clear what the real source of a news item is, as items get reposted and retweeted.

The internet has also increased the opportunities for spreading rumors, arbitrary claims, conspiracy theories, junk science, and deliberate disinformation—the type of content that is often referred to as "fake news." That term originally referred to openly satirical media like *The Onion*, which publishes humorous riffs on the daily news. The term is now applied to a wider range of content; indeed, it is often used loosely to mean anything from out-and-out falsehoods to opinions someone doesn't like. Scholars who research the subject, however, use a narrower definition. Fake news refers to factual-sounding claims that are posted either with indifference to the truth, usually in order to support a point of view; or with a deliberate intent to deceive. Here are some examples from a study by *Buzzfeed News* of the top fake news items on Facebook in 2016 (with the number of engagements):

- Obama Signs Executive Order Banning the Pledge of Allegiance in Schools Nation-wide (2.2 million)
- Actor Bill Murray Announces 2016 Presidential Run (210,000)
- Mike Pence: "Sarah Palin Is My Role Model for Beautiful, Smart American Women" (254,000)

Those who peddle fake news are usually skilled in the technical knowledge of how to exploit the resources of social media to magnify their impact. But there are strategies we can use to protect ourselves.

Plausibility: Consider whether the news item is plausible in light of your background knowledge of the world. Of course some real news is surprising and unexpected; that's what makes it newsworthy. And we have to be careful not to engage in confirmation bias by accepting a fact only if it coheres with our views. But all of us have a large stock of knowledge about science, people, society and politics, and many other things. If a news item conflicts with that knowledge, it should be double-checked before accepting it as true.

This is especially important for items that are passed around on social media. A major 2018 study by scholars at MIT examined stories that circulated on Twitter, focusing on 126,000 that could be verified as true or false.* They found that falsehoods were 70% more likely to be retweeted than truths. "Whereas the truth rarely diffused to more than 1000 people, the top 1% of false-news cascades routinely diffused to between 1000

---

*Soroush Vosoughi, Deb Roy, and Sinan Aral, "The Spread of True and False News Online," *Science* and 100,000 people." Why the difference? The best explanation the researchers could find was that false news was more novel and aroused stronger emotions than the truth. All the more reason, then, to use our background knowledge to assess the initial probability that a news item is true. If a headline is really arresting, there's a chance it should be convicted of deception.

Check the source: When we rely on news items of any kind, we depend on the competence and objectivity of the source. So we should start by checking the source. If the item came in your Facebook or Twitter feed, is it clear where it came from originally? Is the original source mentioned? Is there a link to it? If it's a site that appeared in a Google search, is the site reputable? Many fake news sites mimic major media sites. The fake news example about Obama and the Pledge of Allegiance, for example, came from a site with the URL *abcnews.com.co*. The "co" is a giveaway that this isn't ABC News. To check the credibility of a website, you can use both a "vertical" and a "horizontal" approach. A vertical check means going deeper into the site itself—such as its "About" section—to look for the site's purpose, outlook, ownership, etc. The horizontal approach is to Google the site's name or URL to see what other sites may have said about it, especially sites that you already know are credible.

APPLY Fact-Checking

Fact-checkers are professional journalists who research and report on the truth or falsity of news items and claims. They focus on different areas, and use slightly different ways of ranking items as true, false, misleading, etc.

Snopes.com: The oldest and largest fact-checking site online, Snopes is an independent publication owned by Snopes Media Group. It checks print sources, social media, and urban legends, among other things.

PolitiFact.com: Owned by the nonprofit Poynter Institute for Media Studies, PolitiFact focuses on statements made by politicians and rating them for accuracy.

FactCheck.org: FactCheck.org monitors the factual accuracy of what is said by major U.S. political players in the form of TV ads, debates, speeches, interviews, and news releases. It is a project of the Annenberg Public Policy Center of the University of Pennsylvania.

TruthorFiction.com: This site focuses on stories that are the most widely circulated via forwarded emails on the internet, exposing fake news, myths, hoaxes, etc.

NewsGuard: NewsGuard rates news websites (rather than individual news items) by their adherence to standards of credibility and transparency. It provides a browser plug-in that shows the rating next to news links on search engines and social media feeds.

Wikipedia: Wikipedia is not a fact-checking site per se; it is an online encyclopedia. But it's worth consulting its enormous range of articles to check factual claims. Articles are written collaboratively by volunteer writers and editors. Editorial standards require that content be "verifiable against a published reliable source, thereby excluding editors' opinions."

Use fact-checkers: To check the credibility of a site or of information in general, it's a good idea to use online fact-checkers. These sites serve the same function in the marketplace of ideas that product reviewers like *Consumer Reports* serve in the marketplace of goods. They are not infallible, or immune from their own biases, but their professional skills in journalism and commitment to objectivity give them a high degree of credibility. A list of the best fact-checking sites is in the Apply box nearby.

As we said at the start of this section, confirmation bias is the most important and most pervasive of the cognitive biases we will discuss, not least because it can make us vulnerable to bias in the information sources we use. In the next section, we will review several other general biases that, like confirmation bias, affect thinking in general, whatever the topic or type of reasoning involved.

SOLVE Countering Bias

In this section we covered the chief strategies for countering our own confirmation bias and the biases in the sources we rely on for information:

Confirmation bias

- Talk with people who have different views.
- Consider what evidence would count against your view.

- Shift your focus from proving you're right to "getting it right."

Information credibility

- Distinguish factual statements from opinion.
- Check different sources.
- Consider the plausibility of the item.
- Use fact-checkers.

REVIEW Confirmation Bias and Biased Sources

- Confirmation bias is the tendency to look for and take account of evidence supporting a conclusion, assumption, or hypothesis; while ignoring, downplaying, or failing to seek evidence against it.
  - It is exemplified in thinking that involves inaccurate stereotypes, generalizations, self-worries, and political views, among other things.
  - The bias is caused by both emotional and cognitive factors.
- Relying on news media and other sources for information is a form of testimonial evidence, which is appropriate only if the

source is credible: both competent and objective.

- Objectivity means a commitment to seeking the truth in the *process* of thinking.
- Traditional journalism distinguished between reporting facts and offering opinions, but this distinction has become blurred. Nevertheless, it is important to identify factual information in source material.
  - Online sources, including social media, are more difficult to evaluate for credibility.
  - "Fake news" is a pervasive problem that requires careful fact-checking.

EXERCISE 4.1B

I. For each of the following statements, determine whether it is a statement of fact or an opinion.

*1. George Clooney was the highest-income entertainer in 2018.

2. Global warming will cause economic harm to agriculture.

3. Armadillos always have exactly four babies.

*4. Godiva makes the best chocolates.

5. The giraffe is the largest land mammal.

6. One is the loneliest number.

*7. The Fig Newton is named for Newton, Massachusetts.

8. Houston is the largest U.S. city.

9. The cat is the most popular pet in America.

*10. He who laughs last, laughs best.

11. If you want peace, work for justice.

12. Iodine is necessary for human health.

*13. Crepe myrtles are beautiful trees.

14. Maroon is superior to burnt orange.

15. Vatican City is the world's smallest country.

II. For each of the following issues, you are asked to consider several possible sources of information. State whether each source is more likely to be reliable or biased and why.

*1. Marcos is an employer reviewing applications. He is considering hiring Luke but would like more information. Whom should he consult?
   a. Luke's ex-wife
   b. Luke's previous employers
   c. A trusted current employee who knows Luke
   d. Luke's football teammate

2. After class, you go to the coffee shop with several classmates. One of them mentions a rumor that Kanye West has announced he is running for president. You believe the rumor only after:
   a. A friend retweets the rumor to you.
   b. You ask the barista.
   c. You check Kanye's website.
   d. You check Snopes.

3. You must declare a major this semester. You've narrowed down your options to three possibilities that you find equally appealing. You decide to rank them according to their projected demand. How can you find out which major is most likely to lead to a good job?
   a. Ask some friends.
   b. Ask someone currently working in each field.
   c. Check the U.S. Department of Labor website.
   d. Ask a senior majoring in each department.

*4. Kevin has just been diagnosed with a rare form of cancer. Since he lives in a small town, he decides to travel to a city with a major cancer center to better assess his treatment options. He wants to choose the best hospital he can. What do you think of the sources he consults?
   a. A recommendation from his physician
   b. Hospital ads in popular magazines
   c. Several neighbors
   d. Internet rankings of U.S. cancer centers

5. Melinda and Christie are arguing about whether illegal immigrants are entitled to the wages they earn under U.S. law. They look for information

to settle their dispute. Are their sources reliable or biased? They check:

a. The website of a blogger known for his anti-immigration views
b. FAQs published by the U.S. Department of Labor
c. Other students
d. A lawyer specialiazing in labor law

6. Suppose you are working on a group project for class. You need to determine whether dogs or cats are best at problem-solving. How do you decide?

a. Take a group vote.
b. Email an animal expert at a local vet school.
c. Check the internet for research on animal cognition.
d. Ask a crazy cat lady.

*7. A guest speaker in your philosophy class claims that former slave states are the only states that allow capital punishment. Stunned by this claim, you search for confirmation. You check:

a. A U.S. Department of Justice fact sheet on criminal penalties by state
b. The guest speaker's blog
c. FactCheck.org

d. With a local anti–death penalty activist

8. Could there be intelligent life on other planets? Assess the following sources.

a. NASA
b. Someone who claims to have been abducted by aliens
c. A book on this subject written by a respected astronomer
d. William Shatner

9. You want to know the healthiest diet for weight loss. You consider information from:

a. Your mother
b. A registered dietician
c. A best-selling diet book
d. The receptionist at your gym

*10. Your roommate Carla, who is from Texas, says that Texas has the largest state fair in the country. Where would you look for information to confirm or disconfirm her claim?

a. The *Dallas Morning News*
b. A rodeo rider you saw on ESPN
c. Another classmate from Texas
d. Travel Texas, the state's economic development and tourism bureau

III. Use online resources to assess whether the following statements are true or false.

1. Kellogg's has announced that it is releasing ranch-flavored Pop-Tarts.

2. The United States is the only industrialized nation without universal health care.

3. The average insurance premium doubled under Obamacare.

4. Pokémon creator Satoshi Tajiri has admitted that he originally developed his popular game for Satanists.

5. After an assisted living facility was closed due to bankruptcy, the center's cook and janitor

stayed on without pay to care for residents.

6. High levels of arsenic were found in bottled water sold at major U.S. retailers.

7. Wind turbines cause cancer.

8. A Hawaiian boy found a message in a bottle from a girl in Oregon.

9. The U.S. Food and Drug Administration has confirmed that vaccines cause autism.

10. Aquafina bottled water remains unfrozen even when placed in a freezer overnight.

4.2 Other General Biases

Confirmation bias is a general bias that can affect our thinking whatever the topic or type of reasoning involved (whether deductive or inductive, for example). In this section we discuss two other general biases: belief bias and hindsight bias.

4.2A Belief Bias

Belief bias is the tendency to let agreement or disagreement with a conclusion affect one's evaluation of the validity or strength of the argument for that conclusion. In belief bias, like confirmation bias, we let our preexisting beliefs affect our assessment of the evidence for or against them. But there's a difference: Confirmation bias is the tendency to look only for positive evidence and to ignore or discount contrary evidence. Belief bias is an error in evaluating the evidence we have; it is not a matter of gathering evidence but of assessing whether and to what extent the evidence, stated as premises, supports the conclusion of an argument.

Consider two deductive arguments. In Chapter 2 we saw that a deductive argument is valid when the premises, if true, guarantee the truth of the conclusion. Is either of the following arguments valid?

> No police dog is vicious.
> Some highly trained dogs are vicious.
> Therefore, some highly trained dogs are not police dogs.

> No nutritional thing is inexpensive.
> Some vitamin tablets are inexpensive.
> Therefore, some vitamin tablets are not nutritional.

Both arguments are valid. But it may be easier to see that in the first one than in the second. The conclusion of the first is clearly true—guard dogs, for example, are highly trained but not police dogs. And the premises are plausible. In the second argument, the conclusion is not plausible, nor is the first premise. You have to stop and analyze the argument more carefully to see that the conclusion does follow from the premises. The two arguments have exactly the same logical form:

> No [police dog/nutritional thing] is [vicious/inexpensive].
> Some [highly trained dogs/vitamins] are [vicious/ inexpensive].
> Therefore, some [highly trained dogs/vitamins] are not [police dogs/nutritional things].

These two arguments were used in a classic psychological experiment, in which 86% of the participants correctly identified the first as valid while only 59% recognized that the second is valid. That's still over half, but the difference indicates the role of belief bias.

This bias has been studied primarily with deductive arguments. But there is also evidence that belief bias applies to inductive arguments. As we saw in Chapter 2, the standard of evaluation for induction is not validity but strength. A number of experiments presented participants with arguments of equivalent strength, some with plausible conclusions, others with implausible conclusions. The results showed that participants often judged the plausible ones to be stronger—an indication, once again, of belief bias at work.

In later chapters, we will study in more detail the nature and standards of deductive validity (Part II) and inductive strength (Part III). That knowledge will give you the best tools for evaluating arguments of either type. But the discussion of arguments in general (Chapter 2) has provided the basic guideline. We evaluate arguments by two standards:

1. Are the premises true?
2. How well do the premises—*if* they were true—support the conclusion?

The truth of the premises is a matter of how they relate to the facts of reality. Validity and strength are a matter of how the premises relate to the conclusion. If an argument meets both standards, then it provides good reason for accepting the conclusion. But questions about validity or strength apply *only* to the second question. An argument can be valid or strong even if its conclusion is false or implausible.

4.2B Hindsight Bias

It's often said that hindsight is 20/20. The saying is sometimes used dismissively to mean that there was no way to know what the outcome of a decision would be: "Don't criticize what I did, because I made the best decision I could at that time." Or it is said ruefully to mean "I should have known." But the saying is a half-truth. The part that is not true has been investigated by psychologists, who have identified several forms of hindsight bias.

Before we discuss that bias, let's recognize the part that is true. Hindsight is another name for memory, which is a vital cognitive asset. Memory is the vast store of all our knowledge, everything we have learned in the course of our lives, only a tiny fraction of which can be held in conscious awareness at any moment. Without memory, we could not engage in speech or reasoning at all. Memories of your life—your experiences, family and friends, actions and reactions, struggles and successes, growth as a person—all of that and more makes up your sense of your unique individual identity. That's what makes the loss of memory in Alzheimer's and other conditions such a tragedy for the victims.

But memory is fallible. Sometimes people "remember" something that never happened, due to wishful thinking, suggestive questioning, or other causes. People can distort or edit their memories of events, especially important events in their lives. When something with personal significance is recalled and told to others repeatedly, the narrative can easily be edited for coherence, or to show oneself in the best light, and the edited version makes it difficult to be sure how true it is. Another error is mixing up past events, combining elements from each, in what psychologists call a conjunction error. One of your authors (David Kelley) got in touch with a high-school girlfriend after many years and remembered a movie they saw at the time. It was a crystal clear memory, but when he went to watch the film again, he found that he had mixed up two movies, combining the actors and story from one and the title and music from the other.

Psychologists have studied these and many other forms of memory error. And they have real-world consequences. Eyewitness testimony in trials, for example, has been shown to be unreliable in many cases; as a result, police and courts have adopted measures to enhance reliability. Another consequence may be of particular interest if you are a student. Writers sometimes credit a thought or insight to themselves when they actually came across the point from someone else in the course of research, even to the extent of reproducing the actual words written by an author. Such unconscious plagiarism is an example of mistaking the source of a memory.

APPLY The Seven Sins of Memory

In his engaging book of this title, Daniel Schacter describes seven ways our memory is vulnerable to problems, including hindsight bias.

1. Transience: Weakening of memory over time

2. Absent-mindedness: Failure to remember because attention is elsewhere

3. Blocking: Thwarted search for info even when attention is focused on trying to find it

4. Misattribution: Assigning a memory to the wrong source, including fantasy and attributing info to a friend when it actually came from a newspaper

5. Suggestibility: Misattribution due to leading questions

6. Bias: Editing or making up past events due to present knowledge; hindsight bias

7. Persistence: Repeated recall of disturbing info

Schacter is not a skeptic about the value of memory: "I suggest that the seven sins are by-products of otherwise adaptive features of memory, a price we pay for processes and functions that serve us well."

These memory errors may reflect biases or may result from the limitations of memory itself. What psychologists call **hindsight bias**, however, is a particular kind of error, in which knowing the outcome of an event distorts one's view of the sequence leading up to that outcome. The distortion takes several forms.

I knew it all along.

The first is misrepresenting what you predicted in advance after you found out what the outcome actually was. Suppose you are asked before a final exam: What do you think are your chances of getting an A, a B, and a C? We write down your answers. Then you take the exam, you get the grade a week later, and a month after *that* you are asked to recall the probabilities you estimated before the exam. Whatever your actual grade, it's likely that you would recall your estimate for that grade as higher than it was, and your estimates for the other grades as lower. Psychologists have performed many experiments of this type, and the consistent result is that knowing the outcome of an event tends to bias hindsight about one's previous estimates and expectations. This is the "I knew it all along" form of hindsight bias.

It had to happen.

There is also what can be described as the "It had to happen" form. After we know the outcome, we tend to regard it as deterministic, inevitable, or more predictable than it was. In the 2016 presidential election, most commentators expected Hillary Clinton to win. After the surprise victory of Donald Trump, commentators began explaining why it was virtually certain to occur. The same thing happens daily with the stock market: Traders in the market are quick to explain market moves after the fact. As you might expect, this form of hindsight bias is also a temptation in history, the study of the past. Historian Wilfred M. McClay, for example, speaking about the events leading up to the Civil War, points out that students of history are susceptible to "the illusion that it was written in advance." He urges readers to "remember that people at the time had no foresight to match our hindsight."

I should have predicted it.

Finally, as a result of the two preceding forms of the bias, there is the tendency to think one could have or should have predicted the outcome. In other words, we tend to evaluate a decision process by the outcome. In a baseball game that is tied at the beginning of the ninth inning, the manager of the visiting team puts in a left-handed pitcher

---

APPLY Hindsight Bias and Survivor's Guilt

In *The Hunger Games*, Katniss Everdeen is thrust into a kill-or-be-killed situation through no fault of her own. We don't condemn her efforts to stay alive. In fact, we regard her as a heroine. Our hearts ache at the choices she's forced to make; we know she's not to blame. She believes that as well. But later, she's haunted by her actions. Katniss suffers from survivor's guilt, a mental condition that sometimes occurs for people who have survived a traumatic event in which others died. Though generally associated with grief, survivor's guilt is *not* part of a normal, healthy grieving process.

The syndrome was first identified in the 1960s by therapists working with Holocaust survivors. Symptoms may include anxiety, depression, and social withdrawal—and especially feelings of guilt and helplessness. Victims may find themselves constantly reliving the event. Worst of all, since they feel guilty for surviving, they may seek to "right the wrong," by bringing about their own death. Suicides and sudden, violent deaths, in particular, may cause a survivor to fantasize about dying in a similar manner.

Survivor's guilt is as individual as the people who experience it, but at least three distinct reactions have been noted. Survivors may experience:

- Guilt about being alive: Survivors may wonder why they lived when others died. Unable to deal with the random nature of events, they may feel unworthy of life.

- Guilt about what they did: Like Katniss, some survivors may blame themselves for taking actions to save their own lives. More commonly, the guilt involves remembering and inflating the importance of prior events such as arguments, unkind words, and perhaps childhood fights.

- Guilt about what they failed to do: "I should have told her I loved her." "I should have warned him not to go." Coulda, woulda, shoulda . . . normal thoughts in normal situations, but for someone with survivor's guilt, these thoughts can become a relentless form of self-torture.

Notice that at least the last two reactions involve hindsight bias. Survivors reach back into the past and imagine that they should have used present knowledge to prevent past events. Hindsight bias in such cases may be too deeply rooted to avoid. Survivor's guilt is a complex and serious psychological condition often requiring professional intervention. We hope you never experience survivor's guilt or the trauma that causes it. But if you do, please take care of yourself, surround yourself with supportive friends, stay involved in life, and seek professional help. And, as you are able, at least consider the possibility that your thinking may be distorted.

to face a left-handed batter—who proceeds to hit a home run. You can imagine the next day's talk on sports channels about what a bad decision that was. But neither the manager nor the fans could have known ahead of time that a home run was coming. The manager was playing the odds appropriately. Another example, with more serious social consequences, happens with juries in medical malpractice cases. Even if the doctor was performing a routine procedure with little known risk of injury to the patient, but something went wrong, juries can make the hindsight judgment that the doctor should have known.

One of the consequences of hindsight bias is that it impairs our ability to learn from experience. Making decisions is one of the most important ways we exercise our ability to think and reason, using all the skills that this book teaches. But the link between thinking and deciding is two-way: We reason about the best decision to make in light of the circumstances, but we can also use the outcome to improve our ability to think through future decisions. A key lesson in this respect is that circumstances are always complex. We rarely if ever know *ex ante* (before the event) what we come to know *ex post*, when the outcome is known. The hindsight bias that makes the outcome seem inevitable and predictable can interfere with the ability to appreciate the multiple factors that led to that outcome. As psychologist Daniel Schacter says, "If we feel that we knew all along what would happen, then we may be less inclined to profit from the lessons a particular event or incident can teach us" [*The Seven Sins of Memory*, 149].

A good way to counter hindsight bias, accordingly, is to consider what *other* outcomes a decision or event might have had. We can imagine ourselves back in time, at the point where we made the decision or observed the event, and think about the range of possible outcomes. That's what we normally do, after all, in making a decision: We ask whether an action will lead to the result we want or fail to do so, whether there might be unintended consequences, etc. The same process can help avoid hindsight bias even after we know the outcome.

REVIEW Belief and Hindsight Biases

Belief bias is the tendency for agreement or disagreement with a conclusion to affect one's evaluation of the validity or strength of the argument for that conclusion.

Hindsight bias is the tendency for knowledge of the outcome of an event to affect one's judgment about the antecedent likelihood of that outcome and one's memory of one's prior estimate of its likelihood.

EXERCISE 4.2

I. Evaluate the validity or strength of the following arguments. For deductive arguments, the options are valid or invalid. For inductive arguments, the options are weak or strong.

*1. No philosopher is a blue-collar worker.
Some college professors are philosophers.
Some college professors are not blue-collar workers.

2. If you boil water, then it freezes.
If water freezes, then it forms ice crystals.
If you boil water, then it forms ice crystals.

3. All poodles are dogs.
Some animals are dogs.
Some animals are not poodles.

*4. The bartenders at my favorite bars chat with customers.
Chatting with customers requires an outgoing personality.
An outgoing personality is necessary for success as a bartender.

5. All politicians are congressmen.
All politicians are crooks.
All crooks are congressmen.

6. No business owner is a veteran.
Some ex-marine is a business owner.
Some ex-marine is not a veteran.

*7. Either global warming is not real or we should protect the environment.
We should protect the environment.
Global warming is real.

8. No vegan is a Republican.
Some vegans are vegetarians.
Some vegetarians are not Republicans.

9. Iron is a good insulator and it is transparent.
Windows should be transparent and provide good insulation.
Iron is a good material for windows.

*10. Some women are religious.
No Christian is a woman.
Some Christians are not religious.

11. If the Eagles win their conference, then they will play in the finals.
If the Eagles play in the finals, then they will win the championship.
If the Eagles win their conference, then they will win the championship.

12. Some trees are deciduous.
No rose is a tree.
Some roses are not deciduous.

*13. Some cats are calicos.
No dog is a cat.
Some dogs are not calicos.

14. If cats are felines, then dogs are canines.
Dogs are not canines.
Cats are not felines.

15. I have a handgun and have never shot anyone.
No one at my gun club has ever shot anyone.
No one is killed by guns.

*16. Cell phones require the use of rare earth elements.
Most of these elements are mined in China.
Manufacturing cell phones depends on trade with China.

17. Some well-educated people are financially literate.
No accountant is well-educated.
Some accountants are not financially literate.

18. Interest rates will rise if and only if inflation increases.
Interest rates are decreasing.
Inflation will not increase.

II. Think of two decisions you have made, one that you consider a good decision, and one that you consider bad. In each case, (a) explain why it was good or bad; and (b) explain how and why the outcome might have been different.

III. | Integrative Exercise | Determine whether each of the following scenarios involves one of the biases we have discussed so far (confirmation, belief, and hindsight biases). If so, identify the bias.

∗1. The farm crisis of the 1930s was a direct result of a decade of over-production. American farmers had increased food production during World War I in order to feed our European allies and U.S. troops. When the war ended, the sudden decrease in demand led to rapidly falling prices. In an attempt to maintain their incomes, farmers increased production even further resulting in more oversupply and falling prices. The U.S. Department of Agriculture obviously behaved irresponsibly by failing to subsidize farmers in order to reduce crop production at the end of the war.

2. Kira is writing a paper on global warming. Before writing her essay she consults articles on FoxNews.com, *The National Review*, and the Global Climate Coalition, an organization of businesses opposed to regulation of greenhouse gases.

3. John and Jeff are discussing immigration. Jeff favors opening borders but John is unsure. Jeff says, "Look, either we subject undocumented immigrants to unsanitary conditions or we allow open immigration. You know the detention centers are overcrowded and unsanitary." John: "You're right. Open immigration is the only thing that makes sense."

∗4. In 2017, Hurricane Harvey threatened the Texas Gulf Coast. The storm conformed to no known historical patterns, making its landfall nearly impossible to predict. The entire Texas coast prepared for the worst. After the devastating storm made landfall at San Jose Island, coastal residents unaffected by the storm were interviewed. "Yes, I prepared to be on the safe side," said one Brownsville, Texas, resident, ". . . but I knew it wouldn't hit here. I knew it all along."

5. "Of course God doesn't exist," Rachel argues. "The life of Anne Frank is all the proof we need. A perfectly good, benevolent God would never allow such a tragedy."

6. Andrew is taking a college admissions exam. He is asked to determine whether the following argument is valid.

> All billionaires are wealthy.
> Some fashion designers are not billionaires.
> ———————————————
> Some fashion designers are not wealthy.

"Younger, unknown fashion designers are usually not wealthy," reasons Andrew. "They have to work hard and wait for their designs to catch on. The argument must be valid."

∗7. Zack often checks his horoscope for the day, believing it's always correct. Last Tuesday it read, "Romance is looking positively wonderful today, with a couple of positive aspects pointing the way for some tender moments for you." Sure enough, he got a date with a woman he liked.

8. Rafael, a college student, enjoys reading true crime books and decides to sign up for a course in criminal psychopathology. He notices that, when he reads the assigned text, much of the information seems familiar to him. He decides he already knows the material and doesn't need to study for his first exam. On the day of the exam, however, he finds he is unable to recognize the correct answers on the multiple choice test. Later, when he sees his F, he tells his friend, "I knew I should have studied."

4.3 Heuristic Biases

A heuristic is a strategy for reaching a conclusion or making a decision quickly, without having to analyze all the relevant issues in detail. It is a "mental shortcut" or rule of thumb for getting an answer quickly and efficiently. For example, common advice on student loans is that you should not borrow more than you expect to make in your first working year. That rule is based on the financial experience of many people, including financial advisors; it may or may not apply to you but it's a place to start.

Heuristics can often provide good answers and solutions. But they can also lead to cognitive biases. Psychologists Amos Tversky and Daniel Kahneman pioneered the study of these biases, including three that we will discuss in this section, based on heuristics called representativeness, availability, and anchoring. Research on these biases is ongoing, and psychologists disagree on many of the details. But our concern is with the basic, well-established tendencies these biases reveal.

The heuristics in this section have to do with *quantitative* issues, such as probability estimates. So far we have dealt mainly with *qualitative* issues: arguments and fallacies involving statements about the traits of individuals ("Annette must be wealthy") or about generalizations ("Water flows downhill"). We will cover quantitative issues in more depth in later chapters on statistical reasoning and probability. But nothing in the heuristics we'll cover in this section requires such advanced knowledge.

4.3A Stereotypes and Representativeness

A stereotype is a conception of the features common to members of a group. The stereotype of a bird, for example, is an animal that flies and is fairly small compared with most mammals. A robin is a stereotypical bird, a penguin is not. A stereotype goes beyond the definition of the group, which must be true of every member; it includes features that are common but not universal to that group. The common stereotype of a CEO, for example, is someone who is decisive, well-paid, and comfortable exercising authority. Many CEOs fit that description, but the description goes beyond the definition (the person in an organization with the ultimate responsibility and authority to make decisions).

As we discussed in the first section of this chapter, stereotypes can be grounded in confirmation bias. They can also reflect racial, ethnic, sexual, or other prejudices. But stereotypes as such can be useful cognitive devices. If you go to a movie theater, for example, you expect a stereotypical seat, padded, with armrests; if you found instead a straight-backed, wooden dinner table chair, you would be surprised.

If you know that a person belongs to a certain group, therefore, you can make an initial inductive inference that he or she has many of the features of that stereotype. As you get to know the person as an individual, of course, you should revise your conclusion accordingly. The logic works in reverse as well: If you know the features of a person, you can infer that the person belongs to the group whose stereotype includes those features. Suppose I give you this profile of a professional person named Jack:

> Jack is a 45-year-old man. He is married and has four children. He is generally conservative, careful, and ambitious. He shows no interest in political and social issues and spends most of his free time on his many hobbies which include home carpentry, sailing, and mathematical puzzles.

Is Jack more likely to be an engineer or a lawyer? The profile clearly fits the stereotype of an engineer better than the stereotype of a lawyer. But the inference that he is an engineer is fairly weak.

To see why, consider a classic experiment by Kahneman and Tversky. Subjects in the experiment were given the profile of Jack. They were also told that the profile was of a person randomly selected from a total of 100 people. One group of subjects was told that 30 of the 100 were engineers, 70 were lawyers. The other subjects were given the opposite proportions, 70 engineers and 30 lawyers. Those proportions are called the base rates, the proportions of engineers and lawyers in the total. If we knew the base rate and had no further information about Jack, we would naturally infer that the probability of his being an engineer is 30% or 70%, depending on which base rate we were given. But subjects in the experiment gave essentially the same probability for Jack's being an engineer, regardless of which base rate they were given. They were going just by the profile, which makes Jack seem more similar to—more representative of—the engineer stereotype.

The **representativeness** heuristic, then, is the tendency to estimate the probability that a thing or event belongs to a class primarily by the similarity of the thing or event to the stereotype of that class—without taking sufficient account of other relevant evidence such as base rates.

Subjects in the experiment were given made-up information that was precise but limited: the choice of only two professions, and a sample with a precise number of people in each profession. In real life, there are more alternatives to consider, and we have to estimate base rates. But we still need to be careful to avoid the representativeness bias. Suppose we are told that a student named Francine is fluent in French, having taken many courses in French and spent her junior year in France; that she loves opera; and that she tends toward liberalism in her political views. Suppose we then ask what her major is. The information suggests that it might be French. A safer bet would be literature or modern languages in general, since those categories include French as well as other languages. Or, safer still, one of the humanities as opposed to the physical or social sciences or a technical field like computer science. We might conclude that there's a better than even chance she's in the humanities, say 65%.

But now we need to consider the base rate—the proportion of students majoring in one of the humanities. If Francine is at your school, you have some sense of the most popular majors. At most colleges there are more students majoring in psychology, economics, and other fields outside the humanities, so we would need to lower our probability estimate about Francine. If she is not at your school, it will take a little more work to find the base rates. But they are easy to find from the National Center for Education Statistics—according to which the number of humanities majors in the United States is dwarfed by business, health professions, social sciences, and engineering, among others.

Major	Bachelor Degrees, 2015–16
Business	371,694
Psychology	117,440
Engineering	106,850
English language and literature/letters	42,795
Foreign languages, literatures, and linguistics	18,427

U.S. Department of Education, National Center for Education Statistics, 2017

The point is that what we know about Francine fits the stereotype of a literature major, or at least a student in the humanities, but nothing in the information we have excludes the possibility that she's in another field. Without considering the base rates, any inference about her major would be very weak.

In short, similarity to a stereotype is not adequate support for an inference that a person, event, or thing is an instance of the class.

4.3B Availability

Availability is the tendency to estimate the frequency or likelihood of an event on the basis of how quickly instances or associations come to mind. For example, if we are asked whether cars or planes are the safer mode of transportation, we might say cars. Airplane crashes come to mind easily because they are dramatic, widely reported events, whereas car accidents are less memorable. Plane crashes are more available to memory than traffic fatalities, and that can easily influence a judgment about relative risks. As with representativeness, the problem here involves base rates. But the availability heuristic is not the failure to consider base rates; the base rate in this example—the frequency of accidents—is the very thing we are trying to estimate. The problem is that the information most available to memory is not necessarily a reliable guide to actual base rates. In this case, the base rate used by most transportation experts is deaths and injuries per mile traveled. By that measure, planes are much safer.

Availability is not inherently a bias. If you are consciously thinking about an issue, or engaged in discussion or debate about it, your memory will naturally call up relevant information—past observations, reasons, conclusions you have reached. If your prior thinking was objective, that background information can be trustworthy. As we discussed in connection with hindsight bias, memory is an essential cognitive function. We can check it when necessary, but if we can't trust it in general, then we can't trust any of our thinking.

That said, memory *is* fallible. As we discussed in connection with confirmation bias, we tend to remember confirming evidence for a belief more readily than disconfirming evidence. And hindsight bias can lead us to misremember a previous decision or prediction when we learn the outcome later. The availability heuristic is another distorting factor—a bias when irrelevant factors influence the ease of recall from memory. This can happen in a number of ways.

Dramatic events covered by the media: Airplane crashes are an example. There are many others. A shark sighting off an ocean beach is reported; it's scary and memorable. But the risk of a shark attack is much lower than other risks at ocean beaches; in the United States, for example, drowning in rip currents is 45 times more frequent than fatal shark attacks. A case of child abuse or kidnap makes the news, but the many more cases of children walking safely to school do not. Campus rallies that turn violent are headlines; peaceful rallies, not so much. The media tend to cover unusual and dramatic things, which are more easily recalled, feeding the availability bias.

Personal experience: Events and experiences in our own lives that have strong feelings attached are more easily recalled than other, more routine, experiences. A breakup in a relationship, for example, is easier to recall than the many happy dates and conversations along the way. The salience of the breakup makes it easier to recall, and so can bias your judgment about relationships.

Repetition: "Repeat something long enough and people will believe it." When we hear a statement repeatedly, it becomes more familiar than something we hear for the first time; it comes to mind more readily, and thereby seems more credible. Repetition is another way the availability heuristic can lead to bias. It is a factor, for example, in the spread of fake news on social media. As we noted in the first section of this chapter, the internet makes it easy to circulate a claim so widely, through so many channels, that it is often not clear what its real source is. So the claim lodges in memory through repetition, without any assessment of the source, and is easily available to us. Repetition is also used deliberately by advertisers to promote brand recognition. (Name a facial tissue: For most of us, Kleenex is the first—and probably the only—brand that comes to mind.) In the same way, politicians and others who wish to persuade us have standard talking points they keep repeating in hopes the points will stick.

A special form of repetition is called an "availability cascade," in which repetition expands in a kind of chain reaction. A cascade typically begins with an event that catches public attention when it is reported—an oil spill, for example, or a mass shooting. The report spawns public concern, which leads to more coverage, which leads to more concern, and so on. The concern is often reasonable, as in the examples. But the increase in availability can result in an exaggerated sense of how frequent events of that type are.

To counter the availability bias, we should be aware, first of all, that availability can mislead us in judging how frequently something occurs; and then seek additional information as needed by consulting sources other than our own memories. The actual frequencies of things like oil spills or school shootings can be found online with a bit of searching.

4.3C Anchoring

At the San Francisco Exploratorium museum, psychologists Karen Jacowitz and Daniel Kahneman asked a group of visitors to estimate the height of the tallest redwood tree. Half of them were asked whether that height is greater or less than 1,020 feet; the other half were asked whether the height is greater or less than 180 feet. Then people in each group were asked to give their best estimate. The experiment was designed to test whether the estimates would be influenced by the "greater or less than" numbers—the so-called anchors. The answer was clearly Yes:

Anchor (ft)	Average Estimate (ft)
1,020	844
180	282

(The actual height of the tallest redwood is 380 feet.)

This experiment is one of many that test how we make quantitative estimates; they show that we are easily influenced by a numerical starting point, an anchor, which we then adjust to reach an estimate. As with other heuristics, this can be a reasonable method of getting to a plausible estimate—if the anchor has some basis in reality. If you were asked, for example, what is the average height of professional (male) basketball players, 6′ 6″ would be a pretty good anchor. But arbitrary or irrelevant factors, as in the experiment, can turn the heuristic into a bias called anchoring. **Anchoring** is the tendency to estimate a quantity by starting with a reference point (the anchor) and moving away from the anchor insufficiently.

Researchers have noted the many ways anchoring operates in everyday life. For example, if you are buying a used car, the salesperson offers a price that sets an anchor; and many of us, in making a counteroffer, do not adjust far enough down—we don't ask for the lowest price the dealer would accept. The same pattern applies to buying a house and to other purchases where the price is negotiable. Skilled negotiators know that the first side to name a price usually comes off better.

Another common example of anchoring is restaurants that feature high-priced entrées. Very few customers may order those meals, but the high price sets an anchor that makes the lower-cost entrées seem like a bargain. In the same way, a shoe salesperson may bring out the most expensive shoes first; with those as an anchor, you might be willing to pay a little more for mid-priced shoes.

Kahneman provides an explanation of how anchoring works:

Start from an anchoring number, assess whether it is too high or too low, and gradually adjust your estimate by mentally "moving" from the anchor. The adjustment typically ends prematurely, because people stop when they are no longer certain that they should move further. [*Thinking Fast and Slow*, 120]

Here's a simple illustration of the process: Using a straightedge but not a ruler, draw a vertical line that is 2½ inches long on a sheet of paper, starting from the bottom. On another sheet, covering up the first, draw a line from the top that *ends* 2½ inches from the bottom. Now compare the lines side by side. It's likely that there's a gap between the lines. Starting from the bottom of the sheet as an anchor, you probably stopped too soon; you stopped when you became uncertain how much longer your line had to be. Starting from the top, you stopped when you became uncertain how much further down you had to go. For both lines, adjustment from the anchors (the bottom and top of the sheets) was inadequate.

Drawing up from the bottom   Drawing down from the top

2½ inches

For factual estimates like the height of the tallest redwood, the best way to counter the anchoring bias is simply to look for information on the issue. In most cases, a quick Google search will give you at least a plausible range for tree heights, prices, average SAT scores at colleges, salary ranges in professions, and other estimates. In negotiating a price, you can counter the seller's offer with your own anchor: What is the most I would pay before I walk away? What is the least the seller would take before he or she walks away? And in all cases, it helps to step back from the immediate issue and consider how anchoring might be involved. With your knowledge of anchoring, for example, you can see through the shoe salesperson's strategy in bringing out the expensive shoes, and thereby neutralize it. Forewarned is forearmed.

REVIEW **Heuristic Biases**

Representativeness is the tendency to estimate the probability that a thing or event belongs to a class primarily by the similarity of the thing or event to the stereotype of the class.

Availability is the tendency to estimate the frequency or likelihood of an event on the basis

of how quickly instances or associations come to mind.

Anchoring is the tendency to estimate a quantity by starting with a reference point (the anchor) and moving away from the anchor insufficiently.

4.3D Taking the Outside View

We have discussed the importance of base rates for the representativeness and availability heuristics. They are also relevant to anchoring. Suppose you plan to buy a new computer, configure it, and transfer your files. How long will that take? You might make different estimates depending on what anchor you start from: a low anchor ("Will it take more or less than 2 days?") or a high one ("More or less than 10 days?"). The base rate here would be the frequency of different setup times, information you might get from an IT professional.

But base rates are only one type of information in a more general category called the *outside view*, as opposed to the *inside view*. The inside view is concerned with the particular case at hand: an individual person with features that fit a stereotype, an airplane crash, a project you are working on, a forthcoming exam in a college course, a case of alleged sexual harassment, a summer travel plan, etc. The outside view is the wider context of information about people and stereotypes, airplane crashes, projects, harassment, etc. Taking the outside view means stepping back from the particular case to consider that wider context. The outside view includes base rates when they are relevant, as in using stereotypes (representativeness), but it includes other kinds of information that is relevant to other cognitive tasks.

For example, Jenny is a college student who needs to decide on a major. She's learning toward biology. She's taken four biology courses already. The subject matter engages her interest; she is fascinated by the theory of evolution and other theoretical issues; she enjoys the lab work; the instructors were great; she got As in all of the courses. That's the inside view. What about the outside view? It would include a base rate: How many people who declare biology as a major complete the requirements? The outside view might also include other factors such as:

- What professions would a biology major prepare her for? Medicine, biological research, the pharmaceutical industry, environmental work?
- What would be the requirements of postgraduate work toward these professions—an M.D., a Ph.D. in biology? How much are they likely to cost?
- What are the income prospects in these professions?

In taking the outside view, Jenny would need to look beyond her experience in her courses so far. The information to answer the outside questions is available in sources such as data on salaries, on graduate and medical schools, etc.

Choosing a major in college is an important decision, but it doesn't determine the rest of your life. We are not suggesting that you choose a major you don't enjoy just because of future job prospects. Whatever you concentrate in, you will have many and varied opportunities after school. But many of the projects we pursue in our work and personal life are much more complicated, such as launching a new business, buying a house, getting married, and starting a family; the planning involves much more thought and information. The more complex the project is, the greater is the tendency to become trapped in the inside view and the greater the need, by contrast, to consider the outside view as well.

Researchers have found, for example, that entrepreneurs launching a new business regularly overestimate their chances of success. They may have a well-developed plan for financing, production, and sales, and focus on that inside view of their venture; but do not take account of the failure rate of new businesses like theirs, which is typically much higher than their estimates. As Kahneman (who coined the inside/outside distinction) observes:

> The inside and outside views draw on different sources of information, and apply different rules to its use. An inside view forecast draws on knowledge of the specifics of the case, the details of the plan that exists, some ideas about likely obstacles

and how they might be overcome. In an extreme form, the inside view involves an attempt to sketch a representative scenario that captures the essential elements of the history of the future [i.e., how the business plan will work out]. [Daniel Kahneman and Dan Lovallo, "Timid Choices and Bold Forecasts: A Cognitive Perspective on Risk Taking," *Management Science*]

In contrast, the outside view includes the rate of success and failure for new ventures in that line of business, as well as statistical data on the likelihood of specific components, such as obtaining finances and finding the needed specialists to hire. Even when entrepreneurs are queried on such outside factors, their estimates tend to be higher than is actually the case.

On a lighter note, Harvard economist Greg Mankiw relates a story from when he was a grad student working under professor Larry Summers (who later served as president of Harvard and an advisor to President Obama):

Larry told me that his research assistants always vastly underestimated how long any task would take. His rule of thumb: Double the estimate the RA gives, and then move to the next higher time unit. So, if the RA says the task will take an hour, it will take two days. If the RA says it will take two days, it will take four weeks.

The outside view is relevant not only to the heuristics we have reviewed in this section. It applies across the range of cognitive biases we have reviewed. In the case of confirmation bias, for example, the inside view is the evidence you have for a belief and would cite in defending it. The outside view would mean looking for evidence against that view, as we discussed in Section 4.1. And, as we will see, it also applies to the biases we discuss in the next section.

APPLY Will This Marriage Last?

Philip Tetlock is a psychologist who has studied the cognitive traits and strategies of "superforecasters," people who are unusually accurate in predicting political and other events. In a radio interview, he gave an amusing example of taking the outside view.

Let's say you're at a wedding, and you're sitting next to somebody who has the bad taste to ask you, how likely do you think it is this couple's going to stay married? . . . It's bad taste and all that. But you see how happy the couple is, and you can see it's a joyous occasion. You say, I can't imagine these people who are so happy together getting divorced. I think maybe a 5 percent chance they're going to get divorced.

Your 5% guesstimate at the wedding is a case of representativeness: The couple looks similar to cases of happy, enduring marriages. By contrast, Tetlock explains, one of his superforecasters would start with the outside view. What is the frequency of divorce among couples in this demographic group? Say it's 40% in the first 10 years. Starting your estimate with the base rate "puts you in the ballpark of plausibility right away." Then you could adjust that estimate by taking the inside view. You would raise or lower the probability depending on what you know or learn about this particular couple—their personalities, previous relationships, mutual commitment, etc.

[National Public Radio, *Hidden Brain*, "Degrees of Maybe: How We Can All Make Better Predictions," June 26, 2017]

SOLVE Heuristic Biases

Heuristics can be valuable rules of thumb in reaching conclusions, but they can also lead to cognitive biases. Here are some strategies for countering those biases.

- Representativeness: Consider base rates in dealing with stereotypes.

- Availability: Seek information beyond what is immediately available from memory to estimate event frequencies.
- Anchoring: Consider a different anchor.
- Take the outside view, putting the particular details of an issue in a wider context.

EXERCISE 4.3

I. Which heuristic is most likely to be involved in each of the following examples?

∗1. Alicia, a third grader, asks her mother if she can start walking the three blocks to school with her best friend. Mom and Dad discuss her request but, even though they live in a quiet suburban neighborhood, decide that the risk of abduction is too high.

2. Newlyweds Jack and Rosalind are shopping for a refrigerator. They have agreed on a budget of $700. They are greeted at the door by a salesperson who shows them several models, ranging from $1500 to $2500 in price. Feeling self-conscious but wanting to save some money, Jack asks if there are any less expensive options. The salesperson shows them a very nice refrigerator on sale for $999. Jack and Rosalind agree immediately, saying it's a bargain.

3. Angela is planning a Caribbean vacation. She makes a reservation at an all-inclusive resort and books a flight. In the weeks leading up to her vacation, Angela sees several internet stories about passengers insulted, abused, and even assaulted by airline personnel. Angela begins to worry about her trip, eventually canceling her reservations and staying home.

∗4. After a hurricane, an animal rescue organization is handing out emergency pet food at an evacuation center. They have dog food, cat food, and bird seed. Miranda is the last person in line. She is a 50-year-old woman who checked into the center alone. Before Miranda says a word, the volunteer smiles and tells her, "Just a minute, I'll get some more cat food."

5. Jaime's criminal justice professor asks him to rank common dangers associated with firearms by frequency. He lists them from the most to least unlikely as: getting killed in a mass shooting, suicide, accidental shooting. He's surprised to learn that accidental shooting is the most—not least—frequent of the options.

6. Cindy is a realtor in a mid-sized city. She meets with a client who wants to buy a three-bedroom house with a

large back yard for around $100,000. Cindy meets her client and arranges tours of five three-bedroom houses on half-acre lots, ranging in price from $200,000 to $500,000. She then shows him a three-bedroom house on a quarter-acre, listed for $148,000. Her client offers the full asking price the very next day.

*7. After graduation, Tobias needs to look for a job. The employment outlook is not so good in his region of the country, but Tobias has an advantage: two uncles, each of whom is able and willing to help him get a job. Uncle Ralph is a police officer in a neighboring city; Uncle Eric works for a local logging company. Should Tobias seek a career in logging or law enforcement? Tobias reasons, "I hear about cops getting killed in the line of duty all the time. I think I'll ask Uncle Eric to get me a job as a logger." [Note: Loggers are more likely to die on the job than cops.]

8. Stuart is a representative for VoteNow, a nonpartisan organization formed to educate voters about upcoming elections. He is on campus at Fredricks University to distribute information about upcoming town hall events sponsored by the candidates. He knows that the faculty and students at Fredricks U self-identify as 70% conservative, 20% libertarian, and 10% progressive. He is approached by Professor Kovacs. She tells Stuart that she teaches anthropology. Professor Kovacs is wearing a long, full print skirt, beads, and Birkenstocks. Stuart looks through his information, hands her a flyer about local progressive political events, and reminds her to register to vote.

9. Keith is asked to give a campus tour to a visiting logician. When he arrives at the philosophy department, he finds three professors engaged in small talk. Not wanting to interrupt, he waits patiently, listening to their conversation. One professor, Dr. Manning, is a small, bookish looking guy who says he enjoys sudoku puzzles and organizes his weekly television viewing by highlighting programs in the listings, then creating a chart for his wall. The second professor, Dr. Garcia, is tall, well-dressed, and says that his hobbies are chess and photography. There is also a short, middle-aged professor, Dr. Murray, who says that she likes to make jelly, bake, and spend time with her cats. Taking advantage of a break in the conversation—and considering himself quite clever—Keith turns to Dr. Manning and asks if he's ready for his tour. Dr. Manning replies, "No, I'm not the person you're looking for." Before he can continue, Keith turns to Dr. Garcia. The three professors laugh, then explain that Dr. Murray is the logician.

*10. For most investors, expenses are one of the few factors they can control. Two common types of mutual fund expenses are the load, or sales commission, and the expense ratio. Suppose you are given information about several funds with a 5.75% load and a 1.9% expense ratio. You know very little about investing but have been warned that you should keep costs down. You ask the broker if there are similar, cheaper funds and she shows you one with a 2.0% load and a 1.2% expense ratio. You choose that fund, never realizing that there are many no-load funds with expense ratios less than one percent.

II. ┃Integrative Exercise┃ Match bias names to definitions (use all biases so far).

*1. Availability _____

2. Hindsight bias _____

3. Belief bias _____

*4. Representativeness _____

5. Confirmation bias _____

6. Anchoring _____

a. The tendency for knowledge of the outcome of an event to affect one's judgment about the antecedent likelihood of that outcome and one's memory of one's prior estimate of its likelihood.

b. The tendency to estimate a quantity by starting with a reference point (the anchor) and moving away from the anchor insufficiently.

c. The tendency to estimate the frequency or likelihood of an event on the basis of how quickly instances or associations come to mind.

d. The tendency to estimate the probability that a thing or event belongs to a class primarily by the similarity of the thing or event to the stereotype of the class.

e. The tendency for agreement or disagreement with a conclusion to affect one's evaluation of the validity or strength of the argument for that conclusion.

f. The tendency to look for and take account of evidence supporting a conclusion, assumption, or hypothesis; while ignoring, downplaying, or failing to seek evidence against it.

4.4 Self-Defensive Biases

In this section, we will examine two cognitive biases that are often motivated by the effort to preserve our self-regard. The first is cognitive dissonance, a tendency that leads to a biased way of dealing with conflicts between our behavior and our standards and beliefs. The second is attribution bias, which has to do with judgments of self and others. Both of these biases have been well established by research in psychology. But both can be countered through self-awareness and objectivity regarding oneself.

4.4A Cognitive Dissonance

The theory of cognitive dissonance was introduced by social psychologist Leon Festinger and remains an active topic of research. Festinger's definition, still used today, involves three elements:

1. A person experiences a conflict, a dissonance or inconsistency, between two cognitions: two of his ideas, observations, beliefs, or opinions.
2. This conflict produces an aversive state; the experience of cognitive dissonance is unpleasant.
3. In light of that aversive state, people are motivated to reduce the conflict in some way.

Formulated in this abstract way, inconsistency among our ideas *should* be aversive. The core of logical thinking is to maintain consistency in our beliefs and avoid contradictions. As we saw in Chapter 2, for example, the standard of validity in a deductive argument is that one cannot accept the premises and deny the conclusion without contradiction. If you believe, for example, that all math majors are introverts, but you also like your friend Rosa, who is majoring in math, because she is so extroverted, there's a contradiction in your thoughts that needs to be resolved.

But cognitive dissonance in psychology is normally given a narrower definition, as a conflict between one's behavior and one's standards, beliefs, or expectations of oneself. The conflict is thus a threat to one's self-esteem, creating a desire to explain away the conflict. The bias is the tendency to do so by nonrational means, such as reinterpreting the behavior, altering the standards, or making up extenuating circumstances. A common example is smoking. A smoker is obviously aware of his habit. He also knows that smoking is harmful to his health, and (let's assume) he wants to promote his health. He could reconcile the conflict by quitting, or by deciding the risk is worth taking. But if he is unwilling to do so, he may deny or minimize the evidence that smoking is harmful; he may minimize the amount he smokes; he may take comfort in thinking of other people who smoke. The problem here does not lie in the effort to maintain consistency. It lies in the effort to remove the conflict—and thereby justify the behavior—by falsifying the other factors. If the smoker denies or minimizes the health risk, for example, he is evading or falsifying a huge body of evidence.

For our purposes, then, **cognitive dissonance** may be defined as the tendency to experience discomfort about the discrepancy between one's actions and one's standards, and to reduce or remove the discrepancy by nonrational means. The bias takes many common forms.

BUYER'S REMORSE The common experience of "buyer's remorse" can lead to cognitive dissonance. I am making a major purchase, such as a new car. I have considered various alternatives and chosen the car that I think best fits my needs and budget. I'm excited as I drive off in my new set of wheels. But then the excitement fades. Before my decision to purchase, I was focused on the good points in this car and the shortcomings in the alternatives. Now it's the reverse. I'm noticing shortcomings in the car I bought—the acceleration isn't great, the back seats are a bit cramped—and thinking of benefits the other cars had to offer. So now I have a conflict: "I make good decisions," but "I made a bad decision with this car." The rational way to deal with this negative state of mind is to review the reasons I made the choice, including the actual good and bad points of each alternative, in order to counter the worry that my choice was wrong. But instead I might engage in the cognitive dissonance bias by exaggerating the defects of the other cars and exaggerating the benefits of mine. (If that doesn't work, there are other ways to reduce dissonance: claiming that the dealer misled me, noticing other people driving the same model, "If so many people made the same purchase, it can't be a bad decision," etc.)

ATTITUDE CHANGE Research on cognitive dissonance has often focused on changes in attitude. In a typical experiment, subjects are told that the researcher is gathering arguments pro and con about some issue—whether a school should raise tuition 10%, for example, or whether the government should ban alcohol. The experiment is designed so that some subjects are asked to write arguments against their own position; they are either assigned to write for the opposite view or asked to volunteer to do so. Afterward, the experimenters ask them whether and to what degree they support that view. The goal is to create cognitive dissonance: The subjects are acting in conflict with their own beliefs; the question is whether they will reduce the dissonance by changing their view. A regular finding is that subjects who are *assigned* to write the arguments do not change their view; they can easily reduce the dissonance because they were forced to write what they did. But subjects who *volunteered* did tend to change views, or at least lower their opposition, as a way to rationalize their choice to write.

A FOOT IN THE DOOR Salespeople, political campaigners, and others who want us to take an action often start small, to get a foot in the door. A campaigner might ask a voter to put a small sign for the candidate in his yard. If the voter agrees, then to avoid cognitive dissonance that small action leads him to strengthen his support for the candidate, and thus to become more amenable to requests for money, and then to volunteer, in an upward spiral of commitment to maintain consistency. As another form of this technique, consider contests run by consumer-product companies. The company offers a big prize for the best short testimonial of its product, with no purchase needed to enter the contest. What's the point? The company is giving out money but not making any. Robert Cialdini explains the rationale, in *Influence: The Psychology of Persuasion*:

> Participants write essays for attractive prizes that they have only a small chance to win. But they know that for an essay to have any chance of winning at all, it must include praise for the product. So they find praiseworthy features of the product. . . .

Having taken the action to praise the product, the pull of consistency leads to a positive view of the product—and then, the company hopes, a purchase.

These are a few of the many situations in which cognitive dissonance can operate. The best way to counter it is to go back to the initial action and examine your reasons for taking it. Can you endorse those reasons? Would you do the same thing again? Is it really better to maintain a false sense of consistency than to admit a mistake (if it was a mistake)? This can be hard in cases where the action was unworthy of oneself, or a major violation of one's moral standards, and one has a strong incentive to rationalize the conflict away. But rationalizing won't change the facts.

4.4B Attribution Bias

In psychology, the term "attribution" refers to the judgments we make to interpret the causes or reasons for peoples' behavior—both our own actions and those of others. It would be hard to exaggerate the importance of attribution. We spend a large part of our lives in social circumstances, interacting with others—with families and friends, in class, in the workplace, and in the broader circles of community and politics. To make sense of our social environment, we need to make sense of the people involved in terms of their goals, convictions, personalities, circumstances, and pressures. That's attribution.

The main distinction in psychological research on attribution is between internal and external factors. Internal factors are traits of the person, including beliefs, goals, personality, and character. External factors are things about the circumstances in which the person acts. Why did the teacher give you a low grade in the course? Was it that the teacher didn't like you, or that you didn't do well on the final? If you attribute your low grade to the teacher's bias, you are assigning the outcome to an external factor; if you assign it to your performance on the final, the attribution is internal, your own performance or lack of preparation. Why did Nadine storm out of the room after you said something to her? Did she react that way because she's highly emotional, or because you said something truly offensive to her? Being highly emotional is an internal personality trait; reacting to what you said is an external cause.

Attribution biases are errors in attributing internal and external factors to explain behavior. In psychology, the usual point of departure in discussing attribution biases is the *fundamental attribution error*, the tendency, when interpreting another person's action, to underestimate the role of external circumstances, usually by *overestimating* the role of internal factors such as character. I'm a guest of Lorenzo at dinner, he leaves a generous tip, and I infer that he's a generous person—a trait of character. I don't consider the external circumstances that may have affected the tip. Perhaps he is trying to impress me. Perhaps he's a regular at this place and expects his tip to generate future favors from the restaurant.

There are reasons why we may be inclined to interpret the behavior of others in terms of traits rather than circumstances. One reason is the way we observe their actions; we typically begin by classifying the action we observe in terms of traits. Lorenzo did something generous, so he must be a generous person. Giselle reacted in a hostile way, so she must be a hostile person. In other words, a trait analysis is built into our initial observation of the action.

But there are problems in calling such attributions *errors*. By what standard? There is a deep question about causality here, quite apart from human action: Both internal and external causes are involved in virtually every action, by any object, and we can't have a full explanation without considering both types of causes. Suppose you drop an egg on the kitchen floor and it breaks. What was the cause? The immediate cause was that it hit the floor, an external factor. But if you had dropped a tennis ball, it would have bounced. The difference is explained by internal factors—the fragility of the eggshell versus the resilience of the rubber ball. In the case of human action, what we do is normally a function of both internal and external factors. A generous person like Lorenzo is generous in certain circumstances, like the restaurant scenario we sketched. But he might not be generous toward a co-worker who couldn't get his or her work done on time—a difference in circumstances. Philosophers as well as psychologists differ about the relative importance of internal traits versus external circumstances in human behavior. So we have to put psychological findings in that wider context.

To be sure, some psychological experiments support the fundamental attribution error by revealing the power of circumstances in surprising ways, such as Yale professor Stanley Milgram's famous experiment on obedience. In that experiment, subjects were recruited for what they were told would be a study of the effects of punishment on learning word associations. The "learners" were given word pairs; then the subjects, the "teachers," gave them a word and asked for the pair, giving an electric shock if the learner got it wrong, using a machine with increasing voltage levels. With repeated errors, the subject was told by the experimenter to increase the voltage of the shock, which ranged from 15 to 450 volts, namely, from "slight shock" to "strong shock" to "extreme intensity shock," to "XXX," at the high (and deadly) end. Actually, the learners were confederates, who deliberately gave wrong answers; and the machine gave no shocks. But subjects, urged by the experimenter to increase the shock level with every error, kept increasing it, despite the "screams" of the learners. Some 65% went all the way to the highest shock level.

The experiment was designed to study obedience to authority; as such it has implications for many issues. For our purposes, it is evidence about the impact of circumstances on behavior. Yale psychiatrists consulted about the experiment before it was run predicted that few if any subjects would administer the high voltages; surely, they thought, personal traits of sympathy and reluctance to do harm would lead the subjects to opt out. And afterward, many of subjects themselves were disturbed by their behavior. The Milgram experiment indicates that the fundamental attribution error is real. In some circumstances, like the demand of an authority figure, an external, circumstantial factor can be the real cause of behavior that we would otherwise attribute to internal traits such as character. At the same time, however, there is abundant evidence about the reality of stable personal traits such as temperament and personality.

In any case, there are attribution phenomena that are clearly biases. They involve discrepancies in the way we attribute the causes of action to ourselves as opposed to others. Let's consider three types.

ACTOR-OBSERVER BIAS Consider the difference in attributions—internal vs. external— we make about others and ourselves. The fundamental attribution error is the tendency to overestimate the role of personal traits in the actions of others. But we also tend to *underestimate* those traits in understanding our own actions. This tendency is the actor-observer bias. It is not clear from the evidence how common this tendency is. To whatever extent it may influence our judgments, however, there is a plausible explanation. It is difficult to put ourselves in the other person's shoes and see his circumstances as fully as he does, so we take a shortcut of attributing the person's actions to internal factors. But we are aware of our own circumstances in much more detail, and aware of how we act differently in different situations, so situational explanations of our actions seem more natural. Nathan failed the mid-term exam; he is probably not a good student. I failed the exam; I was studying hard for another course, my parents were on my case about choosing a major, I had a cold, ...

FALSE CONSENSUS A corollary of the actor-observer bias is false consensus. As Lee Ross, a prominent researcher, describes it, people tend:

> to see their own behavioral choices and judgments as relatively common and appropriate to existing circumstances while viewing alternative responses as uncommon, deviant, and inappropriate. . . .

The corollary is that one:

> judges those responses that differ from [one's] own to be more revealing of the actor's stable dispositions than those responses which are similar to one's own. [Lee

Ross, "The Intuitive Psychologist and His Shortcomings: Distortions in the Attribution Process," *Advances in Experimental Social Psychology*]

In other words, we tend to see our own actions as the normal, rational response to the circumstances at hand. Those who respond in the way we do confirm that view. Assuming that that response is obviously right, why would anyone respond differently? It must be because of some difference internal to them—a perspective, attitude, or bias distinctive to them. This reaction can easily lead to dismissing such people as threats to one's self-confidence.

SELF-SERVING BIAS The actor-observer and false consensus biases may be simply cognitive shortcuts, not necessarily self-defensive. But the self-serving bias has a clear role in preserving one's self-regard. This bias is the tendency to attribute our successes to our personal traits, such as ability, and our failures to external circumstances. To take an earlier example, if you ace the final it's because of your ability and study habits; if you do poorly, it's because of the teacher's bias or some other circumstance. An invidious corollary of this bias is to reverse the attribution for others: If Carlos got a good grade on the test, it's because the teacher likes him, or some other external circumstance; but if he did poorly, it's because of his own traits: he's not very smart, he's too lazy to study, etc.

To counter attribution biases, we can use the method we discussed in regard to confirmation bias: Consider a different viewpoint. To use that method in this case, consider how another person's action might have been a response to his circumstances. We cannot see the world entirely as that person does, but with a bit of empathy we can try to put ourselves in his shoes. If Carlos did poorly on the test, what external factors might have played a role? Can we be sure he's a poor student who would have failed in *every* circumstance? Conversely, we can consider how our own traits might have affected our response to the circumstances in which we acted; and, in particular, how our traits might have contributed to a failure rather than blaming it on external factors. We can also ask whether another person might have acted differently in the same circumstances, drawing attention to the role of internal factors through the difference between ourselves and someone else. Suppose I am working with someone—call her Talia—who has treated me unfairly. I let it slide; I don't call her on it. I attribute my response to external factors: we're working on the same team, she might retaliate, etc. But what if I imagine another person who would call her out? It might highlight a fear of confrontation on my part, an internal factor, as opposed to another person's self-confidence.

REVIEW **Self-Defensive Biases**

Cognitive dissonance is the tendency to experience discomfort at the inconsistency between one's actions and one's standards, and to reduce or remove the dissonance by nonrational means.

Attribution biases are tendencies to misattribute internal and external causes of action to others and to oneself.

EXERCISE 4.4

I. Answer the following multiple-choice questions about self-defensive biases.

*1. A conflict between personal beliefs and actual behavior may result in
   a. Reconciliation bias
   b. Actor-observer bias
   c. Attribution bias
   d. Cognitive dissonance

2. Self-serving bias and false consensus are both examples of
   a. Cognitive dissonance
   b. Actor-observer bias
   c. Attribution bias
   d. Adaptability bias

3. Which of the following might be a good way to deal with cognitive dissonance rationally?
   a. Find a way to maintain psychological consistency.
   b. Go back to the initial action and examine the reasons for that action.

c. Try to determine whether other people have made the same decision.
d. There is no way to mitigate cognitive dissonance.

*4. Attribution bias involves
   a. Judgments about our own actions and motives
   b. The tendency to ignore evidence against a conclusion
   c. Judgments about the actions and motives of others
   d. Both a and c

5. We tend to see our own choices and judgments as common and appropriate and alternate judgments as deviant and inappropriate due to
   a. Cognitive dissonance
   b. Self-serving bias
   c. False consensus
   d. Dissociative attitude bias

II. What self-defensive biases are involved in the following situations?

*1. Alice is a member of a sorority that prides itself on its honor code. Every week, members renew their vow that they will not lie, cheat, steal, or associate with those who do. Several friends invite Alice to join them in Fort Lauderdale for spring break. Her parents agree she can go but only if she raises the money herself. Alice works hard but is still $100 short of the amount she needs. The night before the trip, she takes $100 from the cookie jar where she knows her mother keeps some money. During her flight to Florida, Alice starts to feel guilty. She thinks, "It's not like its really stealing. That money is for family expenses. I'm a member of this family, so I'm entitled to at least a little of the money."

2. Fatima and Omar are on their first date. When Omar arrives to pick her up, Fatima notices how polite and deferential he is to her parents and how he helps her grandmother rise from her chair. At dinner, Omar is consistently polite and helpful to everyone they meet. Fatima thinks to herself, "He's obviously a kind and generous person," not realizing he's trying to impress her.

3. Jeremiah's speech class is having debates; students are asked to pair up and take opposing views on a variety of topics. Jeremiah would like to debate his friend Wayne. But they agree on almost everything. So Jeremiah volunteers to argue against free speech zones even though he would prefer the "pro" position.

Both students research thoroughly and argue their cases well. Both receive As on the assignment. After their debate, Jeremiah tells Wayne that he is now opposed to free speech zones.

*4. At the Acme Corp. all promotions are publicly announced at the monthly staff meeting. Chloe and Abdulla, two members of the marketing department, sit together during the meeting. As the first few promotions are announced, Abdulla whispers to Chloe, "Same as always, the brownnosers get the promotions." Chloe rolls her eyes and nods in response. They are both visibly surprised when Chloe's name is called next; she's finally received a long-desired promotion. As the group applauds, Abdulla pats her on the back and says, "See, all your hard work paid off." Chloe nods and smiles gratefully.

4.5 Countering Bias

At the beginning of this chapter, we distinguished between cognitive biases and fallacies. Fallacies are logical errors that can be avoided by understanding why the conclusion is not supported by the premises. Begging the question, for example, is the fallacy of trying to support a proposition with an argument in which that proposition is a premise. The argument is circular; it goes nowhere. That's a logical error. Though fallacies seem plausible—that's why people commit them—they don't need special psychological techniques to avoid them. Biases do. They are psychological tendencies that typically operate beneath the surface of conscious awareness. To avoid them, we need to be self-aware of the cognitive and motivational factors at work.

But biases are just tendencies, and they are avoidable. They can be countered by knowledge of how they arise and operate, and by employing the counterstrategies we discussed. We always have the choice to review our beliefs and decisions to look for the effects of bias. Even when the biases operate automatically, we can deal with them as we do with optical illusions, like the Poggendorff illusion:

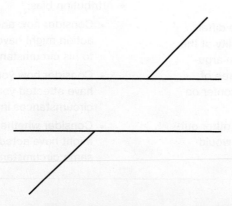

The two diagonal line segments do not look aligned; if each were extended across the blank space between the vertical bars, it looks as if the line segments would not meet in a single straight line. In fact, they would. You can't help seeing them as nonaligned, but you can counter the optical illusion by using a straightedge that crosses the blank space. In the same way, there are strategies for countering cognitive biases even when those biases are deeply rooted in our psychology.

In earlier sections, we considered a number of strategies to counter specific biases. They are summarized in the Solve box nearby. But some of the strategies can be applied more generally, to a range of different biases, and therefore have a special importance for us. In this section we will review those general strategies and add a few more to expand our toolkit.

SOLVE Countering Cognitive Biases

Confirmation bias

- Talk with people who have different views.
- Consider what evidence would count against your view.
- Shift your focus from proving you're right to "getting it right."

Information credibility

- Distinguish factual statements from opinion.
- Check multiple sources.
- Consider the plausibility of the item.
- Use fact-checkers.

Other general biases

- Belief bias: Be clear about the difference between (a) the plausibility of the premises and conclusion of an argument and (b) the internal degree of support the premises would confer on the conclusion.
- Hindsight bias: Consider how other outcomes of a decision or event would have been possible.

Heuristic biases

- Representativeness: Consider base rates in dealing with stereotypes.
- Availability: Seek information beyond what is immediately available from memory to estimate event frequencies.
- Anchoring: Consider a different anchor.
- Take the outside view, putting the particular details of an issue in a wider context.

Self-defensive biases

- Cognitive dissonance: Review the initial action and your reasons for taking it. Admit mistakes instead of rationalizing past actions.
- Attribution bias:
  - Consider how another person's action might have been a response to his circumstances.
  - Consider how your own traits might have affected your response to the circumstances in which you acted.
  - Consider whether another person might have acted differently in the same circumstances.

CONSIDER THE OPPOSITE We discussed this strategy in connection with confirmation bias, but it can be applied to many of the other biases as well. In the case of hindsight bias, for example, the specific strategy of considering how other outcomes of a decision or event were possible is a form of "consider the opposite"; the strategy is to consider the opposite of what actually happened as a possibility. With attribution bias, as another example, we can counter the tendency to attribute another person's actions to internal traits by considering how external factors might have been involved. That, too, is a form of considering the opposite. The general value of this strategy is that it helps us to pause in our automatic reactions and thoughts, to step back and be more aware of why we came to a given conclusion, and to ask whether the reasons stand up to examination by confronting alternative conclusions.

A special form of this strategy called a *premortem* can be applied to projects and decisions. The strategy, created by psychologist Gary Klein, is to imagine yourself into the future: A project you are planning has been implemented, and has failed utterly; now generate reasons why it failed. The technique is often used by project teams in business, but it is applicable to any decision. You have just graduated college, for example, and have several job offers. You are leaning toward one of them—say it's a programming job in a start-up tech company. Now imagine that a year later the job has turned out to be a dead end. Explain why that happened. The point of this exercise is not to create pessimism. The point is to improve our decision-making. In deciding, we look to the future, anticipating steps to the goal, obstacles that may occur, and so forth. But that's all hypothetical, and confirmation bias encourages us to look for reasons to expect success. A premortem of failure shifts our focus; in imagination, we take the failure as an outcome that has occurred and we engage hindsight to explain it. In effect, we turn hindsight bias into a positive device. The evidence indicates that this strategy counters the confirmatory optimism of advance planning by highlighting potential obstacles.

WANNA BET? Annie Duke is a world-class poker champ and business consultant. In her book *Thinking in Bets*, she explains the value of asking how much you would be willing to bet that your belief is true.

> Being asked if we are willing to bet money on [a belief] makes it much more likely that we will examine our information in a less biased way, be more honest with ourselves about how sure we are of our beliefs, and be more open to updating and calibrating our beliefs. The more objective we are, the more accurate our beliefs become.

Thinking in bets means estimating the probability that a belief is true. Turning that estimate into a bet, even an imaginary one, adds a money incentive; but the essence of the technique is to bring to the fore your degree of confidence in the belief. This has an obvious value in dealing with confirmation bias. It complements the "consider the opposite" strategy, which asks us to consider rival positions and contrary evidence, by asking us to evaluate the strength of the evidence for our own belief.

Thinking in bets also encourages us to take the outside view, which we discussed as a way to counter biases that arise from heuristics. By contrast with the inside view, which is focused on the particular case or issue at hand, the outside view is the wider context of information. It includes base rates when they are relevant, as in using stereotypes (representativeness), as well as other kinds of information that is relevant to other cognitive tasks—and other biases. Thinking in bets, Duke observes, raises such outside-view questions as:

How do I know this?

How much information do I have that's relevant to the belief?

What is the quality of my sources?

What other things like this have I been confident about that turned out not to be true? [65]

These questions, and the degree of confidence in our beliefs they help us estimate, apply to most of the cognitive biases we have reviewed. They encourage us to be more self-aware about the sources of our beliefs, to be alert to possible biases, and to weigh the evidence in a more rational way.

CHAPTER REVIEW

Summary

- Cognitive biases are systematic psychological tendencies to make errors in seeking and interpreting information.
- Some biases are tendencies that can affect thinking in general, whatever the topic or type of reasoning involved, including confirmation bias, belief bias, and hindsight bias.
- Heuristic biases are cognitive rules of thumb that are often useful but can lead us astray,

including representativeness, availability, and anchoring.
- Self-defensive biases are systematic errors in judgments about oneself and others, often motivated by self-regard and defensiveness, including cognitive dissonance and attribution biases.
- Cognitive biases can be countered by awareness of our vulnerability to them and by specific strategies to avoid them.

Key Terms

cognitive biases (p. 147)

confirmation bias (p. 148)

belief bias (p. 161)

hindsight bias (p. 163)

representativeness (p. 169)

availability (p. 170)

anchoring (p. 172)

cognitive dissonance (p. 179)

attribution bias (p. 181)

Putting It All Together

I. **Integrative Exercise** Match bias names to definitions.

✳1. Availability ____

2. Hindsight bias ____

3. Attribution bias ____

✳4. Belief bias ____

5. Cognitive dissonance ____

6. Representativeness ____

✳7. Confirmation bias ____

8. Anchoring ____

a. The tendency for knowledge of the outcome of an event to affect one's judgment about the antecedent likelihood of that outcome and one's memory of one's prior estimate of its likelihood.

b. The tendency to experience discomfort at the inconsistency between one's actions and one's standards, and to reduce or remove the dissonance by nonrational means.

c. The tendency to estimate the probability that a thing or event belongs to a class primarily by the similarity of the thing or event to the stereotype of the class.

d. The tendency to estimate the frequency or likelihood of an event on the basis of how quickly instances or associations come to mind.

e. The tendency to estimate a quantity by starting with a reference point (the anchor) and moving away from the anchor insufficiently.

f. The tendency to misattribute internal and external causes of action to others and to oneself.

g. The tendency for agreement or disagreement with a conclusion to affect one's evaluation of the validity or strength of the argument for that conclusion.

h. The tendency to look for and take account of evidence supporting a conclusion, assumption, or hypothesis; while ignoring, downplaying, or failing to seek evidence against it.

II. **Integrative Exercise** What cognitive biases are involved in the following situations?

✳1. In 1959, wild European rabbits were successfully introduced in Australia by English immigrants who wanted to hunt them for sport. It took only 50 years for the rabbits to spread throughout Australia. Today these animals are considered an invasive species, causing widespread crop damage. European settlers should have known better than to import their animals into an alien habitat!

2. Professor Tacelli's philosophy class is waiting for him to arrive when the teaching assistant enters the room and announces that class is canceled because Prof. Tacelli has had an allergic reaction. Shaquille, a nursing major doing a rotation in the emergency room, raises his hand and asks, "When will he be out of the hospital? Anaphylaxis is life-threatening." The TA looks confused and says, "He just has hives, he'll be back tomorrow."

3. Aspen, a college junior, writes an essay claiming that the majority of Americans favor some sort of socialism. His sociology professor says he must support this claim with

evidence and suggests that he do some research. He reports that, according to the Socialism Now! website, 75% of their subscribers say they strongly prefer socialism over capitalism.

*4. In the upcoming election, candidates will probably focus largely on the economy. Indicators suggest that either inflation or unemployment will increase. The best available evidence suggests higher inflation is ahead. Therefore, we should expect unemployment to stay low.

5. The BetterBread Company is expanding to a new region of the country. In order to build brand awareness, they sponsor a contest for the best promotional jingle about one of their products. The Grand Prize winner will receive an all-expense paid vacation for two to Hawaii; runners-up will win cash prizes. Isaiah has never heard of BetterBread but decides to try his luck. After posting his entry, Isaiah goes shopping. When he comes to the bread aisle, he notices BetterBread on the shelf. He grabs a loaf, ignoring his usual bread.

6. Generally speaking, Americans are opposed to any tax on wealth. A recent study shows that 87% of Beverly Hills residents surveyed opposed such a tax.

*7. Corrinne, a 16-year-old female, went to her doctor presenting with jaundice, fatigue, and swelling of the legs and abdomen. She was diagnosed with viral hepatitis. Corrinne was given several prescriptions and told that her illness would probably resolve itself in four to eight weeks. But when her psychiatric symptoms began, it was discovered that she had Wilson's disease, a rare genetic disorder. When they received this diagnosis, her parents were outraged, insisting that Corrine's pediatrician should have considered Wilson's disease all along.

8. If Republicans win the White House, then the border will be closed and trade between the United States and Mexico will decrease. Studies show that trade between the two countries has already begun to decrease and construction on the wall has started. Guess the Republicans will win the presidency.

9. Two departments of Food-X Corp. are presenting a new employee compensation plan. The plan is the same for both departments. Each year, every employee receives a two percent "step"—a raise intended to reward experience and longevity. Sometimes, they also receive a raise on top of the step, usually as result of the rising cost of living. Mr. Savonaroli, the manager of the quality control department, tells his staff, "Good news, this year our facility will be receiving a three percent raise." Production-floor manager Ms. Bloch tells her staff, "Good news, this year, everyone will receive a one percent raise on top of their step." Ms. Bloch's staff is happy and grateful. Mr. Savonaroli's staff is unhappy when they receive their contacts; they were expecting three percent on top of their annual step.

*10. Quanhua loves animals and opposes any kind of cruelty to them. He volunteers at a local animal shelter, supports a dog-rescue organization, and assists with the feral cat colony on campus. One day in the school cafeteria, he notices a poster sponsored by a local animal rights organization that says, "Go Cruelty Free. Go Vegan." As Quanhua walks to his seat, he feels troubled. He reasons to himself, "Dogs and cats are pets, they're not meant to be food. Cows are livestock; that's what they're raised for." He eats his burger and fries, then goes to class.

III. You are working in the traffic division of your town's government, considering whether to increase the number of streets that have bike lanes, shown on the map below. But a council member is concerned that bike lanes may increase the number of pedestrian accidents above the normal level. So far you have only fragmentary information, shown in the table: for some streets, whether there's a bike lane or not; for other streets, the level of accidents, normal or higher. For which streets do you need to get information in order to confirm or disconfirm the council member's claim? Put a Y in the "Information needed?" column for that street.

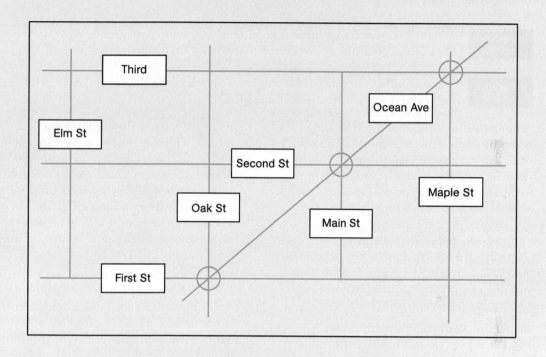

Street	Information You Have	Information Needed?
Elm	Normal accidents	
Oak	Bike lane	
Main	No bike lane	
First	Bike lane	
Second	Higher accidents	
Third	Higher accidents	
Ocean	No bike lane	
Maple	Normal accidents	

IV. For each claim, state at least two reliable sources you might use to evaluate whether the claim is true or false.

*1. Ariana Grande is a Princeton graduate.

2. Thomas Jefferson signed the U.S. Constitution.

3. Authorities found the bodies of 300 children who had been frozen alive so that their organs could be harvested.

*4. Texas is the only state allowed to fly its state flag at the same height as the U.S. flag.

5. In U.S. law, hate speech is not free speech.

V. `Integrative Exercise` Imagine that you are a journalist employed by a national magazine. Write a brief article, incorporating at least one cognitive bias into your story.

VI. `Integrative Exercise` For each of the following situations, you are given a specific cognitive bias. How might you invoke that bias in another person?

1. You are a waiter at a popular restaurant. One week, you are instructed to push a somewhat expensive weekly special. A couple comes in, looks at the menu, and asks you for recommendations. How do you make the special seem attractive? (anchoring)

2. You are trying to get a dedicated space for smokers by convincing university administrators that there is widespread approval for your proposal. How can you make sure your informal faculty/student survey supports your case? (confirmation bias)

3. You want to start your own business selling kitchen supplies. Since you are part of a multilevel marketing company, part of your success depends on building your network by recruiting other people. (cognitive dissonance)

4. You are trying to gain support for a dedicated LGBT+ student center. You are talking to a friend who asks, "Isn't it true that most students oppose this idea?" You know from polls that many of the opponents are majors in criminal justice, fashion merchandising, or theology. How can you convince your friend to ignore their opinions? (representative bias)

5. You're selling program ads for the drama department's next performance. You hope to sell at least a $200 ad to Kampus Korner, a convenience store near campus. You worry that the owner, Mr. Rainwater, might think this is too much money to spend on a single ad. Persuade him to buy the ad. (anchoring)

VII. Test people you know for cognitive bias. Ask at least 6 people the following questions and record their answers. Did they exhibit cognitive biases? In questions with dollar amounts, use each amount with half of your test subjects.

Anchoring

1. Do you think the average textbook costs more or less than $50/$100? How much would you estimate the average price is?

2. Our school is thinking of increasing the fee for parking permits in order to raise money for a new parking garage. Surveys of colleges and universities show that the average parking fee is ($100/$200) a year. What do you think would be fair?

Availability

3. Gun control is in the news again. What is the biggest danger posed by allowing gun ownership? [After you've collected your answers, fact-check them for accuracy. List any reasons people gave for saying a given danger is the biggest.]

Representativeness

4. Surveys of incoming freshmen indicate that 20% say they would like to be lawyers while

10% say they would like to go into elementary education. Can you guess whether each of the following is a pre-law student, an elementary education major, or is majoring in some other subject?

a. Valerie is a friendly, bubbly woman who wears bright colors and loves children.

b. Leo is an easygoing guy who enjoys watching football and reading the *Wall Street Journal*.

c. Esmer is a serious, articulate young woman who enjoys debates.

PART TWO

Deductive Logic

In Chapter 2, we identified the two broad kinds of inference, deductive and inductive. The role of a deductive argument is to draw a conclusion that is contained implicitly in the premises. A deductive argument is either valid or invalid; there are no intermediate degrees of partial validity. If the argument is valid, then the conclusion follows necessarily from the premises. In an inductive argument, by contrast, the conclusion amplifies—it goes beyond—what the premises state. Inductive arguments have degrees of strength, depending not only on the relationship between premises and conclusion but also on the context of other information available.

We now begin our study of deduction, which is the subject of Part 2. We are going to examine two approaches, two different ways of analyzing deductive arguments and evaluating them for validity. In the first half of Part 2 (Chapters 5–7), we will examine the traditional approach, first developed by the ancient Greek philosopher Aristotle. Then, in the second half of Part 2 (Chapters 8–10), we will turn to the modern approach, developed mainly in the 20th century. While both approaches use symbols to represent certain aspects of deductive arguments, the traditional method is more closely related to ordinary language and is still valuable for analyzing and evaluating the forms of deductive reasoning we use most often. The modern approach is more thoroughly symbolic. It's more like algebra, which means that we have to invest in learning the symbolic notation. But the reward is the ability to analyze and evaluate a wider range of deductive arguments.

Categorical Propositions

5

At a certain point in our understanding of the natural world, we learned that whales are mammals. Since we also know that all mammals breathe by means of lungs, we can infer that whales breathe by means of lungs. Using the method of argument analysis we learned in Chapter 2, we would diagram this inference as follows:

1. Whales are mammals.
2. All mammals breathe by means of lungs.
3. Whales breathe by means of lungs.

This is an example of the inference pattern known as the categorical syllogism. A categorical syllogism is a deductive argument with two premises, in which the premises and the conclusion are categorical propositions. In this chapter, we examine the basic structure of categorical propositions. We will turn to the syllogism itself in the next chapter.

LEARNING OBJECTIVES

On successful completion of the chapter, you will be able to:

✓ Identify the components of categorical propositions and translate them into standard form. (5.1)

✓ Demonstrate mastery of both the traditional and modern squares of opposition. (5.2–5.3)

✓ Construct Venn diagrams. (5.4)

✓ Test immediate inferences. (5.5)

5.1 Standard Form

5.1A Components of Categorical Propositions

A **categorical proposition** can be regarded as an assertion about the relations among classes. This is easy to see in the example above. Whales are a species of animal; mammals are the genus to which that species belongs. The proposition "Whales are mammals" says that the first class is included in the second. Every categorical proposition says that a certain relationship exists between two classes (or categories). The parts of the proposition that refer to the classes are called the *terms* of the proposition, and there are two terms: the *subject* and the *predicate*, symbolized by *S* and *P*. In our example, the subject is "whales" and the predicate is "mammals."

It isn't always so obvious that we are talking about classes of things. In the proposition "Whales breathe by means of lungs," the phrase "breathe by means of lungs" indicates a property that some objects have. But for any property there's a class of things that have the property—in this case, things that breathe by means of lungs. So we would rewrite the proposition as "Whales are things that breathe by means of lungs," in order to make it clear that we are talking about two classes. In the same way, we would rewrite the proposition "Whales are large" as "Whales are large things." In general, we revise each proposition (without changing the meaning) so that it has the form "*S* is *P*" or "*S*s are *P*s."

The subject and predicate are not always single words. In fact, that is rarely the case. More often, one or both of the terms is a complex phrase. But phrases can designate classes of things just as well as individual words can. In each of the following examples, the subject and predicate terms are set off by parentheses.

(Computers) are (electronic machines that can be programmed to follow a sequence of instructions).

(Soldiers who have won the Medal of Honor) are (heroes).

(Commodities such as corn and wheat) are (economic goods subject to the law of supply and demand).

In the first example, the subject is a single word, but the predicate is not. The opposite is true in the second. And in the third neither term is a single word. But all three have the same basic form: *S*s are *P*s.

In addition to the subject and predicate, there is a third element of categorical propositions, indicated by the words "is" or "are." This element—called the **copula**—links subject and predicate. In all the examples so far, the copula has been *affirmative*. We said that *S* is *P*. But the copula can also be *negative*, as in the propositions:

Whales *are not* fish.

Copper *is not* a precious metal.

Private schools *are not* required to have a pension plan.

In terms of classes, we can make both the affirmative statement that *S* is included in *P* and the negative statement that *S* is excluded from *P*. The affirmative or negative character of a proposition is called its **quality**.

The fourth and final element of a categorical proposition, **quantity**, is a little less obvious than the others. The subject of "Whales are mammals" is "whales," and it is clear that we are talking about all of them. But sometimes we make statements about only *some* members of a class: Some whales are fish-eating carnivores, some politicians are crooks, some of Spike Lee's movies are not comedies. In ordinary language, we often do not say "all" or "some" explicitly; the context makes it clear which we mean. But the difference is crucial in logic, and we need to make it explicit.

A proposition with the form "All *S* are *P*" is **universal** in quantity. A proposition with the form "Some *S* are *P*" is **particular**. The distinction between universal and particular also applies to negative as well as affirmative propositions. Thus, "Some good tablet computers are not Apple products" is a particular negative proposition. "No freshman is a varsity player" is a universal negative proposition. Notice that the word "No" does double duty: It indicates both the negative quality and the universal quantity of the proposition.

A categorical proposition, then, has four components: (1) a subject term; (2) a predicate term; (3) a copula, which is either affirmative or negative in quality; (4) one or more words indicating quantity, universal or particular. The quality and quantity, taken together, determine the logical *form* of a proposition; the subject and predicate determine its *content*. Thus, the two statements "All whales are mammals" and "All snakes are reptiles" have the same logical form—affirmative and universal—although their content is quite different. Since there are two possible qualities, and two possible quantities, there are altogether just four standard logical forms for categorical propositions, no matter how complex their subject and predicate terms may be. These four forms are:

	Affirmative	Negative
Universal	All S are P	No S is P
Particular	Some S are P	Some S are not P

Each of these standard forms has a traditional label that we will use as a shorthand reference to the form. The two affirmative forms are A and I, the first two vowels of the Latin word *affirmo* ("I affirm"). The negative forms are E and O, the vowels in *nego* ("I deny").

	Affirmative	Negative
Universal	A	E
Particular	I	O

EXERCISE 5.1A

I. For each of the following propositions, identify the subject and predicate terms, the copula, the quality, and the quantity. Then name the form (A, E, I, or O).

＊1. Some movie stars are good actors.

2. Some movie stars are not good actors.

3. Some baseball players are not golfers.

＊4. All graduate students are broke people.

5. All phones are communication devices.

6. Some phones are landlines.

＊7. No phones are laptops.

8. Some people who have Ph.D.s are airheads.

9. No self-respecting person is a liar.

＊10. No one who laughs at my teddy bear is a friend of mine.

11. All discoveries are additions to the stock of human knowledge.

12. No person over the age of 60 is an Olympic marathon champion.

＊13. Some arguments in the works of great philosophers are fallacies.

14. All paintings are works of art.

15. Some works of art are not beautiful things.

II. Change the quantity, but not the quality of the following statements.

*1. All students who skip class are people who lack motivation.

2. No violins are percussion instruments.

3. Some political scientists are professional pollsters.

*4. Some dogs are not animals that enjoy swimming.

5. Some Canadians are people who value free speech.

III. Change the quality but not the quantity of the following statements.

*1. All convicted felons are deranged individuals.

2. Some politicians are dishonest opportunists.

3. Some birds are not carnivorous animals.

*4. No student who has been convicted of a drug-related crime is a student eligible for financial aid.

5. All good books are things that get better with age.

IV. Change both the quantity and the quality of the following statements.

*1. All fish are animals with gills.

2. Some college students are not vegans.

3. No persons under the age of 21 are persons who are allowed to purchase alcohol.

*4. Some businessmen are people who owe their success to a novel idea.

5. No mammals are animals that lay eggs.

V. For each of the following, you are given either a subject or a predicate term. Use the given term to construct a standard form categorical proposition of the type indicated in the parentheses.

*1. Subject term: students with an average of B or higher (A)

2. Predicate term: mammals (E)

3. Predicate term: older Americans with disabilities (O)

*4. Subject term: classic movies (I)

5. Predicate term: mammals that lay eggs (I)

6. Subject term: U.S. representatives serving more than one term (A)

*7. Predicate term: animals with wings (A)

8. Subject term: birds (E)

9. Subject term: dogs weighing over 5 pounds (O)

*10. Predicate term: applicants with more than ten years' experience (I)

5.1B Translating into Standard Form

To work with a categorical statement, we need to formulate it as one of the four standard forms: A, E, I, or O. The quantity must be explicitly indicated by a quantifier—a word such as "all," "no," or "some." The subject and predicate terms must be words or phrases designating a class of objects. And the copula must always be some form of the verb "to be": "is," "are," "was," "were," "will be" (and their negative forms).

Quantifier	Subject Class	Copula	Predicate Class
[All]		[Are, were, will be, are not, were not, will not be]	
[No]	S	[Is, was, will be, is not, was not, will not be]	P
[Some]		[Are, were, will be, are not, were not, will not be]	

If a categorical statement is already in standard form, then all we need to do is look for words that indicate logical form. But in most cases we have to rework the sentence a bit in order to get it into standard form. If the predicate of a sentence is not a term designating objects, we have to turn it into one. "All whales are large" must be rewritten as "All whales are large things." Similarly, "Some blondes have more fun" becomes "Some blondes are people who have more fun"; "No mammal can breathe under water" becomes "No mammal is a thing that can breathe under water"; and so on. The goal is always to arrive at the basic form: *[quantifier] S [copula] P*, where *S* and *P* are nouns or phrases referring to things, types of things, or classes of things.

As we go along, we will point out other problems connected with putting statements in standard form, as well as the techniques for dealing with them. But let's take care of some of the easier problems now.

Subject–predicate order. In English, the subject normally comes first in a sentence, with the predicate following it. But there are exceptions. In the statement "Tender is the night," for example, "the night" is the subject; that is what the statement is about. Similarly, the subject of the sentence "In the middle of the table were some pears" is "pears." In both of these cases, the order of subject and predicate is simply reversed. But consider another nonstandard statement: "No code has been made that cannot be broken." What is the subject term? "Codes." But which codes? "Codes that cannot be broken." The subject has been split in half, with the predicate ("has been made") coming in between the two halves of the subject. In standard form, this statement would be "No code that cannot be broken is a thing that has been made." In all cases of nonstandard order, you can identify the subject by asking what the statement is about.

Singular terms. Some categorical propositions have subject terms referring to a single person, place, or thing rather than to a class. For example:

New York is a large city.

Ellie is a good basketball player.

I am not a coward.

The third car in the lot is a clunker.

In logic, a statement of this sort is called a **singular proposition**. The mark of a singular proposition is that the subject term is a name, pronoun, or phrase standing for a single object. Even though these propositions do not refer to classes, they have traditionally been treated as having universal quantity, and in this chapter we will follow that tradition. Thus an affirmative singular statement is an A proposition, and a negative one is an E proposition. The rationale is that a singular term may be thought of as naming a class with one member, and so of course the statement is about all the members of that class. To make this explicit, we could recast the examples above:

> All cities identical to New York are large cities.
>
> All people identical to Tom are good basketball players.
>
> No person identical to me is a coward.
>
> All cars identical to the third car in the lot are clunkers.

Such rephrasing is cumbersome, though. From here on out, we will leave singular statements as is, but remember that they are to be treated as universal.

Nonstandard quantifiers. Words that indicate quantity are called **quantifiers**. So far we have considered only the standard ones: "all," "some," and "no." But English (like any other language) has many nonstandard quantifiers in addition to the standard ones. Here are some of the ways to indicate universal quantity, with the quantifier indicated in bold:

Universal Propositions

Affirmative	Negative
All whales are mammals.	**No** dinosaur ate sushi.
A cat is a predator.	Not **a** creature was stirring.
Every president faces unexpected challenges.	**None** of the telephones is working.
Each item on the menu must have a price.	
Any student using the gym must show an ID.	

Particular propositions can also be expressed in various ways:

Particular Propositions

Affirmative	Negative
Some apples are good for baking.	**Some** apples are not good for baking.
A car is parked outside.	**A** wire is not plugged in.

Notice that the indefinite article "a" can mean either universal or particular quantity, depending on the context. It can mean any instance of a category such as cats, but it can also mean some instance, as in our example: "A car is parked outside."

As we noticed before, statements do not always contain an explicit quantifier, so we often need to determine from the context which one to insert. The statement that whales are mammals, for example, is clearly meant as a universal statement. So is the statement "Objects heavier than air must fall when unsupported"; if such objects *must* fall, then all of them do. In contrast, when you stay at a friend's house and he says, "Beer is in the refrigerator," it's a safe bet he means some beer, since the refrigerator has not been built that would hold all the beer that exists.

A special problem arises with statements that have the form "All *S* are not *P*." Despite its appearance, this is not a standard form. It is ambiguous. Consider the statement "All politicians are not crooks." Does this mean that no politicians are crooks (an E proposition) or that some politicians are not crooks (an O proposition)? It could mean either. So when you encounter a statement with that form, you will need to decide from the context whether an E or an O statement is intended and translate it accordingly.

In regard to particular quantifiers, remember that "some" means "at least one." "Some" is an extremely unspecific quantifier. It says, in effect: We know that at least one *S* is/is not *P*, but we don't know (or we're not saying) how many are. Certain other non-universal quantifiers are much more specific than "some"—for example, "few," "several," "many," "most." But they should all be translated as "some," and the statements containing them should be treated as particular propositions. To be sure, this can change the meaning of the statement; sometimes important information is lost. But the logic of the syllogism recognizes only two degrees of quantity: all and less than all. Reasoning that depends on the more specific degrees of quantity will be treated in Part 3.

APPLY "Some," "Most," and the Law School Admissions Test

You've learned that, in logic, we interpret the word "some" to mean "at least one," and that we translate any word or phrase that means at least one but less than all as a particular statement. This interpretation holds throughout the study of logic. But be careful if you take the LSAT. ETS (the company that administers the LSAT) also interprets "some" as "at least one."

That means it only takes one case to make a "some" statement true. Unlike logicians, however, the LSAT uses the word "most" in our everyday sense of the word; to make a claim about most of a subject class true, the statement must apply to more than half the members of the class.

SOLVE Putting Propositions in Standard Form

To put a categorical proposition in standard form:

1. Identify the subject and predicate terms. Remember that the subject does not always come first in ordinary language.

2. If necessary, reformulate the subject and predicate terms so that they refer to classes.

3. Identify the quantity of the proposition.
   a. Singular propositions about an individual thing are treated as universal.
   b. Nonstandard quantifiers like "every," "any," and "few" must be translated into the standard quantifiers: "all," "no," and "some."

EXERCISE 5.1B

I. Translate each of the following statements into standard form.

＊1. A student who does not complete the appropriate course withdrawal form is at risk of receiving an F for the course.

2. Blessed are the poor in spirit.

3. Not any of the states ban same-sex marriage.

＊4. Some of the conference speakers are eloquent.

5. Some apples are not tart.

6. All states must comply with federal law.

II. Integrative Exercise Put each of the follwing statements into standard form; identify the subject and predicate terms, the quantifier, and the copula; and name the quantity, quality, and form (A, E, I, or O).

＊1. All human beings are rational.

2. No mushrooms that grow in this forest are edible.

3. Some people are born great.

＊4. Some people do not achieve greatness.

5. Some people have greatness thrust upon them.

6. None of the students in my fourth hour class failed the exam.

＊7. Foolish is the man who seeks fame for its own sake.

8. Some of the members of the Capitol Rotunda Exercise and Reducing Club have not been pulling their weight.

9. The political party that wins a presidential election can expect to lose congressional seats two years later.

＊10. Some of the greatest authors in literature did not attend college.

11. Some skiers are out of control.

12. Blessed are the meek.

＊13. Some houses in the area were not affected by the storm.

14. Nobody's perfect.

15. Every rise in the stock market is followed by a fall.

＊16. John F. Kennedy was not successful in his domestic policy.

17. Not a single doctor can figure out what is wrong with my son.

18. A family that plays together stays together.

＊19. Some of the furniture is not on sale.

20. The window in my study is open.

5.2 The Square of Opposition

If you are given a subject term *S* and a predicate term *P*, there are four possible categorical propositions you can form with them: the four standard forms A, E, I, and O. Each of these propositions is logically related to the others, and traditional logicians organized these relationships into what they called the square of opposition. In this section, we explore the traditional square of opposition. In the next section, we will consider a modern challenge to it.

5.2A Contraries

Let's start with the two universal propositions, A and E. Consider "All bread is nutritious" and "No bread is nutritious." Obviously, these are opposing statements. They cannot both be true. Even if you don't know what S and P stand for, you can tell in the abstract that "All S are P" and "No S is P" cannot both be true. But notice that they could both be false. If some types of bread are nutritious and others are not—if some S are P and some S are not P—then both universal statements would be false. In general, an A proposition and an E proposition that have the same subject and predicate terms cannot both be true, but they could both be false. We identify this relationship in logic by calling A and E contrary propositions, or **contraries**. We can enter this relationship on a diagram that has the four standard forms of proposition arranged in a square:

A: All *S* are *P* ⟵————— contraries —————⟶ **E**: No *S* is *P*

I: Some *S* are *P*   **O**: Some *S* are not *P*

5.2B Contradictories

Our discussion of contraries suggests another possible relationship: statements that cannot both be true *and* cannot both be false. Does this relationship exist in our square? Yes. Look at A and O. If you accept the O proposition "Some bread is not nutritious," then you cannot also accept the A, "All bread is nutritious," and vice versa. They cannot both be true. But they cannot both be false, either. A can be false only if there is at least one S that is not P—some bread that is not nutritious—and in that case O is true. (Remember that "some" means "at least one.") Similarly, O can be false only if all S are P—all bread, every loaf without exception, is nutritious. So A and O cannot both be true, and they cannot both be false. If one is true, the other is false, and vice versa. Propositions that have this relationship are called **contradictories**.

It should be easy to see now that E and I are also contradictories. They cannot both be true and they cannot both be false. If it is false that no bread is nutritious, this could only be because at least some bread is nutritious, in which case I is true. In contrast, if I is false, that means not even one S is P, and thus it would be true to say that no S is P—E would be true. So our diagram now looks like this:

A: All *S* are *P* ⟵————— contraries —————⟶ **E**: No *S* is *P*

contradictories
contradictories

I: Some *S* are *P*   **O**: Some *S* are not *P*

It's important to be clear about the difference between contrary and contradictory propositions. If you want to challenge a universal statement that someone else has made, you do not have to prove the contrary statement; you just have to prove the contradictory. Suppose someone says that all men are male chauvinists, and you object. You don't have to show that *no* man is a male chauvinist, only that *some* men are not. For the same reason, if you're the one claiming that all men are sexist and someone else objects, you can't say, "Oh, you think no man is a sexist?" You would be committing the fallacy of false dichotomy, because you would be ignoring the possibility that some men are not chauvinists—a claim that is more limited, but still incompatible with your own assertion.

5.2C Subalternates

Let's consider now the relationship between A and I, a vertical relation on the diagram. Both A and I are affirmative propositions; they differ only in quantity. A is the more sweeping statement, because it makes a claim about all Ss. I is more cautious: When we say that some *S* are *P*, we are not committing ourselves to any claim about the whole class of Ss. We can see from this that if A is true, I must be true as well. If *all* Ss are *P*, then it is safe to say that *some* Ss are *P*—though we usually wouldn't bother to say it.

What about going in the opposite direction? Here we have to be careful. Normally when a person says "Some *S* are *P*," we take him to mean also that some Ss are not *P*. If *all S* were *P*, we assume he would have said so. Thus, in everyday speech, an I proposition is often taken to imply that the corresponding O proposition is true, and the corresponding A false. But in logic we do not make this assumption. We take the I proposition quite literally as a statement that at least one *S* is *P*. That leaves it an open question whether the other Ss are *P* or not. It might turn out that the others are not *P* (in which case the O proposition would be true). But it also might turn out that all the others *are P*, in which case the A proposition would be true. We don't know. So the truth of the I proposition leaves the truth or falsity of the corresponding A and O propositions *undetermined*.

In logic, the I proposition is called a **subalternate** to the A. This technical term is drawn from the military hierarchy, where "subaltern" means "lower in rank," and this gives us a good analogy. A general can issue orders to a private, but not vice versa; in the same way, the truth of an A proposition implies the truth of the I, but not vice versa. For exactly the same reasons, the O proposition is subalternate to the E. In this case, both propositions are negative, but that doesn't matter; the universal one always implies the particular, but not vice versa.

Before we leave the subalternate relation, notice what happens when we consider false statements instead of true ones. Now the tables are turned. If the I proposition is false, then the A must be false as well. If not even one S is P, then it is certainly false that all S are P. In the same way, on the negative side of the square, if not even one S is *not* P, then it is certainly false that no S is P: If O is false, E is false as well. But suppose that A is false. Does that mean I must be false as well? No. Even if it isn't true that all politicians are honest, it might still be true that some are. Similarly, the falsity of an E proposition leaves the truth or falsity of the O undetermined. It would be false, for example, to say that no natural substances cause cancer but it is still possible that some do not.

5.2D Subcontraries

There is only one relationship we haven't considered yet: the relationship between I and O. Can they both be true? Yes—that happens quite often. Some movie stars are good actors; some are not. Some clothes are made of wool; some are not. But can they both be false? No. Any given object in the class of Ss must either be P or not be P. If it is P, that makes the I proposition true. If it is not P, that makes the O proposition true. So I and O cannot *both* be false. Notice that this is the mirror image of the relationship between A and E, which cannot both be true but can both be false. A and E are contraries, so I and O are called **subcontraries**.

When we add this relationship to our diagram, we have the full traditional square of opposition.

In laying out the square of opposition, we have used fewer examples than usual, and we've generally explained the logical relationships in a more abstract way as relationships among S and P. This was deliberate, and the reason can best be conveyed by an analogy. When you learned arithmetic, you learned a set of rules about specific numbers: $1 + 1 = 2$, $3 \times 7 = 21$, $8 - 5 = 3$, and so forth. When you went on to algebra, you had to master the idea of variables (x, y, z), which stand for any number, so that you could learn rules applying to all numbers: $x + x = 2x$, $x + y = y + x$, and so on. A number like 4 is abstract because it can stand for anything that has four units or members. But the variable x represents a higher level of abstraction, because it can stand for any number.

In the same way, a specific proposition is abstract because it contains concepts: WHALES, MAMMALS, etc. As we saw in Chapter 1, these are abstract terms. But S and P represent a higher level of abstraction because they are variables: S stands for a class of things, any class, just as x in algebra stands for a number, any number. What we are doing now is the algebra, not the arithmetic, of concepts. And the relationships in the square of opposition are like the laws of algebra, not like the rules for adding or subtracting specific numbers. Thus, in order to grasp these relationships, you need to be able to think at the higher level of abstraction, in terms of the variables S and P. The more you practice this, the easier it will be for you to spot logical relationships in concrete examples.

REVIEW   The Traditional Square of Opposition

A : All S are P   **E** : No S is P
I : Some S are P   **O** : Some S are not P

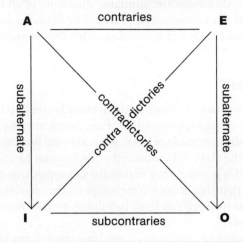

EXERCISE 5.2

I. Replace each of the following propositions with the related proposition indicated in the parentheses.

✶1. All S are P. (contrary)

2. Some S are not P. (contradictory)

3. No S is P. (subalternate)

✶4. Some S are P. (contradictory)

5. All S are P. (subalternate)

6. No S is P. (contrary)

✶7. Some S are P. (subcontrary)

8. No S is P. (contradictory)

9. Some S are not P. (subcontrary)

✶10. All S are P. (contradictory)

II. For each pair of propositions, given that the first one is true, determine whether the second is true, false, or undetermined, in accordance with the traditional square of opposition.

✶1. All S are P. Some S are P.

2. All S are P. No S is P.

3. No S is P. All S are P.

✶4. Some S are P. All S are P.

5. Some S are not P. All S are P.

6. No S is P. Some S are P.

✶7. Some S are not P. No S is P.

8. All S are P. Some S are not P.

9. Some S are P. Some S are not P.

✶10. Some S are P. No S is P.

11. Some S are not P. Some S are P.

12. No S is P. Some S are not P.

5.3 Existential Import

In discussing the relationships that make up the square of opposition, we have been assuming that subject and predicate terms stand for categories of things in reality. But some terms, such as "unicorn" and names of other mythological beings, are vacuous: They do not have any referents in reality. How does this affect the truth or falsity of categorical statements involving these terms? It seems natural to say that the A proposition "All unicorns have horns" is true, at least as a statement about mythology. In the same way, when a teacher issues the warning, "All students who miss three or more classes will fail the course," the statement may be true even if there aren't any students who miss three or more classes. Indeed, the whole point of the warning is to discourage anyone from becoming an instance of the subject term.

These statements seem to lack what logicians call **existential import**, because their truth doesn't depend on the existence of unicorns or students who miss three or more classes. A statement has existential import only when its truth depends on the existence of things in a certain category—in the case of a categorical proposition, the existence of things in the category signified by its subject term. A statement with existential import implies that things in that category exist, so if they do not exist, the statement is false.

In modern logic, existential import is a function of a statement's logical form. According to this view, universal categorical statements (A and E) always lack existential import, just because they are universal, whereas particular statements (I and O) always have existential import. Propositions of the form *All S are P* and *No S is P* do not imply that there are any *S*s, but propositions of the form *Some S are P* and *Some S are not P* do have that implication.

	Affirmative	Negative
Universal statements *lack* existential import: Their truth does *not* depend on the existence of *S*s	**A**: All *S* are *P*	**E**: No *S* is *P*
Particular statements *have* existential import: Their truth *does* depend on the existence of *S*s	**I**: Some *S* are *P*	**O**: Some *S* are not *P*

Because this distinction is based on logical form, it doesn't matter what the subject term is. The principle that universal propositions lack existential import is not limited to statements like "All unicorns have horns." It also applies to statements like "All dogs are animals," which is clearly about a class of existing things. According to the modern view, however, the statement does not *logically* imply their existence; it would be true even if there were no dogs. In contrast, the statements "Some dogs are animals" and "Some unicorns have horns" do have existential import because of their logical form. Since dogs exist but unicorns don't, the first statement is true but the second is false. The same distinction applies to negative propositions. The universal E proposition "No perpetual motion machine has been patented" is true, even though there are no perpetual motion machines. But the particular O statement "Some perpetual motion machines have not been patented" is false.

The issue of existential import has major implications for the square of opposition. The traditional square presupposes that the terms of any categorical proposition do have referents. If we adopt the modern doctrine about existential import, however, then some of the relations in the traditional square no longer hold. Let's start with subalternation. On the traditional view, an A proposition of the form *All S are P* entails the corresponding I proposition *Some S are P*. Now suppose there are no *S*s. On the modern view, the I proposition would be false, but the A proposition could still be true. So the truth of the A proposition does not imply the truth of the corresponding I. The same is true for E and O. Subalternation must therefore be removed from the square.

The next casualty is the relation between A and E. On the traditional view, these propositions are contraries: They cannot both be true. If all *S*s are *P*, then it cannot also be true that no *S* is *P*. On the modern doctrine, however, neither of these universal statements has existential import, so they could both be true in the case where there are no *S*s. For example, "All unicorns have horns" and "No unicorns have horns" are both true by default because there are no unicorns.

Finally, the I and O propositions no longer fit the definition of subcontraries. Two statements are subcontraries if, in virtue of their logical form, they could both be true but could not both be false. If no *S*s exist, however, then both particular statements are false. To stay with our mythological example, the absence of unicorns means that both "Some unicorns have horns" and "Some unicorns do not have horns" are false statements.

The only relationship that survives in the modern square of opposition is that of contradictories. If there exists a single thing that is both *S* and *P*, then the I proposition is true and the E is false. But if nothing is both *S* and *P*, then the I proposition is false and the E is true—even if the absence of things that are both *S* and *P* is due to the fact that there aren't any *S*s at all. The same reasoning applies to the A and O propositions. So E is true if and only if I is false, and A is true if and only if O is false.

The modern square of opposition, then, is quite different from the traditional square. All of the horizontal and vertical relationships in the traditional square are removed, leaving only the diagonal relationship between contradictory statements.

Which version of the square of opposition—the traditional or the modern—should we adopt? Our answer depends on which is the correct view of existential import, and that remains a controversial issue. Something can be said on both sides. Against the

REVIEW **The Modern Square of Opposition**

A: All *S* are *P*   **E**: No *S* is *P*

contradictories
contradictories

I: Some *S* are *P*   **O**: Some *S* are not *P* modern doctrine, it can be argued that it's unfair to deprive all universal statements of existential import just because of a few unusual cases. Normally, we do take such statements to be about a class with real members. For example, if we said that everyone convicted of terrorism last year was sentenced to life in prison, you would feel cheated if we went on to claim that the statement is true only because no one was convicted of terrorism last year. However, the exceptions do exist—there are statements that lack existential import—and we want our principles of logical form to be true without exception.

In light of this unresolved theoretical issue, it is useful for you to be familiar with both the traditional and the modern square of opposition. If you are dealing with a universal statement that clearly refers to a class of actual things, it is safe to use the traditional version of the square in deriving implications. But if there is any question about the existence of *S*s or *P*s, then you should rely on the modern version of the square.

EXERCISE 5.3

For each pair of propositions, given that the first one is true, determine whether the second is true, false, or undetermined, in accordance with the modern square of opposition.

✳1. All *S* are *P*. Some *S* are *P*.

2. All *S* are *P*. No *S* is *P*.

3. Some *S* are not *P*. All *S* are *P*.

✳4. Some *S* are *P*. All *S* are *P*.

5. No *S* is *P*. Some *S* are *P*.

6. Some *S* are not *P*. Some *S* are *P*.

✳7. All *S* are *P*. Some *S* are not *P*.

8. Some *S* are *P*. Some *S* are not *P*.

9. Some *S* are *P*. No *S* is *P*.

✳10. No *S* is *P*. Some *S* are not *P*.

11. Some *S* are not *P*. No *S* is *P*.

12. No *S* is *P*. All *S* are *P*.

5.4 Venn Diagrams

It is often helpful to think of a term in a proposition as a circle containing the members of the relevant class. There is in fact a systematic way of doing this: the method of Venn diagrams, invented by the English mathematician John Venn. This method gives us a way to represent each of the different forms of categorical proposition.

Venn diagrams use two overlapping circles, representing the subject and predicate terms:

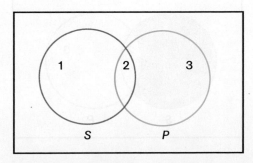

Since the circles overlap, there are three areas in the diagram, and we represent what a proposition asserts by marking the diagram in certain ways.

The simplest case is the I proposition. "Some *S* are *P*" says that at least one member of *S* is also a member of *P*. We can represent this by putting an X in area 2, where the *S* and *P* circles overlap, to mark the existence of at least one *S*:

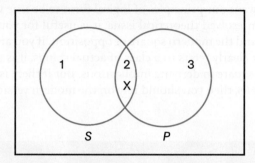

In the same way, the O proposition "Some *S* are not *P*" means that at least one member of *S* is not a member of *P*, so we put the X in area 1:

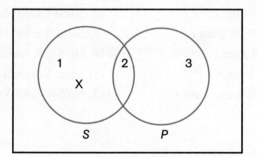

The representation of the universal propositions is a little different. For the A proposition "All *S* are *P*," we can't just add more Xs to area 2. That would not capture the universality of the proposition because it would leave open the possibility that some *S*s are not *P*. To capture the universality of the proposition, we need to rule out that possibility. We do so by shading out area 1 to indicate that it is empty:

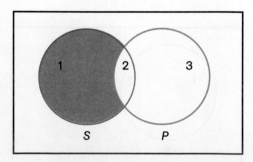

What this diagram tells us is that if there are any *S*s, they will be in area 2 (i.e., they will be *P*). But does the diagram say that there *are* any *S*s? No. Venn diagrams are based on the modern view of existential import, which holds that universal propositions do not imply the existence of any referents for the subject term.

In the same way, the E proposition "No *S* is *P*" is represented by shading out area 2 to indicate that it is empty:

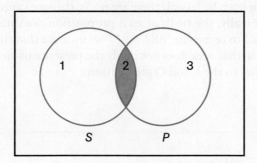

This diagram says that if there are any *S*s, they will be in area 1 (i.e., they will not be *P*), but it does not assert that there are any *S*s. Once again, in accordance with the modern doctrine of existential import, the universal E proposition does not imply the existence of referents for its subject term.

When the diagrams for the four categorical propositions are arranged in a square, they show very clearly the logical relationships in the modern square of opposition:

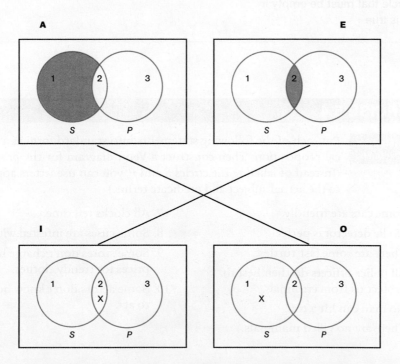

The diagrams for the A and O propositions are exact opposites, as they should be, since these propositions are contradictories: The diagram for the O proposition says there is something in area 1, while the A proposition says there is nothing there. The same relationship clearly exists between the E and I propositions.

On the modern view of existential import, A and E are not contrary propositions, since they can both be true if there are no Ss. The Venn diagrams make this clear: If both A and E are true, the entire S circle is shaded out, meaning that there are no Ss at all. Similarly, I and O can both be false: If there are no Ss, then we cannot put an X in either area of the S circle. Finally, the truth of an A proposition does not imply the truth of the I. By shading area 1 to represent "All S are P," we indicate that that area is empty. The absence of anything in that area does not imply the presence of anything in area 2. The same reasoning applies to the E and O propositions.

SOLVE Using Venn Diagrams

To construct a Venn diagram for a categorical proposition:

1. Draw two overlapping circles, representing the subject and predicate terms.

2. If the proposition is universal, shade out the area of the S circle that must be empty if the proposition is true.

3. If the proposition is particular, put an X in the area of the S circle where something must exist for the proposition to be true.

EXERCISE 5.4

I. **Integrative Exercise** Put each of the following statements into standard form as a categorical proposition. Then construct a Venn diagram for the proposition. (Instead of labeling the circles S and P, you can use letters appropriate to the actual subject and predicate terms.)

✳1. Some cats are friendly.

2. No lie detector is perfect.

3. There are some fast turtles.

✳4. All police officers do their best to protect us from criminals.

5. No man can lift a ton.

6. There are no gilled mammals.

✳7. All clocks tell time.

8. Some cities are infested with crime.

9. Some stores don't charge high prices for trendy clothes.

✳10. Some actors don't know how to act.

II. For each pair of Venn diagrams, determine whether the propositions represented by the diagrams are consistent or inconsistent—that is, if one of the propositions is true, could the other be true as well?

✱1.

2.

3.

✱4.

5.

 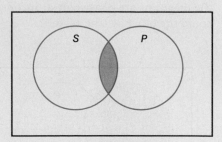

III. [Integrative Exercise] Write standard form categorical propositions for each set of Venn diagrams in the previous section. Be sure that each set of statements reflects the consistency or inconsistency of the diagrams.

5.5 Immediate Inference

The square of opposition expresses the relationships of compatibility or incompatibility among the four standard forms of categorical proposition. These propositions have the same subject and predicate terms, but they make different assertions about the relationship between the subject class and the predicate class. For any two of the propositions, the question is: Are they compatible? Could they both be true? Could they both be false? But there are also relationships of logical equivalence among categorical propositions.

Equivalence is the relationship two propositions have when they say the same thing. In Chapter 2, we saw that statements can be equivalent if they use synonymous words (e.g., "Sally bought a car" and "Sally purchased a car") or if they differ only in grammatical structures such as active versus passive—"Sally purchased a car" and "A car was purchased by Sally." Now we are going to consider some of the ways categorical propositions can be equivalent in virtue of their logical form rather than the specific meaning of words or the grammar of English. In logic, two propositions are equivalent if the truth of each necessarily implies the truth of the other, and the falsity of each necessarily implies the falsity of the other. Logically equivalent propositions, in other words, must be either both true or both false. Categorical propositions can be transformed into logically equivalent propositions by means of various operations. Three particular operations—*conversion*, *obversion*, and *contraposition*—have traditionally been singled out for special attention. An understanding of these operations—known as *immediate inferences*—will give you a better feel for the logical features of categorical statements.

5.5A Conversion

The first immediate inference is called conversion, or taking the **converse**. The converse of a proposition is the result of switching its subject and predicate terms. Thus the converse of the I proposition "Some Englishmen are Scotch drinkers" is "Some Scotch drinkers are Englishmen"—another way of saying the same thing. The changes required for conversion are highlighted in this table:

	Quantifier	Subject	Copula	Predicate
Proposition	Some	Scotch drinkers	are	Englishmen
Converse	Some	Englishmen	are	Scotch drinkers

Notice that the converse is itself an I proposition. Taking the converse of a proposition does not alter its quality or quantity, so the form of the proposition remains the same.

If the first proposition is true, the second must be true as well, and vice versa. Venn diagrams help make this equivalence clear. If two propositions are equivalent, their diagrams must be the same, and that's exactly what we find when we diagram an I proposition and its converse:

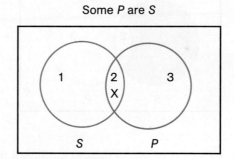

You might have thought that, to diagram the converse, we have to switch the S and P circles, since the P term is now the subject of the proposition. You could do that, but you don't have to; and keeping the circles in the same place makes it easier to use the diagrams as a test for equivalence. But that policy requires a small change in the way we approach the diagram. To diagram the standard form proposition "All S are P," we start with the S circle and ask: What does this proposition assert about things in the class of Ss? To diagram the converse, we follow the same process of thought. But since P is now the subject of the proposition, we start with that circle and ask: What does this proposition assert about things in the class of Ps?

The converse of the E proposition "No Norwegians have been U.S. presidents" is "No U.S. presidents have been Norwegians." Once again, the converse has the same form as the original proposition, and once again the statements are equivalent. An E proposition says that S is excluded from P, which implies that P is excluded from S.

No *S* is *P*

No *P* is *S*

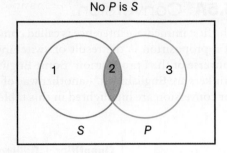

Since an E proposition is equivalent to its converse, it is legitimate to infer one from the other.

It is not legitimate, however, to infer the converse of an A proposition. The converse of "All pickpockets are criminals" would be "All criminals are pickpockets." As you can see, the converse here is not equivalent: The first statement is true, but its converse is false. *All S are P* does not imply *All P are S*, because saying that *S* is included in *P* does not imply that *P* is included in *S*.

All *S* are *P*

All *P* are *S*

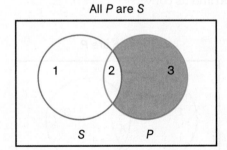

"All *S* are *P*" might seem to imply "All *P* are *S*" when *S* and *P* are terms standing for the same class. Consider the definition of "human beings" we discussed several chapters ago. Both of the following propositions are true: (1) "All human beings are rational animals," and (2) "All rational animals are human beings." The fact remains, however, that 2 does not logically follow from 1. If it seems to follow, that is because we know that there are no rational animals other than human beings. But that information is not contained in 1; it is extra information we happen to have in this case.

Taking the converse of an A proposition is sometimes called the fallacy of **illicit conversion**. Have you ever heard someone say, when he was being ridiculed for a new or unconventional idea, "Yeah, well they laughed at Columbus, too?" In saying that, he is appealing to the proposition "All brilliant new ideas were ridiculed," which may well be true. But he is implicitly inferring the converse, namely, "Any idea that is ridiculed is a brilliant new idea," and that proposition is almost certainly false. In any case, it does not follow. Be careful, then, to avoid illicit conversion. As we will see in the next chapter, it is a common error in syllogistic reasoning.

Finally, let's look at the O proposition. Venn diagrams tell us that the converse is not equivalent.

Some *S* are not *P*

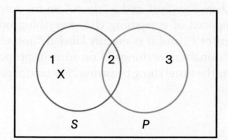

Some *P* are not *S*

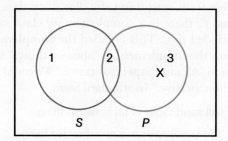

It often happens that an O proposition and its converse are both true. For example: some officers are not gentlemen and some gentlemen are not officers; some teachers are not gifted people and some gifted people are not teachers. Nevertheless, an O proposition is not logically equivalent to its converse, as we can see from another example: "Some human beings are not Americans" does not imply "Some Americans are not human beings." You can generate other examples like this if you use a genus as the subject term and a species as the predicate term. (Try it with "Some animals are not dogs," "Some legislators are not senators.")

Thus conversion is a legitimate immediate inference only for E and I propositions.

EXERCISE 5.5A

State the converse of each of the following propositions, and indicate whether the proposition and its converse are equivalent.

✳1. Some trees are leaf-shedding plants.

2. All stickers are scented.

3. All shrimp are crustaceans.

✳4. All green vegetables are things that contain beta-carotene.

5. Some books are not ebooks.

6. Some poor neighborhoods are safe areas.

✳7. No candidates for the legislature this year were adherents of Zoroastrianism.

8. All passenger trains are enterprises that depend on government subsidies.

9. All geniuses struggle with madness.

✳10. Some video games are not violent.

11. Some tornadoes move in a straight line.

12. Some copiers do not work properly.

✳13. Some poor neighborhoods are not safe areas.

14. None of my children is a married person.

15. Nothing you read on the internet is trustworthy.

5.5B Obversion

The second type of immediate inference—obversion, or taking the **obverse**—is based on a fact about classes. When we group things together into a class, we are distinguishing them from everything else. For every class, there's an "us" and a "them." So for every class *C*, there is a complementary class composed of everything else, everything not included in *C*. This is called the **complement** of *C*, and it is usually labeled "non-*C*." Thus the complement of "abrasive things" is "nonabrasive things." Consider the proposition "All sandpaper is abrasive." We could say the same thing by saying "No sandpaper is nonabrasive." In standard form:

All sandpaper is an abrasive thing.

No sandpaper is a nonabrasive thing.

The second proposition is called the obverse of the first.

We arrive at the obverse of a proposition by making two changes: We replace the predicate term with its complement, and we change the quality of the proposition—affirmative to negative or negative to affirmative. Thus the obverse of an A proposition, "All *S* are *P*," is always an E proposition, "No *S* is non-*P*." The changes required for obversion are highlighted in this table:

	Quantifier	Subject	Copula	Predicate
Proposition	All	sandpaper	is	an abrasive thing
Obverse	No	sandpaper	is	a nonabrasive thing

Notice that the subject term remains unchanged and that the quantity also stays the same. (Remember that in a universal negative proposition, "No" does double duty; it signifies both universal quantity and negative quality. So when we take the obverse of the A proposition, "No *S* is non-*P*" changes the quality of the A proposition but the quantity remains universal.) If the predicate term already has the form "non-*P*," we follow the same rule: "Non-*P*" is changed to its complement, which is "*P*." Thus the obverse of "All heavy elements are unstable things" is "No heavy element is a stable thing."

For all four types of proposition, obversion results in an equivalent proposition. In each case, the obverse follows logically. The two changes we make—replacing *P* with non-*P* and switching the quality—cancel each other.

Proposition	Obverse
A: All sandpaper is an abrasive thing.	**E**: No sandpaper is a nonabrasive thing.
I: Some people are kind persons.	**O**: Some people are not unkind persons.
E: No machine is a conscious being.	**A**: All machines are nonconscious beings.
O: Some chemicals are not toxic substances.	**I**: Some chemicals are nontoxic substances.

To diagram these equivalences, we first need to understand how to diagram the complement of a term. The complement of *P*, non-*P*, includes everything outside the

P circle. That includes not only area 1 in the *S* circle, but also the region outside both circles, which we have labeled area 4.

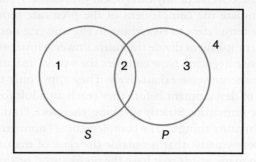

So let's take the A proposition "All *S* are *P*." Its obverse is "No *S* is non-*P*." Since this is an E proposition, we diagram it by shading out the area of overlap between subject and predicate. The subject term is represented by areas 1 and 2. The predicate term, non-*P*, is represented by areas 1 and 4. The area of overlap is obviously area 1, so we shade it out.

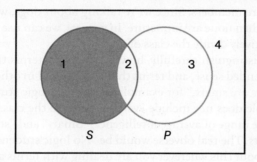

You can see that this Venn diagram is identical to the standard diagram for the A proposition, which means the proposition and its obverse are equivalent.

Let's try this with one of the particular propositions: "Some *S* are *P*" and its obverse "Some *S* are not non-*P*." The obverse is an O proposition, so we will need to put an X in the subject circle outside its overlap with the predicate. Once again, the subject term *S* is represented by areas 1 and 2 and the predicate term non-*P* by areas 1 and 4, so the overlap is again area 1. That leaves area 2 as the only part of *S* that is outside the area of non-*P*, so that's where we put our X. The result is identical with the standard diagram for I propositions.

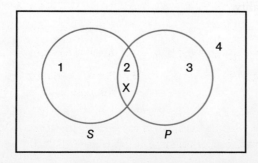

Having seen how to prove equivalence of the obverse for the A and I propositions, you should now be able to apply the technique to E and O.

When you take the obverse of any categorical proposition, you need to be careful about how you formulate the complement of the predicate term. Strictly speaking, the complement of a term refers to everything in the universe not included under the term. A term and its complement divide the entire universe into two mutually exclusive and jointly exhaustive categories. Now consider the words "mature" and "immature." These do not divide the universe exhaustively. They apply only to living things that pass through stages of development before they reach an adult form. A six-penny nail is neither mature nor immature. Strictly speaking, therefore, "immature things" is not the complement of "mature things." The complement is "nonmature," which refers to anything—even six-penny nails—that is outside the class of mature living things. The same point applies to many words that have the prefix "im-," or similar prefixes such as "a-" and "un-."

Nevertheless, when we take the obverse of the proposition "All the dogs in Fleabite Kennels are mature things," it would be acceptable to use "None of the dogs in Fleabite Kennels are immature things." That's because the subject term, "dogs in Fleabite Kennels," restricts the universe of discourse to a genus that *can* be exhaustively divided into mature and immature members. Since we're talking about dogs, we can be sure that if they are all mature, then none are immature. In general, we can use obversion whenever *P* and non-*P* exhaustively divide the class of *S*s.

We do need to distinguish carefully, however, between terms that are complementary, even in this extended sense, and terms that are opposed in other ways. The obverse of "All logic students are smart," for example, is not "No logic student is stupid." The class of stupid people does not include everyone outside the class of smart people; it leaves out the middle range of average intelligence. "Smart" and "stupid" are opposites, but not complements. The real obverse would be "No logic student is non-smart." You need to be careful about this wherever you are dealing with terms at opposite ends of a spectrum—black and white, tall and short, fat and thin. The fallacy of false dichotomy is often committed in such cases. "No one in that family is thin," says Joe. "You mean," says Martha, "everyone in the family is fat?" No. All Joe said is that everyone in the family is non-thin.

When you take an obverse, finally, be sure to distinguish between the word "not" and the prefix "non-" "Not" is a mark of quality and is part of the form of a proposition. "Non-" is part of the predicate term. With the I proposition, it is easy to forget that we need both: *P* must become non-*P* and "are" must become "are not." Notice also that the obverse of an O proposition is an I proposition. "Some *S* are non-*P*" is affirmative, even though it sounds negative, because the "non-" is part of the predicate term and does not indicate negative quality.

APPLY Venn Diagrams

Many people think Venn diagrams are useful only for math and logic. But that's not true! Venn diagrams are a useful tool for analyzing relationships of all sorts. That's why they're used in fields ranging from astronomy to zoology. Here's an example comparing republics and democracies.

Next time you need to write a compare and contrast essay, try using a Venn diagram to organize your work.

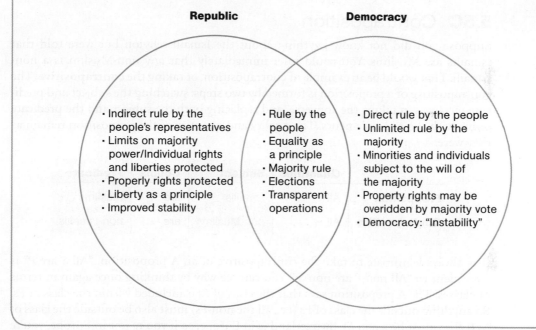

Republic

- Indirect rule by the people's representatives
- Limits on majority power/Individual rights and liberties protected
- Properly rights protected
- Liberty as a principle
- Improved stability

- Rule by the people
- Equality as a principle
- Majority rule
- Elections
- Transparent operations

Democracy

- Direct rule by the people
- Unlimited rule by the majority
- Minorities and individuals subject to the will of the majority
- Property rights may be overidden by majority vote
- Democracy: "Instability"

EXERCISE 5.5B

State the obverse of each of the following propositions. Make sure that you use genuinely complementary terms.

✳1. None of the athletes is an injured person.

2. Some of the beans are cooked foods.

3. All of the dishes are washed things.

✳4. All of Alister's friends are students.

5. Some gamblers are lucky people.

6. Some criminals are not insane people.

✳7. Some policies are wise things.

8. No sighting of a UFO is a thing that has been confirmed.

9. All of the campers were happy people.

*10. Some companies were not enter-
     prises that made a profit this year.

11. Some proponents of the legaliza-
    tion of marijuana are unkempt
    people.

12. Some snakes are not poisonous
    beings.

*13. No one in this room is a suspect.

14. All of the rooms with an ocean view
    are reserved places.

15. Some of the planes are things
    unable to take off.

5.5C Contraposition

Suppose you did not know anything about the Ismaili religion but were told that
Ismailis are Muslims. You could infer immediately that any non-Muslim is a non-
Ismaili. That would be an example of contraposition, or taking the **contrapositive**. The
contrapositive of a proposition is formed by two steps: switching the subject and predicate terms, as in taking the converse, and replacing both the subject and the predicate
terms with their complements. The quality and quantity of the proposition remain as
they were.

	Quantifier	Subject	Copula	Predicate
Proposition	All	Ismailis	are	Muslims
Contrapositive	All	non-Muslims	are	non-Ismailis

It is always legitimate to take the contrapositive of an A proposition. "All *S* are *P*" is
equivalent to "All non-*P* are non-*S*." You can see why by thinking once again in terms
of classes. The A proposition says that the class of *S*s is included within the class of *P*s.
So anything outside the class of *P*s (i.e., all the non-*P*s) must also be outside the class of
*S*s (i.e., it must be a non-*S*). Switzerland is in Europe, so if you're not in Europe, you're
not in Switzerland.

Diagramming the equivalence can be challenging because we have to deal with the
complements of both the subject and the predicate terms. So let's start by listing the
areas that represent the terms and their complements:

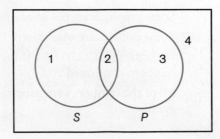

Term	Areas of Diagram
S	1 and 2
Non-*S*	3 and 4
P	2 and 3
Non-*P*	1 and 4

Using the table on the right as our guide, we diagram "All non-*P* are non-*S*" in the usual way by looking first to the subject of the proposition, non-*P*. Since this is an A proposition, we must shade out the area of non-*P* that is not included in the predicate term, non-*S*. Of the two areas that make up the class of non-*P*s, area 4 is the one that it shares with non-*S*—4 is the area of overlap between non-*P* and non-*S*—which leaves area 1 as the area of non-*P* outside non-*S*. That's the area we can now shade out.

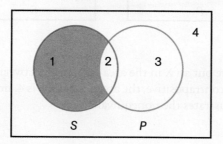

This diagram is identical to the standard diagram for the A proposition, which means the proposition and its contrapositive are equivalent.

Contraposition is not a legitimate operation for E and I propositions. For example, the E proposition "No primate is an aquatic animal" is clearly not equivalent to its contrapositive, "No nonaquatic animal is a nonprimate," because the first is true and the second false (cows are nonaquatic animals but they are nonprimates). Venn diagrams reveal why an E proposition is not equivalent to its contrapositive:

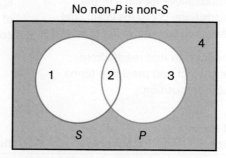

The diagram on the left is the standard one for the E proposition, with the area of overlap between *S* and *P*—area 2—shaded out. In the diagram on the right, for the contrapositive, the shaded area of overlap between non-*P* and non-*S* is not area 2 but area 4.

Similarly, the I proposition, "Some humans are giraffes," is clearly not equivalent to its contrapositive, "Some nongiraffes are nonhumans." In this case the first is false while the second is true (monkeys are nongiraffes and also nonhumans).

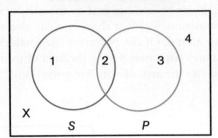

For an I proposition, we put an X in the area of overlap between subject and predicate. In the diagram for the contrapositive, the area of overlap is 4, not 2. Once again the difference in diagrams illustrates the nonequivalence.

REVIEW Immediate Inferences

The table that follows summarizes the key information about the three immediate inferences. For the converse and contrapositive, the nonequivalent propositions are crossed out. In order to test your understanding, try to reproduce the table without looking at it. List the converse, obverse, and contrapositive for each of the four types of propositions (12 items in all), and determine whether they are equivalent or not.

Converse: the proposition that results from switching the subject and predicate terms in a categorical proposition.

Obverse: the proposition that results from changing the quality of a categorical proposition and replacing the predicate term with its complement.

Contrapositive: the proposition that results from replacing the subject term in a categorical proposition with the complement of the predicate and the predicate with the complement of the subject.

Standard Form Proposition	Converse	Obverse	Contrapositive
A: All S are P	~~All P are S~~	No S is non-P	All non-P are non-S
E: No S is P	No P is S	All S are non-P	~~No non-P is non-S~~
I: Some S are P	Some P are S	Some S are not non-P	~~Some non-P are non-S~~
O: Some S are not P	~~Some P are not S~~	Some S are non-P	Some non-P are not non-S

The O proposition is the only one, besides the A, that is equivalent to its contrapositive. It is rarely used in ordinary speech. The closest we can come to a natural-sounding example would be something like the following. If we were considering candidates for some job or office, we might say with a sigh, "Some talented candidates are not acceptable." The contrapositive would be "Some unacceptable people are not untalented." (You can test this equivalence yourself by constructing the Venn diagrams.) The A proposition, however, is far and away the most common case in which we use the contrapositive.

EXERCISE 5.5C

I. State the contrapositive of each of the following propositions and indicate whether the proposition and its contrapositive are equivalent.

∗1. All tenors are singers.

2. Some jeans are not flattering garments.

3. No whales are fish.

∗4. All noncitizens are nonvoters.

5. Some non-tulips are not non-flowers.

6. All almonds are nuts.

∗7. No non-novels are non-poems.

8. Some cats are not tigers.

9. Some nuts are almonds.

II. **Integrative Exercise** For each proposition below, find the converse, obverse, or contrapositive as indicated in parentheses, identify the form of the resulting categorical proposition, and determine whether the resulting proposition is equivalent to the original.

∗1. Some *S* are *P*. (contrapositive)

2. All *S* are *P*. (converse)

3. No *S* is *P*. (converse)

∗4. Some *S* are not *P*. (obverse)

5. Some *S* are not *P*. (converse)

6. All *S* are *P*. (obverse)

∗7. Some *S* are *P*. (obverse)

8. No *S* is *P*. (obverse)

9. Some *S* are non-*P*. (obverse)

∗10. Some non-*S* are *P*. (converse)

11. All non-*S* are non-*P*. (obverse)

12. Some *S* are non-*P*. (converse)

∗13. No non-*S* is non-*P*. (contrapositive)

14. All non-*S* are *P*. (converse)

15. All *S* are non-*P*. (contrapositive)

∗16. Some non-*S* are not non-*P*. (contrapositive)

17. No non-*S* is *P*. (converse)

18. Some non-*S* are non-*P*. (obverse)

∗19. No *S* is non-*P*. (contrapositive)

20. Some *S* are not *P*. (contrapositive)

III. **Integrative Exercise** Construct Venn diagrams to check your answers for the previous section.

CHAPTER REVIEW

Summary

- A categorical proposition has a subject and a predicate term, which give it its content.
- Each categorical proposition also has an affirmative or negative quality and a universal or particular quantity.
- The quality and quantity together determine the form of a categorical proposition—A, E, I, or O.
- In traditional logic, the four standard forms can be arranged in a square of opposition, which exhibits the following logical relationships: contraries, contradictories, subalternates, and subcontraries.
- If we hold that A and E propositions lack existential import, then all relationships except contradictories must be omitted from the square of opposition.
- Each term (*S* and *P*) also has a complementary term (non-*S*, non-*P*).

- Some forms of categorical propositions can be transformed into equivalent propositions through immediate inferences, but we must be careful to avoid illegitimate transformation.
- Only I and E propositions can legitimately be transformed through conversion; only A and O propositions can legitimately be transformed through contraposition; all four forms of the propositions can legitimately be transformed through obversion.
- If we accept the view that universal propositions lack existential import, we can use Venn diagrams, in which the subject and predicate terms of a proposition are represented by overlapping circles, to represent the meaning of any categorical proposition and to determine whether two propositions are equivalent.

Key Terms

categorical proposition (p. 197)
copula (p. 198)
quality (p. 198)
quantity (p. 198)
universal proposition (p. 198)
particular proposition (p. 198)
singular proposition (p. 201)
quantifier (p. 202)
contraries (p. 205)

contradictories (p. 205)
subalternates (p. 206)
subcontraries (p. 207)
existential import (p. 209)
converse (p. 217)
illicit conversion (p. 218)
obverse (p. 220)
complement (p. 220)
contrapositive (p. 224)

Putting It All Together

I. The following statements are in standard form. Name the form of the proposition (A, E, I, or O). Then reformulate each proposition so that it is less awkward and more concise (see how many words you can eliminate).

*1. Some large corporations are not things that paid any income tax last year.

2. No Spanish playwright is a person who has won the Nobel Prize in Literature.

3. All planets are things whose motion is governed by the gravitational attraction of the sun.

*4. Some statistics that indicate economic growth are statistics that can be misleading.

5. All persons who chronically tell lies are persons who feel insecure about their ability to succeed on the basis of the truth.

6. Some academic subjects are branches of study that require the use of mathematical techniques.

*7. Some proponents of radical economic change are not thinkers who have carefully considered the consequences of their ideas.

8. Some fast-food restaurants are establishments in which you are permitted to have a hamburger prepared "your way."

9. No automobile produced in the United States as a standard factory model is a vehicle that can safely be driven at over 200 miles per hour.

*10. No Friday is a day on which my family ate meat.

II. **Integrative Exercise** Translate each of the following statements into standard form and identify the form. Then find the logically related proposition mentioned in the parentheses.

*1. All sonnets have 14 lines. (contrary)

2. Some metals rust. (converse)

3. That man in the corner is drunk. (obverse)

*4. Some fish are not carnivores. (obverse)

5. Nobody knows the trouble I've seen. (subalternate)

6. At the edge of the clearing were some deer. (subcontrary)

*7. Big girls don't cry. (contrary)

8. "War is hell."—General Sherman (contradictory)

9. Sugar is sweet. (subalternate)

*10. So are you. (obverse)

11. "Construction crew at work"—highway sign (contradictory)

12. Alice doesn't live here any more. (contrary)

*13. Real men don't eat quiche. (converse)

14. Students who return after midnight are required to sign in. (obverse)

15. No one has run a mile in less than 3:40. (contradictory)

*16. Every country with the word "Democratic" in its official name is a dictatorship. (contrapositive)

17. Someone is knocking at my door. (subcontrary)

18. Some criminals don't come from poor families. (contrapositive)

*19. No law is just that forces a person to act against his judgment. (contrapositive)

20. Some proposals put forward for the control of nuclear arms would not affect the levels of submarine-based missiles. (contradictory)

III. For each Venn diagram below, name the categorical proposition it represents.

*1.

5.

2.

6.

3.

*7.

*4.

8.

IV. **Integrative Exercise** Name the logical relationship that exists between each pair of propositions below. If the two propositions are not equivalent, does the second follow from the first? In any case where existential import makes a difference, give both the traditional and the modern interpretation.

∗1. No man is an island. Some men are not islands.

2. Some water is not fit to drink. Some water is unfit to drink.

3. All sailors are swimmers. All swimmers are sailors.

∗4. Some cases of cancer are conditions hard to diagnose. Some cases of cancer are not conditions hard to diagnose.

5. Some people are persons unlucky in love. Some people are not persons lucky in love.

6. None of my acquaintances is in trouble with the law. No one who is in trouble with the law is an acquaintance of mine.

∗7. No dishonest person is a happy person. No unhappy person is an honest person.

8. Some of the union members were not pleased with the new contract. Some people who were pleased with the new contract were not union members.

9. All voluntary actions are actions for which we can be held responsible. All actions for which we cannot be held responsible are involuntary actions.

∗10. All medical expenses are deductible items. Some deductible items are medical expenses.

V. **Integrative Exercise** For each pair of propositions in Exercise IV, use Venn diagrams to determine whether they are equivalent. In both diagrams, the *S* circle represents the subject of the first proposition and the *P* circle represents the predicate of the first proposition.

VI. Find a literal translation for each of the following proverbs. Your translation should be a universal categorical proposition (A or E).

∗1. Every cloud has a silver lining.

2. Nothing ventured, nothing gained.

3. Birds of a feather flock together.

∗4. Rome wasn't built in a day.

5. People in glass houses shouldn't throw stones.

6. A penny saved is a penny earned.

∗7. Forewarned is forearmed.

8. A rolling stone gathers no moss.

9. Uneasy lies the head that wears a crown.

∗10. Money talks.

VII. **Integrative Exercise** The passages below contain immediate inferences. Put the premise and conclusion in standard form, and determine whether the conclusion is a legitimate inference.

∗1. "[A]ll revolutionaries in the domain of thought, from Galileo and Columbus to Wagner and Manet, have been for a time persecuted and derided. Ergo, since the Post-Impressionists have provoked a vast amount of scornful mirth, they are necessarily great men." [Art critic Royal Corissoz speaking ironically, "The Post-Impressionist Illusion," *Century* magazine]

2. "He said he would acquire no knowledge which did not bear upon his object. Therefore all that knowledge which he possessed was such as would be useful to him." [Arthur Conan Doyle, *A Study in Scarlet*]

3. "The East Coast was hammered by its second snowstorm in a week yesterday. . . . Most intriguing of all was the word out of

Washington, D.C., possibly the most snow-fearing town anywhere in the U.S. . . . All 'nonessential federal workers' were allowed to go home. So that means those who lashed themselves to their desks during the 10-inch 'blizzard' are essential. Did anyone make the list?" [*Wall Street Journal*]

∗4. "The chief foundations of all states, new as well as old or composite, are good laws and good arms; and as there cannot be good laws where the state is not well armed, it follows that where they are well armed they have good laws." [Niccolo Machiavelli, *The Prince*]

5. Just as my fingers on these keys
   Make music, so the selfsame sounds
   On my spirit make a music, too.
   Music is feeling, then, not sound;
   And thus it is that what I feel, . . .
   desiring you, . . .
   Is music.
   [Wallace Stevens, "Peter Quince at the Clavier"]

VIII.   The operation of contraposition can be deconstructed into a sequence of simpler operations. If we take the obverse of a proposition, and then apply conversion to the result, and then take the obverse again, we will arrive at the contrapositive of the original proposition. Use this to explain why contraposition is legitimate for A and O propositions, but not for E and I.

Categorical Syllogisms

Now that we understand the logical structure of categorical propositions, we can turn to the categorical syllogism, which is one of the basic types of deductive argument. In this chapter, we learn how to analyze and evaluate arguments of this type. The first section reviews the logical structure of syllogisms, and the remainder of the chapter describes two different methods for evaluating them.

6.1 The Structure of a Syllogism

Let's begin with an example from the previous chapter—the inference that whales breathe by means of lungs because they are mammals. When we put the premises and conclusion into standard form as categorical propositions, the argument may be expressed as follows:

> All whales are mammals.
> All mammals are animals that breathe by means of lungs.
> ————————————————
> All whales are animals that breathe by means of lungs.

LEARNING OBJECTIVES

On successful completion of the chapter, you will be able to:

✅ Translate categorical syllogisms into standard form. (6.1)

✅ Analyze the mood and figure of categorical syllogisms. (6.1)

✅ Determine the validity of categorical syllogisms and identify missing statements in enthymemes. (6.2–6.3)

✅ Test categorical syllogisms for validity using both rules and Venn diagrams. (6.4–6.5)

If we were diagramming this argument using the techniques we learned in Chapter 2, we would join the premises with a plus sign. But in deductive reasoning the premises always work together, so we don't need a special symbol to represent that fact. All we need is the line between the premises and the conclusion.

This argument is a **categorical syllogism**. The term **syllogism** refers to various types of deductive argument that have two premises and a conclusion. In a *categorical* syllogism, both of the premises and the conclusion are categorical propositions. Since every categorical proposition has two terms, there could be six distinct terms here. But there aren't. There are only three, "whales," "mammals," and "animals that breathe by means of lungs"—each term occurring twice. This pattern exists in every categorical syllogism, and each of the three terms has a distinct name.

The term that occurs in the predicate of the conclusion ("animals that breathe by means of lungs") is called the **major term** of the syllogism. This term also occurs in one of the premises (2), which is therefore called the **major premise**. The term that occurs in the subject of the conclusion ("whales") is called the **minor term**. This term occurs as well in the other premise (1), which we therefore label the **minor premise**. That leaves "mammals," which is not part of the conclusion, but occurs once in each of the premises. It is called the **middle term**, because it links together the major and minor terms. Schematically, the pattern of repetition is

Major premise:	All *M* are *P*	All mammals are animals that breathe by means of lungs.
Minor premise:	All *S* are *M*	All whales are mammals.
Conclusion:	All *S* are *P*	All whales are animals that breathe by means of lungs.

Notice that we have switched the order of the premises. This makes no difference in the logic of the argument, but it is a convention that when we put a categorical syllogism into standard form, we always put the major premise first. The schematic argument on the left is the logical form of the argument on the right; the left side represents the structure of the right side, in the same way that "All *S* are *P*" represents the structure of any universal affirmative proposition. We always use *S* and *P* to stand for the terms in the conclusion—*S* for the minor term (the subject of the conclusion), *P* for the major term (the predicate). And we always use *M* for the middle term.

An argument need not have exactly this structure in order to be a categorical syllogism. Suppose that you didn't know whether moose were predators or not, but you did know that antlered animals are not predators. Then you might reason as follows:

No *M* is *P*	No antlered animal is a predator.
All *S* are *M*	All moose are antlered animals.
No *S* is *P*	No moose is a predator.

In this argument, the conclusion and one of the premises are E propositions, but it is still a categorical syllogism, for we can still identify a major, a minor, and a middle term.

The premises and conclusion of a categorical syllogism, in fact, can have any of the standard forms: A, E, I, or O. A categorical syllogism also has a form as a syllogism. The form of a syllogism is a function of both the forms of its propositions and the arrangement of its constituent terms. There are 256 possible syllogistic forms. Most of these forms are invalid; only 24 forms, at most, are valid. The lesson to be learned is that validity—a necessary requirement for good reasoning—is not only valued but *rare*. It might sound like we're searching for a needle in a haystack but we're not condemned to relying solely on good luck. Understanding the structure of categorical syllogisms can help us formulate valid arguments; learning to evaluate syllogisms can help us avoid bad ones.

To identify a syllogism's form, we start by listing the letters that identify the standard forms of the propositions in the following order: major premise, minor premise, conclusion. This list is called the **mood** of the syllogism. The mood of the argument about whales is AAA; the mood of the argument about moose is EAE.

Syllogisms can also vary in the way their terms are arranged. Notice the arrangement in the following argument:

No *P* is *M*	No Marxist is an advocate of private property.
All *S* are *M*	All conservatives are advocates of private property.
No *S* is *P*	No conservative is a Marxist.

The mood of this argument is also EAE. But the terms are arranged differently: The middle term is now the predicate in both premises, whereas in the argument about moose it was the subject of the major premise.

The position of the middle term in the premises is called the **figure** of the syllogism. Since there are two premises, and two possible positions for the middle term in each premise, there are four figures. They are identified by number, as follows:

Figures of Categorical Syllogisms

	1st		2nd		3rd		4th	
Major	*M*	*P*	*P*	*M*	*M*	*P*	*P*	*M*
Minor	*S*	*M*	*S*	*M*	*M*	*S*	*M*	*S*
Conclusion	*S*	*P*	*S*	*P*	*S*	*P*	*S*	*P*

Within each figure, the premises and the conclusion can have any of the standard forms for categorical propositions. That is, within each figure, a syllogism can have any mood. Conversely, any given mood describes four different syllogisms, one in each figure. To identify a syllogism completely, therefore, we must indicate figure as well as mood. The argument about whales is AAA-1, the argument about moose is EAE-1, and the argument about private property is EAE-2. In this way mood and figure together uniquely identify the form of any categorical syllogism, just as the letters A, E, I, and O uniquely identify the form of a single categorical proposition.

In each figure, the middle term serves as a link between major and minor terms. But in everyday reasoning, the different figures are typically used to express different kinds of links. The first figure, for example, is a natural way to express a species–genus relationship. Thus we inferred that whales have a certain property (they breathe by means of lungs) because they belong to a genus (mammals) that has the property. And we inferred that moose do not have a certain property (they are not predators) because they belong to a genus (antlered animals) that lacks the property. In both cases, the minor term *S* was the species, the middle term *M* its genus.

In the second figure, the middle term is the predicate of both premises. It is therefore commonly used when we try to find out the relation between two classes, *S* and *P*, by seeing whether there is some property *M* that one has and the other lacks. In the example above, we inferred that conservatives (*S*) cannot be Marxists (*P*) because one group believes in private property and the other doesn't.

In the third figure, the middle term is the subject of both premises. Thus it can be used to show that there is some overlap between two classes, *S* and *P*, by pointing out that *M*s are members of both groups. Suppose we were wondering whether any great plays (*S*) had been written in blank verse (*P*). We might think of Shakespeare, and reason thus:

All *M* are *P*	All of Shakespeare's dramas are plays written in blank verse.
Some *M* are *S*	Some of Shakespeare's dramas are great plays.
Some *S* are *P*	Some great plays are plays written in blank verse.

The form of this argument is AII-3.

The fourth figure is somewhat odd. In structure it is the mirror image of the first figure, and perhaps because the first figure strikes us as a natural way to reason, the fourth seems very unnatural. You will probably not encounter it often in everyday speech. Nevertheless, it can be a valid mode of inference, as in the following syllogism:

Some *P* are *M*	Some crimes against property are frauds.
All *M* are *S*	All frauds are felonies.
Some *S* are *P*	Some felonies are crimes against property.

This has the form IAI-4.

Of course, these examples are merely the typical uses of the different figures. In each figure there are also many atypical examples. Moreover, in all the examples we've considered so far, the conclusion followed from the premises, but this is not always the case. In the next section, we discuss the standard for evaluating syllogistic arguments.

SOLVE Identifying a Syllogism's Form

A categorical syllogism is a deductive argument containing two categorical premises, a categorical conclusion, and three terms—major, minor, and middle—with each term occurring in two propositions. To identify the logical form of a syllogism:

1. Put each of the propositions into standard form as a categorical proposition.
2. Determine which proposition is the conclusion; the other two are the premises.
3. Arrange premises and conclusion in the standard order:
   a. On the first line, put the major premise: the premise containing the predicate term of the conclusion (i.e., the major term).

   b. On the second line, put the minor premise: the premise containing the subject term of the conclusion (i.e., the minor term).
   c. On the third line, put the conclusion.
4. Mood: Identify the logical form of the premises and conclusion as A, E, I, or O propositions. Write down the letters in order: major premise, minor premise, conclusion.
5. Figure: Determine whether the syllogism is first, second, third, or fourth figure by noting the location of the middle term in the two premises. Write the figure down after the mood.

EXERCISE 6.1

I. Identify the major, minor, and middle terms of each of the following standard form syllogisms.

✴1. All honor students are students with consistently high grades.
   Some honor students are student athletes.
   Some student athletes are students with consistently high grades.

2. All pesticides are hazardous materials.
   All fungicides are pesticides.
   All fungicides are hazardous materials.

3. No man is an island.
   All barrier islands are islands.
   No barrier island is a man.

✴4. All mice are rodents.
   All deer mice are mice.
   All deer mice are rodents.

5. No senior is a freshman.
   All cadets with boots and spurs are seniors.
   No cadet with boots and spurs is a freshman.

II. Put each of the following syllogisms into standard form (remember to put the major premise first), and then identify the mood and figure.

✴1. Any ambitious person can learn logic, and anyone reading this book is ambitious. So anyone reading this book can learn logic.

2. No Greek poet was a genius, because no Greek poet was eccentric, and all geniuses are eccentric.

3. Some kids who play video games have poor language skills. No person with poor language skills does well in school. So some kids who play video games do poorly in school.

✴4. Some books about vampires are not great works of literature. After all, no *Twilight* book is a work of great literature, and all the *Twilight* books are about vampires.

5. Some dresses with tulle are red. No red dress is a wedding dress, so some dresses with tulle are not wedding dresses.

6. Some promilitary advertisements are not propaganda, because some of them are truthful, and no truthful advertisement is propaganda.

✴7. Some essential nutrients are not organic, because no mineral is an organic substance, and some minerals are essential nutrients.

8. Some bureaucrats are not chosen on the basis of their ability, and all bureaucrats are civil servants. Therefore some civil servants are not chosen on the basis of their ability.

9. No machine is capable of perpetual motion, because every machine is subject to friction, and nothing that is subject to friction is capable of perpetual motion.

*10. Any good poem is worth reading, but some good poems are difficult to interpret. Thus some things worth reading are difficult to interpret.

III. For each mood and figure, write out the syllogism it describes. Hint: Start with the figure, and lay out the positions of *S*, *M*, and *P*; then use the mood to fill in the quantifier and copula for each proposition.

*1. AII-1

  2. AEE-2

  3. IAI-1

*4. EAE-1

  5. EIO-3

  6. IEO-2

*7. IOO-4

  8. AAI-4

  9. AOO-3

*10. AEO-2

6.2 Validity

A syllogism is a type of deductive argument. As we saw in Chapter 2, validity is the standard for evaluating such arguments. In a valid deductive argument, the conclusion draws out information that is implicit in the premises, making it explicit; so there is no internal gap between premises and conclusion. Thus, if the premises are true, the conclusion must be true; you cannot accept the premises and deny the conclusion without contradicting yourself. In an invalid syllogism, however, the truth of the premises does not guarantee the truth of the conclusion; one could affirm the premises and deny the conclusion without contradiction. Validity does not come in degrees. But it is still a matter of the relation between the premises and the conclusion, not between the premises and reality. A valid argument can have false premises, a false conclusion, or both. And an argument whose premises and conclusion are all true can nevertheless be invalid. The only relationship between validity and truth is that a valid syllogism cannot have true premises and a false conclusion.

In this way, the standards of logical validity are like the rules of arithmetic. If you wanted to know the number of square feet in a floor, you would measure the length and width, and then multiply. To get the right answer, you have to measure accurately and also multiply correctly. So there are two kinds of error you could make. You could start with the right measurements but do the multiplication wrong; that would be like a syllogism that has true premises but is invalid. Or you could make a mistake in measuring but still multiply correctly; that would be like a valid syllogism whose premises are false. Just as we can multiply any two numbers, regardless of whether they accurately represent the object we measured, so we can derive valid conclusions from a set of premises even if they are false.

The validity of a syllogism is determined by its form. If two syllogisms have the same form, they are either both valid or both invalid, even if one has true premises and the other has false ones. Consider, for example, two syllogisms that have the form AAA-1:

All fish are animals.	All *M* are *P*	All bananas are animals.
All trout are fish.	All *S* are *M*	All trout are bananas.
All trout are animals.	All *S* are *P*	All trout are animals.

As you can see, the two arguments have the same form. The only difference is that the middle term has been changed in the right-hand argument from "fish" to "bananas," making the premises of that argument false—indeed, preposterous. The fact remains that if all bananas were animals, and all trout bananas, then all trout would have to be animals. AAA-1 is a valid form of syllogism, and so any syllogism that has this form is valid.

But not all forms are valid. In fact, if you chose a form at random, your chances of picking a valid one would be pretty small. There are three propositions in a syllogism, each of which can have any of four forms (A, E, I, or O). That's $4 \cdot 4 \cdot 4 = 64$ possible syllogisms within a given figure. With four figures, we have 256 syllogistic forms. But, again, at most only 24 of them are valid. So we need a way to distinguish the valid from the invalid forms. We could rely on our intuitive sense of whether a given argument seems valid, by reflecting on the three terms and how they are related. In some cases, such as AAA-1, this works for most people. And as you become more familiar with syllogisms, your intuitive feel for their validity will get better and better. That's all to the good. But there are some valid syllogisms that will always seem unnatural and some plausible-sounding arguments that are in fact invalid. Another method would be to memorize all 24 forms, and then check every argument we encounter to see whether it fits one of them. This method also has its value. Some forms are so common—AAA-1 is again the best example—that it is worth getting to know them individually. But memorizing all the valid forms would be far too cumbersome.

What we need is a general method that we can apply to any syllogism to tell whether it is valid or not. Logicians have devised a number of tests for validity. In the remainder of this chapter, we are going to examine two of them. The first method involves a set of rules of validity. The second uses Venn diagrams, with circles representing the major, minor, and middle terms.

Before we examine these methods, however, we need to add a refinement to our understanding of syllogistic structure.

EXERCISE 6.2

Relying on your sense of the logical relationships among terms, try to determine whether the following syllogisms are valid or invalid.

✻1. All *P* are *M*
    No *S* is *M*
    No *S* is *P*

2. All *M* are *P*
   No *S* is *M*
   No *S* is *P*

3. All *M* are *P*
   Some *S* are *M*
   Some *S* are *P*

✻4. No *P* is *M*
    No *S* is *M*
    No *S* is *P*

5. Some *M* are not P
   All *M* are *S*
   Some *S* are not *P*

6. All *P* are *M*
   All *M* are *S*
   All *S* are *P*

∗7. All *P* are *M*
    Some *S* are *M*
    Some *S* are not *P*

9. No *M* is *P*
   Some *M* are *S*
   Some *S* are not *P*

8. All *M* are *P*
   No *M* is *S*
   Some *S* are not *P*

∗10. Some *M* are not *P*
     All *S* are *M*
     Some *S* are not *P*

6.3 Enthymemes

As we saw in Chapter 2, arguments in real life often have implicit premises. We normally do not make explicit mention of all the premises required to support a given conclusion, especially when the premises are obvious or noncontroversial. A syllogism with an unstated premise is called an **enthymeme**. For example, suppose someone infers that Jane's new car gets poor gas mileage because it has a V-8 engine. In standard form:

> (All cars with V-8 engines get poor gas mileage.)
> Jane's car is a car with a V-8 engine.
> Jane's car gets poor gas mileage.

We use parentheses around the major premise to indicate that it was not stated explicitly. We don't use letters to identify implicit premises here, as we did in Chapter 2, because we aren't using numbers to represent explicit ones.

(Notice also that we did not put the major term in strict standard form: "Get poor gas mileage" designates a property, not the class of things that have the property. This is a shortcut we can allow ourselves, now that we understand the structure of syllogisms, in order to avoid cumbersome formulations such as "All cars with V-8 engines are vehicles that get poor gas mileage.")

The term "enthymeme" is also applied to a syllogism in which the conclusion is left unstated. For example, "Anyone who drives his car across the police department lawn is looking for trouble, right? Well, that's what Mitch did last night." The conclusion here (Mitch is looking for trouble) is so obvious that it's rhetorically more powerful to leave it unspoken. But this is a rare case. The more common type of enthymeme has a missing premise.

We identify the missing premise by looking for a premise that will make the syllogism valid. In some arguments, like the one about Jane's car, it is obvious what the missing premise is. If you are not sure, however, you can use what you know about the internal structure of syllogisms. The first step is to lay out the conclusion and the one premise that is given. We can tell from the conclusion what the major and minor terms are, and the premise will give us the middle term. So we know what terms are contained in the missing premise: *P* and *M* if it is the major premise, *S* and *M* if it's the minor.

Most of the syllogisms you will encounter in everyday discourse will be enthymemes. This is not a defect of such discourse; on the contrary, it makes our reasoning more efficient. We state only the new or nonobvious parts of an argument, so that we can focus attention on them.

But it is important to identify missing premises because sometimes they are controversial, dubious, or false. A businessman might argue in favor of a government subsidy program on the grounds that it kept his firm from bankruptcy. If we lay out the argument, we can see that the implicit premise is "Any program that keeps my business from going bankrupt is a good program." It is not obvious, to say the least, that this proposition states a good criterion for public policy. The argument as a whole is less plausible than it may have seemed at first now that we have made the assumption explicit. The ability to identify assumed premises, then, is an important skill to develop. Without this skill, we would rarely be able to use the rest of what we have learned about syllogistic reasoning.

Until now, we've said that categorical syllogisms, including enthymemes, properly consist of just two premises and a conclusion. A special sort of enthymeme, **sorites** arguments, consist of chains of interlocking syllogisms in which the intermediate conclusion has been omitted. In the next chapter, you'll learn more about sorites and other extended arguments.

EXERCISE 6.3

I. Determine whether each of the following enthymemes is missing a premise or the conclusion. Supply the missing statement, making the syllogism valid if possible.

*1. All cats are irrational by nature so Boots must be irrational by nature.

2. All cellular providers add on unnecessary fees and SureCell is a cellular provider.

3. Nobody who eats meat is a vegan, so Carlos is not a vegan.

*4. Some college students are humanities majors, so some college students will not be high earners.

5. Libby is a Libertarian, therefore Libby believes in free speech.

II. Rewrite the following sorites by supplying the intermediate conclusions. You may find it helpful to rearrange the premises.

*1. No dogs are cats.
   Some mammals are cats.
   All poodles are dogs.
   Some mammals are not poodles.

2. Some fish are trout.
   No trout are bass.
   Some cold-blooded animals are reptiles.
   All fish are cold-blooded animals.
   Some reptiles are not bass.

3. Anything that increases happiness promotes human flourishing.
Marijuana increases happiness.
<u>Nothing that promotes human flourishing should be illegal.</u>
Marijuana should not be illegal.

✶4. Nothing that is sweet is salty.
All peanuts are nuts.
Only salty things cause thirst.
<u>Nuts are sweet.</u>
Peanuts do not cause thirst.

5. Whoever cheats on his taxes depletes public revenue.
Some accountants are dishonest people.
All those who deplete public revenue are criminals.
<u>All dishonest people cheat on their taxes.</u>
Some accountants are criminals.

III [Integrative Exercise] Find the missing premise (or conclusion) in each of the following enthymemes, put the argument into standard form, and identify its mood and figure. Be sure to complete the syllogism so that it is valid, if that is possible.

✶1. Any food that generates stomach acid is bad for an ulcer patient, and fried foods generate stomach acid.

2. Squares are rectangles, since they have four sides.

3. Economic arrangements are important because they affect the distribution of power.

✶4. No one who trades stocks on the basis of proprietary information is an honest person. Some investment bankers, therefore, are not honest people.

5. Some Europeans are Muslims, since some Cypriots are.

6. Some of the articles were written in Spanish, so Jacob could not read them.

✶7. Some entertaining movies are not moral, because no moral movie is violent.

8. It isn't true that all politicians are honest, for some have taken bribes.

9. Some parents spank their children, so there are some bad parents out there.

✶10. Some self-determined nations are unstable, so they must not be democracies.

6.4 Rules of Validity

The first method for assessing validity is based on the fact that valid syllogisms share certain properties. These properties can be used to formulate a set of four rules—four tests that a syllogism will pass if it is valid. Two of the rules, however, involve a property called "distribution" that we have not yet discussed. Once we have seen what it's all about, we will return to the rules of validity.

SOLVE Distribution

In universal (A and E) statements the subject term is distributed, while the predicate term is distributed in negative (E and O) statements. You may find this mnemonic device helpful:

Underachieving **S**tudents **N**ever **P**repare. (**U**niversals distribute **S**ubjects, **N**egatives distribute **P**redicates.)

6.4A Distribution

A categorical statement makes an assertion about the members of the two classes represented by the subject and predicate terms. In some cases, the statement asserts something about every member of the class. If we say that all porcelain vases are fragile, we are making a claim about the entire class of porcelain vases, each and every one of them. But if we say that some porcelain vases are fragile, we are not claiming anything about the entire class. To mark this distinction, which is crucial for the traditional analysis of categorical reasoning, we need to introduce the concept of **distribution**.

A term is distributed in a categorical statement if the statement makes an assertion about all members of the class designated by the term. If not, the term is undistributed. The concept of distribution applies to the terms in all categorical propositions—E, I, and O, as well as A—and we need to learn the rules for telling whether a given term is distributed or undistributed.

The rule for the subject term is easy. The subject term is distributed if the proposition is universal (A or E) and undistributed if the proposition is particular (I or O). As we have just seen, a statement of the form *All S are P* makes a claim about the whole class of *S*s, so *S* in this case is distributed. The same is true for *No S is P*, because this statement excludes each and every member of the *S* class from the *P* class. In contrast, *Some S are P* does not claim something about all *S*s, and neither does *Some S are not P*. For the subject term, what matters is quantity. Quality is irrelevant.

The rule for the predicate term is different and not quite as obvious. Let's start by considering the E proposition. When we say "No dictatorship is a democracy," we are drawing a line between dictatorships and democracies. We are saying that the first class lies completely outside the second. We are saying that no dictatorship is identical with any democracy. But this also means we are saying something about each and every member of the class of democracies, because it implies that none of them is identical with any dictatorship. In general, when we say that no *S* is *P*, we are excluding all the *P*s from the class of *S*s just as much as we are excluding all the *S*s from the class of *P*s. So in this case *P* is distributed.

What about the predicate in an A proposition? When we say "All whales are mammals," have we made a claim about the entire class of mammals, each and every one? No. The statement leaves it open whether or not there are any other mammals besides whales—any other species in that genus. We know that there are, but we haven't said it. A statement of the form *All S are P* says that each member of *S* is identical to some member of *P*. But it does not imply that each member of *P* is identical to some member of *S*. There may be *P*s that are not *S*. We don't know whether there are or aren't. The same is clearly true for the predicate in an I proposition. A statement of the form *Some S are P* makes a claim neither about all the *S*s nor about all the *P*s. So in both affirmative propositions, the predicate term is undistributed.

Of the four standard forms, the only one left is O. In a statement of the form *Some S are not P*, the subject term is undistributed because we are talking only about some members of *S*. But those members are being excluded from the class of *P*s in the same way that, in the E proposition, all the members were being excluded. Suppose the statement is "Some stockbrokers are not very bright." Which stockbrokers? We don't know, but let's suppose there's just one, and let's call him Tom. We are saying that Tom is not identical with anyone in the class of bright people. This implies that no one in the class of bright people is identical with Tom. Here again we are making a claim about the entire class of bright people, so the predicate of our statement is distributed.

For the predicate, then, what matters is quality, not quantity. The predicate term is distributed if the proposition is negative (E or O) and undistributed if the proposition is affirmative (A or I).

Before we leave the topic of distribution, a word of warning about two common errors. The first is to think that a proposition as a whole can be distributed or undistributed. Unlike quality and quantity, distribution is not a feature of the proposition as a whole. It is a feature of its terms. The second mistake is to treat distribution as a feature that a term has in and of itself. The term "whales," standing by itself and not part of any proposition, is neither distributed nor undistributed. It simply picks out a certain class of animals and stands for all the members of that class. It is only when the term is used as the subject or the predicate of a proposition that it acquires a distribution, for only then is it being used to make a statement about all or some members of that class.

REVIEW Two Rules for Distribution

In a categorical proposition:

The subject term is distributed if the proposition is universal (A or E) and undistributed if the proposition is particular (I or O).

The predicate term is distributed if the proposition is negative (E or O) and undistributed if the proposition is affirmative (A or I).

Distributed terms are highlighted.

A: All   **S**   are   P   **E**: No   **S**   is   **P**

I: Some   S   are   P   **O**: Some   S   are not   **P**

EXERCISE 6.4A

I. Put the following propositions into standard form (if they are not already), then identify the subject and predicate terms, and mark each term with a D if it is distributed or a U if it is undistributed.

*1. All machines are manufactured objects.

2. No inanimate object is conscious.

3. Some countries are not at peace.

*4. Some trees are deciduous.

5. Every day is a new beginning.

6. Some of my best friends are trapeze artists.

*7. Some cars are lemons.

8. Some materials are not flammable.

9. Some bachelors wish they were married.

*10. No one with any manners would clean his teeth at the dinner table.

II. Integrative Exercise Each of the following propositions is in standard form. Identify the letter name (A, E, I, or O), quantity, and quality of each proposition. Then state whether the subject and predicate terms are distributed.

*1. No drunk is a person with good judgment.

2. Some college students are not people obsessed with texting.

3. All cats are animals that are gray in the dark.

*4. Some married men are men who wish they were bachelors.

5. All circles are geometric shapes.

6. Some spring break vacations are not bacchanalian parties.

*7. No bird is an animal.

8. Some successful plays are Broadway musicals.

9. Some categorical propositions are not statements in standard form.

*10. All spiders are arachnids.

6.4B The Rules

Now that we understand the concept of distribution, we can examine the rules for determining whether a categorical syllogism is valid:

1. The middle term must be distributed in at least one of the premises.
2. If either of the terms in the conclusion is distributed, it must also be distributed in the premise in which it occurs.
3. The premises cannot both be negative.
4. If either premise is negative, the conclusion must be negative; and if the conclusion is negative, one premise must be negative.

If a syllogism complies with all four, it is valid; if it violates even one of the rules, it is invalid. Let's examine each of these rules in turn.

1. In a valid syllogism, the middle term must be distributed in at least one of the premises.

This rule means that at least one of the premises in a syllogism must make a statement about the entire class designated by the middle term *M*. If *M* is undistributed in both premises, it will not provide a strong enough link between the other two terms, *S* and *P*, to guarantee that the conclusion follows from the premises.

Consider the following argument, which has the form AAA-2:

All *P* are *M*	All conservatives believe in private property.
All *S* are *M*	All people who defend capitalism believe in private property.
All *S* are *P*	All people who defend capitalism are conservatives.

If we look at the abstract form on the left, we can see that in each premise, *M* is the predicate of an affirmative proposition. *M* is therefore undistributed in both premises, and the argument violates the rule. If we look at the example on the right, we can see why an argument of this form is invalid. The fact that conservatives believe in private property does not mean that they are the *only* people who do. So the fact that people who defend capitalism believe in private property does not necessarily mean that they are conservatives. They may or may not be. The premises locate the two classes. *P* (conservatives) and *S* (procapitalists), within the wider class (*M*) of believers in private property. But that doesn't tell us whether *S* is included in *P*, or *P* in *S*, or whether there is any overlap at all. Again, there may or may not be.

A syllogism that violates rule 1 commits the fallacy of the undistributed middle, and AAA-2 is the classic example, one that occurs fairly often. The reason that people often take such an argument to be valid is probably that they switch *M* and *P* in the major premise. They hear "All *P* are *M*," but switch it to "All *M* are *P*." They hear "All conservatives believe in private property" but take it to mean "Anyone who believes in private property is a conservative"—treating the belief as a defining trait of conservatives. If this transformation were legitimate, it would change the argument from the invalid form AAA-2 to the valid form AAA-1:

AAA-2	**AAA-1**
All *P* are *M*	All *M* are *P*
All *S* are *M*	All *S* are *M*
All *S* are *P*	All *S* are *P*

But this transformation is not legitimate. The major premise on the right is the *converse* of the major premise on the left, and we know that an A proposition and its converse are not equivalent.

The fallacy of the undistributed middle is often committed when people attribute guilt by association—for example, the accusation that someone is a terrorist because he supports the same causes as some terrorists. The fallacy is clear when we put this inference into standard form:

Some terrorists support an independent Palestinian state.
So-and-so supports an independent Palestinian state.
So-and so is a terrorist.

This syllogism has the logical form IAA-2 (remember that singular propositions are treated as universals). The middle term (people who support an independent Palestinian state) is not distributed, so the conclusion doesn't follow.

2. In a valid syllogism, if either of the terms in the conclusion is distributed, it must also be distributed in the premise in which it occurs.

Once again, the rationale for this rule is based on the nature of distribution. If the predicate of the conclusion (the major term) is distributed, then the conclusion is making a statement about all members of that class. If that term is not distributed in the major premise, then the premise is not making a statement about the entire class. So the conclusion is making a stronger claim than the premise can support—it goes beyond the information in the premise. The same reasoning applies to the minor term: If the minor term is distributed in the conclusion, it must be distributed in the minor premise too. A syllogism that violates this rule is said to have an *illicit major* or *illicit minor*, depending on which term is at fault. The following argument has an illicit minor:

All *M* are *P*	All vertebrates reproduce sexually.
All *M* are *S*	All vertebrates are animals.
All *S* are *P*	All animals reproduce sexually.

S is distributed in the conclusion, but not in the minor premise. The minor premise says that vertebrates are a species of the genus animals, and it is not valid to assume that what is true of all vertebrates (that they reproduce sexually) must be true of other species in the same genus, such as lower invertebrates. At most we can conclude that *some* animals reproduce sexually. That is, we must keep *S* undistributed in the conclusion.

The classic example of an illicit major is the syllogism AEE-1, and it occurs often in political debate. Here's an example:

Supporters of national health insurance want to make medical care more widely available.
None of the doctors I know support national health insurance.
None of the doctors I know want to make medical care more widely available.

Here the major term (people who want to make medical care more widely available) is distributed in the conclusion but not in the major premise. The argument boils down to the claim that if you don't agree with these policies (e.g., that national health insurance is a good idea), then you don't accept these goals (making medical care more widely available). And of course that isn't true. People can share a goal but disagree about the best means of achieving it.

It is important to remember that rule 2 applies only if a term in the conclusion is distributed. If the term is undistributed in the conclusion, then it doesn't matter whether or not it is distributed in the premise.

3. No valid syllogism can have two negative premises.

In syllogistic reasoning, two negatives don't make a positive. They don't make anything. If both premises are negative, they tell us that both the major and the minor term are excluded, wholly or in part, from the middle term. And that won't tell us how the major and minor terms are related to each other.

No *S* is *M*	No chiropractor has sung for the Metropolitan Opera.
No *M* is *P*	No one who has sung for the Metropolitan Opera has been in Kuala Lumpur.
No *S* is *P*	No chiropractor has been in Kuala Lumpur.

Thus knowing that no chiropractor has sung for the Metropolitan Opera and that no one who has sung for the Metropolitan Opera has been in Kuala Lumpur will not tell us that no chiropractors have been in Kuala Lumpur or that some have, or anything else.

4. If either premise of a valid syllogism is negative, the conclusion must be negative; and if the conclusion is negative, one premise must be negative.

If a premise is negative, it tells us that one class (either *S* or *P*, depending on which premise it is) is excluded from another class (*M*). From this information, we might be able to infer that *S* is *excluded* from *P*—if the other rules are satisfied. But we could not correctly infer that *S* is *included* in *P*. Conversely, if the conclusion is negative, it says that *S* is excluded from *P*. The only information that would justify this conclusion is the information that *S* is excluded from *M* (which is included in *P*) or that *S* is included in *M* (which is excluded from *P*). In either of those cases, we have one negative premise.

Violations of rules 3 and 4 occur much less often than violations of 1 and 2. In most cases, syllogisms that commit either of the fallacies of negation are so obviously invalid that we avoid them instinctively. But there are a few contexts in which syllogisms that violate rules 3 or 4 do seem plausible, and we have to be careful. Here's an example:

No *P* is *M*	No one who competes for money is an amateur.
No *S* is *M*	No member of the Bush League is an amateur.
All *S* are *P*	All members of the Bush League compete for money.

This syllogism violates rules 3 and 4: It has two negative premises and an affirmative conclusion. By our rules, it is invalid. Yet the conclusion seems to follow. Why is that?

Well, for one thing, we assume that members of the Bush League are involved in some competitive sport and are thus either amateur or professional players. But that information is not actually given in the minor premise; it is merely suggested by the name "Bush League." We also assume that competing for fun (or whatever) rather than money is the defining trait of an amateur, so that any nonamateur competitor must be competing for money. That, too, is not given or implied by the premises. What makes the argument seem valid, therefore, is that in our minds we substitute for it the following syllogism, which is valid (it is our old friend AAA-1):

All *M* are *P*	All nonamateur competitors compete for money.
All *S* are *M*	All members of the Bush League are nonamateur competitors.
All *S* are *P*	All members of the Bush League compete for money.

As always, it is important to focus on what the premises actually say and to be careful not to read into them any background knowledge we happen to possess.

When we apply the rules of negation, we need to remember to watch out for complementary terms, such as *S* and non-*S*. Suppose someone says that Ruth does not make friends easily because she is not communicative, and uncommunicative people do not make friends easily. We might represent this syllogism as follows:

No uncommunicative people make friends easily.
Ruth is not communicative.
Ruth does not make friends easily.

Intuitively, this argument seems valid, and indeed it is. Yet both premises are negative, and so you might conclude that it is invalid. The problem is that the syllogism is not in standard form, so we can't apply the rules just yet.

Since "communicative" and "uncommunicative" are complementary terms—logically related, to be sure, but still distinct—the argument has four terms altogether, whereas a syllogism can have only three. Because those two terms are logically related, however, we can change one into the other by using an immediate inference. What we do in this case is take the *obverse* of the minor premise, so that we now have the syllogism in standard form:

> No uncommunicative people make friends easily.
> Ruth is uncommunicative.
> Ruth does not make friends easily.

We now have just three terms, so the argument is in standard form. And the minor premise is now affirmative, so that the syllogism satisfies all the rules. When you encounter complementary terms, you will have to use the obverse, or occasionally the contrapositive, to change one of them into the other before you can apply the rules.

The four rules we have discussed provide a complete test for the validity of categorical syllogisms—with one caveat. Consider the following syllogism:

> All cars are designed for personal transportation.
> All cars are motor vehicles.
> Some motor vehicles are designed for personal transportation.

This syllogism satisfies all of our rules. But notice that its conclusion is particular, while both premises are universal. This raises the issue of existential import, discussed in the previous chapter. If we adopt the traditional view, which presupposes referents for all terms in categorical propositions, there is no problem here. But if we adopt the modern view, which says that universal propositions lack existential import while particular ones have it, then the conclusion makes an assertion not justified by the premises. The premises do not actually assert the existence of any motor vehicles, while the conclusion does.

The logicians who identified the rules of validity usually held the traditional view of existential import. As a method of determining whether a syllogism is valid, the rules are indeed better suited to the traditional view. Conversely, if we adopt the traditional view of existential import, the rules provide the most natural way to assess validity. It is not difficult, however, to adapt this method for the modern view. Since existential import is a function of quantity—universal versus particular—we just need to add a fifth rule dealing with quantity:

5. *If the conclusion of a valid syllogism is particular, one premise must be particular.*

In effect, the rule says that if the conclusion has existential import—if it implies the real existence of things in the class of Ss—it must get that import from one of the premises. Otherwise the conclusion makes a claim that goes beyond what is given in the premises. The syllogism about cars obviously violates the rule, so it would be invalid on the modern view. When you include this rule in order to test for validity on the modern view, it is best to start by applying the first four rules. If a syllogism violates any of them, it is invalid on both the traditional and the modern view of existential import. If it satisfies those rules, then check whether it has a particular conclusion; if it does, then it must have a particular premise in order to be valid on the modern view.

The syllogism about cars has the form AAI-3. It is one of nine forms that are "conditionally valid"—on the traditional view of existential import but invalid on the modern view:

Conditionally Valid Traditional Syllogisms That Are Invalid on the Modern View

1st figure	2nd figure	3rd figure	4th figure
AAI-1	AEO-2	AAI-3	AAI-4
EAO-1	EAO-2	EAO-3	EAO-4
			AEO-4

There are also fifteen "unconditionally valid" forms. Syllogisms having any of these forms are valid on both the traditional *and* the modern view:

Unconditionally Valid Syllogisms

1st figure	2nd figure	3rd figure	4th figure
AAA-1	AEE-2	AII-3	AEE-4
AII-1	AOO-2	EIO-3	EIO-4
EAE-1	EAE-2	IAI-3	IAI-4
EIO-1	EIO-2	OAO-3	

REVIEW Rules for Testing Validity

	Rule	Violation
Distribution	1. The middle term must be distributed in at least one of the premises.	Undistributed middle term
	2. If either the major or the minor term in the conclusion is distributed, it must also be distributed in the premise in which it occurs.	Illicit major term, illicit minor term
Negation	3. The premises cannot both be negative.	Two negative premises
	4. If either premise is negative, the conclusion must be negative; and	Negative premise, affirmative conclusion
	If the conclusion is negative, one premise must be negative.	Affirmative premises, negative conclusion
Quantity	5. If the conclusion is particular, one premise must be particular. (Required only on the modern view of existential import.)	Universal premises, particular conclusion

EXERCISE 6.4B

I. For each of the following invalid categorical syllogisms, state whether it commits a fallacy of distribution, negation, or quantity.

*1. All professors are people who are highly educated.
   All engineers are people who are highly educated.
   All engineers are professors.

2. All students are people who desire knowledge.
   All students are novices.
   All novices are people who desire knowledge.

3. All opponents of free speech are people who support speech codes.
   No philosopher is an opponent of free speech.
   No philosopher is a person who supports speech codes.

*4. All mammals are warm-blooded animals.
   All mammals are animals that give live birth.
   Some animals that give live birth are warm-blooded animals.

5. No convicted felon is a person who has been elected president.
   No person who has been elected president has been a person under the age of forty.
   No convicted felon has been a person under the age of forty.

6. All snakes are reptiles.
   All snakes are cold-blooded animals.
   Some cold-blooded animals are reptiles.

*7. All hip-hop artists are musicians.
   All violinists are musicians.
   All violinists are hip-hop artists.

II. Use the rules to test the validity of the following syllogisms. (These are the same syllogisms you evaluated intuitively in Exercise 6.2.) If the syllogism is invalid, state the reason.

*1. All *P* are *M*
   No *S* is *M*
   No *S* is *P*

2. All *M* are *P*
   No *S* is *M*
   No *S* is *P*

3. All *M* are *P*
   Some *S* are *M*
   Some *S* are *P*

*4. No *P* is *M*
   No *S* is *M*
   No *S* is *P*

5. Some *M* are not *P*
   All *M* are *S*
   Some *S* are not *P*

6. All *P* are *M*
   All *M* are *S*
   All *S* are *P*

*7. All *P* are *M*
   Some *S* are *M*
   Some *S* are not *P*

8. All *M* are *P*
   No *M* is *S*
   Some *S* are not *P*

9. No *M* is *P*
   Some *M* are *S*
   Some *S* are not *P*

*10. Some *M* are not *P*
   All *S* are *M*
   Some *S* are not *P*

III.   **Integrative Exercise**   First put each of the following syllogisms into standard form, and identify its mood and figure. Then use the rules to determine whether it is valid or invalid. If it is invalid, state the rule that it violates.

✳1. It's obvious that Tom has something to hide. He pled the Fifth Amendment in court last week; people with things to hide always plead the Fifth.

2. Protestant churches do not accept the authority of the pope. Since the United Church of Christ does not accept the pope's authority, it must be a Protestant church.

3. Some of the students in this class are freshmen, and of course no freshman will graduate this year. So none of the students in this class will graduate this year.

✳4. Some things that are well made are not expensive, for paperback books are inexpensive, and some of them are well made.

5. Some developing countries that need AIDS medication are places with poor manufacturing standards, because no developing country that needs AIDS medication can produce it and no country that can produce the medication has poor manufacturing standards.

6. No one who makes a profit cares about people, and lots of pharmaceutical companies make a huge profit. So those companies must not care about people.

✳7. None of the developing countries can afford the AIDS medications that they need. Many countries that can afford AIDS medicines are capitalist, so some of the developing countries must not have a capitalist system.

8. Any tax that discourages productive activity harms the economic growth of the country. Hence a tax on income, which obviously discourages productive activity, harms the country's economic growth.

9. All journalists are people with low salaries, and some people with low salaries are freelance writers, so at least some journalists must be freelance writers.

✳10. Some of the proposals before this committee, I have to conclude, are not inspired. All of the proposals are reasonable, but some inspired ideas are not reasonable.

11. Some flowers that bloom all season flourish in the shade, and thus some shade-loving flowers are not perennials (since no perennial blooms all season).

12. Pharmaceutical companies that aid developing countries give their products as charity, and they will raise their prices. So some of the companies that are giving their products as charity will raise their prices.

✳13. Some countries that can participate in the global market flout drug patent laws, and all countries that can participate in the global market get the imports that they need. So some countries that get the imports they need are countries that flout drug patent laws.

14. Some countries whose people need AIDS medications have illegitimate governments, and no legitimate government neglects the needs of its poor populations. So some countries that neglect the needs of their poor are countries whose people need AIDS medication.

15. No country that can afford preventative medicines is a country where the number of people with AIDS will increase, but many countries with an AIDS population can't afford preventative medicine, so these countries will see an increase in the numbers of their people with AIDS.

6.4C Enthymemes and Rules

We can use the four rules of validity to help us analyze enthymemes. When we are given a syllogism with a missing premise, as we have seen, we can always determine what terms must be involved in the missing premise. For example, suppose a literature professor says, "Some works of epic narrative are poetry because they are in rhymed stanzas." Putting this inference into standard form, we have a conclusion and one premise:

(?)	(?)
Some works of epic narrative are works written in rhymed stanzas.	Some S are M
Some works of epic narrative are poetry.	Some S are P

Since the missing premise is the major one, it must be a proposition relating P (poetry) and M (works written in rhymed stanzas). In this case, we can see that M is not distributed in the minor premise: That premise does not make a claim about all works in rhymed stanzas. So rule 1 requires that the term be distributed in the major premise. Since the conclusion is affirmative, rule 4 requires that the major premise be affirmative as well. There is only one way to have M distributed in an affirmative premise: the proposition "All works written in rhymed stanzas are poetry" (All M are P).

Let's try another example. Someone observes that since all banks have government-insured deposits, no hedge fund is a bank. Once again we start by putting the conclusion and the stated premise into standard form:

All banks are institutions with government-insured deposits.	All P are M
(?)	(?)
No hedge fund is a bank.	No S is P

In this case, the missing premise is the minor one, involving the terms S (hedge funds) and M (institutions with government-insured deposits). Since the major premise is affirmative but the conclusion is negative, the minor premise must be negative as well (rule 4). And both terms in that premise must be distributed, M because it is not distributed in the major premise (rule 1) and S because it is distributed in the conclusion (rule 2). Only two premises satisfy all these conditions:

No S is M No hedge fund is an institution with government-insured deposits.

No M is S No institution with government-insured deposits is a hedge fund.

Each of these E propositions is the converse of the other and thus they are equivalent. Either one would give us a valid syllogism.

EXERCISE 6.4C

Integrative Exercise For each of the following enthymemes, use what you have learned about the rules of validity to supply the missing premise or conclusion that will result in a valid syllogism.

✳1. Trees need water because they are plants.

2. No one who is dishonest will be happy, since a dishonest person lacks character.

3. Because all government agencies are spending other people's money, none can be truly entrepreneurial.

✳4. Some water is unsafe to drink, because anything containing coliform bacteria is unsafe.

5. Some exceptional people are not eligible to vote, since everyone eligible to vote is a citizen.

6. Not one of the union demands deserves any serious consideration, since none of them is compatible with the labor contract that is still in effect.

✳7. No creature whose actions are wholly determined by heredity and environment is a moral agent. Thus no non-human animal is a moral agent.

8. The plan to build a new factory is flawed because it does not have a provision for construction delays.

6.5 Venn Diagrams

6.5A Diagramming Syllogisms

In the previous chapter, we learned how to draw Venn diagrams for categorical propositions. These diagrams provide another test for validity on the modern view. To create a Venn diagram for a syllogism, we do not need three separate diagrams for the premises and conclusion. We can represent the argument as a whole in a single diagram using *three* overlapping circles, one for each term. We always use the following structure:

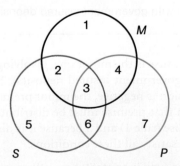

The three circles divide the space into seven different areas, instead of the three areas in the simpler diagrams we used to represent individual propositions. But any two of these circles overlap in the same way as the simpler diagrams. That means we can diagram any of the propositions in a syllogism by focusing just on the relevant pair of circles and ignoring the third one.

The technique of Venn diagrams is based on the fact that in a valid syllogism, the conclusion asserts no more than what is already contained, implicitly, in the premises. If the conclusion asserts more than that, it does not follow from the premises, and the syllogism is invalid. The technique is to diagram the premises, and then see whether anything would have to be added in order to diagram what the conclusion asserts. If so, the syllogism is invalid; if not, it is valid.

Let's take an example we've used before:

No antlered animal is a carnivore.	No *M* is *P*
All moose are antlered animals.	All *S* are *M*
No moose is a carnivore.	No *S* is *P*

The first step is to diagram the major premise, using just the circles representing *M* (antlered animals) and *P* (carnivores). So we shade out the area of overlap between *M* and *P*, which includes areas 3 and 4.

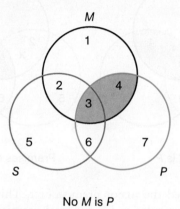

No *M* is *P*

The second step is to add the minor premise to our diagram, using the circles representing *S* (moose) and *M*. Since this is an A proposition, we shade out the region of *S* outside *M*—areas 5 and 6.

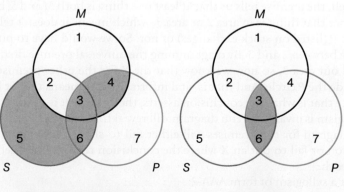

Premises combined   Conclusion

The final step is to examine the completed diagram of the premises and determine whether it contains the information asserted by the conclusion. The conclusion, *No S is P*, requires that the overlap between *S* and *P* (areas 3 and 6) be shaded out. The premises taken together do shade out that region: 3 was shaded by the first premise, 6 by the second. So the syllogism is valid. For a syllogism to be valid, the combined diagram must contain all the information asserted by the conclusion. It may contain more information, but it cannot omit anything.

Now let's try a syllogism with a particular premise:

No privately held company is listed on stock exchanges.	No *M* is *P*
Some privately held companies are large corporations.	Some *M* are *S*
Some large corporations are not listed on stock exchanges.	Some *S* are not *P*

First we diagram the premises:

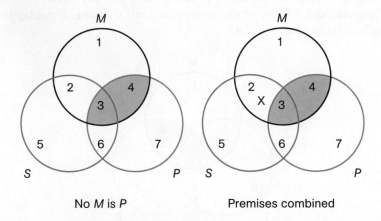

No *M* is *P*   Premises combined

Notice that we diagrammed the major premise first. This is not required logically, but whenever there is a particular and a universal premise, it is best to diagram the universal one first because that will usually help us in placing the X for the particular premise. Suppose we had started with the particular premise. The diagram for *Some M* (privately held companies) *are S* (large corporations) requires an X in the region of overlap between *M* and *S*. But that region is divided into two areas, 2 and 3, by the *P* circle. Taken by itself, the premise tells us that at least one thing is both *M* and *S*, but it doesn't tell us whether that thing is in area 2 or area 3—which means it doesn't tell us whether that thing is *P* (listed on stock exchanges) or not. So we would have to put a tentative X on the line between 2 and 3. By diagramming the universal premise first, however, we have shaded out area 3, so now we know that the X for the other premise must go in area 2, outside the *P* circle. And that is vital information; it means that at least one *S* is not a *P*. Since that is what the conclusion asserts, the argument is valid.

If a syllogism is invalid, a Venn diagram will reveal that fact in one of two ways. The combined diagram for the premises will either fail to shade out an area excluded by the conclusion or fail to put an X where the conclusion requires one. Let's look at an example of each.

Consider a syllogism of form AAA-2:

All athletes are people in good physical condition.	All P are M
All fitness instructors are people in good physical condition.	All S are M
All fitness instructors are athletes.	All S are P

The Venn diagram reveals the invalidity by failing to shade out the right areas:

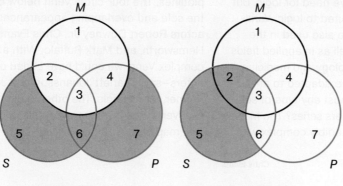

Premises combined   Conclusion

In the combined diagram, areas 6 and 7 have been shaded to represent the major premise, *All P* (athletes) *are M* (people in good physical condition). To diagram the minor premise, *All S* (fitness instructors) *are M*, we need to shade out the region of *S* outside *M*; since area 6 is already shaded, we just need to shade out area 5. But one area in the region of *S* outside *P*, area 2, has not been shaded. Thus the premises leave open the possibility that *some S are not P*; they do not guarantee that *all S are P*. So the conclusion does not follow; the syllogism is invalid.

Now let's examine a case in which the problem is revealed by the placement of Xs:

No member of the Green Party was elected to Congress.	No M is P
Some candidates who favor strong environmental regulation are not members of the Green Party.	Some S are not M
Some candidates who favor strong environmental regulation were elected to Congress.	Some S are P

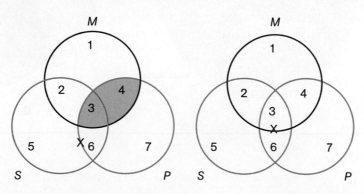

Premises combined   Conclusion

APPLY Diagraming the Avengers

In this book, we've used two- and three-circle Venn diagrams; that's all we need for logic. But Venn diagrams are not limited to logic. Variations of Venn diagrams are also used in the theoretical sciences as well as in applied fields such as information technology and medicine. In fact, Venn diagrams can be adapted to analyze relationships between almost any type of set. Are you a fan of the Avengers series? The Marvel Cinematic Universe is incredibly complex with many reoccurring characters and interesting plotlines. The four-circle Venn below depicts the sole and overlapping appearances of MCU actors Robert Downey Jr., Chris Evans, Chris Hemsworth, and Mark Ruffalo. With a more complex Venn, we could have added other MCU actors—say, Scarlett Johansson and Jeremy Renner, for example. The other diagram is a five-oval Venn. See if you can find sets of information that map onto it. But no Marvel—that's our thing!

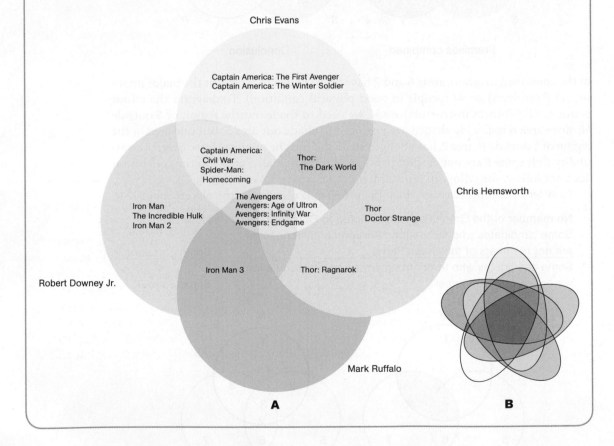

Chris Evans

Captain America: The First Avenger
Captain America: The Winter Soldier

Captain America:
Civil War
Spider-Man:
Homecoming

Thor:
The Dark World

Chris Hemsworth

The Avengers
Avengers: Age of Ultron
Avengers: Infinity War
Avengers: Endgame

Thor
Doctor Strange

Iron Man
The Incredible Hulk
Iron Man 2

Robert Downey Jr.

Iron Man 3

Thor: Ragnarok

Mark Ruffalo

A

B

The conclusion requires an X in the overlap between *S* (candidates who favor strong environmental regulation) and *P* (people elected to Congress). It could be either in area 3 or in area 6, so we put it on the line between the areas. But the premises do not justify putting an X in either area. The major premise, *No M* (member of the Green Party) *is P* (a person elected to Congress), tells us that area 3 is empty, so it has been shaded out. To justify the conclusion, the minor premise would therefore need to give us an X in area 6. But the minor premise does not give us that information. It tells us that some *S* are not *M*, which means there is at least one such candidate in either area 5 or area 6. We cannot put the X inside area 6. It has to go on the line between 5 and 6. Locating the X on the line means: We know that at least one *S* is not an *M*, but we don't know whether that *S* is also a *P*. All that the premises tell us is: There's an *S* that may or may not be a *P*. The conclusion doesn't follow.

Remember that the premises of a valid syllogism may contain more information than the conclusion, but they cannot contain less. The combined diagram may shade out areas that the conclusion leaves open, but it cannot leave open the areas that the conclusion says are shaded out. In the same way, the combined diagram may locate an X inside an area while the conclusion says merely that the area *may* contain one. But if the conclusion requires an X inside an area, the premises must put one there; otherwise the syllogism is invalid.

SOLVE Testing Validity by Venn Diagrams

1. Draw three overlapping circles, representing the major, minor, and middle terms.

2. Diagram each of the premises:
   a. Using just the two circles representing the terms in that premise, diagram the proposition as you would on a two-circle diagram.
   b. If one premise is universal and the other is particular, diagram the universal one first.
   c. In diagramming a particular premise, if there are two possible regions in which to put the X, put it on the line separating the regions.

3. Determine whether anything would have to be added to the diagram to represent the claim made by the conclusion: Would any additional areas need to be shaded out? Would an X need to be placed in an area where the premises do not require one? If nothing needs to be added, the syllogism is valid. If anything needs to be added, it is invalid.

EXERCISE 6.5A

I. For each of the following syllogisms, diagram the premises and the conclusion to determine whether the syllogism is valid.

*1. No *M* is *P*
 Some *M* are not *S*
 Some *S* are *P*

 2. No *M* is *P*
 All *M* are *S*
 All *S* are *P*

 3. All *P* are *M*
 No *M* is *S*
 No *S* is *P*

*4. Some *P* are *M*
 No *M* is *S*
 Some *S* are not *P*

 5. Some *P* are not *M*
 No *S* is *M*
 Some *S* are *P*

 6. Some *P* are not *M*
 Some *S* are not *M*
 Some *S* are not *P*

*7. Some *M* are *P*
 All *M* are *S*
 Some *S* are *P*

 8. Some *M* are *P*
 All *S* are *M*
 Some *S* are not *P*

 9. Some *P* are not *M*
 All *S* are *M*
 Some *S* are not *P*

*10. All *M* are *P*
 All *S* are *M*
 All *S* are *P*

 11. No *P* is *M*
 Some *M* are *S*
 Some *S* are not *P*

 12. All *P* are *M*
 Some *M* are *S*
 Some *S* are *P*

*13. No *M* is *P*
 Some *S* are *M*
 Some *S* are not *P*

 14. All *P* are *M*
 No *S* is *M*
 No *S* is *P*

 15. All *M* are *P*
 Some *M* are *S*
 Some *S* are *P*

II. **Integrative Exercise** Use rules to check your answers for the previous section. Remember that you are checking for validity on the modern view.

6.5B Enthymemes and Venn Diagrams

Now that we know how to construct Venn diagrams, we can put them to a further use: finding the missing premise (or conclusion) in an enthymeme. Remember that to find the missing element, our goal is to make the syllogism valid if possible. Since Venn diagrams test for validity, they can reveal what the missing element must be.

The first step is to diagram the premise that is given and compare it with the conclusion. Suppose we have an argument of the form "Since no *S* is *M*, no *S* is *P*." To diagram the premise, we shade out the region of overlap between *S* and *M*:

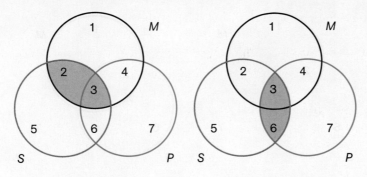

Given premise: No *S* is *M*   Conclusion: No *S* is *P*

Now we look at the conclusion. If "No *S* is *P*" is true, then the region of overlap between *S* and *P* must be shaded out. Area 3 has already been shaded out by diagramming the premise we were given. The missing premise, therefore, must be one that will let us shade out area 6. The missing premise involves the terms *M* and *P*. Of all the possible propositions involving these terms, "All *P* are *M*" is the only one that allows us to shade out area 6:

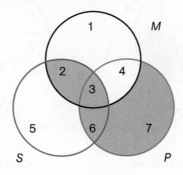

Premises combined: No *S* is *M* + All *P* are *M*

Thus the syllogism is:

(All *P* are *M*)
No *S* is *M*
No *S* is *P*

Let's try this strategy with an enthymeme that has a particular conclusion: "Some *S* are not *P*, because no *M* is *P*." Once again, we diagram the premise that we are given:

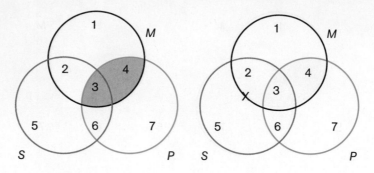

Given premise: No *M* is *P*   Conclusion: Some *S* are not *P*

The conclusion requires an X in the region of *S* that is outside *P*, either in area 2 or in area 5. Is there a missing premise that could give us an X in either area? We know that the missing premise must involve the terms *S* and *M*. And since it must give us an X to put in the diagram, we know that it must be a particular proposition. The obvious candidate is "Some *S* are *M*." Since area 3 has already been shaded out, the X for this premise must go in area 2. Since this is one of the regions of *S* outside *P*, the premise makes the syllogism valid.

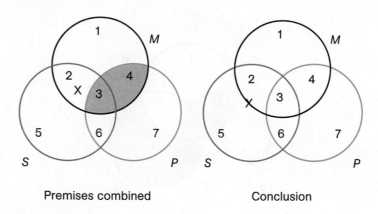

Premises combined   Conclusion

We would get the same result if we used the converse proposition, "Some *M* are *S*." But the premise "Some *S* are not *M*" would *not* give us a valid syllogism. The X for that proposition would go on the line between areas 5 and 6, which means we have not established the existence of any *S*s that are not *P*.

Occasionally, as we saw in discussing enthymemes previously, we will be given the premises, and the conclusion will be left unstated. Suppose we are given the premises:

No *P* is *M*
All *S* are *M*

What conclusion, if any, follows validly from these propositions? To answer that question, we diagram both premises:

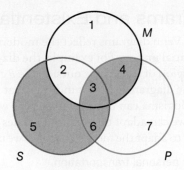

Premises combined
No *P* is *M* + All *S* are *M*

The conclusion will be a proposition about *S* and *P*. Since there are no Xs in the diagram, we know that the conclusion will be universal, not particular. And since both areas in the overlap between *S* and *P* have been shaded out, the appropriate conclusion is "No *S* is *P*."

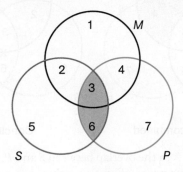

Conclusion
(No *S* is *P*)

EXERCISE 6.5B

Integrative Exercise   For each of the enthymemes that follow, use what you have learned about Venn diagrams to find the missing element and to prove that the resulting syllogism is valid.

*1. Some *S* are *P*, because some *S* are *M*

2. All *S* are *M*, and all *M* are *P*, so . . .

3. All *M* are *P*, so some *S* are *P*

*4. Since some *M* are S, some *S* are *P*

5. Since no *P* is *M*, some *S* are not *P*

6. Since no *P* is *M*, no *S* is *P*

*7. No *S* is *P*, because all *S* are *M*

8. Some *S* are *P*, since all *M* are *P*

9. All *M* are *S* and some *M* are not *P*, which means that . . .

*10. Some *S* are not *P*, because no *P* is *M*

6.5C Venn Diagrams and Existential Import

As we learned in Chapter 5, Venn diagrams reflect the modern view that universal propositions do not have existential import. For example, the diagram for an A proposition, *All S are P*, shades out the region of the S circle outside the P circle but does not put an X in the region of overlap. The diagram does not indicate that there are any Ss. Nevertheless, Venn diagrams for syllogisms can be adapted for use with the traditional view of existential import—just as we can adapt the method of rules for the modern view.

When we discussed how to adapt the method of rules, we used the following example:

All cars are designed for personal transportation.	All M are P
All cars are motor vehicles.	All M are S
Some motor vehicles are designed for personal transportation.	Some S are P

The standard Venn diagrams for premises and conclusion would be

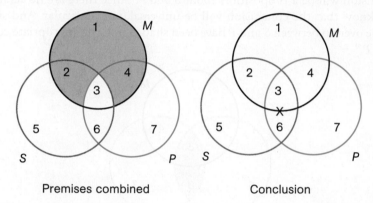

Premises combined   Conclusion

The conclusion requires an X in the overlap between S and P; it goes on the line between areas 3 and 6 because the existence of an S in either area would make the conclusion true. But the premises do not give us an X anywhere in the diagram. They shade out areas 1, 2, and 4, but that is all they do.

To reflect the traditional view, we need to modify the way universal propositions are diagrammed. On both the traditional and the modern views of existential import, a proposition of the form *All S are P* excludes the possibility of Ss that are not P. It is this negative aspect of the universal propositions that we represent by shading out area 1 in the diagram on the left. On the traditional view, however, the universal proposition also has a positive aspect: It implies that some Ss exist and that those Ss are P. In addition to shading out area 1, therefore, we need to put an X in area 2.

All S are P   No S is P

Exactly the same reasoning applies to a proposition of the form *No S is P*, which requires an X in area 1. But a proposition of this form is equivalent to its converse, *No P is S*. That means we are assuming the existence of *P*s as well as *S*s, and we need a second X in area 3.

How does this work in a diagram for a syllogism? Let's return to our example. The diagram on the left represents the major premise, *All M are P*. The X would have to go on the line between areas 3 and 4 because the premise says there are *M*s in the overlap with *P*, but it does not tell us whether those *M*s are *S* (area 3) or non-*S* (area 4). In the same way, the diagram on the right represents the minor premise, *All M are S*, with an X on the line between areas 2 and 3.

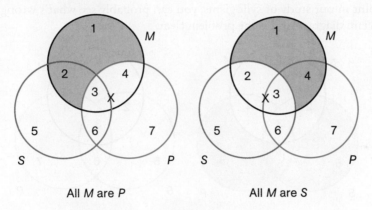

All *M* are *P*   All *M* are *S*

When we combine the premises into a single diagram, however, areas 2 and 4 are shaded out, so the Xs that indicate existential import have to go in area 3. Since that area is in the overlap between *S* and *P*, we know that some *S* are *P*—exactly what the conclusion says. The diagram tells us that the syllogism is valid, as it is on the traditional view.

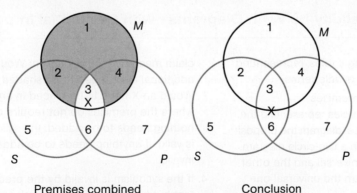

Premises combined   Conclusion

The issue of existential import is relevant to validity only when both premises of a syllogism are universal and the conclusion is particular. In all other cases, standard Venn diagrams yield the same results on both the traditional and the modern views, without having to put in Xs for universal propositions. When you do have universal premises with a particular conclusion, it is best to do the shading for both premises before trying to locate the Xs. As our example illustrated, the shading will often allow us to put the X in a particular area rather than on the line between areas. Thus to use Venn diagrams with the traditional view of existential import, we should test them first by the standard procedure. If a syllogism is invalid by that procedure and has two universal premises and a particular conclusion, it may still be valid on the traditional view of existential import. In this case, insert Xs in the appropriate regions of the diagram and reapply the standard procedure.

Of course, not every syllogism with two universal premises and a particular conclusion is valid, even on the assumption of existential import. Here's an example:

All rock stars are skilled musicians.   All *P* are *M*
All band leaders are skilled musicians.   All *S* are *M*
Some band leaders are rock stars.   Some *S* are *P*

By this point in our study of syllogisms, you can probably see what's wrong with this one. The Venn diagram makes the problem clear.

      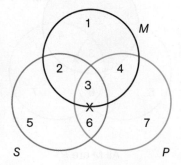

Premises combined   Conclusion

SOLVE Testing Validity by Venn Diagrams—with Existential Import

1. Draw three overlapping circles, representing the major, minor, and middle terms.

2. Diagram each of the premises:
   a. Using just the two circles representing the terms in that premise, diagram the proposition as you would on a two-circle diagram.
   b. If one premise is universal and the other is particular, diagram the universal one first.
   c. In diagramming a particular premise, if there are two possible regions in which to put the X, put it on the line separating the regions.

3. Determine whether anything would have to be added to the diagram to represent the claim made by the conclusion: Would any additional areas need to be shaded out? Would an X need to be placed in an area where the premises do not require one? If nothing needs to be added, the syllogism is valid. If anything needs to be added, it is invalid.

4. If the syllogism is invalid by the preceding test but has two universal premises and a particular conclusion, it may still be valid on the traditional view of existential import. In this case: For each universal premise, add an X to the diagram in the appropriate region. Then repeat step 3.

The conclusion that some band leaders (*S*) are rock stars (*P*) requires an X in the overlap between *S* and *P*. It doesn't matter whether it is in area 3 or area 6. But area 6, along with 5 and 7, will be shaded out by the two universal premises. So the premises are going to have to give us an X in area 3. Both premises are affirmative, so the Xs that represent their existential import will go in the areas of overlap: 3 and 4 for the major premise *All P are M*, 2 and 3 for the minor premise *All S are M*. Since none of these areas has been shaded out, both Xs have to go on the lines dividing area 3 from the adjacent areas. And that means the conclusion does not follow. The band leaders (*S*) who are skilled musicians (*M*) are represented by the X on the line between 2 and 3. Since we don't know whether they are in area 3, we can't infer that those band leaders are also rock stars (*P*), which is what the conclusion asserts. In the same way, rock stars who are skilled musicians are represented by the X on the line between 3 and 4. Since we don't know whether they are in area 3, we can't infer those rock stars are also band leaders.

EXERCISE 6.5C

Use Venn diagrams to determine whether each of the following syllogisms is valid (a) on the modern view of existential import and (b) on the traditional view.

✱1. No *P* is *M*
 All *S* are *M*
 Some *S* are not *P*

Premises combined   Conclusion

2. All *M* are *P*
 No *S* is *M*
 Some *S* are not *P*

Premises combined   Conclusion

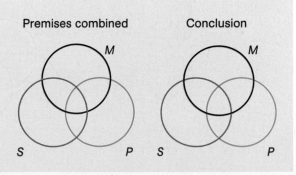

3. No *P* is *M*
   <u>All *S* are *M*</u>
   Some *S* are *P*

Premises combined   Conclusion

*4. All *P* are *M*
    <u>No *M* is *S*</u>
    Some *S* are not *P*

Premises combined   Conclusion

5. All *P* are *M*
   <u>All *M* are *S*</u>
   Some *S* are *P*

Premises combined   Conclusion

6. All *P* are *M*
   <u>No *S* is *M*</u>
   No *S* is *P*

Premises combined   Conclusion

*7. Some *M* are not *P*
   All *S* are *M*
   ────────────
   Some *S* are not *P*

Premises combined

Conclusion

8. All *M* are *P*
   All *M* are *S*
   ────────────
   Some *S* are *P*

Premises combined

Conclusion

9. No *M* is *P*
   Some *M* are *S*
   ────────────
   Some *S* are not *P*

Premises combined

Conclusion

*10. No *M* is *P*
   No *S* is *M*
   ────────────
   Some *S* are *P*

Premises combined

Conclusion

CHAPTER REVIEW

Summary

- This chapter covered the analysis and evaluation of categorical syllogisms.
- The two premises and the conclusion of a categorical syllogism are categorical propositions, and they contain three terms: the major, the minor, and the middle.
- We analyze a categorical syllogism by identifying its logical form, which is determined by its mood and figure.
  - The mood identifies the logical form of the component propositions
  - The figure identifies the position of the middle term in the premises.
- A syllogism with a premise or the conclusion left unstated is called an enthymeme; to analyze such an argument, we must identify the missing element.
- Sorites are a variety of enthymeme consisting of a chain of categorical syllogisms with omitted intermediate conclusions.
- We evaluate a syllogism by testing for validity.
  - A syllogism is valid if the truth of the premises would guarantee the truth of the conclusion.

- A syllogism is either valid or invalid; there are no intermediate degrees of strength.
- Validity depends on the logical form of the argument.
- We can test for validity in two ways.
  - The first test for validity uses a set of rules that a syllogism must satisfy to be valid. If we assume the traditional view of existential import, we use four rules regarding distribution and negation; for the modern view, we need an additional rule regarding quantity.
  - The second method uses Venn diagrams with three overlapping circles representing the terms.
- Basic Venn diagrams presuppose the modern view that universal propositions lack existential import, but the diagrams can be adapted for use with the traditional view.

Key Terms

categorical syllogism (p. 233)

syllogism (p. 233)

major term (p. 233)

major premise (p. 234)

minor term (p. 234)

minor premise (p. 234)

middle term (p. 234)

mood (p. 234)

figure (p. 235)

enthymeme (p. 240)

sorites (p. 241)

distribution (p. 243)

Putting It All Together

I. **Integrative Exercise** Using any of the methods discussed in this chapter, determine whether the following argument forms are valid.

✳1. All *M* are *P*
Some *S* are *M*
Some *S* are *P*

2. No *M* is *P*
Some *S* are not *M*
Some *S* are *P*

3. No *M* is *P*
Some *M* are not *S*
Some *S* are *P*

✳4. All *P* are *M*
Some *S* are not *M*
Some *S* are *P*

5. Some *M* are *P*
Some *M* are not *S*
Some *S* are not *P*

6. Some *P* are *M*
No *S* is *M*
Some *S* are not *P*

✳7. No *P* is *M*
All *S* are *M*
No *S* is *P*

8. All *M* are *P*
Some *S* are not *M*
Some *S* are not *P*

9. All *P* are *M*
Some *M* are *S*
Some *S* are *P*

✳10. No *P* is *M*
All *M* are *S*
No *S* is *P*

11. Some *M* are *P*
No *M* is *S*
Some *S* are not *P*

12. No *P* is *M*
Some *S* are *M*
Some *S* are not *P*

✳13. Some *M* are not *P*
All *M* are *S*
Some *S* are not *P*

14. Some *M* are *P*
All *S* are *M*
Some *S* are *P*

15. No *M* is *P*
All *M* are *S*
Some *S* are not *P*

II. **Integrative Exercise** Put each of the following statements into standard form as a categorical proposition, and determine whether the subject and predicate terms are distributed.

✳1. Some children broke the dishes.

2. Every toy under the tree was wrapped.

3. Some people don't like hot food.

✳4. Some of the president's nominees were not confirmed.

5. No warrant is issued without a judge's order.

6. Some evenings are enchanted.

✳7. There are no stupid questions.

8. Some restaurants that serve liquor do not have a license.

9. Dead men tell no tales.

✳10. All terms in the subject position of a universal categorical proposition are distributed.

III. **Integrative Exercise** Put each of the following syllogisms into standard form, supply the missing proposition if it is an enthymeme, and determine whether it is valid or not.

✳1. Walleyes are fish, so they live in the water.

2. Amy must have done all her studying at the last minute, for anyone who crams like that does poorly on the final exam, and Amy certainly did poorly.

3. Amoebas are not plants, because they are capable of locomotion, and no plant has that capacity.

*4. No friend of mine is a friend of Bill's, but Mary is not a friend of Bill's, so she is a friend of mine.

5. Every economist understands how markets work, but some economists advocate socialism. Some advocates of socialism, therefore, understand how markets work.

6. Any office equipment worth buying will make workers more productive, but some computers do not do so. Some computers, therefore, are not worth buying.

*7. Some democracies are tyrannies, because any country that ignores human rights is tyrannical, and some democracies do just that.

8. Those who supported the Voting Rights bill were opposed to racial discrimination. So conservatives, who did not support the bill, do not oppose discrimination.

9. A person who overreacts to the charge that he is motivated by envy invariably is envious. But people with a strong sense of justice are not motivated by envy, and so they don't overreact that way.

*10. No nonprofit organization sells stock, but some hospital organizations do sell stock, and are therefore for-profit.

11. No building constructed before 1850 is earthquake-proof, because all of them were built without steel, and no structure built without steel is earthquake-proof.

12. Any syllogism of the form AAA-3 has an illicit minor term, and any syllogism with such a form is invalid. Thus any syllogism with an illicit minor term is invalid.

*13. Some actions that are expedient in the short term are not moral. We can see this from the fact that some dishonest means of gaining wealth, which are immoral by nature, are expedient in the short term.

14. All depression involves a profound sense of loss, but this patient's condition does not involve any such sense. It is therefore not a case of depression.

15. No job providing health care benefits is unacceptable to me, but some white collar jobs do not provide such benefits. So some white collar jobs are not acceptable to me.

*16. Some international conflicts arise from just motives, but no aggressive war arises in that way. Hence some aggressive wars are not international conflicts.

17. All great orchestra conductors are flamboyant, but none of them is careless. Thus some flamboyant people are not careless.

18. Some politicians are dishonest, for politicians by nature depend on reputation for their offices, and some people who depend on reputation are not honest.

*19. We should never confuse music and noise: Music is an orderly progression of sounds, noise a disorderly one.

20. Some philosophy courses are graded objectively, for while any course in which the grade is based exclusively on essays is graded nonobjectively, some of those courses, at least, are not in philosophy.

IV. **Integrative Exercise** Put each of the following statements into standard form as a categorical proposition. Then devise a valid syllogism that uses the statement as a premise.

*1. "No Civil War picture ever made a nickel." [Irving Thalberg to Louis B. Mayer, advising him not to make *Gone with the Wind*. Otto Friedrich, *City of Nets*.]

2. "He that speaks much, is much mistaken." [Benjamin Franklin, *Poor Richard's Almanac*]

3. "Not all who have vices are contemptible." [La Rochefoucauld, *Maxims*]

*4. "Some books are undeservedly forgotten; none are undeservedly remembered." [W. H. Auden, *Apothegms*] (Find two syllogisms, one for each part of the sentence.)

V. For each mood and figure, write out the syllogism in standard form using S, M, and P as terms. Then devise a syllogism with that form. Try to find terms for S, P, and M that give you a plausible argument.

✳1. AAA-1
  2. AEE-2
  3. IEO-3

✳4. EAE-1
  5. EIO-3

VI. [Integrative Exercise] Put each of the propositions below into standard form, and identify the subject and predicate terms. Then use either a genus or a species of the subject as the middle term in a syllogism that supports the given proposition as a conclusion. For example, if the given proposition is "Bears are warm-blooded," the subject term is "bears," a possible genus is "mammals," and a possible syllogism using that genus as a middle term is:

> All **mammals** are warm-blooded.
> All bears are **mammals**.
> _____
> All bears are warm-blooded.

✳1. Some bonds yield tax-free interest.

  2. Trees need water.

  3. Women have rights to life, liberty, and the pursuit of happiness.

✳4. Some blue-collar workers are highly paid.

  5. Electrons do not travel faster than the speed of light.

  6. No car trip is free of the risk of an accident.

✳7. Some relationships are lifelong.

  8. Some methods of doing research are not ethical.

VII. [Integrative Exercise] Put each of the following syllogisms into standard form, filling in the missing premise or conclusion if it is an enthymeme; identify mood and figure; and determine whether it is valid or invalid.

✳1. "Thus, a minimum wage is nothing more than a price control. Price controls have always been disastrous, so a minimum wage must be harmful." [Stephan Kinsella, "Simple Economics Goes Against It," _Morning Advocate_]

  2. "Dear Connoisseur:
"Like me, you probably first came across the 'syllogism' in an introductory course on logic.
"Let me share with you one of our favorites:
"'You appreciate the finer things in life. The Glenlivet is one of the finer things. Therefore, you will appreciate The Glenlivet.'"
[Glenlivet advertisement]

  3. "First, there is an argument from the universality of physical laws. It runs: All material systems are governed by the laws of physics. All living systems are material. Therefore, all living systems are governed by the laws of physics." [Marjorie Grene, "Reducibility: Another Side Issue?" in _Interpretations of Life and Mind_]

✳4. "That man must be tremendously ignorant: he answers every question that is put to him." [Voltaire, _Dictionnaire Philosophique_]

  5. "A member of a free democracy is, in a sense, a sovereign. He has no superior." [William Graham Sumner, _What the Social Classes Owe to Each Other_]

  6. "I want to believe I'm losing my mind. But I can't believe it. Then I say that people who are crazy can never believe they are, and that means I . . . am." [John D. MacDonald, _The Turquoise Lament_]

✳7. "He who would rejoice loudly of his victories cannot expect to thrive in the world of men, for he who rejoices over victory does so at the expense of other men." [_Tao Te Ching_]

8. "The Constitution suggests that what must be proscribed as cruel [punishment] is (a) a particularly painful way of inflicting death, or (b) a particularly undeserved death; and the death penalty, as such, offends neither of these criteria and cannot therefore be regarded as objectively 'cruel.'" [William F. Buckley, "Capital Punishment," in *Execution Eve and Other Contemporary Ballads*]

9. "Because no man by merit has a right to the grace of God, I, having no merit, am entitled to it." [C. S. Lewis, *The Four Loves*]

*10. "Certainly some individuals who suffer organic abnormalities or psychoses that produce rage attacks can properly be diagnosed as insane; they do not, for one thing, revert to normalcy after a violent episode." [Carol Tavris, *Anger*]

11. "There was no wound upon the dead man's person, but the agitated expression upon his face assured me that he had foreseen his fate before it came upon him. Men who die from heart disease, or any sudden natural cause, never by any chance exhibit agitation upon their features." [Arthur Conan Doyle, *A Study in Scarlet*]

12. "My contention is that no good thing harms its owner, a thing which you won't gainsay. But wealth very often does harm its owners . . . ." [Boethius, *Consolation of Philosophy*]

*13. "Observation implies movement, that is locomotion with reference to the rigid environment, because all observers are animals and all animals are mobile." [James J. Gibson, *The Ecological Approach to Visual Perception*]

14. "Ms. Swift explained why she fights [against Apple, Spotify, and others squeezing musicians on royalties]. 'Music is art, and art is important and rare. Important, rare things are valuable. Valuable things should be paid for.'" ["In Support of Taylor Swift, Economist," *Wall Street Journal*]

15. ". . . we yield, of course, to this short syllogism. Man was created for social intercourse; but social intercourse cannot be maintained without a sense of justice; then man must have been created with a sense of justice." [Thomas Jefferson, *On Civil and Natural Rights*]

VIII. For each of the following propositions, (a) create a valid syllogism with the proposition as its conclusion; (b) create an invalid syllogism with the proposition as its conclusion; (c) create a valid syllogism with the contradictory proposition as its conclusion; and (d) create an invalid syllogism with the contradictory proposition as its conclusion.

1. All women should have careers.

2. Some lies are morally permissible.

3. Some courses should not be graded.

4. No dictatorship is truly benevolent.

5. All true art is representational.

IX. Integrative Exercise Using what you know about categorical syllogisms, particularly the rules of validity, explain why each of the following statements is true.

*1. A valid syllogism in the second figure must have a negative conclusion.

2. In a valid syllogism of the first figure, the minor premise must be affirmative.

3. In a valid syllogism of the third figure, the conclusion must be particular.

*4. No valid syllogism has two particular premises.

5. If either premise of a valid syllogism is particular, the conclusion must be particular as well.

Reasoning with Syllogisms

The categorical syllogism is a form of deductive reasoning that we use fairly often, as should be clear from all the examples we considered in the previous chapter. But those examples were carefully chosen to illustrate the logical form of the syllogism, and we studied each form in isolation. It is time now to leave the laboratory, so to speak, and observe the behavior of these arguments in their natural environment: the context of everyday reasoning. In addition, not all syllogisms are categorical. There are other types of syllogism that we use frequently in everyday reasoning, and we need to understand how they work.

In the first two sections, we'll learn about noncategorical syllogisms that have disjunctive or hypothetical propositions as premises. Then, in Section 7.3, we'll learn more about how to spot the logical form—the skeleton of a syllogism—beneath the flesh it is wearing. This is similar to the process of distilling an argument, which we studied in Chapter 2, but here we'll need to incorporate what we've learned about deductive logic. In the final section, we examine deductive arguments that have more than a single step—extended arguments that involve *chains* of syllogisms.

To introduce the new forms of syllogism that we will examine in the first two sections, compare these three propositions:

> Whales are mammals.
>
> Whales are mammals or they are very large fish.
>
> If whales are mammals, then they cannot breathe under water.

The first is a categorical proposition, but the other two are not. They are compound propositions. As we learned in Chapter 1, a compound proposition combines two or more component propositions by means of a connective. Compound propositions that use the connective *or*, as in the second example, are called **disjunctive propositions**. Compound propositions that use the connective *if . . . then*, as in the third example, are called **hypothetical propositions**.

Both the second and third examples contain the first proposition as a component, but neither asserts that it is true. These are statements in which the components are expressed but *not* asserted. What the compound statement asserts is that a certain relationship

CHAPTER OUTLINE

7.1 Disjunctive Syllogisms

7.2 Hypothetical Syllogisms

7.3 Distilling Deductive Arguments

7.4 Extended Arguments

LEARNING OBJECTIVES

On successful completion of the chapter, you will be able to:

- Identify valid and invalid forms of disjunctive and hypothetical syllogisms. (7.1–7.2)
- Translate hypothetical propositions into standard form. (7.2)
- Distill disjunctive, hypothetical, and categorical arguments. (7.3)
- Analyze extended arguments containing disjunctive and hypothetical, or categorical syllogisms. (7.4)

exists between the components. The disjunctive proposition says that whales belong to one or the other of two wider classes—without saying which one. The hypothetical proposition tells us what the implication would be if whales are mammals—without actually saying that they are. When we use compound propositions in our reasoning, it is the relationship among the components that is important.

To put these propositions into standard form, therefore, we don't need to break down the component propositions into subject and predicate terms. We use single letters to represent the components, along with the connective:

Compound Proposition	Logical Form
Whales are mammals or they are very large fish.	p or q
If whales are mammals, then they cannot breathe under water.	If p, then q

Notice that we use lowercase letters to stand for the components, whereas we used uppercase letters to stand for the subject and predicate terms in categorical propositions. That is a convention logicians have adopted to make it clear whether a letter stands for a term within a proposition (uppercase letters) or for a whole component proposition (lowercase letters).

As in the case of categorical reasoning, our goal is to identify the logical *forms* of compound propositions and then to identify which propositions are *equivalent*, and which arguments are *valid*, in virtue of their logical forms. Traditional logic never developed a systematic theory of equivalence or validity for compound propositions; for a systematic theory, we must turn to modern propositional logic, the subject of Chapters 8 and 9. But there are certain forms of reasoning with disjunctive and hypothetical premises that we're going to study here because they are easily grasped and are frequently encountered in everyday thought and speech. We will see that even though these arguments use compound propositions, the corresponding syllogisms are simpler to analyze and evaluate than are categorical syllogisms.

7.1 Disjunctive Syllogisms

The components of a disjunctive proposition (p and q) are called **disjuncts**. Such a statement does not actually assert that p is true, or that q is, but it does say that one or the other (or both) of them is true. So if we know independently that one of the disjuncts is *not* true, we can infer that the other must be true. If you know that the meeting will be either in room 305 or in room 306, and you find that it is not in 305, you can infer that it is in 306.

The meeting is in room 305 or the meeting is in room 306.	p or q
The meeting is not in room 305.	Not-p
The meeting is in room 306.	q

This argument is a **disjunctive syllogism**: a deductive argument with a disjunctive premise, a premise negating one of the disjuncts, and a conclusion affirming the remaining disjunct. You can see that the argument is valid. If the premises are both true, then the conclusion must be true as well. It does not matter which disjunct we deny in the second premise. If we checked the other room first and found it empty, we could have reasoned: either *p* or *q*, but not-*q*, therefore *p*. This too is valid.

It is important to understand that *p* and not-*p* are contradictory propositions. If one is true, the other is false; they cannot both be true, nor can they both be false. Since we will be dealing with such negations frequently in this chapter, let's pause to clarify how to state them correctly.

First, if we negate a proposition that is itself a negation, the strict formulation is a double negative: not-not-*p*. In modern propositional logic (see Chapters 8 and 9), we insist on strictness. But as with numbers, two negatives make a positive. So for our purposes here, we will treat the negation of a negative proposition as affirmative. Thus:

Proposition	Negation
p	Not-*p*
It is raining.	It is not raining.
It is not snowing.	It is snowing.

Second, in compound propositions, the component propositions *p* and *q* are usually categorical. For example, in the proposition "Whales are mammals or they are very large fish," the first disjunct is implicitly about all whales; it is an A (universal affirmative) categorical proposition. Its negation is "Some whales are not mammals," not "No whales are mammals." In other words, we need to remember what we learned about contradictories versus contraries and subcontraries (see Chapter 5).

Quantity	Proposition	Negation
Universal	All whales are mammals. No whales are fish.	Some whales are not mammals. Some whales are fish.
Particular	Some mushrooms are hallucinogens. Some cats are not pets.	No mushrooms are hallucinogens. All cats are pets.
Singular	Tom is a rich man.	Tom is not a rich man.

A disjunctive syllogism, then, is a deductive argument with a disjunctive premise, a premise negating one of the disjuncts, and a conclusion affirming the remaining disjunct. Is it equally valid to argue by *affirming* a disjunct?

p or *q*

p

Not-*q*

No. Affirming a disjunct is not a valid form of inference. The reason is that a disjunctive statement, in claiming that at least one of the disjuncts is true, does not rule out the possibility that they are both true. The truth of one does not entitle us to deny the other. Of course, we do sometimes use "or" in what is called the *exclusive* sense to mean "*p* or *q* but not both," as in "Tom is either asleep or reading." We also use "or" in the *inclusive* sense to mean "*p* or *q* or both," as in "She's either tired or confused." An argument that denies a disjunct is valid in either case, but when an argument that affirms a disjunct seems valid, it is because of the specific content of the disjunctive premise, not the logical form of the argument. Consider the arguments:

Argument 1	Argument 2
Tom is asleep or Tom is reading.	The meeting is in room 305 or the meeting
Tom is asleep.	is in room 306.
Tom is not reading.	The meeting is in room 305.
	The meeting is not in room 306.

In argument 1, we know that a person cannot be asleep and reading at the same time. That's a fact about the nature of sleep. In argument 2, we know that meetings are normally held in a single place where people can see and hear each other, so this meeting is not in both rooms. That's a fact about human conventions. In both cases, what makes the argument seem valid is a fact that is not actually stated and is not a matter of logical form. For logical purposes, therefore, we always assume that "or" is used inclusively, so that affirming a disjunct is fallacious.

In cases where such an argument seems valid intuitively, it is easy to translate the argument into a different form that makes the validity clear. Suppose someone has just given birth. We know the child is either a boy or a girl. If we find out that it is a girl, can we infer that it is not a boy? Of course we can. But that's because we know that male and female are mutually exclusive possibilities. A child cannot be both a boy and a girl—which means it is either not a girl or not a boy. That's a disjunctive proposition, and it is the real premise at work in our inference:

The child is not a girl or the child is not a boy.	*p* or *q*
The child is a girl.	Not-*p*
The child is not a boy.	*q*

This is a case of denying a disjunct and therefore is valid.

There's another lesson to be drawn from this example. When we say that a child cannot be both a boy and a girl, the statement has the logical form:

Not-(*p* and *q*)

which is always equivalent to:

Not-*p* or not-*q*

A proposition of the form *p and q* is true if and only if both components are true. So if we *deny* such a proposition, then we are saying that at least one component must be false. There's an old saying that "You can't have your cake and eat it, too." What this means is that you can keep the cake (i.e., have it on hand) only if you don't eat it, but that if you eat the cake, you no longer have it. Thus the proverb can be put into standard disjunctive form as: "Either you don't have the cake or you don't eat it."

In ordinary reasoning, disjunctive syllogisms often have more than two disjuncts. It is simpler to deal just with two, but this is a game that any number can play. Suppose we have four: We know that either p or q or r or s. Then we could reason:

p or (q or r or s)
Not-p
q or r or s
    q or (r or s)
    Not-q
    r or s
        r or s
        Not-r
        s

As long as we eliminate all the disjuncts but one, that one must be true—assuming, of course, that the disjunctive premise is true to begin with.

We use the disjunctive syllogism when we know that there is a certain range of possibilities and we want to find out which one is actual. If we want to know who committed a crime, for example, we might start out with a list of suspects and then cross them off the list one by one, as we acquired more evidence, until we were left with just one. As Sherlock Holmes said, when you have eliminated the impossible, what is left, however improbable, must be true. Again, in making a personal decision, we might start with a set of alternatives and then, by a process of elimination, narrow the set down to one. We also use disjunctive reasoning when we try to explain something: a person's behavior, a rise in the stock market, or a rise or fall in average temperatures. Various theories are proposed, and the process of establishing one particular theory usually involves the use of evidence to rule out its rivals.

It is quite common with the disjunctive syllogism, as with the categorical, to leave one of the premises unstated. If you are looking for a book and decide that it must be

---

APPLY Solve a Mystery . . .

. . . or at least write one. Arthur Conan Doyle's Sherlock Holmes denies the disjunct when he says, "Eliminate all other factors, and the one which remains must be the truth." Holmes is probably more closely associated with deductive reasoning than any other fictional detective. But he's not alone. From G. K. Chesterton's Father Brown to his spiritual successor Father Dowling (created by philosopher Ralph McInerny), other sleuths have illustrated the problem-solving potential of logic. Each has his own individual talents: Holmes has keen powers of observation;

Brown has astute understanding of human psychology; and Dowling has superior knowledge of theology and philosophy. But their shared respect for logic and rationality is evident. Consider Father Brown's declaration when he unmasks an imposter, "As a matter of fact, another part of my trade, too, made me sure you weren't a priest. . . . You attacked reason. . . . It's bad theology." Want to create the next Sam Spade or Adrian Monk? If you're an aspiring writer—at least of mysteries—master the art of reasoning as well as the elements of writing.

at the library because it isn't in your bag, you are using a disjunctive syllogism with an implicit premise:

(Either my book is in my bag or I left it in the library.)
My book is not in my bag.
_____
I left it in the library.

It is usually the disjunctive premise, as in this example, that is left implicit. Indeed, the fallacy of false dichotomy is often committed because we rely implicitly on a disjunctive premise that does not identify all the possible alternatives. In the argument above, for example, it might occur to you, once you have identified the implicit assumption, that there are other places you might have left the book.

EXERCISE 7.1

Put each of the following disjunctive syllogisms into standard form, identify the disjuncts and any implicit elements, and determine whether the syllogism is valid.

✳1. Either I'm hearing things or someone is out in the hall singing "Jingle Bells." I know I'm not hearing things. So there's someone out there singing.

2. Either the circuit is broken or the light bulb is dead. But I know the bulb isn't dead, so the circuit must be broken.

3. I have to get the book here in town or else in New York next weekend. But I can't get it here; therefore I will have to get it in New York.

✳4. There are only two possible responses to this threat: We send in the troops or we negotiate. Negotiation is out of the question, so we must send in the troops.

5. I can't both go to the movies with you tonight and study for the exam, and I have to study for the exam. So I can't go.

6. We need Brody or Emily to play for the Red Team. Brody can't play, so Emily will.

✳7. Either marriage is sacrosanct or gay people can get married. Gay people can get married, so marriage isn't sacrosanct.

8. Jackson must be a liberal because he certainly isn't a conservative.

9. According to the union contract, either we have to close the plant on Labor Day or we have to pay the workers twice the regular wage. But we have too much work to close the plant, so we'll have to pay the workers double time.

✳10. Either Paul will win this case or he won't be promoted to partner. He wasn't promoted to partner, so he must have lost the case.

11. Either human beings have free will or they are not responsible for their actions. But they are responsible, so they do have free will.

12. NASA and the private sector are the only viable options for space travel. NASA has shown that it's capable of piloting missions into space, so it looks like the commercial firms are out.

✳13. Kids shouldn't ever have access to guns. So if we're choosing between kids being around guns or kids being able to play violent video games, then I guess they can play all the violent games they want.

14. Either I'm out of money or I made a mistake in my checkbook. I'm sure I made a mistake, though, so I'm not out of money.

15. I only have two hands: I can't make dinner and take out the trash, too.

Since I'm making dinner, I am not going to take out the trash.

✳16. I only have two alternatives: I work hard or I fail this course. But I am working hard, so I won't fail.

17. Some economists believe that we can't have both low inflation and low unemployment. If that assumption is true, inflation must be low, because unemployment is high.

7.2 Hypothetical Syllogisms

Hypothetical propositions have the form "If *p*, then *q*," and they serve as premises in several types of inference that we use quite often. In this section, we look first at the structure of hypothetical propositions and some of the differing ways they can be expressed in language. We will then turn to the inferences—the forms of hypothetical syllogism—and distinguish the valid ones from the invalid.

7.2A Hypothetical Propositions

Like a disjunctive proposition, a hypothetical proposition has two components that we represent with lowercase letters. But in this case they are not called disjuncts. The "if" component is called the **antecedent** and the "then" component is the **consequent**. Thus, in this statement:

If it rains, then the graduation will be held in the gym.

the antecedent is "it rains" and the consequent is "the graduation will be held in the gym." In a hypothetical proposition, we are not actually asserting the truth of the antecedent or the consequent. We are saying that the truth of the first would be sufficient to guarantee the truth of the second. Until we know that it actually is raining, the possibility that the graduation will be held in the gym is merely hypothetical. It is not something we can assert categorically.

Hypothetical propositions are used pervasively in ordinary speech to identify relationships of dependence among facts, events, or possibilities. The statement "If you leave your bike out in the rain, it will rust" identifies the consequence of a certain action. The statement "If it's four o'clock, then I'm late for class" says that the existence of one fact ("It's four o'clock") implies the existence of another ("I'm late"). The statement "If I want to pass the course, then I need to study" expresses the recognition that achieving a goal ("I will pass the course") depends on a certain means ("I will study").

A hypothetical proposition is similar to an A categorical proposition. We have seen that the proposition "All *S* are *P*" is not equivalent to its converse, "All *P* are *S*," so we cannot infer one from the other. In the same way, "If p, then q" is not equivalent to "if q, then p." Consider the statements:

> If I were president of the United States, I would be a politican.

> If I were a politician, I would be president of the United States.

These are clearly not equivalent; the first is true by definition (anyone who holds elective office must be a politician), whereas the second is dubious to say the least.

Another point of similarity between A categorical propositions and hypothetical propositions is that both have a valid contrapositive. "All S are P" is equivalent to "All non-P are non-S." In the same way, "if p, then q" is equivalent to "if not-q, then not-p." For example:

> If it rained last night, then the ground is wet this morning.

> If the ground is not wet this morning, then it did not rain last night.

These propositions are clearly equivalent, and it's easy to see why the equivalence holds as a general rule. A hypothetical proposition says that the truth of p is sufficient to guarantee the truth of q. If that's the case, then the only way q could fail to be true is for p to be false as well.

Hypothetical propositions can be expressed in a variety of nonstandard forms. The easiest of the nonstandard cases to translate occurs when the consequent is stated first, the antecedent second, as in:

> I'll stay home tomorrow if I still feel sick.

The component proposition "I still feel sick" is the antecedent, even though it comes second, because it is the "if" component. Thus, in standard form the proposition is: "If I still feel sick, then I will stay home tomorrow." In general "p if q" should be translated "If q, then p."

What about a statement with the form "p only if q," such as:

> I'll stay home tomorrow only if I'm sick.

Does this say the same thing as the preceding statement? Is it saying that if I am sick I will stay home tomorrow? No—it is saying that if I am *not* sick, then I will *not* stay home. Being sick is the only thing that would keep me home. Think of it as a promise I've made to you. Now suppose I am sick, but I show up anyway. Have I broken my promise? No—but I would break the promise if I stayed home and was not sick. Thus the statement "p only if q" can be translated in either of two equivalent ways:

$$p \text{ only if } q \quad \begin{matrix} \text{If not-}q\text{, then not-}p \\ \text{If } p\text{, then } q \end{matrix}$$

One translation may sound more natural than the other in certain contexts. But since they are contrapositives, they are logically equivalent. Note also that "If p, then q" is the converse of "I'll stay home tomorrow if I still feel sick." We have already seen that a hypothetical proposition is not equivalent to its converse.

When we want to claim that the truth of either p or q implies the truth of the other, we combine the preceding forms: p if and only if q. As the word "and" suggests, we are making two statements:

SOLVE Putting Hypothetical Propositions into Standard Form

The standard form of hypothetical propositions is:

    If [antecedent], then [consequent].

    The antecedent and consequent are component propositions that we represent by lowercase letters: p, q, r, . . . , not-p, not-q, not-r, ...

    Nonstandard hypothetical propositions can be put into standard form according to the following equivalences:

Nonstandard Form	Standard Form
p if q	If q, then p
p only if q	If p, then q
p if and only if q	If q, then p If p, then q
p unless q	If not-p, then q
Without X, q	If X does not exist (occur), then q

    p if q $\longrightarrow$ if q then p

and

    p only if q $\longrightarrow$ if p then q

The analysis on the right makes it clear that in the "if and only if" construction, both p and q serve as antecedents, and both also serve as consequents. But that's because we have two statements, not one.

    Another nonstandard hypothetical statement has the form "p unless q." For example, "The plant will die unless you water it." This means the plant will die if you do not water it: "Unless" means "if not." Thus the following three propositions are equivalent:

    p unless q

    p if not-q

    If not-q, then p

Does "p unless q" also imply "if q, then not-p"? Are we also saying that if you do water it, the plant will not die? No—in some contexts it might be assumed that we are also saying this, but it is not asserted by the original statement. Once again, think of the statement as a promise I have made to you. If you water the plant and it still dies, I haven't broken my promise, strictly speaking; I didn't promise that water alone would keep the plant alive, only that the absence of water would kill it. Consequently, "p unless q" is exactly equivalent to "if not-q, then p" and should be translated that way.

    Finally, consider a statement like the following:

    Without distribution requirements, most students would take too narrow a range of courses.

Here we do not have two component propositions: The phrase beginning "without" does not contain a whole statement. Yet it is easy to turn that phrase into a whole statement—"distribution requirements do not exist"—which can be made the antecedent in a standard-form hypothetical statement:

> If distribution requirements did not exist, then most students would take too narrow a range of courses.

In general, "Without X, q" can be translated "If X does not exist (or occur), then q."

Of course there are other nonstandard ways of expressing disjunctive and hypothetical propositions. Our language is far too rich and subtle for us to capture every possibility in a small set of rules. But the rules we've just learned will allow us to put a great many statements occurring in everyday speech into standard form.

EXERCISE 7.2A

Identify the antecedent and consequent in each of the following statements, then put the statement into standard form (if it is not in standard form already).

*1. If you miss your first serve in tennis, then you get a second try.

2. You lose the point if you miss the second try.

3. If a categorical syllogism has two negative premises, then it is not valid.

*4. A married couple filing a joint return may deduct certain child-care expenses if they itemize their deductions.

5. People will want to protect animals in nature only if they can form a connection to animals at the zoo.

6. Prices rise if demand increases.

*7. Without the presence of antibodies in the patient, doctors cannot detect a virus.

8. Average levels of education in Ethiopian villages will increase if and only if the people have access to clean water.

9. If you don't start saving now, then you will not be able to buy a car when you're 16.

*10. Without a cooling mechanism, a car's engine would rapidly overheat.

11. I'll call you unless you call me first.

12. You may not take this course unless you have satisfied the prerequisites.

*13. Without an understanding of deductive validity, we would probably commit fallacies in our reasoning.

14. If we don't punish the use of cell phones with fines and tickets, then drivers won't pay attention to simple safety reminders.

15. I will go to the party only if you go.

*16. I'll only go out with you tonight if you promise not to wear your Nehru jacket.

17. The subject term of a categorical proposition is distributed if and only if the proposition is universal.

18. We will lower the occurrence of STDs in teenagers if and only if we teach them about using condoms.

*19. People will not buy a product unless it is safe.

20. We cannot change the fashion industry's presentation of impossibly thin bodies unless consumers do not value thinness.

7.2B Forms of Hypothetical Syllogism

Now that we understand the logical form of hypothetical propositions, let us turn to the inferences we can make with them. The first is the **pure hypothetical syllogism**, in which the conclusion and both of the premises are hypothetical propositions. For example:

Logical Form	Example
If *p*, then *q*	If my wallet is not in my apartment, then I lost it.
If *q*, then *r*	If I lost my wallet, then I will have to cancel my credit cards.
If *p*, then *r*	If my wallet is not in my apartment, then I will have to cancel my credit cards.

Notice that the component proposition *q*—in our example, "I lost my wallet"—plays the same role as the middle term in a categorical syllogism. It serves to link the other components, *p* and *r*, which appear together in the conclusion. Any argument with the same logical form is valid.

It's essential to the validity of the pure hypothetical syllogism that the component occurring in both premises be the consequent in one premise and the antecedent in the other. If it is the antecedent in both premises, or the consequent in both, the conclusion will not follow. Thus each of the following argument forms is invalid:

Logical Form	Example
If *q*, then *p*	If I lost my wallet, then it is not in my apartment.
If *q*, then *r*	If I lost my wallet, then I will have to cancel my credit cards.
If *p*, then *r*	If my wallet is not in my apartment, then I will have to cancel my credit cards.

Suppose you are away from your apartment but your wallet is in your pocket or purse. The conclusion is false, but both premises could be still be true, which could not be the case if the argument were valid. The same applies if *q* occurs in the consequent of both premises:

Logical Form	Example
If *p*, then *q*	If the wind blows hard, then my hair will get mussed.
If *r*, then *q*	If Dad pats my head, then my hair will get mussed.
If *p*, then *r*	If the wind blows hard, then Dad pats my head.

We often use pure hypothetical syllogisms in describing chains of events in which each event causes the next. For example, if we asked an economist how government deficits are related to inflation, he might say: "If the government runs a deficit, then the Federal Reserve Bank creates more money; if the Federal Reserve Bank creates more money, prices will eventually rise; so if the government runs a deficit, prices will eventually rise." We also use these syllogisms in thinking about what implication a state of affairs might have for our lives, as in the example above; and in planning strategies to achieve our goals in games or in real life. A chess player, for example, might reason: "If I move my queen here, he will move his rook there. But if he moves his rook there, I will have to sacrifice a pawn. So if I move my queen there, I will have to sacrifice a pawn."

In a pure hypothetical syllogism, both premises are hypothetical, and so is the conclusion. At no point do we assert that p, q, or r is actually the case. Our reasoning is, so to speak, purely hypothetical. But there is another sort of inference that allows us to derive a nonhypothetical conclusion:

If p, then q	If you play with fire, you will get burned.
p	You played with fire.
q	You got burned.

In an argument of this form, the second premise is categorical; it affirms the antecedent of the hypothetical premise. This entitles us to infer the consequent, which is also categorical. Such inferences are called **mixed hypothetical syllogisms**.

Any argument of this form is valid because it merely unfolds what is implicit in the meaning of the hypothetical premise. That premise says that the truth of p would be sufficient for the truth of q. If we then assume that p is true, we may conclude that q is true as well. We can also work this in the opposite direction. If we assume that q is false, we can infer that p is false—for if p were not false (i.e., if it were true), then q could not have been false either. Thus the following mixed hypothetical syllogism is valid:

If p, then q	If God had wanted us to fly, He would have given us wings.
Not-q	He has not given us wings.
Not-p	He did not want us to fly.

In this case, we denied the consequent, and that allowed us to deny the antecedent. Once again, the conclusion is a categorical proposition.

Thus there are two valid mixed hypothetical syllogisms. The medieval logicians called the first one *modus ponens*: the method of **affirming the antecedent**. They called the second one *modus tollens*: the method of **denying the consequent**. Both are valid for the same reason: They spell out the implications of the hypothetical premise. Indeed, by using contraposition, we can transform any *modus tollens* argument into *modus ponens*:

Modus tollens (denying the consequent)		*Modus ponens* (affirming the antecedent)
If p, then q	$\longleftarrow$ contrapositive $\longrightarrow$	If not-q, then not-p
Not-q		Not-q
Not-p		Not-p

Merely by taking the contrapositive of the hypothetical premise, but leaving everything else the same, we have changed the *modus tollens* argument on the left into the *modus ponens* argument on the right.

There are two other possible forms of mixed hypothetical syllogism: **denying the antecedent** and **affirming the consequent**. Both of them are invalid:

Denying	If *p*, then *q*	If my car is out of gas, it will stop running.
the	Not-*p*	My car is not out of gas.
antecedent	Not-*q*	It will not stop running.
Affirming	If *p*, then *q*	If my car is out of gas, it will stop running.
the	*q*	My car stopped running.
consequent	*p*	It is out of gas.

In each case, the hypothetical premise says that being out of gas is sufficient to make my car stop running. Both arguments assume, however, that being out of gas is the *only* thing that can do so. That is not true, of course, and it is not implied by the hypothetical premise. Suppose the tank is full but the battery is dead. That would make the premises of both arguments true, but the conclusion in each case would be false. A valid deductive argument cannot have true premises and a false conclusion.

There are circumstances in which these inferences may *seem* valid. Suppose someone says "If I get a C on the next exam, then I'll pass the course." Someone else who is skeptical of the first person's chances might reason:

> If he gets a C on the exam, he will pass the course.
> But he won't get a C.
> So he won't pass.

This is a case of denying the antecedent, and it is invalid as stated. What makes it seem valid is the background knowledge that if he *does not* get a C, he will not pass. If we used this premise, then the argument would be a case of affirming the antecedent, which is valid. But this premise is not contained in or implied by the one that was actually asserted; it is extra information.

We have now covered all the possibilities for mixed hypothetical syllogisms. There are two valid forms and two invalid ones. We don't need a separate set of rules for testing validity; we just need to remember these forms, which are summarized in the Review box.

REVIEW Mixed Forms of Hypothetical Syllogisms

Valid		**Invalid**	
Affirming the antecedent (*modus ponens*)	If *p*, then *q* *p* *q*	Affirming the consequent	If *p*, then *q* *q* *p*
Denying the consequent (*modus tollens*)	If *p*, then *q* Not-*q* Not-*p*	Denying the antecedent	If *p*, then *q* Not-*p* Not-*q*

Like the other types of syllogism, a hypothetical syllogism may leave a premise unstated. Suppose you are indoors and cannot see the sky, but you infer that the sun isn't shining because there are no shadows on the ground outside. Your reasoning contains an implicit hypothetical premise:

> (If the sun were shining, there would be shadows.)
> <u>There are no shadows.</u>
> The sun is not shining.

In other cases, both premises are given but the conclusion is left implicit; this is more common with the hypothetical than with other syllogisms. If you can find an example of this, you have grasped the material in this section—and we're sure you *can* find an example.

EXERCISE 7.2B

I. For each of the following standard form syllogisms, identify its type and determine whether the syllogism is valid.

＊1. If you wanted to marry him, then you wouldn't be running around with other men.
<u>You are running around with other men.</u>
You do not want to marry him.

2. If I did not hurry, then I would be late.
<u>I hurried.</u>
I was not late.

3. If we do not complete the project on schedule, then we will pay a penalty.
<u>If we pay a penalty, then the project will not be profitable.</u>
If we do not complete the project on schedule, then the project will not be profitable.

＊4. If Frank was jealous of Cindy, then he would follow her around with a sour expression.
<u>Frank followed Cindy around with a sour expression.</u>
Frank is jealous of Cindy.

5. If the lights are still working, then the battery is not dead.
<u>The lights are still working.</u>
The battery is not dead.

6. If Rome had enlisted the efforts of all citizens, it could have repelled invaders.
<u>Rome did not enlist the efforts of all its citizens.</u>
It could not resist invasion.

II. | Integrative Exercise | Put each of the following hypothetical syllogisms into standard form, identify any implicit premise or conclusion, identify what type of hypothetical syllogism it is, and determine whether the syllogism is valid.

＊1. If he had even mentioned her name, I would have hit him. But he didn't, so I didn't.

2. If children are deprived of affection as infants, they will learn not to expect it; and if they learn not to expect it, they won't seek it out later in life. So if children are deprived of affection early in life, they won't look for it later on.

3. If I take the new job, I'll have a longer commute, and if I have a longer commute, I will need a new car. So I'll need a new car if I take the new job.

*4. "There's milk in the refrigerator if you want some."
"But I don't want any, Mom."
"Then there isn't any milk there, wise guy."

5. If you leave the milk out of the refrigerator, it will sour. The milk soured, so you must have left it out.

6. Jan made it to her appointment, if the train was running on time. The train was running on time, so Jan made it to her appointment.

*7. If salmon reliably return from the ocean to the streams in which they were spawned—and they do—then they must have some means of detecting subtle differences in the chemical composition of the water of those streams at the point where they flow into the ocean.

8. If I wait until Wednesday to take my suit to the cleaners, it will not be ready until Saturday. If so, I will not be able to wear it to the wedding on Thursday. So if I wait until Wednesday to take the suit to the cleaners, I will not be able to wear it to the wedding.

9. If the time it takes Mercury to rotate around its axis (its period of rotation) is the same as the time it takes to revolve once around the Sun (its period of revolution), it always presents the same side to the Sun. And if it always presents the same side to the Sun, then that's the only side we can see. So if Mercury's period of rotation equals its period of revolution, we can see only one side.

*10. If you install an electrical outlet with a grounding wire, you reduce the risk of shorting the circuit. You also comply with the building code. In other words, if you comply with the building code, you reduce the risk of shorting the circuit.

11. Unless we reduce the interest rate by 2%, it doesn't make sense to refinance the mortgage, and there's no way we're going to get a rate that is lower by that much.

12. If the plan to build grocery stores in low-income areas is successful, then deaths from heart disease will decrease. Deaths from heart disease have decreased, so the plan to build grocery stores was successful.

*13. Anarchy would be a fine and beautiful system for society to adopt—if men were angels. Alas, they are not.

14. If someone had been snooping around here last night, there would be footprints, right? Well there are. So someone was snooping around here last night.

15. If God had wanted people to fly, He would not have given us Buicks. But He has given us Buicks; therefore . . .

*16. Our visual system must have some way of detecting edges. If we did not have such a capacity, we would not perceive objects.

17. Unless we adopt this proposal, the company will go bankrupt. So we must adopt the proposal.

18. You won't be able to master logic unless you are serious about it. But if you have read this far, you

must be serious. So if you have read this far, you will be able to master logic.

∗19. If the errors and distortions in television news were not the result of political bias, but merely sloppy reporting, they would be randomly distributed across the political spectrum. But in fact they are all slanted in a particular direction.

20. If beauty pageants for young girls allow tight outfits, then this encourages girls to be sexual at too young an age. If pageants encourage girls to be sexual at too young an age, the girls who participate will develop low self-esteem. So if the girls who participate in beauty pageants develop low self-esteem, the beauty pageants allowed tight outfits.

7.3 Distilling Deductive Arguments

Like any other language, English offers an endless variety of ways to express our thoughts. By choosing words carefully, we can capture subtle shades of meaning that do not affect the logic of an argument but are important in other ways. By varying the grammatical structure of our sentences, we can focus attention on different parts of the same argument. These resources of our language often enable us to convey our reasoning more powerfully—and sometimes more clearly—than if we put it into standard form. But those same resources can make it difficult to evaluate the validity of an argument, and they can be used to disguise poor reasoning. To analyze and evaluate a deductive argument, therefore, we need to distill the logical form of the argument from the words used to express it. Distilling the logical form requires that we identify what *kind* of syllogism it is—disjunctive, hypothetical, or categorical. And, in the case of categorical syllogisms, it requires that we identify the *quantity* of the premises and conclusion: universal or particular. In this section, we discuss the challenges you may face in these tasks.

7.3A Identifying the Form of a Syllogism

The syllogisms we encounter in everyday thought and speech do not wear labels identifying themselves as disjunctive, hypothetical, or categorical. But we need to know this in order to know which standard form is appropriate. To distinguish among the types of syllogism, we rely on two basic criteria. We use *linguistic* clues: connectives like "if . . . then" and "either . . . or," quantifiers like "all" and "some," and so on. And we look at the *substance* of the argument, its content. What is it about? What kinds of facts does it use as premises? What kind of conclusion is it trying to establish?

To see how this works, let's begin with the disjunctive syllogism, which is the easiest to spot. The abstract logical form of this syllogism, as we saw, is:

p or *q*

Not-*p*

q

If the disjunctive premise in such an argument is stated explicitly, it is easy to iden-tify. We have seen that there are just a few nonstandard ways in which to express a dis-junctive proposition. If the disjunctive premise is not stated explicitly, there's another linguistic feature to look for. A disjunctive syllogism usually has a negative premise and a positive conclusion. So we can look for the pattern "not-*p*, therefore *q*." In a mixed hypothetical syllogism, by contrast, the second premise and the conclusion are usually either both positive or both negative. Suppose, for example, that you are driving on a highway at night and see a vehicle with a single light approaching. Here are two deduc-tive inferences you might make:

> I don't hear engine noise from the vehicle, so it is not a motorcycle.

> The vehicle is not a motorcycle, so it must be a car with a headlight missing.

In the first, both the stated premise and the conclusion are negative, whereas the sec-ond has a negative premise but a positive conclusion. That's an indication that the first inference is a mixed hypothetical syllogism, whereas the second is a disjunctive syllo-gism, and we would fill in the implicit premises accordingly:

(If the vehicle were a motorcycle, I would hear engine noise from the vehicle.)	If *p*, then *q*
I don't hear engine noise from the vehicle.	Not-*q*
The vehicle is not a motorcycle.	Not-*p*
(The vehicle is either a motorcycle or a car with a headlight missing.)	*p* or *q*
The vehicle is not a motorcycle.	Not-*p*
The vehicle is a car with a headlight missing.	*q*

Hypothetical and categorical syllogisms come in a greater variety of nonstandard forms, but the same kinds of criteria will help distinguish between them. The hypo-thetical syllogism is used primarily to deal with relationships of dependence among facts, events, and possibilities. We typically use it in reasoning about cause and effect or means and ends. The categorical syllogism is used primarily to deal with relation-ships among classes of things. We typically use it in applying a general rule to a specific instance and in connection with genus–species hierarchies.

Corresponding to that substantive distinction is a linguistic one: the pattern of rep-etition in the argument. In a hypothetical syllogism, *propositions* are repeated as units, as wholes: *p*, *q*, not-*p*, not-*q*. In a categorical syllogism, in contrast, the *terms—S, P,* and *M*—are repeated.

Suppose a parent says to a teenager:

> You can go to Zelda's party as long as you're home by midnight. And you under-stand—right?—that to get home by then, you'll have to catch the 11:15 bus from Glendale.

The parent is saying that going to the party depends on the child's being home at a certain time, which in turns depends on catching a certain bus. The obvious conclusion to be drawn is that the child can go to the party only if he or she agrees to catch the bus home. Since we are dealing here with relationships among actions, we might expect that the inference is a hypothetical syllogism. But what kind of hypothetical syllogism? The parent's instruction does not contain any of the forms of the *if–then* connective we have studied. In the first sentence, what connects the component propositions *p* ("You can go to Zelda's party") and *q* ("You are home by midnight") is the expression *as long as*. This is clearly equivalent to *only if*, and we have seen that *p only if q* is equivalent to *if p then q*. In the same way, the second sentence asserts that *q* ("You are home by midnight") *only if r* ("You catch the 11:15 bus"). So we would put the inference into standard form as a pure hypothetical syllogism with an implicit conclusion:

> If you go to Zelda's party, then you will be home by midnight.
> <u>If you will be home by midnight, then you will catch the 11:15 bus.</u>
> (If you go to Zelda's party, then you will catch the 11:15 bus.)

By contrast, consider an argument that you might hear in a courtroom:

> Some of the witnesses who have testified so far on behalf of the accused cannot be considered reliable—not because they are dishonest, but because reliability in a matter as complex as this requires a level of training and experience that some of the witnesses do not possess.

No proposition is repeated in this argument, but there is a repetition of the terms "witnesses" and "reliable [people]."

This argument also contains a second linguistic mark of a categorical syllogism: the explicit use of a quantifier, "some." As we have seen, the quantity of a proposition is an essential element in a categorical syllogism, but it does not play an essential role in a hypothetical syllogism. This is not a criterion that works in every case. For one thing, the quantifier in a categorical proposition may be implicit (e.g., "Whales are mammals"). In addition, a hypothetical proposition has categorical components, and those components may contain explicit quantifiers (e.g., "if all whales are mammals, then they cannot breathe under water"). But a categorical syllogism is more likely to mention and stress the quantity of its premises than is a hypothetical syllogism.

In order to put a categorical syllogism into standard form, it is best to begin with statements that contain an explicit quantifier. Thus, in our example, the first part of the sentence, which is the conclusion, is the easiest to put into standard form: "*Some* of the witnesses are not reliable." A quantifier also appears in the last clause, which tells us that *some* of the witnesses do not possess an adequate level of training and experience. In standard form:

> (?)
> Some witnesses are people who do not possess an adequate level of training and
> <u>experience.</u>
> Some witnesses are not reliable people.

The remaining part of the sentence—"reliability in a matter as complex as this requires a [an adequate] level of training and experience"—must be the major premise. This statement contains no quantifier. And it is a statement about attributes—reliability, training, and experience—whereas the minor premise and conclusion are about classes of people. But if attribute A (reliability) depends on attribute B (training and experience), then all people who have A must have B. So the major premise can be formulated:

> All reliable people are people who possess an adequate level of training and experience.

In the same way, a statement to the effect that attribute A is incompatible with attribute B can be translated as a universal negative proposition: No thing with A is a thing with B. Thus the statement "Good teaching is incompatible with ideological indoctrination" might be recast as "No good teacher engages in ideological indoctrination."

When you distill an argument with a hypothetical premise, you may need to restate that premise as a categorical statement before you can put the argument into standard form. Consider the following argument:

> If a dog's tail is between its legs, it is fearful. Well, look at Spot. He must be scared of something.

We might try to put the argument into standard form as a mixed hypothetical syllogism—*modus ponens*, or affirming the antecedent:

If *p*, then *q*	If a dog's tail is between its legs, then it is fearful.
p	(Spot's tail is between his legs.)
q	Spot is fearful.

In order to connect the hypothetical statement with the conclusion, we filled in an implicit premise that Spot's tail is between his legs. But that premise will not actually make the connection. In a *modus ponens* syllogism, the categorical premise *p* must be the same as the antecedent of the hypothetical premise. In this case, the categorical premise is about Spot, while the hypothetical premise is about dogs in general. In making the argument about Spot, we are applying a generalization about the behavior of dogs to the case of a particular dog. To capture the logic of the argument, we should recast it as a categorical syllogism:

> All dogs who have their tails between their legs are fearful.
> (Spot is a dog who has his tail between his legs.)
> Spot is fearful.

SOLVE Identifying the Form of a Syllogism

The following strategies are useful for identifying the form of a syllogism:

1. If any of the statements in the argument is compound, try to cast the argument as a disjunctive or hypothetical syllogism.

2. Look at the patterns of repetition. If terms are repeated, the argument is likely to be a categorical syllogism; if propositions are repeated, it is likely to be a disjunctive or hypothetical syllogism.

3. Look for the presence of explicit connectives such as "or" and "if."

4. Look for the presence of explicit quantifiers such as "all" and "some," which are signs of a categorical syllogism.

5. If the argument applies a generalization to a particular case, it is likely to be a categorical syllogism.

7.3B Nonstandard Quantifiers

In distilling the logical form of an argument, the presence of quantifiers is an important clue that the argument is a categorical syllogism. But English contains many quantifiers in addition to the standard ones: "all," "some," and "no." In Chapter 5 we looked at a few nonstandard quantifiers:

	Affirmative	**Negative**
Universal	**All** whales are mammals. **A** cat is a predator. **Every** president faces unexpected challenges. **Each** item on the menu has a price. **Any** student using the gym must show an ID.	**No** dinosaur ate sushi. Not **a** creature was stirring. **None** of the telephones is working.
Particular	**Some** apples are good for baking. **A** car is parked outside. A **few** people at the conference got sick.	**Some** apples are not good for baking. **A** wire is not plugged in.

We also learned that a singular proposition, about a particular person or thing (e.g., Spot), is to be treated as universal. But there are other nonstandard ways to indicate quantity. Let's look at three:

1. "There is . . ."
2. "Always," "never," "sometimes," "occasionally"
3. "Only"

1. "There is . . ."

The subject term in English normally comes at the beginning of a sentence, before the verb. But when a sentence begins "There is . . . ," the subject is not "there." In the sentence "There is soot in the fireplace," the subject is "soot," so in standard form this would be "Some soot is (a thing that is) in the fireplace." The quantity in such sentences is usually particular, as in this example, but not always. The statement "There are no snakes in Ireland" is universal: "No snake (is a thing that) exists in Ireland." Once you have identified the subject term in such sentences, the quantity will normally be obvious.

2. "Always," "never," "sometimes," "occasionally."

These, and others like them, are words indicating quantity pertaining to time. In some cases, the reference to time is not really essential, and the statement can easily be put into standard form. "Triangles always have three sides" means "All triangles have three sides." "Syllogisms in the fourth figure are never easy to analyze" means "No syllogism in the fourth figure is easy to analyze."

In other cases, however, the reference to time is essential. Suppose it occurs to you that your friend Sally won't be coming to the party because it's –20°F outside, and she never leaves home when the temperature falls that low. What you are doing here is applying a generalization about Sally's behavior. To put the inference into standard form, we need to state the generalization in terms of classes of times or occasions:

> All times when it's extremely cold are times when Sally does not leave home.
> Now is a time when it's extremely cold.
> _____
> Now is a time when Sally won't leave home.

This formulation of the major premise is rather awkward and pedantic, but it's necessary in order to convey the logical form of the inference. Note that the minor premise and conclusion are singular propositions because the subject term, the pronoun "now," refers to a unique time. These propositions are thus to be treated as universal in quantity.

We would use the same technique for statements like "He is never willing to admit he made a mistake," or "My car sometimes won't start when it's cold." In standard form:

> No time is a time when he is willing to admit he made a mistake.

> Some times when it's cold are times when my car won't start.

And we can use the same technique for quantifiers relating to place instead of time, quantifiers like "everywhere," "anywhere," "nowhere," "somewhere." For example, the complaint "You can't find a decent meal anywhere in this town" would be put into standard form as:

> No place in this town is a place where you can find a decent meal.

In all of these examples of quantifiers for time and place, we are of course dealing with categorical propositions. In some cases, however, a statement with this kind of quantifier could equally well be treated as a hypothetical proposition. Consider the following argument:

> It rains whenever a mass of hot, humid air collides with a high-pressure mass of colder air. Since it has been hot and muggy, and a cold front is moving in from the west, I expect it will rain.

The component proposition "It rains/will rain" is contained in each sentence. And saying that a hot, humid air mass collides with a mass of colder air describes the same situation as saying that it has been hot and muggy and that a cold front is moving in. So the argument looks like a hypothetical syllogism. But the word "whenever" in the first sentence is a universal quantifier, and the statement is about a certain kind of weather condition that can occur at various times; whereas the second sentence is about the specific weather condition at the moment. This is a subtle example of the issue we discussed a few pages ago, with the argument that Spot is fearful because his tail is between his legs. A general proposition about the weather is being applied to a particular situation. So we might analyze the argument as either a categorical or a hypothetical syllogism.

Categorical	**Mixed hypothetical**
All times when a mass of hot, humid air collides with a high-pressure mass of colder air are times when it rains.	If a mass of hot, humid air collides with a mass of cold air, then it rains.
Now is a time when a mass of hot, humid air is colliding with a high-pressure mass of colder air.	A mass of hot, humid air is colliding with a mass of cold air.
Now is a time when it will rain.	It will rain.

We prefer the mixed hypothetical version of the argument. It captures the essential logic of the inference, and it is simpler. But either version would be correct.

3. "Only."

We have seen that the word "only" is used in hypothetical propositions of the form "*p* only if *q*." It is also used to indicate quantity in categorical propositions such as:

Only a fool would believe that story.

Only people with self-esteem are happy.

These propositions have the form "Only *S* are *P*." This is not the same as saying that all *S* are *P*. The first proposition does not mean that all fools believe the story: Some may never have heard it. The second proposition does not say that everyone with self-esteem is happy: There may be other factors that are also necessary for happiness. Instead, we must translate such statements in one of two equivalent ways.

In cases like the first, the most natural translation is "All people who believe that story are fools": All *P* are *S*. In cases like the second, the most natural translation is "No one who lacks self-esteem is happy": No non-*S* is *P*. These two modes of translation are logically equivalent, as we can prove by immediate inferences:

All *P* are *S*

No *P* is non-*S* (taking the obverse)
No non-*S* is *P* (taking the converse)

In distilling a categorical syllogism, however, it's a good idea to use the "All *P* are *S*" translation in all cases, even if it seems less natural. Some other proposition in the argument is likely to contain the term *S*, and this way you won't have to translate *S* into non-*S* or vice versa.

In both examples above, the word "only" occurred at the beginning of the sentence. But it can occur elsewhere in a sentence, and in those cases you need to make sure you understand what the sentence means—what statement is being made—before you try to put it into standard form. By the rules of English grammar, "only" normally modifies the word or phrase that follows it, and that makes a difference in what the sentence means. To illustrate, consider the rules that a recreational center might have for using the various swimming pools. The statements in the following table differ only in the placement of "only," but they do not have the same meanings.

Statement	Meaning	Standard Form
Only children under 5 may swim in the kiddie pools.	No one 5 or older may swim in the kiddie pools.	All people who may swim in the kiddie pools are children under 5.
Children under 5 may swim **only** in the kiddie pools.	Children under 5 may not swim anywhere else (e.g., the big pool).	All places where children under 5 may swim are the kiddie pools.
Children under 5 may **only** swim in the kiddie pools.	Children under 5 may not do anything in the kiddie pools except swim (e.g., they can't fight, eat, throw balls, . . .).	All things that children under 5 may do in the kiddie pools are (acts of) swimming.

In the topmost example, "only" occurs at the beginning, so we apply our formula: *Only S are P* becomes *All P are S*. In standard form:

All people who may swim in the kiddie pools are children under 5.

The middle example makes a very different statement because "only" modifies the pools rather than the children. To put it into standard form, we can begin by recasting the sentence so that "only" occurs at the beginning: "Only kiddie pools are places where children under 5 may swim." We can then apply our formula to put the statement into standard form:

All places where children under 5 may swim are kiddie pools.

The final example might be taken as equivalent to this; in casual speech, that would be a reasonable interpretation. Strictly speaking, however, "only" modifies the verb "swim," and thus quantifies things one can do in kiddie pools rather than the pools themselves, as in the middle example. It means that swimming is the only thing that children under 5 may do in the pools; they are not allowed to do anything else, such as fighting, eating, throwing balls, or whatever. So once again we recast the sentence to put "only" at the beginning—"Only swimming is a thing that children under 5 may do in kiddie pools"—and then apply our formula to put that into standard form:

All things that children under 5 may do in the kiddie pools are (acts of) swimming.

The guidelines for distilling syllogisms we discussed in this section do not cover all the problems you will encounter. The resources of our language are too rich and varied for us to list all the possible nonstandard ways of expressing a deductive argument. We have discussed only the major ones. But if you understand these, you should be able to handle the others by common sense.

EXERCISE 7.3

Integrative Exercise   Put each of the following syllogisms into standard form, and determine whether each is valid. Be sure to identify any implicit premises or conclusions.

*1. Only computers with at least 1 gigabyte of internal memory can run Microsoft Windows 10, and my computer doesn't have that much memory. So I can't run Windows.

2. Were the earth's crust a single rigid layer, the continents could not have shifted their positions in relation to each other, but such "continental drift" has clearly occurred.

3. Only U.S. citizens can vote in U.S. elections. Since you're a citizen, you can vote.

*4. Without some mechanism of natural selection, there would be no way for new species of organisms to arise—as they have. So clearly there is a mechanism of natural selection.

5. It's raining today, and whenever it rains, the traffic slows to a crawl.

6. You can't get a decent meal anywhere in this town, but we have to eat here somewhere, so let's forget about a decent meal.

*7. Anyone who can strike a log with an ax in just the right place can split it with one blow. But it takes a good eye to hit the log just right, so only someone with a good eye can split logs in a single blow.

8. Photosynthesis must occur as far down as 250 meters below the surface of the ocean, for there are algae that live at those depths.

9. Many immigrants are here illegally! In order to preserve the law, we need to expel them, make them pay fines, or grant them amnesty. We can't possibly expel them, and we can't grant them all amnesty, so we'll have to fine them.

*10. I'd be willing to take statistics only if I could take it in the morning, when my brain is functioning. But it isn't offered in the morning, so I won't take it.

11. Current will not flow unless the circuit is unbroken, and this circuit is broken. So the current isn't flowing.

12. The book cannot be published. The agreement was that it would not be published unless there was no objection from the review committee, and the review committee did object.

*13. Under the "bubble" concept of air pollution regulation, a new factory in a given area can emit a given quantity of pollutants into the air only if it purchases the right to emit that quantity from some other factory, and another factory is willing to sell the right only if it is willing to reduce its emissions by the same quantity. So if a new factory emits a given quantity of pollutants, some other factory is emitting less of that pollutant by the same quantity.

14. Robin wasn't really embarrassed, because the blotch she gets whenever she's embarrassed wasn't there.

15. If we don't allow drilling in the Arctic National Wildlife Refuge, we'll remain dependent on foreign oil. And we can no longer afford to depend on foreign oil.

7.4 Extended Arguments

In our study of argument structure in Chapter 2, we saw that arguments often involve more than a single step. Premises combine to support an intermediate conclusion, which is then used as a premise to support an ultimate conclusion. Or, moving in the opposite direction, a conclusion is supported by premises that are themselves supported by further premises. When such an extended argument is deductive, we can use what we know about syllogisms to analyze it in more depth than was possible in Chapter 2.

Consider the following argument:

> A nervous system contains many individual cells, so no one-celled animal, by definition, could have one. But only something with a nervous system could be conscious, so no one-celled animal is conscious.

This is certainly a deductive argument, and it has the marks of a categorical syllogism. There's an explicit quantifier, "no," and various terms are repeated: "one-celled animal," "conscious [beings]," and so on. Notice, however, that the argument has two conclusions, both introduced by the word "so." It is clear that the first one (no one-celled animal has a nervous system) is an intermediate conclusion, because a further inference is drawn from it. The ultimate conclusion of the argument is "no one-celled animal is conscious." The argument, then, has more than one step and must be analyzed accordingly.

We begin our analysis by isolating and numbering the propositions that play a role in the argument. Thus:

> (1) A nervous system contains many individual cells, so (2) no one-celled animal, by definition, could have one. But (3) only something with a nervous system could be conscious, so (4) no one-celled animal is conscious.

Before we start looking for syllogisms in an argument like this, it's a good idea to step back and try to get a feel for the flow of the argument as a whole. It seems clear that 1 is a premise used to support 2, and that 2 and 3 together support the ultimate conclusion. So we would diagram this argument as follows:

As the diagram reveals, the argument has two steps: from 1 to 2 and from 2 + 3 to 4. So now we need to look at each step individually. It doesn't matter which one we do first, but since the second step has two premises and looks as if it is a syllogism, let's start there. Putting everything into standard form, we have:

3. All conscious organisms have nervous systems.
2. No one-celled animal has a nervous system.
4. No one-celled animal is conscious.

Let's go back to the first step, from 1 to 2. The apparent subject term in 1 is "nervous systems," but the argument is clearly about classes of organisms that do or do not have them, so we would put 1 in standard form accordingly:

1. All organisms with nervous systems have many cells.
2. No one-celled animal has a nervous system.

This is clearly an enthymeme. More specifically, this is a sorites argument and the missing premise is this: (*a*) No one-celled animal has many cells. (Since we are using the numbering technique of Chapter 2, we use letters instead of parentheses to indicate implicit premises.)

The argument as a whole then looks like this:

1. All organisms with nervous systems have many cells.
a. No one-celled animal has many cells.
2. No one-celled animal has a nervous system.

3. All conscious organisms have nervous systems.
2. No one-celled animal has a nervous system.
4. No one-celled animal is conscious.

What we have done here is to break up a single chain of reasoning into its component syllogisms, so that we can evaluate each step for validity. This process is like that of

---

APPLY Tired of All Those Pop Quizzes?

Use your knowledge of logic to avoid them. Here's how. Imagine that some members of the class—not you, of course!—haven't been keeping up with the reading. Your frustrated professor announces, "Sometime next week, I will give this class a surprise exam." Can she do that? Well, the rules at your college or university probably say "yes," but let's see if you can convince her that reason says "no." Suppose your class meets three times a week on Monday, Wednesday, and Friday. Try this line of reasoning: "Professor, you can't possibly surprise us with an exam on Friday because, when we get to the end of class on Wednesday without an exam, we'll know that it must be on Friday, so no surprise. That just leaves Monday or Wednesday. And once we've eliminated Friday, we can see that Wednesday is impossible as well. Because if we make it to the end

of class on Monday without an exam, we'll know that you're planning it for Wednesday, so no surprise there either! Only Monday's left, we'll all know that, so you can't surprise us on Monday either."

This scenario is a version of the sorites problem known as the Paradox of the Surprise Exam. A paradox is a nonsensical or contradictory result from seemingly correct reasoning. In this one, we see the inconsistency between our commonsense knowledge that students are often surprised by pop quizzes and the reasonableness of the student's argument. If you like puzzles of this sort, you might enjoy reading *Paradoxes* by Mark Sainsbury or *A Brief History of the Paradox* by Roy Sorensen.

Will this argument persuade your teacher to suspend pop quizzes? Maybe not. But it's worth a try!

addition. To add a column of numbers, you first add two of them, then add their sum to the third, and that sum to the fourth, and so on. Similarly, in an extended argument, we combine two premises in a single syllogism to derive a conclusion, then combine that conclusion with the next premise to yield a further conclusion, and so on until we reach the ultimate conclusion. Just as we can add a column of numbers of any length, so we can have an argument with any number of steps. And just as we must add each pair of numbers correctly for the final sum to be correct, so each step must be valid if an argument as a whole is to be valid.

But the analogy is not perfect. When you are given a column of numbers, the intermediate sums are never part of the column itself, whereas intermediate conclusions are often given in the statement of an argument. Thus we need to distinguish premises from intermediate conclusions. Moreover, you can add numbers in any order and get the same final sum, but in an argument you have less freedom: To break it down into the correct individual steps, you must put the premises together in the right order.

So analyzing extended arguments is a little more difficult than adding numbers. No single procedure will work in every case. What we need is a set of procedures from which we can pick and choose, adapting our method to the circumstances of the particular case. In the remainder of this section, therefore, we will look at a variety of specific arguments that illustrate common problems and the techniques we can use to solve them.

7.4A Categorical Syllogisms in Extended Arguments

In the example we just analyzed, the intermediate conclusion was stated explicitly. Let's look at a somewhat more difficult example in which the intermediate conclusions are *not* stated:

> Since (1) values are nothing more than our own evaluations of the facts, (2) they are not objective. (3) Knowledge of the facts is based on empirical evidence, and (4) anything based on such evidence is objective. But (5) evaluating facts is different from knowing them.

The ultimate conclusion here is 2: "No values are objective." Four premises are used to support the conclusion, whereas a single syllogism can have only two premises, so we know that this is an extended argument. Premise 1 is directly related to the conclusion, but the others aren't, so where do we go from here?

Let's try working backward from the conclusion. Since 1 contains the minor term ("values"), we will assume that it is the minor premise of a syllogism. What major premise would be needed to complete the syllogism? It must contain the major term "objective (state of mind)" and the middle term "evaluation of the facts." None of the other statements in the argument contains these two terms, so we need to supply a major premise that makes this step of the argument valid. Using the techniques we learned for enthymemes, and labeling the new premise as *a*, we have:

a. No evaluation of the facts is objective.
1. All values are evaluations of the facts.
2. No values are objective.

If this were an enthymeme—that is, if 1 were the only premise we were given—then we would treat *a* as an implicit premise, and our job would be done. But since there are other premises in the argument—3, 4, and 5—we should see whether they provide support for *a* as an intermediate conclusion. We cannot combine these premises in a single step. But 3 and 4 look like the premises of a syllogism, so let's see what conclusion we get by putting them together.

4. All things based on empirical evidence are objective.
3. All knowledge of the facts is based on empirical evidence.
b. All knowledge of the facts is objective.

The conclusion (*b*) is not explicitly stated, so we have to give it a letter, but it follows validly from 3 and 4, which were stated.

We are almost done now. Working down from the top (from premises 3 and 4), we found that *b* followed as an intermediate conclusion. Working up from the bottom (from the ultimate conclusion), we saw that we would have to get to *a* as an intermediate conclusion. So the question is whether *b*, together with the remaining premise 5, will support *a*. That is, we now know that the argument has the structure:

We identified *b* as the intermediate conclusion that follows from 3 and 4, so we know that step *i* is valid. Likewise, we supplied *a* as a premise that would make step *iii* valid. So everything turns on the middle step. Writing it out as a standard form syllogism, we have:

b. All knowledge of the facts is objective.
5. No evaluation of the facts is knowledge of the facts.
a. No evaluation of the facts is objective.

This syllogism is invalid. In terms of the rules of validity for categorical syllogisms, it has an illicit major term, "objective (states of mind)," distributed in the conclusion but not in the major premise. You can easily confirm its invalidity by using Venn diagrams. The argument tries to show that no evaluation of the facts is objective by distinguishing evaluation from knowledge of the facts. For that line of argument to work, we would need the additional premise that *only* knowledge of the facts is objective. In accordance with the rule we learned earlier in the chapter, this "only" statement means: "All objective states of mind are knowledge of the facts." This statement is not equivalent to premise *b*. (It is the converse of *b*, and the converse of an A proposition is not equivalent to it.) Nor can the statement be derived from premises 3 and 4. So the argument as a whole is invalid.

7.4B Hypothetical Syllogisms in Extended Arguments

Extended arguments need not be categorical. Hypothetical syllogisms can also be combined into longer arguments. Suppose that during a shortage of consumer goods, the government issued this statement:

> As unpleasant as the current shortage is, it means (1) we are consuming less. And so (2) in the long run our standard of living will rise. For (3) in order to improve our standard of living, we must save, and (4) in order to save, we must forgo current consumption.

If this argument sounds fishy to you, that's because it is. Let's see why.

The speaker here is trying to convince us that because we are consuming less at the moment, our standard of living will rise in the long run: 1 is being offered as a reason for 2. The link between them is provided by 3 and 4, both of which are hypothetical propositions about means and ends and can easily be combined into a pure hypothetical syllogism:

> 3. If we are to improve our living standards, we must save.
> 4. If we are to save, we must forgo current consumption.
> _____
> a. If we are to improve our living standards, we must forgo current consumption.

The question now is whether *a*, together with 1, will support the conclusion. The statement that we are consuming less is categorical, and it is just another way of saying what the consequent of *a* says. So these premises together give us a mixed hypothetical syllogism:

> a. If we are to improve our living standards, we must forgo current consumption.
> 1. We are forgoing current consumption.
> _____
> 2. We will improve our living standards.

And since it isn't valid to affirm the consequent, as this step does, the argument as a whole is invalid.

Notice that for this example, we did not use a diagram. That's because it would not have been much help. It would have told us that 1 + 3 + 4 support 2, but it would not have told us how to break the argument down into steps. Once we put the two hypothetical premises together, however, the analysis was straightforward. Remember that diagrams are like maps. They are useful for keeping track of where we are in an argument, and in many cases we would be lost without them. But just as you don't always need a map to reach your destination, you won't always need a diagram to see how to reach a conclusion.

7.4C Extended Arguments with Elements of Different Types

It is possible to combine hypothetical with categorical elements in an argument—indeed, this is quite common. Consider the following:

> (1) Certainty would be possible in human knowledge only if some method of ascertaining the facts were infallible. But (2) all of our methods are subject to the influence of emotion, bias, peer pressure, and other subjective factors. Hence (3) certainty is impossible.

At first glance, the structure of this argument is simple: 1 and 2 together support 3. But the structure is actually a little more complex. Premise 1 is a hypothetical proposition of the form *p only if q*, which we put into standard form as *if p, then q*. Since the conclusion is categorical, let's try to formulate it as a mixed hypothetical syllogism:

> 1. If certainty is possible, then some method is infallible.
>   (?)
>   _____
> 3. Certainty is not possible.

Since the conclusion is the negation of the antecedent in 1, it looks as if the argument is an instance of denying the consequent (*modus tollens*). Thus the second premise must be the negation of "some method is infallible," which would be the E proposition "no method is infallible." And that is not what premise 2 says. But premise 2 can be used in a categorical syllogism to establish the E proposition as an intermediate conclusion. Thus the argument as a whole would be:

> a. No method subject to the influence of emotion, etc., is infallible.
> 2. All of our methods are subject to emotion, etc.
> _____
> b. No method is infallible.

> 1. If certainty is possible, then some method is infallible.
> b. No method is infallible.
> _____
> 3. Certainty is not possible.

So the actual structure of the argument consists of one categorical syllogism and one mixed hypothetical syllogism, both valid.

Let's work through another example, drawn from the Sherlock Holmes novel *A Study in Scarlet*, in which Holmes is trying to solve a case of murder. In the following passage, he explains why he came to believe that the killer's motive was revenge for a personal wrong, presumably involving a woman.

> And now came the great question as to the reason why. (1) Robbery had not been the object of the murder, for (2) nothing was taken. Was it politics, then, or was it a woman? That was the question which confronted me. I was inclined from the first to the latter supposition. (3) Political assassins are only too glad to do their work and to fly. (4) This murder had, on the contrary, been done most deliberately, and the perpetrator had left his track all over the room, showing that he had been there all the time. (5) It must have been a private wrong, and not a political one, which called for such a methodical revenge.

The conclusion appears in 5, which we can state more simply as the proposition

> 5. The murderer was someone seeking private revenge.

Holmes reaches this conclusion by excluding the other possible motives, robbery and assassination. So let's start at the top and analyze his arguments for excluding these motives.

The case against robbery as the motive is contained in the first two statements:

> *a.* (?)
> 2. No thing was taken.
> _____
> 1. The murderer was not a robber.

The implicit premise *a* is clearly that if the murderer had been a robber, something would have been taken. Premise 2 denies the consequent: "No thing was taken" is the contradictory proposition to "Some thing was taken." So in standard form we have a *modus tollens* syllogism:

> *a.* If the murderer had been a robber, then something would have been taken.
> 2. No thing was taken.
> _____
> 1. The murderer was not a robber.

To explain why he ruled out political assassination, Holmes makes a general claim about assassins (3) and then applies it to the murderer (4). So we would formulate his argument as a categorical syllogism:

> 3. All political assassins work quickly.
> 4. The murderer did not work quickly.
> _____
> *b.* The murderer was not a political assassin.

So far, then, we could diagram the first steps of the argument as follows:

The question now is how we get from 1 and *b* to the conclusion, 5. Both 1 and *b* are negative statements, whereas the conclusion is the positive claim that the murder was someone seeking private revenge. As we observed in the previous section, that pattern is a mark of a disjunctive syllogism. And indeed, when we step back from the details of Holmes's argument and consider the basic flow, it is clear that he is considering various possibilities and ruling out all but one. The disjunctive premise is partially suggested by the question in the middle of the paragraph ("Was it politics, then, or was it a woman?"), but we need to add robbery as a further disjunct. So the final step of the argument is:

> *c.* The murderer was a robber, or a political assassin, or someone seeking private revenge.
> 1. The murderer was not a robber.
> *b.* The murderer was not a political assassin.
> _____
> 5. The murderer was someone seeking private revenge.

(Remember that a disjunctive proposition can have more than two disjuncts, but then it needs more categorical premises to rule out all but one of the disjuncts.)

You can confirm for yourself that each step of this argument, and thus the argument as a whole, is valid. You can also see the value of analyzing the argument as we have, for in doing so we found that it depends crucially on the disjunctive premise *c*. And once we have made that assumption explicit, we can go on to ask whether it is true—whether there really are just three possible motives for murdering someone. Sherlock Holmes may be guilty of the fallacy of false dichotomy. At the very least, the argument loses some of its plausibility when it is spelled out in full.

7.4D Compound Components

When we discussed disjunctive and hypothetical propositions, we assumed that their components, *p* and *q*, were categorical propositions. That is not always the case. The components can themselves be compound, as in the following examples, where the compound component is indicated by parentheses:

If it rains or is cold, we will cancel the camping trip.	If (*p* or *q*), then *r*
If interest rates rise, then if corporate profits remain the same, their stocks will decline.	If *p*, then (if *q*, then *r*)
Some people are frightened if a dog approaches.	Some *S* are (if *P*, then *Q*)
All of the therapists at LiveWell Clinic are either psychologists or psychiatrists.	All *S* are (*P* or *Q*)

The first two statements are hypothetical propositions; in number one, the antecedent is a disjunctive proposition, while in number two, the consequent is an embedded hypothetical proposition. Statements three and four are categorical rather than compound propositions, but they have compound predicate terms, and arguments involving such propositions may require that we take account of the disjunctive or hypothetical structure of the predicate.

To see how this works, consider an argument involving the last example:

> All of the therapists at LiveWell Clinic are either psychologists or psychiatrists.
> Tess, a therapist at LiveWell, must be a psychologist since she isn't a psychiatrist.

The conclusion is that Tess is a psychologist. To derive that conclusion, we first have to apply the universal statement about therapists at LiveWell clinic to Tess. That will be a categorical syllogism:

> All therapists at LiveWell Clinic are either psychologists or psychiatrists.
> Tess is a therapist at LiveWell Clinic.
> _____
> Tess is a psychologist or she is a psychiatrist.

Once we have that intermediate conclusion, the rest of the argument is obvious: Tess is not a psychiatrist, so she is a psychologist.

Here's another example, drawn once again from a Sherlock Holmes story. In the following passage, Holmes is trying to find out who was with the murdered man on the night of his death; he already knows that the two drank rum together in the victim's cabin.

> You remember that I asked whether whiskey and brandy were in the cabin. You said they were. How many landsmen are there who would drink rum when they could get these other spirits? Yes, I was certain it was a seaman. [Arthur Conan Doyle, "Black Peter"]

The conclusion is that (1) the visitor was a seaman—a sailor. The first two sentences together tell us that (2) whiskey and brandy were available in the cabin. What about the rhetorical question in the third sentence? The most accurate way to formulate Holmes's assumption here would be as a compound hypothetical proposition:

> 3. If whiskey and brandy were available in the cabin, then if the visitor were a landsman, he would not have had rum.

This proposition has the form: if p, then (if q, then r)—a hypothetical proposition in which the consequent is itself hypothetical. And since premise 2 affirms the antecedent of 3, we can formulate the first step of the argument as a mixed hypothetical syllogism:

> 3. If whiskey and brandy were available in the cabin, then if the visitor were a landsman, he would not have had rum.
> 2. Whiskey and brandy were available.
> _____
> a. If the visitor were a landsman, he would not have had rum.

Since Holmes has already established that (4) the visitor *did* drink rum, the consequent of *a* is false, so we can formulate the second step of the argument as another mixed hypothetical syllogism (in this case, denying the consequent):

> a. If the visitor were a landsman, he would not have had rum.
> 4. The visitor had rum.
> _____
> 1. The visitor was not a landsman.

SOLVE Analyzing Extended Arguments

1. Identify the conclusion.
2. Label as many of the premises in the passage as you can.
3. Diagram as much of the structure as possible.
4. If this is not sufficient to identify the whole structure, then use what you know about syllogisms to find missing premises and

intermediate conclusions. Work up from the ultimate conclusion or down from the premises. Remember that the individual steps of the argument need not all be syllogisms of the same type.

5. Evaluate each step for validity. The argument as a whole is valid if—but only if—every step is valid.

The conclusion here is the obverse of the conclusion as stated in the passage—on the assumption that landsmen and seamen are complementary classes. If we want to make this assumption explicit, we would have to add a disjunctive premise. But we need not bother with that here.

7.4E Distilling an Extended Argument

The examples we have discussed illustrate the basic method for analyzing extended deductive arguments. But these examples have been fairly self-contained and easy to follow. In everyday speech and thought, extended arguments are normally embedded in a context of descriptions, examples, rhetorical asides, disclaimers, and other material that is not directly relevant to the argument itself. In order to analyze such arguments, you need to extract them from this context. So as our final illustration, let's look at a more realistic case. The two passages below are from a key chapter in John Kenneth Galbraith's *The Affluent Society*. Together they constitute his central argument for the claim that, in our society, private production is no longer urgent and that more resources should be transferred to the public sector (government).

> If the individual's wants are to be urgent, they must be original with himself. They cannot be urgent if they must be contrived for him. And above all, they must not be contrived by the process of production by which they are satisfied. For this means that the whole case for the urgency of [private] production, based on the urgency of wants, falls to the ground. One cannot defend production as satisfying wants if that production creates the wants.
>
> The even more difficult link between production and wants is provided by the institutions of modern advertising and salesmanship. These cannot be reconciled with the notion of independently determined desires, for their central function is to create desires—to bring into being wants that previously did not exist.

Let's go through each of these passages in turn, trying to follow the drift of Galbraith's argument. In the first passage, he is criticizing the economists who say that an increase in production is highly valuable ("urgent") because it will satisfy consumer desires. Even though Galbraith doesn't say it in so many words, his conclusion is clearly that increased production is not highly valuable. And his basic reason is indicated by the first three sentences: An increase in production is valuable only if the desires it will satisfy are "original with" the consumer—that is, only if the consumer has those desires independently, not because they have been "contrived" for him by the producers of the goods. Galbraith does not say whether he is talking about all desires or only some, but the latter is the more plausible interpretation of his argument.

So far, then, we have a hypothetical premise and a conclusion:

1. If an increase in production is valuable, then some of the desires it satisfies must be original with the consumer.
2. (None of the desires it satisfies are original with the consumer.)
3. An increase in production is not valuable.

Galbraith does not actually assert premise 2 in the first passage, but it is necessary for his argument, and it seems clear that he is gearing up to try to prove it.

Let's turn, then, to the second passage, which introduces his discussion of advertising. Advertising is the key "link between production and wants"; its "central function is to create desires" that did not exist before. Galbraith takes it as obvious that no desire instilled by advertising is "original with" the consumer. And he assumes that any desire that an increase in production *would* satisfy would have to be instilled by advertising. Thus he is giving us a categorical syllogism in support of 2:

4. No desire instilled by advertising is original with the consumer.
5. All desires that would be satisfied by increased production must be instilled by advertising.
2. (No desire that would be satisfied by increased production is original with the consumer.)

As a result of our analysis, then, we can see that Galbraith's argument is an inference in two steps. The analysis required that we read between the lines, distilling the essential points he was making to a much greater extent than in previous examples. (And of course we performed part of the "distillation" for you by isolating those two passages; had you been given the whole chapter to analyze, you would have had to pick them out yourself.) A good deal of interpretation was involved here, which means that you might have come up with a different wording for some of the premises. This will generally be the case with extended arguments in real life. But different formulations will not affect the basic logic of the argument.

This example illustrates the value of identifying the basic logic of an argument. Both steps of Galbraith's argument are valid. So the soundness of the argument depends on the truth or falsity of the premises—specifically on 1, 4, and 5. (Statement 2 is an intermediate conclusion.) Knowing that those are the key premises would help you in reading the text, because you would then be on the lookout for the evidence he offers in support of those premises. In addition, Galbraith's argument has been criticized by many other writers, so if you know the basic structure of his argument, you can organize and evaluate the counterarguments by asking which premises they are directed against.

EXERCISE 7.4

Integrative Exercise   Analyze each extended argument that follows: Identify the structure of the argument, formulate each step as a syllogism, adding implicit premises as needed, and determine whether the argument is valid.

✳1. The killer left fingerprints all over the place, so he couldn't have been a pro. A pro would not have been so sloppy.

2. It isn't true that only conscious beings can manipulate symbols, because some computers can do that, and computers aren't conscious—only living organisms are.

3. If Jones was not at the meeting, then all the witnesses have been lying. But some of the witnesses, at least, have been clergymen.

✳4. Any metal that can oxidize at normal temperatures will rust. But some steel contains chromium and is therefore rustproof.

5. Non-human animals do not have a sense of humor, because humor presupposes a rational faculty, which only human beings possess.

6. Roy's temperature is over 100°F. If a person's temperature is above 100°F, he either is sick or has been recently engaged in some strenuous activity. Roy isn't sick, so he must have been doing something strenuous.

✳7. Price controls will not work in controlling inflation. They would work, perhaps, if every law of economics were false, but some of those laws are supported by overwhelming evidence.

8. Liberals believe in government support for academic research. Since no one who favors liberty can accept interference by the state in the realm of ideas, liberals do not really favor liberty.

9. If the direction of the flow of time, from past to present to future, depends on the expansion of the universe, then time will reverse its direction if the expansion stops and the universe begins contracting—as current evidence from astrophysics suggests it will.

✳10. The law that requires that one have a driver's license in order to drive in this state implies that illiterate people cannot drive, since they would obviously fail the test one must pass to get a license.

11. In the early 1770s, the American colonies came to a crisis point: They would obtain full and fair representation in the English Parliament, or else they would seek independence. But they would receive full representation only if the existing Parliament was willing to accept a diminution of its power, and it was not. So the outcome was rebellion.

CHAPTER REVIEW

Summary

- In order to analyze deductive arguments as they occur in ordinary language, identify the kind of syllogism involved.
- In addition to the categorical syllogisms discussed in Chapter 6, there are disjunctive and hypothetical syllogisms.
- A disjunctive syllogism employs a disjunctive proposition *p or q* as a premise.
- It is valid to deny one disjunct and infer that the other is true. Because we interpret the conjunction "or" in the inclusive sense, however, it is not valid to affirm one disjunct and infer that the other is false.
- A hypothetical syllogism employs a hypothetical proposition *if p, then q* as a premise.
    - In a pure hypothetical syllogism, both premises and the conclusion are hypothetical propositions.
    - In a mixed hypothetical syllogism, one premise is hypothetical; the other premise either affirms or denies one of the components, and the conclusion affirms or denies the other.
    - A syllogism that affirms the antecedent or denies the consequent is valid, and a syllogism that denies the antecedent or affirms the consequent is invalid.

- To determine whether a given argument is a categorical, hypothetical, or disjunctive syllogism, we rely on linguistic criteria of various kinds, such as the presence or absence of explicit quantifiers and connectives.
- We also rely on substantive criteria: Disjunctive syllogisms typically deal with alternative possibilities, hypothetical syllogisms with relationships of dependence, and categorical syllogisms with relationships among classes.
- Deductive arguments in everyday thought and speech are normally extended. To analyze and evaluate them, break the arguments down into component steps, identifying implicit premises and intermediate conclusions.
- Deductive reasoning is used pervasively in politics, law, ethics, and the sciences, as well as in everyday thinking.
- Deductive reasoning allows us to apply the knowledge embodied in all of our concepts for classes of things; to draw conclusions about cause and effect, or means and ends; and to find our way among the alternatives set by a given situation.

Key Terms

disjunctive proposition (p. 275)

hypothetical proposition (p. 275)

disjunct (p. 276)

disjunctive syllogism (p. 276)

antecedent (p. 281)

consequent (p. 281)

pure hypothetical syllogism (p. 285)

mixed hypothetical syllogism (p. 286)

affirming the antecedent (*modus ponens*) (p. 286)

denying the consequent (*modus tollens*) (p. 286)

denying the antecedent (p. 286)

affirming the consequent (p. 286)

Putting It All Together

I. **Integrative Exercise** Determine whether the following argument forms are valid.

＊1. If p, then q
   $\dfrac{q}{p}$

2. p or q
   $\dfrac{\text{Not-}q}{p}$

3. If p, then q
   $\dfrac{\text{Not-}p}{\text{Not-}q}$

＊4. If p, then q
   $\dfrac{p}{q}$

5. p if q
   $\dfrac{\text{Not-}q}{\text{Not-}p}$

6. p unless q
   $\dfrac{\text{Not-}p}{q}$

＊7. p or q
   $\dfrac{q}{p}$

8. p or q
   $\dfrac{p}{\text{Not-}q}$

9. p only if q
   $\dfrac{p}{q}$

＊10. Not (p and q)
   $\dfrac{\text{Not-}p}{q}$

11. p unless q
   $\dfrac{q}{\text{Not-}p}$

12. p only if q
   $\dfrac{\text{Not-}p}{\text{Not-}q}$

II. **Integrative Exercise** Create arguments by following the instructions for each of the problems below.

1. Construct a *modus ponens* syllogism to support this conclusion: The economy will go into a recession next year.

2. Construct an invalid mixed hypothetical syllogism with this conclusion: Jane does not speak Spanish.

3. Use a pure hypothetical syllogism to explain why pushing down the accelerator makes the car go faster.

4. Construct a valid disjunctive syllogism to support this conclusion: Honesty is the best policy.

5. Construct the most plausible argument you can that commits the fallacy of affirming the consequent.

III. **Integrative Exercise** Put each of the following arguments into standard form and determine whether it is valid.

＊1. "If the Moral Law was one of our instincts, we ought to be able to point to some one impulse inside us which was always what we call good. . . . But [we] cannot. . . . The Moral Law is not any one instinct." [C.S. Lewis, *Mere Christianity*]

2. "Faith is not reason, else religion would be . . . a part of philosophy, which it assuredly is not." [Richard Taylor, "Faith"]

3. "How often have I said to you that when you have eliminated the impossible, whatever remains, however improbable, must be

the truth? We know that he did not come through the door, the window, or the chimney. We also know that he could not have been concealed in the room, as there is no concealment possible. Whence, then, did he come?"

"He came through the hole in the roof!"

"Of course he did. He must have done so." [Arthur Conan Doyle, *The Sign of Four*]

∗4. "At present, then, there is no evidence on the effects of imitation [on language learning] that is very conclusive. This in itself is somewhat surprising in view of the importance that many theorists have attributed to imitation. If it is an important factor in language development, it should be relatively easy to find evidence of its importance. We are forced to conclude that imitation . . . does not contribute importantly to language development." [Donald J. Foss and David T. Hakes, *Psycholinguistics*]

5. "The tax benefit [for energy-related investments by businesses] only helps if you're paying taxes, and you're only paying taxes if you're making money." [National Public Radio, "Marketplace"]

6. "The Air Force has a saying that if you're not catching flak, you're not over the target. I'm catching the flak, I must be over the target." [Mike Huckabee, Republican primary debate, 2008]

∗7. "For if we cannot be sure of the independent existence of objects, we cannot be sure of the independent existence of other people's bodies, and therefore still less of other people's minds, since we have no grounds for believing in their minds except such as are derived from observing their bodies. Thus if we cannot be sure of the independent existence of objects, we shall be left alone in a desert—it may be that the whole outer world is nothing but a dream, and we alone exist." [Bertrand Russell, *Problems of Philosophy*]

IV. An article in a science magazine ("Neutrino Astronomy Born in a Supernova," *Science News*) contained the following statement:

"If neutrinos have a small rest mass, they will have a small magnetic moment, a small intrinsic magnetism. (The converse is not true, so a zero magnetic moment does not necessarily mean no mass.)"

A letter to the editor in a subsequent issue took issue with the statement:

"Let 'neutrino has non-zero rest mass' be statement A, and 'neutrino has non-zero magnetic moment' be statement B. You are saying that 'A implies B' does not necessarily imply 'non-B implies non-A.' But that is wrong. 'A implies B' does necessarily imply 'non-B implies non-A.' Particle physics may be counterintuitive at times, but it doesn't overthrow the rules of logic.

"I think you probably meant 'A implies B' does not necessarily imply 'B implies A,' which is certainly true. . . ."

The author of the original article then replied:

"The statement was in error. It should have read: 'If the neutrino has a magnetic moment, it will also have mass. But it can have mass without having a magnetic moment."

Use what you have learned in this chapter to identify the logical error of which the original article was accused. Was the letter to the editor correct in what it says about logic? Is the author's reply correct?

V. Integrative Exercise Put each of the following statements into standard form as a categorical, hypothetical, or disjunctive proposition.

✱1. Pride goeth before a fall.

2. "Separate educational facilities are inherently unequal." [Chief Justice Warren, Opinion of the Court, *Brown v. Board of Education*, 1954]

3. "A man who does not think for himself does not think at all." [Oscar Wilde]

✱4. "Curiosity is one of the permanent and certain characteristics of a vigorous mind." [Samuel Johnson, *Rambler*]

5. "Where there's marriage without love, there will be love without marriage." [Ben Franklin, *Poor Richard's Almanack*]

6. "Were we faultless, we would not derive such satisfaction from remarking the faults of others." [La Rochefoucauld, *Maxims*]

✱7. "Not to know what happened before one was born is to remain a child." [Cicero, *De Oratore*]

8. "The whole of science is nothing more than a refinement of everyday thinking." [Albert Einstein, *Physics and Reality*]

9. "You can't think and hit at the same time." [Yogi Berra]

✱10. "The people never give up their liberties but under some delusion." [Edmund Burke, *Speech at County Meeting of Buckinghamshire*]

VI. Integrative Exercise The syllogisms that follow are taken from previous exercises. Each is in standard form (or very close to it). Translate it into ordinary language. Use what you have learned in this section to express the argument in a more natural, idiomatic way: Reformulate the propositions, leave an obvious premise unstated, but above all make them sound like things people would actually say!

1. Some bureaucrats are not chosen on the basis of ability.
   All bureaucrats are civil servants.
   Some civil servants are not chosen on the basis of ability.

2. All geniuses are eccentric.
   No Greek poet was eccentric.
   No Greek poet was a genius.

3. If the circuit is broken, current will not flow.
   The circuit is broken.
   The current will not flow.

4. Any state that ignores human rights is a tyranny.
   Some democracies ignore human rights.
   Some democracies are tyrannies.

5. If children are deprived of affection early in life, they will learn not to expect it.
   If children learn not to expect affection, they will not seek it out later in life.
   If children are deprived of affection early in life, they will not seek it out later in life.

VII. Integrative Exercise Put each of the following arguments into standard form as a categorical, hypothetical, or disjunctive syllogism, supplying any missing premise or conclusion. Then determine whether it is valid.

✱1. "The wound upon the dead man was, as I was able to determine with absolute confidence, fired from a revolver at the distance of something over four yards. There was no powder-blackening on the clothes." [Arthur Conan Doyle, "The Reigate Puzzle"]

2. "If we look at the actual tasks of working science, we shall find that not all prediction is scientific—or horserace tipsters would be scientists—and not all science is predictive, or evolutionary biologists would not be scientists." [Stephen Toulmin, "From Form to Function: Philosophy and History of Science in the 1950s and Now"]

3. "Saccadic eye movements occur whenever the eyes move without a [moving] target to follow. In reading, of course, there is no moving target to follow; so reading involves saccadic eye movements." [Donald J. Foss and David T. Hakes, *Psycholinguistics*]

*4. "As it is impossible for the whole race of mankind to be united in one great society, they must necessarily divide into many." [William Blackstone, *Commentaries on the Laws of England*]

5. "The fish which you have tattooed immediately above your wrist could only have been done in China. . . . That trick of staining the fishes' scales of a delicate pink is quite peculiar to China." [Arthur Conan Doyle, "The Red-Headed League"]

6. "In all the world, only mammals have true hair and produce milk, so [duckbills] have been classified as mammals." [Isaac Asimov, "What Do You Call a Platypus?" in *National Wildlife Magazine*]

*7. "It is only about the things that do not interest one, that one can give a really unbiased opinion; and this is no doubt the reason why an unbiased opinion is always absolutely valueless." [*More Letters of Oscar Wilde*, ed. Rupert Hart-Davis]

8. "Had we but world enough, and time, This coyness, lady, were no crime . . . But at my back I always hear Time's winged chariot hurrying near; . . ." [Andrew Marvell, "To His Coy Mistress"]

9. "This gain [in entropy] occurs every time heat flows from a higher to a lower temperature, and since nothing interesting or useful happens unless heat does make this descent, all interesting and useful things are accompanied by an irreversible increase in entropy." [Jeremy Campbell, *Grammatical Man*]

*10. "A prince should therefore have no other aim or thought, nor take up any other thing for his study, but war and its organization and discipline, for that is the only art necessary to one who commands." [Niccolo Machiavelli, *The Prince*]

11. "If a moving object does possess acceleration, that is, if a in formula (1) [$F = ma$] is not zero, then the force F cannot be zero. Now an object falling to Earth from some height does possess acceleration. Hence some force must be acting." [Morris Kline, *Mathematics in Western Culture*]

12. "It is well known that quantitative differences ultimately pass into qualitative differences. This is true everywhere, and is therefore true in history." [George Plekhanov, *Essays in Historical Materialism*]

*13. "A clown is someone who stands before a crowd and gestures wildly to get their attention. So is a politician." ["Today's Chuckle"]

14. "Some philosophers have, in the past, leaped . . . to what they take to be a proof that the mind is *essentially non-physical* in character. . . . No physical object can, in itself, refer to one thing rather than to another; nevertheless, *thoughts in the mind* obviously do succeed in referring to one thing rather than another. So thoughts . . . are of an essentially different nature than physical objects." [Hilary Putnam, *Reason, Truth, and History*]

15. "Observation implies movement, that is locomotion with reference to the rigid environment, because all observers are animals and all animals are mobile." [Gibson, *Ecological Approach to Visual Perception*]

VIII. For each of the statements that follow, (a) find a syllogism to support the statement, (b) find a syllogism to support one of the premises of the syllogism in (a), and (c) write out the complete argument in a short paragraph.

1. Mary will win the election for student body president.

2. Dancing is good exercise.

3. If interest rates decline, stock prices will rise.

4. Cheating is wrong.

5. Nothing ventured, nothing gained.

IX. Analyze each of the arguments that follow: Identify the structure of the argument, formulate each step (there may be one or more) as a syllogism, and determine whether the argument is valid.

∗1. "Appellant's conduct is not a nuisance unless it is unreasonably noisy for an industrial area. What a reasonable amount of noise will be depends on the character of the neighborhood. Although appellant produces more noise in the area of the industrial park than any other source, it has not been shown that the level of noise it produces is out of keeping with the character of its location. Since it has not been shown that the noise from appellant's operation is out of keeping with its industrial location, it cannot be found to be a nuisance." [Legal brief]

2. "Since happiness consists in peace of mind, and since durable peace of mind depends on the confidence we have in the future, and since that confidence is based on an understanding of the nature of God and the soul, it follows that true happiness requires that understanding." [Gottfried Leibniz, *Preface to the General Science*]

3. "[Milton] identifies four reasons why [censorship will not work]. First, the decisions of the censor cannot be trusted unless the censor is infallible and beyond corruption. No mortal possesses such grace; therefore no mortal is qualified to be a censor." [Irving Younger, "What Good Is Freedom of Speech?" *Commentary*]

∗4. Touchstone: . . . Wast ever in court, shepherd?
Corin: No, truly.
Touchstone: Then thou art damned. . . .
Corin: For not being at court? Your reason.

Touchstone: Why, if thou never wast at court, thou never saw'st good manners; if thou never saw'st good manners, then thy manners must be wicked; and wickedness is sin, and sin is damnation. Thou art in a parlous state, shepherd. [Shakespeare, *As You Like It*]

5. "Anything that changes over time has, by definition, a history—the universe, countries, art and philosophy, and ideas. Science also, ever since its emergence from myths and early philosophies, has experienced a steady historical change and is thus a legitimate subject for the historian." [Ernst Mayr, *The Growth of Biological Thought*]

6. "But the secular power has no legal right to coerce heretics unless heresy is a crime. And heresy is not a crime, but an error; for it is not a matter of will." [J.B. Bury, *A History of Freedom of Thought*]

∗7. Robespierre's opponents accused him of having treated his personal enemies as enemies of the state. "I deny the accusation," he answered, "and the proof is that you still live."

8. "The fifth way [of proving that God exists] is taken from the governance of the world. We see that things which lack knowledge, such as natural bodies, act for an end, and this is evident from their acting always, or nearly always, in the same way, so as to obtain the best result. Hence it is plain that they achieve their end, not fortuitously, but designedly. Now whatever lacks knowledge cannot move

towards an end, unless it be directed by some being endowed with knowledge and intelligence as the arrow is directed by the archer. Therefore some intelligent being exists by whom all natural things are directed to their end; and this being we call God." [Thomas Aquinas, *Summa Theologica*]

[Note: The last sentence is included for the sake of completeness, but it raises problems for analysis that we have not yet discussed. For the purposes of this exercise, therefore, assume that Aquinas's conclusion is "some things are directed by a being with knowledge and intelligence."]

9. "Between these alternatives there is no middle ground. The constitution is either a superior paramount law, unchangeable by ordinary means, or it is on a level with ordinary legislative acts, and, like other acts, is alterable when the legislature shall please to alter it.

"If the former part of the alternative be true, then a legislative act contrary to the constitution is not law: if the latter part be true, then written constitutions are absurd attempts, on the part of the people, to limit a power in its own nature illimitable." [Chief Justice John Marshall, Opinion of the Court, *Marbury v. Madison*, 1803]

*10. "Every man has a property in his own person. This nobody has any right to but himself. The labour of his body and the work of his hands, we may say, are properly his. Whatsoever, then, he removes out of the state that nature hath provided and left it in, he hath mixed his labour with it, and joined to it something that is his own, and thereby makes it his property. . . . For this labour being the unquestionable property of the labourer, no man but he can have a right to what that is once joined to. . . ." [John Locke, *Second Treatise of Civil Government*]

8 Propositional Logic

LEARNING OBJECTIVES

On successful completion of the chapter, you will be able to:

✓ Demonstrate an understanding of logical connectives. (8.1)

✓ Translate English sentences into logical notation. (8.2)

✓ Master the truth functions that define the logical operators and compute truth values of compound propositions. (8.3)

✓ Construct and use both long and short-form truth tables to classify and test formal properties of propositions. (8.4)

✓ Construct and use both long and short-form truth tables to test propositional arguments for validity. (8.5–8.6)

The principles of deductive reasoning we have studied so far represent a portion of traditional logic as it was developed by ancient and medieval logicians. We've seen that these principles allow us to analyze and evaluate many of the arguments we encounter every day. But they are incomplete in certain respects. Consider this argument:

> If there is a recession this year or a foreign affairs fiasco, then the president will not be reelected.
> There will be a recession.
> The president will not be reelected.

This is a deductive argument. It's rather simple, and it's obviously valid. But it does not fit any of the argument forms we studied in Chapter 7. It has the logical form:

> If *p* or *q*, then *r*
> *p*
> *r*

This may look like an example of *modus ponens* (affirming the antecedent), but the antecedent is the disjunctive proposition *p or q*, and the second premise affirms *p*, not the disjunction as a whole. In Chapter 7 we learned to recognize disjunctive and hypothetical arguments, but we didn't learn how to analyze arguments that *combine* disjunctive and hypothetical elements. Since these arguments involve more complex relationships among propositions, we need a more elaborate system of rules. Logicians have devised such a system, called *propositional logic*.

Propositional logic is one main branch of what is known as symbolic logic. In earlier chapters, we used symbols such as *p* and *q* to represent propositions, regardless of their content. But we did not symbolize the logical forms of propositions; we used words like "all," "some," "if . . . then," and "or." Modern symbolic logic replaces all of these with symbols. In this respect it is like mathematics, which not only uses variables to represent numbers but also uses special symbols for operations like addition or multiplication that we can perform on numbers. Logicians have introduced the new symbols and rules to serve many purposes. The analysis of complex arguments is only one of these purposes. But it's the one that concerns us, given the focus of this book on thinking skills. In this chapter and the next, we will study propositional logic, and we'll see that the patterns of inference we learned in Chapter 7 are part of a larger system. As you go through these chapters, you will notice that the term "statement" is used more often than "proposition." For most purposes, the terms are interchangeable (see Chapter 1). Both terms designate the content of a complete thought. But now we will be concerned with the symbolic expression of such contents, so "statement" will usually be the better term.

8.1 Connectives

Propositional logic is the logic of compound statements—statements that are made up of other, simpler propositions. Here are some examples:

My brother is *not* driving to school.

My sister is happy, *and* she's throwing a party.

The Democrats will win *or* the Republicans will win.

If the Democrats win, *then* my sister will be happy.

The party will be fun *if and only if* Buzz shows up.

Each of these statements has one or more component statements along with an italicized expression, called a connective, which tells us how the components are related.

The first statement is a **negation**. Negation is a unary, or one-place, connective, as it operates on only one component statement. Nevertheless, the negation word "not" is still called a connective because it transforms the component into a more complex proposition. Negation is the only unary connective; all other logical connectives are binary, or two-place connectives, meaning they connect two component statements. In the second example, the connective is "and"; statements of this form are called **conjunctions**. We're already familiar with statements like the third example—a disjunctive statement, or **disjunction**; and the fourth—a hypothetical statement, or **conditional**, as it is usually called in symbolic logic. In the fifth, the connective "if and only if" is called a **biconditional**.

These are the basic types of compound statements in propositional logic, and each connective has a symbol, shown in the box below. Let's look closely at each of them.

REVIEW **Five Connectives in Propositional Logic**

Type	Connective	Statement Form
Negation (not)	~	$\sim p$
Conjunction (and)	•	$p \cdot q$
Disjunction (or)	$\vee$	$p \vee q$
Conditional (if–then)	⊃	$p \supset q$
Biconditional (if and only if)	≡	$p \equiv q$

8.1A Negation, Conjunction, and Disjunction

NEGATION   Imagine the tail end of the classic children's quarrel: "It is." "It isn't." "It is so." "It is not." We don't know from this excerpt what the children are arguing about, but one is asserting something that the other is denying. We represent the denial of a proposition by the negation sign ~, called the "tilde." If T is the statement "The temperature is rising," then ~T ("not T") could be expressed in any of the following ways:

It's not the case that the temperature is rising.   ~T

It's false that the temperature is rising.   ~T

The temperature is not rising.   ~T

Since T and ~T are contradictory propositions, they cannot both be true, and they cannot both be false. It can't be raining *and* not raining—not at the same time and same place. But it must be *either* raining *or* not raining. It is useful to formulate this relationship graphically through a diagram called a **truth table**. The letter *p* stands for any statement that can be true or false. The truth or falsity of any statement is called its **truth value**, represented by T and F, as on a true-false test. Thus the statement "Lemons are fruit" has the truth value T; "Lemons grow in the Arctic" has the truth value F. The truth table for negation therefore has just two lines:

Negation

p	~*p*
T	F
F	T

If *p* is true, then ~*p* is false, and vice versa.

Since a negation sign reverses truth value, two negation signs cancel out. For example, the statements:

It's not the case that Larry will not come.   ~~L

and

Larry will come.   L

are equivalent. In other words, a double negation has the same truth value as the original proposition. Negation is an on/off switch; flip it twice and you're back where you started. Our other logical connectives allow us to express two component propositions in a single statement.

CONJUNCTION   A conjunction is a way of expressing two component statements, called *conjuncts*, in a single statement. For example:

The rent is due, and I have no money.

For the statement to be true, both conjuncts must be true. And if the conjuncts are both true, the conjunction is true. The conjunction sign • (called the "dot") represents this relationship between the truth of the components and the truth of the compound statement as a whole. In ordinary speech and thought, of course, the word "and" may indicate a richer connection. It may suggest a time relation between the conjuncts, as in "I went upstairs and went to bed." Or the conjuncts may both be reasons for a certain conclusion or decision. For example, someone explaining why he did not buy an SUV might say, "An SUV would be too big, and it would be too expensive." In propositional logic, however, we are not concerned with these further connotations. We use the symbol "•" to abstract from them and consider only the fact that a conjunction is true whenever both conjuncts are true.

With two component statements, and two possible truth values for each, we have four possible combinations in our truth table.

p	$p \bullet q$	q
T		T
T		F
F		T
F		F

We are going to be using truth tables a lot in this chapter, and they will get more complicated than this simple example, so it's important to be clear about how they work. Each row represents one of the four possible combinations of truth values for p and q. By convention, we use the first two rows for the cases in which p is true, while q varies—true in the first row, false in the second. The two remaining rows are for the cases in which p is false, and q once again varies—true in the third row, false in the fourth.

Now we can use the column under the connective to show the truth value of the compound statement for each combination of component truth values.

Conjunction

p	$p \bullet q$	q
T	**T**	T
T	**F**	F
F	**F**	T
F	**F**	F

The table shows that $p \bullet q$ is true only in the first case, where each of the component statements, p and q, has the truth value T. In all other cases, $p \bullet q$ is false.

This truth table may strike you as a complicated way of stating the obvious. But we will see that truth tables are valuable because they give us a systematic way of describing and relating all the connectives to one another. It will also give us one basic test for the validity of propositional arguments. We will get to all of this in due course. Meanwhile, there are two important points to note regarding conjunction.

First, this connective may be indicated by other words in English besides "and." Consider the following:

I want to go skydiving, *but* I have a sprained ankle.	S • A
Although steel rusts, it is often used in underwater construction.	R • U
Julie worked hard to pass the course; *nevertheless* she failed.	W • F

In the symbolic formulation on the right, we use capital letters to abbreviate the components in the statements on the left: S for "I want to go skydiving," A for "I have a sprained ankle," etc. In those statements, the italicized word suggests some incongruity between the component propositions, but the sentence still asserts both components; the sentence is true as long as the components are both true. Each of these sentences, therefore, has the logical form of a conjunction.

Second, remember that the conjuncts in a statement of the form $p • q$ must be separate statements. The word "and" can be misleading in this respect. Compare the following statements, which are grammatically similar:

Renee and Tom took logic.

Tony and Samia got married.

The first statement is a normal conjunction: It is shorthand for "Renee took logic and Tom took logic." But the second is different. It does not mean merely that Tony got married (to someone) and that Samia also got married (to someone). It means that Tony and Samia got married to each other. So the sentence makes a single statement about a pair of people; it is not a pair of statements that can be joined by conjunction or represented by the truth table for the dot.

DISJUNCTION   A disjunctive statement asserts that either p or q is true. The component statements p and q are called the *disjuncts*, and the connective "or" is represented by ∨—the "vee" or "wedge" sign. It is used to symbolize statements such as the following:

We will grow corn in our field or we will let it lie fallow.	G ∨ L
Ramla got a job with Goldman Sachs or Morgan Stanley.	G ∨ M
Either the Yankees or the Twins will win the American League pennant.	Y ∨ T
I will buy you onion rings unless you brought your lunch.	O ∨ B

In the first example, we have two component statements joined by the connective "or," and the symbolic formula mirrors the structure of the English sentence. In the second, the disjunction occurs in the predicate of a sentence with a single subject, so we have to do a bit of revising before we put it into symbolic notation. The two components in this statement are:

Ramla got a job with Goldman Sachs.
Ramla got a job with Morgan Stanley.

In this next statement, the disjunction occurs in the subject, and again we revise to extract the component statements:

The Yankees will win the American League pennant.
The Twins will win the American League pennant.

Disjunction can also provide an easy way to translate the English connective "unless." The last example says that, if I don't buy you onion rings, it is because you brought your own lunch. While it may not yet be obvious to you, this statement is logically equivalent to the disjunction of the components.

I will buy you onion rings.
You will bring your lunch.

In the next section, we will see that "unless" may also be translated as a conditional and, in the next chapter, we will see how the resulting two statements are logically equivalent.

As with conjunction and negation, the truth value of $p \vee q$ is determined by the truth values of its components. The disjunction is true as long as at least one of the disjuncts is true. The truth table for disjunction, therefore, is as follows:

Disjunction

p	$p \vee q$	q
T	**T**	T
T	**T**	F
F	**T**	T
F	**F**	F

Notice how this truth table is different from the one for conjunction. A conjunction is true for only one pair of component truth values and false for all the others. A disjunction is *false* for only one pair of component truth values and *true* for all the others.

The second, third, and fourth lines of the table are pretty obvious. If p and q are both false, then $p \vee q$ is false. If only one of them is true (it doesn't matter which one), then the disjunction is true. What about the first line, where both components are true? Disjunction is normally used to state alternatives, such as alternative actions you can choose (go the party or watch television at home), or alternative explanations for someone's behavior (she is mad because I'm late or because I said something wrong). In some cases, the alternatives are mutually exclusive. When you tell someone "I will go to the party or I will watch television at home," part of what you mean to say is that it's one or the other but not both; you have to choose. The same is true in our first example earlier, where the choice is between one use of a farm field and another, incompatible use. So it seems odd to say that the disjunctive statement would be true if both disjuncts were true. In other cases, however, the alternatives are *not* mutually exclusive, but rather inclusive. For example, she could be mad because I'm late *and* because of something I said. Similarly, a case of emphysema can be caused both by smoking *and* by inhaling coal dust. In everyday thought and speech, it is usually clear from the context whether we are dealing with exclusive or inclusive alternatives. But in propositional logic, we abstract from the specific content of statements in order to isolate their logical form. To avoid any ambiguity, the disjunctive connective is always treated as inclusive. If we need to assert that p and q are not both true, we can add a statement to that effect.

EXERCISE 8.1A

For each of the following statements, identify the component propositions and the logical connective. Then put the statement in symbolic form, using the letters indicated in parentheses.

✱1. Roses are red, and violets are blue. (R, V)

2. I am not a crook. (C)

3. Mickey heard the story, and he is angry. (M, A)

✱4. I can pay the rent or I can buy groceries. (R, G)

5. It's not the case that time is on my side. (T)

6. She's either a lunatic or a genius. (L, G)

✱7. Jerry will either win the race or take second place. (W, S)

8. War is not the solution. (S)

9. Either we pay the fine now or we pay a larger fine later. (N, L)

✱10. The Cucumber County seed-spitting contest is not a world-class event. (C)

11. The campers were tired, but they were happy. (T, H)

12. The Batman action figure has two accessories, while the Spider-man toy has only one. (B, S)

✱13. Either the guest of honor wore brown or he fell in the mud on the way to the party. (B, M)

14. Color film is good for outdoor shots, but black-and-white is best for portraits. (C, B)

15. He is an excellent cook, although he hates food. (C, F)

✱16. Gracie is a cat yet she eats hummus. (C, H)

17. Tippy is a cat but she thinks she's human. (C, H)

18. I'll buy you dinner unless you already ate. (B, A)

✱19. The statement "All poems are sonnets" is false. (P)

20. Rolando is an electrician; Thomas is also. (R, T)

8.1B Conditional and Biconditional

CONDITIONAL A conditional statement has the form *if p then q*. In such a statement *p* is called the *antecedent* and *q* the *consequent*. The connection between them, the if–then relationship, is represented by the symbol ⊃, called the "horseshoe." A statement involving this connective says that if the antecedent is true, the consequent is true as well. The statement does not assert that the antecedent is true, nor does it assert that the consequent is true. All it asserts is that there's a relationship between the two. Conditional statements are used to describe various relationships, such as means and ends (if you study hard, you will pass the test); cause and effect (if the jet stream shifts to the north, there will be drought in the Midwest); policy and consequence (if the city imposes rent control, there will be a housing shortage); or moves in a game (if I expose my king, my opponent will attack). But just as we use the letters *p* and *q* to abstract from the particular content of individual propositions, we use the symbol ⊃ to abstract from the particular nature of the relationship between them, in order to study the logical form of conditional statements. Thus the horseshoe would be used to translate each of our examples into symbolic notation:

If you study hard, you will pass the test.	S ⊃ P
If the jet stream shifts to the north, there will be drought in the Midwest.	J ⊃ D
If the city imposes rent control, there will be a housing shortage.	R ⊃ H
If I expose my king, my opponent will attack.	E ⊃ A

In propositional logic, the horseshoe connective is defined by a truth table:

Conditional

p	p ⊃ q	q
T	T	T
T	F	F
F	T	T
F	T	F

The important line in the table is the second one. To see why, let's work with the first example. When we make this statement to someone, we are not asserting that the person actually will study hard or pass the test. But we are committing ourselves to the claim that studying hard will result in passing the test. If the person does study hard and yet fails, then our statement is false. That's what the second line of the truth table means: If *p* is true but *q* is false, the conditional statement itself is false. Now suppose that the person studies hard and passes the test, the situation represented in the first line of the table. That's certainly consistent with the truth of the conditional. Likewise if he doesn't study hard and doesn't pass—the last line of the table. What about the third line? Suppose he doesn't study hard but still passes. Would that prove our conditional statement false? No: The statement doesn't say that studying hard is the *only* way to pass; perhaps the exam was easy or perhaps the person already knew the material well.

In other words, every combination of truth values for *p* and *q* is consistent with the truth of *p* ⊃ *q* except for the case represented on line 2, where *p* is true and *q* false. The fact that the other combinations of truth values are *consistent* with *p* ⊃ *q* may not seem enough to establish that the conditional *has* to be true in these cases, rather than having an undetermined truth value. There is a real issue here, and we will discuss it soon. For now, we will have to treat it as a simplifying assumption in propositional logic that a conditional statement is regarded as true in these cases.

When we discussed conditional statements in Chapter 7 (where we called them hypothetical statements), we noted that *if p then q* is not equivalent to *if q then p*, and neither one implies the other. For example, suppose we reverse the antecedent and consequent in the third conditional statement above:

If the city imposes rent control, there will be a housing shortage.	R ⊃ H
If there is a housing shortage, the city has imposed rent controls.	H ⊃ R

The original statement states that rent control will result in a housing shortage. It does not state that rent controls are the *only* cause of shortages. But that's exactly what the reversed example says. If a shortage occurs in the absence of rent controls, this version of the statement is false, but the original may still be true.

We can now use truth tables to understand why any statement of the form $p \supset q$ is different from the corresponding statement $q \supset p$.

p	$p \supset q$	q		q	$q \supset p$	p
T	**T**	T		T	**T**	T
T	**F**	F		F	**T**	T
F	**T**	T		T	**F**	F
F	**T**	F		F	**T**	F

$p \supset q$ is false only on the second row, where p is true and q is false. But for those truth values of the components, $q \supset p$ is true. q is now the antecedent and p the consequent, and in that case the conditional is true. $q \supset p$ is false only on the third row, where q is true and p false; and on that row $p \supset q$ is true. This asymmetry in conditional statements makes them different from conjunctions and disjunctions, which are symmetrical: $p \cdot q$ and $q \cdot p$ always have the same truth value, as do $p \vee q$ and $q \vee p$.

Conditional statements in English need not take the form *if p then q*. Each of the following is also a conditional:

> I will go camping this weekend if I finish my work.

> I will go camping this weekend only if I finish my work.

> Finishing my work is a necessary condition for going camping this weekend.

> Finishing my work is a sufficient condition for going camping this weekend.

> I will go camping this weekend unless it rains.

In the first example, the "if" component is placed second in the sentence rather than first. But it is still the antecedent, and so in standard form, it is:

> If I finish my work, then I will go camping this weekend. F ⊃ C

The second example looks similar, but the word "only" changes everything. To see the difference, suppose you have invited me to go camping this weekend. If I tell you "I'll go if I finish my work," and I do finish it, then my promise commits me to going with you; not going would mean breaking a promise; my statement to you would be proven false. But if I tell you "I'll go *only if* I finish my work," and I do finish it, does this promise commit me to going? No. Finishing is a necessary condition for going, but perhaps there are factors I didn't mention. All that I actually promised is that not finishing my work would guarantee I don't go. So if I *do* go, then I have finished my work:

> If I go camping this weekend, then I will have finished my work. C ⊃ F

SOLVE Putting Conditional Statements into Standard Form

Conditional statements can be put into standard form according to the following rules of equivalence:

Nonstandard form	Standard form	Symbolic form
p if q	If q then p	$q \supset p$
p only if q	If p then q	$p \supset q$
p if only q	If q then p	$q \supset p$
p unless q	If not q then p	$\sim q \supset p$
	If not p, then q	$\sim p \supset q$

In the third and fourth examples, the conditional relation is represented by the phrases "necessary condition" and "sufficient condition." It's important to distinguish between these two phrases in order to understand why we translate both as conditionals. An event, A, is a necessary condition for event B if and only if B cannot occur unless A occurs also. For example, breathing is a necessary condition for living; if I stop breathing, I die. Likewise, in the third example, I am saying that if I'm to go camping, it's necessary that I finish my work. If I don't, the camping trip is off, no exceptions. The necessary condition of a statement is always the consequent of a conditional. Therefore, in standard form it is this:

> If I go camping this weekend, then I finished my work.   C $\supset$ F

The fourth example is also a conditional, but it tells us the sufficient rather than the necessary condition. An event, A, is sufficient condition for event B if and only if A alone is enough to bring about B all by itself. For example, decapitation is sufficient to bring about my death, nothing else is needed. Is it necessary? Of course not. Many things could cause my death: stabbing, shooting, suffocation, maybe even natural causes. But decapitation is sufficient. If you cut off my head, I die. Likewise, the fourth example states that finishing my work—all by itself—is a sufficient condition for my camping trip. The sufficient condition is always the antecedent of a conditional. Thus, in sandard form:

> If I finish my work, then I'll go camping this weekend.   F $\supset$ C

In our fifth example, finally, the component statements "I will go camping this weekend" (C) and "It is raining (this weekend)" (R) are joined by the word "unless." As a general rule, *p unless q* can be taken to mean *if not q then p*. Thus I am saying that I will go camping if it does not rain. I am not saying that rain will necessarily keep me from going; I'm leaving myself that option. But I *am* saying that in the absence of rain, I will definitely go; and that if I do not go, then it is raining. If it doesn't rain and I still do not go camping, then my statement was false. So we can put the statement into standard form as a conditional in either of two equivalent ways, as shown in the following example.

SOLVE **Translating Conditional Statements**

Many English phrases other than "if . . . then" may be translated as conditionals. Be on the lookout for phrases such as:

- provided that
- implies

- sufficient condition
- given that
- in case
- necessary condition

If it does not rain this weekend, I will go camping.	~R ⊃ C
If I do not go camping this weekend, it is raining.	~C ⊃ R

(Later in this chapter, we will learn how to prove that statements of the forms $\sim q \supset p$ and $\sim p \supset q$ are indeed equivalent.)

BICONDITIONAL The fifth and final connective, the biconditional, is illustrated by the statement that I will teach a certain class if and only if 10 or more students enroll. The symbol for *if and only if* is ≡, a "triple bar":

I will teach the class if and only if 10 or more students enroll.	T ≡ E

This statement can be understood as a conjunction of two conditional statements, one of them indicated by the "if," the other by the "only if":

If 10 or more students enroll, then I will teach the class ("if").	E ⊃ T
If I teach the class, then 10 or more students are enrolled ("only if").	T ⊃ E

We typically use the biconditional to state:

- A "go/no go" criterion for an action or a decision, as in our example.
- The criteria for inclusion in a category (the platypus is a mammal if and only if it is warm blooded and produces milk for its young).
- The terms of a contract (the renter's security deposit will be returned at the end of the lease if and only if the apartment is left in good repair).
- The causal factors governing an event (a match will ignite if and only if it is struck in the presence of oxygen).

The triple bar is not the same as the equals sign, which we do not use as a connective in propositional logic, but there is a similarity. A biconditional statement is true when the two components have identical truth values; they are either both true or both false. Suppose it turns out that I teach the class but fewer than 10 students have enrolled. That would prove the statement false. And if 10 or more students do enroll but I don't teach the class, that too would prove the statement false. Thus the truth table for the biconditional is:

Biconditional

p	p ≡ q	q
T	T	T
T	F	F
F	F	T
F	T	F

SOLVE Translating Biconditionals

Use the biconditional to translate these English phrases in addition to "if and only if":

- just in case
- necessary and sufficient condition

EXERCISE 8.1B

For each of the following statements, identify the component propositions and the logical connective. Then put the statement in symbolic form, using the letters indicated in parentheses.

*1. If these shoes go on sale, I'll buy two pairs. (S, B)

2. If the cat's away, the mice will play. (C, M)

3. If you put your hand in the candle flame, you will get burned. (C, B)

*4. I'll scratch your back if and only if you'll scratch mine. (I, Y)

5. You will succeed only if you work hard. (S, W)

6. I'll get an A for the course if I get 90% or better on the final exam. (A, F)

*7. I'm ready if you are. (I, Y)

8. If you're in a jam, I'm your man. (J, M)

9. The polar ice caps will start melting if average temperatures on Earth rise by 5°F. (P, T)

*10. We will launch the new website next month if and only if the shopping cart function passes the security test. (W, S)

11. If terrorists sabotage the Niger Delta oil pipeline, Nigerian oil shipments will be reduced by half. (T, O)

12. If you wait in line a long time, there is a good chance you are in the wrong line. (W, C)

*13. The litmus paper in the beaker will turn red if the liquid is acidic, and only if it is. (L, A)

14. You and I can be friends unless you take advantage of me. (F, A)

15. He'll go away if you ignore him. (G, I)

✳16. The plant will die unless you water it. (P, W)

17. Only if oxygen is present will iron rust. (O, R)

18. Unless the Astros put their best starting pitcher in the first game of the World Series, they will lose the series. (B, L)

✳19. I'll go swimming only if I can wear my water wings. (S, W)

20. I'll stand by what I said unless you prove I'm wrong. (S, P)

21. You will pass if only you study. (P, S)

✳22. The presence of oxygen is a necessary condition for iron to rust. (O, R)

23. Matt will sing given that Bao will dance. (M, B)

24. A stake through the heart is both necessary and sufficient for killing a vampire. (S, K)

✳25. Jane will go to the zoo provided that Dan goes also. (J, D)

26. Passing all three exams is a sufficient condition for passing the course. (E, C)

APPLY Truth Tables Revolutionized Our World

If you've ever played *Minecraft*, you'll recognize the basic idea behind a switching circuit. Use Redstone to power a block. You can then switch on adjacent blocks to achieve a variety of results. You may know that the computer you're playing on operates in a similar fashion by sending electricity through circuits. But did you realize that it's modern logic that made it all possible? Advances in logic led to the development of much of the technology we now take for granted, including the telephone and the computer.

Truth tables, electronic circuits, set theory, and Boolean algebra are equivalent systems for proving theorems. But many people are unaware that the roots of modern technology date back to 18th century philosophy. In 1705,

the philosopher Gottfried Wilhelm Leibniz showed that it's possible to combine logic and arithmetic using the binary number system. In 1886 another philosopher, the American logician and pragmatist Charles Sanders Peirce, described how logical operations could be carried out by electrical switching circuits. After World War II, switching circuit theory allowed technological innovation to proceed at an unprecedented rate. Logic circuits are composed of multiple logic gates which represent the same logical relationships as the truth tables. In fact, each of the operators we've discussed corresponds to a logic gate or gates. Here are the operators expressed in symbolic notation, truth tables, and logic gates.

Operator	Symbolic Notation	Truth Table Notation	Logic Gate
Negation	~p	<table><tr><td>p</td><td>~p</td></tr><tr><td>T</td><td>F</td></tr><tr><td>F</td><td>T</td></tr></table>	A —▷o— Ā NOT

Conjunction $p \cdot q$

p	$p \cdot q$	q
T	T	T
T	F	F
F	F	T
F	F	F

AND

Disjunction $p \vee q$

p	$p \vee q$	q
T	T	T
T	T	F
F	T	T
F	F	F

OR

Biconditional $p \equiv q$

p	$p \equiv q$	q
T	T	T
T	F	F
F	F	T
F	T	F

XNOR

What about the conditional logic gate? Switching circuit theory represents the conditional by combining two logic gates, the negation and the disjunction.

Conditional $p \supset q$

p	$p \supset q$	q
T	T	T
T	F	F
F	T	T
F	T	F

In the next chapter, we will learn the rule of inference that shows that $\sim p \vee q$ is equivalent to $p \supset q$ thus justifying this interpretation.

8.1C Truth Functions

We have defined each of the connectives in terms of a truth table. Compound statements involving these connectives are therefore *truth-functional*. That is, the truth or falsity of the compound statement is a function solely of the truth values of its components and does *not* depend on any other connection between the components. We need to appreciate the implications of this way of defining the connectives, including some of the problems it poses.

We saw that a statement of the form $p \bullet q$ is true as long as p and q are both true, even if those component statements have no other relationship. In real life, we would be puzzled if someone said something like:

Apples are red and the United Nations was formed in 1945.

The word "and" carries at least the suggestion that the elements it joins have some relevance to each other, however remote. But if we treat this compound statement truth-functionally, then the truth of the components is all that matters. This is not much of a problem with conjunction. The statement above is odd, but if someone pressed us, we would acknowledge that it is true. An "and" statement is nothing more than the sum of its parts, and both parts in this case are true.

A disjunctive statement in ordinary language, however, is not merely the sum of its parts, and the truth-functional interpretation is less natural here. We have already discussed the fact that the connective $\lor$ is inclusive rather than exclusive: The disjunction is true if p and q are both true as well as when just one of them is true. That's one point of difference from at least some uses of "or" in everyday speech. But the truth-functional definition raises additional questions. When we assert a statement of the form p *or* q, it's normally because p is related to q in some way that makes them alternatives in a given situation. We also assume that p and q are both genuine possibilities. But the truth-functional connective $\lor$ is not bound by these constraints. We can take any true statement and combine it with any other statement whatever to form a true disjunction. Thus:

Napoleon was French $\lor$ Caffeine is addictive

is true even though the components are not related in any way that makes them alternatives to each other. And:

Earth is spherical $\lor$ 2 + 2 = 5

is true even though the second disjunct is mathematically impossible. These statements would seem more than odd if we encountered them outside a logic text; we might well hesitate to call them true.

We would be even more hesitant about comparable examples of conditional statements. As we noted, the connective $\supset$ is a way of abstracting from the particular nature of the connection—causal, logical, means–end, etc.—between p and q. As a truth-functional connective, however, it does not require the existence of any connection between the propositions. Let's look at the truth table again:

p	p ⊃ q	q
T	T	T
T	F	F
F	T	T
F	T	F

The table shows that $p \supset q$ is true in both cases where p is false: the third and fourth rows. Thus a conditional with a false antecedent is true even if there is no connection between antecedent and consequent, as in:

If grass is red, then humans can breathe under water.   R ⊃ B

The table also shows that $p \supset q$ is true in both cases where q is true. So a conditional with a true consequent is true, again regardless of any connection, as in:

If water runs uphill, then grass is green.   W ⊃ G

These two examples are bizarre statements. They are extreme cases that illustrate the purely formal nature of the truth-functional connective. But even in cases closer to ordinary thought and speech, the same issues arise. In our initial discussion of conditionals, we considered the statement:

If you study hard, you will pass the test.

S	S ⊃ P	P
T	T	T
T	F	F
F	T	T
F	T	F

We saw that the statement is clearly false in the case where you have studied hard but do not pass (line 2 of the table). In every other case, the truth values of S and P are consistent with the truth of the conditional. Intuitively, though, the fact that they are consistent does not seem to guarantee the truth of the conditional, not in the way that the truth values on line 2 guarantee that the conditional is false. In line 1, for example, you study hard and pass the test. Does that make the conditional statement true? What if the instructor intended to give you a passing grade no matter how you did? Would the conditional statement still seem true?

In all of these examples, the hesitation to say that the statements are true arises from the sense that what makes a conditional true is some real connection between the conditions referred to by the component propositions. Since the truth-functional analysis of conditionals does not require any such connection, it seems to miss something relevant to their truth. It is only when the antecedent is true and the consequent false that the truth-functional analysis is clearly in line with our normal understanding of what makes conditional statements true or false. For on that line of the truth table, the truth values imply the absence of the connection that would make the conditional true.

The examples we have used so far have been indicative statements—the kind that purport simply to state what *is* the case. In English and other languages, however, we also make subjunctive statements about what *would be*, or *would have been*, the case. To see the difference, consider an earlier example:

> If grass is red, then humans can breathe under water.
> If grass were red, then humans could breathe under water.

The first statement is indicative, the second subjunctive. The first seems odd because there's no apparent connection between the color of grass and human respiratory abilities. But this statement does not explicitly assert such a connection. The second statement does. The subjunctive form states what would be true if some fact or circumstance were different from what it is, and we can make such a statement only on the assumption that there's some real connection between antecedent and consequent. So the mere fact that the antecedent is false is not enough to make a statement like the second example true. Subjunctive statements, which are also called *contrary-to-fact* or *counterfactual* statements, are not truth-functional and can't be symbolized by ⊃.

All of these points regarding conditionals apply equally to the biconditional, which is also a truth-functional connective. The symbol ≡ stands for a relationship among truth values; it does not imply any further connection between the components. The statement

> Squirrels eat nuts if and only if London has a subway.   S ≡ L

is true because both components are true. And

> Tom Clancy wrote Hamlet if and only if triangles have four sides.   C ≡ T

is true because both components are false. The lack of any connection in either case is irrelevant. But a subjunctive statement like

> I would have won the Olympic marathon if and only if I had had Wheaties every morning for breakfast.

is clearly false even though both components have the same truth value (false).

So you can see there's a problem with interpreting compound statements, especially conditionals, in a truth-functional way. The problem is quite complex; it touches on a number of basic issues concerning logic and language; and there is no consensus among specialists who have explored these issues in depth. We can't go into all the issues and theories in an introductory text, but we can say this: The if–then structure in language is used to make various types of statements, all of which are truth-functional in one respect: If the antecedent is true and the consequent false, then the conditional must be false—the situation described in line 2 of the truth table. On the other lines, where the antecedent is false or consequent true—their truth values are at least consistent with the truth of the conditional. For most of the things we are concerned with in propositional logic, consistency is enough. When we study propositional inferences, for example, as we will do in the next chapter, we will be concerned with how to tell whether an inference is valid or invalid and how to derive conclusions from premises in a valid way. Validity, as we know, means that if the premises of an argument are true then the conclusion must be true as well, and the test for whether an inference is valid or invalid is whether we could consistently affirm the premises and deny the conclusion.

So even if conditional statements in ordinary language assert something more than the truth-functional analysis captures, this "something more" is not relevant for most inferences. We can regard it as a simplifying assumption that the conditional is true on lines 1, 3, and 4 of the truth table for conditionals. This assumption allows us to use the truth table method as a systematic and powerful device for argument analysis. In the vast majority of cases, it is a reliable test for the validity of propositional inferences.

With these caveats about truth functions in mind, let us go on now to look at more complex statements involving the connectives.

APPLY Wason Selection Task

Imagine you are shown four cards with a letter on one side and a number on the other, and told, "If the card has a vowel on one side, then it has an even number on the other side." You are asked to test the statement by turning over only the cards to show the statement is false. How many—and which—card or cards do you flip?

| E | T | 2 | 5 |

If there is a vowel on one side, there is an even number on the other.

Most people answer either the E card alone or both the E and the 2 cards. Both answers are incorrect; they are examples of the confirmation bias we studied in Chapter 4. Don't feel bad if you chose incorrectly. As few as four percent of the population gets it right. We can use our knowledge of truth functions to avoid such errors. A conditional is false if and only if it has a true antecedent and a false consequent. To test the statement for falsity, we must turn over any card that has a vowel (true antecedent) or an odd number (false consequent). In other words, we must flip the E and 5 cards. This puzzle was first introduced by Peter Wason in the 1960s. It is studied by cognitive psychologists, neuroscientists, and philosophers in an attempt to better understand human reasoning.

EXERCISE 8.1C

Identify the components and the connective in each of the following statements. Then put the statement into symbolic form. For this exercise, it will be up to you to pick appropriate letters to stand for the components.

*1. Holly or Dexter will take your call.

2. Angel will buy a car provided he finds a job.

3. Either Spitball Harry gets his act together or we're going to lose this game.

*4. If Brazil was settled by aliens, water runs uphill.

5. Winning isn't the important thing.

6. If God is dead, everything is permitted.

*7. Jackson will work on Saturday if and only if he is paid overtime.

8. You can't hide your lying eyes, and your smile is a thin disguise.

9. Mason will tutor Reo given that there is no soccer match scheduled.

*10. I love Karen and Karen loves Abdul.

11. If it is raining in Seattle, copper conducts electricity.

12. Although the beach was beautiful, the water was shark-infested.

*13. Water freezes at 50°F or Canada is in North America.

14. Starting the charcoal with napalm is not a good idea.

15. Art is long but life is short.

*16. A bank will lend you money only if you're able to repay it.

17. The French Revolution was either an act of liberation or an act of destruction.

18. If Morley won the lottery, he is being unusually quiet about it.

*19. Swallows are nesting in the barn if and only if Congress is in session.

20. Decapitation is sufficient to bring about Patricia's death.

21. You should insert the disk if and only if you are ready to proceed.

*22. I'll ask his advice if and only if I consider him to be a worthy sage.

23. The penny-stock market is thinly traded and will soon collapse.

24. Gainor is a brilliant scholar of ancient languages, though she is so absentminded she needs business cards to remember her own name.

*25. Heating water to 212°F is both necessary and sufficient for boiling it.

26. The doctors X-rayed my head and did not find anything.

27. The defendant was not gone from his desk long enough to have killed the victim and returned to work.

*28. If you come to a fork in the road, [you should] take it.

29. I will definitely come to your party, unless something better comes along.

30. Daniel will submit a proposal just in case John agrees to help with the presentation.

8.2 Statement Forms

So far we have dealt chiefly with statements containing a single connective and two components (or just one in the case of negation). We can also put together much more complex statements, involving any number of connectives and components. Indeed, that is one of the chief advantages of a symbolic notation for connectives. To do so, however, we first need to talk about a distinction that has been implicit in what we have covered so far.

You may have noticed that we use capital letters as well as the lowercase letters p and q to represent statements. The capital letters are abbreviations for actual statements, so that we don't have to keep writing them out. We use lowercase letters when we want to talk about statements in general, so that we can identify the logical forms that compound statements can take. Consider the statement:

Either the car is out of gas or the fuel line is blocked.   C $\vee$ F

$p \vee q$

If we represent it as C $\vee$ F, we are symbolizing this particular statement, and the letters C and F stand for its particular component statements. However, we would use $p \vee q$ when we want to talk about this or any other disjunctive statement, with any pair of components. In logic we refer to the lowercase letters as **statement variables** and to a compound formula like $p \vee q$ as a **statement form**. Like the variable x in a mathematical equation, which can stand for any number, the statement variables p, q, r, etc., stand for any actual or possible statement. Together with the connectives, they are used to represent the abstract logical form of compound statements. An actual statement like 1 is a particular instance or example of the abstract form. The distinction between a statement form and its instances is like the distinction between a concept and the things it stands for. The concept DOG represents any and all particular dogs, abstracting from the differences among them in order to identify what they have in common as a type of animal. In the same way, a statement form abstracts from the differences among a class of actual statements in order to identify the logical form they have in common.

When we are dealing with simple components like C and F as instances, the distinction doesn't make much difference for understanding the logical form of statements. But it is vital when we deal with statements with components which are themselves complex.

Either I'll go home and watch television or I'll think about the election.

I'll go home, and I'll either watch television or think about the election.

These statements involve the same component propositions: I'll go home; I'll watch television; I'll think about the election. We can abbreviate them with the letters H, T, and E, respectively. And both have the same connectives: one conjunction and one disjunction. But they don't say the same thing. The second statement implies that H is true (i.e., that I will go home), while the first statement does not imply this.

That's a substantial difference. The reason for it becomes clear when we identify the logical form of each statement:

Statement 1			Statement 2		
H • T	∨	E	H	•	T ∨ E
p	∨	q	p	•	q

Like the earlier statement about the car, 1 has the basic logical form of a disjunction; it is also an instance of $p \vee q$. Unlike the earlier statement, the first disjunct in 1 is itself compound, with its own internal connective linking H and T. But disjunction is the *main* connective, and anything true of disjunction as such will be true of 1. However, as shown in the columns on the right, the main connective in 2 is conjunction. Statement 2 is an instance of $p \cdot q$, in which the q conjunct is itself compound.

So far we have identified the *core* logical form of these statements. But since the components are themselves compound and include internal connectives, we need to do more to capture the fully specific logical form. To do so, we need two rules of punctuation to avoid ambiguity. The first rule is to use parentheses so that the connectives •, ∨, ⊃, and ≡ join two and only two components, where one or both components may themselves be compound statements marked off by parentheses. The main connective stands outside all parentheses. Thus statements 1 and 2, and their fully specific logical forms, become:

$$(H \cdot T) \vee E \qquad H \cdot (T \vee E)$$
$$(p \cdot q) \vee r \qquad p \cdot (q \vee r)$$

In 1 and 2, the grouping makes a difference because the statements involve different connectives. If the connectives are all the same, it doesn't always matter how we group the components or which connective we treat as the main one. For example:

I'm going home, and I'm going to bed, and I'm going to sleep until Wednesday.

We could represent this statement either as H • (B • S) or as (H • B) • S. The statement forms

$$p \cdot (q \cdot r)$$

and

$$(p \cdot q) \cdot r$$

are equivalent. Just as you can add three numbers in any order and still get the same sum, you can group three conjuncts in any order and get equivalent statements. The same is true for disjunction: $(p \vee q) \vee r$ is equivalent to $p \vee (q \vee r)$. But it isn't true for conditionals. Compare the following statements:

If I have a million dollars, then if I am happy, I have nothing to complain about.	M ⊃ (H ⊃ C)
If it's true that if I have a million dollars, I am happy, then I have nothing to complain about.	(M ⊃ H) ⊃ C

These are clearly not equivalent. Even when the grouping does not make a difference, however, as with conjunction and disjunction, we must still group the components one way or the other, in accordance with the strict rule that connectives (other than negation) connect two and only two components.

The second rule of punctuation has to do with negation. A negation sign in front of a component statement is a denial of that component only, while a negation sign in front of a compound statement marked off by parentheses is a denial of the compound statement as a whole. The difference is illustrated by the following examples:

Either Leslie is not sad or she's a good actor.   ~S ∨ A

Leslie is neither sad nor a good actor.   ~(S ∨ A)

In the second one, notice that negation is the main connective, applied to the component S ∨ A as a whole. So when you are translating from English into symbolic notation, you'll need to decide whether the verbal indicators of negation ("not," "isn't," "neither . . . nor," etc.) apply to individual component statements or to compound ones.

Since we are now dealing with compound statements whose components can be internally complex, we need a way of referring specifically to the simple components that we represent with letters. Traditionally they are called **atomic statements**, by analogy with the atoms that make up molecules. Atomic statements do not have any internal connectives. They are the building blocks from which we can assemble compound statements by using connectives, and then use those compound statements in turn as components to build more complex statements. Using an example from the previous page, we can illustrate the terminology in a diagram. Each element in the symbolic formulation is labeled by the kind of element it is (top row) and by the role it plays in the statement (bottom row):

When you are given a complex statement to translate into symbolic form, you will need to rely on common sense and your knowledge of the English language. Your goal is to be able to answer three questions:

1. What are the atomic statements, the ones that will be assigned capital letters?
2. What is the main connective?
3. What are the other connectives, and how should they be grouped with the atomic statements?

Let's work through a few examples.

If the new video game is a big seller, we will make a lot of money; but if not, we will still have learned something about the market, and we will be able to use many of the techniques we invented for other products.

At first glance, it may look as if the main connective is a conditional, since the statement begins with "If." When we get to the semicolon, however, we can see that there's a second conditional, and that it is joined to the first one by conjunction. As a first step toward identifying the logical form, we can recognize that this sentence is saying "If X happens, then Y; but if ~X, then Z." The main connective is "but," which we know to translate as conjunction. Now let's identify and label the atomic components:

V   The new video game is a big seller.

M   We will make a lot of money.

L   We will learn something about the market.

I   We will be able to use many of the techniques we invented for other products.

Having answered questions (i) and (ii), it's pretty clear how to put it all together:

$$(V \supset M) \cdot [{\sim}V \supset (L \cdot I)]$$

Notice that we use square brackets around the second conjunct because we used parentheses around one of its components. This is a convenience to help us keep our groupings clear. If we needed to group bracketed statements together, we would use braces: { }.

Let's try another:

If the seller delivers the goods to the purchaser's warehouse by May 1, and either the purchaser or an authorized agent of the purchaser signs an invoice for said goods, then purchaser owes seller a sum of $1,000 unless said goods are found to be defective within 30 days.

In this case, the "If" at the beginning is not misleading: The statement does have the overall form of a conditional; in essence it says that if delivery is made, then money is owed. If you can see that right away, you can follow the same top-down strategy as in the previous example. But here the antecedent has a number of components, and we don't get to the consequent for quite a while. So you might find it easier to follow a bottom-up strategy, identifying and grouping the components as they come. Initially we can isolate three components:

G   The seller delivers the goods to the purchaser's warehouse by May 1.

P   The purchaser signs an invoice for said goods.

A   An authorized agent of the purchaser signs an invoice for said goods.

REVIEW Translating Complex Statements

When translating complex English statements into symbolic form, you should be able to answer three questions.

1. What are the atomic statements that will be assigned statement letters?

2. What is the main connective?

3. What are the other connectives, and how should they be grouped with the atomic statements?

What this part of the statement says is "G and either P or A." The meaning makes it clear how this should be punctuated:

G • (P ∨ A)

Now we can deal with the rest of the sentence, beginning with "then." There are two more simple components:

O   The purchaser owes seller a sum of $1,000.

D   The goods are found to be defective within 30 days.

This part of the statement says "O unless D." As we have seen, *p* unless *q* is to be translated if not *q* then *p*. So the consequent is a conditional and would be symbolized as ~D ⊃ O. Finally, we put the pieces together: Having analyzed the two halves of it separately, it should be clear that the statement as a whole is a conditional, so the main connective is a horseshoe:

[G • (P ∨ A)] ⊃ (~D ⊃ O)

Now, what is the logical form of this statement? One answer is:

[*p* • (*q* ∨ *r*)] ⊃ (~*s* ⊃ *t*)

This is the fully specific logical form. Each atomic statement has been replaced with a statement variable, and all of the connectives are included—the main connective as well as the connectives within the compound component statements. Any statement with the same structure would have the same logical properties, no matter what simple statements we substitute for *p*, *q*, *r*, *s*, and *t*. But it would also be true to say that our example has the logical form:

p ⊃ *q*

This is the core logical form, including only the main connective and using the variables *p* and *q* to stand for the main components. Our statement is an instance of both forms.

This simplified formula helps us to realize that our particular statement has the logical properties common to all conditionals, regardless of the fact that its antecedent and consequent are themselves compound. Suppose we want to know whether the following argument is valid:

[G • (P ∨ A)] ⊃ (~D ⊃ O)
G • (P ∨ A)
―――――――――――――
~D ⊃ O

If we start by looking for the main connective in the first premise, we can see that the premise has the form *p* ⊃ *q*. It then becomes obvious that the argument as a whole is a case of *modus ponens*:

p ⊃ *q*
p
―――――
q

which is a valid argument form. The internal structure of the antecedent and the consequent is irrelevant to the validity of the argument.

In the next chapter, we're going to learn how to analyze arguments involving rather complex propositions. Our tools of analysis, however, will be some fairly simple rules like *modus ponens*. So it's important that you learn to spot these simple patterns even when they are embedded within a more complex structure. The way to do that is to keep in mind the difference between actual statements and statement forms.

SOLVE Punctuation Rules

1. Use parentheses, brackets, and braces so that the connectives •, ∨, ⊃, and ≡ join two components, where one or both of the components may themselves be compound statements marked off by parentheses or brackets.

2. To negate a compound statement, enclose the compound statement within parentheses (or brackets) and place the negation sign in front of the left parenthesis (or bracket).

EXERCISE 8.2

I. **Integrative Exercise** Identify the main connective in each of the following statements.

∗1. (H • R) ≡ T

2. (N ∨ Q) ∨ Z

3. ~B ⊃ C

∗4. ~(B ⊃ C)

5. (J ∨ T) ∨ (K • G)

6. [(J ∨ T) ∨ K] • G

∗7. [(C • W) ⊃ I] • Q

8. L ⊃ [(U • T) ∨ (F ⊃ G)]

9. [(~J ⊃ K) ≡ (R ∨ B)] ≡ (R • K)

∗10. ~{[(J ⊃ K) ≡ (R ∨ B)] ⊃ (R • K)}

II. **Integrative Exercise** Put each of the following statements into symbolic notation, using appropriate letters to abbreviate atomic components.

∗1. You may have a dog only if you get straight As this year.

2. Publicity stunts are effective only if they are comprehensible.

3. If you have to ask, then you'll never know.

∗4. If the model is ready and the cameras are working, we should start shooting the photo.

5. You'll have fun if you just relax.

6. If you work hard and long, you'll find success in the end.

∗7. If Brooklyn is in California, then either California has become larger or Brooklyn has moved.

8. Raul will propose marriage if only he can talk to Maria alone.

9. Government is not the solution; it's the problem.

✳10. If you convinced me and I convinced you, then there would still be two points of view.

11. Both Mississippi and Oklahoma are not high-paying states for teachers.

12. The wedding will be perfect unless it rains or the groom doesn't show.

✳13. If a subatomic particle has a charge, the charge is either positive or negative.

14. Jada will apply to Michigan State in case Deandre does, but Jane will apply only to LSU.

15. If Paula's coming to the party implies that Evelyne will also, then Nellie will tag along.

✳16. Either you'll come to the barbecue and enjoy yourself or you'll stay at home and be depressed all day.

17. Neither Bill nor Lucy has indicated that they will attend the wedding.

18. It's not the case that if men were angels, government would not be necessary.

✳19. Your package will be there on Wednesday morning or my company isn't the best mailing service on the West Coast.

20. We may lose or we may win, but we will never be here again.

21. If you can't swim or dive, you are better off walking or running.

✳22. I'll tell it to a priest or I'll tell it to a bottle, but I won't go to see a shrink.

23. It isn't true that he quit his job, but if he did I'd be the first to know.

24. It's my party and I'll cry if I want to.

✳25. If you don't feel guilty about lying, then either you have a good reason for lying or you don't have a conscience.

26. The woods are lovely, dark and deep. But I have promises to keep.

27. If deuterium did change to helium, then fusion did take place, and we have discovered a new source of energy.

✳28. If you stand I will stand with you, and if you fall I will trip over you.

29. If soup is in short supply, then we will serve salad only if demand is great and it is included in the price of the meal.

30. The stock market will go up or it will go down, but if we can't know in advance which way it will move, it is better to stay invested.

✳31. If the weather is good and we leave early, then if we don't hit any bad traffic, we will arrive on time.

32. If an object is dropped, it will fall unless some other force counteracts gravity.

33. A labor is not worth doing unless it is worth doing passionately.

✳34. If you violate the law, you will go to jail, unless you are very rich or a politician.

35. We can visit your family on Christmas or we can visit my family in summer, but I won't go to Iowa in the winter or Arizona in the summer.

36. You should fill out either the singles' form or the married form, but not both.

✳37. The fire will be put out only if a fresh water supply is found, but it won't be found if we don't have more men searching.

38. Matt will sing given that Jose will dance if and only if Raul plays drums only if Dixie does.

39. Taken together, hard work and talent are sufficient for success.

*40. This liquid is water if and only if it will freeze if we chill it to 32°F and will boil if we heat it to 212°F.

41. If an overheated ocean and Earth's eastward rotation imply increased hurricane formation, then the U.S. Gulf Coast is in danger this summer.

42. He's either a knave or a fool, but he isn't both a knave and a fool.

*43. If nominated, I will not run, and if elected I will not serve.

44. If a student utilizing a university laboratory damages any equipment, then if the student is shown to be negligent, then the student will be held responsible for replacing the damaged equipment or will be suspended.

45. This visit is covered by your insurance if the doctor is in the network and you have paid your deductible, unless you've exceeded 40 visits or it's a new year.

*46. If the apartment allows pets and has a fitness room, we will take it today, unless it doesn't have on-site parking, in which case we'll have to wait until next month.

47. Taking the final exam is a necessary condition for passing the course according to the student handbook; moreover, passing all the exams and completing all other assignments is a sufficient condition for receiving a C.

48. Mrs. Goldberg will purchase a new winter coat at Filene's department store if Esmeralda invites her to come to Texas for the winter, provided that Jane offers to pay for the plane tickets and baggage fees.

*49. Lee's introducing the speaker implies that JuJu gives the closing remarks given that Sean's attending the afternoon sessions implies that neither Andres nor Aaron will give a presentation.

50. If ticket offices are open or ticket vending machines are available, and you buy your ticket on the train, you will be charged an additional $1.00, but you will not be charged the additional dollar if the station is not open.

8.3 Computing Truth Values

We have learned that a compound statement is truth-functional: Its truth or falsity is a function of the truth or falsity of its component statements. Now we will learn how to compute the truth value of a statement from information about the truth values of its components. For a statement with just one connective, the truth table column for that connective tells us how to make the computation. But we can also construct truth tables for more complex statements, with more than one connective, like the ones we discussed in the previous section. Knowing how to do this will enhance your understanding of complex statements and lay the ground for the next chapter, where we will learn how to construct and evaluate arguments involving such statements.

Let's begin by revisiting a previous example:

If the new video game is a big seller, we will make a lot of money; but if not, we will still have learned something about the market, and we will be able to use many of the techniques we invented for other products.

$(V \supset M) \bullet [\sim V \supset (L \bullet I)]$

Suppose it turns out that the game was not a big seller, but that it still made a lot of money; and that, while the company did not learn anything about the market, it did use the invented techniques for other products. In other words, M and I are true, V and L are false. What do these facts tell us about the truth or falsity of the entire statement?

To answer that question, let's create an abbreviated truth table and put in the truth values for the atomic statements. Notice that V occurs twice, so it has to have the same truth value in both places.

(V	⊃	M)	•	[~	V	⊃	(L	•	I)]
F		T			F		F		T

This truth table has a different format from the ones we have used previously. For simple compound statements with only one connective, we used columns for the atomic statements and put the compound statement at the head of its own column. For example:

p	p • q	q
T		T
T		F
F		T
F		F

With longer compound statements, it is easier to put just the relevant connective at the head of the column rather than repeating the whole statement. Thus in the abbreviated table above, the highlighted column with the main connective represents the truth value of the whole statement.

To compute the truth value of the whole statement, we must first compute the truth values of the components, starting with the connectives that apply directly to the atomic statements, putting T or F under those connectives. The first component, V ⊃ M, is true because V is false and M is true. Thus we put T under the horseshoe for that component. The second main component is internally complex, so the procedure is to work from the inside out, establishing truth values at each level of grouping before going on to higher levels. The conjunctive component L • I is false, since L is false. That conjunction is the consequent of a conditional statement whose antecedent, ~V, is true; so the conditional statement is false.

(V	⊃	M)	•	[~	V	⊃	(L	•	I)]
F	**T**	T		**T**	F	**F**	F	**F**	T

SOLVE Alternative Truth Table Methods

There are many acceptable methods for constructing truth tables. In this book, we have chosen to use the most efficient method, reducing the number of required columns to a minimum. But each method has its advantages and disadvantages. Using initial setup columns for establishing truth value assignments, while less efficient, may be a more effective way of

learning truth tables for some people. Let's look at the two methods side by side. The table on the left is the method this textbook uses, the one on the right is the alternative method.

Your instructor may choose to use either of these methods or another alternative. But whichever method you use, you can be certain your tables contain the same information.

P	⊃	(R	•	S)
T	T	T	T	T
T	F	T	F	F
T	F	F	F	T
T	F	F	F	F
F	T	T	T	T
F	T	T	F	F
F	T	F	F	T
F	T	F	F	F

P	R	S	P	⊃	(R	•	S)
T	T	T	T	T	T	T	T
T	T	F	T	F	T	F	F
T	F	T	T	F	F	F	T
T	F	F	T	F	F	F	F
F	T	T	F	T	T	T	T
F	T	F	F	T	T	F	F
F	F	T	F	T	F	F	T
F	F	F	F	T	F	F	F

We have now computed the truth values of the two main components of the statement, so we can take the final step of determining the truth value of the statement as a whole. The statement has the core logical form of a conjunction, $p • q$; since q is false, the conjunction is false.

(V	⊃	M)	•	[~	V	⊃	(L	•	I)]
F	T	T	**F**	T	F	F	F	F	T

In this case, we knew whether each of the components is true or false. But what if we don't know? Then we need to expand the truth table to include all the possible combinations of truth values for the atomic statements. Consider the conditional statement A ⊃ (A • B). Since the statement includes two atomic statements, we need four lines:

A	⊃	(A	•	B)
T		T		T
T		T		F
F		F		T
F		F		F

As in the previous example, the next step is to compute the truth value of the compound component (A • B in this case), but to do it for each line of the table, as indicated in bold below. We can then compute the truth value of the statement as a whole, as indicated under the main connective, ⊃.

A	⊃	(A	•	B)
T	**T**	T	**T**	T
T	**F**	T	**F**	F
F	**T**	F	**F**	T
F	**T**	F	**F**	F

Because this example involved just two atomic components, A and B, we could work with the familiar four-line truth table. But now we need to understand how to construct truth tables for statements with more atomic components. Remember that a truth table must represent every possible combination of truth values. Since each atomic statement can be either true or false, every additional atomic component requires that we double the number of lines in the table:

Atomic Statements	Rows in Truth Table
1	2
2	4
3	8
4	16
⋮	⋮
n	2^n

To ensure that we represent every possible combination of truth values, without repeating any combination or leaving any out, we fill in the truth values systematically. To illustrate the procedure, let's take a statement with three atomic components: ~A ⊃ (B ∨ C). The truth table will have eight rows.

~	A	⊃	(B	∨	C)
	T		T		T
	T		T		F
	T		F		T
	T		F		F
	F		T		T
	F		T		F
	F		F		T
	F		F		F

In each column for an atomic statement, the cells where we put T are highlighted. We start on the right, with the last statement, C, and alternate T and F in its column. Then we move left to the previous statement, B, and alternate two rows of T and two rows of F. Finally, in the column for A, we put T in the first four rows, F in the last four. If we had a compound statement with four atomic components, we would follow the same procedure, starting on the right with alternating rows of T and F, and moving left until we reached the first atomic statement. With four atomic components, the table will have 16 rows, so the column under the first component will have eight rows of T followed by 8 rows of F.

Now let's use the truth table to determine whether ~A ⊃ (B ∨ C) is true or false for each combination of atomic truth values.

~	A	⊃	(B	∨	C)
F	T	T	T	T	T
F	T	T	T	T	F
F	T	T	F	T	T
F	T	T	F	F	F
T	F	T	T	T	T
T	F	T	T	T	F
T	F	T	F	T	T
T	F	F	F	F	F

The main connective is a conditional, and both antecedent and consequent are compound, so we start by computing their truth values. The column under the tilde is determined by the column under A together with the rule for negation. The column under the vee is determined by the columns under B and under C together with the rule for disjunction. And the column under the horseshoe, representing the truth value of the statement as a whole, is determined by the columns under ~ and under ∨, together with the rule for conditionals, as shown in the shaded column.

Now let's look at the other punctuation rule from the preceding section, the one concerning negation. When the negation sign is attached to an atomic statement, it negates that statement only, but when it is outside the parentheses indicating a compound statement, the truth value under the negation sign in the table will be the opposite of the truth value under the connective in the compound component. To see the difference this makes, consider the statements ~(A • B) and ~A • B:

~	(A	•	B)
F	T	T	T
T	T	F	F
T	F	F	T
T	F	F	F

~	A	•	B
F	T	**F**	T
F	T	**F**	F
T	F	**T**	T
T	F	**F**	F

SOLVE Constructing Truth Tables

To construct the truth table for a statement with more than one connective:

1. Write the statement at the top of a table.
   a. Make enough rows to include every possible combination of truth values for the atomic component statements: for 1 atomic statement, 2 rows; for 2 statements, 4 rows; for 3 statements, 8 rows; etc.
   b. Make a column under each atomic statement and each connective, including negation signs.
2. In the column under the atomic statement farthest to the right, fill in alternating T and F from the first to the last row. In the column under the next atomic statement to the left, put T in the first two rows, F in the next two, and so on to the last row. Under the next atomic statement to the left, put T in the first four rows, F in the next four,

and so on to the last row. Continue in this fashion until you have put truth values in the columns under each atomic statement.
3. On each row, identify the connectives that apply directly to the atomic statements. Determine the truth value of the compound components involving just that connective, and put T or F in the column under that connective.
4. Identify the connectives that apply to the compound components identified in step 3. Determine the truth value of the higher-level compound components involving just *that* connective, and put T or F in the column under that connective. Repeat this step with each level of compound components until you reach the main connective (the one outside all parentheses). The truth values in its column are the truth values of the statement as a whole.

You can see from the columns under the main connectives that the placement of the negation sign results in different truth values for the two statements in the second and fourth rows.

EXERCISE 8.3

For each statement below, classify the statement by identifying the main connective and construct a truth table.

∗1. A ∨ (B ∨ A)

2. ~C ≡ D

3. ~(E ∨ F)

∗4. G • ~G

5. H ⊃ (I ⊃ H)

6. J ⊃ (K • L)

∗7. (M ∨ N) ≡ O

8. (P ⊃ Q) ≡ (~Q ⊃ ~P)

9. (R ⊃ ~S) ∨ (T • R)

∗10. [(U ⊃ V) • (~V ∨ W)] ≡ (U ⊃ W)

11. (A • B) ⊃ (C ∨ D)

12. ~(F • G) ⊃ (H ∨ I)

∗13. ~[K ∨ (L ⊃ ~M)]

14. ~[(~N ∨ ~O) ∨ (N ∨ O)]

15. (P • Q) ⊃ ~(R • S)

8.4 Formal Properties and Relationships

So far in this chapter we have learned about the connectives that bind atomic statements into compound statements. We have learned how to use these connectives to translate English sentences into symbolic form. We have seen that the connectives are truth-functional: The truth or falsity of a compound statement is determined solely by the truth values of its atomic components; for each combination of those truth values, the connectives specify whether the compound statement is true or false. The connectives determine the logical form of a statement, and we have seen how statements with the same logical form have certain features in common. In this section of the chapter, we are going to learn about some additional features that truth-functional statements have in virtue of their logical form.

8.4A Tautologies, Self-Contradictions, and Contingencies

In a truth table for a compound statement, each row represents a specific combination of truth values for the atomic statements, and the rows taken together represent every possible combination of atomic truth values. In the examples we have considered so far, the compound statement is true on some rows, false on others. But now we need to identify two special cases.

Consider the statements below:

A	≡	A		A	•	~	A
T	**T**	T		T	**F**	F	T
F	**T**	F		F	**F**	T	F

Both statements have a single atomic statement, A, so there are just two rows in the truth tables. The statement on the left, A ≡ A, has to be true by the very nature of the biconditional connective, regardless of what statement A says, and regardless of whether A is true or false. In other words, A ≡ A is true in virtue of its logical form, independently of the truth or falsity of its component. For example, you may not know how many floors there are in the Empire State Building, but you do know that the statement

> The Empire State Building has 97 floors if and only if the Empire State Building has 97 floors.

is true. A statement that has this property is called a **tautology**. A tautology is a compound statement that is true for every combination of truth values of its atomic components. In the truth table for a tautology, therefore, the column under the main connective will have only Ts, no Fs.

The statement on the right has the opposite property. It is false on each row of the table. By the very nature of negation, A and ~A cannot both be true, so the statement contradicts itself. Statement A may be true or it may be false, but A • ~A *has* to be false. For example, you may not know whether vinegar is an acid, but you do know that the statement

> Vinegar is an acid and vinegar is not an acid.

is false. Statements that have this property are called **self-contradictions**. As with tautologies, a statement is self-contradictory in virtue of its logical form, regardless of the truth values of its components. In the truth table for a self-contradiction, the column under the main connective will have only Fs, no Ts.

Tautologies and self-contradictions are not always so easy to identify. Let's consider a few more examples. (Since we are dealing with issues of logical form, our examples will be statement forms, using statement variables p, q, r, etc.).

p	⊃	(q	∨	p)
T	**T**	T	**T**	T
T	**T**	F	**T**	T
F	**T**	T	**T**	F
F	**T**	F	**F**	F

If you think about the truth-functional character of the connectives, you can see why a statement of this form will always be true. Since the statement is a conditional, it could be false only if the antecedent p is true and the consequent $q \lor p$ is false. But in every row where p is true in the antecedent, it is true in the consequent as well, which guarantees that $q \lor p$ is true. So there's no way the statement as a whole could be false. This statement is a tautology.

Now, consider this statement:

(p	⊃	q)	•	(p	•	~	q)
T	**T**	T	**F**	T	**F**	F	T
T	**F**	F	**F**	T	**T**	T	F
F	**T**	T	**F**	F	**F**	F	T
F	**T**	F	**F**	F	**F**	T	F

As you can see from the column under the main connective, a statement of this form is a self-contradiction. The main connective is conjunction, so both conjuncts would have to be true for the statement as a whole to be true. But there is no row in which that is the case, and once again you can see why. The first conjunct states that if p is true, then q is true as well. In other words, it denies that $p • \sim q$ is true. But that is exactly what the other conjunct affirms, making this statement a self-contradiction.

Compound statements that are neither tautologies nor self-contradictions are called **contingent statements** (or contingencies). Contingent statements are true for some combinations of atomic truth values, false for others. Their truth value, in other words, is contingent on the truth or falsity of their atomic components as well as their logical form, so they are true on some rows of their truth table but false on others.

EXERCISE 8.4A

Identify whether each of the statements below is a tautology, a self-contradiction, or a contingency by creating a truth table for the statement.

✱1. (A • B) ∨ A

2. (A ∨ B) ∨ ~A

3. (A ∨ B) ∨ A

✱4. ~A ⊃ (B ⊃ ~A)

5. (D • ~E) ⊃ E

6. (A ⊃ B) ∨ ~B

✱7. (A ⊃ B) • (A • ~B)

8. (A ⊃ B) • ~ (~A ∨ B)

9. ~(A ⊃ B) • B

✱10. (~A ∨ B) ∨ (~B • A)

11. (A ≡ B) ⊃ (A ∨ ~B)

12. [(A ⊃ B) • (A ⊃ ~B)] ≡ (A • B)

✱13. ~(P ⊃ Q) ≡ (~P ⊃ ~Q)

14. (A ⊃ B) • (B ⊃ C)

15. ~(A ∨ C) ≡ [(A ∨ B) • (B ⊃ C)]

✱16. [(A ≡ B) • (C ⊃ A)] • (C ⊃ ~B)

17. (P ⊃ Q) • (R ⊃ S)

18. (D ⊃ F) ⊃ (M ⊃ N)

8.4B Equivalence, Contradiction, and Consistency

In addition to revealing certain properties of individual statements, truth tables can reveal certain formal *relationships* between compound statements. The first of these relationships is **equivalence**, and we will see in the next chapter that it is extremely important for analyzing arguments. Two statements are equivalent when they have exactly the same truth values on each row of their respective truth tables (i.e., the same truth values in the column under their main connectives). For example, we have observed time and again that conditional statements are true whenever the antecedent is false or the consequent is true. We can now express that observation in terms of equivalence: $p \supset q$ is equivalent to $\sim p \lor q$.

p	⊃	q		~	p	∨	q
T	**T**	T		F	T	**T**	T
T	**F**	F		F	T	**F**	F
F	**T**	T		T	F	**T**	T
F	**T**	F		T	F	**T**	F

Any statement with the disjunctive form of $\sim p \lor q$ is false in the second row, where both disjuncts, $\sim p$ and q, are false—and that is the one row on which the conditional statement $p \supset q$ is false. The two statements are true on all other rows. Because the main connectives of these two statements have the same set of truth values, the statements are equivalent.

In Chapter 7, we discussed another case of equivalence: *not both p and q* is equivalent to *not-p or not-q*. We can now put these statement forms into symbolic notation and show their equivalence in a truth table:

~	(p	•	q)	~	p	∨	~	q
F	T	T	T	F	T	**F**	F	T
T	T	F	F	F	T	**T**	T	F
T	F	F	T	T	F	**T**	F	T
T	F	F	F	T	F	**T**	T	F

The opposite relationship to equivalence is **contradiction**. Two statements are contradictory when they have *opposite* values on every row of their respective truth tables (i.e., opposite truth values on each row under their main connectives). Here's a simple example:

~	p	∨	q		p	•	~	q
F	T	**T**	T		T	**F**	F	T
F	T	**F**	F		T	**T**	T	F
T	F	**T**	T		F	**F**	F	T
T	F	**T**	F		F	**F**	T	F

The truth table shows that the two statements have opposite values on all rows. If ~p ∨ q is true, then p • ~q has to be false. Once again, this is true in virtue of the logical form of the statements. Any pair of statements with the same logical forms as these will be contradictory.

Let's try one more example, this one with three atomic components:

(p • q) ⊃ r

~r ⊃ (~q ∨ ~p)

To determine whether these statement forms are equivalent, contradictory, or neither, we will need a truth table with eight rows:

(p	•	q)	⊃	r		~	r	⊃	(~	q	∨	~	p)
T	**T**	T	**T**	T		F	T	**T**	F	T	**F**	F	T
T	**T**	T	**F**	F		T	F	**F**	F	T	**F**	F	T
T	**F**	F	**T**	T		F	T	**T**	T	F	**T**	F	T
T	**F**	F	**T**	F		T	F	**T**	T	F	**T**	F	T
F	**F**	T	**T**	T		F	T	**T**	F	T	**T**	T	F
F	**F**	T	**T**	F		T	F	**T**	F	T	**T**	T	F
F	**F**	F	**T**	T		F	T	**T**	T	F	**T**	T	F
F	**F**	F	**T**	F		T	F	**T**	T	F	**T**	T	F

Both statement forms are conditionals. In (p • q) ⊃ r, the antecedent is a conjunctive statement that is true only in the first two rows. On the first row, where r is true, the conditional statement as a whole is true; on the second row, where r is false, the conditional is false. On all the remaining rows, the conditional is true simply because the antecedent is false. In ~r ⊃ (~q ∨ ~p), each of the atomic statement variables is negated, so the first step is to fill in the columns under the negation signs. In the four rows where the antecedent ~r is false, the conditional statement is true. In the other four rows, where ~r is true, the conditional is true in all the rows where the consequent, ~q ∨ ~p, is true. And that is the case in all the rows except the second. So the second statement is false only in that row, as is the first. The columns under the main connective of each statement are identical; the statements are equivalent.

To understand equivalence and contradiction, it is useful to consider how they relate to tautology and self-contradiction. Tautology and self-contradiction are features of individual statements, whereas equivalence and contradiction are relationships between two statements. Nevertheless, there's an important connection between equivalence and tautology and a similar connection between contradiction and self-contradiction.

If two statements are equivalent, we can connect them in a single biconditional statement that will be a tautology. A biconditional statement is true on a given row of its truth table when its components have the same truth value. If its components have the same truth values on *every* row of the truth table, then it is a tautology—and that will be the case whenever those components are equivalent. Thus, to take our first examples of $p \supset q$ and $\sim p \vee q$, the following statement form is a tautology:

(p	⊃	q)	≡	(∼	p	∨	q)
T	**T**	T	**T**	F	T	**T**	T
T	**F**	F	**T**	F	T	**F**	F
F	**T**	T	**T**	T	F	**T**	T
F	**T**	F	**T**	T	F	**T**	F

In the same way, connecting two contradictory statements into a single biconditional statement results in a self-contradiction. A biconditional statement is false on any row of its truth table where its components have different truth values. If the components are contradictory statements, they have opposite truth values on every row of their truth tables. So the biconditional must be false on each row, and that makes it a self-contradiction, as we can see by combining previous examples $\sim p \vee q$ and $p \bullet \sim q$ into a single biconditional:

(∼	p	∨	q)	≡	(p	•	∼	q)
F	T	**T**	T	**F**	T	**F**	F	T
F	T	**F**	F	**F**	T	**T**	T	F
T	F	**T**	T	**F**	F	**F**	F	T
T	F	**T**	F	**F**	F	**F**	T	F

There are two other relationships among statements that we need to understand: consistency and inconsistency. Like equivalence and contradiction, these are relationships that hold in virtue of the logical forms of the statements involved. Two statement forms are **consistent** if it is possible for instances of those forms to both be true. When statements are consistent, they do not contradict each other—the truth of one statement does not rule out the possibility that the other is true as well. As with the other relationships, we test for that possibility by means of truth tables. Each row of a truth table represents a possible combination of atomic truth values. For statements to be consistent, there must be at least one row on which both statements are true. Here's an example:

q	∨	(p	•	~	q)		p	•	q
T	**T**	T	F	F	T		T	**T**	T
F	**T**	T	T	T	F		T	**F**	F
T	**T**	F	F	F	T		F	**F**	T
F	**F**	F	F	T	F		F	**F**	F

Both statements are true in the first row, where their atomic components p and q are both true, so these statement forms are consistent. By contrast, the following statements are inconsistent:

p	≡	q		p	•	~	q
T	**T**	T		T	**F**	F	T
T	**F**	F		T	**T**	T	F
F	**F**	T		F	**F**	F	T
F	**T**	F		F	**F**	T	F

For p ≡ q to be true, p and q must both be true or both be false—the possibilities represented on the first and last rows of the table. For p • ~q to be true, p must be true and q false, as represented on the second row. Whatever actual statements we substitute for p and q, the logical forms of the compound statements make it impossible for them both to be true. Note that the statements are not contradictory: They could both be false, as on the third row, but they cannot both be true. However, two contradictory statements will necessarily be inconsistent. Because contradictory statements have opposite truth values on each row of their truth tables, there cannot be any row on which both statements are true.

As formal relationships among statements, consistency and inconsistency differ from equivalence and contradiction in several ways.

- *The criteria for equivalence and contradiction involve every row of the truth tables for the statements*: The statements must have the same truth value (for equivalence) or opposite truth values (for contradiction) on *all* rows of the tables. By contrast, the criterion for consistency can be met if the statements are both true on *some* rows (i.e., at least one).
- *For equivalence and contradiction, it does not matter whether the statements are true or false on any row of their truth tables*; what matters is whether they have the same truth

value (for equivalence) or opposite truth values (for contradiction) on every row. For consistency and inconsistency, by contrast, truth is precisely what matters. The criterion for consistency is not merely that the statements have the same truth value on at least one row, but that that value be T.

- *Unlike equivalence and contradiction, consistency and inconsistency are relationships that apply not only to pairs of statement forms but to sets of three or more.* For any set of statements, it is possible to construct truth tables like the ones we have used so far, and then determine whether there is any row where all the statements are true. As an example, let's take two of our earlier statements, which we saw were consistent. Notice what happens when we add a third statement:

q	∨	(p	•	~	q)	p	•	q	p	⊃	~	q
T	T	T	F	F	T	T	T	T	T	F	F	T
F	T	T	T	T	F	T	F	F	T	T	T	F
T	T	F	F	F	T	F	F	T	F	T	F	T
F	F	F	F	T	F	F	F	F	F	T	T	F

These three statements are inconsistent, since there is no combination of truth values for which they are all true. Though the third statement is consistent with the first, it is not consistent with the second, so the set of statements is inconsistent.

When you are given a pair of statements and want to know which of these relationships applies, the first step is to create the truth tables for the statements. Looking at the columns under the main connectives in each statement, you can then use the three points in the previous bulleted list, as well as the definitions of the relationships in the Review box. A good strategy to follow is first to check for equivalence and contradiction; if the statements have neither of those relationships, you can then check for consistency and inconsistency. The Solve box on the next page spells out the procedure as a kind of flowchart.

REVIEW Formal Relationships Among Statements

Two statements are:

- *equivalent* if and only if they have the *same* truth values for *all* combinations of their atomic truth values;
- *contradictory* if and only if they have *opposite* truth values for *all* combinations of their atomic truth values.

Two or more statements are:

- *consistent* if and only if there is *some* combination of their atomic truth values that makes all of them true;
- *inconsistent* if and only if there is *no* combination of truth values for their atomic component statements that makes all of them true.

SOLVE Identifying Formal Relationships

To identify the relationships among pairs of statements:

1. Create truth tables for the statements and examine the truth values under their main connectives.

2. Check for the formal relationships in the following order:

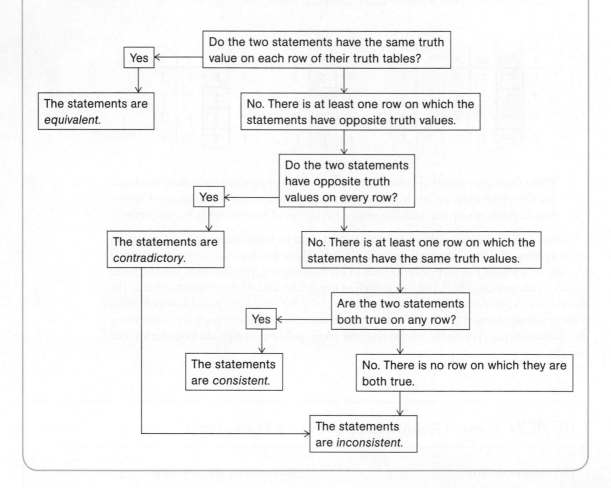

EXERCISE 8.4B

Determine whether the statements in each of the following sets are equivalent, contradictory, consistent, or inconsistent by creating truth tables for the statements.

*1.	~(A • B)	~A ∨ ~B	
2.	~(A • B)	~ (~A ∨ ~B)	
3.	~(A • B)	A ∨ B	
*4.	~(A ∨ B)	~(~A • ~B)	
5.	C ⊃ D	~(C • ~D)	
6.	C ⊃ D	C • ~D	
*7.	C ⊃ D	C ∨ ~D	
8.	Y ⊃ Z	~Z ⊃ ~Y	
9.	~ (Y ⊃ Z)	~(Z ∨ Y)	
*10.	Y ⊃ (Z • W)	~(Z • W) ⊃ ~Y	
11.	(Y ∨ W) ⊃ (Z • W)	~(Z • W) ⊃ ~(Y ∨ W)	
12.	~(A ⊃ C)	A ⊃ (C • B)	
*13.	E • (F ∨ G)	(E • F) ∨ (E • G)	
14.	E ∨ (F • G)	(E ∨ F) • G	
15.	J ≡ K	~ [(J ⊃ K) • (K ⊃ J)]	
*16.	(J ⊃ K) • (K ⊃ J)	(J • K) ∨ (~J • ~K)	
17.	(L • M) ⊃ N	L ⊃ (M ⊃ N)	
18.	(L ∨ M) ⊃ N	L ∨ (M ⊃ N)	
*19.	(A ⊃ B) ∨ (C • A)	~(A ⊃ B) • ~(C • A)	
20.	~[(Z ∨ Y) ⊃ W]	~W ⊃ ~(Z ∨ Y)	
21.	~[(C ⊃ E) ∨ (D • E)]	~[(C ⊃ E) • ~ (D • ~E)]	
*22.	(A • B) ⊃ C	B • ~ C	A ≡ C
23.	E • [F ∨ (G • H)]	(E • F) ∨ [E • (G • H)]	

8.5 Truth Table Test of Validity

In the previous sections, we learned how to put compound statements into symbolic form, using letters to represent the atomic component statements and connectives to represent the relationships among them. Now we will learn how to analyze and evaluate *arguments* involving compound statements. Here's an example of such an argument:

If Shakespeare did not write the plays attributed to him, scholars would have discovered the real author by now. But they haven't done so.	~W ⊃ D
	~D
Therefore, Shakespeare did write those plays.	W

The first sentence is a conditional statement involving the atomic statements W (Shakespeare wrote the plays attributed to him) and D (scholars have discovered the real author of those plays). The second sentence denies the consequent of the conditional. Those two statements function as premises in support of the conclusion, W.

As in traditional deductive logic, we evaluate arguments by the standard of validity. An argument is valid when the conclusion follows necessarily from the premises; that is, you cannot accept the premises as true but deny the truth of the conclusion without contradicting yourself. Conversely, an argument is invalid when the premises could be true while the conclusion is false. In deductive logic, whether traditional or modern, arguments are either valid or invalid: There is no middle ground; validity doesn't come in degrees.

In modern deductive logic, however, we can establish an argument's validity by methods that apply to more complex arguments than traditional logic was capable of handling. We're going to learn two of these methods. The first uses truth tables to find out whether the premises of an argument could all be true while the conclusion is false. The second, which we will learn in the next chapter, uses rules of inference to prove, step by step, that the conclusion follows from the premises.

In Section 8.3, we learned how to construct a truth table to compute the truth or falsity of a compound statement for all possible combinations of truth values of its atomic component statements:

- Create a column under each atomic statement and each connective.
- Create just enough rows to include every possible combination of truth values for the atomic statements: for 1 atomic statement, 2 rows; for 2 atomic statements, 4 rows; for 3 atomic statements, 8 rows; etc.
- Insert truth values for the atomic statements systematically, with alternating T and F in the column under the rightmost atomic statement, alternating TT and FF under the next statement to the left, and so on.

We can adapt this procedure to test for the validity of an argument. Let's work with the argument about Shakespeare:

~W ⊃ D
~D
W

If we were creating a truth table for the first premise alone, it would look like this:

~	W	⊃	D
F	T	**T**	T
F	T	**T**	F
T	F	**T**	T
T	F	**F**	F

To create a truth table for the *argument*, we create additional columns to represent the second premise and the conclusion, with a forward slash before the conclusion in order to separate it from the premises:

		Premise 1			Premise 2		/	Conclusion
~	W	⊃	D		~	D	/	W
	T		T			T		
	T		F			F		
	F		T			T		
	F		F			F		

As with truth tables for individual statements, each atomic component that appears more than once must have the same truth value on each row. So in the columns under premise 2 and the conclusion, the atomic statements D and W must have the same truth values on each row that each has in premise 1.

We now compute the truth values of each premise and of the conclusion, putting the result under the main connective for each statement. The procedure is exactly the same as with truth tables for single statements, except that now we have three different statements, whose truth values are represented in the three shaded columns.

		Premise 1			Premise 2		/	Conclusion
~	W	⊃	D		~	D	/	W
F	T	**T**	T		**F**	T		**T**
F	T	**T**	F		**T**	F		**T**
T	F	**T**	T		**F**	T		**F**
T	F	**F**	F		**T**	F		**F**

The test for validity is whether the conclusion can be false while the premises are both true. So the first step is to look at the column under the conclusion and flag the rows on which it is false—rows 3 and 4:

		Premise 1			Premise 2		/	Conclusion
~	W	⊃	D		~	D	/	W
F	T	**T**	T		**F**	T		**T**
F	T	**T**	F		**T**	F		**T**
T	F	**T**	T		**F**	T		**F**
T	F	**F**	F		**T**	F		**F**

Now we check the premises on those rows in order to see whether they are both true.

		Premise 1			Premise 2	/	Conclusion
~	W	⊃	D	~	D	/	W
F	T	**T**	T	**F**	T		**T**
F	T	**T**	F	**T**	F		**T**
T	F	**T**	T	**F**	T		**F**
T	F	**F**	F	**T**	F		**F**

In row 3, the premise ~D is false, and in line 4 the premise ~W ⊃ D is false. Since the truth table shows us every combination of possible truth values, we have just established that there's no way this argument could have true premises and a false conclusion, which is the standard for validity. So this argument is valid.

When we use truth tables to determine whether an argument is valid or invalid, we are concerned only with the truth values of the premises and conclusion as whole statements—the truth values in the shaded columns. For compound statements such as premises 1 or 2 in the previous argument, we disregard the truth values of their components and take account only of the columns under their main connectives. It's not that the truth values of the components are irrelevant: We had to take account of them in computing the truth value of the compound statement. But once we have done so, it is only the truth value of the statement as a whole that matters for validity; the truth values of the components have no further relevance.

Let's see how the truth table test identifies an invalid argument:

> If Iran is enriching uranium in order to make a bomb, it will hide the enrichment facility from satellite observation. That's exactly what Iran is doing, so its goal is to make a bomb.

$$B \supset H$$
$$\underline{H\qquad}$$
$$B$$

This argument is a case of affirming the consequent, which is fallacious. The truth table shows why. As before, we write the premises at the top, with the conclusion marked off by the slash; and we fill in the truth values on each row:

B	⊃	H	H	/	B
T	**T**	T	**T**		**T**
T	**F**	F	**F**		**T**
F	**T**	T	**T**		**F**
F	**T**	F	**F**		**F**

The conclusion is false in the third and fourth rows, and in row 3, both premises are true. It only takes one such case to show that the argument is not valid.

The truth table test for validity will work with arguments of any complexity. Let's try the argument:

A ⊃ B
C ⊃ B
A ⊃ C

We have three atomic components here (A, B, and C), so to represent all the possibilities we need a truth table with eight lines:

A	⊃	B	C	⊃	B	/	A	⊃	C
T	**T**	T	T	**T**	T		T	**T**	T
T	**T**	T	F	**T**	T		T	**F**	F
T	**F**	F	T	**F**	F		T	**T**	T
T	**F**	F	F	**T**	F		T	**F**	F
F	**T**	T	T	**T**	T		F	**T**	T
F	**T**	T	F	**T**	T		F	**T**	F
F	**T**	F	T	**F**	F		F	**T**	T
F	**T**	F	F	**T**	F		F	**T**	F

The conclusion is false on rows 2 and 4. On row 4, the first premise is false, so there is no problem. But on row 2, both of the premises are true. So that row establishes that the premises could be true while the conclusion is false. The argument is not valid.

So far we have been working back from the conclusion to the premises. We can also work forward from premises to conclusion: We flag the rows on which all the premises are true, and then check to see whether the conclusion is false on any of those rows. We will reach the same result regardless of where we start, but sometimes it is easier to work forward. Consider the argument:

(A ∨ B) ⊃ C
A
C   1

(A	∨	B)	⊃	C	A	/	C
T	T	T	**T**	T	**T**		**T**
T	T	T	**F**	F	**T**		**F**
T	T	F	**T**	T	**T**		**T**
T	T	F	**F**	F	**T**		**F**
F	T	T	**T**	T	**F**		**T**
F	T	T	**F**	F	**F**		**F**
F	F	F	**T**	T	**F**		**T**
F	F	F	**T**	F	**F**		**F**

There are just two rows on which the premises are both true, and the conclusion is true on both rows. So the argument is valid. To double-check that it's valid, notice that the conclusion is false on four other rows, and on each of those rows at least one premise is false.

SOLVE Truth Table Test of Validity

To determine whether a propositional argument is valid:

1. Create a truth table for the argument.
   a. Put the premises and the conclusion in the top row of a truth table, with a forward slash before the conclusion.
   b. Make columns under each connective and each atomic statement contained in the premises and conclusion.
   c. Create just enough rows to include every possible combination of truth values for the atomic statements that are components of the premises and conclusion: for 1 atomic statement, 2 rows; for 2 atomic statements, 4 rows; for 3 atomic statements, 8 rows; etc.
   d. Insert truth values for the atomic statements systematically, with alternating T and F in the column under the rightmost

atomic statement, alternating TT and FF under the next statement to the left, and so on, until you have inserted truth values in every column under an atomic statement.

2. Test for validity:
   a. Identify each row in which the conclusion is false. If there is at least one false premise in every such row, the argument is valid. If the premises are all true in any row where the conclusion is false, the argument is invalid.

   OR

   b. Alternative: Identify each row in which the premises are all true. If the conclusion is false in any such row, the argument is invalid. If the conclusion is true in all rows where the premises are all true, the argument is valid.

EXERCISE 8.5

For each of the following arguments, construct a truth table to determine whether it is valid. If it is invalid, indicate which row or rows have true premises and a false conclusion.

✽1. A ⊃ B
    B
    A

2. C ∨ D
    D
    ~C

3. E ⊃ F
    ~E
    ~F

✽4. F ≡ G
    F ∨ G
    F • G

5. ~A ≡ ~B
    B ∨ A
    ~A

6. A • B
    B ∨ A

✽7. G ⊃ H
    G ⊃ (G • H)

8. A ⊃ ~A
    (B ⊃ A) ⊃ B
    A ≡ ~B

9. J ⊃ K
    K ⊃ L
    J ⊃ L

✽10. ~(M ∨ N)
    ~N

11. D ⊃ E
    E ⊃ D
    (D • E) ∨ (~D • ~E)

12. P • Q
    Q • R
    P ⊃ R

✽13. S ⊃ (T • V)
    ~V
    ~S

14. A ⊃ ~(B ⊃ C)
    A
    B

15. (J ⊃ K) ⊃ J
    (K ⊃ J) ⊃ K
    ~J ∨ ~K

✽16. (M ∨ N) ⊃ S
    ~S ∨ O
    ~O
    ~M • ~N

17. (P ≡ T) ⊃ ~M
    R ∨ ~M
    ~R
    P ≡ T

18. D ∨ ~(S ≡ T)
    D ⊃ T
    S ⊃ (~T • ~S)
    S
    ~(S ≡ T)

✽19. P ⊃ R
    X ⊃ ~M
    R ⊃ M
    M ⊃ X
    P ⊃ ~M

20. P ⊃ (S • R)
    R ∨ ~P
    ~R ∨ T
    ~T
    P • R

APPLY **A Truth Table Might Save Your Life Someday**

No, really. Current research on molecular logic gates is making nanomedicine a reality. By designing an injectable molecule using chemical or physical "statement letters," to produce outputs corresponding to truth functions, scientists may be able to treat illnesses and prevent tissue damage before we even know it's happening. Chances are, these logic gates will be constructed out of DNA. In the April 2004 edition of *Nature*, it was announced that scientists at the Weizmann Institute successfully constructed a DNA computer. Family history of cancer? A biocomputer could detect cancer cells as they develop and dispense anticancer drugs thus preventing tumors before they can form. In other cases, oncologists may treat cancer by injecting DNA logic gates that work in sequence to deliver multistep therapies. Nanosurgery might even be customized according to occupational risk factors. For example, ironworkers or others whose jobs require them to work at dangerous heights may soon be able to be injected with a DNA logic gate capable of sensing and reducing the presence of thrombin, a blood-clotting enzyme which causes brain damage following a head injury.

8.6 Truth Table Test: Short Form

It's rather cumbersome to work with an eight-row truth table, and for every additional atomic component statement, we double the number of rows we need. The problem gets worse exponentially: For an argument with n components, we need a table with 2^n lines. Fortunately, there's a shorter and more efficient way to construct and use truth tables. This shortcut method can, in many cases, reduce our truth tables to a single line. In the following sections, we will learn how to construct short-form truth tables and use them to test for both validity and consistency.

8.6A Validity

We've seen that in a valid argument the truth of the premises guarantees the truth of the conclusion. This means that an argument in which it's possible for all the premises to be true, and the conclusion still to be false, is invalid. For practical purposes, this means that we can simply check for an invalidating truth value assignment—a line in which all the premises are true and the conclusion is false—when using a truth table to test for validity. In a properly constructed truth table, finding such a line shows the argument is invalid. By contrast, if there is no such line, the argument is valid. Thus we're always looking for confirmation that the argument is invalid; failure to find that confirmation is, by default, conclusive proof of validity.

   This suggests a shortcut: instead of writing out the whole truth table for an argument, we can simply attempt to construct a row where all the premises are true and the conclusion is false. If we can find a consistent truth value assignment that satisfies this requirement, the argument's invalid. If there is no such line, it's valid.

Let's do this for an argument that has four atomic components, for which the complete truth table would require 16 lines.

(G ⊃ H) • (J ⊃ K)
G ∨ J
———————————
H ∨ K

We start in the usual way, putting the premises and conclusion in a row. We put the letter T under the main connective in each premise and F under the main connective in the conclusion to indicate our goal: We are looking for a way to assign truth values to individual components that will make the premises true and the conclusion false. In other words, we are going to work back from the truth values under the main connectives in order to see whether any assignment of truth values to the components could give rise to that result. It's a bit like doing a crossword or sudoku puzzle.

(G	⊃	H)	•	(J	⊃	K)	G	∨	J	/	H	∨	K
			T					T				F	

We will begin with the conclusion since it is a disjunctive statement, and a disjunction is false only if both disjuncts are false. So we put an F under H and K in the conclusion—and then under those letters wherever else they occur, since we must assign truth values to letters consistently.

(G	⊃	H)	•	(J	⊃	K)	G	∨	J	/	H	∨	K
		F	T			F		T			F	F	F

Notice that the first premise is a conjunction, so it can be true only if each conjunct is true. And each conjunct is a conditional statement with a false consequent (H in the first case, K in the second), so it will be true only if the antecedents (G and J) are also false.

(G	⊃	H)	•	(J	⊃	K)	G	∨	J	/	H	∨	K
F	T	F	T	F	T	F		T			F	F	F

To be consistent, of course, we need to put an F under G and J in the second premise. But that would make the premise itself false. So we can see that there is simply no way to make both premises true and the conclusion false. We have established that the argument is valid without needing to lay out all 16 lines of the truth table.

The short method worked out very easily with this argument because there is only one pair of truth values for H and K that makes the conclusion false. This will not always be the case. In the argument:

A ∨ C
C ⊃ D
<u>D • B</u>
A • B

the conclusion is a conjunction, which can be false in three different ways. If we start there, we have three lines to consider. It would be more efficient to start with the third premise. It too is a conjunction, but since it is a premise, we are trying to make it true. There's only one way to do that:

A	∨	C	C	⊃	D	D	•	B	/	A	•	B
	T		T	T	T	T	T	T			F	T

Since B is true, the only way to make the conclusion false is to make A false:

A	∨	C	C	⊃	D	D	•	B	/	A	•	B
F	T			T	T	T	T	T		F	F	T

Now we can see that the only way to make the first premise true is to make C true, and that makes the second premise true as well. So we have found a set of component truth values that make all the premises true and the conclusion false—which proves that the argument is invalid.

APPLY A Truth Table Might Rob You of Your Humanity Someday

Well, maybe. Some people believe that advances in technology, including nanotechnology utilizing DNA truth tables, may allow us to enhance (or eliminate) our bodies, improve our cognition, and delay or prevent aging to such an extent that we direct our own evolution to a new species. These posthumans may take one of several forms. Our descendants might be biological, though radically augmented, humans or cyborgs. Or maybe the posthuman will be a symbiosis of human and artificial intelligence consisting of a brain–computer interface. Post-

humans might even exist solely as uploaded consciousnesses. Most futurists think there will be one or more transitional species, trans-humans, as we use emerging fields such as nanotechnology, genetic engineering, and bio-engineering to create beings that are smarter, stronger, longer-lived, and more durable than we are. Sound far-fetched? Maybe so, but some transhumanists argue that we are already seeing signs of the future in the growing use of mediated reproduction, reconstructive surgery, and gene therapies.

It will not always be possible to test validity by considering only a single line. Sometimes it is necessary to examine several possible sets of component truth values. Here's an example:

(L ∨ M) ⊃ N
~N ∨ O
(O • L) ⊃ M
M ≡ N

Each of the premises can be true with more than one combination of component truth values, and the conclusion can be false with more than one combination. So we will have to try more than one set of truth values. Let's start with the conclusion. A biconditional statement is false if its components have opposite truth values. We need two lines in the table to capture both of the ways that can happen:

(L	∨	M)	⊃	N		~	N	∨	O		(O	•	L)	⊃	M	/	M	≡	N
		T	**T**	F			F	**T**						**T**	T		T	**F**	F
			T					**T**						**T**			F	**F**	T

In row 1, we can see right away that if M is true and N false, there is no way to make the first premise true:

(L	∨	M)	⊃	N		~	N	∨	O		(O	•	L)	⊃	M	/	M	≡	N
		T	**T**	F			F	**T**						**T**	T		T	**F**	F
			T					**T**						**T**			F	**F**	T

Since that premise is a conditional with a false consequent (N), it can be true only if the antecedent is false. Since M is true on this line, however, the disjunctive antecedent is true, which makes the premise false. We need not go further. No matter what values O and L have, we have established that there's no way to make both premises true in row 1.

So we can turn to row 2, where M is false and N true. We can start with the second premise: For the disjunction to be true, O must be true.

(L	∨	M)	⊃	N		~	N	∨	O		(O	•	L)	⊃	M	/	M	≡	N
		T	**T**	F			F	**T**						**T**	T		T	**F**	F
F		T	**T**	T		F	T	**T**	T		T			**T**	F		F	**F**	T

The third premise is a conditional whose consequent, M, is false. So the premise will be true only if we can make the antecedent of the conditional false. Since O is true, L must be false. And that makes the antecedent of the first premise false and the premise itself true.

(L	∨	M)	⊃	N		~	N	∨	O		(O	•	L)	⊃	M	/	M	≡	N
			T	**T**	F		F	**T**						**T**	T		T	**F**	F
F	F	F	**T**	T		F	T	**T**	T		T	F	F	**T**	F		F	**F**	T

The result is that all the premises are true on this line. Since we have this one case in which the premises are true and the conclusion false, the argument is invalid. Even though we had to consider two different cases, the short method was easier and faster than constructing the entire truth table for this argument.

SOLVE Truth Table Test: Short Form

To use the short form of the truth table test for validity:

1. Put the premises and the conclusion in the top row of a truth table, with a slash mark before the conclusion. Make columns under each atomic statement and each connective.

2. Put T under the main connective in each premise and F under the main connective in the conclusion.

3. Identify each combination of truth values for the atomic components of the conclusion that will make it *false*. Create a row for each combination. If there are more than a few such combinations, then try to identify one of the premises that can be made *true* by fewer combinations of atomic truth values.

4. In either case, put each combination of truth values in its own row, making sure that in each row, each atomic component has the same truth value wherever it occurs in the argument.

5. Determine whether any combination of truth values is consistent with the truth of the premises and the falsity of the conclusion. If so, the argument is invalid. If not, the argument is valid.

EXERCISE 8.6A

Integrative Exercise Test each of the following arguments for validity by using the short form of the truth table test. (If you are uncertain of your answer, create a full truth table for the argument.)

＊1. A • B
  C ∨ B
  ~C

2. D ∨ (E • F)
  ~E
  D

3. F ⊃ (G ⊃ H)
  F • H
  G

＊4. J ⊃ K
  K ⊃ L
  ~L
  ~J

5. (C ⊃ D) ⊃ (D ⊃ B)
   D _____
   C ⊃ B

6. (M • N) ∨ (N • O)
   N ⊃ ~M _____
   O

*7. W ⊃ Y
   (W ⊃ Z) ∨ (Y ⊃ Z)
   ~Z _____
   ~(W • Y)

8. (C • D) ⊃ (P • M)
   P ∨ C
   ~P • D
   T ∨ ~D _____
   P • M

9. (J ⊃ K) ⊃ J
   (K ⊃ J) ⊃ K _____
   ~J ∨ ~K

*10. (A • C) ∨ (B ⊃ C)
   ~C ∨ B _____
   ~B ∨ C

11. S ⊃ T
   V ⊃ W
   S ∨ V
   ~W _____
   T

12. R ≡ T
   ~R ∨ O
   O ⊃ S
   C ∨ ~S
   ~C • N _____
   ~T

*13. (E ⊃ F) ∨ [E ⊃ (G • H)]
   H ⊃ (F ∨ G) _____
   E ⊃ H

14. (J ⊃ K) • (L ⊃ M)
   ~K ∨ ~M _____
   ~J ∨ ~L

15. [(J • T) • Y] ∨ (~J ⊃ ~Y)
   J ⊃ T
   T ⊃ Y _____
   Y ≡ T

*16. ~[A ∨ ~(B ∨ ~C)]
   D ⊃ (A ⊃ C) _____
   ~A ≡ ~B

17. (R • C) ⊃ ~E
   ~(C • R) ⊃ S
   ~F ⊃ ~S _____
   E ⊃ F

18. P ⊃ T
   T ⊃ N
   P ∨ ~F
   R ⊃ F
   T ∨ R
   D • ~T _____
   P ≡ T

*19. N ∨ O
   P ∨ Q
   ~Q ∨ N
   P ⊃ (N ∨ R) _____
   O

20. (A ∨ B) ⊃ [C • (D ⊃ E)]
   A _____
   D ⊃ E

8.6B Consistency

We can also use short-form truth tables to test pairs or sets of compound statements. The short-form test for propositions is similar to that for arguments except, of course, for the fact that there is no conclusion since we are examining single statements. Remember that two statements are consistent if and only if it's possible for them to both be true, that is, they don't contradict each other. We may test for consistency by constructing a short-form truth table showing that it's possible for the main operators of the statements to both be true. If it's not possible for the two statements to be simultaneously true, they are inconsistent. Here's an example:

$$(M \cdot R) \supset (M \cdot S) \qquad\qquad M \cdot R$$

Let's test for consistency using the short-form method. We'll start by assigning each of the main operators' truth values. Since we are trying to find a truth value assignment showing that the two statements are consistent, we must make each of the main operators true.

(M	•	R)	⊃	(M	•	S)	M	•	R
			T					T	

There are three ways a conditional can be true but only one way a conjunction can be true, so we'll start with the conjunction. For the conjunction to be true, each conjunct must be true.

(M	•	R)	⊃	(M	•	S)	M	•	R
			T				T	T	T

Values must be assigned consistently in order to provide a fair test; we'll fill in the values of M and R in the conditional.

(M	•	R)	⊃	(M	•	S)	M	•	R
T	T	T	T	T			T	T	T

Since a true antecedent with a false consequent is false, we must make S true to preserve the truth of the conditional. We are able to do so without contradiction, so the two statements are consistent.

(M	•	R)	⊃	(M	•	S)	M	•	R
T	T	T	T	T	T	T	T	T	T

Let's look at another example. Consider the following set of statements:

$$C \supset (S \lor F) \qquad\qquad F \lor C \qquad\qquad S \supset {\sim}C \qquad\qquad {\sim}F$$

Again, we want each of the main operators to be true.

C	⊃	(S	∨	F)	F	∨	C	S	⊃	~	C	~	F
	T					T			T			T	

We then need to compute the values for the components. There's only one way for the fourth statement to be true; let's start there and assign the values for all occurrences of F.

C	⊃	(S	∨	F)		F	∨	C		S	⊃	~	C		~	F
T				F		F	T				T				T	F

There is now only one way for the disjunction to be true: C must be true. We can now fill in the values for C.

C	⊃	(S	∨	F)		F	∨	C		S	⊃	~	C		~	F
T	T			F		F	T	T			T	F	T		T	F

Look carefully at the first statement. A conditional with a true antecedent and a false consequent is false. We must make S true in order for the first statement to be true. But, since we must assign values consistently, we are unable to make the third statement true.

C	⊃	(S	∨	F)		F	∨	C		S	⊃	~	C		~	F
T	T	T	T	F		F	T	T		T	T	F	T		T	F

Therefore the statements are inconsistent.

When we used short-form truth tables to test for validity, we saw that more than a single line was sometimes necessary. It's the same when testing statements for consistency. Consider the following set of statements.

$$P \supset (R \bullet S) \qquad P \lor R \qquad \sim R \supset (S \bullet T)$$

We want to make each of the main operators true as in the previous examples.

P	⊃	(R	•	S)		P	∨	R		~	R	⊃	(S	•	T)
	T						T					T			

Each of the statements can be true in three different ways. We'll select one of the statements and figure out all the ways it can be true.

P	⊃	(R	•	S)		P	∨	R		~	R	⊃	(S	•	T)
	T					T	T	T				T			
						T	T	F							
						F	T	T							

We now know the values for P and R on each line. Let's fill in those values for the first line.

P	⊃	(R	•	S)		P	∨	R		~	R	⊃	(S	•	T)
T	T	T				T	T	T		F	T	T			
						T	T	F							
						F	T	T							

Notice that the last statement has a false antecedent. A false antecedent conditional is always true. Thus we may assign any values we like to the consequent as long as they don't conflict with those we have already assigned. So how do we know which values to assign? A look at the first statement gives us the answer. In order for a true antecedent conditional to be true, it must also have a true consequent. In this case, the consequent is the conjunction R • S. The only way to make this consequent true is to make both conjuncts true. Once we fill in the truth value for S, we simply make an arbitrary truth value assignment (you may select either true or false) for T. We'll make it true this time.

P	⊃	(R	•	S)		P	∨	R		~	R	⊃	(S	•	T)
T	T	T	T	T		T	T	T		F	T	T	T	T	T
						T	T	F							
						F	T	T							

We have shown that it is possible for all these statements to be simultaneously true; therefore they are consistent, and we don't need to fill out the other lines. We must fill out each line of multiline truth tables until we find a truth value assignment that shows the given statements are consistent or until we reach a contradiction for every possible truth value assignment.

EXERCISE 8.6B

Integrative Exercise Use the short form of the truth table test to determine whether the following sets of statements are consistent or inconsistent.

❋1. A ⊃ B
  A • B
  ~A ∨ B

2. D ∨ H
  ~D • (H ⊃ L)
  M ⊃ L
  L • ~D

3. P ⊃ K
 P • ~K
 P ⊃ (P • K)

∗4. D ⊃ G
 (D • F) ∨ G
 ~G • ~F

5. R ≡ S
 ~R ∨ S
 ~S ∨ R

6. C ⊃ G
 (C ≡ G) ⊃ N
 ~N • ~G

∗7. F ⊃ G
 G ∨ ~F
 F ≡ G

8. ~D ∨ ~F
 ~(D • F) ∨ T
 T ⊃ ~F
 ~T ⊃ (D • ~F)

9. ~T
 M ⊃ ~T
 T ⊃ ~M
 S ⊃ T

∗10. (P ∨ Q) • R
 (R • P) ∨ (R • Q)
 ~R • D
 D ⊃ R

11. C ⊃ ~A
 ~C ∨ (~A ∨ T)
 C • R
 (C • S) ∨ (R • S)
 ~A

12. P ⊃ T
 S ⊃ (M • O)
 ~T ∨ S
 T ⊃ (~S • ~P)

∗13. R ⊃ P
 T ⊃ P
 Q ⊃ P
 ~P • (~Q • ~T)
 ~P ∨ (S • ~R)
 ~Q ∨ (A • B)

14. P ⊃ Q
 Q ⊃ R
 T ∨ ~R
 P ⊃ T
 ~T ⊃ S

15. (H ⊃ T) ⊃ (T ⊃ H)
 H ≡ T
 H • T
 ~(H ∨ T)
 (H ∨ T) ⊃ (A • B)
 A ⊃ (H • T)

CHAPTER REVIEW

Summary

- Propositional logic is the logic of compound statements. Compound statements are made up of atomic statements linked together by connectives.
- We defined five basic forms of compound statements, involving five different connectives: $\sim p$ (negation), $p \bullet q$ (conjunction), $p \vee q$ (disjunction), $p \supset q$ (conditional), and $p \equiv q$ (biconditional).
- The basic forms, together with the rules of punctuation, allow us to construct more complex compound statements.
- The truth value of a compound statement is a function of the truth values of its components in accordance with the truth table for the connectives involved.
- We can construct more complex truth tables for compound statements involving more than one connective. These truth tables show whether the statement is true or false for each combination of truth values of its atomic components.
- Two special types of compound statements have truth values determined by their logical form, regardless of the truth values of their atomic components. Tautologies are true for every combination of atomic truth value; self-contradictions are false for every combination.
- There are also relations that hold among statements by virtue of their respective logical forms: equivalence, contradiction, consistency, and inconsistency.
- We can also construct truth tables to test arguments for validity. We simply construct a table in which the truth values of the premises and conclusion are computed for each possible combination of truth values of the atomic statements.
- In a shorter version of this method, we look for assignments of truth values that will make premises true and the conclusion false. If there is such an assignment, the argument is invalid; otherwise it is valid.
- This short-form method can also be used to check sets of statements for consistency. To test for consistency, we try to find a consistent truth value assignment showing that the main operators for each statement can be simultaneously true.

Key Terms

negation (p. 319)
conjunction (p. 319)
disjunction (p. 319)
conditional (p. 319)
biconditional (p. 319)
truth table (p. 320)
truth value (p. 320)
statement variables (p. 337)

statement form (p. 337)
atomic statement (p. 339)
tautology (p. 351)
self-contradiction (p. 351)
contingent statement (p. 352)
equivalence (p. 353)
contradiction (p. 353)
consistent (p. 355)

Putting It All Together

I. Put each of the following statements into symbolic form, replacing English words and punctuation with connectives and parentheses.

∗1. *p* if *q*

2. Either *p* or *q*

3. It's not the case that *p*

∗4. *p* and either *q* or *r*

5. Not both *p* and *q*

6. *p* unless *q*

∗7. Neither *p* nor *q*

8. If *p* and *q*, then not *r*

9. Either *p* or *q*, although if *p* then not *r*

∗10. *p* or *q* if and only if *r*

11. If *p* and either *q* or *r*, then *s*

12. If neither *p* nor *q*, then if *r* or *s*, *t*

∗13. It's true that if *p*, then *q*, if and only if it's also true that if *r*, then *s*

14. If not *p* and not *q*, then *r*, *s*, and *t*

15. If not both *p* and *q*, then *r*, and if *p* or *q*, then *s*

II. Find statements in English that have the following logical forms.

∗1. ~*p* ∨ *q*

2. *p* • *q*

3. *p* ⊃ *q*

∗4. *p* • (*q* ∨ *r*)

5. ~(*p* ∨ *q*)

6. (*p* ∨ *q*) • *r*

∗7. *p* ⊃ (*q* ∨ ~*r*)

8. (*p* • *q*) ∨ (*r* • *s*)

9. (*p* • ~*q*) ⊃ *r*

∗10. (*p* ∨ *q*) • (*r* ∨ *s*)

11. *p* ⊃ (*q* ⊃ *r*)

12. ~*p* ⊃ (*q* ∨ *r*)

∗13. *p* ⊃ ~(*q* • *r*)

14. ~(*p* • *q*) ⊃ (*r* ⊃ *s*)

15. [*p* ⊃ ~(*q* ∨ *r*)] • *s*

III. Each of the following statements is taken from a legal document. Translate the statement into symbolic notation.

∗1. *Employee handbook*: Employees must work their scheduled work day before and after the holiday if he or she is to be paid for the holiday, unless he or she is absent with prior permission from a supervisor.

2. *Publishing contract*: If the Author shall not have delivered the final manuscript by the date stipulated, and if within six months of written notice from the Publisher to the Author said delivery shall not have been made or a new delivery date mutually agreed to, the Publisher may terminate this agreement and recover any advances made to the Author hereunder.

3. *U.S. Constitution (I, 7)*: If any Bill shall not be returned by the President within ten Days . . . , the Same shall be a Law . . . unless the Congress [has adjourned], in which Case it shall not be a Law.

∗4. *Credit card agreement*: If we find that we made a mistake on your bill, you will not have to pay any finance charges related to any questioned amount. If we didn't make a mistake, you may have to pay finance charges, and you will have to make up any missed payments on the questioned amount. In either case, we will send you a statement of the amount you owe and the date that it is due. (Treat this as a single conjunctive statement.)

5. *State penal code*: A person is guilty of murder in the first degree when [i.e., if and only if]:

a. With intent to cause the death of another person, he causes the death of such person; and

  i. The defendant was more than eighteen years old at the time of the commission of the crime; and . . .

  ii. Either:

   1. the victim was a police officer . . . who was killed in the course of performing his official duties, and the defendant knew . . . that the victim was a police officer; or

   2. the victim was an employee of a correctional institution . . . who was killed

in the course of performing his official duties, and the defendant knew . . . that the victim was an employee of a correctional institution; or

  3. at the time of the commission of the crime, the defendant was confined in a state correctional institution . . . upon a sentence for the term of his natural life . . . , or at the time of the commission of the crime, the defendant had escaped from such confinement.

IV. For each of the following, classify the statement by identifying the main connective and construct a truth table.

✳1. ~A • B

 2. ~(A ≡ B)

 3. ~(A ⊃ ~B)

✳4. (C ∨ D) • ~E

 5. (F • G) ⊃ ~H

 6. J • (K ⊃ L)

✳7. (M • N) ⊃ O

 8. P ≡ ~(Q ∨ R)

 9. S ⊃ (T ∨ ~U)

✳10. (V ∨ W) • ~(V • W)

V. | Integrative Exercise | Construct a long form truth table to determine whether the following sets of statements are consistent. Check your work by constructing a short-form truth table for each set of statements.

✳1. B ≡ C
  (B ≡ C) ⊃ ~A
  ~A • ~D

 2. D ⊃ E
  D • R
  ~R ∨ ~E

 3. A • G
  (F ∨ A) ⊃ S
  ~G ∨ B
  B ⊃ A

✳4. (D ⊃ E) ⊃ (D ⊃ C)
  ~D • ~F
  D ∨ F
  C ∨ ~D

 5. G ⊃ H
  H ⊃ J
  ~G ⊃ H
  H ∨ J

 6. R ⊃ S
  ~T ⊃ ~S
  ~T ∨ M
  M ⊃ Q
  R • ~Q

✳7. ~(R ≡ T)
  R ⊃ T
  ~T ⊃ R
  R • T

 8. (R ⊃ Q) ⊃ (Q ⊃ R)
  R ≡ Q
  ~R

 9. ~W ⊃ (L • I)
  (~W • A) ⊃ (L • I)
  ~L ∨ ~I
  ~A • ~W

✳10. (P • Q) ⊃ (S • T)
  S ⊃ (T ⊃ V)
  P ∨ S
  Q ∨ T
  S • ~Q

VI. [Integrative Exercise] Use the truth table method, either the full or the short form, to determine whether the following arguments are valid.

∗1. A ⊃ B
   ~B ∨ C
   ~A ∨ C

2. D • (E ∨ F)
   ~F
   D ⊃ E

3. G ⊃ H
   ~G ⊃ H
   H

∗4. (M • N) ∨ (M • O)
   N ≡ O
   M

5. A ≡ B
   (A • C) ⊃ D
   B ∨ E
   D ∨ E

6. [(K ∨ L) • M] ⊃ N
   (L • M) ⊃ O
   ~O ⊃ K

∗7. (K ⊃ L) ⊃ (M ⊃ N)
   (K ⊃ M) ⊃ (L ⊃ N)

8. (A • B) ≡ (C • D)
   ~B ∨ ~D
   ~A • ~C

9. (F • G) ⊃ [H ⊃ (I • J)]
   G ⊃ H
   F ⊃ ~J
   ~F ∨ ~G

∗10. E ⊃ (F • G)
   H ⊃ (I ∨ J)
   F ⊃ (~I • ~J)
   ~(E • H)

11. A ⊃ [B ⊃ (C ⊃ D)]
   (C ⊃ D) ⊃ E
   F ∨ A
   F ∨ (B ⊃ E)

12. (G ⊃ H) • [(I ∨ J) ⊃ K]
   (G • I) ∨ (G • J)
   H • K

∗13. [A ∨ (B • C)] ⊃ D
   ~(D • E)
   A ⊃ E
   B • C

14. {F • [(G ∨ H) ⊃ (I • J)]} ⊃ (F ∨ G)
   F • I
   G ⊃ ~L
   ~K ⊃ (H ∨ ~J)

VII. [Integrative Exercise] Translate the following arguments into symbolic notation. Test the validity of each argument by constructing either a full or short-form truth table.

∗1. Either you will study, or you will fail. You will study so, obviously, you will not fail.

2. If utilitarianism is correct, the happiness of the majority should always take precedence over individual rights. But individual rights must not be violated merely for the happiness of others. Utilitarianism is not correct.

3. If an omniscient, omnipotent, and omnibenevolent God exists, then there can be no evil. But evil clearly exists. Therefore, an omniscient, omnipotent, omnibenevolent God does not exist.

∗4. Either we regard convicted felons as willful criminals or as mentally ill. If they are willful, we must incarcerate them for the good of society. If they are mentally ill, we must incarcerate them for their own protection. Either way they must be incarcerated.

5. If Esmeralda goes to the racetrack, she gambles too much. But Jane will drink too much if she goes. Esmeralda will gamble too much so you can be sure that either one or the other will go to the races.

9

Natural Deduction in Propositional Logic

LEARNING OBJECTIVES

On successful completion of the chapter, you will be able to:

- Identify substitution instances of the rules of implication. (9.1)

- Use implication rules to construct propositional proofs. (9.1)

- Identify substitution instances of replacement rules. (9.2)

- Construct propositional proofs using implication and replacement rules. (9.2)

- Construct proofs using conditional proof and indirect proof. (9.3)

- Demonstrate an understanding of tautologies by constructing proofs with or without premises. (9.3)

In the previous chapter, we learned how to use truth tables to test arguments for validity. But for arguments that involve complex statements or more than a few premises, even the short version of the truth table method can be cumbersome. Natural deduction gives us a proof procedure that is both less unwieldy and more informative than the truth table method. Truth tables give us a *semantic* demonstration of validity. That is, truth tables show an argument is valid by showing that it's impossible for all the premises to be true and the conclusion to be false. Natural deduction—proofs—show us exactly how the conclusion of an argument can be derived from its premises. That's why proofs of this sort are sometimes called derivations. Proof in logic is like proof in geometry. It is a series of small steps, each of which is a valid inference. If we can get from premises to conclusion by valid steps, then we have shown that the conclusion follows necessarily from the premises, and thus that the argument as a whole is valid.

In this chapter, we will learn how to establish validity by constructing proofs. It often takes some ingenuity to come up with a proof, so the fact that you haven't found one for a given argument does not establish that the argument is invalid. Perhaps you haven't looked hard enough. Unlike the truth table method, therefore, the method of proof won't establish that an argument is invalid. If an argument *is* valid, however, a proof will often reveal why the conclusion follows from the premises more clearly than the truth table method does.

Learning to prove arguments can be challenging and frustrating but it can also be fun and immensely satisfying. It helps to understand the nature of the task ahead. Logic is, of course, a body of theoretical knowledge, but success in logic is not just about learning theory or memorizing rules. When we learn to prove arguments valid, we are learning a practical *skill* akin to learning how to play a musical instrument, a sport, or a craft such as woodcarving or knitting. Theoretical knowledge may be necessary for success in these fields, but it's not sufficient. To be a good violinist, *you must first play the violin.* So remember that to be successful at proofs, you must practice effectively, consistently, and extensively. In the following sections, we'll discuss the tools, strategies, and methods that lead to successful proofs.

REVIEW **Validity**

Validity is the central concept in the study of logic. An argument is valid if and only if the truth of the premises guarantees the truth of the conclusion. In other words, a valid argument is truth preserving: if the premises are true, the conclusion must be true as well. All deductive arguments are either valid or invalid. There is no middle ground; validity doesn't come in degrees.

9.1 Natural Deduction and the Rules of Inference

To understand the method of proof, we need to begin with the rules for taking a single step. The most basic requirement is that each step of a proof must itself be a valid inference. The rules of inference are the tools we use to produce effective proofs. But it would be impossible to remember all the valid forms, even the simpler ones. Ideally we want a toolbox equipped with enough tools to make our job easier, but not so many that we can't properly master them all. We will learn 19 rules of two different types: the rules of implication and the rules of replacement. These two types of rules function somewhat differently so it's important to know which is which. We'll learn the more powerful set, the rules of implication, first.

9.1A The Rules of Implication

The rules of implication are the most fundamental and powerful tools in natural deduction. We are going to work with nine argument forms that are commonly used in propositional logic. Each of these forms will serve as a rule for taking a single step in a proof. All the rules of implication have two distinctive characteristics. First, each one is itself a valid argument form. This can be demonstrated using the truth table method. In fact, we've already seen several examples. The second characteristic is the overarching requirement that the rules of implication must be applied to whole lines of proof only; they may never be applied to a component of a statement. Let's start with four hypothetical and disjunctive forms of inference.

It's important to understand that these are argument *forms* rather than actual arguments. The difference is the same as the difference between a statement form and an actual statement. As we saw in the previous chapter, a statement form is an abstract way to represent the logical form that a class of actual statements has in common, using variables (*p, q, r,* etc.) for the component statements. Any actual statement in that class is an instance of the statement form. The same distinction carries over to arguments—as you might expect, since arguments are made up of statements. An argument form is an abstract way to represent a certain logical structure that a whole class of actual arguments have in common, and any actual argument in that class is an instance of the form. Thus the argument:

That fabric is either silk or rayon.	S ∨ R
It is not silk.	~S
It is rayon.	R

is an instance of the argument form DS.

For statement forms, as we saw, the instances of the variables *p, q, r,* etc., need not be simple component statements. The same is true for argument forms. Each of the following arguments, for example, has the form *modus ponens:*

In the same way, each of the following arguments is an instance of one of the other argument forms:

SOLVE Recognizing Substitution Instances

Understanding the reasoning behind the implication rules is essential for mastering propositional logic. It's just as important to be able to recognize argument forms regardless of the complexity of the substitution instance. Recognizing the form of an argument is recognizing the pattern of reasoning. If you're having trouble recognizing substitution instances, here are three methods that may help. If you would like more examples, look at the sections where we introduce the implication rules. You'll notice that we've combined methods one and two by using both colors and shapes.

1. Consistently assign a shape to each component of the argument and use it as a template. Take a moment to look at how we've used this method when introducing the rules. In the simpler rules, each statement has its own shape.

Consistently assign a shape to each component of the argument form and use it as a template. Every shape of the same sort (square, oval, triangle, etc.) must contain the same statement.

You can then apply the same shape pattern to the more complex statements:

2. If you prefer, substitute colors for shapes. Just remember to highlight each occurrence of a statement—and only occurrences of that statement—with the same color.

$$p \supset q$$
$$q \supset r$$
$$\overline{p \supset r}$$

$$(T \equiv S) \supset \sim R$$
$$\sim R \supset (M \cdot N)$$
$$\overline{(T \equiv S) \supset (M \cdot N)}$$

3. Pencil in the *p*'s and *q*'s of the rule.

$$\overset{p}{}\qquad\overset{q}{}$$
$$(\sim T \vee U) \vee (R \cdot S)$$
$$\overset{\sim q}{\sim (R \cdot S)}$$
$$\overset{p}{(\sim T \vee U)}$$

You can then check your *p*'s and *q*'s against the rules.

Try all three methods and use the one that works best for you; soon you'll find identifying substitution instances of the rules natural and easy!

To use these argument forms in building proofs, you will need to be able to spot the argument form embodied in complex instances like these.

So how do we build a proof? Let's work through a simple example that will give you an overview, and then look at each of the elements in the process.

Interest rates have increased (I). If so, according to economic theory, then either demand for credit has increased (D) or the supply of credit has decreased (S). The supply would have fallen only if people were saving less (L). But savings have not declined. So the demand must have gone up.	1. I 2. I ⊃ (D ∨ S) 3. S ⊃ L <u>4. ~L</u> 5. D

The argument is not a simple instance of any of the four argument forms above. It is an extended argument in which we will need to apply several of the implication rules in separate steps to get from premises to conclusion, as we can see if we construct an argument diagram by the method of Chapter 2:

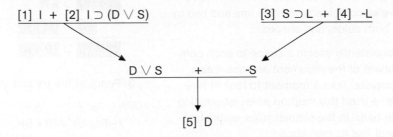

Premises 1 and 2 can be combined by *modus ponens* to infer the intermediate conclusion D ∨ S, and premises 3 and 4 can be combined by *modus tollens* to infer ~S. Those intermediate conclusions, finally, can be combined in a disjunctive syllogism to yield our ultimate conclusion.

Diagrams can sometimes be useful as an aid in constructing a proof, but in symbolic logic we represent the steps in a proof in a different notation that is more explicit. We start by listing the premises, as before, but we don't give the conclusion a number; instead, we put it on the same line as the last premise, separated by a slash mark, as in the truth table method. The slash mark indicates that we have listed the conclusion merely as a note to ourselves that D is the statement we are trying to derive from premises 1–4.

1. I		Premise
2. I ⊃ (D ∨ S)		Premise
3. S ⊃ L		Premise
4. ~L	/ D	Premise / Conclusion

Now we put in the three steps of the proof:

5. D ∨ S	1,2 MP
6. ~S	3,4 MT
7. D	5,6 DS

Line 5 is our first inference from the premises, our first intermediate conclusion. To show that we inferred it from premises 1 and 2, we don't use an arrow. We just name

SOLVE Constructing Proofs

Working backward from the conclusion is generally the easiest and most efficient way to construct a proof. If, however, you have tried reasoning backward from the conclusion and are still having difficulty, try working forward from the premises. The following strategies are sometimes useful:

1. Look for pairs of premises to which the rules of *modus ponens, modus tollens,* hypothetical syllogism or disjunctive syllogism can be applied.

2. Observe whether the result can be combined with a further premise in a way that takes you closer to the conclusion.

After you've applied one of these suggestions, try reevaluating your strategy by working backward from the conclusion again.

those premises off to the right, where we also state the argument form we used. We do the same for the two other steps. When we reach the line that states the conclusion, we're done.

Thus, a proof consists entirely in statements. Each line is either a premise, an intermediate conclusion, or the final conclusion. As in a board game, we have a starting position (the premises) and we take one step at a time, in accordance with a rule, until we reach the goal. The basic argument forms serve as implication rules. Since the argument forms are valid, any line that we derive from previous lines in accordance with the rules is a valid inference from the premises—up to and including the final line, the conclusion.

There may be more than one path from premises to conclusion. So as we add more rules to the four we have learned so far, and as we work with proofs requiring a larger number of steps, the possibility of multiple paths from premises to conclusion will only increase. In fact, there are infinitely many possible proofs for every valid argument.

9.1B Constructing a Proof

We now have a few tools to get us started constructing proofs. Each of these tools, each rule of implication, is an argument form that we know to be valid, ensuring that each line we add to a proof follows validly from statements on previous lines. The more familiar you are with these rules, the easier you will find it to recognize patterns in the arguments you are given, and that will make it easier to find the steps by which you can derive the conclusion from the premises.

We have also learned two overarching rules about constructing proofs. First, an implication rule must be applied to the entire statement on a previous line. For example, *modus tollens* is used correctly for the statement on the left but not for the one on the right:

1. D ⊃ E			1. (D ⊃ E) ∨ F	
2. ~E			2. ~E	
3. ~D	1,2 MT		3. ~D	1,2 MT [error]

Second, implication rules must be applied one at a time. For example, consider the argument:

1. A ⊃ B   Premise
2. B ⊃ C   Premise
3. C ⊃ D   / A ⊃ D   Premise / Conclusion

It is obvious that the conclusion A ⊃ D follows by the rule of hypothetical syllogism. But we cannot derive the conclusion in a single step. That would not result in a fallacious "proof," as was the case when we tried to apply an implication rule to part of a statement. But it is still an error because HS applies to only two statements at a time. So our proof will need two separate steps:

4. A ⊃ C   1,2 HS
5. A ⊃ D   3,4 HS

With the first four implication rules and the overarching rules in hand, we can now consider the strategies for constructing proofs. An understanding of the rules is crucial since they are the tools you will use to derive the conclusion from the given premises. That's why it's a good idea to master a few rules at a time, adding others as your skills improve. Good tools are important; knowing how to use those tools is the first step to becoming a master craftsman. But a skilled craftsman needs more than good tools, he needs a plan or design to guide his work. Likewise, we need a strategy for finding proofs as well as a knowledge of the rules. Think of the difference between rules and strategies in a game: The rules are fixed; they define the activity, and you must comply with them. Strategies, however, are guidelines you can use to best achieve the goal. The process of constructing a proof is not mechanical. You have to think about what steps, in what order, will get you to the conclusion.

Every proof has to begin with the premises. Sometimes there is only one inference you can draw directly from the premises, one step you can take by applying an implication rule. As the number of premises increases, however, there will normally be more than one possible inference. In that case, the order in which you draw the inferences does not matter, as long as you put each statement you derive on its own numbered line and indicate the justification. Nor does it matter if you make an inference that turns out not to be of any further use in the proof. It may be a "false start" in terms of reaching the conclusion, but it is not actually incorrect if it follows from the premises. Having unnecessary lines makes a proof less elegant than it might be, but it does not invalidate the proof.

REVIEW Two Overarching Rules for Constructing Proofs

Don't forget these two rules for constructing proofs. First, the rules of implication apply to whole lines only, never to a component of a statement. Second, all implication rules must be applied one at a time.

Memorizing rules is fairly easy. Applying the rules in a manner that leads to the conclusion of an argument is less so. One of the most common student complaints is "I know all the rules, I just don't know where to start." This complaint reveals the lack of an effective proof strategy. So, where do we start? One possibility can be illustrated by a game you may remember from childhood. Can you help the mouse find the cheese?

Did you ever learn the trick to solving the maze? It's easy if you work backward from the cheese to the mouse. The same idea applies in logic. It's usually easier for beginners to reason backward from the conclusion to the premises. At first, this process might seem awkward. But if you take the time to practice this way of thinking, you will eventually learn to "see" proofs with little difficulty. Here's how it works. Consider the following argument:

1. P ⊃ T   Premise
2. T ⊃ S   Premise
3. M ∨ ~S   Premise
4. ~M   / ~P   Premise / Conclusion

You usually won't know how long a proof will be in advance but, for now, we'll work with proofs that can be done in a set number of steps to make it easier to grasp the strategy. We know that the last line of a proof is always the conclusion, so we can fill that in right away. But what about the justification? First, we need to figure out from which line the conclusion will come. Look at the conclusion and try to find it in the premises, perhaps as a component of a statement. The desired conclusion, ~P, does not occur in the premises but we have P as the antecedent of line 1. Which rule would allow us to derive ~P from line 1? In other words, which rule gives us the negation of the antecedent of a conditional? Clearly, it's *modus tollens*.

1. P ⊃ T		Premise
2. T ⊃ S		Premise
3. M ∨ ~S		Premise
4. ~M	/ ~P	Premise / Conclusion
5. _____	_____	
6. _____		
7. ~P		1,_ MT

What would we need in addition to line 1 to do MT? To apply *modus tollens*, we need both a conditional and the negation of the consequent of that conditional—in this case ~T—as a separate line of proof. We don't have ~T; we'll have to prove it. Since it's all we need to prove ~P, we know it will be the last line of proof before the conclusion. Treat ~T as an intermediate conclusion and try to find it in the premises. Line 1 has T, but we know that that's not our line for two reasons. First, there is no rule that lets us derive the negation of the consequent of a conditional statement. Second, we want ~T in order to use it *with* line 1 so it's probably not going to come *from* line 1. That leaves line 2. Is there a rule that allows us to derive the negation of the antecedent of a conditional statement? Yes, MT is the rule we're going to use. We can complete our justification for line 7 and fill in line 6 of our proof.

1. P ⊃ T		Premise
2. T ⊃ S		Premise
3. M ∨ ~S		Premise
4. ~M	/ ~P	Premise / Conclusion
5. _____	_____	
6. ~T		2,_ MT
7. ~P		1,6 MT

Look at line 2: what additional formula would we need to apply MT to line 2? We would need ~S, right? We can treat ~S as another intermediate conclusion, one that will help us prove ~T. We're in luck; ~S occurs as a component of line 3 of the proof. Which rule would allow us to derive ~S? In other words, which rule allows us to derive one disjunct of a disjunction? It's obviously disjunctive syllogism. We can use ~M on line 4 along with line 3 to apply DS. This allows us to complete the proof.

1. P ⊃ T		Premise
2. T ⊃ S		Premise
3. M ∨ ~S		Premise
4. ~M	/ ~P	Premise / Conclusion
5. ~S		3,4 DS
6. ~T		2,5 MT
7. ~P		1,6 MT

In conclusion, you should always remember that, with simple proofs, you may be able to derive the conclusion in a few steps by applying implication rules directly to the premises. But with longer, more complex proofs, you will normally have to make a series of inferences, using each intermediate conclusion as a premise for a further inference in a sequence that gets you to the conclusion. The strategy of working backward from the conclusion means asking yourself what intermediate steps would enable you to derive the conclusion, and then asking how those intermediate statements themselves could be derived. The strategy is like planning a trip. If you wanted to get to Los Angeles, for example, you might reason: "If I can get to Denver, I know how to get from there to Los Angeles. So how can I get to Denver?" Just take it step by step and focus on the process. You'll soon build speed.

EXERCISE 9.1B

I. Each of the following arguments is an instance of one of the four implication rules we have learned (MP, MT, HS, DS). Identify the rule.

∗1. $C \lor D$
   $\underline{\sim C}$
   D

2. $E \supset F$
   $\underline{\sim F}$
   $\sim E$

3. $M \supset N$
   $\underline{M}$
   N

∗4. $H \supset K$
   $\underline{K \supset J}$
   $H \supset J$

5. $M \supset \sim D$
   $\underline{\sim \sim D}$
   $\sim M$

6. $A \lor B$
   $\underline{\sim B}$
   A

∗7. $(D \lor E) \supset F$
   $\underline{D \lor E}$
   F

8. $(N \bullet O) \lor M$
   $\underline{\sim M}$
   $N \bullet O$

9. $(A \bullet B) \supset (C \bullet D)$
   $\underline{A \bullet B}$
   $C \bullet D$

∗10. $(H \lor J) \supset K$
   $\underline{\sim K}$
   $\sim (H \lor J)$

11. $\sim M \supset [(N \bullet O) \lor P]$
   $\underline{\sim M}$
   $(N \bullet O) \lor P$

12. $(H \lor J) \lor K$
   $\underline{\sim (H \lor J)}$
   K

∗13. $A \supset (B \equiv C)$
   $\underline{\sim (B \equiv C)}$
   $\sim A$

14. $A \supset (B \bullet C)$
   $\underline{(B \bullet C) \supset (D \lor E)}$
   $A \supset (D \lor E)$

15. $(E \bullet F) \supset (G \lor H)$
   $\underline{\sim (G \lor H)}$
   $\sim (E \bullet F)$

∗16. $(M \supset N) \supset (L \bullet N)$
   $\underline{(L \bullet N) \supset (L \supset O)}$
   $(M \supset N) \supset (L \supset O)$

17. $[\sim (N \bullet O) \supset L] \lor (M \bullet N)$
   $\underline{\sim [\sim (N \bullet O) \supset L]}$
   $M \bullet N$

18. $[(H \bullet \sim J) \supset K] \supset (L \bullet \sim M)$
   $\underline{(L \bullet \sim M) \supset (J \lor K)}$
   $[(H \bullet \sim J) \supset K] \supset (J \lor K)$

∗19. $[\sim M \bullet (N \supset \sim K)] \supset [N \equiv \sim (M \lor J)]$
   $\underline{\sim M \bullet (N \supset \sim K)}$
   $N \equiv \sim (M \lor J)$

20. $(A \bullet B) \supset (C \equiv A)$
   $\underline{(C \equiv A) \supset D}$
   $(A \bullet B) \supset D$

II. Answer the questions about each of the following arguments. You may then use your answers to help you get started on the next section of exercises.

*1. 1. A ⊃ B
    2. ~A ⊃ C
    3. ~B   / C
    a. Look at the conclusion and try to find it in the premises. Where is it?
    b. Which rule would allow you to derive C from the premise?
    c. What additional statement is needed along with the premise to apply the rule? Do you have it? If not, is there a premise from which it can be derived as an intermediate conclusion?
    d. Which rule would allow you to derive your intermediate conclusion?
    e. What additional statement is needed to derive the intermediate conclusion? Do you have it as a separate line of proof?

2. 1. A ∨ B
   2. A ⊃ C
   3. ~C   / B
   a. Look at the conclusion and try to find it in the premises. Is it a component of one of the premises?
   b. Which rule would let you derive B from the premise?
   c. What additional statement is needed to apply the rule? Do you have it? If not, is there a premise from which it can be derived as an intermediate conclusion?
   d. Which rule would allow you to derive your intermediate conclusion?
   e. What additional statement is needed to prove your intermediate conclusion?

3. 1. D ∨ ~E
   2. E ∨ ~B
   3. ~D   / ~B
   a. Look at the conclusion and try to find it in the premises. Where is it?
   b. Which rule would allow you to derive ~B from the premise?
   c. What additional statement is needed to apply the rule? Do you have it? If not, can it be derived as an intermediate conclusion?
   d. Which rule would allow you to derive your intermediate conclusion?
   e. What additional statement is needed to prove your intermediate conclusion?

*4. 1. E ⊃ D
    2. ~D
    3. ~E ⊃ C   / C
    a. Look at the conclusion and try to find it in the premises. Is it a component of one of the premises?
    b. Which rule would allow you to derive C from the premise?
    c. What additional statement is needed to apply the rule? Do you have it in a separate line of proof? If not, can it be derived as an intermediate conclusion from any of the premises?
    d. Which rule would allow you to derive your intermediate conclusion?
    e. What additional statement is needed to derive the intermediate conclusion? Do you have it?

5. 1. J ∨ K
   2. ~J
   3. K ⊃ L   / L
   - a. Look at the conclusion and try to find it in the premises. Is it a component of one of the premises?
   - b. Which rule would allow you to derive L from the premise?
   - c. What additional statement is needed to apply the rule? Do

you have it as a separate line of proof? If not, can it be derived as an intermediate conclusion?
   - d. Which rule would allow you to derive your intermediate conclusion?
   - e. What additional statement is needed to prove your intermediate conclusion?

III. For each of the following arguments, complete the proof using the four implication rules we have learned (MP, MT, HS, and DS). Be sure to include the justification. (For 1–5, the numbered lines following the final premise/conclusion indicate the number of steps required for the proof. For 6–16, you will need to determine that on your own.) You may refer to the previous exercise for help with the first five arguments.

*1. 1. A ⊃ B
    2. ~A ⊃ C
    3. ~B   / C
    4. _____ _____
    5. _____ _____

2. 1. A ∨ B
   2. A ⊃ C
   3. ~C   / B
   4. _____ _____
   5. _____ _____

3. 1. D ∨ ~E
   2. E ∨ ~B
   3. ~D   / ~B
   4. _____ _____
   5. _____ _____

*4. 1. E ⊃ D
    2. ~D
    3. ~E ⊃ C   / C
    4. _____ _____
    5. _____ _____

5. 1. J ∨ K
   2. ~J
   3. K ⊃ L   / L
   4. _____ _____
   5. _____ _____

6. 1. B ⊃ C
   2. D ⊃ B
   3. A ⊃ D   / A ⊃ C

*7. 1. B ≡ C
    2. (B ≡ C) ⊃ ~A
    3. A ∨ D   / D

8. 1. (B • C) ⊃ D
   2. (B • C) ∨ A
   3. ~D.   / A

9. 1. (A ⊃ B) ⊃ (C ∨ D)
   2. ~ (C ∨ D)
   3. ~ (A ⊃ B) ⊃ E   / E

*10. 1. ~D
     2. D ∨ (A ⊃ D)
     3. B ⊃ A   / ~B

11. 1. H ⊃ I
    2. J ⊃ K
    3. H ∨ J
    4. ~K   / I

12. 1. (A ∨ B) ⊃ (C • D)
    2. ~ (C • D)
    3. ~ (A ∨ B) ⊃ E   / E

*13. 1. G ⊃ H
     2. ~H
     3. I ⊃ G   / ~I

14. 1. ~B ⊃ ~C
    2. (~B ⊃ ~D) ⊃ ~A
    3. ~C ⊃ ~D   / ~A

15. 1. A ⊃ B
    2. ~B
    3. ~A ⊃ ~D
    4. D ∨ E   / E

*16. 1. (A ∨ B) ∨ (B ⊃ C)
     2. (A ∨ B) ⊃ (~H ≡ ~J)
     3. C ⊃ ~D
     4. G ⊃ B
     5. ~(~H ≡ ~J)   / G ⊃ ~ D

9.1C Rules of Implication (Continued)

The first four implication rules are not enough to construct proofs for all valid arguments. We will need some additional rules. We can begin with three rules that involve basic operations with conjunction and disjunction:

Simplification (Simp) | **Conjunction (Conj)** | **Addition (Add)**

As argument forms, simplification and conjunction are based on the fact that a conjunction is true if and only if both conjuncts are true. So if we already have a conjunctive statement, then of course we can infer either of its component statements (Simp). Conversely, if we already have both conjuncts independently, then of course their conjunction follows (Conj). In the context of proof, Simp is useful when we need to eliminate a conjunction. For example, we might be given a conjunction as a premise and can see that one conjunct is not relevant to the conclusion. Conjunction, on the other hand, allows us to introduce a conjunction, putting together two statements into a single conjunctive statement.

Addition allows us to introduce a new statement by adding it, in the form of a disjunction, to a statement we already have. This rule may be a little less obvious than the other two because we start with a given statement p and can add any other statement whatever, regardless of whether it has any relationship to p. But remember the truth table for disjunction: A disjunctive statement is true as long as one or the other of the disjuncts is true (or both). This means that if we are given p as a premise or have derived it by a series of valid steps in a proof, then we can infer the disjunction of p with any other statement.

An example of how Add is used in proof is the argument at the very beginning of the previous chapter:

If there is a recession this year or a foreign affairs fiasco, the president will not be reelected. Since there will be a recession, the president will not be reelected.

    1. (R ∨ F) ⊃ ~P
    2. R   / ~P

From premise 2, we would use Addition to infer R ∨ F, which can then be combined with 1 to derive the conclusion by *modus ponens*:

1. (R ∨ F) ⊃ ~P		Premise
2. R	/ ~P	Premise / Conclusion
3. R ∨ F		2 Add
4. ~P		1,3 MP

Simp, Conj, and Add are often used in proofs when we need to break a compound statement down into its components and then reassemble the components into a new compound statement. Here's an example:

1. A • B		Premise
2. C	/ (A ∨ D) • C	Premise / Conclusion

Notice that the conclusion includes a disjunctive component, but there is no disjunction in the premises, nor any occurrence of D. That suggests we will need to use Add to infer A ∨ D from A. But A is conjoined with B in premise 1, so we will first need to use Simp to extract it. Once we have A ∨ D, finally, we can use Conj to combine it with C from premise 2. Thus, the proof will use all three of our new rules:

3. A	1 Simp
4. A ∨ D	3 Add
5. (A ∨ D) • C	2,4 Conj

The last two implication rules are called dilemmas. Argument by dilemma is a common tactic in debates, and we sometimes use inferences of this form in thinking about alternative courses of action. Here's an example:

> If I go to bed early (E), I'll be unprepared for the test (U); but if I stay up late studying (L), I'll be too tired to do well (T). Those are my choices: either I go to bed early or I stay up late studying. So either I'll be unprepared for the test or I'll be too tired to do well.

If we put this into symbolic notation, we can see that it involves a combination of conditional and disjunctive elements:

(E ⊃ U) • (L ⊃ T)
E ∨ L
─────────────
U ∨ T

The first premise conjoins two conditional statements; the second premise says that at least one of the two antecedents is true; and the conclusion is that at least one of the two consequents is true. This argument is an instance of a form called constructive dilemma (CD).

Destructive dilemma (DD) is the parallel form in which we argue that one of the two consequents is *false* and therefore that one of the two antecedents is false, as in the example below:

> If conservatives are right (C), welfare breeds dependency (D); while if liberals are right (L), it is merely a temporary transition to self-supporting work (T). But either welfare does *not* breed dependency or it is *not* merely a temporary transition. So either the conservatives or the liberals are not right.

(C ⊃ D) • (L ⊃ T)
~D ∨ ~T
~C ∨ ~L

Generalizing from the examples, the implication rules are:

As with the first set of implication rules, each of the rules we have just learned identifies a form of valid inference, using the letters *p*, *q*, etc., for the component propositions. We must remember that instances of these components may themselves be compound statements. Thus, each of the following arguments is an instance of the argument form indicated beside it:

(A • B) ――――――― (A • B) ∨ Ⓒ	Add
(D ⊃ Ⓔ) • [(F ∨ G) ⊃ Ⓗ] ~Ⓔ ∨ ~Ⓗ ――――――――――――― ~ D ∨ ~ (F ∨ G)	DD
(J ⊃ K) • L M ≡ N ――――――――――― [(J ⊃ K) • L] • M ≡ N	Conj
[(P • R) ⊃ Ⓢ] • (T ⊃ ~W) (P • R) ∨ T ――――――――――― Ⓢ ∨ ~W	CD
(A ⊃ B) • [D ∨ (~E • F)] ――――――――――――― [D ∨ (~E • F)]	Simp

As with the first set of implication rules, moreover, each of the rules we have just learned must be applied to the whole statement on a given line of a proof, not to a component of the statement. This overarching rule is very important to remember; applying an implication rule to a component of a statement is one of the most common errors in constructing proofs. Here's another example of the error:

If I got the breaks and had the talent, I'd be a Hollywood star. But I'm not a star, so obviously I haven't had the breaks.

1. (B • T) ⊃ S   Premise
2. ~S   / ~B   Premise / Conclusion
3. B ⊃ S   1 Simp [error]
4. ~B   2,3 MT

In line 3, simplification is being applied to the antecedent of premise 1, in an effort to reduce B·T to the simpler component B, and thus replace (B • T) ⊃ S with B ⊃ S, so that a *modus tollens* inference in line 4 will yield the conclusion. But B • T is not itself stated as a premise. It is only one component of a conditional statement, and implication

---

REVIEW Nine Basic Implication Rules

Modus ponens (MP)

$$\boxed{p} \supset \widehat{q}$$
$$\boxed{p}$$
$$\widehat{q}$$

Modus tollens (MT)

$$\boxed{p} \supset \widehat{q}$$
$$\sim\widehat{q}$$
$$\sim\boxed{p}$$

Hypothetical syllogism (HS)

$$\boxed{p} \supset \widehat{q}$$
$$\widehat{q} \supset \boxed{r}$$
$$\boxed{p} \supset \boxed{r}$$

Disjunctive syllogism (DS)

$$\boxed{p} \vee \widehat{q} \qquad\qquad \boxed{p} \vee \widehat{q}$$
$$\sim\boxed{p} \qquad \text{or} \qquad \sim\widehat{q}$$
$$\widehat{q} \qquad\qquad\qquad \boxed{p}$$

Simplification (Simp)

$$\boxed{p} \bullet \widehat{q} \qquad \text{or} \qquad \boxed{p} \bullet \widehat{q}$$
$$\boxed{p} \qquad\qquad\qquad \widehat{q}$$

Conjunction (Conj)

$$\boxed{p} \qquad\qquad\qquad \boxed{p}$$
$$\widehat{q} \qquad \text{or} \qquad \widehat{q}$$
$$\boxed{p} \bullet \widehat{q} \qquad\qquad \widehat{q} \bullet \boxed{p}$$

Addition (Add)

$$\boxed{p} \qquad\qquad\qquad \boxed{p}$$
$$\boxed{p} \vee \widehat{q} \qquad \text{or} \qquad \widehat{q} \vee \boxed{p}$$

Constructive dilemma (CD)

$$(\boxed{p} \supset \widehat{q}) \bullet (\boxed{r} \supset \widehat{s})$$
$$\boxed{p} \vee \boxed{r}$$
$$\widehat{q} \vee \widehat{s}$$

Destructive dilemma (DD)

$$(\boxed{p} \supset \widehat{q}) \bullet (\boxed{r} \supset \widehat{s})$$
$$\sim\widehat{q} \vee \sim\widehat{s}$$
$$\sim\boxed{p} \vee \sim\boxed{r}$$

rules like simplification may not be applied to a component of a previous line in a proof. You can see why the result is an invalid argument. I'm admitting at the outset that becoming a Hollywood star depends on two factors: having talent and getting the breaks. In blaming my lack of stardom on not getting breaks, however, I am conveniently forgetting the talent factor. This is illicit simplification.

EXERCISE 9.1C

I. Each of the following arguments is an instance of one of the basic implication rules we learned in this section (Simp, Conj, Add, CD, or DD). Identify the rule in each case.

*1. A • B
   B

2. (G ⊃ H) • (I ⊃ J)
   ~H ∨ ~J
   ~G ∨ ~I

3. K
   K ∨ L

*4. D
   E
   D • E

5. (F ⊃ G) • (H ⊃ I)
   F ∨ H
   G ∨ I

6. A • (B ∨ C)
   A

*7. (A ⊃ B) • (C ⊃ ~D)
   ~B ∨ ~ ~D
   ~A ∨ ~C

8. K
   G • H
   K • (G • H)

9. (A ⊃ B) • (C ⊃ B)
   C ⊃ B

*10. (G ⊃ H) • (I ⊃ J)
   G ∨ I
   H ∨ J

11. (K • L) • M
   M

12. (F ⊃ G)
   (F ⊃ G) ∨ H

*13. [H ⊃ (I ∨ K)] • (J ⊃ L)
   H ∨ J
   (I ∨ K) ∨ L

14. I ∨ J
   K ∨ L
   (I ∨ J) • (K ∨ L)

15. (A ⊃ B) • (C ⊃ D)
   ~B ∨ ~D
   ~A ∨ ~C

*16. (A ⊃ B) • (B ⊃ C)
   A ∨ B
   (A ∨ B) • [(A ⊃ B) • (B ⊃ C)]

17. M ∨ (L ⊃ N)
   (~O • M) ∨ [M ∨ (L ⊃ N)]

18. [(A ≡ B) ⊃ F] • [D ⊃ (B ∨ E)]
   ~F ∨ ~ (B ∨ E)
   [~ (A ≡ B) ∨ ~D]

*19. J ∨ K
   (J ∨ K) ∨ ~ (L ⊃ M)

20. [N ⊃ (O • P)] • (N ⊃ ~S)
   N ∨ N
   (O • P) ∨ ~S

II. Answer the questions about each of the following arguments. You may then use your answers to help you get started on the next section of exercises.

*1. 1. A   / (A ∨ B) ∨ C
   a. Look at the conclusion and try
      to find it in the premise. Do you

have it? Are there statements
in the conclusion that aren't in
the premise?

b. Which rule would allow you to introduce the new atomic statements into your proof?

c. What is your intermediate conclusion?

d. Which rule will allow you to move from your intermediate conclusion to your final conclusion?

2. 1. (A • B) • C   / A

a. Look at the conclusion and try to find it as a component of the premise. Where is it?

b. Which rule would allow you to derive an intermediate conclusion from the premise?

c. What is your intermediate conclusion?

d. Which rule will allow you to derive the desired conclusion from your intermediate conclusion?

3. 1. A • B   / A ∨ C

a. Look at the conclusion and try to find it in the premise. What do you notice? (Consider proving A as an intermediate conclusion.)

b. Which rule would allow you to derive A from the premise?

c. Which rule would allow you to infer A ∨ C from your intermediate conclusion?

✷4. 1. A
2. (A ⊃ B) • (C ⊃ D)   / B ∨ D

a. Look at the conclusion and try to find it in the premises. Do you have it? Do you have the individual disjuncts as components of a premise?

b. Which rule would allow you to derive B ∨ D from the premise?

c. What additional statement would you need to apply that rule? Do you have it as a separate line of proof? If not, is there a premise that allows you to derive it as an intermediate conclusion?

d. Which rule would allow you to derive your intermediate conclusion?

5. 1. (A ⊃ B) • (C ⊃ D)
2. C   / B ∨ D

a. Look at the conclusion and try to find it in the premises. Do you have it? Do you have the individual disjuncts as components of a premise?

b. Which rule would allow you to derive B ∨ D from the premise?

c. What additional statement would you need to apply that rule? Do you have it as a separate line of proof? If not, is there a premise that allows you to derive it as an intermediate conclusion?

d. Which rule would allow you to derive your intermediate conclusion?

III. Construct a proof for each of the following arguments using *only* the implication rules you learned in this section (Add, Simp, Conj, CD, and DD). (For 1–5, the numbered lines following the final premise/conclusion indicate the number of steps required for the proof. For 6–22, you will need to determine that on your own.) You may refer to the previous exercises for help with the first five arguments.

✷1. 1. A   / (A ∨ B) ∨ C

2. _____   _____

3. _____   _____

2. 1. (A • B) • C   /A
   2. _____   _____
   3. _____   _____

3. 1. A • B   /A ∨ C
   2. _____   _____
   3. _____   _____

*4. 1. A
   2. (A ⊃ B) • (C ⊃ D)   /B ∨ D
   3. _____   _____
   4. _____   _____

5. 1. (A ⊃ B) • (C ⊃ D)
   2. C   /B ∨ D
   3. _____   _____
   4. _____   _____

6. 1. (A ⊃ C) • (B ⊃ D)
   2. (A ∨ B) • (B ∨ D)   /C ∨ D

*7. 1. (A ⊃ C) • (B ⊃ D)
   2. ~C   / ~A ∨ ~B

8. 1. A
   2. B
   3. C   /(C • A) • B

9. 1. (A ⊃ B) • (D ⊃ E)
   2. A ∨ D   /(B ∨ E) ∨ D

*10. 1. (D ⊃ E)
   2. (F ⊃ G)
   3. D ∨ F   /E ∨ G

11. 1. A ∨ C
   2. (A ⊃ B) • (C ⊃ D)
   3. (B ⊃ E) • (D ⊃ G)   /E ∨ G

12. 1. A • D
   2. B   /(D • B) ∨ A

*13. 1. B • C
   2. ~A • D   / ~A • B

14. 1. B
   2. A   /(A ∨ D) • (B ∨ C)

15. 1. (D ⊃ B) • (C ⊃ A)
   2. (E ⊃ D) • (B ⊃ C)   /(E ⊃ D) • (D ⊃ B)

*16. 1. A ⊃ D
   2. B ⊃ C
   3. B ∨ A   /C ∨ D

17. 1. A ⊃ B
   2. ~E ⊃ D
   3. (~E ∨ A) • (~E ∨ B)   /D ∨ B

18. 1. B ⊃ (A ∨ C)
    2. D ⊃ E
    3. B   / (A ∨ C) ∨ E

✳19. 1. (A ⊃ C) • (B ⊃ D)
    2. ~C ∨ ~D
    3. [(~A ∨ ~B) ⊃ E] • (~E ⊃ F)   / E ∨ F

20. 1. A ⊃ B
    2. C ⊃ D
    3. C • A   / B ∨ D

21. 1. ~C • E
    2. A ⊃ C
    3. B ⊃ D   / ~A ∨ ~B

✳22. 1. (D ∨ A) ⊃ ~C
    2. (D • B) ⊃ A
    3. D • ~B   / ~C ∨ A

IV. [Integrative Exercise] For each of the following proofs, state the justification for each step. You will need all the implication rules.

✳1. 1. A ⊃ B   Premise
    2. ~A ⊃ C   Premise
    3. ~B   / C   Premise / Conclusion
    4. ~A   _____
    5. C   _____

2. 1. A ∨ B   Premise
   2. A ⊃ C   Premise
   3. ~C   / B   Premise / Conclusion
   4. ~A   _____
   5. B   _____

3. 1. (F • G) ∨ H   Premise
   2. H ⊃ I   Premise
   3. ~ (F • G)   / I ∨ G   Premise / Conclusion
   4. H   _____
   5. I   _____
   6. I ∨ G   _____

✳4. 1. (M • O) ⊃ (L ∨ K)   Premise
    2. O • (L ∨ B)   Premise
    3. M • ~H   / (L ∨ K)   Premise / Conclusion
    4. M   _____
    5. O   _____
    6. M • O   _____
    7. (L ∨ K)   _____

5. 1. (E ⊃ F) • (~F ∨ ~G)   Premise
  2. H ⊃ I   Premise
  3. I ⊃ G   / ~E ∨ ~H   Premise / Conclusion
  4. H ⊃ G   _____
  5. E ⊃ F   _____
  6. (E ⊃ F) • (H ⊃ G)   _____
  7. ~F ∨ ~G   _____
  8. ~E ∨ ~H   _____

V. | Integrative Exercise | Show that each of the following arguments is valid by constructing a proof.

✳**1.** 1. A
  2. A ⊃ ~B
  3. B ∨ C   / C

2. 1. E ⊃ (F ∨ G)
  2. ~ (F ∨ G)   / ~E ∨ G

3. 1. D ⊃ E
  2. F ⊃ G
  3. D ∨ F   / E ∨ G

✳**4.** 1. D ⊃ E
  2. D ∨ A
  3. ~E   / A

5. 1. [(B • A) • (C • D)] • [(E • ~D) ∨ G]   / B

6. 1. ~B
  2. (~B ∨ ~C) ⊃ ~D   / ~D

✳**7.** 1. (A ∨ B) ⊃ C
  2. E ⊃ (A ∨ B)
  3. C ⊃ D   / E ⊃ D

8. 1. (A ∨ B) ⊃ [C • (D ⊃ E)]
  2. A   / D ⊃ E

9. 1. (P ∨ K) ⊃ ~H
  2. P • M   / ~H

✳**10.** 1. A ⊃ B
  2. C ⊃ D
  3. ~B   / ~A ∨ ~C

11. 1. A ∨ (B ∨ C)
  2. (B ⊃ E) • (C ⊃ G)
  3. ~A   / E ∨ G

12. 1. (B ⊃ G) • (A ⊃ ~E)
  2. C
  3. C ⊃ (B ∨ A)   / G ∨ ~E

*13. 1. B ⊃ C
    2. B ∨ (A • E)
    3. ~C   / A • E

14. 1. [B ∨ (A • E)] • [C ⊃ (B ∨ A)]
    2. ~B   / A • E

15. 1. (~A ∨ G) ⊃ (B • D)
    2. ~C
    3. C ∨ (~A ∨ G)   / B

*16. 1. ~(A ⊃ B)
    2. (A ⊃ B) ∨ C
    3. G ⊃ (A ⊃ B)   / ~G • C

17. 1. ~E
    2. ~D
    3. B ⊃ D   / (~E ∨ ~C) • ~B

18. 1. (~B ⊃ A) • (~C ⊃ D)
    2. ~A
    3. ~B   / D

*19. 1. E ⊃ B
    2. B ⊃ C
    3. A ⊃ E
    4. C ⊃ G   / A ⊃ G

20. 1. A ⊃ B
    2. E ⊃ G
    3. (A ⊃ B) ⊃ (C ⊃ D)
    4. E ∨ C   / G ∨ D

21. 1. H ⊃ I
    2. J ⊃ K
    3. H ∨ J
    4. ~K   / I

*22. 1. ~C
    2. B ⊃ C
    3. B ∨ A
    4. A ⊃ E   / E

23. 1. (A ≡ B) ⊃ [B ⊃ (C ⊃ D)]
    2. B
    3. A ≡ B
    4. C   / D

24. 1. (A ≡ B) ⊃ (E ∨ C)
    2. ~E
    3. A ≡ B
    4. C ⊃ D   / D

✳25. 1. (A ≡ B) ⊃ (E ∨ C)
2. (B ⊃ D) ⊃ (A ≡ B)
3. (E ∨ C) ⊃ ~G
4. ~G ⊃ A   / (B ⊃ D) ⊃ A

26. 1. A ⊃ B
2. (A ⊃ ~C) ⊃ ~D
3. B ⊃ ~C
4. E ⊃ D   / ~E

27. 1. J ⊃ H
2. ~C ⊃ D
3. J ∨ ~C
4. ~H   / D

✳28. 1. E ⊃ A
2. B ⊃ E
3. A ⊃ ~C
4. B   / ~C

29. 1. (J ⊃ K) ⊃ (L • M)
2. (N ∨ O) ⊃ (J ⊃ K)
3. N   / L

30. 1. ~A ⊃ (~B ⊃ ~C)
2. ~B
3. C ∨ D
4. A ⊃ B   / D

✳31. 1. A ∨ B
2. C ⊃ D
3. ~A • ~D   / B • ~C

32. 1. A
2. (B ∨ C) ∨ (D ∨ ~E)
3. A ⊃ ~(B ∨ C)
4. A ⊃ ~D   / ~E

33. 1. A ⊃ B
2. A ∨ C
3. B ⊃ D
4. ~C   / E ∨ D

✳34. 1. (B • A) ⊃ (C • D)
2. E ≡ F
3. (~C ⊃ ~G) ⊃ [F ⊃ (D ⊃ H)]
4. [F ⊃ (D ⊃ H)] ⊃ [(E ≡ F) ⊃ (B • A)]
5. ~C ⊃ ~G   / C • D

35. 1. F ⊃ G
2. G ⊃ H
3. ~I
4. H ⊃ I
5. F ∨ J   / J

36. 1. (A ∨ B) • ~C
    2. ~B • (C ∨ D)   / D • A

*37. 1. D ⊃ B
    2. C ⊃ A
    3. E ⊃ D
    4. B ⊃ C
    5. E ∨ B   / (B ∨ A) • (D ∨ C)

38. 1. B ∨ (D • E)
    2. (G ∨ C) ⊃ ~B
    3. (D ∨ H) ⊃ J
    4. G   / J

39. 1. A ∨ (B ∨ C)
    2. D ⊃ ~E
    3. ~A ⊃ (C ⊃ F)
    4. B ⊃ D
    5. ~A   / ~E ∨ F

*40. 1. (A ∨ D) ⊃ [(B ⊃ G) • (C ⊃ E)]
    2. A • ~G
    3. ~C ⊃ D
    4. B ∨ E   / E

41. 1. A ⊃ (B ⊃ C)
    2. A ∨ D
    3 (D ⊃ E) • (E ⊃ F)
    4. G ⊃ (~F • ~C)
    5. G   / ~B

9.2 Equivalence and the Rules of Replacement

The implication rules are the basic tools we use in constructing proofs. In this section, we will acquire some additional tools that involve logical equivalence. As we saw in the previous chapter , two statements are logically equivalent when they have the same truth value for every combination of truth values their atomic component statements can have. We show that two statements are equivalent by constructing truth tables for each of them. If both statements are true on the same rows and false on the same rows, then they are equivalent; if their truth values differ on even a single row, then they are not equivalent. The statement forms $p • q$ and $q • p$ provide a simple example:

p	•	q		q	•	p
T	**T**	T		T	**T**	T
T	**F**	F		F	**F**	T
F	**F**	T		T	**F**	F
F	**F**	F		F	**F**	F

So how do we use equivalent statements in proof? Consider the following argument:

(B • A) ⊃ C
A • B
―――――
C

This looks like a simple case of *modus ponens*, but it isn't, because the second premise is not identical to the antecedent of the first. We need to replace the second premise with the equivalent statement B • A. We could do so using the implication rules simplification and conjunction:

1. (B • A) ⊃ C		Premise
2. A • B	/ C	Premise / Conclusion
3. A		2 Simp
4. B		2 Simp
5. B • A		3,4 Conj
6. C		1,5 MP

We could accomplish the same thing more easily if we could just replace A • B with B • A in one step:

1. (B • A) ⊃ C		Premise
2. A • B	/ C	Premise / Conclusion
3. B • A		2 [?]
4. C		1,3 MP

The replacement does not affect the validity of the argument, but it does make the proof much easier.

9.2A Rules of Replacement

How shall we describe our justification for step 3? We could adopt a general rule allowing any statement to be replaced by any other statement equivalent to it. But there are many such equivalences, too many to remember. So once again, as with implication rules, it is customary to work with a limited set. Each replacement rule specifies a pair of equivalent statement forms, and the rule authorizes us to replace any instance of one statement form with the corresponding instance of the other. We are going to use 10 replacement rules altogether.

The equivalence we used in the proof above is the replacement rule called commutation:

Commutation (Com): $(p \cdot q) :: (q \cdot p)$

$(p \lor q) :: (q \lor p)$

The double colon, ::, is the symbol we use to assert the logical equivalence of two statement forms. As the name implies, this equivalence is like the commutative law for numbers: *x times y = y times x* and *x plus y = y plus x*. In the argument above, we used the conjunctive form of commutation, and we would put "Com" as our justification on line 3. Another replacement rule that you may recognize from mathematics is:

Association (Assoc): $[p \cdot (q \cdot r)] :: [(p \cdot q) \cdot r]$

$[p \lor (q \lor r)] :: [(p \lor q) \lor r]$

Whereas the commutation rules say that the *order* of conjuncts or disjuncts makes no difference in truth value, the association rules say that the *grouping* makes no difference, either. Note that Com and Assoc apply only to conjunction and disjunction, not to conditionals: $p \supset q$ is not equivalent to $q \supset p$, and $p \supset (q \supset r)$ is not equivalent to $(p \supset q) \supset r$.

The next equivalence is one we've seen before:

Double negation (DN): $p :: \sim\sim p$

As we noted, negation is an on/off switch, so the two signs on the right cancel out. You'll need to use DN more often than you might think. If you had the two premises $\sim A \lor B$ and A, for example, it would be natural to infer B by disjunctive syllogism. Strictly speaking, however, DS can be applied only when you have the negation of one of the disjuncts. The negation of $\sim A$ is $\sim\sim A$, so you cannot use the implication rule DS until you have used the replacement rule DN to replace A with $\sim\sim A$.

Disjunctive syllogism	Proof		
$p \lor q$	1. $\sim A \lor B$		Premise
$\sim p$	2. A	/ B	Premise / Conclusion
q	3. $\sim\sim A$		2 DN
	4. B		1,3 DS

The next two rules are a little trickier, because they involve more than one kind of connective, but they should be obvious when you think them through. One is called distribution, and it may also be familiar from mathematics. The distributive law for numbers is that:

$a \times (b + c) = (a \times b) + (a \times c)$

For example:

$8 \times (5 + 7) = (8 \times 5) + (8 \times 7) = 96$

The multiplier *a* distributes across both of the numbers in the sum. A parallel principle of equivalence holds for the connectives conjunction and disjunction, and (unlike with numbers) it works both ways.

Distribution (Dist): $[p \cdot (q \lor r)] :: [(p \cdot q) \lor (p \cdot r)]$

$[p \lor (q \cdot r)] :: [(p \lor q) \cdot (p \lor r)]$

We can illustrate the first distributive rule with an earlier example:

I'll go home and either watch television or think about the election.	H • (T ∨ E)
I'll go home and watch television or I'll go home and think about the election.	(H • T) ∨ (H • E)

The two statements are obviously equivalent; they are just different ways of saying the same thing.

Another very important replacement rule is named after the 19th-century logician Augustus De Morgan. There are two formulations of this rule as well:

De Morgan's law (DM):   ~(p • q) :: ~p ∨ ~q
                              ~(p ∨ q) :: ~p • ~q

An example of the first formulation is the statement "You can't have your cake and eat it too," ~(H • E), which means that either you don't have your cake or you don't eat it: ~H ∨ ~E. The second formulation of De Morgan's law is equally obvious. A statement of the form ~(p ∨ q) would normally be expressed in English by "neither . . . nor," as in:

Cheating is neither honest nor smart.	~(H ∨ S)
Cheating is not honest, and cheating is not smart.	~H • ~S

De Morgan's law is useful because it allows us to get rid of a negated compound statement, which is often hard to work with in a proof.

Replacement rules are based on the equivalence of two statement forms, using p, q, and r for the component propositions. As with the implication rules we learned in the previous section, the instances of these components may themselves be compound rather than atomic statements. Thus, each of the following equivalences is an instance of the replacement rule beside it in the list below:

(A ∨ B) • C :: C • (A ∨ B)	Com
[F ∨ (G ⊃ H)] ∨ K :: F ∨ [(G ⊃ H) ∨ K]	Assoc
L ⊃ (N ∨ P) :: ~~[L ⊃ (N ∨ P)]	DN
(A • B) ∨ (C • D) :: [(A • B) ∨ C] • [(A • B) ∨ D]	Dist
~[(O ⊃ R) ∨ (O ⊃ S)] :: ~(O ⊃ R) • ~(O ⊃ S)	DM

When we use replacement rules in a proof, the basic procedure is the same as when we use implication rules: We add a new line to the proof and state the justification. For example:

1. (G ⊃ K) • (J ⊃ L)		Premise
2. ~L ∨ ~K	/ ~G ∨ ~J	Premise / Conclusion
3. ~K ∨ ~L		2 Com
4. ~G ∨ ~J		1,3 DD

Before we could draw a destructive dilemma inference from the two premises, we had to switch the order of disjuncts in premise 2, replacing ~L ∨ ~K with ~K ∨ ~L. The latter is entered as a new line (3), with the notation that it was derived from 2 by the replacement rule of commutation.

Despite that broad similarity in the procedures for using implication and replacement rules, however, there are two very important differences.

The first difference is that an implication rule is a one-way street. It authorizes a step from premises to conclusion but not in the other direction. If we have the premises A ⊃ B and A, we can derive B by *modus ponens*, but from B alone we obviously cannot derive A ⊃ B or A. By contrast, a replacement rule is a two-way street. If we have the statement K • (L ∨ M) on some line in a proof, we can use distribution to replace it with (K • L) ∨ (K • M). But if we have the latter, distribution allows us to replace it with the former.

The second difference is that we can apply replacement rules to components of a statement on a previous line in a proof as well as to the statement as a whole. We cannot do this with implication rules. As we saw in the previous section, applying an implication rule to a component does not guarantee a valid inference. When we use a replacement rule, however, we are simply replacing one statement with its logical equivalent. Whether we apply the rule to the whole statement on a previous line or to a component of a statement, the new statement has exactly the same truth conditions as the statement it replaces, and it will thus have all the same logical implications. Here is a simple example:

1. A • ~ (C ∨ D)   / ~D   Premise / Conclusion
2. A • (~C • ~D)   1 DM
3. (A • ~C) • ~D   2 Assoc
4. ~D   3 Simp

In step 2, we used De Morgan's law to replace the component ~ (C ∨ D) in premise 1 with ~C • ~D. Since these are equivalent, and thus have the same truth values, we are guaranteed that the whole statement on line 2 has the same truth values as the whole statement on line 1. Replacing one with the other cannot affect the validity of the argument as a whole (as we could easily confirm by the truth table test of validity). But the replacement does enable us—with the help of association in step 3—to use the implication rule simplification to derive ~D.

REVIEW Implication Rules versus Replacement Rules

There are two major differences between implication rules and replacement rules:

- Implication rules can only be applied in one direction. Replacement rules are all bidirectional.

- Implication rules apply to whole lines of proof only. Replacement rules can be applied to whole lines or to statement components.

EXERCISE 9.2A

I. For each of the following statements, find a statement that is equivalent by the specified rule. Since replacement rules apply to component parts of a statement as well as to the statement as a whole, there may be more than one right answer.

✱1. (B • D) • F   Assoc

  2. A ∨ D   Com

  3. C ∨ (F ∨ G)   Assoc

✱4. ~E • ~N   DM

  5. H ⊃ J   DN

  6. ~A • ~F   DM

✱7. A • (K ∨ M)   Dist

  8. (J ⊃ L) • (~J ⊃ M)   DN

  9. (F ⊃ G) • (H ⊃ I)   Com

✱10. ~[(A ≡ B) • O]   DM

 11. (B ∨ F) ∨ [(E ⊃ ~G) • (E ⊃ H)]   Dist

 12. (K ∨ L) • [K • (M ≡ N)]   Assoc

II. Each of the following statements is an instance of one of the replacement rules we've examined so far (Com, Assoc, DN, Dist, or DM). Identify the rule.

✱1. (A ∨ B) :: (B ∨ A)

  2. [C ∨ (D • E)] :: [(C ∨ D) • (C ∨ E)]

  3. ~ (F • G) :: (~F ∨ ~G)

✱4. H :: ~ ~H

  5. [J ∨ (K ∨ L)] :: [(J ∨ K) ∨ L]

  6. ~F ⊃ (A ⊃ M) :: ~F ⊃ (A ⊃ ~ ~M)

✱7. (A • B) :: (B • A)

  8. [(M ⊃ N) • O] :: [O • (M ⊃ N)]

  9. [B • (C • D)] :: [(B • C) • D)]

✱10. [F • (G ∨ H)] :: [(F • G) ∨ (F • H)]

 11. (H ∨ I) :: ~ ~ (H ∨ I)

 12. C ∨ (A • B) :: [(C ∨ A) • (C ∨ B)]

✱13. [~H • ~ (G ≡ I)] :: ~[H ∨ (G ≡ I)]

 14. [(A ∨ ~B) ⊃ (C • D)] ::
     [(A ∨ ~B) ⊃ (~ ~C • D)]

 15. [~C • ~ (D ∨ E)] :: ~[C ∨ (D ∨ E)]

✱16. {~ ~D ∨ [(A • B) ≡ ~C]} ::
     {[(A • B) ≡ ~C] ∨ ~ ~D}

 17. {~L • [(M ⊃ N) ∨ (M ⊃ ~N)]} ::
     {[~L • (M ⊃ N)] ∨ [~L • (M ⊃ ~N)]}

 18. {[(H • J) ∨ ~K] ∨ (G ⊃ K)} ::
     {(H • J) ∨ [~K ∨ (G ⊃ K)]}

✱19. ~[(F ⊃ E) ∨ ~ (C ∨ E)] ::
     ~ (F ⊃ E) • ~ ~ (C ∨ E)

 20. ~{[(K ∨ L) ⊃ (M • ~N)] • O} ::
     {~[(K ∨ L) ⊃ (M • ~N)] ∨ ~O}

 21. {(E ⊃ H) • [(F ⊃ I) ∨ G]} ::
     {[(E ⊃ H) • (F ⊃ I)] ∨ [(E ⊃ H) • G]}

III. | Integrative Exercise | Construct a proof for each of the following arguments, using the rules of replacement we learned in this section (Com, Assoc, DN, Dist, and DM) along with the rules of implication from Section 9.1.

✳1. 1. (A • A) ∨ ~~B   / A ∨ B

2. 1. ~(A ∨ B)   / ~B • ~A

3. 1. A ∨ (D ∨ C)   / C ∨ (A ∨ D)

✳4. 1. ~(D ∨ E)   / ~D

5. 1. D ∨ (E • G)   / D ∨ E

6. 1. ~(~D ∨ E)   / D • ~E

✳7. 1. A • (B ∨ C)
    2. ~(A • B)   / A • C

8. 1. ~~[A • (B ∨ C)]   / (A • B) ∨ (A • C)

9. 1. (A • B) ∨ (C • D)   / (A • B) ∨ C

✳10. 1. C ∨ ~D   / ~(~C • D)

11. 1. A • (B ∨ C)]   / [(A • B) ∨ (A • C)] ∨ ~F

12. 1. ~[A • ~ (B • C)]   / (~A ∨ B) • (~A ∨ C)

✳13. 1. (B ∨ C) ∨ D
    2. ~B   / C ∨ D

14. 1. ~P ∨ (Q • R)
    2. ~Q   / ~P

15. 1. (A • B) ∨ (C • D)   / C ∨ A

✳16. 1. A • G
    2. ~G ∨ B   / B ∨ F

17. 1. A ⊃ B
    2. ~B ∨ C
    3. A   / C

18. 1. ~A ∨ ~C
    2. ~B ⊃ C
    3. A   / B

✳19. 1. E ∨ F
    2. ~G ∨ H
    3. ~ (E ∨ H)   / F • ~G

20. 1. (D • E) ∨ (F • G)
    2. (D ⊃ H) • (F ⊃ I)   / H ∨ I

21. 1. (D ⊃ C) ∨ (B ⊃ C)
    2. ~ (E • A) ⊃ ~(D ⊃ C)
    3. ~E • ~C   / ~B

9.2B Rules of Replacement (Continued)

The preceding replacement rules dealt with conjunction, disjunction, and negation. Another group of rules we're going to use pertains to conditionals and biconditionals. The first is:

Transposition (Trans): $(p \supset q) :: (\sim q \supset \sim p)$

We dealt with transposition in Chapter 7 when we discussed the contrapositive of conditionals. You may recall our example:

If it rained last night, the ground is wet.	$R \supset W$
It the ground is not wet, it did not rain last night.	$\sim W \supset \sim R$

These statements are obviously equivalent. We use transposition in proofs when it is easier to work with the transposed statement than with the statement itself. Suppose, for example, that we want to derive the statement R ⊃ S, either as the conclusion or as a step on the way to the conclusion. And suppose that earlier lines in the proof included the statements W ⊃ S and ∼W ⊃ ∼R. We could use transposition to set up a hypothetical syllogism:

1. W ⊃ S	Premise or already derived from premises
2. ∼W ⊃ ∼R	Premise or already derived from premises
3. R ⊃ W	2 Trans
4. R ⊃ S	1,3 HS

APPLY Conditional Reasoning and the LSAT

Many questions in the logical reasoning section of the Law School Admissions Test rely on conditional reasoning. Here's one type of question you might see:

> Lawson cuts the grass every Saturday. He drinks iced tea every time he cuts the grass. Therefore, if it's not Saturday he doesn't drink iced tea.

Does the conclusion follow from the premises? Let's symbolize the argument so its form is clearer. Each statement can be translated as a conditional statement. We'll let S = It is Saturday, C = Lawson cuts the grass, and D = Lawson drinks iced tea.

$$S \supset C$$
$$C \supset D \qquad / \sim S \supset \sim D$$

By HS, the premises lead naturally to the conclusion S ⊃ D (If it's Saturday, Lawson drinks iced tea). By negating both the antecedent and consequent of the conclusion, the question tries to make you think they've applied HS and Trans to arrive at the conclusion. That would be a valid argument with the conclusion ∼D ⊃ ∼S (If Lawson doesn't drink iced tea, it's not Saturday). But this is not the given conclusion; the argument is invalid. Taking a minute to symbolize the conditionals and their transposed versions (contrapositives) can help you achieve your best score.

Another rule was mentioned in connection with the truth-functional character of the conditional. We noticed that a conditional statement is true if either the antecedent is false or the consequent true. In other words, $p \supset q$ is equivalent to $\sim p \vee q$:

Implication (Imp): $(p \supset q) :: (\sim p \vee q)$

An example of this equivalence in ordinary language would be:

If I stay for dinner, I'll have to listen to my uncle doing his Elvis Presley impression.	S ⊃ L
Either I don't stay for dinner or I'll have to listen to my uncle doing his Elvis Presley impression.	~S ∨ L

The rule is so named because "implication" (or "material implication") is another name for the conditional.

Next we have a replacement rule telling us how to transform a biconditional into equivalent statements.

Equivalence (Equiv): $(p \equiv q) :: [(p \supset q) \bullet (q \supset p)]$
$$:: [(p \bullet q) \vee (\sim p \bullet \sim q)]$$

The first formulation of this rule captures the meaning of the biconditional: *p if and only if q*. The second formulation follows from the truth table for the connective "≡": A biconditional is true if and only if both components have the same truth values. These rules are essential when we encounter a biconditional statement in a proof because (as you may have noticed) none of the basic implication rules include biconditional statements. So to work with a biconditional statement in a proof, whether it is a premise or the conclusion, we normally have to replace it with one of the equivalent statements. Here's an example:

A ∨ (D ≡ C)
~A
―――――――
~C ⊃ ~D

It is easy to see that the two premises can be used in a disjunctive syllogism to derive D ≡ C. But then what do we do? We need to use the material equivalence rule to replace the biconditional connective. Which version of the rule should we use? Since the conclusion is a conditional statement, the natural choice is the first one. That will give us D ⊃ C, from which we can derive the conclusion by using transposition:

1. A ∨ (D ≡ C)		Premise
2. ~A	/ ~C ⊃ ~D	Premise / Conclusion
3. D ≡ C		1,2 DS
4. (D ⊃ C) • (C ⊃ D)		3 Equiv
5. D ⊃ C		4 Simp
6. ~C ⊃ ~D		5 Trans

The next rule of replacement is an obvious one known as tautology. When Robert Frost says he has "miles to go before I sleep, and miles to go before I sleep," the repetition is merely for dramatic effect. The conjunction of a statement with itself, $p \bullet p$, says nothing more or less than p. The same is true for the disjunction of a statement with

---

SOLVE **Proving Biconditionals**

The easiest way to prove a biconditional is almost always to prove each of the corresponding conditionals separately, conjoin them, then apply equivalence.

---

itself: $p \lor p$. (Imagine a child being offered the following "choice" by a parent: You can clean your room, or you can clean your room.) So the rule is:

Tautology (Taut): $p :: (p \bullet p)$
                          $p :: (p \lor p)$

Our final rule is:

Exportation (Exp): $[(p \bullet q) \supset r] :: [p \supset (q \supset r)]$

This looks a little strange, but it makes sense when you think about it. Here is an example we have used before:

If I got the breaks, and had the talent, I'd be $(B \bullet T) \supset S$
a Hollywood star.

The same statement in a different form would be:

If I got the breaks, then if I had the talent I'd be $B \supset (T \supset S)$
a Hollywood star.

If we have a statement of the form $(p \bullet q) \supset r$ in a proof, exportation allows us to isolate p as an antecedent; if we have already derived p, we can then infer $q \supset r$. Conversely, if we have a statement of the form $p \supset (q \supset r)$, exportation allows us to isolate r as a consequent; if we have already derived $\sim r$, we can infer $\sim (p \bullet q)$; or, if we have derived $p \bullet q$, we can infer r.

We now have nine implication rules and ten replacement rules with which to construct proofs. As with the implication rules, the more familiar you are with the replacement rules, the easier you will find it to recognize patterns in the arguments you are given, and that will make it easier to find the steps by which you can derive the conclusion from the premises. For both kinds of rules, the most important thing is to understand the logic of the rule—to understand why it allows a valid step in a proof. The deeper your understanding, the easier you will find it to construct proofs. The replacement rules we have learned in this section do not change the basic strategy for constructing proofs that we discussed in connection with implication rules: to work backward from the conclusion we are trying to reach. What replacement rules add to the process is a way to streamline proofs and—in some cases—to construct proofs that would not be possible without them.

The replacement rules are stated in full in the Review box that follows. One way to think about them is in terms of the functions they can perform in proofs:

- Commutation and association allow us to rearrange the elements in conjunctive or disjunctive statements, with no change in the connectives involved.
- Double negation and transposition allow us to introduce negation or eliminate it.
- Tautology allows us to simplify a statement or to duplicate it.
- The other rules allow us to replace one connective with another:
- Distribution allows us to interchange conjunction with disjunction as the main connective.
- De Morgan's law allows us to replace a negated conjunction with a disjunction of negated components or a negated disjunction with a conjunction of negated components.
- Implication allows us to interchange a conditional with a disjunction.
- Equivalence allows us to interchange a biconditional with conjoined conditionals or disjoined conjunctions.
- Exportation allows us to alter a conditional statement, exchanging a conjunctive antecedent with a conditional consequent.

REVIEW Ten Rules of Replacement

Commutation (Com)

$(p \bullet q) :: (q \bullet p)$
$(p \lor q) :: (q \lor p)$

Association (Assoc)

$[p \bullet (q \bullet r)] :: [(p \bullet q) \bullet r]$
$[p \lor (q \lor r)] :: [(p \lor q) \lor r]$

Double negation (DN)

$p :: \sim\sim p$

Distribution (Dist)

$[p \bullet (q \lor r)] :: [(p \bullet q) \lor (p \bullet r)]$
$[p \lor (q \bullet r)] :: [(p \lor q) \bullet (p \lor r)]$

De Morgan's law (DM)

$\sim(p \bullet q) :: (\sim p \lor \sim q)$
$\sim(p \lor q) :: (\sim p \bullet \sim q)$

Transposition (Trans)

$(p \supset q) :: (\sim q \supset \sim p)$

Implication (Imp)

$(p \supset q) :: (\sim p \lor q)$

Equivalence (Equiv)

$(p \equiv q) :: [(p \supset q) \bullet (q \supset p)]$
$(p \equiv q) :: [(p \bullet q) \lor (\sim p \bullet \sim q)]$

Tautology (Taut)

$p :: (p \bullet p)$
$p :: (p \lor p)$

Exportation (Exp)

$[(p \bullet q) \supset r] :: [p \supset (q \supset r)]$

EXERCISE 9.2B

I. For each of the following statements, find a statement that is equivalent by the specified rule. Since replacement rules apply to component parts of a statement as well as to the statement as a whole, there may be more than one right answer.

✻1. A ⊃ B   Trans

  2. B   Taut

  3. (K • L) ⊃ J   Exp

✻4. F ⊃ ~G   Imp

  5. [M • ~ (J ∨ K)] ⊃ (B ∨ N)   Exp

  6. ~ (F ⊃ H) ⊃ (M ∨ ~N)   Trans

✻7. F ≡ (G ≡ H)   Equiv

  8. ~ (K ∨ L) ∨ [(L • N) ⊃ O]   Imp

  9. (A ⊃ B) ≡ ~A   Equiv

✻10. ~(F ⊃ H) ⊃ (M ∨ ~N)   Imp

  11. E ≡ M   Equiv

  12. A • (D ⊃ J)   Taut

II. Each of the following statements is an instance of one of the replacement rules we've examined so far (Trans, Imp, Equiv, Taut, or Exp). Identify the rule.

✻1. A :: (A • A)

  2. (C ⊃ D) :: (~D ⊃ ~C)

  3. [F ⊃ (G ⊃ H)] :: [(F • G) ⊃ H]

✻4. (C ≡ D) :: [(C • D) ∨ (~C • ~D)]

  5. (E ⊃ F) :: (~F ⊃ ~E)

  6. [~G ⊃ (H ⊃ I)] :: [(~G • H) ⊃ I]

✻7. (J ⊃ ~K) :: (~J ∨ ~K)

  8. [(L • M) ⊃ (N ∨ O)] ::
     [~(N ∨ O) ⊃ ~(L • M)]

  9. [(~A ⊃ ~B) • (~B ⊃ ~A)] :: (~A ≡ ~B)

✻10. [(C • D) ⊃ E] :: [~ (C • D) ∨ E]

  11. (~A ∨ B) :: (A ⊃ B)

  12. {[(E • G) • (G ⊃ ~H)] ⊃ ~(F • H)} ::
      {(E • G) ⊃ [(G ⊃ ~H) ⊃ ~ (F • H)]}

✻13. (A • B) :: [(A • B) ∨ (A • B)]

  14. {~[(L • J) ⊃ K] ∨ ~[(L • J) ⊃ H]} ::
      {[(L • J) ⊃ K] ⊃ ~[(L • J) ⊃ H]}

  15. [(A • ~B) ∨ (~A • ~~B)] :: (A ≡ ~B)

✻16. [~(M ⊃ N) ∨ (I ∨ J)] ⊃ (H • N) ::
      [(M ⊃ N) ⊃ (I ∨ J)] ⊃ (H • N)

  17. [(F ⊃ E) ∨ ~(C ∨ E)] ::
      [(~F ∨ E) ∨ ~(C ∨ E)]

III. **Integrative Exercise** Construct a proof to show that each of the following arguments is valid, using the implication and replacement rules. (For the first five problems, you will need only the new replacement rules from this section—Trans, Imp, Equiv, Taut, and Exp. For the remaining problems, be prepared to use all of the replacement rules, as well as the implication rules.)

✻1. 1. (A • A) ∨ ~~B   / A ∨ B

  2. 1. A ⊃ B   / ~~B ∨ ~A

  3. 1. $(A \cdot B) \supset C$ / $\sim(B \supset C) \supset \sim A$

∗4. 1. $\sim A \lor (B \supset C)$ / $(A \cdot B) \supset C$

  5. 1. $(A \supset B) \cdot (\sim B \lor A)$ / $A \equiv B$

  6. 1. $A \supset (A \supset C)$ / $A \supset C$

∗7. 1. $A \cdot G$
    2. $\sim G \lor B$ / $B \lor F$

  8. 1. $C \equiv D$ / $(C \supset D) \cdot (\sim C \supset \sim D)$

  9. 1. $(G \cdot H) \supset J$
    2. $J \supset K$ / $G \supset (K \lor \sim H)$

∗10. 1. $C \equiv D$ / $(C \cdot D) \lor \sim(C \lor D)$

 11. 1. $(F \supset G) \cdot (H \supset J)$
    2. $\sim F \supset H$ / $G \lor J$

 12. 1. $C \supset (D \cdot E)$ / $(C \supset D) \cdot (C \supset E)$

∗13. 1. $E \supset (F \supset G)$ / $F \supset (E \supset G)$

 14. 1. $\sim(H \cdot J)$
    2. $\sim J \supset K$ / $H \supset K$

 15. 1. $\sim L \supset (M \supset N)$
    2. $\sim N$ / $L \lor \sim M$

∗16. 1. $\sim(G \equiv M)$ / $(G \lor M) \cdot \sim(G \cdot M)$

 17. 1. $[(A \cdot B) \supset C] \cdot (E \supset C)$
    2. $(A \cdot B) \lor (E \cdot A)$ / C

 18. 1. $(A \cdot B) \lor C$
    2. $C \supset D$
    3. $A \supset \sim B$ / D

∗19. 1. $(E \supset K) \cdot (K \supset O)$
    2. $O \supset E$ / $O \equiv E$

 20. 1. $A \supset (H \lor J)$
    2. $J \equiv H$
    3. $\sim J$ / $\sim A$

 21. 1. $A \lor (B \supset C)$
    2. $\sim C$ / $B \supset A$

∗22. 1. D
    2. $\sim D \lor (E \equiv F)$ / $\sim E \supset \sim F$

 23. 1. $(J \supset K) \supset (J \supset L)$
    2. $J \cdot \sim L$ / $\sim K$

 24. 1. $A \supset B$ / $(A \cdot C) \supset B$

∗25. 1. $A \supset (H \lor J)$
    2. $J \equiv H$
    3. $\sim J$ / $\sim A$

26. 1. (E ∨ F) ⊃ G
    2. H ⊃ E
    3. ~H ⊃ F   / G

27. 1. (A ⊃ B) • (A ⊃ C)
    2. (B • C) ⊃ (D • E)
    3. ~D   / ~A

*28. 1. (I ∨ J) ⊃ K
    2. (L ∨ M) ⊃ ~K
    3. M   / ~J

29. 1. (L • C) ⊃ ~E
    2. ~(C • L) ⊃ G
    3. ~F ⊃ ~G   / E ⊃ F

30. 1. (F • G) ⊃ H
    2. F
    3. (I ⊃ ~H) • (F ⊃ G)   / G ≡ H

*31. 1. (A ∨ B) ⊃ (C ∨ D)
    2. E • [E ⊃ (C ⊃ G)]
    3. (B ∨ A) ⊃ (D ⊃ H)
    4. (F ∨ E) ⊃ (A ∨ B)   / G ∨ H

9.3 Conditional Proof and Indirect Proof

In this section, we're going to learn two additional techniques that can be used in proofs. Given the rules we're using, these techniques are necessary in order to construct proofs for certain valid arguments. And even where they are not necessary, they can make life easier by reducing the number and complexity of the steps we need to derive a conclusion.

9.3A Conditional Proof

The first technique is called **conditional proof (CP)**, and we can see the rationale for it if we examine the following argument:

A ⊃ (B ⊃ C)
B
―――――――――
A ⊃ C

Intuitively, this argument seems valid. The first premise doesn't tell us whether A is true, but suppose it is. On that supposition, B ⊃ C would follow. From B ⊃ C, together with the second premise (B), we could derive C. If A is true, therefore, C must be true as well—and that's exactly what the conclusion says. The method of conditional proof is a way of capturing this process of thought. The method is used to prove a conditional statement. We start by assuming the antecedent (in this case A), then we use that assumption (along with the premises we are given) to derive the consequent (C), and this justifies the conclusion (A ⊃ C).

To keep track of what we're doing, it helps to use a special notation. A conditional proof for the argument above would be formulated as follows:

1. A ⊃ (B ⊃ C)		Premise
2. B	/ A ⊃ C	Premise / Conclusion
3. A		Assumption
4. B ⊃ C		1,3 MP
5. C		2,4 MP
6. A ⊃ C		3–5 CP

The indented lines (3–5) are the conditional part of the proof. This is the subproof in which we assume that A is true and show that C follows. But the premises *do not* tell us that A is true. It is an assumption we have made. So we cannot end the proof on line 5. We have borrowed A, and now we have to pay it back. We do that on line 6. At this point in the proof, we are no longer assuming that A is true; we have discharged that assumption. We are saying that *if* A is true, C is true as well. This conditional statement is justified by the fact that C follows from A, along with the other premises. So line 6 is not indented, and we note the justification in the column to the right: Line 6 is justified by the conditional proof in lines 3 through 5.

APPLY Implication Rules and the LSAT

If you're thinking about law school, you'll want to be prepared for the Law School Admissions Test. Reviewing MP and MT is sure to help. Let's review the forms:

MP	**MT**
$p \supset q$	$p \supset q$
p	$\sim q$
q	$\sim p$

We affirm the antecedent or deny the consequent. There are two fallacies associated with MP and MT: denying the antecedent and affirm-ing the consequent. Neither of those forms is valid and the LSAT will try to determine if you know the difference. More difficult questions may combine the fallacious conclusion with transposition to make it trickier. Many of these questions are quite short. Use your knowledge of the argument forms, rather than the content of the statements, to lead you to the correct answer. If you see conditional statements with negated antecedents and consequents, try applying transposition, $(p \supset q) :: (\sim q \supset \sim p)$, then checking for the valid (or fallacious) forms of MP and MT.

To see the value of this technique, compare the conditional proof above with the kind of proof we would need if we used only the implication and replacement rules:

1. A ⊃ (B ⊃ C)		Premise
2. B	/ A ⊃ C	Premise / Conclusion
3. ~A ∨ (B ⊃ C)		1 Imp
4. ~A ∨ (~B ∨ C)		3 Imp
5. (~A ∨ ~B) ∨ C		4 Assoc
6. (~B ∨ ~A) ∨ C		5 Com
7. ~B ∨ (~A ∨ C)		6 Assoc
8. ~~B		2 DN
9. ~A ∨ C		7,8 DS
10. A ⊃ C		9 Imp

You can see that the conditional proof is much simpler. It saves us all the trouble of translating the first premise into a disjunction and rearranging all the terms.

This brings us to another point about conditional proof. Consider the following argument:

P ⊃ Q   / P ⊃ (P • Q)

By now, you can probably see that the argument is obviously valid. Try proving it using only the 19 inference rules. Couldn't do it, could you? The point is our 19 rule system is incomplete without CP. With the addition of CP, however, we can prove any valid argument.

A conditional proof can be used only to prove a conditional statement. But that conditional statement need not be the conclusion of the argument as a whole. We can use the method at any point in a proof to derive a conditional that will help us get to the ultimate conclusion. For example:

K • H
(F • K) ⊃ G
~F ∨ G

Here we have a disjunctive conclusion. Neither premise involves that connective, but we know that ~F ∨ G is equivalent to F ⊃ G, so we might try deriving the latter statement. And since it is a conditional, we might consider using conditional proof:

1. K • H		Premise
2. (F • K) ⊃ G	/ ~F ∨ G	Premise / Conclusion
3. F ⊃ (K ⊃ G)		2 Exp
4. K		1 Simp
5. F		Assumption
6. K ⊃ G		3,5 MP
7. G		4,6 MP
8. F ⊃ G		5–7 CP
9. ~F ∨ G		8 Imp

When we use conditional proof to derive a conditional statement that is not the conclusion but only a step toward the conclusion, we have to obey an important restriction. Once we discharge the assumption in the indented subproof and get back to the main proof, as we did above in line 8, we can no longer use any line that is part of the subproof. Any such line depends on an assumption we are no longer making. Once you repay a loan, the money is no longer in your account for you to use. To maintain the validity of your proofs, therefore, be careful to discharge any assumption you have made in a conditional subproof, and then seal off that subproof from any further use.

We can also use one conditional proof inside another, as long as we are careful to pay back all our loans. In the following example, the conclusion is a conditional statement whose consequent is an embedded conditional. We can use a secondary conditional proof to derive the consequent, F ⊃ H, within the primary conditional proof that establishes the conclusion, D ⊃ (F ⊃ H).

1. (D • E) ⊃ [F ⊃ (G • H)]		Premise
2. D ⊃ E	/ D ⊃ (F ⊃ H)	Premise / Conclusion

Primary CP

3. D	Assumption
4. E	2,3 MP
5. D • E	3,4 Conj
6. F ⊃ (G • H)	1,5 MP

Secondary CP

7. F	Assumption
8. G • H	6,7 MP
9. H	8 Simp

10. F ⊃ H	7–9 CP
11. D ⊃ (F ⊃ H)	3–10 CP

Lines 7 through 9 are a secondary conditional proof within the primary conditional proof (lines 3 through 10). The rule that we cannot use any line in a conditional proof once we have completed the proof and discharged its assumption applies in layers when we embed one conditional proof inside another. Thus we had to close the secondary conditional proof on line 10 in order to get back to the primary one, and from that point on we can no longer use lines 7–9 in any further step. Then of course we had to close the primary conditional proof on line 11 by discharging its assumption.

REVIEW Conditional Proof

Consider using the method of conditional proof when it would help to derive a conditional statement. To use the method:

1. Enter the antecedent of the conditional statement you want to derive on a new line, indenting the line and labeling it as an assumption.

2. Derive the consequent of that conditional statement, using the assumption together with any previous line in the proof (including premises, but not including any line in a previous conditional proof). Indent these lines, noting your justification in the normal way.

3. Enter the conditional statement as a nonindented line. As justification, enter the lines of the conditional proof and the method, CP.

4. Statements derived within the conditional portion of the proof cannot be used after that portion has been completed.

EXERCISE 9.3A

Construct proofs for the following arguments, using conditional proof (CP).

*1. 1. H ⊃ (I • G)   / H ⊃ I

 2. 1. A ⊃ (B ∨ C)
     2. ~C   A ⊃ B

 3. 1. K ⊃ J
     2. J ⊃ (L • M)   / K ⊃ M

*4. 1. D ⊃ (E ⊃ F)
     2. D ⊃ (F ⊃ G)   / D ⊃ (E ⊃ G)

 5. 1. K ⊃ (L ≡ M)
     2. ~L   / K ⊃ ~M

 6. 1. [A ⊃ (B • C)] • [B ⊃ (D • C)]   / (A ∨ B) ⊃ C

*7. 1. A ⊃ B
     2. (B • A) ⊃ D
     3. [(B • A) • D] ⊃ E   / A ⊃ E

 8. 1. (~A • B) ∨ (D • C)   / A ⊃ (C ∨ E)

 9. 1. ~(A ∨ B) ∨ C
     2. C ⊃ D   / ~B ∨ D

*10. 1. ~(N • P)
     2. T ∨ P
     3. (T • ~P) ⊃ O
     4. ~N ⊃ (M • S)
     5. O ⊃ ~M   / N ≡ O

11. 1. ~A ∨ [~B ∨ (C • D)]   / (A • B) ⊃ C

12. 1. ~(A • B) ∨ (C ⊃ D)
    2. A ∨ ~C
    3. C   / B ⊃ D

✱13. 1. (E ⊃ F) • (G ⊃ H)
     2. E ∨ (I ⊃ G)   / I ⊃ (F ∨ H)

14. 1. F ⊃ ~S
    2. (A • N) ∨ (A • F)
    3. S ⊃ ~N   / ~S

15. 1. (F • G) ∨ (H • ~I)
    2. I ⊃ ~ (F • E)   / I ⊃ ~E

✱16. 1. (~A ⊃ ~B) ⊃ (C • D)
     2. D ⊃ (C • E)   / ~(A • ~E)

17. 1. [K ⊃ (L ⊃ K)] ⊃ (~M ⊃ M)   / M

18. 1. (A ∨ B) ⊃ C
    2. ~A ⊃ (D • E)   / C ∨ D

✱19. 1. (A ⊃ B) ⊃ ~C   / ~(C • B)

20. 1. [(P ∨ M) • (G ∨ L)] ⊃ T   / P ⊃ (G ⊃ T)

21. 1. [A ⊃ (B ⊃ C)] • [A ⊃ (C ⊃ B)]
    2. (C ≡ B) ⊃ ~D   / D ⊃ ~A

✱22. 1. T • ~W   / S ⊃ [S ⊃ (R ⊃ S)]

23. 1. (P ⊃ S) ⊃ ~S
    2. ~R ⊃ M
    3. T ∨ ~R
    4. ~T   / M • ~S

24. 1. B ⊃ ~(~E ∨ R)
    2. (D • E) ⊃ {E ⊃ [C • (~M ⊃ ~D)]}
    3. R ∨ D
    4. M ⊃ (G • ~T)
    5. ~(~T • ~B)   / B ≡ M

9.3B Indirect Proof

The second additional technique we're going to use is called **indirect proof (IP)**. This proof strategy takes its name from the fact that we attempt to prove the conclusion indirectly rather than directly. This distinguishes IP from all the previous methods we have learned—including implication rules, replacement rules, and conditional proof. Instead of proceeding step by step toward a conclusion, we take a detour: We assume the opposite of what we are trying to derive. If we are trying to derive some statement *p*, and we have shown that assuming ~*p* leads to a contradiction, we go back to the assumption and reject it. We can therefore enter *p* as a line in the main proof. (Because this method of proof hinges on the fact that a contradiction can never be true, it is sometimes known by its Latin name *reductio ad absurdum*.) Here's an argument for which indirect proof is the most useful method:

$(A \lor B) \supset D$
~$B \supset D$
D

It's hard to see where to begin with this argument. The conclusion D is the consequent of both premises, but there's no apparent way to derive D from those premises. But if we assume ~D, then we can use that assumption in *modus tollens* inferences with each premise. Let's see where this leads us. The first step is to enter ~D as an assumption, indenting it as we did with conditional proof:

1. $(A \lor B) \supset D$		Premise
2. ~$B \supset D$	/ D	Premise / Conclusion
3. ~D		Assumption
4. ~$(A \lor B)$		1,3 MT
5. ~A • ~B		4 DM
6. ~B		5 Simp
7. ~ ~B		2,3 MT
8. B		7 DN
9. A $\lor$ B		8 Add
10. D		1,9 MP
11. D • ~D		3,10 Conj
12. D		3–11 IP

As with conditional proof, we indent the portion of the proof in which we are relying on the assumption. Within that subproof, we use the assumption together with the premises to derive two contradictory statements, in this case our original assumption ~D and the D we derived on line 10. It is a requirement of *indirect proof* that we combine these statements into a single self-contradiction. Since the assumption of ~D led to a contradiction, we can enter D as a line in the primary proof and note that it is justified by the *indirect proof* in lines 3 to 11.

REVIEW The Law of Non-Contradiction

Indirect proof is based on the fact that a contradiction—any statement of the form *p* • ~*p*—is necessarily false. This idea, known as the law of non-contradiction, is a fundamental principle of rationality that makes

knowledge possible. How important is it? So important that the Greek philosopher Aristotle said, "The most certain of all basic principles is that contradictory propositions are not true simultaneously."

Indirect proof is a natural method to consider using when the conclusion is an atomic statement, but it can be used with compound statements as well. Here is an example:

(A • B) ⊃ (C ⊃ D)
B ⊃ ~D
<u>A ⊃ C</u>
~(A • B)

Notice that the conclusion is the negation of the antecedent in the first premise. What the argument is saying is that if A • B were true, then C ⊃ D would be true (by MP); that C ⊃ D is somehow incompatible with the other two premises; and therefore A • B can't be true. *Indirect proof* is a way to capture this line of thought in a formal proof.

1. (A • B) ⊃ (C ⊃ D)   Premise
2. B ⊃ ~D   Premise
3. A ⊃ C   / ~(A • B)   Premise / Conclusion
    4. A • B   Assumption

Since the conclusion is a negation, inserting *its* negation as our assumption would give us ~~(A • B), and we would have to use the double negation rule to get A • B. But since line 4 is an assumption rather than a derived statement, we can simplify the procedure by adopting the rule that to derive a negated statement by IP, we simply remove the negation sign in our assumption.

Our goal now is to show how the assumption in line 4 leads to contradictory results, using the other premises of the argument. Following our initial line of thought, we would use the assumption with premise 1 to derive C ⊃ D. Then we can break A • B down into its components, and use A and B separately to draw conclusions from premises 2 and 3:

    5. C ⊃ D   1,4 MP
    6. A   4 Simp
    7. C   3,6 MP
    8. D   5,7 MP
    9. B   4 Simp
    10. ~D   2,9 MP
    11. D • ~D   8,10 Conj

There's our contradiction: We derived both D and ~D by valid steps and conjoined them as a single contradictory statement. The contradiction proves that the assumption in line 4 is false. So, to wrap things up, we now enter the negation of line 4 in the main (not indented) proof.

12. ~(A • B)   4–11 IP

That's our conclusion, so we're done.

When you use indirect proof, you need to keep certain things in mind.

We begin an indirect proof segment by taking the statement we want to prove and putting the contradictory statement on an indented line as an assumption. If the statement to be proved is not a negation, our assumption will be its negation: assume ~*p* to prove *p*. If the statement to be proved is already a negated statement, our assumption will be the unnegated statement: assume *p* to prove ~*p*.

Ultimately, of course, what we want to prove is the conclusion of the argument, so we often begin by assuming its negation, as in our example. But we can also use indirect proof to derive some other statement that we need as an intermediate conclusion from which the main conclusion can be derived by further steps.

The contradiction you derive within the indirect proof may or may not have the initial assumption as one of its components. In some cases, we assume p and derive $\sim p$. In other cases, we assume p and derive some other contradiction $q \bullet \sim q$. That's what happened in our example, where we assumed A $\bullet$ B but the contradiction was D $\bullet$ $\sim$D. In such cases, be sure that when you return to the main argument (as in line 12 above), what you enter is the negation of the initial assumption. That's what you have proved in the indirect proof.

The indirect proof segment must end with a self-contradictory statement of the form $q \bullet \sim q$. The self-contradiction can involve a simple atomic component, like D in our example, but it can also be internally complex. For example, [G ⊃ (H ∨ K)] $\bullet$ $\sim$[G ⊃ (H ∨ K)] is an instance of $q \bullet \sim q$ and would be legitimate as the final line of an indirect proof.

As with conditional proof, we can no longer use any line in an indirect proof segment once we have finished it and returned to the main proof.

As with conditional proof, we can use one indirect proof inside another. We can also use an indirect proof inside a conditional proof, and vice versa. Because both techniques are self-contained modules within a proof, we can use them at any point as long as we comply with the internal logic of the techniques.

Let's walk through one more example that illustrates these points.

A ⊃ [~D ∨ (~B • C)]
A ⊃ (E • F)
_____
A ⊃ ~[(D • B) ∨ ~E]

Notice that both of the premises and the conclusion are conditional statements. They even have the same antecedent. This argument is just begging for us to use conditional proof. So let's assume A and use it to derive the consequent.

1. A ⊃ [~D ∨ (~B • C)]		Premise
2. A ⊃ (E • F)	/ A ⊃ ~[(D • B) ∨ ~E]	Premise / Conclusion
3. A		Assumption
4. ~D ∨ (~B • C)		1,3 MP
5. E • F		2,3 MP

Now what? To complete the conditional proof, we need to derive the consequent of the conclusion, ~[(D • B) ∨ ~E]. Nothing in lines 1–5 seems to offer a direct route to that statement. So let's try using indirect proof as an indirect route, embedded within the conditional proof. We begin this segment by assuming the statement (D • B) ∨ ~E. Since line 5 gives us E, we can go on to derive D • B by a disjunctive syllogism.

6. (D • B) ∨ ~E	Assumption
7. E	5 Simp
8. ~~E	7 DN
9. D • B	6,8 DS

To complete the *indirect proof*, we need to generate a contradiction. From line 9, we can get both D and B by simplification. Now look at line 4. D contradicts the first disjunct, and B contradicts the second. So we can spell out that reasoning in formal steps and close the indirect proof segment.

10. D	9 Simp
11. ~~D	10 DN
12. ~B • C	4,11 DS
13. B	9 Simp
14. ~B	12 Simp
15. B • ~B	13,14 Conj
16. ~[(D • B) ∨ ~E]	6–15 IP

We are now back in the conditional proof that began on line 3. We have discharged the assumption in line 6, and we can no longer use any of the lines that depend on it (through line 15). The last step is to close out the conditional segment by bringing back A as the antecedent of the conditional statement we were trying to prove:

17. A ⊃ ~[(D • B) ∨ ~E]	3–16 CP

This brings us to a final point about conditional proof and IP. These two strategies can also be used, singly or jointly, to prove a special class of arguments. Consider this argument from Exercise 9.3A:

1. T • ~W / S ⊃ [S ⊃ (R ⊃ S)]	

Did this one stump you? If you followed our basic strategy of reasoning backward from the conclusion, you noticed immediately that the single premise is not related to the conclusion in any way at all. At this point, you hopefully decided to assume for conditional proof. What happened then?

1. T • ~W / S ⊃ [S ⊃ (R ⊃ S)]	
2. S	

You were stuck again. At this point, you learned that you would need to assume for CP at least once more. Here's one possible proof:

1. T • ~W / S ⊃ [S ⊃ (R ⊃ S)]	Premise / Conclusion
2. S	Assumption
3. S	Assumption
4. ~R ∨ S	3 Add
5. R ⊃ S	4 Impl

6. S ⊃ (R ⊃ S)	3–5 CP
7. S ⊃ [S ⊃ (R ⊃ S)]	2–6 CP

Your proof may have been somewhat different from this one but, however you solved it, you didn't rely on the given premise. In Chapter 8, we constructed truth tables showing that some propositions are true under all circumstances, regardless of the truth values of their components. As a consequence, they are true no matter what other statements may be true or false. Thus these logical truths, or tautologies, may be proven with any premise or with no premises at all. Here's another example:

/ T ⊃ (S ⊃ T)

Without premises, we must start our proof with an arbitrary assumption. We're trying to prove a conditional statement; assuming for CP should lead us to a proof.

/ T ⊃ (S ⊃ T)

1. T	Assumption
2. ~S ∨ T	1 Add
3. S ⊃ T	2 Imp
4. T ⊃ (S ⊃ T)	1–3 CP

Notice that, although our proof begins inside an indented sequence, our initial assumption is line 1, and all lines fall within the indented sequence until we have discharged our initial assumption. As you practice the next set of exercises, remember that you may be asked to prove a tautology from unnecessary premises, unrelated premises, or no premises at all. Just remember our basic strategies. Our system is now complete; CP and IP, along with the 19 rules of inference ensure that we can prove every valid argument.

REVIEW Indirect Proof

Consider using the method of indirect proof when it would help to derive a statement indirectly. That statement may be the conclusion of the argument or an intermediate conclusion. To use the method:

1. Enter the negation of the statement you want to derive on a new line, indenting the line and labeling it as an assumption. If the statement to be derived is itself a negation ~p, the assumption can be the unnegated statement p.

2. Derive a contradictory statement, using the assumption together with any previous line

in the proof (including premises, but not including any line in a previous conditional or indirect proof). Indent these lines, noting your justification in the normal way.

3. Enter the negation of the assumption as a non-indented line. As justification, enter the lines of the indented sequence and the method, IP.

4. Statements derived within the indented portion of the proof cannot be used after that portion has been completed.

EXERCISE 9.3B

Integrative Exercise

Construct proofs for the following arguments using conditional proof (CP) or indirect proof (IP) along with the 19 rules of inference.

✳**1.** 1. A ∨ B
     2. B ⊃ (C • ~C)   / A

2. 1. D ⊃ E
    2. ~D ⊃ E   / E

3. 1. ~ (O • M) ⊃ (L • ~G)
    2. G   / O • M

✳**4.** 1. (N ⊃ O) ⊃ P
     2. (N • ~O) ⊃ P   / P

5. 1. F ⊃ ~S
    2. (A • N) ∨ (A • F)
    3. S ⊃ ~N   / ~S

6. 1. (F ⊃ G) ⊃ H
    2. ~F   / H

✳**7.** 1. ~J ⊃ (K ∨ L)
     2. J ⊃ M
     3. ~K • ~L   / M

8. / S ⊃ [P ⊃ (P ⊃ P)]

9. 1. (A ⊃ B) ⊃ ~C   / ~(C • B)

✳**10.** 1. (R ∨ S) ⊃ T
      2. V ⊃ T
      3. S ∨ V   / T

11. 1. (A ∨ B) ⊃ (C • D)
     2. ~(D • A)   / ~A

12. 1. T ⊃ P
     2. M • S   / (~F ⊃ ~F) ∨ (~R • ~T)

✳**13.** / ~ (R • ~R) ≡ ~ (T • ~T)

14. 1. F • (G ⊃ H)
     2. ~I ⊃ (F ∨ H)
     3. F ⊃ G   / I ∨ H

15. / (P ⊃ ~Q) ≡ (~P ∨ ~Q)

✳**16.** 1. (A ⊃ B) ⊃ (C • D)
      2. B ⊃ E
      3. C ⊃ ~E   / ~B

17. / (C ⊃ C) ⊃ (A ∨ ~A)

18. / S ⊃ {S ⊃ [S ⊃ (S • S)]}

✳**19.** 1. (A ⊃ B) ⊃ C
      2. (A ⊃ D) • (~B ⊃ ~D)   / E ∨ C

20. 1. M ⊃ (N • ~L)
    2. X ⊃ ~(S ∨ ~L)   / (R • M) ⊃ (T ∨ ~X)
21. 1. N ⊃ [(L ∨ ~L) ⊃ S]
    2. S ⊃ {[T ⊃ (P ⊃ P)] ⊃ ~(~R ∨ R)}   / ~N
✱22. 1. (R ∨ M) ⊃ N
    2. (T • N) ⊃ ~(B ⊃ B)   / R ⊃ ~T

SOLVE Constructing Proofs

The following strategies are useful in constructing proofs:

1. Working forward from the premises:
   a. Look for pairs of premises to which the rules of *modus ponens*, *modus tollens*, disjunctive syllogism, hypothetical syllogism, or constructive or destructive dilemma can be applied.
   b. Then see whether the result can be combined with a further premise in a way that takes you closer to the conclusion.

2. Working backward from the conclusion:
   a. If the conclusion is an *atomic* statement, identify the premise(s) in which that statement occurs and look for ways to get from that premise(s) to the conclusion.
   b. If the conclusion is a *compound* statement, identify the main connective and the elements it connects.
   c. If the main connective is a conditional, look for a way to derive it by hypothetical syllogism or by conditional proof.
   d. If the main connective is conjunction, look for ways to derive each conjunct separately and use the rule of conjunction.
   e. If the main connective is disjunction, look for a way to derive one of the disjuncts and then use the rule of addition. Or look for a way to derive it by constructive or destructive dilemma.

3. If you reach an impasse in which you cannot identify a path from the premises to the conclusion, consider using indirect proof.

4. Use rules of equivalence to make changes that advance the proof:
   a. Use commutation and association to rearrange the elements in conjunctive or disjunctive statements, with no change in the connectives involved.
   b. Use transposition to introduce negation or double negation to eliminate it.
   c. Use tautology to simplify a statement or to duplicate it.
   d. Use distribution to interchange conjunction with disjunction as the main connective.
   e. Use De Morgan's law to replace a negated conjunction with a disjunction of negated components or a negated disjunction with a conjunction of negated components.
   f. Use implication to interchange a conditional with a disjunction or negated conjunction.
   g. Use equivalence to interchange a biconditional with conjoined conditionals or disjoined conjunctions.
   h. Use exportation to alter a conditional statement, exchanging a conjunctive antecedent with a conditional consequent.

CHAPTER REVIEW

Summary

- In the previous chapter, we learned to test validity using truth tables. In this chapter, we learned to prove validity using natural deduction proofs.
- Use natural deduction to derive the conclusion of an argument from its premises, using a sequence of steps.
- Each step of a proof must be justified by one of the 19 rules of inference.
  - There are nine implication rules; each is a basic inference form we know to be valid.
  - There are 10 replacement rules allowing us to replace one statement with another that is logically equivalent.

- Use conditional proof to prove conditionals by assuming the antecedent and deriving the consequent of the desired conditional.
- Use indirect proof by assuming the negation of the desired statement, along with the given premises, to derive a contradiction.
- The construction of a proof establishes the validity of the argument, but the failure to find a proof does not establish that the argument is invalid.

Key Terms

Note: All of the implication and replacement rules defined by logical forms appear in the box that follows this list.

modus ponens **(MP)** (p. 381)

modus tollens **(MT)** (p. 381)

hypothetical syllogism (HS) (p. 381)

disjunctive syllogism (DS) (p. 381)

simplification (Simp) (p. 392)

conjunction (Conj) (p. 392)

addition (Add) (p. 392)

constructive dilemma (CD) (p. 394)

destructive dilemma (DD) (p. 394)

commutation (Com) (p. 405)

association (Assoc) (p. 405)

double negation (DN) (p. 405)

distribution (Dist) (p. 405)

De Morgan's law (DM) (p. 406)

transposition (Trans) (p. 410)

implication (Imp) (p. 411)

equivalence (Equiv) (p. 411)

tautology (Taut) (p. 412)

exportation (Exp) (p. 412)

conditional proof (CP) (p. 416)

indirect proof (IP) (p. 421)

Rules of Implication and Replacement

Implication Rules

Modus ponens (MP)

$p \supset q$

$\underline{p}$

q

Modus tollens (MT)

$p \supset q$

$\underline{\sim q}$

$\sim p$

Hypothetical syllogism (HS)

$p \supset q$

$\underline{q \supset r}$

$p \supset r$

Disjunctive syllogism (DS)

$p \vee q$ $\qquad\qquad p \vee q$

$\underline{\sim p}$ or $\quad \underline{\sim q}$

q $\qquad\qquad\qquad p$

Simplification (Simp)

$\underline{p \bullet q}$ or $\quad \underline{p \bullet q}$

p $\qquad\qquad q$

Conjunction (Conj)

p or $\qquad p$

$\underline{q}$ $\qquad\quad \underline{q}$

$p \bullet q$ $\qquad\quad q \bullet p$

Addition (Add)

$\underline{p}$ or $\quad \underline{p}$

$p \vee q$ $\qquad\quad q \vee p$

Constructive dilemma (CD)

$(p \supset q) \bullet (r \supset s)$

$\underline{p \vee r}$

$q \vee s$

Destructive dilemma (DD)

$(p \supset q) \bullet (r \supset s)$

$\underline{\sim q \vee \sim s}$

$\sim p \vee \sim r$

Replacement Rules

Commutation (Com)

$(p \bullet q) \quad :: \quad (q \bullet p)$

$(p \vee q) \quad :: \quad (q \vee p)$

Transposition (Trans)

$(p \supset q) \quad :: \quad (\sim q \supset \sim p)$

Association (Assoc)

$[p \bullet (q \bullet r)] \quad :: \quad [(p \bullet q) \bullet r]$

$[p \vee (q \vee r)] \quad :: \quad [(p \vee q) \vee r]$

Implication (Imp)

$(p \supset q) \quad :: \quad (\sim p \vee q)$

Double negation (DN)

$p \quad :: \quad \sim\sim p$

Equivalence (Equiv)

$(p \equiv q) \quad :: \quad [(p \supset q) \bullet (q \supset p)]$

$(p \equiv q) \quad :: \quad [(p \bullet q) \vee (\sim p \bullet \sim q)]$

Distribution (Dist)

$[p \bullet (q \vee r)] \quad :: \quad [(p \bullet q) \vee (p \bullet r)]$

$[p \vee (q \bullet r)] \quad :: \quad [(p \vee q) \bullet (p \vee r)]$

Tautology (Taut)

$p \quad :: \quad (p \bullet p)$

$p \quad :: \quad (p \vee p)$

De Morgan's law (DM)

$\sim(p \bullet q) \quad :: \quad (\sim p \vee \sim q)$

$\sim(p \vee q) \quad :: \quad (\sim p \bullet \sim q)$

Exportation (Exp)

$[(p \bullet q) \supset r] \quad :: \quad [p \supset (q \supset r)]$

Putting It All Together

I. Each of the following is an instance of one of the basic implication rules. Identify the rule.

*1. $(A \equiv B) \bullet [C \supset (D \bullet {\sim}E)]$
$\underline{}$
$A \equiv B$

2. $[(F \supset G) \vee H] \vee (G \bullet I)$
$\underline{{\sim}[(F \supset G) \vee H]}$
$G \bullet I$

3. $\underline{[J \vee (K \bullet L)]}$
$[J \vee (K \bullet L)] \vee (J \supset L)$

*4. ${\sim}I \supset [J \bullet (K \vee L)]$
$\underline{J \supset (K \vee I)}$
$\{{\sim}I \supset [J \bullet (K \vee L)]\} \bullet [J \supset (K \vee I)]$

5. $(A \vee B) \supset {\sim}(C \vee D)$
$\underline{{\sim}(C \vee D) \supset (A \vee E)}$
$(A \vee B) \supset (A \vee E)$

6. $[(A \bullet B) \supset C] \bullet [(C \vee D) \supset B]$
$\underline{[(A \bullet B) \vee (C \vee D)]}$
$C \vee B$

*7. ${\sim}(E \bullet F) \supset [(E \supset G) \bullet (F \supset H)]$
$\underline{{\sim}(E \bullet F)}$
$(E \supset G) \bullet (F \supset H)$

8. $(M \bullet N) \supset [(M \vee O) \bullet (N \vee O)]$
$\underline{{\sim}[(M \vee O) \bullet (N \vee O)]}$
${\sim}(M \bullet N)$

9. $[(F \vee G) \supset (G \vee H)] \bullet [(H \bullet I) \supset J]$
$\underline{{\sim}(G \vee H) \vee {\sim}J}$
${\sim}(F \vee G) \vee {\sim}(H \bullet I)$

*10. $(K \bullet L) \supset [M \bullet (N \vee O)]$
$\underline{(K \bullet L) \supset (M \supset O)}$
$\{(K \bullet L) \supset [M \bullet (N \vee O)]\} \bullet [(K \bullet L) \supset (M \supset O)]$

11. $(A \bullet B) \vee [(A \bullet C) \supset (B \bullet C)]$
$\underline{{\sim}[(A \bullet C) \supset (B \bullet C)]}$
$A \bullet B$

12. $\underline{[(D \bullet E) \vee (D \bullet F)] \bullet [(E \bullet F) \vee (E \bullet D)]}$
$(E \bullet F) \vee (E \bullet D)$

*13. $[G \supset (H \bullet I)] \supset [J \bullet (I \supset K)]$
$\underline{[J \bullet (I \supset K)] \supset [(K \bullet G) \supset I]}$
$[G \supset (H \bullet I)] \supset [(K \bullet G) \supset I]$

14. $\{(L \vee M) \supset [N \supset (O \supset M)]\} \bullet [(L \bullet N) \supset {\sim}O]$
$\underline{(L \vee M) \vee (L \bullet N)}$
$[N \supset (O \supset M)] \vee {\sim}O$

15. $[(A \vee B) \bullet (C \vee D)] \supset \{A \supset [D \bullet (E \vee C)]\}$
$\underline{{\sim}\{A \supset [D \bullet (E \vee C)]\}}$
${\sim}[(A \vee B) \bullet (C \vee D)]$

II. Each of the inferences below can be justified by one of the rules of replacement. (The rule may have been applied to the whole premise or only to a component of the premise.) Name the rule.

*1. $\underline{(A \bullet B) \vee C}$
${\sim}{\sim}[(A \bullet B) \vee C]$

2. $[(D \vee E) \vee F] \supset G$
$[D \vee (E \vee F)] \supset G$

3. ${\sim}\{(H \supset I) \vee [J \bullet (K \vee L)]\}$
${\sim}(H \supset I) \bullet {\sim}[J \bullet (K \vee L)]$

*4. $\underline{[(A \vee B) \supset C] \supset (D \vee E)}$
${\sim}[(A \vee B) \supset C] \vee (D \vee E)$

5. $[(F \bullet G) \bullet H] \supset (I \bullet J)$
${\sim}(I \bullet J) \supset {\sim}[(F \bullet G) \bullet H]$

6. $(K \vee L) \bullet [M \supset (N \bullet O)]$
$[M \supset (N \bullet O)] \bullet (K \vee L)$

*7. $\underline{(A \vee B) \supset (C \supset D)}$
$[(A \vee B) \supset (C \supset D)] \vee [(A \vee B) \supset (C \supset D)]$

8. $\underline{[(E \vee F) \bullet G] \supset [(H \bullet I) \supset (I \supset J)]}$
$[(E \vee F) \bullet G] \supset [\sim(H \bullet I) \vee (I \supset J)]$

9. $\underline{[(A \vee B) \supset C] \equiv (C \vee D)}$
$\{[(A \vee B) \supset C] \supset (C \vee D)\} \bullet \{(C \vee D) \supset [(A \vee B) \supset C]\}$

*10. $\underline{[(E \bullet F) \bullet G] \supset [(E \vee H) \bullet (E \vee I)]}$
$(E \bullet F) \supset \{G \supset [(E \vee H) \bullet (E \vee I)]\}$

11. $\underline{(K \bullet L) \vee [(M \supset N) \bullet O]}$
$[(K \bullet L) \vee (M \supset N)] \bullet [(K \bullet L) \vee O]$

12. $\underline{\{(J \supset K) \supset [L \equiv (M \vee N)]\} \supset [J \supset (N \vee K)]}$
$\{(J \supset K) \supset [(L \vee L) \equiv (M \vee N)]\} \supset [J \supset (N \vee K)]$

*13. $\underline{[(A \bullet B) \vee C] \bullet [(A \vee C) \bullet (C \vee D)]}$
$[(A \bullet B) \vee C] \bullet [(C \vee A) \bullet (C \vee D)]$

14. $\underline{[(E \bullet F) \vee (G \bullet H)] \bullet [(E \bullet F) \vee (I \supset J)]}$
$(E \bullet F) \vee [(G \bullet H) \bullet (I \supset J)]$

15. $\underline{\sim\{[(K \vee L) \supset M] \bullet (N \vee O)\} \bullet [(L \bullet M) \supset N]}$
$\{\sim[(K \vee L) \supset M] \vee \sim(N \vee O)\} \bullet [(L \bullet M) \supset N]$

III. Integrative Exercise   For each of the following proofs, state the justification for each line, giving the line(s) from which it was derived and the implication or replacement rule by which it was derived.

*1. 1. $A \supset (B \vee C)$ Premise
    2. $\sim B$ / $\sim(A \bullet \sim C)$ Premise / Conclusion
    3. $\sim A \vee (B \vee C)$ _____
    4. $\sim A \vee (C \vee B)$ _____
    5. $(\sim A \vee C) \vee B$ _____
    6. $\sim A \vee C$ _____
    7. $\sim A \vee \sim\sim C$ _____
    8. $\sim(A \bullet \sim C)$ _____

2. 1. $(H \bullet J) \supset K$ Premise
    2. $\sim H \supset L$ Premise
    3. $\sim(J \supset L)$ / $J \supset K$ Premise / Conclusion
    4. $\sim(\sim J \vee L)$ _____
    5. $\sim\sim J \bullet \sim L$ _____
    6. $J \bullet \sim L$ _____
    7. $\sim L$ _____
    8. $\sim\sim H$ _____
    9. H _____
    10. $H \supset (J \supset K)$ _____
    11. $J \supset K$ _____

3. 1. $(D \supset E) \bullet (F \supset G)$ Premise
    2. $D \equiv \sim G$ Premise
    3. D / $E \bullet \sim F$ Premise / Conclusion
    4. $(D \supset \sim G) \bullet (\sim G \supset D)$ _____
    5. $D \supset \sim G$ _____

6. ~G   _____
7. F ⊃ G   _____
8. ~F   _____
9. D ⊃ E   _____
10. E   _____
11. E • ~F   _____

✳4. 1. (A • B) ⊃ ~C   Premise
    2. (C ⊃ E) ⊃ D   Premise
    3. ~D • B   / ~A   Premise / Conclusion
    4. ~D   _____
    5. ~(C ⊃ E)   _____
    6. ~(~C ∨ E)   _____
    7. ~~C • ~E   _____
    8. ~~C   _____
    9. ~(A • B)   _____
    10. ~A ∨ ~B   _____
    11. B   _____
    12. ~~B   _____
    13. ~A   _____

5. 1. (M ∨ N) ∨ (P • R)   Premise
    2. S ⊃ ~P   Premise
    3. M ⊃ R   Premise
    4. N ⊃ Q   / S ⊃ (R ∨ Q)   Premise / Conclusion
    5. S   _____
    6. ~P   _____
    7. ~P ∨ ~R   _____
    8. ~(P • R)   _____
    9. M ∨ N   _____
    10. (M ⊃ R) • (N ⊃ Q)   _____
    11. R ∨ Q   _____
    12. S ⊃ (R ∨ Q)   _____

IV.   <u>Integrative Exercise</u>   Translate each of the arguments below into symbolic notation and test it for validity by the truth table method. If it is valid, construct a proof.

✳1. It's possible that the earth's continents were once joined in a single giant landmass. The reason is that the earth's crust is divided into separate tectonic plates. If earthquakes occur, and they do, then the plates must be moving. If the crust is divided into separate plates and the plates are moving, then it's possible that the continents were once joined in a single giant landmass.

2. The patient reported headaches, fatigue, and loss of interest in normal activities. When these symptoms occur, the condition is either sleep deprivation or depression. If he is sleep-deprived, sleeping pills would eliminate his symptoms; but they did not. Therefore he is depressed.

3. If the boss snaps at you if you make a mistake, he's irritable. So, if he's irritable and you make a mistake, he'll snap at you.

✳4. Smith is guilty of burglary if and only if he took the goods from Jones's residence and she did not consent to their removal. Smith did take the goods, but Jones consented. So Smith is not guilty of burglary.

5. Either human beings as a species evolved in Africa and later dispersed in migration to various other regions or their precursors migrated at an earlier time and modern humans evolved independently in various regions. If the precursors of humans migrated at an earlier time, then it should not be the case—and it is—that we find their remains only in Africa. Therefore humans evolved in Africa.

6. Identical twins are formed 5 days after conception, when the cell cluster divides in two and each half attaches separately to the uterine wall. If personhood begins at conception, then there is a person present before the cell division. If so, that person either (a) is identical with both of the persons who come to exist after cell division; or (b) dies and is replaced by those two persons; or (c) is identical with one but not the other of those persons. But none of those alternatives can be the case. Therefore personhood does not begin at conception.

∗7. Either human choices are determined by antecedent factors or they are free. If human choices are determined by antecedent factors, then we cannot act in any way different from the way we do act. If so, then we are not morally responsible for our actions. But we are morally responsible for our actions, so our choices must be free.

8. Either human choices are determined by antecedent factors or they are free. If human choices are free, then they are uncaused; if they are uncaused, they are random; and if they are random, then we are not responsible for them. Since we are responsible for our choices, they must be determined by antecedent factors.

9. Gravity is solely an attractive force. If so, then if the universe is not expanding, it is contracting due to gravitational attraction. But if the universe were contracting, the average density of matter in space would be increasing, and it isn't. So the universe is expanding.

∗10. At the trial of Ken Giscan for the murder of Alice Lovelace, the judge instructed the jury that Giscan is guilty if and only if he had a motive, he possessed the murder weapon, and he was not with Sally Alibi at the time of the murder. The facts established at trial were these: Lovelace had ended her relationship with Giscan; Giscan was with Alibi at the time of the murder only if Alibi was telling the truth; if Alibi is jealous, she was not telling the truth; if Lovelace ended the relationship, then Giscan had a motive and Alibi was jealous; Giscan possessed the murder weapon. Therefore, Giscan is guilty.

11. It's a sure bet that the antacid division of the Hi-5 corporation is going to be sold. Hi-5 stock is going to decline unless the company improves its profits or the economy as a whole improves. The company will not improve its profits unless it sells the antacid division. However, if Hi-5 stock declines, the company will be taken over and its antacid division will be sold.

12. Mauritius has threatened to attack our commercial vessels in the shipping lanes off its shores. If we take preventive action and the threat is not real, we will be denounced for aggression. If the threat is real and we do not take preventive action, the attack will succeed; and if it succeeds, lives will be lost and further attacks will be encouraged in the future. None of these consequences is acceptable. We shall not be denounced for aggression, and we shall neither lose lives nor encourage future attacks. Therefore we will take preventive action if and only if the threat is real.

∗13. Why read books? Either a book repeats what is in the Bible, in which case, if you read it, you are wasting your time; or it contradicts what is in the Bible, in which case, if you read it, you are committing a sin. One should neither waste time nor commit a sin. Therefore one should not read a book.

14. If the traditional religious view is correct, God is both omnipotent and perfectly benev-

olent. If God is omnipotent, He is capable of preventing evil, and if He is perfectly benevolent, he would want to prevent evil. But if God wanted to prevent evil, and was capable of doing so, then there would be no evil, and there is. So the traditional religious view is not correct.

15. If I take his pawn with my knight, he will either take my knight or move his bishop to the space my knight is now guarding. If he takes my knight, I'll lose a valuable piece, but his queen will be exposed. If he moves his bishop to that space, my queen will be exposed. But if I don't take his pawn with my knight, my queen will be exposed anyway. I'm going to either take his pawn or not take it. So either his queen or mine will be exposed.

V.   Integrative Exercise   Show that each of the following arguments is valid by constructing a proof. Be sure to assign a line number to each premise and separate the conclusion from the premises with a slash.

✻1. ~C
   ___
   C ⊃ D

2. (A ≡ B) • C
   ___
   (A ≡ B) ∨ C

3. ~ (A ∨ B)
   ___
   ~B

✻4. B ⊃ D
   ___
   B ⊃ (B ⊃ D)

5. A ⊃ B
   ___
   B ∨ ~A

6. D ∨ E
   ___
   ~D ⊃ E

✻7. A ⊃ ~F
   ___
   F ⊃ ~A

8. B • {[~(D ≡ E) • (B ≡ C)] ∨ (G ⊃ A)}
   ___
   B ∨ (A • E)

9. H ⊃ (I • G)
   I ⊃ (G ⊃ F)
   ___
   H ⊃ F

✻10. (A ⊃ C) • (B ⊃ C)
   A ∨ B
   ___
   C

11. C
   ___
   D ⊃ C

12. ~B ∨ (C • D)
   ___
   B ⊃ C

✻13. E ⊃ (F ⊃ G)
   ___
   F ⊃ (E ⊃ G)

14. ~D
   (A • B) ∨ (C ∨ D)
   ___
   (A • B) ∨ C

15. (A ≡ B) • C
   D
   ___
   (A ≡ B) • D

✻16. ~C ∨ ~D
   C
   ___
   ~D

17. ~(D • G)
   ~~G
   ___
   ~D

18. (D ∨ E) ∨ H
   ___
   (D ∨ H) ∨ E

✻19. [~(D ≡ E) • (B ≡ C)] ∨ (G ⊃ A)
   ~[~(D ≡ E) • (B ≡ C)]
   G
   ___
   A

20. A ⊃ (B ≡ C)
   ~(D ≡ E)
   A
   ___
   ~(D ≡ E) • (B ≡ C)

21. (A • B) ∨ (C ∨ D)
   ~A
   ___
   C ∨ D

✻22. W ⊃ X
   ~Y ⊃ ~X
   ___
   W ⊃ Y

23. (D • E) ⊃ F
   (D ⊃ F) ⊃ G
   ___
   E ⊃ G

24. (H ∨ I) ⊃ [J • (K • L)]
   I
   ___
   J • K

✷25. A ⊃ B
(C ⊃ D) • (E ≡ G)
A ∨ C
_____
B ∨ D

26. ~[(A • B) ∨ C]
(A • B) ∨ (C ∨ D)
_____
D

27. D
~D ∨ (E ≡ F)
_____
~E ⊃ ~F

✷28. A ⊃ (B • C)
~(A ⊃ D)
_____
B

29. (E ∨ F) ⊃ G
~H ⊃ F
~G
_____
H • ~E

30. A ⊃ (B ⊃ C)
(~D ∨ E) ⊃ (F ∨ G)
~(D ⊃ E) ⊃ (B • ~C)
_____
A ⊃ (F ∨ G)

✷31. (H • I) ⊃ J
(I ⊃ J) ⊃ (K ∨ L)
_____
~L ⊃ (H ⊃ K)

32. A • (B ⊃ C)
(B • ~A) ∨ (B • D)
_____
C • D

33. [(A ∨ B) • C] ⊃ [(A ∨ D) • (A ∨ E)]
C • ~A
_____
B ⊃ (D • E)

✷34. (~E • F) ⊃ G
(H • J) ⊃ (E ∨ J)
~E • (F ∨ ~J)
_____
H ⊃ (J ⊃ G)

35. (F • G) ⊃ [H ⊃ (I • J)]
G ⊃ ~J
F ⊃ H
_____
~F ∨ ~G

36. ~(A • B) ⊃ [C ⊃ (D ⊃ E)]
[(A • B) ∨ F] ⊃ (G • H)
[(C • D) ⊃ E] ⊃ I
J ⊃ (G ⊃ ~H)
_____
J ⊃ I

✷37. [K ⊃ (L ⊃ K)] ⊃ (~M ⊃ M)
_____
M

38. [(G • H) ⊃ (I ∨ J)] ⊃ ~G
(K ∨ G) ⊃ (I • L)
_____
~G

39. (A ⊃ B) • ~(C ⊃ D)
~A ⊃ D
[(A • C) ∨ B] ⊃ E
_____
G ⊃ E

✷40. [(A • B) ∨ C] ⊃ [D ⊃ (E • F)]
B • ~(A ⊃ E)
_____
D ⊃ F

41. (G • H) ∨ [(I ∨ J) • (K ⊃ L)]
(J ⊃ M) • ~I
G ≡ N
_____
M ∨ N

42. A ≡ B
[(C ⊃ D) • ~D] ∨ [A • ~ (C • ~D)]
(B ∨ E) ⊃ F
_____
C ⊃ F

✷43. (A ∨ B) ⊃ [~(C • D) ⊃ E]
B • C
E ⊃ (F ∨ G)
(B ⊃ ~F) • (C ⊃ ~G)
_____
D

44. H ≡ {I • [(J • K) ∨ (L • M)]}
[I • (K ∨ L)] ⊃ N
_____
H ⊃ N

45. (A • ~B) ⊃ (C • D)
E • ~F
(G • E) ⊃ ~(A ≡ B)
(B • ~A) ⊃ F
_____
G ⊃ C

✷46. H ⊃ {I • [(J • K) ⊃ (L • M)]}
K ⊃ ~(I • L)
_____
J ⊃ ~(H • K)

47. (H ≡ J) ∨ (H ≡ K)
J ⊃ (L • M)
K ⊃ (N • M)
H
_____
M

Predicate Logic 10

Propositional logic allows us to analyze arguments that depend on logical relationships among propositions. The units of analysis are component propositions—p, q, r, etc.—along with the truth-functional connectives that create compound propositions. But some arguments require a finer-grained analysis. An obvious example is the categorical syllogism:

> No herbivore eats meat.
> <u>All horses are herbivores.</u>
> No horse eats meat.

Neither the premises nor the conclusion of this argument is compound, so the representation of the argument in propositional logic would be:

> p
> q
> r

which gives no clue that the argument is valid. To understand its validity, we need to break the propositions down into their elements, and this is the function of *predicate logic*.

Like the traditional logic of categorical syllogisms (see Chapter 6), predicate logic breaks a proposition down into a subject and a predicate. The subject is what the statement is about; the predicate is what the statement says about the subject. But predicate logic analyzes the subject–predicate relationship in a way that is different from traditional logic. In the first three sections of this chapter, we'll go over the symbolic notation that is used to represent the inner structure of propositions. Then we'll go on to learn a few new rules of inference and see how to use them (along with the propositional rules from the past chapter) in constructing proofs. We will also see how predicate logic can handle statements about relationships among things and, with the addition of the identity operator, allow us to translate and prove arguments involving definite descriptions, superlatives, and numerical statements. Finally,

LEARNING OBJECTIVES

On successful completion of the chapter, you will be able to:

- Translate singular, quantified, categorical, and compound statements from English into symbolic notation. (10.1–10.3)

- Construct proofs using propositional and predicate rules of inference. (10.4)

- Construct translations and proofs containing relational or overlapping predication. (10.5)

- Demonstrate an understanding of identity relations by translating statements and constructing proofs using the identity operator. (10.6)

- Use the counterexample method and the finite universe method to prove invalidity in predicate logic. (10.7) we will learn two ways to test predicate arguments for invalidity, namely, the counterexample and finite universe methods.

10.1 Singular and Quantified Statements

10.1A Singular Statements

To understand how to analyze statements in predicate logic, we begin by distinguishing the subject of a statement from the predicate. The subject is the part of the sentence that specifies what the statement is about; the predicate is the part that specifies what we are saying about the subject. In the following examples, the subject is in boldface, and the rest of the sentence is the predicate.

1. **London** is a city.
2. **Jane** got married last Saturday.
3. **Our family** lives in a white house.
4. **Our house** is the last one on the right.
5. **The Civil War** was caused by many factors.
6. Totally unprepared am **I**.
7. **The Milky Way galaxy** is immense.
8. Down the chimney came **Santa**.
9. **Cyprus** was a major source of copper in the Bronze Age.
10. On my left is **Mr. Keith Richards**.

In English, the subject normally comes first, but that is not always the case. In 6, the phrase "totally unprepared" is not the subject; it designates a property of the actual subject, "I" (actually, Liesl in *The Sound of Music*). In the same way, the subject comes last in 8 and 10. Nevertheless, "Santa" and "Mr. Keith Richards," respectively, are the subjects of the statements because they name the things that we're talking about. In each of the examples, the rest of the statement is the predicate, whose function is to say something about what is named. The predicate may indicate a category to which the thing belongs (as in 1), an attribute of the thing (as in 4, 6, 7, 9, and 10), an action (as in 2, 3, and 8), or a causal explanation (as in 5)—there are many kinds of statements we can make about things.

Every statement has a subject–predicate structure. But each of our examples belongs to the subcategory of **singular statements**. A singular statement is about a single thing, as opposed to a general statement about a class of things. The thing can be a person (Jane, Keith Richards), a place (London, Cyprus), an event (the Civil War), or an object (our house). It can be a group that is treated as a single unit, like "our family" in 3. Even 7 is a singular statement; although our galaxy contains a great many things, the statement treats it as a single unit. Hence, we have a particular statement about our galaxy, as opposed to a general statement about galaxies (e.g., galaxies tend to have spiral shapes). And even if the thing does not actually exist, as in 8 (you knew that, right?), the statement at least purports to refer to an individual.

To represent singular statements symbolically, we need two symbols, one for the subject, and one for the predicate. It is conventional to use capital letters for predicates, lowercase letters for subjects, with the predicate letter given first. Thus our examples would be put into predicate notation as follows:

Subject	Predicate	Symbolic
london	is a **C**ity.	Cl
jane	got **M**arried last Saturday.	Mj
we	**L**ive in a white house.	Lw
our **h**ouse	is the last one on the **R**ight.	Rh
the **c**ivil war	was **C**aused by many factors.	Cc
i	am totally **U**nprepared.	Ui
the **m**ilky way	is **I**mmense.	Im
cyprus	was a major source of **C**opper in the Bronze Age.	Cc
santa	**C**ame down the chimney.	Cs
mr. **k**eith richards	is on my **L**eft.	Lk

This notation may seem foreign at first, since it reverses the order of English grammar. It's a bit like Yoda-speak in *Star Wars* ("Strong am I with the Force"). It may help to think of the symbolic formula as saying that the predicate is true of the subject: Being a city (C) is true of London (l); getting married last Saturday (M) is true of Jane (j), and so on.

In the 10 examples of actual statements, we used letters keyed to the subject and predicate. When we are working with statement *forms* rather than actual examples, it is customary to use $a, b, c, \ldots$ as subjects and $P, Q, R, \ldots$ as predicates. Thus we can say that singular statements have the form "*a* is *P*," where *a* is the name of something and *P* is what we're saying about it, so the statement will look like this: *Pa*. These subject–predicate pairs are the atomic statements in predicate logic, just as p, q, r, etc., are the atomic statements in propositional logic. And, as in propositional logic, singular statements can be combined into compound statements by means of propositional connectives. Indeed, everything we learned about propositional logic applies to them. Here are some examples:

Statement	Symbolic
If London is a city, it has a mayor.	Cl ⊃ Ml
Scotland is not a city.	~Cs
If Cyprus was a major source of copper in the Bronze Age, then Egypt imported copper.	Cc ⊃ Ie
Jane got married last Saturday and so did Tamara.	Mj • Mt
Harry's car is an orange convertible.	Oc • Cc
I will be either at home or in New York.	Hi ∨ Ni
If the moon is out tonight and the sea is calm, I'll go for a sail or a walk on the beach.	(Om • Cs) ⊃ (Si ∨ Wi)

Note that the atomic components in these compound statements may have the same subject, as in 11, 15, and 16. The atomic components can also have the same predicate, as in 14, or differ in both subject and predicate, as in 13. In 15, we could have treated "orange convertible" as a single predicate, but since the color and the type of car are independent characteristics, we can also make them separate predicates ascribed to the car. These differences in structure would not be evident if we represented the statements simply as propositions—*p*, *q*, *r*, etc. The predicate notation includes more of the statement's structure than does the propositional notation we studied in the preceding two chapters. We will make use of that additional structure in a moment. But for now the important point is that everything we learned about using connectives to combine atomic statements applies to predicate as well as propositional notation.

EXERCISE 10.1A

Put each of the following statements into symbolic notation.

٭1. Tobias is bored.

2. Governor Smith is a crook.

3. The solar system is billions of years old.

٭4. London Bridge is falling down.

5. Tom's car is a Volkswagen but Sally's car is a Rolls.

6. I'm confused and she is not helping.

٭7. Randy Newman is not a short guy but Napoleon was.

8. The ninja kicked and spun.

9. Monaco is either a big city or a small nation.

٭10. Jim Jones is either crazy or thirsty.

11. I am sick and tired.

12. If the paint is dry, the wall is finished.

٭13. Luminous beings are we, not this crude matter. [Yoda]

14. The printer works but the fax is broken.

15. If we win, we'll either go dancing or go to a movie.

٭16. Macbeth was a tyrant with a conscience.

17. I am firm, you are stubborn, and he is obstinate.

18. If I fail this course or get a low grade, I will change my major.

٭19. If either Sarah or Isaiah majors in philosophy, then Orlando will minor in mathematics.

20. If Julius Caesar crosses the Rubicon and maintains his popular support, then Pompey will rally his forces if he has Senate support.

21. If Sofia didn't answer my e-mail, she didn't receive it or she is mad.

٭22. If the streets are clear, I'll drive, but if not, I'll take the train.

23. If Angelina Jolie retires or has a baby, then she will not make movies.

24. If Ashwin runs any faster, he'll break the record or at least win.

٭25. Whether the baby is a boy or a girl, its name will be Jamie.

10.1B Quantified Statements

Suppose we want to make a statement about a class of things rather than an individual object—for example, "All cities have mayors." How can we formulate that statement in the notation of predicate logic? We can't take the predicate C ("is a city") and make it the subject: MC. The literal translation of this would be "is a city has a mayor," which doesn't make any sense. Instead, predicate logic uses a device called the bound variable. In this section, we see how the device works. In Section 10.2, we will see how it applies to statements like "All cities have mayors."

Suppose someone says, "It is a city." The subject term "it" is a pronoun without an antecedent. We would assume that "it" stands for something, but we wouldn't know what; it could stand for anything. In logic, we would represent such an "it" by the letter x, and the statement "it is a city" would be symbolized Cx. The letter x functions as a **variable**, as in an algebraic equation. In the equation $x + x = 2x$, for example, x stands for *any* number, without specifying which number. In the same way, the x in Cx can stand for any individual thing without specifying which thing.

The formula Cx—"x is a city"—is not a complete statement. A statement has to say something that is either true or false, but that is not the case with Cx (imagine seeing "x is a city" on a true–false test—quick, which is it, true or false?). The variable x can stand for anything that exists, so we at least need to specify whether our statement concerns everything that exists or only some things. We can accomplish this by introducing a **quantifier**, which tells us whether Cx is being asserted of all x (everything in the world) or of some x (at least one thing in the world).

In the first case, we use a **universal quantifier**, symbolized by an x in parentheses at the front of the statement: $(x)Cx$. Any of the following would be a literal translation of this formula:

For all x, x is a city.

Take anything whatever: it is a city.

"It is a city" is true of everything.

All of these are ways of saying that everything is a city. Of course this statement is quite false. The authors of this book, your professor, and the Liberty Bell are all individual things in the world, and none of us is a city. At most we can say that some things are cities. To make this statement, we use the **existential quantifier**, symbolized by a backward E and placed, once again, in parentheses at the front of the statement: $(\exists x)Cx$. Any of the following would be a literal translation:

For some x (one or more), x is a city.

There exists something such that it is a city.

"It is a city" is true of at least one thing.

All of these are equivalent to the statement in ordinary English that something is a city.

An expression of the form Px is called an **open sentence**, and its variable is said to be a **free variable**. When we preface the sentence with a quantifier, the variable is said to be a **bound variable**. The quantifier binds the variable by telling us how to interpret it, and the result is a **closed sentence** or statement. The use of a quantifier, then, completes a statement containing a variable. It turns an open sentence, which has no truth value, into a statement that is either true or false.

The universal and existential quantifiers are the only ones used in the basic-level predicate logic we are studying. As with the traditional logic of syllogisms, predicate logic recognizes only two degrees of quantity: all, and at least one. In ordinary language, of course, we have terms for many intermediate degrees, such as "few," "many," or "most." But statements involving such terms must be put into symbolic form using the existential quantifier.

It is important to distinguish both kinds of quantified statement from singular statements. A singular statement is about a particular thing, and we refer to the subject by name or by a description such as "our house," "the dog," or "that man I met last night." In symbolic notation, we use a lowercase letter as the subject of the statement, and we do not use a quantifier of either kind. In a quantified statement, by contrast, the subject is a variable that can stand for anything. So we must use a quantifier to specify whether the statement applies to everything or only to some things. Thus, predicate logic uses three types of statement:

Type	Example	Symbolic Notation	Quantifier	Predicate	Subject
Singular	My father is alive.	Af	None	A	f
Quantified, Existential	Some things are alive. There are living things.	$(\exists x)Ax$	$(\exists x)$	A	x
Quantified, Universal	Everything is alive.	$(x)Ax$	(x)	A	x

In principle, we could use any letter in the alphabet as a variable. To avoid confusing variables with names, however, it is conventional to reserve the last three letters for variables: x, y, z. It does not matter which one we use. What does matter is that the quantifier use the same letter: $(x)Px$, $(y)Ry$, $(\exists z)Qz$, etc. If the quantifier does *not* use the same letter, the result is not a statement. Thus in the formula $(\exists z)Sy$, the existential quantifier does not bind the variable y, which therefore remains free; Sy remains an open sentence; and it has no truth value because we do not know whether we are asserting the predicate S of all y or only of some.

EXERCISE 10.1B

Put each of the following statements into symbolic notation.

*1. Everything is illuminated.

2. Something smells.

3. Everything has a purpose.

*4. Everything is groovy.

5. Everything is edible.

6. All things change.

*7. There's something coming for us.

8. Everything is for sale.

9. Some things are falling apart.

*10. Everything is made of atoms.

11. There was an explosion.

12. Some things are lighter than air.

*13. There's a reason for everything.

14. There are ghosts.

15. Some things are better left unsaid.

10.2 Categorical Statements

Now that we understand how variables and quantifiers work, let's return to the question of how to symbolize a statement about the members of a class of things—a statement such as:

All cities have mayors.

"Cities" is the grammatical subject of the statement, but it cannot be the subject in logical notation. The only things that can be subjects in predicate logic are (a) names or phrases that refer to a particular individual thing and (b) variables that can stand for any individual thing. But "city" is a general term referring to a certain category or class of places. It can be part of the predicate in a statement like "London is a city" (Cl). As we saw in the previous section, however, we can't take that predicate and make it the subject—MC. So how can we translate 1a into predicate notation?

The first clue is the word "all," which suggests that a universal quantifier is involved, which in turn implies that we will need to use a variable. But remember that a variable can stand for anything whatever and the universal quantifier represents the entire universe of discourse. Our example does not say that everything is a city, nor that everything has a mayor. But it does imply that *if* something is a city, *then* it has a mayor. This is the second clue to the symbolic translation. A statement of this form is treated as a conditional statement, with the same variable used as the subject in both antecedent and consequent, bound by the universal quantifier. Thus:

$(x)(Cx \supset Mx)$ For all x, if x is a city, then x has a mayor.

Here, "is a city" is a predicate, as it has to be, and the subject of both Cx and Mx is the variable x. The translation uses both the bound variable of predicate logic and a connective from propositional logic.

The two atomic statements in which the variable occurs, Cx and Mx, are placed within a pair of parentheses immediately after the quantifier. This is to indicate that the quantifier applies to the entire statement and binds the variable in both occurrences. If we did not use parentheses—$(x)Cx \supset Mx$—the quantifier would apply only to Cx, and Mx would remain an open sentence with a free variable since a quantifier governs only the statement immediately following it. To have a closed sentence, or statement, we must use parentheses to bring both variables within the **scope** of a quantifier. In this respect, a quantifier is like a negation sign. The difference between

$(x)Cx \supset Mx$ and $(x)(Cx \supset Mx)$

is like the difference between

~C ⊃ M and ~(C ⊃ M).

In traditional syllogistic logic, the statement form "All *S* are *P*" is one of the four basic types of categorical statement. The four types are distinguished in terms of their quantity (universal or particular) and their quality (affirmative or negative):

	Affirmative	*Negative*
Universal	All *S* are *P*.	No *S* is *P*.
Particular	Some *S* are *P*.	Some *S* are not *P*.

We have just seen how modern predicate logic would deal with universal affirmative statements. What about the others? A statement such as:

No city is entirely fireproof

is also universal but it is negative. In traditional logic, the word "No" serves two functions: It indicates both universal quantity and negative quality. In modern predicate logic, we separate those functions, as we would in English if we had expressed this statement as "*Every* city is *not* entirely fireproof." So we use the universal quantifier, but we negate the consequent:

(*x*)(C*x* ⊃ ~F*x*)   For all *x*, if *x* is a city, then *x* is not entirely fireproof.

For particular statements, the word "some" suggests that we use the existential quantifier. And the connective has to be conjunction rather than the conditional. For example:

Some tests are difficult

tells us that something—at least one thing in the world—is both a test and difficult. So the symbolic translation would be the existential statement:

(∃*x*)(T*x* • D*x*)   For some *x*, *x* is a test and *x* is difficult.

The negative statement

Some tests are not difficult

would be translated in a similar way:

(∃*x*)(T*x* • ~D*x*)   For some *x*, *x* is a test and *x* is not difficult.

Why do we use different connectives for universal and existential statements? Why not use the same connective? Well, let's try it. The way to tell whether a symbolic formula is a good translation of an English sentence is to ask whether they have the same truth value. If the English sentence is true but the symbolic formula is false, or vice versa, then we don't have an accurate translation. Suppose, then, that we use conjunction for a universal statement. For example:

Every accountant understands arithmetic.   (*x*)(A*x* • U*x*) [error]

This won't work because the English statement is true, but the symbolic statement is obviously false. It says that everything in the universe is both an accountant and understands arithmetic. What the English statement actually means is that if something is an accountant, then it (he or she) understands arithmetic. That's why we have to treat these universal statements as conditionals. The symbolic representation of this example is therefore $(x)(Ax \supset Ux)$.

Conversely, suppose we try to translate a particular statement as a conditional. It's a little trickier to see why this won't work. Consider first a true English sentence:

> Some rocks are sedimentary. $(\exists x)(Rx \supset Sx)$ [error]

The symbolic statement says that for some x, if x is a rock, then x is sedimentary. And that's true. The problem is that the symbolic statement is true not only of certain rocks (the ones that are sedimentary) but also of anything that is not a rock at all. For something that is not a rock, the antecedent of the conditional is false, which makes the conditional itself true. To see why this difference between the English and the symbolic statements is a problem, let's take a sentence that is clearly false:

> Some rocks are lighter than air. $(\exists x)(Rx \supset Lx)$ [error]

Both the English sentence and the symbolic formula are false in regard to the category of rocks. For any x that is a rock, the antecedent of the symbolic formula, Rx, is true but the consequent Lx is false, which makes the conditional statement false. But for something that is *not* a rock, the antecedent of the conditional is false, which makes the conditional *true* even though the English sentence is false. So we cannot translate particular statements as conditionals; we have to use conjunction, $(\exists x)(Rx \bullet Lx)$.

For predicate logic, then, the diagram for the four statement types is as follows:

	Affirmative	Negative
Universal	$(x)(Sx \supset Px)$ For all x, if x is S, then x is P.	$(x)(Sx \supset {\sim}Px)$ For all x, if x is S, then x is not-P.
Existential	$(\exists x)(Sx \bullet Px)$ For some x, x is S and x is P.	$(\exists x)(Sx \bullet {\sim}Px)$ For some x, x is S and x is not-P.

Notice that in modern predicate logic we refer to "some" statements as *existential* rather than *particular*—which is the term used in syllogistic logic. The terminology indicates that the quantifier $(\exists x)$ does double duty: It is a statement of quantity (some x rather than all x) and it is a statement of existence (there exists at least one x). The existence

---

REVIEW   The Meaning of "Some"

In logic, the meaning of the word "some" is somewhat different than in everyday English. Two points to remember:

- We interpret "some" to mean "at least one."

- Any word or phrase signifying at least one but not all of a subject class should be translated as "some." Examples include "most," "a few," or "several."

APPLY **Predicate Logic and the Law School Admissions Test**

You've learned that, in logic, we interpret the word "some" to mean "at least one," and that we translate any word or phrase that means at least one but less than all with the existential quantifier. This interpretation holds throughout the study of logic. But be careful if you take the LSAT. ETS (the company that administers the LSAT) also interprets "some" as "at least one." That means it only takes one case to make a "some" statement true. Unlike logicians, however, the LSAT uses the word "most" in our everyday sense of the word; to make a claim about most of a subject class true, the statement must apply to more than half the members of the class.

component raises the issue of existential import (discussed previously in Chapter 5). A categorical statement has existential import if its truth depends on the existence of objects in the subject category. Traditional logic tended to assume that all four of the standard categorical statements have existential import. Modern logic holds that particular/existential statements have existential import but that universal ones do not. One can make a case for either view, depending on which examples one chooses. On the one hand, the statement "No flying saucers were sighted over Atlanta last night" seems true even if there are no flying saucers at all; on the other hand, the statement "All of our first edition books were stolen" seems false if we never had any first edition books. Among particular/existential statements, there are similar contrasting cases. A statement of the form *Some S is (or is not) P* normally implies that the S or Ss in question exist. But what about "Some witches are good" and "Some witches are bad," as in the world of *Wizard of Oz*? If the universal statement "All witches can fly" is true despite the nonexistence of witches, why not the nonuniversal ones?

The point to be made here is that the modern view is built into the structure of modern predicate logic. Because universal statements are conditionals, they do not assert the existence of any Ss; all they say is that if any x is an S, then it is (or is not) a P. If there are no Ss, then any statement of the form $(x)(Sx \supset Px)$ is true by default, regardless of the consequent, because the antecedent is not true of anything. That follows from the nature of the conditional as defined by its truth table. So universally quantified statements necessarily lack existential import. By contrast, existential statements necessarily have existential import. By the nature of conjunction, any statement of the form $(\exists x)(Sx \bullet Px)$ is true only if some x is S.

If a universal statement in English seems to have existential import, then to capture this fact in a symbolic translation, we must combine a universally quantified formula with an existentially quantified one. For example, the translation of "All of my first edition books were stolen" would include two components: $(x)(Bx \supset Sx)$, and $(\exists x)(Bx)$. (In the next section, we will see how to combine two quantified statements like these into a single statement.)

The final point to keep in mind about translating into predicate notation is that English (like any other language) has many different ways of indicating universal or existential quantity. Some of the more common ones are summarized in the following table.

Universal		Existential	
Affirmative	**Negative**	**Affirmative**	**Negative**
All	No	Some are	Some are not
Any	None	There is (are)	There is (are) . . . not
A (A cat is a predator)	Not a (Not a creature was stirring)	A (A car is parked outside)	A (A student is not present)
Every, Everything	Nothing	Something	Something
Everyone (people)	No one	Someone	Someone
Always (time)	Never	Sometimes	Sometimes
Everywhere (place)	Nowhere	Somewhere	Somewhere
		Any	

The table illustrates several things you need to keep in mind in translating English sentences into predicate notation:

- The indefinite article "a" can mean either universal or existential quantity, depending on the context. It can mean any instance of a category such as cats, but it can also mean some particular instance, as in our examples: "A car is parked outside" and "A student is not present."
- Although we most often see the word "any" used to indicate the universal quantifier, it is sometimes (most often in conditionals) an existential indicator. For example, "Any blank can be filled" is obviously a statement about a universal quantity—all blanks—while the statement "If any mechanic can fix your car, Akara can" seems equivalent to saying "If there is a mechanic who can fix your car, it's Akara," a clearly existential statement.
- The word "there" at the beginning of a sentence normally indicates existential quantity. In a negative statement, however, it can indicate either existential or universal quantity, depending on where the mark of negation occurs, as in the following examples:

There is **not** milk in the refrigerator.

There is milk **not** in the refrigerator.

The first example is a universal negative statement. It says that no milk is to be found in the refrigerator: $(x)(Mx \supset {\sim}Rx)$. The second, however, is an existential negative statement. It says that some of the milk is not in the refrigerator: $(\exists x)(Mx \bullet {\sim}Rx)$.

- The last three rows of the table are quantifiers keyed to certain general classes of existents: people, times, and places. In the case of "everyone" and "someone," we would simply use a predicate for person, as in:

Everyone laughed. $(x)(Px \supset Lx)$

Someone laughed. $(\exists x)(Px \bullet Lx)$

SOLVE Translation into Predicate Notation

Statements in predicate logic are composed of subjects, predicates, quantifiers, and connectives. Subjects are either (a) names or phrases that refer to a specific individual thing and (b) variables that can stand for any individual thing. To translate a statement in ordinary language into predicate notation:

1. If the sentence is a singular statement, naming a specific person, place, or thing, then assign a lowercase letter to the subject of the sentence and assign an uppercase letter to the predicate describing the subject; for example, *Pa.*

2. If the sentence is a quantified statement, referring to all or some members of a class, use the device of variable and quantifier: Use a variable (*x, y, z, . . .*) as the subject of the symbolic notation, with an uppercase

letter for the predicate; for example, *Px.* Next,

a. If the statement is about all members of the class, use the universal quantifier, (*x*)*Px.*

b. If the statement is about some members of the class, use the existential quantifier, (∃*x*)*Px.*

3. If the statement is one of the four standard categoricals—A, E, I, or O—then

a. For universal statements (All *P* are *Q* and No *P* is *Q*) use the universal quantifier and a conditional for the connective [(*x*) (*Px* ⊃ *Qx*) and (*x*)(*Px* ⊃ ~*Qx*), respectively].

b. For existential statements (Some *P* are *Q* and Some *P* are not *Q*) use the existential quantifier and a conjunction for the connective [(∃*x*)(*Px* • *Qx*) and (∃*x*)(*Px* • ~*Qx*), respectively].

In the case of "always/never" and "sometimes," if the quantifier is specifically about times, then we usually need to use the more complex statement forms we will discuss later. The same is true for quantifiers keyed to places. But these quantifiers of time or place are often just variant ways of saying "all" or "some," and then we put them into symbolic form as such. For example:

Triangles always have three sides.   (*x*)(T*x* ⊃ S*x*)

Inflation is everywhere a monetary phenomenon.   (*x*)(I*x* ⊃ M*x*)

As in all issues of translating from English to symbolic notation, deciding which quantifier to use should depend ultimately on your understanding of what the sentence is about and what it is saying.

EXERCISE 10.2

Put each of the following statements into symbolic notation.

✳1. All skyscrapers are buildings.

2. Some buildings are skyscrapers.

3. Some cars are turbocharged.

✳4. Some knights wore armor.

5. All good things in life are free.

6. No fallacy is sound.

*7. Some ketones are used as solvents.

8. No person is omniscient.

9. Some people are not sensible.

*10. Some pitchers are good hitters.

11. No freshman can take this course.

12. All squares are rectangles.

*13. Some rectangles are squares.

14. All of my children are home from school.

15. Some galaxies do not have a spiral shape.

*16. Every cloud has a silver lining.

17. The quadruple axel jump has never been completed.

18. There are many thatched roofs in England.

*19. Not a coin was found in the sunken ship's treasure chest.

20. Sometimes suspects are not perpetrators.

10.3 Quantifier Scope and Statement Forms

So far we have seen how statements of certain kinds can be translated into the standard forms of predicate logic. For singular statements, we use lowercase letters as names of particular things and uppercase letters as predicates—*Pa, Qb, Rc,* etc. Atomic singular statements like these can be combined by connectives into compound statements such as *Pa ⊃ Qb*. For quantified statements, we use variables instead of names as subject terms, along with a universal or existential quantifier to bind the variable. The simplest quantified statements have a single predicate: $(x)Px$, $(\exists y)Qy$, etc. For categorical statements, we use a quantifier and two predicates that are both within the scope of the quantifier: $(x)(Sx ⊃ Px)$, $(\exists x)(Qx \bullet Rx)$, etc. In this section, we will see how quantifiers and connectives are used in two other, more complex kinds of statements.

10.3A Compound Statements Within the Scope of a Quantifier

Categorical statements are a special case of a more general kind of statement in predicate logic: statements with a quantifier whose scope includes the entire statement. A categorical statement includes just two predicates with the same variable as subject, and one of two connectives. But a quantifier can apply to a compound sentence that has more than two predicates, linked by more than one connective. For example:

All banks that are chartered by the federal government can borrow from the Federal Reserve System. $(x)[(Bx \bullet Cx) ⊃ Fx]$

This is clearly a universal affirmative statement, so we have to treat it as a conditional. Unlike the categorical statements we studied in the previous section, however, the subject category is defined by two features: being a bank (B*x*) *and* being chartered by the federal government (C*x*). Since these features seem independent, it is best to treat them as separate predicates rather than the single predicate "banks chartered by the federal government." So B*x* and C*x* must be conjoined as the antecedent of the conditional. To put this statement into predicate notation, we interpret it as saying that for all *x*, if *x* is a bank and *x* is chartered by the federal government, then *x* can borrow from the Federal Reserve System.

Here's another case of a compound subject:

Butter and eggs are rich in cholesterol. $(x)[(Bx \lor Ex) \supset Cx]$

"Butter and eggs" looks like a conjunction, but this appearance is deceptive. The same substance cannot be both butter and eggs. The point is that if something falls into either category, then it is rich in cholesterol, so we translate "and" as disjunction rather than conjunction. The statement says that for all *x*, if *x* is butter or *x* is eggs, then *x* is rich in cholesterol. We would use the same form for other statements about what two different kinds of thing have in common, such as "Dogs and cats make good pets."

Some plants will grow only if they are fertilized. $(\exists x)[Px \cdot (Gx \supset Fx)]$

In this case we are talking about some plants, so we would expect to use an existential quantifier, with conjunction as the main connective inside the parentheses: "For some *x*, *x* is a plant and . . ." And what? The second conjunct says that *x* will grow only if *x* is fertilized. We have to remember how to represent an "only if" statement as a conditional. In our study of propositional logic, we saw that *p only if q* means *if p then q*. In the same way, G*x* only if F*x* is equivalent to *if Gx then Fx*. So the second conjunct is G*x* ⊃ F*x*. Notice that even though this statement involves a conditional element, the main connective is conjunction. We're saying of something that it has two properties: It's a plant, and if it grows then it has been fertilized.

All goods except foods are subject to sales tax. $(x)[(Gx \cdot {\sim}Fx) \supset Sx]$

Here we have another universal statement with a compound antecedent, but the qualifying phrase "except foods" is negative; it excludes a subcategory from the category of goods. We are saying that anything that is a good and isn't a food is subject to the tax.

Those who doubt the existence of God are $(x)[(Px \cdot Dx) \supset (Sx \lor Ax)]$
skeptics or atheists.

The consequent of this statement is compound: *x is a skeptic or x is an atheist*. The subject category is defined by doubt in the existence of God, which looks like a single feature, not a compound. But the word "those" is an implicit reference to people. Remember that variables in predicate logic range over everything, so if a statement is clearly about people as opposed to other things, we should indicate that by including the symbolic predicate P in the translation: For all *x*, if *x* is a person and *x* doubts the existence of God, then *x* is either a skeptic or an atheist. In the same way, when we are talking specifically about events, we need to include the predicate "is an event," as in the statement:

Something happened on the way to the forum. $(\exists x)(Ex \cdot Fx)$

Here, E*x* means "*x* is an event" and F*x* means "*x* happened on the way to the forum."

10.3B Combining Quantified Statements

The examples we just discussed involved compound statements within the scope of a single quantifier. Quantified statements can also be modified and combined by connections that lie outside their scope. That is, quantified statements, like any other kind, can be put together by means of connectives into compound statements, and this often provides us with the most natural translation of a sentence in English.

Consider the statement:

If everything is physical, then some things have mass.

This is clearly a conditional statement. But instead of a single quantifier with a connective inside its scope, the antecedent "Everything is physical" and the consequent "Some things have mass" each has its own quantifier, and the horseshoe connecting antecedent and consequent is *outside* the scope of either quantifier:

If everything is physical, then some things have mass. $(x)Px \supset (\exists y)My$

See now a more complex example, in which we have connectives both inside and outside the scope of the quantifiers:

Either all the gears are broken or a cylinder $(x)(Gx \supset Bx) \lor (\exists y)(Cy \cdot My)$
is misfiring.

Here we have a disjunction of two separately quantified statements. Each disjunct is a compound statement with a connective within the scope of its quantifier, but the disjunctive connective is outside the scope of either.

In the examples before, we used different variables to indicate that the components of the compound statement are separately quantified. This isn't really necessary. The universal quantifier in the previous example applies only to Px; its scope does not include "things [that] have mass," so we could have used x as the variable for those things. Here, though, the parenthesis after Bx tells us that that is where the scope of the universal quantifier ends. Its scope does not overlap with that of the existential quantifier governing the second disjunct. So by the time we get to the misfiring cylinder, we're free to use x again to refer to it; there would be no ambiguity about which quantifier governed the variable. Later in the chapter, however, we will deal with quantifiers that *do* overlap in scope. In that case, it will be necessary to use different variables, so we might as well adopt this practice from the outset.

In both of these examples, there was no option about where to place each connective. By the meaning of the statement, it had to be either inside the scope of a quantifier or outside. In some cases, however, there are options.

Negating quantified statements. The antecedent of the statement "If everything is physical, then some things have mass" is:

Everything is physical. $(x)Px$

Suppose we wanted to deny this statement. Where would we put the negation sign, before the quantifier or after it?

For all *x*, *x* is not physical. $(x){\sim}Px$
It is not the case that for all *x*, *x* is physical. ${\sim}(x)Px$

The first option clearly goes too far: To deny that everything is physical, we don't need to say that there are no physical things whatsoever. We just need to say that not everything is physical, and that's what the second one says. The general rule is that to negate a quantified statement, we put the negation sign at the beginning, in front of the quantifier. But we do have a further option. The second option says that not all things are physical. We can make the same assertion by saying that some things are not physical:

Not all things are physical.	~(x)Px
Some things are not physical.	(∃x)~Px

The first statement here is the negation of a universal statement, and the negation sign is outside the scope of the quantifier. The second is an existential statement, and the negation sign is *inside* the scope of the quantifier. Both versions are equivalent; either would be a valid formulation.

The same principle applies to existential statements. For example:

Statement	Something is broken.	(∃x)Bx
Negation	It's not the case that something is broken.	~(∃x)Bx
Negation	Nothing is broken.	(x)~Bx

If we deny that even a single thing is broken, we are thereby asserting that everything is unbroken; both formulations are equivalent. In the next section, we will see that these equivalences are examples of a more general principle.

Conjoining and disjoining quantified statements. Consider the statement:

Everything has a location in space and time.

Using S for "has a location in space" and T for "has a location in time," we could translate this in either of two ways:

(x)(Sx • Tx)   or   (x)Sx • (y)Ty

Option one says that for each thing, it has a location in space and a location in time. Option two says that for each thing, it has a location in space, and for each thing, it has a location in time. These are clearly equivalent.

But now consider a different statement:

Everything is either mental or physical.

Once again we might think of two possible translations:

(x)(Mx ∨ Px)   or   (x)Mx ∨ (y)Py

These are *not* equivalent: the first says of each thing that it is either mental or physical and thus allows that the universe might contain two different kinds of things; the second says that the universe is monolithic—either everything is mental or everything is physical.

REVIEW Types of Statements in Predicate Logic

Type	Predicate Notation	Meaning	Example
Atomic singular statement	Pa	a is P	London is a city.
Truth-functional compounds of singular atomic statements	$Pa \supset Qa$ $Pa \cdot Qb$, etc.	If a is P, it is Q a is P and b is Q	If London is a city then it is large. Tom is healthy but Sue is sick.
Quantifier applied to atomic open sentence Px	$(x)Px$ $(\exists x)Px$	For all x, x is P There exists an x that is P	Everything is material. Something is on fire.
Truth-functional compounds of open sentences within the scope of a quantifier	$(x)\sim Px$ $(\exists x)\sim Px$ $(x)(Px \supset Qx)$ $(\exists x)(Px \cdot Qx)$ $(x)[Px \lor (Qx \cdot Rx)]$	Nothing is P Something is not P For all x, if x is P then it is Q Some x is P and it is Q For all x, x is P or it is Q and R	Nothing is infinite. Something is not infinite. All men are mortal. Some birds are carnivores. Everything is either scary or warm and fuzzy.
Truth-functional compounds of quantified statements. Scope of quantifiers does not cover connective.	$\sim(x)Px$ $(x)Px \supset (y)Qy$ $(x)Px \supset (\exists x)Qx$ $(\exists x)Px \lor (\exists y)Qy$	It is not the case that all x are P If all x are P, then all y are Q If all x are P, then some x is Q Either something is P or something is Q	It is not the case that everything is physical. If everything is physical, then everything has mass. If everything is created, then there is a God. There was either an explosion or a collision.

Thus with a universal quantifier, it doesn't matter where we put a sign of conjunction, but it does matter where we put a sign of disjunction. The opposite is true for the existential quantifier:

Something is hot and cold.	$(\exists x)(Hx \cdot Cx)$
Something is hot and something is cold.	$(\exists x)Hx \cdot (\exists y)Cy$
Something is hot or cold.	$(\exists x)(Hx \lor Cx)$
Something is hot or something is cold.	$(\exists x)Hx \lor (\exists y)Cy$

Can you see why the last two statements are equivalent, but the first two are not?

It is usually obvious which connectives to use in symbolizing a statement. But in order to tell whether they belong inside or outside the scope of the quantifiers, you need to think carefully about what the statement means and to practice putting statements of various types into predicate notation.

EXERCISE 10.3

I. **Integrative Exercise**   Put each of the following statements into symbolic notation.

✳1. A poodle is a dog.

2. A poodle won best of show.

3. Someone got hurt, and no one helped.

✳4. Some students are passing, but some are not.

5. If Mary is safe, then everything is fine.

6. Owls exist, but witches do not.

✳7. Marco is either at the office or on his way home.

8. Some laws are not enforced.

9. Not every law is enforced.

✳10. If everyone cheated, no grades would be meaningful.

11. Some tamales are not spicy.

12. There's something rotten in the state of Denmark.

✳13. Whoever stole my purse is a criminal.

14. Some things are not explainable.

15. Not all cats are Siamese.

✳16. Nothing is infinite.

17. Both Flutie Flakes and Rice Krispies are breakfast cereals.

18. There is no such thing as a free lunch.

✳19. Nothing is lost.

20. Some highways are one-way streets, but Highway 6 runs both ways.

21. Every corporation is either making money or losing money.

✳22. Blessed are the poor in spirit.

23. If anyone cheats, everyone loses.

24. If a photograph is black and white, it will have good contrast.

✳25. If one of the tourists is late, all the tourists on the bus must wait.

26. Everyone can go home only if all the work is done.

27. If every cat has nine lives, Felix does.

✳28. Dobermans and German Shepherds are loyal and fierce.

29. Professors and students at the college are listed in the school directory if they are teaching or enrolled in classes.

30. Quitters never win, winners never quit, but those who never win and never quit are idiots.

II. **Integrative Exercise**   Put each of the following into symbolic notation.

✳1. Someone is drinking and driving.

2. No fish are mammals.

3. A building collapsed.

*4. Not all priests are Jesuits.

5. Any car that is turbocharged is fun to drive.

6. There isn't any beer in the refrigerator.

*7. Angie likes to dance but Vince doesn't.

8. Nothing is cheap.

9. Some nearsighted people can't wear soft lenses.

*10. Someone is either whistling or playing a radio.

11. Some great books are not remembered or appreciated.

12. Every great book is appreciated if it is remembered.

*13. Not all students are angels.

14. Not any of the students using the laboratory was injured in the explosion.

15. All trees are either evergreen or deciduous.

*16. There are no ghosts.

17. If everything is physical, then there are no ghosts.

18. Only freshmen can take this course.

*19. None but the brave deserve the fair.

20. A tree, if properly cultivated, will live for a long time.

21. Every physical object has a size and a mass.

*22. If any dog can do a trick, any dog can do a trick.

23. None of my children is married or engaged.

24. All government is an ugly necessity. [G.K. Chesterton, *A Short History of England*]

*25. Anyone caught cheating will forfeit the game.

26. Tests and homework both improve understanding and motivate study.

27. Korey, Lindsay, and Ryan tried to find the prize, but someone beat them to it.

*28. If oranges and limes are citrus fruits, then not all citrus is yellow.

29. If all the tables and booths are taken, then some customers will have to wait to be seated or eat at the bar.

30. Every secret of a writer's soul, every experience of his life, every quality of his mind is written large in his works. [Virginia Woolf, *Orlando*]

10.4 Proof

In predicate as in propositional logic, we use proofs to establish that a conclusion follows validly from a set of premises. We proceed step by step from the premises, in accordance with rules of inference, until we reach the conclusion. The rules we learned in propositional logic, along with the techniques of conditional and indirect proof, are used for proofs in predicate logic as well. To work with quantifiers, we will also need to learn one additional replacement rule and four additional implication rules.

10.4A Using Propositional Rules

Predicate logic deals with two sorts of statements: singular and quantified. Singular statements contain only names and predicates; quantified statements contain variables and quantifiers as well. The rules of propositional logic can be applied in a straightforward way to singular statements. Here's a simple example:

> If Silver Blaze is lame, he will not win the derby.
> Silver Blaze is lame.
> Silver Blaze will not win the derby.

We could put the inference into either propositional or predicate notation:

Propositional	Predicate
L ⊃ ~W	Ls ⊃ ~Ws
L	Ls
~W	~Ws

Either way, the inference is a case of *modus ponens*. There's no need to use the predicate notation, since the validity of the inference does not depend on the internal subject–predicate structure of the atomic statements. But the point is that both versions have the same MP argument form:

$$p \supset q$$
$$\underline{p}$$
$$q$$

If an argument consists entirely of singular statements, moreover, we can analyze and evaluate it using only the methods of propositional logic. For example:

> John's car is not an orange convertible. If his car is not a   ~(Oc • Cc)
> convertible, it gets hot in the summer sun. John's car is   ~Cc ⊃ Hc
> orange. So it gets hot in the summer sun.   Oc
>   Hc

We can prove that the argument is valid using the propositional rules of implication and replacement:

1. ~(Oc • Cc)		Premise
2. ~Cc ⊃ Hc		Premise
3. Oc	/Hc	Premise / Conclusion
4. ~Oc ∨ ~Cc		1 DM
5. ~~Oc		3 DN
6. ~Cc		4,5 DS
7. Hc		2,6 MP

The propositional rules are also sufficient for some arguments involving general statements, when the validity of the argument depends *only* on connectives outside the scope of any quantifier. An example would be the following argument:

| If all actions have causes, then no action is voluntary. If no action is voluntary, then no person is either morally good or bad. So if all actions have causes, no person is morally good or bad. | $(x)(Ax \supset Cx)$
 $(y)(Ay \supset {\sim}Vy)$
<hr> $(x)(Ax \supset Cx)$ | $\supset$

 $\supset$

 $\supset$ | $(y)(Ay \supset {\sim}Vy)$
 $(z)[Pz \supset {\sim}(Gz \lor Bz)]$
<hr> $(z)[Pz \supset {\sim}(Gz \lor Bz)]$ |

Here we have two premises and a conclusion, each of which is a conditional statement; and in each statement, both antecedent and consequent are universally quantified. The main connectives are shaded to emphasize that they are outside the scope of the quantifiers. So despite the internal complexity of the premises and conclusion, the argument is an instance of the hypothetical syllogism inference form:

$p \supset q$
$q \supset r$
$p \supset r$

And the proof would involve a single step:

1. $(x)(Ax \supset Cx) \supset (y)(Ay \supset {\sim}Vy)$ Premise
2. $(y)(Ay \supset {\sim}Vy) \supset (z)[Pz \supset {\sim}(Gz \lor Bz)]$
       / $(x)(Ax \supset Cx) \supset (z)[Pz \supset {\sim}(Gz \lor Bz)]$ Premise / Conclusion
3. $(x)(Ax \supset Cx) \supset (z)[Pz \supset {\sim}(Gz \lor Bz)]$ 1,2 HS

Most arguments in predicate logic, however, require some additional rules. The system of proof we're going to adopt uses one additional replacement rule and four new rules of implication. We will discuss those new rules in the remainder of this section on proof—after a pause for some practice on using just the propositional rules.

EXERCISE 10.4A

Integrative Exercise   Use the rules of propositional logic to construct proofs for the following arguments. Do not use CP or IP.

∗1. 1. $(x)Hx \supset {\sim}(\exists y)My$
   2. $(\exists y)My$ /${\sim}(x)(Hx)$

2. 1. $Pa \supset (Qa \supset Sb)$
   2. ${\sim}Sb$ /${\sim}(Pa \bullet Qa)$

3. 1. $(x)Lx \lor (y)Ny$
   2. ${\sim}(x)Lx \bullet (x)Kx$ /$(y)Ny$

∗4. 1. $[{\sim}(x)Bx \lor (x)Cx] \supset {\sim}(x)Dx$
   2. ${\sim}(x)Bx$ /${\sim}(x)Dx$

5. 1. $(Bf \supset En) \bullet (Cf \supset Gn)$
   2. $Ag \lor ({\sim}En \lor {\sim}Gn)$
   3. ${\sim}Ag$ /${\sim}Bf \lor {\sim}Cf$

  6. 1. ~Fi ∨ (Cd • Dd)   / Fi ⊃ Cd

✶**7.** 1. Cl ≡ Dt   /(Cl ⊃ Dt) • (~Cl ⊃ ~Dt)

  8. 1. (∃x)Mx ⊃ (y)Ly   /~(∃x)Mx ∨ [(z)Rz ∨ (y)Ly]

  9. 1. (x)Hx ⊃ (∃y)Ly

      2. (∃y)Ly ⊃ ~(Ie • Je)

      3. (x)Hx   /~Ie ∨ ~Je

✶**10.** 1. ~Ga ∨ Ha

      2. Fa ⊃ Ha

      3. Ga ∨ Fa   /Ha

10.4B Replacement Rule: Quantifier Negation

In the past section, we noted that the negation of a quantified statement can be formulated in two equivalent ways.

Not all things are physical.	~(x)Px
Some things are not physical.	(∃x)~Px

and

It's not the case that something is broken.	~(∃x)Bx
Nothing is broken.	(x)~Bx

These equivalences are two forms of what is called the rule of **quantifier negation (QN)** in predicate logic. The rule says that we can switch the order of negation and quantifier as long as we switch quantifiers. When the negation sign passes across the quantifier, in other words, it is like a current that changes the quantifier into its opposite.

In these two examples, the quantified statements involve a single predicate. But the rule is true in virtue of the nature of quantifiers and negation, and therefore applies no matter how many predicates and connectives fall within the scope of the quantifier. In the previous section, for example, we discussed the statement "Those who doubt the existence of God are skeptics or atheists." If we were to deny the statement, the QN rule says that the following expressions are equivalent:

~(x)[(Px • Dx) ⊃ (Sx ∨ Ax)]	It is not the case that for all x, if x is a person and x doubts the existence of God, then x is a skeptic or x is an atheist.
(∃x)~[(Px • Dx) ⊃ (Sx ∨ Ax)]	For some x, it is not the case that if x is a person and x doubts the existence of God, then x is a skeptic or x is an atheist.

The first formulation is the direct negation of the statement; the second makes the equivalent claim that there are exceptions to the statement.

To state the rule in its general form, we will use the notation $(\ldots x \ldots)$ to represent any expression involving x that is bound by a quantifier, where the parentheses include the entire statement within the scope of the quantifier. The QN rule then consists of four formulations:

$\sim(x)(\ldots x \ldots)$ :: $(\exists x)\sim(\ldots x \ldots)$
It is not the case that all x are...   There exists at least one x that is not...

$\sim(\exists x)(\ldots x \ldots)$ :: $(x)\sim(\ldots x \ldots)$
It is not the case that some x is...   All x are non-... OR No x is...

$\sim(x)\sim(\ldots x \ldots)$ :: $(\exists x)(\ldots x \ldots)$
It is not the case that all x are non-...   There exists at least one x that is...

$\sim(\exists x)\sim(\ldots x \ldots)$ :: $(x)(\ldots x \ldots)$
It is not the case that some x is non-...   For all x, x is...

Like the propositional replacement rules, such as double negation (DN) or transposition (Trans), QN can be applied either to a whole statement or to a component. It can therefore be used with statements in which quantified component statements are combined by connectives. For example:

If everything is physical, then there are no ghosts. $(x)Px \supset (y)\sim Gy$

If everything is physical, then it is not the case that some things are ghosts. $(x)Px \supset \sim(\exists y)Gy$

We can also apply QN to a component that is internally complex:

All doctors are licensed but not all are competent. $(x)(Dx \supset Lx) \bullet \sim(y)(Dy \supset Cy)$

All doctors are licensed but for some things it is not the case that if it is a doctor then it is competent. $(x)(Dx \supset Lx) \bullet (\exists y)\sim(Dy \supset Cy)$

The formulation of the consequent in the second version is strange, and the literal English translation is awkward. Since the negation sign is now inside the scope of the quantifier, however, we can use the propositional replacement rules implication (Imp), De Morgan's law (DM), and double negation (DN) to derive a more natural-sounding equivalent:

1. $(x)(Dx \supset Lx) \bullet (\exists y)\sim(Dy \supset Cy)$
2. $(x)(Dx \supset Lx) \bullet (\exists y)\sim(\sim Dy \vee Cy)$ 1 Imp
3. $(x)(Dx \supset Lx) \bullet (\exists y)\sim\sim(Dy \bullet \sim Cy)$ 2 DM
4. $(x)(Dx \supset Lx) \bullet (\exists y)(Dy \bullet \sim Cy)$ 3 DN

Statement 4 says that all doctors are licensed but some doctors are not competent.

As a final point about QN, let's see how it can be combined with the propositional rules of replacement to explain one of the relationships among the standard categorical statements. The four standard forms are often arranged in the square of opposition, with diagonal arrows between contradictory statements:

A: All *S* are *P*

$(x)(Sx \supset Px)$

$(\exists x)(Sx \bullet Px)$

I: Some *S* are *P*

E: No *S* is *P*

$(x)(Sx \supset {\sim}Px)$

$(\exists x)(Sx \bullet {\sim}Px)$

O: Some *S* are not *P*

The statements "All *S* are *P*" and "Some *S* are not *P*" are contradictories, which means that the negation of one is equivalent to the other. If you deny that all *S* are *P*, then you are asserting that some *S* are not *P*. So when we put those statements into predicate notation, we should be able to see *why* the negation of the A statement is equivalent to the O statement. We can prove that equivalence by the following steps (which follow the same path as the previous example about incompetent doctors):

1. ${\sim}(x)(Sx \supset Px)$ Negation of the A statement
2. $(\exists x){\sim}(Sx \supset Px)$ From 1, by QN
3. $(\exists x){\sim}({\sim}Sx \lor Px)$ From 2, using the propositional rule Imp
4. $(\exists x)({\sim}{\sim}Sx \bullet {\sim}Px)$ From 3, using DM
5. $(\exists x)(Sx \bullet {\sim}Px)$ From 4, using DN

Can you see how a similar proof could be constructed for the other pair of contradictories?

EXERCISE 10.4B

I. Which of the following pairs of statements are equivalent by QN?

Statements	
*1. $(x)(Px \supset Qx)$	${\sim}(\exists x){\sim}(Px \supset Qx)$
2. $(x){\sim}(Px \bullet Qx)$	${\sim}(\exists x)(Px \bullet Qx)$
3. $(\exists x){\sim}[Px \bullet (Qx \lor Rx)]$	${\sim}(\exists x){\sim}[Px \bullet (Qx \lor Rx)]$
*4. ${\sim}(x){\sim}[Px \supset (Qx \bullet Rx)]$	$(\exists x)[Px \supset (Qx \bullet Rx)]$
5. $(x){\sim}[(Px \bullet Qx) \bullet Rx]$	${\sim}(\exists x)[(Px \bullet Qx) \bullet Rx]$
6. $(x){\sim}[(Px \bullet Qx) \supset Rx]$	$(\exists x){\sim}[(Px \bullet Qx) \supset Rx]$
*7. ${\sim}(x)[Px \supset (Qx \lor Rx)]$	$(\exists x)[Px \supset (Qx \lor Rx)]$
8. ${\sim}(x)[(Px \lor Qx) \supset (Rx \supset Sx)]$	$(\exists x){\sim}[(Px \lor Qx) \supset (Rx \supset Sx)]$

II. Use the rules of propositional logic along with QN to construct proofs for the following arguments. Do not use CP or IP.

*1.   1. ${\sim}(\exists x)(Sx \bullet Rx) \supset Pa$
      2. $(x)(Sx \supset {\sim}Rx)$ /Pa

2.   1. $(\exists x){\sim}(Ax \supset {\sim}Fx)$ /${\sim}(x)(Fx \supset {\sim}Ax)$

3. 1. $(x)Ax \supset (x)Bx$ $/(x)Bx \lor (\exists x) \sim Ax$

*4. 1. $(x)Hx \supset \sim(\exists y)My$

     2. $(\exists y)My$ $/(\exists x) \sim Hx$

5. 1. $(x)Ax$

     2. $(x)Ax \supset (\exists x) \sim Bx$

     3. $(x)Bx \lor (x)Cx$ $/(x)Cx$

6. 1. $(\exists x) \sim Dx \supset (x)Gx$

     2. $\sim(x)Dx \lor (\exists x)Ax$

     3. $(\exists x) \sim Gx$ $/(\exists x)Ax$

*7. 1. $[(x)Cx \bullet (x)Dx] \lor \sim[(\exists x) \sim Cx \supset (x)Dx]$ $/(x)Cx \equiv (x)Dx$

8. 1. $[(x)(Ax \bullet Bx) \supset (x)Cx] \bullet [(\exists x)Fx \supset (x)Cx]$

     2. $(x)(Ax \bullet Bx) \lor [(\exists x)Fx \bullet (\exists x)Ax]$ $/(x)Cx$

10.4C Implication Rules

The need for some additional rules of implication will be clear if we consider the classic syllogism:

All humans are mortal.	$(x)(Hx \supset Mx)$
Socrates is human.	Hs
Socrates is mortal.	Ms

This argument looks like *modus ponens*, but it isn't. The first premise is not a conditional statement, because the conditional sign occurs within the parentheses, within the scope of the quantifier. And the predicates H and M are ascribed to the variable x rather than to s. To treat the argument as a case of MP, we must first get rid of the quantifier and variable and transform the first premise into the conditional statement $Hs \supset Ms$. Then we *would* have a simple MP proof.

This is the basic strategy of proof in predicate logic. We transform quantified statements into singular statements and then use the rules of propositional logic. If the conclusion we're trying to prove is itself a singular statement, we can stop at this point. If the conclusion is quantified, then we must have some way of transforming singular statements back into quantified ones. So we need additional rules for *instantiation* and *generalization*. Instantiation rules, as the name suggests, allow us to consider particular instances of quantified statements by removing quantifiers. Generalization rules allow us to move in the opposite direction and generalize by adding quantifiers. There are two rules of each type, one for each quantifier. The most important thing to remember is that, while quantifier negation rules are rules of replacement, instantiation and generalization rules are rules of implication and, as such, may be applied only to whole lines of proof.

Let's start with the rule of **universal instantiation (UI)**. In the argument above, the statement $(x)(Hx \supset Mx)$ says that the expression $Hx \supset Mx$ (if x is human, then x is mortal) is true of any x. So it is true of you and me, and Gandhi, and Shakespeare, and everyone else. In short, we can replace the *x* with the name of anything whatever, and the resulting singular statement follows from the universal statement. Thus Hs ⊃ Ms (if Socrates is human, then Socrates is mortal) follows from (*x*)(H*x* ⊃ M*x*) by the rule of universal instantiation, and we would establish the validity of the argument above by the following proof:

1. (*x*)(H*x* ⊃ M*x*)		Premise
2. Hs	/ Ms	Premise / Conclusion
3. Hs ⊃ Ms		1 UI
4. Ms		2,3 MP

In this case we instantiated the universal premise with the name s, because the argument is concerned with Socrates. In other arguments, as we'll see, neither the premises nor the conclusion mentions any particular individual. If we need to use universal instantiation in such a case, we must pick an instantial letter. We may designate a name (lowercase *a–w*) to stand for some arbitrary individual. We're not using *actual* names in the case but, rather, *assigned* names for the sake of convenience. We call these assigned names constants.

Instantiating to constants is useful—sometimes essential—when we need to apply propositional inference rules in a predicate proof. But for reasons we'll discuss in a bit, instantiation to constants can sometimes lead to problems if we later have to apply generalization rules. That's why it's generally better to instantiate to a variable (*x, y, z*) unless a constant is really necessary. When we pick an instantial variable, we can retain the variable from the original line of proof or use one of the other two. The instantiated line (F*y* ⊃ B*y*, for example) is not truly a statement since it has an unbound variable and, consequently, can't have a truth value. It's technically a statement function, a sort of pattern for a statement. Statement functions can legitimately be used in proof since they maintain the truth-preserving character of a valid argument.

The general form of universal instantiation can be represented as follows:

Universal instantiation (UI): $\dfrac{(x)(\ldots x \ldots)}{\ldots a \ldots}$ or $\dfrac{(x)(\ldots x \ldots)}{\ldots y \ldots}$

where the dots stand for any formula inside the scope of the quantifier, and where *a* is an instantial constant or *x* is an instantial variable. All of the following would be examples:

$$\frac{(x)Px}{Pa} \qquad \frac{(x)(Px \lor Qx)}{Px \lor Qx} \qquad \frac{(x)(\sim Px \cdot Qa)}{\sim Pb \cdot Qa} \qquad \frac{(x)(Px \supset Qx)}{Pz \supset Qz}$$

Notice that in the third example, the constant *a* is already present in the universal statement, so when we instantiate, we might want to use another letter to replace *x*, as in the example. But we don't have to; since the statement is about all *x*, it makes a claim about *a* or *b* or whatever letter we choose. In the last example, the variable occurs twice in the universal statement, as the subject of both predicates. So it had to be replaced by *z* in both occurrences. In general, every occurrence of the variable must be replaced by the same instantial letter.

We can now see more clearly why instantiation and generalization rules are rules of implication: UI is permissible only if the universal quantifier occurs at the beginning of the statement and the entire rest of the statement falls with its scope. Here are some examples of inferences that violate the restriction:

$$\frac{(x)Px \supset Qa}{Pa \supset Qa} \qquad \frac{(x)(Px \supset (\exists y)Qy)}{Pa \supset (\exists y)Qy} \qquad \frac{\sim(x)(Px \supset Qx)}{\sim(Py \supset Qy)} \qquad \text{[error]}$$

In the first one, the quantifier begins the statement but applies only to *Px*; *Qa* falls outside the quantifier's scope. The same is true in the second, where the component statement following the conditional sign is bound by a separate quantifier. In the third, the quantifier does not begin the statement: The negation sign precedes it and is thus outside its scope. (To do anything with this one, we would first have to use the QN rule to move the negation sign inside the scope of the quantifier. But in that case the universal quantifier would become an existential quantifier, requiring the use of a different instantiation rule.) The problem in all these cases is that the conclusion doesn't follow from the premise. Thus the premise in the second example says that if everything is *P*, then something is *Q*. For example: if everyone is in favor, then a bridge will be built. It doesn't follow that if Alice is in favor, then a bridge will be built.

The rule of **existential generalization (EG)** allows us to move in the opposite direction, from a singular to a quantified statement. Such an inference has the form:

Existential generalization (EG): $\dfrac{...a...}{(\exists y)(...y...)}$ or $\dfrac{...x...}{(\exists y)(...y...)}$

If we know that object *a* has property *P*, we can certainly infer that *something* has this property. If we know that Tom is both an actor and a waiter, we can infer that some actors are waiters (remembering that "some" means "at least one").

$$\frac{Pa}{(\exists x)Px} \qquad \frac{At \cdot Wt}{(\exists x)(Ax \cdot Wx)}$$

In existential generalization, then, we replace a name with a variable and add an existential quantifier. When we do so, we must be sure to place the quantifier at the beginning of the statement, so that the entire statement falls within its scope. But we do not have to replace every occurrence of the name with the variable. Consider the statement:

Alan is president and either he or Ellen is secretary.   Pa • (Sa ∨ Se)

We could apply EG to the statement in either of two ways:

$$\frac{Pa \cdot (Sa \lor Se)}{(\exists x)[Px \cdot (Sx \lor Se)]} \qquad \frac{Pa \cdot (Sa \lor Se)}{(\exists x)[Px \cdot (Sa \lor Se)]}$$

In the first example, we replaced both occurrences of the name *a* with the variable *x*. The quantified statement says that someone is president and either that person is secretary or Ellen is. In the second, we replaced only the first occurrence of *a* with a variable, and the result is the statement that someone is president and either Alan or Ellen is secretary. The conclusions in these inferences are different, but both are legitimate uses of existential generalization.

Let's see how our two rules, UI and EG, work together in a proof. Consider the argument:

$$\frac{(x)[Px \supset (Qx \lor Rx)]}{Sa \bullet Pa}$$
$$(\exists x)[Sx \bullet (Qx \lor Rx)]$$

Since the second premise is a singular statement about *a*, we will need to instantiate the universal premise using the same name. We will then have two singular statements, to which we can apply the rules of propositional logic. Our goal is to get the statement $Sa \bullet (Qa \lor Ra)$, from which the conclusion will follow by generalization. The proof looks like this:

1. $(x)[Px \supset (Qx \lor Rx)]$		Premise
2. $Sa \bullet Pa$	/ $(\exists x)[Sx \bullet (Qx \lor Rx)]$	Premise / Conclusion
3. $Pa \supset (Qa \lor Ra)$		1 UI
4. Pa		2 Simp
5. $Qa \lor Ra$		3,4 MP
6. Sa		2 Simp
7. $Sa \bullet (Qa \lor Ra)$		5,6 Conj
8. $(\exists x)[Sx \bullet (Qx \lor Rx)]$		7 EG

The two rules we have just learned are natural ones, in the sense that each expresses something essential about the quantifier involved. A universal statement says something about everything, so we may naturally instantiate it with the name of any particular. An existential statement says that something is true of at least one thing, so we can naturally support the claim by inferring it from a particular example. The next two rules are less natural, and the inferences they permit are valid only if we observe certain special restrictions. (Of course, these rules are also subject to the general constraints we've discussed: Names and variables must be interchanged consistently, and the quantifier must cover the entire statement.)

Existential instantiation (EI) is the reverse of existential generalization. It has the form:

Existential instantiation (EI): $\quad \dfrac{(\exists x)(\ldots x \ldots)}{\ldots a \ldots}$

This does not appear to be a valid inference. The premise tells us that *something* in the world fits a certain description, but if *a* is the name of a specific individual we're already familiar with, we cannot infer that *a* fits the description. Suppose we know, for example, that some actors are waiters: $(\exists x)(Ax \bullet Wx)$. Does this imply that Brad Pitt is both an actor and a waiter? Obviously not. Nevertheless, it is valid to reason: At least one thing in the world is both an actor and a waiter. Let's call that thing *a*. We can now assert that $Aa \bullet Wa$. Existential instantiation is valid only if we replace the variable with a name we introduce solely for the purpose of standing for the particular thing—whatever (or whoever) it may be—that makes the premise true. We call this assigned name a constant. Since we can think of a constant as an assumed name, we'll use the two words interchangeably. This means that when we use EI in a proof, the constant we use must be one that has not been used previously in the proof, either in the premises or in a previous step, *and* that does not occur in the conclusion.

To see the importance of this restriction, suppose we try to prove that Devon is a knave because some people are either fools or knaves, and Devon is not a fool.

```
1. (∃x)(Fx ∨ Kx)              Premise
2. ~Fd              / Kd       Premise / Conclusion
3. Fd ∨ Kd                     1 EI [error]
4. Kd                          2,3 DS
```

The use of existential instantiation in line 3 is invalid. The existential premise says only that some people are fools or knaves, so we cannot assume that the statement is true of Devon. To instantiate the premise in line 3, we would need to use another name like *a* that refers to some unspecified person, and then we would not be able to draw any conclusion about Devon.

The full statement of this inference rule, therefore, must include the restriction:

Existential instantiation (EI): $\underline{(∃x)(...x...)}$
$...a...$

Restriction: *a* is a constant not used on any previous line of the proof nor in the conclusion.

This restriction does not apply to universal instantiation, since a universal premise is true of every instance. So if we need to instantiate both a universal and an existential statement in a proof, it's best to instantiate the existential statement first. Then we are free to use the same constant when we instantiate the universal premise. An example would be the argument that some paints are health hazards because some paints contain lead, and anything containing lead is a health hazard.

```
1. (∃x)(Px • Lx)              Premise
2. (x)(Lx ⊃ Hx)    / (∃x)(Px • Hx)    Premise / Conclusion
3. Pa • La                    1 EI
4. La ⊃ Ha                    2 UI
5. La                         3 Simp
6. Ha                         4,5 MP
7. Pa                         3 Simp
8. Pa • Ha                    6,7 Conj
9. (∃x)(Px • Hx)              8 EG
```

To obtain line 8, we had to use the same constant to instantiate both premises (since Ha comes from the second premise, and Pa from the first). If we had tried to instantiate

---

REVIEW Implication Versus Replacement Rules

Implication and replacement rules function differently in both propositional and predicate logic.

- Implication rules can be properly applied to whole lines only.

- Replacement rules can be properly applied either to whole lines or to parts of lines.

UI, EG, EI, and UG are all implication rules while QN is a replacement rule.

the second premise before the first (i.e., if we had tried to obtain line 4 before line 3), we would have been blocked by our restriction: The constant *a* could not have been used for the existential instantiation, because it would already have been used. So we had to proceed in the opposite order.

The fourth rule of inference we need is **universal generalization (UG)**, which has the form:

Universal generalization (UG): $$\frac{...x...}{(y)(...y...)}$$

We typically use this rule when the conclusion of an argument is a universal statement, as in the syllogism: All alcoholic beverages are intoxicating; May wine is an alcoholic beverage; therefore. . . . The proof would be:

1. $(x)(Ax \supset Ix)$ Premise
2. $(x)(Mx \supset Ax)$ / $(x)(Mx \supset Ix)$ Premise / Conclusion
3. $Ax \supset Ix$ 1 UI
4. $Mx \supset Ax$ 2 UI
5. $Mx \supset Ix$ 3,4 HS
6. $(x)(Mx \supset Ix)$ 5 UG

We had to instantiate both premises in order to connect them by a hypothetical syllogism, and then we had to generalize to get our conclusion.

We can maintain the validity of our proof by observing certain restrictions on UG. The easiest way to understand the need for these restrictions is to consider the sorts of fallacies we want to avoid.

It is clear, to begin with, that we cannot use UG on any name, i.e., constant, that already occurs in the premises. The premise that Kenya is an African nation (Ak), for example, does not allow us to infer that every country, or every thing in the world, is an African nation $(x)(Ax)$. Similarly, we cannot generalize on a name that was introduced by existential instantiation. Otherwise we could infer that everything is wet from the premise that something is wet:

1. $(\exists x)Wx$ / $(x)Wx$ Premise / Conclusion
2. Wa 1 EI
3. $(x)Wx$ 2 UG [error]

In this proof, *a* is *not* an arbitrary example of things in the world because the premise doesn't tell us that everything is wet, only that some things are, and *a* has been specially designated as one of them. These examples make it clear that, in fact, we can never universally generalize over a constant; we may apply UG to variables only.

As with existential instantiation, therefore, the full statement of this inference rule must include a restriction:

Universal generalization (UG): $$\frac{...x...}{(y)(...y...)}$$

Restriction: *x* is not a constant.

(We will need to add further restrictions when we get to more advanced forms of proof, but this one restriction is sufficient for now.)

REVIEW Replacement and Implication Rules for Predicate Logic

Replacement Rule

Quantifier negation (QN)

$$\sim(x)(\ldots x \ldots) \quad :: \quad (\exists x)\sim(\ldots x \ldots)$$

$$\sim(\exists x)(\ldots x \ldots) \quad :: \quad (x)\sim(\ldots x \ldots)$$

$$\sim(x)\sim(\ldots x \ldots) \quad :: \quad (\exists x)(\ldots x \ldots)$$

$$\sim(\exists x)\sim(\ldots x \ldots) \quad :: \quad (x)(\ldots x \ldots)$$

Implication Rules

General restrictions:

1. Uniform replacement: (a) In universal generalization, the same variable must replace all occurrences of the same instantial letter. (This restriction does not apply to existential generalization.) (b) In both types of instantiation, the same instantial letter must replace all occurrences of the same variable.

2. Quantifier scope: The quantifier that is added in either type of generalization or dropped in either type of instantiation must include the entire line within its scope.

Universal instantiation (UI):
$$\frac{(x)(\ldots x \ldots)}{\ldots a \ldots}$$

or

$$\frac{(x)(\ldots x \ldots)}{\ldots y \ldots}$$

Existential generalization (EG):
$$\frac{\ldots a \ldots}{(\exists y)(\ldots y \ldots)}$$

or

$$\frac{\ldots x \ldots}{(\exists y)(\ldots y \ldots)}$$

Existential instantiation (EI):
$$\frac{(\exists x)(\ldots x \ldots)}{\ldots a \ldots}$$

Restriction: a is a constant not used on any previous line of the proof nor in the conclusion.

Universal generalization (UG):
$$\frac{\ldots x \ldots}{(y)(\ldots y \ldots)}$$

Restriction: x is not a constant.

EXERCISE 10.4C

I. Each of the following inferences is an attempt to apply one of the implication rules we've discussed (UI, EG, EI, or UG). Identify the rule, and determine whether it has been properly applied.

✳1. 1. $(\exists x)(Px \bullet Qx)$ / $Pa \bullet Qa$

2. 1. $Pa \vee Qa$ / $(\exists x)(Px \vee Qx)$

3. 1. $(x)(Px \bullet Qx) \supset (y)Ry$ / $(Pa \bullet Qa) \supset Ra$

✳4. 1. $Pa \supset (Qb \bullet Ra)$ / $(\exists x)[Px \supset (Qb \bullet Rx)]$

5. 1. $(\exists x)(Px \bullet Qx) \supset (y)(Qy \supset Ra)$ / $(Pb \bullet Qb) \supset (Qb \supset Ra)$

6. 1. $(x)[Px \supset (Qx \vee Rx)]$ / $Pa \supset (Qa \vee Ra)$

＊7. 1. $(Pa \equiv Qa) \cdot (Qa \equiv Ra)$ / $(x)(Px \equiv Qx) \cdot (Qx \equiv Rx)$

8. 1. $(x)(Px \supset Qa)$ / $Pa \supset Qa$

9. 1. $Pa \supset Qa$ / $(x)(Px \supset Qx)$

＊10. 1. $(Pb \cdot Qb) \vee Ra$ / $(\exists x)[(Px \cdot Qx) \vee Rx]$

11. 1. $(\exists x)[(Px \cdot Qx) \supset Ra]$ / $(Pa \cdot Qa) \supset Ra$

12. 1. $Pz \supset Qz$ / $(x)(Px \supset Qx)$

II. Use the rules of propositional logic along with the instantiation and generalization rules to construct a proof for each of the following arguments. Do not use CP or IP.

＊1. 1. $(x)Gx$ / $Ga \cdot Gb$

2. 1. $(x)(Tx \supset Lx)$
   2. $\sim Lb$ / $\sim Tb$

3. 1. Kd
   2. Bd / $(\exists x)(Bx \cdot Kx)$

＊4. 1. $\sim Ca$
   2. $(x)(\sim Bx \supset Cx)$ / Ba

5. 1. $(y)(Ty \supset Hy)$
   2. Tb / $(\exists x)Hx$

6. 1. $(y)(Gy \supset Hy)$
   2. Gy / $(\exists x)Hx$

＊7. 1. $(x)(Hx \supset Mx)$
   2. Hs / $Hs \cdot Ms$

8. 1. $(x)Sx$
   2. $(\exists y)Sy \supset (y)Wy$ / $(y)Wy$

9. 1. $\sim(x)(Kx \cdot Jx)$ / $(\exists x)(\sim Kx \vee \sim Jx)$

＊10. 1. $(\exists x)Bx \cdot (x)(Cx \supset Dx)$
   2. $\sim Da$ / $\sim Ca$

11. 1. Fa
   2. $(x)(Fx \supset Gx)$ / $(\exists x)(Fx \cdot Gx)$

12. 1. $(x)(Ex \supset Px)$
   2. $(x)(Px \supset Tx)$ / $(x)(Ex \supset Tx)$

＊13. 1. $(x)Fx$
   2. $(\exists y)Fy \supset (x)Gx$ / Ga

14. 1. $(x)[Gx \supset (Hx \cdot Tx)]$
   2. $(x)[(Hx \cdot Tx) \supset (Ix \vee Sx)]$ / $(x)[Gx \supset (Ix \vee Sx)]$

15. 1. $(x)[(Bx \cdot Cx) \supset \sim Dx]$
   2. Da / $\sim Ba \vee \sim Ca$

＊16. 1. $(x)Sx$
   2. $(\exists y)Sy \supset (y)Wy$ / Wa

17. 1. $(x)(Ax \supset Bx)$
    2. $(\exists x)Ax$ $/ (\exists x)Bx$
18. 1. $(x) \sim (Ax \vee Bx)$ $/ \sim (\exists x)Bx$
*19. 1. $(\exists x)Tx \supset (y)Gy$
    2. $Ig \vee Tg$
    3. $\sim (\exists x)Ix$
    4. $(x)(Gx \supset \sim Rx)$ $/ (x) \sim Rx$
20. 1. $(x)Rx$
    2. $(x)(Rx \supset Sx)$ $/ (\exists x)(Sx \vee Tx)$

10.4D Strategies for Proof

We now have all the rules we need for proofs in predicate logic. So let us consider some strategies that will help us use the rules in constructing proofs. As with proofs in propositional logic, we work forward from the premises and backward from the conclusion, looking for a route that will get us from the one to the other. We will almost always need to use the propositional rules of replacement and implication, so the strategies we learned for propositional logic are still applicable. But the rules of predicate logic require some additional strategies.

Which rules we apply, and how we apply them, depends on the type of statements we are given as premises and conclusion. We summarized these types at the end of Section 10.3. For our purpose in constructing proofs, we can simplify by reducing the classification to three kinds:

	Type	Examples
1.	Singular statements, whether atomic or compound	Pa $(Pa \vee Qb) \supset Rc$
2.	Quantified statements (statements that are entirely within the scope of an initial quantifier)	$(x)Px$ $(\exists x)(Sx \cdot Tx)$ $(\exists x)[(Pa \vee Qx) \supset Rx]$
3.	Truth-functional compounds of quantified statements	$\sim(x)(Qx)$ $(\exists x)(Px \cdot Sx) \supset (\exists y)Qy$ $Sa \cdot \sim(x)(Px \equiv Qx)$

For an argument with premises and conclusion that are all singular statements, as we saw at the beginning of this section, we do not need any of the rules for predicate logic. If the argument is valid, the proof can be constructed using only the implication and replacement rules of propositional logic. The strategies to follow are therefore the ones we discussed in the previous chapter.

For arguments whose premises include statements of type 2, we normally need to use universal or existential instantiation (UI or EI) to derive singular statements, so that we can then use the rules of propositional logic to move toward the conclusion.

- If the premises include an existential statement with one or more universal statements, we should instantiate the existential statement first. If we instantiate a universal premise first, then the restriction on EI will prevent us from using the constant we used in UI.
- If the conclusion is a singular statement of type 1, then we do not need to invoke either of the generalization rules, EG or UG. If the conclusion is an existential statement, we can generalize without restriction—for example, from $Sa \cdot Ta$ to $(\exists x)(Sx \cdot Tx)$. If the conclusion is a universal statement, however, we must be careful not to violate the restriction on UG.

If one or more premises or the conclusion is a statement of type 3, we cannot use the implication rules of predicate logic directly. Remember that the difference between statements of types 2 and 3 is whether the connectives fall within the scope of a single quantifier (2) or outside (3). The instantiation rules can be applied only to type 2 statements, in which the quantifier comes first in the statement and covers the entire statement. And the generalization rules will give us a type 2 statement, $(x)(\ldots x \ldots)$ or $(\exists x)(\ldots x \ldots)$. So with type 3 statements, we need to use other strategies.

- If a premise is the negation of a quantified statement—for example, $\sim(\exists x)(Px \cdot Qx)$—we can use the replacement rule QN to move the negation sign inside the scope of the quantifier: $(x)\sim(Px \cdot Qx)$. Now we have a statement of type 2, and we can apply UI.
- If a premise is a conjunction of quantified statements—for example, $(\exists x)Px \cdot (\exists y)Qy$—use the propositional rule Simp to derive one or both of the statements.
- If the premise is a disjunction or conditional, look for a way to derive one of the components or a negation of a component, and then use the propositional rules MP, MT, or DS.

Example	Strategy
$(x)(Px \supset Qx) \lor (\exists x)(Px \cdot Rx)$	Look for a way to obtain $\sim(x)(Px \supset Qx)$ or $\sim(\exists x)(Px \cdot Rx)$ then use DS to derive the other disjunct.
$(\exists x)(Px \cdot Qx) \supset (\exists x)Rx$	Look for a way to obtain $(\exists x)(Px \cdot Qx)$ and use MP to derive $(\exists x)Rx$; or $\sim(\exists x)Rx$ and use MT to derive $\sim(\exists x)(Px \cdot Qx)$.

Let's work through a few examples to illustrate these strategies.

$(x)(Px \supset Qx)$
$\underline{\sim[(\exists y)Qy \lor (\exists y)Ry]}$
$\sim(\exists x)Px$

The first premise is a statement of type 2, so we can apply UI to it. But the second premise is of type 3; both the main connective (negation) and the internal connective (disjunction) are outside the scope of either quantifier. Our first question should be what to do with this premise. The statement has the logical form $\sim(p \lor q)$, so we can apply De Morgan's law (DM) to it. The result is:

$\sim(\exists y)Qy \bullet \sim(\exists y)Ry$

Now we can use Simp and QN to derive $(y)\sim Qy$ and $(y)\sim Ry$, statements of type 2 to which we can apply the instantiation rule EI. The predicate R does not occur in either the first premise or the conclusion, so we can probably ignore it. But let's see what we can do with the first conjunct, $(y)\sim Qy$.

1. $(x)(Px \supset Qx)$		Premise
2. $\sim[(\exists y)Qy \lor (\exists y)Ry]$	$/ \sim(\exists x)Px$	Premise / Conclusion
3. $\sim(\exists y)Qy \bullet \sim(\exists y)Ry$		2 DM
4. $\sim(\exists y)Qy$		3 Simp
5. $(y)\sim Qy$		4 QN

We now have a universal statement that we can instantiate, and we can do the same with the first premise. Can you see that once we do that, we will be able to use MT?

6. $Py \supset Qy$	1 UI
7. $\sim Qy$	5 UI
8. $\sim Py$	6,7 MT

Now we have a singular statement that clearly relates to the conclusion in some way, so it is time to apply a generalization rule. If we use existential generalization, the result will be $(\exists x)\sim Px$. But that is not the conclusion, $\sim(\exists x)Px$. Instead, we need to use universal generalization and then QN again to get to the conclusion.

9. $(x)\sim Px$	8 UG
10. $\sim(\exists x)Px$	9 QN

Finally, we need to check that the use of UG in line 9 complies with the restriction. Have we applied UG to a constant? No, we remembered to instantiate to variables. So line 9 is a legitimate inference. Notice that we used the variable x to replace y. We used x because that is the variable in the conclusion we wanted to derive. The general point to remember is that there is no restriction on what variable we use in generalizing with UG or EG.

REVIEW UI and EI

We may instantiate a universal statement to any variable or any constant—no restrictions. An existential statement must be instantiated to a new constant. If the product of UI and EI are to be used together *always do EI first*.

Let's look at a second example:

$(\exists x)(Bx \supset Cx) \supset (x)(Cx \supset Fx)$
$(x)(Bx \supset Dx)$
$\underline{(\exists x)(\sim Dx \lor Cx)}$
$(\exists x)(Bx \supset Fx)$

If we ignore the quantifiers for a moment, we can see in a general way the path that the proof could take. The conclusion is $Bx \supset Fx$. If we could establish the antecedent of the first premise, $Bx \supset Cx$, we could infer the consequent, $Cx \supset Fx$. A hypothetical syllogism would then give us the conclusion. To derive the antecedent of the first premise, we will need to use the second and third premises. We can convert the third premise, $\sim Dx \lor Cx$, into a conditional, $Dx \supset Cx$, using the propositional rule implication, and then combine it with the second premise, $Bx \supset Dx$, in another hypothetical syllogism to derive $Bx \supset Cx$. The question is whether we can construct an actual proof along these lines, taking account of the quantifiers and the rules that apply to them.

We can instantiate the second and third premises but not the first, which is a type 3 statement. And we should begin by instantiating the third premise, since it is an existential statement.

1. $(\exists x)(Bx \supset Cx) \supset (x)(Cx \supset Fx)$		Premise
2. $(x)(Bx \supset Dx)$		Premise
3. $(\exists x)(\sim Dx \lor Cx)$	$/ (\exists x)(Bx \supset Fx)$	Premise / Conclusion
4. $\sim Da \lor Ca$		3 EI
5. $Da \supset Ca$		4 Imp
6. $Ba \supset Da$		2 UI
7. $Ba \supset Ca$		5,6 HS
8. $(\exists x)(Bx \supset Cx)$		7 EG
9. $(x)(Cx \supset Fx)$		1,8 MP

From here, the proof is straightforward. We instantiate 8 and 9, use HS again, and then generalize. When we instantiate 8, however, we need to be careful not to use a, because that name was used in earlier lines; we will have to pick another constant.

10. $Bb \supset Cb$	8 EI
11. $Cb \supset Fb$	9 UI
12. $Bb \supset Fb$	10,11 HS
13. $(\exists x)(Bx \supset Fx)$	12 EG

EXERCISE 10.4D

I. **Integrative Exercise**   Construct a proof for each of the following arguments. Do not use CP or IP.

*1. 1. $(x)(Bx \supset \sim Cx)$
   2. Ba
   3. $(x)(Cx \lor Dx)$ $/ Da$

2. 1. Ba ⊃ (x)(Cx ⊃ Dx)
   2. Ca • Ba   / Da

3. 1. (x)(Tx ⊃ Wx) • Ta   / (∃x)(Wx • Tx)

∗4. 1. (x)(Ax ⊃ Bx)
   2. (x)(Cx ⊃ ~Bx)   / (x)(Cx ⊃ ~Ax)

5. 1. (∃y)Gy ⊃ (z)(Bz ⊃ Cz)
   2. Gd
   3. Bh   / (∃z)Cz

6. 1. (∃x)Kx ⊃ (x)(Lx ⊃ Mx)
   2. Kb • Lb   / Mb

∗7. 1. (x) ~(~Fx ⊃ Gx)   / ~(x)Gx

8. 1. (x)[(Px ∨ Qx) ⊃ Rx]
   2. (∃x)(Px • Sx)   / (∃x)Rx

9. 1. (x)(Px ⊃ ~Qx)
   2. (x)(Rx ⊃ Qx)   / (x)(Rx ⊃ ~Px)

∗10. 1. (∃x)Gx ⊃ (x) ~Bx
    2. Ga   / (∃x) ~(Bx • Ax)

11. 1. (x)(Px ⊃ Qx)
    2. (∃x)(Px • Rx)   / (∃x)(Rx • Qx)

12. 1. (x)(Px ⊃ ~Qx)
    2. (x)(~Qx ⊃ ~Hx)
    3. (∃x)(Rx • Px)   / (∃x)(Rx • ~Hx)

∗13. 1. (x)(Ax ≡ Bx)
    2. (x)(Bx ≡ Cx)   / Ag ⊃ Cg

14. 1. Ma
    2. (x)(Mx ⊃ Gx)   / (∃x)(Gx ≡ Mx)

15. 1. (x)[~(~Fx ⊃ Gx) • ~(Mx • Nx)]   / ~(x)Gx

∗16. 1. Fa
    2. ~(∃x)(Fx • Gx)   / (∃x)(Fx • ~Gx)

17. 1. (x)(Ix • Tx)
    2. (∃y)Iy ⊃ (∃z)Hz   / (∃z)Tz • (∃z)Hz

18. 1. (x)(Dx ⊃ Cx)
    2. (x)(Dx ⊃ Jx)
    3. (∃x)Dx   / (∃x)(Jx • Cx)

∗19. 1. ~(y) ~Ty ⊃ (∃x)Sx
    2. (∃x)Sx ⊃ ~(∃z) ~(Rz • Tz)   / (∃y)Ty ⊃ (z)(Rz • Tz)

20. 1. (x)[Lx ⊃ (Cx • Mx)]
    2. (x)(Mx ⊃ Vx)   / (x)(Lx ⊃ Vx)

21. 1. (x)(Rx ⊃ Sx)
    2. (x)(Px ⊃ Qx)
    3. (∃x)(Px ∨ Rx)   / (∃x)(Sx ∨ Qx)

∗**22.** 1. $(x)(Bx \bullet Ax)$
    2. $(y)(Cy \supset \sim By)$ / $(\exists x)(Ax \bullet \sim Cx)$

23. 1. $(x)(Bx \supset Cx)$
    2. $(\exists x)Bx$
    3. $(x)(\sim Dx \supset \sim Cx)$ / $(\exists x)Dx$

24. 1. $(x)[Qx \supset (Tx \lor Ix)]$
    2. $(\exists x)(Qx \bullet \sim Tx)$ / $(\exists x)(Qx \bullet Ix)$

∗**25.** 1. $Ta \supset (y)Gy$
    2. $Ia \lor Ta$
    3. $\sim Ia$
    4. $(x)(Gx \supset Hx)$ / $(x)Hx$

26. 1. $(x)(Bx \supset Cx) \bullet (x)(Dx \supset Ex)$
    2. $(x)(Dx \lor Bx)$ / $(x)(Cx \lor Ex)$

27. 1. $\sim(\exists x)Ax$
    2. $\sim(\exists x)(Bx \bullet \sim Ax)$ / $\sim(x)Bx$

∗**28.** 1. $(x)\{[Bx \bullet (Cx \lor Dx)] \supset Ex\}$
    2. $(\exists x)(Dx \bullet \sim Ex)$ / $(\exists x)\sim Bx$

29. 1. $(\exists z)Gz \supset (y)Ty$
    2. $(\exists x)Ix \supset (x)Hx$
    3. $Gs \bullet Ig$ / $(x)(Tx \bullet Hx)$

30. 1. $\sim(\exists x)[\sim Bx \bullet (\sim Cx \bullet Dx)]$
    2. $\sim(x)(Dx \supset Cx)$ / $(\exists x)(Dx \bullet Bx)$

∗**31.** 1. $\sim(\exists x)(Rx \bullet Fx)$
    2. $(x)(Tx \supset Rx)$
    3. $(x)(Dx \supset Fx)$ / $(\exists x)(\sim Tx \lor \sim Dx)$

32. 1. $(y)(Dy \supset Ny)$
    2. $\sim Np \lor \sim Ng$ / $\sim Dp \lor \sim Dg$

33. 1. $(x)(Bx \supset Fx)$
    2. $(x)(Bx \supset Sx)$ / $(x)[Bx \supset (Fx \bullet Sx)]$

∗**34.** 1. $(z)(Sz \supset Tz)$
    2. $(z)Sz$ / $Ta \bullet Tb$

35. 1. $(\exists z)Pz \supset (\exists y)My$
    2. $\sim(\exists x)Sx \supset \sim(\exists y)My$ / $(\exists z)Pz \supset (\exists x)Sx$

II. [Integrative Exercise] Translate the following predicate arguments into symbolic notation and construct a proof to demonstrate the validity of each. Do not use CP or IP.

∗1. All philosophers are either Platonists or Aristotelians. Jones is not a Platonist but he is a philosopher. Therefore he must be an Aristotelian.

2. If all Aristotelians are also Thomists, then Professor Jones is a Thomist. If he is a Thomist, he must also be a realist. But Professor Jones isn't a

realist so some Aristotelians aren't Thomists.

3. Some of the students in this class are failing. No student who fails a class makes the dean's list. So there is at least one student in this class who won't make the dean's list.

*4. All engineers are good at math so, if Mark is an engineer, then he must be good at math. But everyone who

is good at math understands basic algebra and he doesn't. So Mark is not an engineer.

5. Either Latesha or Jonathan will be elected president of the SGA. According to the Student Government Association bylaws, only seniors can be elected president and Jonathan is a sophomore, not a senior. So I guess it's Latesha for president.

10.4E Conditional Proof and Indirect Proof

In the previous chapter, we learned how the techniques of conditional proof (CP) and indirect proof (IP) are used in propositional logic. They can also be used in predicate logic. For some valid arguments they provide the only way to construct a proof, and for many other arguments they at least simplify the derivation.

Conditional proof is used to derive a conditional statement. We introduce the antecedent of the statement as an assumption on an indented line; from that assumption, along with previous lines in the proof, we derive the consequent; and then we enter the conditional statement on a non-indented line, with the justification CP. Here is a simple example:

1. $(x)[Px \supset (Rx \bullet Sx)]$	/ $(x)(Px \supset Sx)$	Premise / Conclusion
2. $Pz \supset (Rz \bullet Sz)$		1 UI
3. Pz		Assumption
4. $Rz \bullet Sz$		2,3 MP
5. Sz		4 Simp
6. $Pz \supset Sz$		3–5 CP
7. $(x)(Px \supset Sx)$		6 UG

The use of CP gave us an easy way to extract Sz from the conjunction Rz • Sz in the consequent of 2.

In this example, we used CP with the singular statement we derived by instantiating the universal premise. But we can also use CP with quantified statements, as in the following example:

$$(x)(Px \supset Qx)$$
$$(\exists x)Px \supset (\exists y)Qy$$

The argument seems valid intuitively. The premise says that if anything is P, then that thing is Q. The conclusion says that if there is something that is P, then *something* is Q—a weaker claim that has to be true if the premise is true. How can we construct the proof? If we instantiate the premise, we will have a conditional statement, Pa ⊃ Qa. But there does not seem to be any way forward from that point. Instead, we should notice that the conclusion is a conditional statement. Let's assume the antecedent, the quantified statement $(\exists x)Px$, and use conditional proof.

1. $(x)(Px \supset Qx)$	/ $(\exists x)Px \supset (\exists y)Qy$	Premise / Conclusion
2. $(\exists x)Px$		Assumption
3. Pa		2 EI
4. $Pa \supset Qa$		1 UI
5. Qa		3,4 MP
6. $(\exists y)Qy$		5 EG
7. $(\exists x)Px \supset (\exists y)Qy$		2–6 CP

Using conditional proof in predicate logic is subject to the same restriction as in propositional logic. In the indented subproof, lines 2–6, we assume that $(\exists x)Px$ is true and we derive $(\exists y)Qy$ from that assumption together with the premise. But the proof is not complete until we discharge the assumption. We have borrowed $(\exists x)Px$, and now we have to pay it back. We do that on line 7. At this point in the proof, we are no longer assuming that $(\exists x)Px$ is true; we are saying that *if* $(\exists x)Px$ is true, then $(\exists y)Qy$ is true as well. The restriction is that once we discharge the assumption and get back to the main proof, we can no longer use any line that is part of the subproof. Any such line depends on an assumption we are no longer making. In this case, the proof ended with line 7; no further steps were required, so the restriction does not apply. But remember that a conditional subproof can be used to establish an intermediate step in a proof, and in that case we need to be careful to seal off the subproof from any further use.

There is an additional restriction on conditional proof that applies to universal generalization. We have seen that UG cannot be used to generalize over a constant. Now we must add that UG cannot be used within a conditional subproof if the instantial variable occurs free (unbound by a quantifier) in the assumption. If we need to use UG in this manner, we must discharge the assumption, and return to the main proof

---

SOLVE   Assuming for CP in Predicate Logic

The correct assumption can help you avoid violating restrictions and ensure a successful proof. Here are some tips:

- When proving a conditional governed by a single quantifier, such as $(x)(Px \supset Qx)$, assume the antecedent without the quantifier, derive the consequent without the quantifier, and discharge your assumption. Once your assumption is discharged, you can apply UG without worrying about the second restriction.

- When proving a compound conditional in which the antecedent and consequence each has its own quantifier, such as $(\exists x)Px \supset (x)Qx$, assume the antecedent with its quantifier, derive the consequent with its quantifier. You can usually discharge your assumption without applying UG at all.

before using UG. The following proof illustrates the fallacy we commit if we violate this restriction:

1. $(x)(Lx \supset Mx)$ / $(x)[Lx \supset (y)My]$ Premise / Conclusion
2. Lx Assumption
3. $Lx \supset Mx$ 1 UI
4. Mx 2,3 MP
5. $(y)My$ 4 UG [error]
6. $Lx \supset (y)My$ 2–5 CP
7. $(x)[Lx \supset (y)My]$ 6 UG

Let L stand for leopard, M for mammal. The premise says that all leopards are mammals, which is true. The curious-looking conclusion says that if anything is a leopard, then everything is a mammal, which is certainly false. The problem lies in step 5, where we generalized on x (from line 4) within the scope of the conditional proof. This is *not* to say that we can never use UG inside a conditional segment; it's just that we can't do it if the instantial variable occurs free in the initial assumption (even if it was introduced earlier).

The same restriction on UG applies when we use indirect proof. As we learned in Chapter 9, IP is a technique for demonstrating that a certain statement follows from the premises of an argument by showing that denying the statement leads to a contradiction. To establish p, we assume $\sim p$, entering it as an assumption on an indented line. When we have derived a contradiction, $q \bullet \sim q$, we have completed the IP subproof and we enter p on the next line of the main proof. Once we have discharged the assumption in this way, we can no longer use any line in the indented sequence.

Let's see how this works with an example:

1. $(\exists x)Px \supset Qa$ Premise
2. $(x)(Rx \supset Px)$ Premise
3. $(y)(\sim Ry \supset Py)$ / $(\exists y)Qy$ Premise / Conclusion

We can't do anything with 1, because the quantifier does not cover the whole statement. So let's instantiate 2 and 3, using a for x so that we can eventually connect them with 1.

4. $Ra \supset Pa$ 2 UI
5. $\sim Ra \supset Pa$ 3 UI

Now we can see that Pa must be true, given the premises. If it were not true, then we could infer both $\sim\sim Ra$ and $\sim Ra$ by *modus tollens* (MT), and we would have a contradiction. This suggests that we use an indirect proof to derive that contradiction:

6. $\sim Pa$ Assumption
7. $\sim Ra$ 4,6 MT
8. $\sim\sim Ra$ 5,6 MT
9. $\sim Ra \bullet \sim\sim Ra$ 7,8 Conj
10. Pa 6–9 IP

Now we can go back to 1 and connect P with Q to derive the conclusion:

11. $(\exists x)Px$ 10 EG
12. Qa 1,11 MP
13. $(\exists y)Qy$ 12 EG

Conditional proof and indirect proof are useful techniques in predicate logic. But remember the new restriction they impose on universal generalization. The updated statement of that inference is now:

Universal generalization (UG): $$\frac{...x...}{(y)(...y...)}$$

Restrictions:
   1. x is not a constant.
   2. UG is not used within a conditional or indirect subproof if x occurs unbound on the first indented line of that subproof.

REVIEW UG Restrictions

So far we've learned two restrictions on universal generalization. To summarize:

- We cannot universally generalize over a constant.

- UG can't be used inside an indented sequence if the instantial variable occurs free on the first indented line.

EXERCISE 10.4E

Integrative Exercise   Construct a proof for each of the following arguments, using CP or IP.

*1. 1. $(x)[(Sx \lor Cx) \supset Ex]$ / $(x)(Cx \supset Ex)$

2. 1. $(x)(Bx \supset Ax)$ / $(\exists y)By \supset (\exists y)Ay$

3. 1. $(x)Ax$
   2. $(y)By$ / $\sim(\exists z)(\sim Az \lor \sim Bz)$

*4. 1. $(x)(Dx \supset Ex)$
   2. $(x)[(Dx \bullet Ex) \supset Fx]$ / $(x)(Dx \supset Fx)$

5. 1. $(x)Gx \lor (y)Hy$
   2. $(y)(Gy \supset Iy)$ / $(\exists y)\sim Hy \supset (z)Iz$

6. 1. $(x)[(Gx \lor Hx) \supset Ix]$
   2. $(x)Ix \supset (x)Tx$ / $(x)Gx \supset (x)Tx$

*7. 1. $(x)[(Ax \lor Bx) \supset Cx]$
   2. $(x)[Cx \supset (\sim Ax \lor Dx)]$ / $(x)(Ax \supset Dx)$

8. 1. $(x)[Ax \supset (Bx \lor \sim Cx)]$
   2. $(x)(\sim Bx \lor \sim Ax)$ / $(x)(Ax \supset \sim Cx)$

9. 1. ~(∃z)(~Lz • Pz)
  2. (y)(~Ly ∨ Py) / (z)(~Lz ≡ ~Pz)

✳10. 1. (x)(Px ≡ Tx)
  2. (x)(Tx ≡ Ax) / Pm ⊃ Am

11. 1. (x)(Ax ⊃ Bx) • (x)(Bx ⊃ Cx) / (x)[Ax ⊃ (Dx ⊃ Cx)]

12. 1. (x)(Jx ⊃ Lx)
  2. (y)(~ Qy ≡ Ly) / ~(Ja • Qa)

✳13. 1. (x)[Bx ⊃ (Cx ∨ Dx)]
  2. (x)(Dx ⊃ ~Ex) / (x)[(Bx • Ex) ⊃ Cx]

14. 1. (x){[Bx • (Cx ∨ Dx)] ⊃ ~Ex}
  2. (x)(~Ex ⊃ ~Bx)
  3. Da / ~Ba • Da

15. 1. (x)[Px ⊃ (Qx • Rx)]
  2. (x)(Rx ⊃ Sx) / (x)[(Rx ∨ Px) ⊃ Sx]

✳16. 1. (x)[(Bx • ~Cx) ⊃ Dx]
  2. (x)(Dx ⊃ Cx) / (x)(Bx ⊃ Cx)

17. 1. (y)[(By ∨ Cy) ⊃ (Dy • Ey)]
  2. (y)[(Dy ∨ Ey) ⊃ (By • Cy)] / (x)(Bx ≡ Dx)

18. 1. ~(∃x)[Px • (Sx • Tx)]
  2. (x)[(Sx ∨ Qx) • (Tx ∨ Rx)] / (x)[Px ⊃ (Qx ∨ Rx)]

✳19. 1. (∃x)(Bx • ~Cx)
  2. (x){[Bx • ~(Dx ∨ Ex)] ⊃ Cx} / (∃x)[Dx ∨ (Ex • Bx)]

20. 1. ~(∃x)[Bx • ~(Cx ∨ Dx)]
  2. ~(∃y)(Dy • ~Ey) / ~(∃x)~[(Bx ⊃ Ex) ∨ Cx]

21. 1. [(∃x)Gx ∨ (∃x)Hx] ⊃ (∃x)~Ix
  2. (x)(Ix ∨ Qx)
  3. ~(∃x)(Qx • Rx) / (x)Rx ⊃ (x)~Gx

10.5 Relations and Multiple Quantification

In addition to talking about things and their properties, we can talk about the *relationships* among things. In this section, we will learn how to represent such statements in the notation of predicate logic. Unlike the statements we have dealt with so far, relational statements often have two or more quantifiers that overlap in scope, so we need to learn how overlapping quantifiers work. Finally, we will look at arguments involving statements about relationships. We will not need any new implication or replacement rules to construct proofs, but applying the rules to relational statements will require some new techniques and restrictions.

10.5A Relations

To understand how relationships are represented in predicate logic, let's start with singular statements. Here are some examples of relational statements about individual things:

> Brazil is larger than Uruguay.
>
> Jane married Dan.
>
> Omar is president of the Stanford Chess Club.

Each of these asserts that two things are related in a certain way. Grammatically, the statements have a subject–predicate structure, and in each case the second thing named (Uruguay, Dan, and the Stanford Chess Club) is part of the predicate. And we could follow the grammar when we translate into symbolic notation. In the first statement, for example, the predicate would be "is larger than Uruguay," and we would translate the statement as: Lb.

But we can also break things down in a different way. We could treat Uruguay as a *subject*, alongside Brazil. The predicate would then be "is larger than," and we would interpret the statement as saying that this relational predicate is true of Brazil and Uruguay as a pair. To symbolize the statement using this approach, we need a predicate letter and *two* subject letters: Lbu. In the same way, "Jane" and "Dan" are the subjects in the second statement, and the predicate is "married": Mjd. In the third, "Omar" and "the Stanford Chess Club" are subjects of the relational predicate "is president of": Pos. Notice that we have to be careful about the order in which we list the subject letters. This doesn't matter much in the second example because being married is a symmetrical relationship; if Jane married Dan, then Dan married Jane. But that's a special case. If we reversed the letters in the first, we'd have the false statement that Uruguay is larger than Brazil; if we reversed the letters in the third, we'd be saying that the Stanford Chess Club is president of Omar, which doesn't even make sense. As a general rule of thumb for relational predicates, the subject letter that comes first should be the one that represents the subject of the English sentence.

Once we allow that a statement can have more than one subject, there's no reason to stop at two. Many statements assert that some relationship exists among three or more items. In symbolic form, we use a relational predicate and as many subject letters as we need. Consider the statement:

> Lorna sold the Brooklyn Bridge to June.

Here we have a relationship among three things: two people and a bridge. It would be a little awkward to put the predicate in a phrase, as we have been doing. It's easier to think of it as a sentence structure, with slots in the positions where the subjects go:

> _____ sold _____ to _____.

If we let S stand for this structure, we can symbolize this statement by adding letters for the subjects, in the proper order: Slbj. Lorna is the one who did the selling, so the letter *l* goes in the first slot. The Brooklyn Bridge is what got sold, and June is the one to whom it was sold, so the letters *b* and *j* go in the remaining slots. Since the structure has three slots for subjects, S is called a three-place predicate. By the same token, "is president of" is a two-place predicate, and terms for nonrelational properties such as *white* (e.g., "My car is white"—Wc) are one-place predicates. For more complex relationships, we can have predicates with a greater number of subjects—four, five, and so on indefinitely. In principle, for any number *n* we can have *n*-place predicates.

All of our relational statements thus far have been *singular* statements. Even though they are statements about more than one thing, they say something about particular items that are named as individuals. But we have seen how to form general statements by replacing names with variables. We can do the same for statements involving relations. Suppose we know that Omar is president of *something*, but we don't know what. Instead of using the letter *s*, for the Stanford Chess Club, we use the variable *x*, along with the existential quantifier:

> Omar is president of something. $(\exists x)Pox$

The symbolic expression means that there is an *x* such that Omar is president of *x*.

Here are some other examples of quantified relational statements, with the subject terms underlined. Look them over carefully to make sure you understand the rationale behind each symbolic translation.

<u>Lorna</u> sold <u>something</u> to <u>June</u>.	$(\exists x)Slxj$
Every <u>thing</u> is a product of <u>the Big Bang</u>.	$(x)Pxb$
Some <u>thing</u> caused <u>the explosion</u>.	$(\exists x)Cxe$
No <u>South American country</u> is larger than <u>Brazil</u>.	$(x)(Sx \supset {\sim}Lxb)$
Some <u>thing</u> is rotten in the state of <u>Denmark</u> [where S means ____ is in the state of ____].	$(\exists x)(Sxd \bullet Rx)$
<u>I</u> gave <u>my dog</u> a bone [where B means "is a bone" and G means ____ gave ____ to ____].	$(\exists x)(Bx \bullet Gixd)$

EXERCISE 10.5A

Put each of the following relational statements into symbolic notation.

*1. The Mets lost to the Cubs.

2. The mailman is afraid of my dog.

3. Marilyn Monroe starred in *Some Like It Hot*.

*4. I ran into Alison at Disneyland.

5. Adam ate an apple.
   Hint: Use F (fruit) for "is an apple."

6. Some people are not fans of Bruce Springsteen.

*7. Some actions of the government are capricious.

8. A snake talked to Eve.

9. All roads lead to Rome.

*10. Frankie loved Johnnie.

11. Anyone who marries Albert is crazy.

12. No one is a faster draw than Wyatt Earp.

*13. There's nowhere I feel safe.

(Use a two-place relational predicate S: _____ feel safe at _____.)

14. Memphis is south of St. Louis and north of New Orleans.

15. Memphis is between St. Louis and New Orleans.

*16. I have a dream.

17. Peggy married some guy from Duluth.

18. Mary had a little lamb.

*19. Sally borrowed a pen from Tiffany.

20. If someone enters the premises, an alarm will go off.

21. The dog was playing with a ball.

*22. A dog ate my homework.

23. Mariana beat out Miguel and won the race. (Let g stand for Miguel.)

24. The Chrysler building has a lovely spire.

*25. Mufasa and Sarabi adore each other.

26. Some of the passengers on the *Titanic* drowned.

27. If Kimiko votes for anyone, she will vote for a liberal.

*28. Some trees have aesthetic value and should be saved.

29. Santiago sent a love letter to Violeta.

30. The oracle gave Neo a cookie.

10.5B Overlapping Quantifiers

The relational statements we've examined so far have a variable in one of the subject positions, bound by a single quantifier. But we can also have variables in more than one position, each bound by a separate quantifier, as long as we observe a few simple rules.

At some point in your studies, you may have had the insight that:

Everything is related to everything.

The predicate here is:

_____ is related to _____.

Since we are not talking about particular things as individuals, we need variables rather than names in both of the slots: Rxy. And since we are talking about all x and all y, we use a universal quantifier to bind each of the variables:

$(x)(y)Rxy$

This formula is an example of multiple quantification, but it is different from earlier examples such as:

If everything is physical, then there are no ghosts. $(x)Px \supset \sim(\exists y)Gy$

Here, there is no overlap in the scope of the quantifiers. (x) applies only to Px and $(\exists y)$ applies only to Gy. In our first example, by contrast, the quantifiers do overlap; both (x) and (y) apply to Rxy. Such overlap is typical when we have relational predicates, and it's the reason we must use different variables to represent the different subjects of these predicates. If we used the same variable in both roles—R*xx*—with the single quantifier (*x*), we would change the meaning: We would be saying that each thing is related to itself. That follows from the original statement (if each thing is related to everything, then of course it is related to itself), but it is not equivalent.

It would not change the meaning of "Everything is related to everything" if we switched the order of the quantifiers, as you can see by thinking through the literal meaning of the statements.

> (*y*)(*x*)R*xy*   For any two things, *y* and *x*, *x* is related to *y*.
>
> (*x*)(*y*)R*xy*   For any two things, *x* and *y*, *x* is related to *y*.

These are equivalent ways of saying the same thing. In general, when all the quantifiers are universal, it does not matter which we put first in the formula. The same is true when all the quantifiers are existential, as in the statement:

> Something bumped into something.
>
> (∃*x*)(∃*y*)B*xy*   There is at least one thing *x* and at least one thing *y* such that *x* bumped into *y*.
>
> (∃*y*)(∃*x*)B*xy*   There is at least one thing *y* and at least one thing *x* such that *x* bumped into *y*.

Here again, the two versions are equivalent.

When the quantifiers are different, however, order makes a difference. Suppose we wanted to symbolize the general statement that:

> Everything has a cause.

We would use a two-place predicate, _____ causes _____, in which the first slot is the cause and the second is the effect. The statement asserts that for everything that exists, there's something that causes it: (*y*)(∃*x*)C*xy*. This statement does not say that everything has the same cause. It says that each *y* is caused by some *x*, but not necessarily the same *x* for all of the *y* effects. Reversing the order of quantifiers changes the meaning. (∃*x*)(*y*) C*xy* says: There is an *x* such that for all *y*, *x* causes *y*. Now we *are* saying that there is a single cause for everything.

The ability to symbolize statements about relations and to quantify variables separately makes predicate logic a very flexible and powerful instrument for analyzing arguments. But learning to use these devices properly takes practice. We have been working so far with rather simple statements. To get a better feel for the system, it will help to work through some examples that are more complex.

Consider the statement:

> Everyone is afraid of something.

This looks like the statement about causality, but we can't analyze it in quite the same way. The parallel translation would be (*x*)(∃*y*)A*xy*. But this says that everything—rocks, trees, and hurricanes as well as people—is afraid of something, and we're talking only about people. The most natural way to add this information would be as follows: (*x*)(P*x* ⊃ (∃*y*)A*xy*). This says: It is true of every *x* that if *x* is a person, then there is a *y* such that *x* is afraid of it. The scope of the universal quantifier is the entire statement, so it binds *x* in both occurrences, whereas the scope of the existential quantifier is limited to A*xy*.

That's okay, because A*xy* is the only occurrence of *y*. All that matters is that every occurrence of a given variable fall within the scope of the corresponding quantifier.

The earlier example of Jane and Dan illustrates another important point. The statement "Jane married Dan" had two subjects and a two-place predicate. Suppose we want to say when they got married:

Jane married Dan at 5:00 Saturday afternoon.

Now we can treat the time, 5:00 Saturday afternoon, as a third subject filling a slot in the three-place predicate: _____ married _____ at _____. This predicate is different from the two-place predicate M, which did not have a slot for time. So we will use a different letter, W (for wedding), to represent this predicate: W*jds*. This is still a singular statement, since 5:00 Saturday afternoon is a particular time. But now consider the statement:

Jane married Dan at some point in time.

Now we need a variable in the time slot, and an existential quantifier to bind it: $(\exists x)$ (T*x* • W*jdx*), where T*x* says that *x* is a time. Bound variables for times are used to translate words like "at some time," "once," and "always." In the same way, bound variables for places are used to translate words like "somewhere" and "everywhere." (Be careful, though. These expressions are sometimes used merely as alternative ways of making ordinary universal or particular statements, as in "triangles always have three sides.")

Before we can translate a statement, we need to know how many different things we are referring to and which predicates are being asserted of them in which combinations. With complex statements, this is not always obvious, and it helps to proceed in stages. Consider the statement:

Any undergraduate who excels in a subject knows more about it than some graduate students in that subject.

It is immediately clear that this is about undergraduates who excel, and that it's about all of them. So we can let *x* stand for them and rewrite the sentence in a kind of pidgin English-symbolic form:

(*x*)[(*x* is an undergraduate • *x* excels in a subject) ⊃ (*x* knows more about it than some graduate students in that subject)]

Because this is a universal statement, it is formulated as a conditional.

For the second conjunct in the antecedent, which refers to "a subject," we'll need another variable *y*, and *y* is also referred to in the consequent ("it" and "that subject"). The statement does not limit its claim to any particular subject or subjects, so we should use a universal quantifier for *y*. Now we have:

(*x*)(*y*)[(*x* is an undergraduate • *y* is a subject • *x* excels in *y*) ⊃ (*x* knows more about *y* than some graduate students in *y*)]

Since the statement is also about graduate students, we need a third variable to stand for them; and because the claim is limited to some of them, we bind the variable with an existential quantifier:

(*x*)(*y*)[(*x* is an undergraduate • *y* is a subject • *x* excels in *y*) ⊃ $(\exists z)$(*z* is a graduate student • *x* knows more about *y* than *z* does)]

We have now quantified everything that needs quantifying and used connectives to define the propositional structure of the statement. In doing so, we have isolated the predicate elements, and the only remaining task is to introduce symbols for them:

U: ____ is an undergraduate
S: ____ is a subject
E: ____ excels in ____
G: ____ is a graduate student
K: ____ knows more about ____ than ____ does

In full predicate notation:

$(x)(y)\{[(Ux \bullet Sy) \bullet Exy] \supset (\exists z)(Gz \bullet Kxyz)\}$

SOLVE Punctuating Complex Translations

Placing parentheses in complicated predicate translations doesn't have to be difficult. Quantifiers can be used as indicators of where punctuation should go. Here's our statement about graduate and undergraduate students before it's fully punctuated:

$(x)(y)(Ux \bullet Sy) \bullet Exy \supset (\exists z) Gz \bullet Kxyz$
We know we want to offset the antecedent from the consequent of the conditional. We'll use brackets:

$(x)(y)[(Ux \bullet Sy) \bullet Exy] \supset (\exists z) Gz \bullet Kxyz$
More punctuation is needed. Here's the easy way: start from the end of the proposition and

move backward until you reach a quantifier. The quantifier $(\exists z)$ needs to govern every z that follows it. We need to bind Gz • Kxyz into a single formula. That gives us:

$(x)(y)[(Ux \bullet Sy) \bullet Exy] \supset (\exists z)(Gz \bullet Kxyz)$
Working backward, the next quantifier is (y). This universal quantifier needs to bind every formula that follows. We'll use braces:

$(x)(y)\{[(Ux \bullet Sy) \bullet Exy] \supset (\exists z)(Gz \bullet Kxyz)\}$
The universal quantifier (x) needs to govern every x that follows. It already does; no additional punctuation is necessary.

EXERCISE 10.5B

Put each of the following statements into symbolic notation.

✴1. Someone loves me.

2. Something I ate upset my stomach.

3. Jack Sprat could eat no fat.

✴4. All Wonder-Cure products are available at all drugstores.

5. What goes up must come down.

6. I don't like monkeys.

✴7. I learn something new every day.

8. Every senior is older than every freshman.

9. Some freshman is older than any senior.

✴10. Everyone is someone's fool.

11. A rolling stone gathers no moss.

12. If there were no evil, there would be no good.

∗13. Tiffany stole a bike from someone.

14. No student may cheat at any time.

15. Something there is that does not love a wall.

∗16. There are no resorts in Greenland.

17. Either everyone will go or no one will be happy.

18. Some people are lactose intolerant and can't digest milk products.

∗19. Everywhere that Mary went, the lamb was sure to go.

20. Not a sound was heard by anyone.

21. If whales are mammals, then not all mammals are land animals.

∗22. Rap and heavy-metal music are disturbing to some people.

23. No one can satisfy everyone all of the time.

24. Anyone who buys a used car from Mary is a fool.

∗25. In any stone arch there is a stone such that, if it is removed, all the stones will fall.

26. A deciduous tree has leaves that fall from the tree.

27. If someone steals something, he has broken a law.

∗28. Each man kills the thing he loves. [Oscar Wilde]

29. If you can renovate yourself one day, then you can do so every day. [Chu Hsi, *The Great Learning*]

30. If there is no god, then no action a person takes is immoral.

∗31. "I would not join any club that would have someone like me for a member." [Groucho Marx] (Use g to indicate Groucho Marx.)

32. If the murder weapon is a revolver, then someone shot Mr. Boddy with it in the conservatory. (Use a 4-place predicate: ____ killed ____ with ____ in ____.)

33. If a tree falls in the woods and no one is there [in the woods], no sound is made.

∗34. Everybody loves somebody sometime.

35. Every person is smarter than some animal.

36. If some children are angels or geniuses, then some teachers are amazed and delighted.

∗37. Nobody loves everybody.

38. Some people greet every person they meet.

39. Some students fail every exam they take.

∗40. If there are any students who fail the exam, all students must retake it.

10.5C Proof with Relational Statements

For arguments with relational statements, we use the same rules and strategies for proof that we learned in the previous section. Suppose, for example, that someone made the following inference about the 2011 National Basketball Association playoffs:

> If the Miami Heat beats the Boston Celtics in the Eastern Conference finals, then if the Dallas Mavericks beat the Oklahoma City Thunder in the Western Conference

finals, Miami will play Dallas in the NBA finals. Dallas will beat Oklahoma in the Western Conference, so if Miami beats Boston in the East, it will play Dallas for the NBA championship.

This argument involves two kinds of relationship among teams and playoff finals:

B: ____ beats ____ in ____,
P: ____ plays ____ in ____,

where the first two slots are for teams and the third is for playoff finals. So we would formulate the premises and conclusion as follows:

1. Bmbe ⊃ (Bdow ⊃ Pmdn)		Premise
2. Bdow	/ Bmbe ⊃ Pmdn	Premise / Conclusion

Since the conclusion is a conditional statement, the simplest way to proceed is by way of conditional proof.

3. Bmbe	Assumption
4. Bdow ⊃ Pmdn	1,3 MP
5. Pmdn	2,4 MP
6. Bmbe ⊃ Pmdn	3–5 CP

In that argument, the premises and conclusion were singular statements—the atomic components referred to particular teams and particular payoff events—so we needed only the rules of propositional logic. With quantified relational statements, however, we will usually need the replacement and implication rules for predicate logic. Since relational statements can have multiple overlapping quantifiers, we need to be careful that we apply those rules properly.

Applying quantifier negation to relational statements. If we have more than one quantifier, we can still apply QN, but we have to do it in stages, moving the negation sign one quantifier at a time. Thus a statement of the form $\sim(x)(\exists y)Rxy$ would be transformed first into $(\exists x)\sim(\exists y)Rxy$, and then into $(\exists x)(y)\sim Rxy$. Consider the statement:

1. Not every student owns a computer $\sim(x)(\exists y)[(Sx \cdot Cy) \supset Oxy]$

This is equivalent to the statement that some student does not own any computer. We can establish the equivalence by applying QN twice and then applying the propositional replacement rules Imp, DM, and DN:

2. $(\exists x)\sim(\exists y)[(Sx \cdot Cy) \supset Oxy]$	1 QN
3. $(\exists x)(y) \sim[(Sx \cdot Cy) \supset Oxy]$	2 QN
4. $(\exists x)(y) \sim[\sim(Sx \cdot Cy) \vee Oxy]$	3 Imp
5. $(\exists x)(y)[\sim\sim(Sx \cdot Cy) \cdot \sim Oxy]$	4 DM
6. $(\exists x)(y)[(Sx \cdot Cy) \cdot \sim Oxy]$	5 DN

Like a replacement rule in propositional logic, QN can be applied either to a whole statement or to a component. That principle is especially important with relational statements, since they often have one or more quantifiers inside the statement, including only a component of the whole statement within their scope. Suppose, for example, that we have the following line in a proof:

$(\exists x)[Px \cdot \sim(y)(Qy \supset Rxy)]$

QN could be applied to the portion of the statement following the conjunction sign:

$(\exists x)[Px \bullet (\exists y)\sim(Qy \supset Rxy)]$

Applying instantiation rules to relational statements. The rules for universal instantiation and existential instantiation can be used for statements with overlapping quantifiers, whether or not the statement has a relational predicate. The following are examples:

UI	EI	UI
$(x)(\exists y)Pxy$	$(\exists x)(y)(Px \supset Qy)$	$(x)[Px \supset (\exists y)(Qy \bullet Rxy)]$
$(\exists y)Pay$	$(y)(Pa \supset Qy)$	$Pz \supset (\exists y)(Qy \bullet Rzy)$

Remember that to apply UI and EI properly, we must replace each occurrence of the variable with the same instantial letter. The variable used in the quantifier tells us which variables (of the statement) to replace. Thus in the first example, we want to remove the universal quantifier and replace x. There are no restrictions on UI, so we'll replace x with a. In the second example, the existential quantifier governs every x that follows it. Because of the restrictions on EI, we must instantiate to a new constant; we'll replace Px with Pa. In the third, we'll replace Px with Pz and Rxy with Rzy.

We must also remember that UI and EI are permissible only if the entire statement falls within the scope of the quantifier we instantiate. The implication is that these rules can be used only on the quantifier that begins the statement—the outermost quantifier. In the second statement, for example, we couldn't instantiate (y) because it is embedded within the scope of $(\exists x)$. Once we've instantiated $(\exists x)$, then (y) becomes the outermost quantifier, and we can go on to instantiate (y). In the third, however, when we have instantiated (x), we cannot go on to instantiate $(\exists y)$ because its scope does not include the entire statement. We would first need to detach the consequent—for example by deriving Pz and using *modus ponens.*

When we use existential instantiation with a relational statement, we need to be careful not to violate the restriction that EI is valid only if we replace the variable with a constant we introduce solely for the purpose of standing for the particular thing— whatever (or whoever) it may be—that makes the premise true. This means that when we use EI in a proof, the constant we use must be one that has not been used previously in the proof and that does not occur in the conclusion. To see the importance of this restriction, consider the following statements:

Everyone has a mother.	$(y)(\exists x)Mxy$
Someone is a mother of herself.	$(\exists x)Mxx$

Strictly speaking, the symbolic formulation should include the fact that mothers and children are people: for example, for the first statement, $(y)[Py \supset (\exists x)(Px \bullet Mxy)]$. But we will simplify by assuming that the universe consists solely of people, that is, that variables can refer only to people, so that we don't need to include Px or Py in the formula.

The first statement is true, and the second is false. Yet if we did not observe the restriction on EI, we might try to derive statement two from statement one:

1. $(y)(\exists x)Mxy$ / $(\exists x)Mxx$ Premise / Conclusion
2. $(\exists x)Mxa$ 1 UI
3. Maa   2 EI [error]
4. $(\exists x)Mxx$ 3 EG

The argument is clearly invalid, and the problem in the proof occurs in step 3. We can't use *a* to instantiate *x*, because *a* has already been used to instantiate *y*. Line 2 says that someone is *a*'s mother; this does not imply that *a* is her own mother. To instantiate *x*, we need a fresh constant.

Applying generalization rules to relational statements. Existential generalization has no special restrictions, so we can use it with relational statements to replace constants with variables. We just have to remember to apply EG one constant at a time, as in the following proof:

1. $(\exists x)(Dx \bullet Fx)$		Premise
2. $(y)[Dy \supset (z)Gyz]$	/ $(\exists x)(\exists y)(Dx \bullet Gxy)$	Premise / Conclusion
3. $Da \bullet Fa$		1 EI
4. Da		3 Simp
5. $Da \supset (z)(Gaz)$		2 UI
6. $(z)Gaz$		4,5 MP
7. Gab		6 UI
8. $Da \bullet Gab$		4,7 Conj
9. $(\exists y)(Da \bullet Gay)$		8 EG
10. $(\exists x)(\exists y)(Dx \bullet Gxy)$		9 EG

In line 9, we replaced *b* with the variable *y*, bound by $(\exists y)$. Then, in line 10, we could replace *a* with *x*, bound by $(\exists x)$, and thus complete the process of generalizing to reach the conclusion.

As we saw in the preceding section, universal generalization is subject to two restrictions. It is not valid if it is applied to a constant nor if it is used within a conditional or indirect subproof whose assumption contains the instantial variable unbound by a quantifier. With multiple quantifiers, UI is subject to a third restriction. To understand this restriction and the rationale for it, consider the statements:

Everyone loves someone.	$(x)(\exists y)Lxy$
There is someone everyone loves.	$(\exists y)(x)Lxy$

These are not equivalent statements. The first statement says that everyone loves someone (or other); the second says that there is someone (a particular individual) whom everyone loves. Nor does the first statement, which may we be true, imply the second, which is almost certainly false. But consider the following "proof" that the second statement follows from the first:

1. $(x)(\exists y)Lxy$ / $(\exists y)(x)Lxy$	Premise / Conclusion
2. $(\exists y)Lxy$	1 UI
3. Lxb	2 EI
4. $(x)Lxb$	3 UG [error]
5. $(\exists y)(x)Lxy$	4 EG

In step 2 we used UI to instantiate to *x*; 2 says that *x* loves someone. In step 3 we used EI to introduce *b* as the person *x* loves. Can you see why step 4 is a fallacious inference? Since *b* was introduced specifically as the person *x* loves, we can't infer that *everyone* loves *b*. The problem here, to put it in general terms, is that *b* was introduced on a line where *x* was already present, so we can't apply universal generalization on *x* until we get rid of *b*.

So we now have three restrictions on UG:

Universal generalization (UG): $\dfrac{\ldots x \ldots}{(y)(\ldots y \ldots)}$

Restrictions:
1. x is not a constant.
2. UG is not used within a conditional or indirect subproof with an assumption that contains x unbound by a quantifier.
3. $\ldots x \ldots$ must not contain a constant introduced by EI on a line in which the instantial variable occurs free.

To illustrate how to apply the replacement and implication rules to arguments with relational statements, consider the following argument, which will require a longer proof. As we work through the proof, it might help to have paper and pencil handy so that you can keep track of where we are.

1. $(x)\{Px \supset (y)[(Qy \bullet Ry) \supset Sxy]\}$ Premise
2. $(x)(y)(Txy \supset Qy)$ Premise
3. $(x)(\exists y)Txy$ / $(x)[Px \supset (\exists y)(Ry \supset Sxy)]$ Premise / Conclusion

The three premises and the conclusion are quantified statements, with variables in the subject position and no constants. So we're going to have to instantiate all the variables in order to relate the premises and get to the conclusion. In the case of x, that won't be a problem, since it is bound in each premise by a universal quantifier, and there are no special restrictions on universal instantiation. In premise 3, however, y is bound by an existential quantifier. So let's start with that premise. The first step is to uncover the existential quantifier by instantiating the main quantifier, (x). Then we can apply EI to get a singular statement, and then go on to deal with 1 and 2 by using UI.

4. $(\exists y)Txy$ 3 UI
5. Txb 4 EI
6. $(y)(Txy \supset Qy)$ 2 UI
7. $Txb \supset Qb$ 6 UI
8. $Px \supset (y)[(Qy \bullet Ry) \supset Sxy]$ 1 UI

We cannot instantiate y in line 8 because it does not occur at the beginning of the statement. To detach the consequent from Px, we can use conditional proof with Px as the assumption. This is a reasonable strategy to follow because the conclusion of our proof has the internal structure of a conditional with Px as the antecedent, and the output of the conditional segment will be a conditional with Px as antecedent, from which we can generalize.

9. Px Assumption
10. $(y)[(Qy \supset Ry) \supset Sxy]$ 8,9 MP
11. $(Qb \bullet Rb) \supset Sxb$ 10 UI
12. $Qb \supset (Rb \supset Sxb)$ 11 Exp
13. Qb 5,7 MP
14. $Rb \supset Sxb$ 12,13 MP
15. $(\exists y)(Ry \supset Sxy)$ 14 EG
16. $Px \supset (\exists y)(Ry \supset Sxy)$ 9–15 CP
17. $(x)[Px \supset (\exists y)(Ry \supset Sxy)]$ 16 UG

Let's check, finally, to make sure that we used UG properly. First, was UG applied to a constant? No—it was applied to the variable, *x*, in line 16. Did we use UG inside the conditional subproof (lines 9–15)? No. So we don't have to worry about the second restriction. Did line 16 contain any other constant introduced by EI? No—we got rid of *b*, which was introduced by EI, in line 15. Notice that our use of EG to get rid of *b* occurred inside the conditional segment. That's okay, because there are no special restrictions on EG.

Constructing proofs that involve relational statements, then, is amenable to the same rules and strategies that we learned earlier. There is one new restriction on universal generalization, and the need for extra vigilance in applying all the rules, but otherwise you can simply apply everything you have learned about predicate logic.

REVIEW Replacement and Implication Rules for Predicate Logic

Replacement Rule

Quantifier negation (QN)

$\sim(x)(\ldots x \ldots)$ :: $(\exists x)\sim(\ldots x \ldots)$

$\sim(\exists x)(\ldots x \ldots)$ :: $(x)\sim(\ldots x \ldots)$

$\sim(x)\sim(\ldots x \ldots)$ :: $(\exists x)(\ldots x \ldots)$

$\sim(\exists x)\sim(\ldots x \ldots)$ :: $(x)(\ldots x \ldots)$

Implication Rules

General restrictions:
1. Uniform replacement: (a) in universal generalization, the same variable must replace all occurrences of the same instantial letter. (This restriction does not apply to existential generalization.) (b) In both types of instantiation, the same constant must replace all occurrences of the same variable.

2. Quantifier scope: The quantifier that is added in either type of generalization or dropped in either type of instantiation must include the entire line within its scope.

Universal instantiation (UI):

$$\frac{(x)(\ldots x \ldots)}{\ldots a \ldots}$$

or

$$\frac{(x)(\ldots x \ldots)}{\ldots y \ldots}$$

Existential generalization (EG):

$$\frac{\ldots a \ldots}{(\exists y)(\ldots y \ldots)}$$

or

$$\frac{\ldots x \ldots}{(\exists y)(\ldots y \ldots)}$$

Existential instantiation (EI):

$$\frac{(\exists x)(\ldots x \ldots)}{\ldots a \ldots}$$

Restriction: *a* is a name not used on any previous line of the proof nor in the conclusion.

Universal generalization (UG):

$$\frac{\ldots x \ldots}{(y)(\ldots y \ldots)}$$

Restrictions:
1. *x* is not a constant.

2. UG is not used within a conditional or indirect subproof with an assumption that contains *x* unbound by a quantifier.

3. $\ldots x \ldots$ must not contain a constant introduced by EI in a line in which the instantial variable occurs free.

EXERCISE 10.5C

I. Construct a proof for each of the following arguments.

∗**1.** 1. Ca ⊃ (Mp ⊃ Hap)
   2. ~Hap   / ~Ca ∨ ~Mp

 2. 1. (x)~Jx
   2. (∃y)(Hby ∨ Iyy) ⊃ (∃x)Jx   / (y)~(Hby ∨ Iyy)

 3. 1. (x)(y)Hxy
   2. Hcd ⊃ Kf   / Kf

∗**4.** 1. (∃y)(x)Axy   / (x)(∃y)Axy

 5. 1. (∃x)(Cx ∨ Mxx)
   2. (x)~Cx   / (∃y)Myy

 6. 1. (∃x)(y)Rxy
   2. (x)[Rxx ⊃ (∃y)Sxy]   / (∃x)(∃y)Sxy

∗**7.** 1. Aa   / (x)(Ax ⊃ Bx) ⊃ (∃x)(Ax • Bx)

 8. 1. ~(∃x)(~Ax • Bxx)
   2. Baa   / Aa

 9. 1. (x)[Kxx ⊃ (Lx • Nx)]
   2. (∃x)~Nx   / (∃y)~Kyy

∗**10.** 1. (x)[(~Mxa ∨ Nx) ⊃ Lxx]
   2. (∃y)~Lyy   / (∃x)Mxa

 11. 1. (x)(Exx ∨ Qx)
   2. (y)~Eyy
   3. (z)(Qz ⊃ Kz)   / (x)Kx

 12. 1. (∃x)(Nx • Sx)
   2. (x)[Mxn ⊃ ~(Sx ∨ Dx)]   / (∃y)~Myn

∗**13.** 1. (x)(Exx ∨ Qx)
   2. (y)~Eyy
   3. (z)(Qz ⊃ Kz)   / (x)Kx

 14. 1. Cnn ∨ (Ln • Mj)
   2. ~(z)Nsz ⊃ ~Ln   / (∃x)[~Cxx ⊃ (z)Nsz]

 15. 1. (x)(y)[(Px • Qy) ⊃ Rxy]
   2. (x)(∃y)(Sxy ⊃ Px)   / (x)(∃y)[Sxy ⊃ (Qy ⊃ Rxy)]

∗**16.** 1. (x)[(Hx • Gx) ⊃ Cx]
   2. (y)Gy • ~(x)Mxa   / (x)(Hx ⊃ Cx)

 17. 1. (∃x)[Dx ∨ (y)(Mxy ⊃ Dy)]
   2. (x)(Mxa • ~Da)   / (∃x)Dx

 18. 1. (x)(y)[Hxy ≡ (Ly ⊃ Dx)]
   2. (y)Hiy
   3. (∃z)Lz   / (∃x)Dx

∗**19.** 1. (z)(y)[(∃x)Myx ⊃ Mzy]
   2. Mba   / (∃x)(∃y) Mxy

20. 1. $(x)[Hx \supset (Sxx \supset Gx)]$
  2. $(x)(Gx \supset Cx) \cdot (y) \sim Cy$ $/ (x)(\exists y) \sim (Hy \cdot Syx)$

21. 1. $\sim (\exists y)[Ty \lor (\exists x) \sim Hxy]$ $/ (x)(y)Hxy \cdot (x) \sim Tx$

✳22. 1. $(x)(Cxx \supset Sx)$
  2. $(y)[(Sy \lor Tyy) \supset Wy]$ $/ (x)[(Cxx \cdot \sim Kx) \supset (Wx \cdot \sim Kx)]$

23. 1. $(x)(y)[Kxy \equiv (Lx \cdot My)]$
  2. $(\exists x)(Nx \cdot Mx)$ $/ (x)(\exists y)(Lx \supset Kxy)$

24. 1. $(x)[(\exists y)Mxy \supset (\exists y) \sim Ky]$
  2. $(\exists y)(\exists z)Myz$
  3. $(x)(\sim Kx \equiv Nx)$ $/ (\exists z)Nz$

II. **Integrative Exercise** Translate the following arguments into symbolic notation and then construct a proof to demonstrate the validity of each.

✳1. Every student in the room is older than Danny. If Janet is in the room, she's a student. Janet is in the room so she must be older than Danny.

2. Any human is smarter than any dog. Joe is human and Fido is a dog. Therefore Joe is smarter than Fido.

3. If there are any good books in the library, then *The Scarlet Letter* is one of them. Claudia read *The Scarlet Letter*. There is a least one good book in the library. Therefore, Claudia read at least one good library book.

✳4. A smartphone is an electronic gadget. Therefore anyone who owns a smartphone owns an electronic gadget.

5. Everything that is dented was hit by someone. Everything that is mended was repaired by someone. Something is dented and mended. Therefore there is something hit by someone and something repaired by someone.

10.6 Identity

In the previous section, we saw how predicate logic can be used to express relations between individuals, members of a class, or classes. This gives us a great advantage in symbolizing arguments. But it's still not enough for representing all the sorts of arguments we may encounter. Everyday argumentation frequently involves a special *identity* relation and we need to be able to translate and prove arguments containing such statements.

10.6A Translating Identity Statements

The simplest and most obvious use of the identity operator is for statements in which we want to attribute two different names to the same individual. For example:

Stefani Joanne Angelina Germanotta is Lady Gaga.

We'll borrow the equal sign (=) from arithmetic as our identity operator. We can use the identity relation to translate an array of English statements including: simple identity statements; statements involving expressions such as "only," "the only," "no . . . except," "all . . . except"; as well as superlatives, numerical statements, and **definite descriptions**. Once we've learned to translate these statements into our symbolic notations, we'll learn how to prove arguments containing identity statements.

Simple identity statements. At its most basic, the identity operator is used whenever we want to express that two names denote the same person, place, or thing. For example:

Clark Kent is Superman.	k = s
Texas is the Lone Star State.	t = l
The morning star is the evening star.	m = e

We can also deny that two names designate the same individual by negating the identity operator. Suppose we want to say that Tom Hanks is not Jay Z. We can simply deny the statement that the two are identical: $\sim$(h = j). This is a properly translated logical statement. For convenience's sake, however, we will more often borrow the inequality symbol ($\neq$) from arithmetic. Here are some examples:

Mexico is not Bolivia.	m $\neq$ b
Justin Bieber is not Luis Fonsi.	b $\neq$ f

"Only," "the only," and "no . . . except." When these expressions are followed by a plural noun or pronoun, they should be treated as part of an ordinary categorical proposition. For example, if we say, "Only students will receive the discount," we can translate that statement as $(x)(Rx \supset Sx)$, where Rx stands for "x receives the discount" and Sx stands for "x is a student." But when followed by an individual name, these expressions claim that the individual in question has a quality or characteristic that no other person possesses. We can translate these statements by saying that (1) the individual has the given attribute and (2) if anyone (or thing) has that attribute, it is identical to the designated individual. Multiple conjunctions without parentheses are now allowed, making long identity statements more readable.

No state except for Hawaii is an island.	Sh • Ih • $(x)[(Sx • Ix) \supset x = h]$
Only Richard Nixon resigned the presidency.	Pn • Rn • $(x)[(Px • Rx) \supset x = n]$
Mary Edwards Walker is the only woman to receive the Medal of Honor.	Ww • Mw • $(x)[(Wx • Mx) \supset x = w]$

The first statement is equivalent to saying that Hawaii is the only state that's an island. Our translation states that Hawaii is a state, that it is an island, and that if any state is an island, it's identical to Hawaii. The universal statement is necessary to capture the full meaning of the statement. After all, without it, we're only saying that Hawaii is an island state, perhaps one of many. The universal statement makes it clear that we are claiming an exclusive status for Hawaii.

"All . . . except." Expressions such as "only," "the only," and "no . . . except" single out a designated individual as the only one possessing an attribute. The expression "all . . . except" does the opposite: it singles out an individual as the only member of a class that lacks an attribute. Statements containing "all . . . except" can be translated as follows:

All states except Florida have snow on the ground.	Sf • ~Gf • (x)[(Sx • x ≠ f) ⊃ Gx]
Every student was prepared except Tobias.	St • ~Pt • (x)[(Sx • x ≠ t) ⊃ Px]
Nobody was excluded except Melinda.	Pm • Em • (x)[(Px • x ≠ m) ⊃ ~Ex]

The first example gives us a good template for translating these statements. We've said that Florida is a state and doesn't have snow on the ground and that any state that doesn't have snow on the ground must be identical to Florida. The third example may seem more complicated at first glance due to the negated word "nobody." We are saying that Melinda is excluded but everybody else was not.

Superlatives. Remember your high school yearbook? You probably had pages devoted to students who had won superlatives titles—most musically talented, most athletic, most likely to succeed, etc. Superlatives assert that, of all members of a specified class, the designated member exceeds all others in terms of a particular attribute. Here's how they're translated:

The Pacific Ocean is the world's largest ocean.	Op • (x)[(Ox • x ≠ p) ⊃ Lpx]
Rolando is the oldest senior.	Sr • (x)[(Sx • x ≠ r) ⊃ Orx]
One World Trade Center is the tallest building in the United States.	Bw • Uw • (x)[(Bx • Ux • x ≠ w) ⊃ Twx]

Do you see the pattern? First assign the attribute to the individual and then say that, if anything else also has that attribute, it is exceeded by the named item.

Numerical Statements. In logic, we sometimes want to specify a specific number x of items but must do so without using numerals. While it's not at first obvious, the identity operator can help us do so. We can divide numerical statements into three basic types: those that assign an attribute to at least x items; those that say that at most x items have a certain attribute; and, finally, those that specify that exactly x members of a class have a particular attribute.

We've already seen that the existential quantifier may be read as "at least one." This suggests that we can use it to translate the first type of numerical statement by adding additional quantifiers. Here's the general strategy. (1) Assign a number of quantifiers equal to the number of designated items. (2) Assign the attribute to each existentially quantified variable. (3) Assert that none of the quantified variables designate the same individual. Here are some examples:

There is at least one hairless cat.	(∃x)(Cx • ~Hx)
There are at least two universities in Montana.	(∃x)(∃y)(Ux • Mx • Uy • My • x ≠ y)
There are at least three wise men.	(∃x)(∃y)(∃z)(Mx • Wx • My • Wy • Mz • Wz • x ≠ y • x ≠ z • y ≠ z)

Notice that statements using the phrase "at least" have existential import; they assume that the designated items actually exist. That's *not* the case with "at most," the next type of statement.

When we say that at most x number of individuals have a particular attribute or quality, are we claiming that there is any actually existing thing like the ones described?

The answer—at least in logic—seems to be "no." Here's the reasoning: Suppose your professor says to you "There are at most three students who will receive As in this course." If there are four, she was either lying or mistaken. But what if only two students receive As? Most of us would agree that my original statement was true. What if nobody made an A in the course? The word "most" seems to limit the outcome in one direction only. That's why we use the universal quantifier to translate these statements. Consider the following statements:

There is at most one Santa Claus.	$(x)(y)[(Sx \cdot Sy) \supset x = y]$
There are at most two cats in the room.	$(x)(y)(z)[(Cx \cdot Rx \cdot Cy \cdot Ry \cdot Cz \cdot Rz) \supset$ $(x = y \lor x = z \lor y = z)]$

For any maximum limit we want to set, we need that number of quantifiers and one extra (for x items, $x + 1$ quantifiers). In the second example above, for instance, we are saying that both x and y are cats in the room and that if anything else in the room is a cat, either x and y are identical to each other or z is identical to either x or y. At first this might seem like an unnecessarily complicated and unnatural way to express this concept. But it *does* allow us to express these statements without numerals.

Here are some examples of the third type of numerical statement.

There is exactly one Pope.	$(\exists x)[Px \cdot (y)(Py \supset x = y)]$
There are exactly two men qualified for the job.	$(\exists x)(\exists y)\{Mx \cdot Qx \cdot My \cdot Qy \cdot x \neq y \cdot$ $(z)[(Mz \cdot Qz) \supset (z = x \lor z = y)]\}$
There are exactly two actors in *Greater Tuna*.	$(\exists x)(\exists y)\{Ax \cdot Tx \cdot Ay \cdot Ty \cdot x \neq y \cdot$ $(z)[(Az \cdot Tz) \supset (z = x \lor z= y)]\}$

If you study the examples, you'll see that statements expressing an exact numerical value are conjunctions of existential and universal statements. So a statement about exactly two men, for example, amounts to a claim that there are at least two men, but no more than two men.

Definite Descriptions. One way of identifying an individual is to call him by name. Another way is to use a description that fits only that individual: "the first U.S. president," "the owner of the red Ford," and so on. We call these identifying phrases *definite descriptions.* Statements containing definite descriptions have posed special challenges for philosophers. For example, how should we assign truth values for statements such as, "The U.S. emperor has no clothes"? It would seem strange to say this proposition is true. After all, there is no U.S. emperor—clothed or naked. But it also seems strange to say this statement is false. Do we mean that the U.S. emperor does have clothes? The matter can be debated but, in logic, we accept Bertrand Russell's interpretation. According to Russell, translations of sentences with definite descriptions should (1) assert the existence of the item in question, (2) state that there is only one such item, and (3) state that the item has the assigned attribute. Here are some examples:

The author of *The Scarlet Letter* was an American.	$(\exists x)[Wxs \cdot (y)(Wys \supset y = x) \cdot Ax]$
The winner of the contest was a middle-aged man.	$(\exists x)[Wxc \cdot (y)(Wyc \supset y = x) \cdot Ax \cdot Mx]$

In the last statement, Ax stands for "x was middle-aged."

EXERCISE 10.6A

Translate the following identity statements.

＊1. Katy Perry is Katy Hudson.

2. All states except Louisiana follow the English common law.

3. Mercury is the smallest planet.

＊4. There is at least one male calico cat.

5. No president except Calvin Coolidge was born on the 4th of July.

6. There are exactly two men with the formula.

＊7. The author of *To Kill a Mockingbird* was born in Alabama.

8. Donald Trump is not Brad Pitt.

9. Only Katharine Hepburn has received four Best Actress awards.

＊10. There are at most two mammals that lay eggs.

11. No U.S. president except Franklin Roosevelt served four terms.

12. The largest state is Alaska.

＊13. Natalie Portman is Neta-Lee Hershlag but Mr. Rogers is not Captain Kangaroo.

14. There are at least three men in a tub.

15. The current U.S. president is a Republican.

＊16. Only Matt and Margaret went to the party. (Let r stand for Margaret.)

17. Independence Day is the 4th of July.

18. There are exactly two birds that cannot fly.

＊19. He who drives the Batmobile fights the Joker.

20. Tom is the smartest student.

21. If Virginia is the oldest girl, she gets the prize.

＊22. There are at most two politicians who can be trusted.

23. Snoopy is not Clifford but there is at least one big red dog.

24. There are exactly three mules that are not sterile.

＊25. Didi will wear maroon with white, or maroon with gold; actually, she will wear any color except orange.

10.6B Identity and the Rules of Inference

The identity operator can be combined with the rules of propositional and predicate logic to prove arguments containing identity statements. In order to prove such arguments, we need to add three additional rules of inference. Each of these rules reflects a different property of the identity relation. The first rule reflects the reflexive property of identity.

Identity reflexivity (IR):

$$\frac{\ldots y \ldots}{a = a}$$

This rule expresses the commonsense idea that everything is identical to itself. We may insert a statement to the effect that any individual constant is identical to itself at any point within a proof, justifying it by IR. Since this is a claim about the nature of the objects represented by constants, rather than a substitution instance or inference from other lines of proof, no line number is necessary for our justification.

The second rule of identity is based on the symmetric property of identity.

Identity symmetry (IS): $a = b :: b = a$

As you can see, IS is a rule that requires only a one-line justification. It allows us to switch the order of the statements on each side of the equal sign. So if Clark Kent is identical to Superman, then Superman is identical to Clark Kent.

Our third and last rule of identity is a statement of the transitive property of identity. We will divide this into two formulations.

Identity transitivity (IT):

$$\frac{\begin{array}{l} Fa \\ a = b \end{array}}{Fb} \quad \text{or} \quad \frac{\begin{array}{l} a = b \\ b = c \end{array}}{a = c}$$

The first formulation of this rule is obvious if we think about it in terms of a simple substitution of names. Imagine the same person known by two different names, Mark Twain and Samuel Clemens, for example. If Mark Twain has a mustache and Mark Twain is identical to Samuel Clemens, then Samuel Clemens must have a mustache as well. The second formulation also expresses the transitive property of identity. It should remind you of HS. Suppose you are a detective working on a case. You know your suspect, Robert Jones, sometimes goes by the alias Bob Johnson. That is, you know that Jones and Johnson are the same, identical person. You learn from the sheriff of a neighboring county that Bob Johnson has been using the alias Rob Smith. You reason, "If Robert Jones is identical to Bob Johnson and Bob Johnson is identical to Rob Smith, then Robert Jones must be identical to Rob Smith."

Here are some examples of proofs containing identity statements:

1. $(y)(Py \supset g = y)$		Premise
2. $(y)(Qy \supset h = y)$		Premise
3. $(\exists z)(Pz \bullet Qz)$	$/ h = g$	Premise / Conclusion
4. $Pa \bullet Qa$		3 EI
5. $Pa \supset g = a$		1 UI
6. Pa		4 Simp
7. $g = a$		5,6 MP
8. $Qa \supset h = a$		2 UI
9. Qa		4 Simp
10. $h = a$		8,9 MP
11. $a = g$		7 IS
12. $h = g$		10,11 IT

Be careful to observe all restrictions on instantiation and generalization rules—they still hold for identity proofs. That's why we had to perform EI first. Here's another:

1. $(x)(Px \supset Rx)$		Premise
2. $(\exists x)[(Rx \supset \sim Jx) \bullet x = g]$	$/ \sim(Pg \bullet Jg)$	Premise / Conclusion
3. $(Rb \supset \sim Jb) \bullet b = g$		2 EI
4. $Pb \supset Rb$		1 UI
5. $Rb \supset \sim Jb$		3 Simp
6. $Pb \supset \sim Jb$		4,5 HS
7. $\sim Pb \lor \sim Jb$		6 Imp

8. ~(Pb • Jb)	7 DM
9. b = g	3 Simp
10. ~(Pg • Jg)	8,9 IT

There are no special rules for CP and IP in proofs containing identity statements, but you might want to review the restrictions for universal generalization.

EXERCISE 10.6B

Prove that the following arguments are valid. You may use CP or IP as needed.

✳1. 1. $(x)(Rx \supset x = g)$
    2. Rb   / Rg

2. 1. $(x)(Sx \supset x \neq b)$ / ~Sb

3. 1. $(x)(x = r)$
    2. Tr • ~Kg
    3. $(x)(Wx \supset Kx)$ / Tg • ~Wr

✳4. 1. $(z)(z = g)$
    2. $(\exists z)Fz$ / Fg

5. 1. $(x)(x = c)$
    2. $(z)(z = c)$
    3. Fh   / Fb

6. 1. $(x)\sim Px \vee (\exists x)(Tx • x = d)$ / Ps $\supset$ Td

✳7. 1. $(x)(Tx \vee x \neq p)$ / Tp $\vee$ Rn

8. 1. $(x)[(Sx • Rex) \supset x = c]$
    2. $(\exists x)(Sx • Rex • Tx)$ / Tc

9. 1. Me • $(x)(Cx \supset a = x)$
    2. Cg • $(x)(Mx \supset x = g)$ / Ma • Ce

✳10. 1. Ss • $(x)(Sx \supset f = x)$
    2. Rp • $(x)(Rx \supset x = s)$ / $(\exists x)(Rx • Sx)$

11. 1. $(y)[\sim Fy \vee (Dy • y = s)]$
    2. ~Ds   / ~Fg

12. 1. $(x)[Fx \supset (Px \supset x = e)]$
    2. $(x)[Tx \supset (Px \supset x = f)]$
    3. $(\exists z)(Fz • Tz • Pz)$ / f = e

10.7 Proving Invalidity

In the last chapter, we noted that failure to discover a proof of an argument is not proof that the argument is invalid. Perhaps we haven't been persistent enough or perhaps we've overlooked an obvious solution. So how do we know we've looked long and hard enough? How can we establish that the argument we've been given is invalid? In categorical logic, we can use Venn diagrams to prove that a syllogism is invalid. Let's take this example from Chapter 6.

> All athletes are people in good physical condition.
> All fitness instructors are people in good physical condition.
> All fitness instructors are athletes.

This argument has the form:

> All *P* are *M*
> All *S* are *M*
> All *S* are *P*

We want to know if it is possible for the premises to be true and the conclusion to be false. That is, is all the information in the conclusion implicitly contained within the premises? We can test the argument as follows:

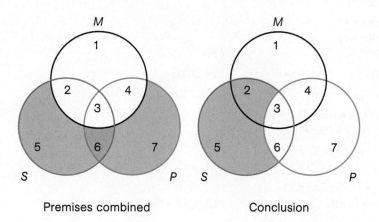

Premises combined   Conclusion

Look at area 2: we can see at a glance that the premises allow for the possibility that some *S* are not *P*. In other words, we have proved that the argument is invalid.

Natural deduction allows us to demonstrate the validity of arguments, not that an argument is invalid. But, as we learned in Chapter 8, we can use truth tables to prove the invalidity of propositional arguments. Here's an example we've seen before:

> B ⊃ H
> H
> B

This is a clear case of affirming the consequent, a fallacious form of argumentation. The following truth table proves its invalidity.

B	⊃	H		H	/	B
T	**T**	T		**T**		**T**
T	**F**	F		**F**		**T**
F	**T**	T		**T**		**F**
F	**T**	F		**F**		**F**

In row 3, both of the premises are true, yet the conclusion is false. Thus the truth of the premises doesn't guarantee the truth of the conclusion; the argument is invalid.

You may have wondered why we haven't used these methods to prove the invalidity of predicate proofs. The answer is simple: neither works in predicate logic. Something else is needed. While there's no way to test predicate proofs for invalidity that is as convenient as these methods, there are two ways that are effective enough for our purpose. In this section, we'll learn them both: the counterexample method and the finite universe method.

10.7A Counterexample Method

If an argument form is valid, any substitution instance of that argument is also valid. Likewise, if we can find any substitution instance of an argument in which all the premises are actually true and the conclusion is actually false, we have shown that the argument is invalid. The counterexample method is just that: an attempt to come up with an example showing that it's possible for the argument to have all true premises and a false conclusion. Here's an example:

$(x)(Hx \supset Mx)$
$(x)(Mx \supset Ax)$
$(x)(Ax \supset Hx)$

APPLY Counterexamples and the GRE

If you're planning on taking the GRE, bone up on counterexamples. The analytical writing sample may require you to construct one. You will be given a sample passage about an issue and asked to construct a counterexample to disprove the argument. While ETS graders don't expect any special technical familiarity with logic, you can use your knowledge of transla-tions and the counterexample method to nail down a high scoring response. Don't get rattled by too much information. Identify the premises and conclusion of the argument, symbolize it, and remember that your goal is just to provide a counterexample of the same form in which all the premises are true and the conclusion is false.

The requirement that the English translation makes both premises obviously true and the conclusion obviously false means we should select statements that are widely known and uncontroversial. Let's let H*x* stand for "*x* is a horse," M*x* stand for "*x* is a mammal," and A*x* stand for "*x* is an animal." We then have the following translation:

> All horses are mammals.
> <u>All mammals are animals.</u>
> All animals are horses.

In a valid argument, the truth of the premises must guarantee the truth of the conclusion. Since we've shown that it's possible for this argument to have true premises and a false conclusion, we've proved that it's invalid.

Coming up with counterexamples can be challenging. It's sometimes possible to let your knowledge of truth functions help you. Suppose you're presented with the following argument:

> ($\exists x$)M*x* $\supset$ ($\exists x$)H*x*
> (*x*)(H*x* $\supset$ Q*x*)
> <u>($\exists x$)H*x*</u>
> ($\exists x$)(M*x* • Q*x*)

Remember, we want to come up with a translation in which all the premises are true and the conclusion is false. Our conclusion is a conjunction. That means we only need to make one of the conjuncts false to make the statement false. Let's see if we can find them in the premises. We have the first conjunct, M*x*, as the antecedent of a conditional statement in the first premise. That's good news; any conditional with a false antecedent is true by default. We'll let M*x* stand for some obviously false statement and make all our other statements true. Let's let M*x* = *x* is a mermaid, H*x* = *x* is a horse, and Q*x* = *x* is a quadruped. We then have the following translation:

> If mermaids exist, then horses exist.
> All horses are quadrupeds.
> <u>There is at least one horse.</u>
> There is something that is a mermaid and a quadruped.

We've shown that it's possible for this argument to have all true premises and a false conclusion so we have proven that it's invalid.

The counterexample method can admittedly be difficult, taxing the creativity and imagination of the user. Thus it's generally best for only relatively simple arguments. For more complex argument forms—or when our resourcefulness fails us—it's better to rely on our second method.

APPLY **Possible Worlds**

Students sometimes confuse the finite universe method with philosophical discussions involving possible worlds. These aren't the same thing, but possible world semantics has been one of logic's contributions to popular culture. The concept of possible worlds is—among other things—a way of discussing propositions about necessity, actuality, and possibility. Possible world theories are too complex and controversial to take up in such a limited space. Just think of it as the general idea that we can imagine distinct alternate worlds representing every way our world might have been. This has been the basis for a variety of stories, novels, movies, and television shows, particularly in science fiction. You're probably familiar with these plots involving parallel or alternate worlds. Examples include movies such as *The One*, popular novels like *Talisman* by Stephen King and Peter Straub, or even episodes of popular television shows such as *Star Trek: The Next Generation*. The Canadian film *Possible Worlds* even makes logic's contribution explicit in the title.

10.7B Finite Universe Method

The finite universe method, like the counterexample method, relies on the fact that an argument is valid by virtue of its form. This means that a valid argument remains valid no matter how the actual world changes. At one time, nobody reading this book existed; that is, the world was different in terms of at least one significant feature, the people who inhabited it. Yet *modus ponens* was obviously valid, even though we had not yet heard of it. Someday, no one reading this book will exist. Do you think MP will cease to be valid once we die? Of course not. MP remains a valid argument form regardless of any change in the world.

The point is that adding or subtracting objects from the world—even people—doesn't affect validity. A valid argument stays valid even in a universe containing a single member. If we can show that in a single-member universe (or two- or three-member universe) it's possible for an argument to have all true premises and still have a false conclusion, we've proven that it's invalid. The finite universe method lets us do just that.

How does the model of a single-member universe help? The rationale becomes clearer when we understand what happens to the meaning of universal and existential quantifiers in a very small universe. Imagine a universe which contains only one object, say, for instance, a kangaroo named Bitsy. In such a universe, the universal statement, "Everything in the universe is a marsupial," is equivalent to saying, "Bitsy is a marsupial," since Bitsy *is* everything in that universe. Now the type of equivalence between these two statements is not exactly logical equivalence. Two logically equivalent statements stay logically equivalent regardless of any changes in the universe. Our two statements are equivalent given a universe of a designated size; they are conditionally equivalent. We'll represent this relationship with a new symbol.

$(x)Mx \therefore Mb$ The statement $(x)Mx$ is conditionally equivalent to Mb
$(\exists x)Mx \therefore Mb$ The statement $(\exists x)Mx$ is conditionally equivalent to Mb

IV. Integrative Exercise   In each of the following "proofs," one line involves an error in the use of a rule of predicate logic. Identify the error.

∗1. 1. $(x)(\exists y)(Px \equiv {\sim}Py)$ / $(Pa \equiv {\sim}Pa)$ Premise / Conclusion
    2. $(\exists y)(Pa \equiv {\sim}Py)$ 1 UI
    3. $Pa \equiv {\sim}Pa$ 2 EI

2. 1. $(x)Px \supset (y)Qy$ / $(x)(Px \supset Qx)$ Premise / Conclusion
    2. Pa Assumption
    3. $(x)Px$ 2 UG
    4. $(y)Qy$ 1,3 MP
    5. Qa 4 UI
    6. $Pa \supset Qa$ 2–5 CP
    7. $(x)(Px \supset Qx)$ 6 UG

3. 1. $(x)(Px \supset Qx) \supset (y)Ry$ Premise
    2. $(\exists x){\sim}Rx$ / $(\exists x)(Px \bullet {\sim}Qx)$ Premise / Conclusion
    3. ${\sim}Ra$ 2 EI
    4. $(Pa \supset Qa) \supset Ra$ 1 UI
    5. ${\sim}(Pa \supset Qa)$ 3,4 MT
    6. ${\sim}({\sim}Pa \vee Qa)$ 5 Imp
    7. ${\sim}{\sim}Pa \bullet {\sim}Qa$ 6 DM
    8. $Pa \bullet {\sim}Qa$ 7 DN
    9. $(\exists x)(Px \bullet {\sim}Qx)$ 8 EG

∗4. 1. $(x)(Px \vee Qx) \supset (\exists y)Ry$ Premise
    2. $(\exists y){\sim}Ry$ / $(\exists x)({\sim}Px \bullet {\sim}Qx)$ Premise / Conclusion
    3. ${\sim}(\exists y)Ry$ 2 QN
    4. ${\sim}(x)(Px \vee Qx)$ 1,3 MT
    5. $(\exists x){\sim}(Px \vee Qx)$ 4 QN
    6. ${\sim}(Pa \vee Qa)$ 5 EI
    7. ${\sim}Pa \bullet {\sim}Qa$ 6 DM
    8. $(\exists x)({\sim}Px \bullet {\sim}Qx)$ 7 EG

5. 1. $(x)[Px \supset (\exists y)(Qy \bullet Rxy)]$ Premise
    2. $(x)(Qx \supset Sx)$ /$(\exists y)(x)[Px \supset (Sy \bullet Rxy)]$ Premise / Conclusion
    3. $Pa \supset (\exists y)(Qy \bullet Ray)$ 1 UI
    4. Pa Assumption
    5. $(\exists y)(Qy \bullet Ray)$ 3,4 MP
    6. $Qb \bullet Rab$ 5 EI
    7. Qb 6 Simp
    8. $Qb \supset Sb$ 2 UI
    9. Sb 7,8 MP
    10. Rab 6 Simp
    11. $Sb \bullet Rab$ 9,10 Conj
    12. $Pa \supset (Sb \bullet Rab)$ 4–11 CP
    13. $(x)[Px \supset (Sb \bullet Rxb)]$ 12 UG
    14. $(\exists y)(x)[Px \supset (Sy \bullet Rxy)]$ 13 EG

6. 1. $(x)[Px \supset (Qx \lor Rx)]$ Premise
    2. $(\exists x)(Sx \bullet \sim Qx)$ Premise
    3. $(x)[Rx \supset (Px \bullet Sx)]$ $/ (x)(Px \supset Sx)$ Premise / Conclusion
    4. $Sa \bullet \sim Qa$ 2 EI
    5. $Pa \supset (Qa \lor Ra)$ 1 UI
    6. $Ra \supset (Pa \bullet Sa)$ 3 UI
      7. Pa Assumption
      8. $Qa \lor Ra$ 5,7 MP
      9. $\sim Qa$ 4 Simp
   10. Ra 8,9 DS
   11. $Pa \bullet Sa$ 6,10 MP
   12. Sa 11 Simp
  13. $Pa \supset Sa$ 7–12 CP
  14. $(x)(Px \supset Sx)$ 13 UG

V.   **Integrative Exercise**   Translate each of the following arguments into symbolic notation, and construct a proof.

∗1. McDonald's hypothesis about the sex life of lizards is a scientific theory, but it is not proven. For it is not consistent with some of the evidence, and a scientific theory is proven only if it is consistent with all the evidence.

2. Anyone who buys a used car from Marty is either a fool or has money to burn. Jamie bought a used car from Marty, and he doesn't have money to burn. So there's at least one fool in the world.

3. Any student who has either taken the prerequisites or received permission from the instructor may take this course. Freshmen are students, and some freshmen got the instructor's permission, so some freshmen may take this course.

∗4. The aerospace plane will have a speed of Mach 4 and will therefore have to use hydrogen fuel. That's because any plane moving at Mach 4 must use a fuel that ignites in air moving at that speed, and only hydrogen will ignite in air moving at Mach 4.

5. Anyone who passes an advanced philosophy course has a logical mind, and anyone with a logical mind can master any field of law. Gabrielle passed metaphysics, which is an advanced philosophy course, so she can master torts, which is a field of law.

6. According to Soviet law, any worker employed by a state-owned enterprise was required to cooperate with the KGB. Since anyone who worked was employed by some state-owned enterprise, all workers were required to cooperate with the KGB.

∗7. People who drink too much are either aggressive or withdrawn. Anyone who's aggressive is dangerous, and anyone who's withdrawn is boring. I don't like dangerous or boring people, so I don't like people who drink too much.

8. One is a member of a club only if the club is willing to have him and if he joins the club. But I wouldn't join any club willing to have me, so I am not a member of any club.

9. All physical things have a finite duration. If everything is physical, then the soul is physical; and the soul, if it has a finite duration, is not immortal. So if everything is physical, the soul is not immortal.

∗10. Every decision is an event, and every event is caused by something. A cause is either an event or an agent. So every decision is caused either by an event or by an agent.

11. For any number there is a number larger than it. Therefore there is no number larger

than every other (assuming it is true of all numbers that if one is larger than another, the second is not larger than the first).

12. All personnel except guards left the building. No executive personnel are guards. Since everyone who left the building was safe, all executive personnel were safe.

∗13. Anyone who aids a criminal is immoral, and every dictatorial government is criminal. No

moral person, therefore, would aid a dictatorial government.

14. If not all actions are determined, then people need some standard of choice, and a standard of choice is a moral code. Since some actions are not determined, every person does need a moral code.

VI.   Integrative Exercise   Show that each of the following arguments is valid by constructing a proof.

∗**1.** 1. $(\exists x)Px \supset (y)Qy$ / $(y)(\exists x)(Px \supset Qy)$

2. 1. Sr
   2. $\sim Sj$ / $r \neq j$

3. 1. $(x)[(Px \lor Qx) \supset Rx]$ / $(x)Px \supset (y)Ry$

∗**4.** 1. $(x)[Px \supset (Qx \lor Rx)]$
   2. $(\exists x)(Px \bullet \sim Rx)$ / $(\exists x)Qx$

5. 1. $(x)[(Qx \bullet Rx) \supset Px]$
   2. $(x)[(Qx \bullet Sx) \supset Tx]$
   3. $(\exists x)[Qx \bullet (Rx \lor Sx)]$ / $(\exists x)(Px \lor Tx)$

6. 1. $(\exists x)(y)[Px \bullet (Qy \supset Rxy)]$
   2. $(x)(Px \supset Qx)$ / $(\exists x)Rxx$

∗**7.** 1. $(x)(Px \equiv Qx)$
   2. $(x)[Px \supset (\exists y)Rxy]$
   3. $(\exists x)Qx$ / $(\exists x)(\exists y)Rxy$

8. 1. $(x)(Px \supset Qx) \supset (\exists y)(Ry \bullet Sy)$
   2. $(x)\sim Sx$ / $(\exists x)(Px \bullet \sim Qx)$

9. 1. $(x)(Px \supset Qx)$
   2. $\sim(\exists x)(Qx \bullet Sx)$
   3. $(x)(Rx \supset Sx)$ / $(x)(Px \supset \sim Rx)$

∗**10.** 1. $Tb \bullet (x)(Tx \supset x = b)$
   2. $b \neq g$
   3. $Rg \bullet Wg$ / $(\exists x)(Rx \bullet \sim Tx)$

11. 1. $(x)[(Px \lor Qx) \supset (\exists y)Sy]$
   2. $(\exists x)[Px \bullet (y)(Sy \supset Rxy)]$ / $(\exists x)(\exists y)Rxy$

12. 1. $(x)[Px \lor (\exists y)Rxy]$
   2. $(x)(Qx \supset \sim Px)$
   3. $(x)(y)(Rxy \supset Sy)$ / $(\exists x)Qx \supset (\exists y)Sy$

∗**13.** 1. $(x)(Pxa \supset Rx)$
   2. $(\exists x)(Qx \bullet Pxb)$
   3. $(x)(Qx \supset \sim Rx)$ / $\sim(x)(Pxb \supset Pxa)$

14. 1. $(x)(Px \lor Qx)$
2. $(x)(\exists y)(Rxy \supset {\sim}Px)$
3. $(x)(y)(Qx \supset Sxy)$ $/ (x)(\exists y)(Rxy \supset Sxy)$

15. 1. $(\exists x)\{Px \bullet (y)(z)[(Qy \bullet Rz) \supset Sxyz]\}$
2. $(x)(Px \supset Rx)$ $/ (y)(\exists x)(Qy \supset Sxyx)$

∗16. 1. $(\exists x)(Px \bullet {\sim}Qx) \supset Ra$
2. $(\exists x)Rx \supset (y)(Py \supset Qy)$ $/ (x)(Px \supset Qx)$

17. 1. $Bf \bullet Sf \bullet (x)[{\sim}(Bx \bullet Sx) \lor x = f]$
2. $Bm \bullet Dm$
3. $(\exists x)(Bx \bullet Sx \bullet {\sim}Dx)$ $/ m \neq f$

18. 1. $(x)[Px \supset (Qa \bullet Rxa)]$
2. $(\exists x)(Qx \lor Sx) \supset (y)(z)(Ryz \supset Tyz)$ $/ (x)(\exists y)(Px \supset Txy)$

∗19. 1. $(\exists x)[Qx \bullet (Rx \lor Sx)]$
2. $(x)[(Qx \lor Sx) \supset Tx]$
3. $(x){\sim}(Px \lor Tx)$ $/ (\exists x)[(Qx \bullet Rx) \bullet {\sim}Px]$

20. 1. $(x)\{Px \supset (y)[(Qy \bullet Ry) \supset {\sim}Sxy]\}$
2. $(x)(y)(Txy \supset Sxy)$
3. $(x)(y)Txy$ $/ (x)[Px \supset {\sim}(\exists y)(Qy \bullet Ry)]$

21. 1. $(\exists x)(Px \bullet Qx) \supset (y)(Ry \supset Sy)$
2. $(\exists x)(Px \bullet Rx)$ $/ (\exists x)(Qx \supset Sx)$

∗22. 1. $(x)\{Px \supset (y)[(Qy \bullet Rxy) \supset (\exists z)(Sz \bullet Txyz)]\}$
2. $(x)(\exists y)(Sx \equiv {\sim}Sy)$ $/ (\exists x)(\exists y)[Px \bullet (Qy \bullet Rxy)] \supset {\sim}(z)Sz$

23. 1. $(x)[Px \supset (\exists y)(z)(Qy \bullet Rxyz)]$
2. $(x)(Qx \supset Sx)$
3. $(x)(y)(z)(Rxyz \supset Txz)$ $/ (\exists x)(\exists y)(z)[Px \supset (Sy \bullet Txz)]$

PART THREE

Inductive Logic

In Chapter 2, we discussed the broad differences between two kinds of argument, deduction and induction. The role of a deductive argument is to draw a conclusion that is contained implicitly in the premises. A deductive argument is either valid or invalid; there are no intermediate degrees of partial validity. If the argument is valid, then it is impossible for the premises to be true and the conclusion false. In an inductive argument, the conclusion amplifies—it goes beyond—what the premises state. As a result, the truth of the premises does *not* guarantee the truth of the conclusion; there is some possibility, however small, that the conclusion is false. Inductive arguments have degrees of strength, depending not only on the relationship between premises and conclusion but also on a wider context of other available information.

In Part 2, we studied deduction in depth. We turn now to *induction*, the other broad category of reasoning. In the following chapters, we will learn how to analyze different types of inductive arguments and how to assess the degree of support their premises confer on the conclusion. The basic mode of inductive reasoning consists of drawing a universal conclusion about a class of things from premises about certain members of that class. We will study this process of generalizing in Chapter 11, with particular attention to generalizations about causality. In Chapter 12, we will study arguments based on analogies, especially the use of analogies in moral and legal reasoning. Chapters 13 and 14 cover statistical inferences and probability, respectively. Finally, in Chapter 15, we will draw on preceding chapters to understand the nature of explanations, especially in science; and we will examine the nature of genuine scientific reasoning as opposed to pseudoscientific "explanations."

11 Generalization and Causality

LEARNING OBJECTIVES

On successful completion of the chapter, you will be able to:

✅ Understand the nature of generalizations and the rules for evaluating them. (11.1)

✅ Understand the difference between necessary and sufficient conditions. (11.2)

✅ Learn to recognize and apply the methods of agreement and difference and their combined use. (11.3)

✅ Learn to recognize and apply the methods of concomitant variations and residues. (11.4)

We use deductive reasoning whenever we act on the basis of general knowledge—knowledge about classes of things and the properties they share. We acquire that knowledge in various ways, but primarily by generalizing from our experience—a form of inductive argument. This process is captured by the old saying "Once burned, twice shy." A child who burns himself on a stove does not treat this as an isolated experience; he draws a general conclusion that will guide his future transactions with hot stoves. In the same way, all of us rely on countless generalizations we have drawn from experience: An egg will break if it's dropped; steel is stronger than wood; we can't breathe under water; shy people tend to be nervous at parties. Imagine trying to live your life without the benefit of such knowledge, treating each experience as a completely new encounter with the world, with no expectations about how things will behave or what the consequences of your actions will be.

In this chapter, we will examine the nature of inductive generalizations and the standards for evaluating them, with special emphasis on generalizations about causality.

11.1 Generalizing

In logical terms, we can see the importance of generalizing by going back to what we learned about deductive arguments. Each of the following propositions was a premise of a deductive argument in a previous chapter:

> All of Shakespeare's plays are in blank verse.
>
> No antlered animal is a predator.
>
> All geniuses are eccentric.
>
> Uncommunicative people do not make friends easily.
>
> Bill never admits he's wrong.
>
> If a mass of hot, humid air collides with a high-pressure mass of cooler air, then it rains.

Each of these is a *general* proposition. It says something about an entire class: Shakespeare's plays, antlered animals, masses of hot, humid air, and so on. When we studied deductive reasoning, we wanted to know what conclusions we could draw from these propositions. Now we want to know how these propositions would themselves be supported by evidence.

Each of them could be treated as the conclusion of a further deductive argument. For example, the second proposition might be supported as follows:

> No herbivore is a predator.
> <u>All antlered animals are herbivores.</u>
> No antlered animal is a predator.

This is a perfectly good argument, but it doesn't really solve the problem, because now we have two new general premises that will need some support. In the same way, the final proposition might be deduced from a more general theory about the properties of air masses, but then we would have to ask what evidence we have for that theory. The implication is that we cannot support a general proposition merely by deducing it from other general propositions. At *some* point in our reasoning, for conclusions like each of these, we have to look at the actual instances of the general propositions. We have to examine Shakespeare's plays, the different species of antlered animals, the geniuses we know or have read about, etc., and then draw the general conclusion from the particular cases.

But there are dangers here, in particular the danger of *hasty generalization*. Hasty generalization is a fallacy because a single instance doesn't necessarily prove a general rule. Suppose we have a general proposition of the form "All S are P." If an individual member of the class of Ss is P, it is called a **positive instance**, and it confirms the generalization; if it is not P, it is a **negative instance** or counterexample, and it disconfirms the generalization. But there is a logical asymmetry here. A single negative instance decisively refutes a general statement. If I say that all athletes are dumb, and you point out that the varsity quarterback is getting excellent grades, you have proved me wrong. A single *positive* instance, however, does not prove that a generalization is *true*. The fact that one athlete is a weak student doesn't prove that all of them are. How is it possible, then, to support a universal proposition merely by looking at examples?

If S stands for a small, delimited class of things, we can solve this problem by examining each member of the class individually to see whether it is P. In the first proposition, for example, the class is Shakespeare's plays—the 37 plays he wrote during his life. It would be feasible to examine each of them and to determine whether it is in blank verse. In fact, this is the *only* way to tell whether the proposition is true, because there's no particular reason why Shakespeare *had* to write all his plays in that form. This is called the method of induction by *complete enumeration*, and it is appropriate when we are dealing with small classes—an author's complete works, the members of a family, the clothes in your closet—where we know something about each member individually.

But most of the generalizations we use in everyday reasoning do not involve classes of that type. They involve classes that are open-ended: There is no limit on the number of members they may have. To claim that all geniuses are eccentric, for example, is to make a statement about the entire class of geniuses—*all* of them, past, present, and future, the obscure ones as well as the famous. Obviously, we cannot examine each member of this class individually. Even in the fifth example, which concerns a single individual, we are still concerned with the open-ended class of occasions on which Bill is wrong. We cannot know anything about the future occasions, and even if we know Bill extremely well, we almost certainly don't know about all the past occasions. With the exception of the first, all the propositions on our list are of this type, and we cannot establish their truth or falsity by the method of complete enumeration.

So we have to rely on an incomplete survey of the class, a *sample* taken from the class as a whole, and infer that what is true of the sample is true of the class. This mode of inference is legitimate when we are dealing with classes of things that possess common traits—properties, relationships, and ways of acting. Those traits are connected in various ways, so that anything possessing a given trait will also possess another one. Members of the same biological species, for example, are alike in their basic survival needs, their method of reproduction, and many other properties. Systems of classification usually pick out classes of objects that share more than a single trait—especially when we classify in accordance with an essential principle. We find the same kind of connection in cause-and-effect relationships. Copper conducts electricity because of its atomic structure, and any substance with the same structure will also conduct electricity. Of course, an object may possess traits that are *not* connected. A given person might have red hair and a short temper, but despite popular mythology, there is no known connection between these properties and thus no reason to expect that all redheads have short tempers.

What we need, therefore, are guidelines to determine whether a sample will give us a well-supported generalization rather than a hasty one. Three rules will help us to decide. These rules are standards for assessing the strength of the inference from sample to generalization, and they are analogous to the rules for determining whether a syllogism is valid. But remember that generalizing is a type of induction, in which—unlike deduction—strength is a matter of degree. So instead of the clear-cut distinction between valid and invalid arguments that we found in studying deduction, we are now going to have to work with a continuum ranging from weak to strong. The rules should be regarded as guidelines to help us locate a given generalization along that continuum.

11.1A Three Rules for Generalizing

1. The sample should be sufficiently numerous and various.

A single instance is usually not enough to support a generalization. In the absence of other knowledge, the fact that a single S is P won't tell us whether S and P are connected, so generalizing that all S are P would be hasty. We need to look at a number of Ss; if all of them are P, then we have better evidence of a connection. But it is even more important to test a *variety* of Ss. If you were buying a car and were considering a Toyota, you might ask people who own Toyotas whether they are satisfied. Suppose that all of them have had problems with the car. If the people all bought cars of the same model year, from the same dealer, with the same package of options, then the problems might be due to one of these other common factors. Your conclusion that Toyotas are poor cars would be stronger if you varied these factors, checking cars of different years, with different options, bought from different dealers.

How much variety is enough? The general rule is that a sample of Ss should vary in every property (other than being S) that *might* be responsible for their being P. Consider the generalization that shy people are nervous at parties. In your sample of shy people, you would certainly want to vary such personality factors as intelligence and degree of interest in people, because these might well affect their nervousness at parties. You would also want your sample to vary in background: Are shy people with lots of social experience as nervous at parties as shy people with little social experience? In contrast, factors such as blood type, political views, or favorite movie do not seem even potentially relevant to the generalization, and there would be no need to vary them.

As the example indicates, deciding whether a given property might be relevant is a judgment call and depends on what other knowledge we have—a point we'll come back to when discussing rule 3. It also depends on how broad or sweeping our conclusion is. A given company, for example, might be classified under concepts of increasing abstractness: STEEL COMPANY, MANUFACTURING FIRM, CORPORATION. A generalization about all manufacturing firms requires a larger and more varied sample than does a generalization about steel companies, and a generalization about all corporations requires an even larger and more varied sample. In general, the more abstract the subject term of the conclusion, the more numerous and varied the sample must be.

2. We should look for disconfirming as well as confirming instances of a generalization.

A generalization is disconfirmed by negative instances or counterexamples: *S*s that are not *P*, Toyota owners who are satisfied with their cars, shy people who are not nervous at parties. If we have looked hard for negative instances and haven't found any, we can be more confident of a generalization than we can if we haven't looked at all.

This rule is important for two reasons, one logical, the other psychological. The logical reason pertains to a key difference between inductive and deductive inference. A deductive argument is self-contained: The premises either do or do not support the conclusion, regardless of what other knowledge we might have. An inductive argument, in contrast, is *not* self-contained. The premises are propositions stating information about the sample, and the degree to which these premises support the conclusion depends on whether we have any *other* information about disconfirming instances. So it's important to look for such information.

The psychological reason is the phenomenon of *confirmation bias*: the tendency to look for and give weight to evidence supporting a conclusion while ignoring, downplaying, or failing to seek evidence against it. As we saw in Chapter 4, confirmation bias is a pervasive problem in many areas of knowledge, caused both by emotional commitments to our beliefs and by cognitive tendencies that make confirming evidence more salient to us than disconfirming evidence. One cognitive factor of particular importance here is that, in everyday contexts, we must find evidence for or against a generalization by searching our memories for positive and negative instances. In most cases, it would be impossible to remember every single experience that might be relevant. What we can extract from memory tends to be influenced by what we are looking for. If we search only for positive cases, those are probably the only ones we're going to find. To avoid this bias, we need to make a special effort to look for counterexamples as well.

How do we look for negative instances? There's no general rule; it depends on each particular case. But one technique is worth mentioning. When we look for instances to test a generalization that all *S* are *P*, we are looking for individual referents of the concept *S*. The easiest referents to recall are the prototypical ones, the central, clear-cut cases. But we should also look for referents close to the borderline of the concept, because many generalizations are true only of the prototypical cases, not of atypical *S*s. If you are wondering whether all birds can fly, don't think just of obvious examples like robins and crows; think also of penguins and ostriches. If you are wondering whether all democracies protect individual rights, don't look just at modern cases like England and the United States; think also of ancient Athens.

3. We should consider whether a link between S and P is plausible in light of other knowledge we possess.

To see the point of this rule, consider two contrasting cases. If chemists discovered a new metal, they would determine its melting point in a laboratory, and a single test would be sufficient to support the generalization that all instances of the metal melt at that temperature. However, the generalization that all swans are white was confirmed by countless instances over a long period of time, yet it was always regarded as somewhat shaky, and eventually black swans were indeed discovered in Australia. Rule 3 explains the difference between these cases. Our scientific knowledge about physical substances tells us that the melting point of a metal is fixed by its atomic structure, which defines that type of metal. So we know ahead of time that all samples of the metal will have the same melting point, whatever it might be, and a single test is enough to identify that point. By contrast, biological theory gives us no reason for thinking that all swans must have the same color, so even a great many positive instances will not make the generalization certain.

These three rules for generalizing, taken together, illustrate a point already mentioned: the open-ended character of induction. Unlike a deductive argument, an inductive one is not self-contained. Its strength is affected by the context of other knowledge we possess. The truth of the premises does not guarantee the truth of the conclusion, and the degree of support the premises provide for the conclusion depends on factors not contained in the argument itself. It is always possible to strengthen an inductive argument further by finding additional positive instances, especially if they increase the variety of the sample (rule 1). But the strength of the argument is dependent on our diligence in looking for disconfirming evidence (rule 2). Its strength also depends on the initial plausibility of the generalization, which is determined by the body of related knowledge we have (rule 3). This is not a defect of induction. But it does mean that inductive reasoning puts a special premium on *integration*, on looking beyond the argument itself to see how it fits with the rest of our knowledge.

The three rules we have just examined are applicable to generalizations of most kinds. Appropriately enough, they are *general* rules. But there are different kinds of generalizations, and for each kind we can formulate more specific rules. In the next section of this chapter, we will study the rules for identifying *causal* relationships. In Chapter 13, we will look at *statistical* generalizations.

EXERCISE 11.1

Use your experience and the rules for generalizing to explain what kind of evidence you would need in order to evaluate each of the following generalizations inductively. In each case, indicate how the rules would guide your reasoning.

*1. The food at restaurant X [pick one you know] is lousy.

2. Italians are hot-tempered.

3. The soil in my garden is highly acidic.

*4. Dogs always go around in circles when they lie down.

5. Ms. or Mr. X [pick someone you know] works well under pressure.

6. None of the clothes in my closet is new.

*7. Doctors have high incomes.

8. Heroes in tragic drama always have a fatal flaw.

9. All religions involve belief in a god or gods.

*10. All geniuses are eccentric.

11. Price controls produce shortages.

12. Without antitrust laws, industries would be dominated by monopolies.

*13. Glass is fragile.

14. All leafy green vegetables contain antioxidants.

15. Wood does not conduct electricity.

11.2 Causality

Generalizing is an effort to identify connections among traits. But the term *connection* is pretty vague. What sort of relationship are we talking about? In most cases, we are talking about *causality*. Causality may involve interactions among things: Collisions between air masses produce rain, a lighted match will set paper on fire. Or it may be a connection between the properties of an object and the way it acts: Uncommunicative people don't make friends easily, a car's design affects its performance, a charged particle will attract or repel other charged particles. Or it may involve a causal link among properties themselves: Steel is hard because of its structure, human beings possess language because they possess reason. In one way or another, many generalizations have to do with causality, and we need to study this relationship more closely.

If you've ever skidded on an icy road, you can imagine what a world without causality would be like. That sudden loss of control, when turning the wheel or pumping the brakes has no effect on the car—imagine the same thing on a wider scale, imagine losing control over *everything*. That thought experiment shows how central causality is to our sense of the world. We expect events to follow regular patterns: Touching a hot stove leads to pain, pumping the brakes makes the car slow down, studying improves our grasp of a subject. We expect objects to act within limits set by their natures: Human beings cannot fly by flapping their arms, rocks don't engage in reasoning, dictators do not welcome opposition. And even if there is no direct causal relation between two traits that seem connected, they may both be effects of a deeper cause. A sore throat and sneezing tend to go together when you have a cold. Neither causes the other; they are both symptoms of the virus at work in your system.

As these examples illustrate, the term *causality* covers a very broad range. Different types of causality can be found in different regions of nature and human life, and the various branches of science have developed specialized techniques for studying causality in their own areas. But we are going to look at a general-purpose technique that will help us identify and analyze causal relationships of any type. The basis of this technique is a distinction between necessary and sufficient conditions.

A given causal factor *a* is a *necessary* condition for an effect *E* when *E* cannot exist or occur without *a*. Factor *a* is a *sufficient* condition for *E* when *a* is enough to guarantee that *E* exists or occurs. To see the difference, let's take a simple example: You drop an egg and it breaks. The effect—condition *E*—is the breaking of the egg. What factors are responsible for making this happen? What factors play the role of *a*? The obvious factor is (1) that you dropped the egg. We would ordinarily think of this as *the* cause, because it is the event that led directly to the effect. But there are other factors involved as well: (2) the hardness of the floor, (3) the fragility of the eggshell, and (4) the fact that the egg is heavier than air. Without 2 and 3, the egg would not have broken when it fell, and without 4 it would not have fallen in the first place. Thus 2, 3, and 4 are all necessary conditions for the effect. What is the sufficient condition? All by itself, 1 is not sufficient—because it would not have produced the effect in the absence of the other conditions. So the sufficient condition is the *combination* of all four factors.

Notice that one condition can be necessary without being sufficient. The fragility of the eggshell is necessary for it to break, but not sufficient—otherwise the egg would break even without being dropped. In contrast, a condition can be sufficient without being necessary. Together with the other factors, factor 1 is a sufficient condition for the effect, but there are other ways in which the eggshell could have broken: It could have been hit with a hammer, the chick inside could have hatched, and so on.

Notice also that 2, 3, and 4 are standing conditions. They are properties of the egg and its environment that endure over time; they were present all along. The act of dropping the egg, by contrast, was a stimulus or *triggering event* that occurred at a specific moment and made the egg break a moment later. In everyday speech, when we speak of *the* cause of an effect, we usually mean the triggering event. But not always. When a bridge with a structural flaw collapses during a high wind, the wind is the triggering event, but we would probably say that the flaw was the cause of the collapse. Why? Because we expect a bridge to be able to withstand winds, and most of them do. It is the flaw that distinguishes this bridge from those that do not fall in high winds. In this way, our notion of *the* cause of an event is governed partly by expectations based on our general knowledge; it is affected by what strikes us as the salient or distinctive feature of a situation. Logically, however, we would analyze this case in exactly the same way as we analyzed the breaking egg.

So far we have been talking about the cause of an *event*, but we can also talk about the cause of a *property*. The fragility of the eggshell, for example, is a standing condition that is partly responsible for its breaking. In that respect we are treating fragility as a cause. But when we ask *why* eggshells are fragile, we are considering the property of fragility as an effect of deeper causes: the shape and composition of the shell. Many of our generalizations involve causal connections of this type. When we conclude that all S are P, it is generally because we are convinced there is something in the nature of Ss that makes them P: Something in the nature of steel makes it stronger than wood, something in Bill's personality makes him unwilling to admit he's wrong, something in the design of a car makes it unreliable. One of the main goals of science is to find the necessary and sufficient conditions for the properties of physical substances, social institutions, individual personalities, and other phenomena.

In short, we study causal relationships by trying to identify the factors that are necessary and/or sufficient for the effect we want to explain. This is what's wrong with the *post hoc* fallacy, the assumption that because *a* preceded *E*, *a* must have caused *E*. The fact that *a* came first is certainly relevant, but all by itself it gives us no reason to think that *a* was either necessary or sufficient for *E*.

What sort of evidence, then, *can* we use? The 19th-century philosopher John Stuart Mill formulated several methods for establishing evidence of a causal connection. They are known as the methods of *agreement*, *difference*, *concomitant variations*, and *residues*. Despite their formidable names, Mill's methods are used in everyday, commonsense reasoning about causality; they are also used by scientists in designing experiments.

11.3 Mill's Methods: Agreement and Difference

Suppose you were trying to figure out why you liked certain courses you've taken. You would probably start by looking for something those courses had in common. Did they share the same subject matter? Were the class discussions interesting? Did all the teachers have the same style, approach, or ability? Suppose the common factor turned out to be lively class discussions. To test the conclusion that this was the source of your enjoyment, the next step would be to look at courses that did *not* have such discussions and see whether you *didn't* enjoy them.

This example illustrates two fundamental techniques for identifying the cause of a given effect. First, we look for a common factor that is present in all the cases in which the effect occurs. When doctors are confronted with a new disease, they typically try to see whether the people who have the disease all ate the same food, or have the same virus in their blood, or are similar in some other way. A detective trying to solve a series of murders might ask whether the victims had something in common. Mill called this technique the **method of agreement**: We look for some respect in which the various cases agree.

Second, to test whether a given factor plays a causal role, we take away that factor, holding everything else constant, and see whether the effect still occurs. If your car makes a funny noise when you accelerate, take your foot off the pedal and see whether the noise goes away. If a baby is crying and you think he might be hungry, see whether the crying stops when you feed him. Scientists use the same technique when they do controlled experiments. In testing the efficacy of a new medicine, for example, they use two carefully matched groups of people. One group gets the drug, the other gets a placebo; the *only* relevant difference between the groups is the presence or absence of the drug, so that any difference in results can then be attributed to that factor. Mill called this the **method of difference**.

To understand these techniques, and to identify their use in different contexts, it helps to represent them schematically.

$$\begin{array}{ll}
& \text{Case 1:} \quad a, b, c \rightarrow E \\
\text{Method of agreement:} & \text{Case 2:} \quad a, d, f \rightarrow E \\
& \underline{\text{Case 3:} \quad a, g, h \rightarrow E} \\
& \text{Therefore, } a \text{ is responsible for } E.
\end{array}$$

Each row represents a separate premise of the argument; it represents a case or situation in which the effect, E, occurs. For example, each row might stand for an individual course, and E would be your response to it. The lowercase letters represent the various factors present in the different situations. There will not always be exactly three cases, or exactly three factors. And it won't always happen that the factors other than a appear only once; b, c, and the others might be present in more than one case. What is crucial to the method of agreement is that only one factor is present in *all* the cases. The conclusion says that the factor present in all cases is responsible for the effect. Notice that this conclusion is a generalization. We are saying that a will cause E in all cases, not just those we have examined, so we are generalizing from a sample to a universal proposition. Indeed, the method of agreement is simply the first rule for generalizing, as applied to the study of causality: We identify a link between a and E by varying the other factors.

The method of difference is depicted similarly.

$$\begin{array}{ll}
& \text{Case 1:} \quad a, b, c \rightarrow \quad E \\
\text{Method of difference:} & \underline{\text{Case 2:} \quad -, b, c \rightarrow \sim E} \\
& \text{Therefore, } a \text{ is responsible for } E.
\end{array}$$

The tilde in front of E in the second line is a sign of negation: It indicates that E does not occur in this case. Once again, there may be any number of factors in each case, but this time there *is* a reason for including just the two cases. The conclusion is a generalization, as before, but we are not generalizing from a sample of positive instances. We are contrasting a single positive instance with a negative instance that is identical except for the absence of one factor, in order to isolate the causal role of that factor. It is crucial, therefore, that all the factors other than a be reproduced in case 2.

The methods of agreement and difference are typically combined, both in everyday reasoning and in science. We will call this combination the **joint method** of agreement and difference (though Mill meant something different by this term), and we can represent its structure as follows:

We have simply taken the method of agreement, as diagrammed above, and contrasted each positive instance with a case that is identical except for the absence of *a*. Not every use of the joint method would be this thorough. We might use the method of difference with only one of the positive instances, or only a few, especially if we have a large number of positive instances. But even a single contrasting case strengthens considerably the evidence provided by the method of agreement.

Let's look at an example of the joint method in action. In the early efforts to find the causes of AIDS, medical researchers found that the disease inhibits certain white blood cells called granulocytes. Why does this happen? Medical researchers found that the inhibiting factor is in the blood serum (the liquid part of blood) rather than in the granulocytes themselves. When they extracted the granulocytes from AIDS patients and combined them with serum from normal donors, the granulocytes were no longer inhibited. But when healthy granulocytes were combined with serum from AIDS patients, the granulocytes *were* inhibited. The effect here is the inhibition of the granulocytes, and we have two factors: the granulocyte cells and the blood serum. In AIDS patients (case 1, below), both the cells and the serum are diseased. The other two cases represent the researchers' results:

Case 1:	sick cells,	sick serum	$\rightarrow$	inhibition of cells
Case 2:	sick cells,	healthy serum	$\rightarrow$	~inhibition of cells
Case 3:	healthy cells,	sick serum	$\rightarrow$	inhibition of cells

Therefore, the cause of the inhibition is in the serum.

Cases 1 and 2 together constitute the method of difference: When sick cells are put into healthy serum, they are no longer inhibited. Cases 1 and 3 together constitute the method of agreement: When the serum is diseased, the granulocytes will be inhibited, regardless of whether they are themselves diseased or healthy.

To see why it is so valuable to combine the methods of agreement and difference, remember the distinction we drew between necessary and sufficient conditions. The method of agreement, by itself, provides evidence that *a* is *sufficient* for *E*. Since the effect can occur in the absence of any other factor, none of the other factors is necessary, so we have reason to think that *a* is sufficient. But we have less reason to think that *a* is *necessary*, since there may be more than one way to bring about the effect. In the case of your course preferences, you might like some courses because of class discussion and others because the subject is especially interesting. To tell whether *a* is necessary, we need to see whether the effect can occur in its absence—and that is what the method of difference tells us. This method provides good evidence that *a* is necessary. If used by itself, however, it does not support very well the conclusion that *a* is sufficient. Why not? Because the two cases:

Case 1: $a, b, c \rightarrow E$
Case 2: $-, b, c \rightarrow \sim E$

leave open the possibility that *b* and *c* are necessary for the effect. (In our example of the egg breaking, *b* might be the fragility of the eggshell and *c* the hardness of the floor.) Thus the methods of agreement and difference have complementary strengths. If we are trying to show that *a* is necessary and sufficient for *E*, we need to use the methods in combination.

Agreement and difference are also used in a negative way to show that a given factor is *not* responsible for an effect. Suppose someone claimed that America's economic wealth was the result of its abundant natural resources. A counterargument would be that some countries with abundant resources, such as Sierra Leone, are *not* wealthy, and that some countries without many resources, such as Luxembourg, *are* wealthy. The first part of this argument is a negative use of the method of agreement. It says that the alleged cause is present in cases where we do not find the effect; hence that factor is not sufficient. The second part of the argument is a negative use of the method of difference. It says that we can take away the alleged cause and still have the effect; hence that factor is not necessary. In general, a negative use of agreement has the structure:

Case 1: $a, b, c \rightarrow E$
Case 2: $a, d, f \rightarrow E$
Case 3: $a, g, h \rightarrow \sim E$
Therefore, a is not sufficient for E.

And a negative use of difference has the structure:

Case 1: $a, b, c \rightarrow E$
Case 2: $-, b, c \rightarrow E$
Therefore, a is not necessary for E.

Notice that, to the left of the arrows in both cases, we have the same arrangement of factors as in the corresponding positive arguments. The difference is solely to the right of the arrows—in whether the effect does or does not occur.

The methods of agreement and difference can provide very strong evidence of a causal connection. If we know all the factors involved, if we have varied all of them in accordance with the methods, and if a is the only factor in whose presence the effect always occurs and in whose absence it does not occur—then the evidence may be decisive. But these are very big *if*s. Sometimes there is more than one factor common to all the cases—and sometimes there isn't *any* single common factor. It often happens that we cannot vary all the factors exhaustively. And we are rarely if ever in a position to be sure that we know what all the factors are. Let's look at four of the more common problems in this regard.

Choosing the factors. We have been assuming so far that there is a definite number of antecedent factors, and a small number at that—perhaps three or four. Strictly speaking, however, there is always an indefinitely large number of factors in the environment of the effect, and in paying attention to only a few of them, we are making a selection. Scientists studying a chemical reaction, for example, will attend to the chemicals involved and the temperature at which the reaction occurs. They will ignore such factors as what they had for breakfast that morning or the price of gold on the London market. So the use of Mill's methods involves *plausibility* judgments. Is it plausible that a given factor could be related to the effect? Do we need to vary it or can it safely be ignored? Plausibility judgments in turn are guided by the knowledge we already possess. In the above example, chemical theory gives ample reason for ignoring the price of gold. But we need to remember that these judgments are fallible. At one time, for instance, no one realized that air pressure might affect the temperature at which water boils, so no one thought to do the experiment at different altitudes above sea level.

Levels of causality. Causal relationships exist at many different levels in the world, from the interactions of subatomic particles, to the chemical structure of a substance, to the biological activity of a single cell, to the behavior of an individual person, to the economy of an entire nation. The problem this poses is that we may look to the wrong level in selecting the factors to study. The problem can be illustrated by an old joke in inductive logic. A man says, "Last weekend I had scotch and soda and got drunk. Monday I had brandy and soda and got drunk again. Yesterday I had bourbon and soda and got drunk again. Obviously the soda is what's making me drunk." The point of the joke is that the type of hard liquor is not the level at which to look for the cause; the real causal factor, the alcoholic content of the drinks, is at the chemical level.

To take a more serious example, researchers trying to isolate the causes of cancer need to consider both genetic factors and lifestyle. These potential causes exist at different levels—the biochemistry of DNA and the behavior of the person, respectively—and require different kinds of experimental evidence. In the same way, historians trying to explain the rise of Nazism disagree about what kind of explanation to look for: economic conditions, cultural trends, or some other type of factor. In such cases, the ideal procedure would be to vary factors at all the levels in a comprehensive fashion. But this is extremely difficult to do, and often impossible; scientists typically choose some particular level to study, on the assumption that the causes will be found there. So we need to be aware of the issue, and we should try to identify those assumptions whenever possible.

Conceptualization. When we notice that a particular effect occurs in a certain situation, we know that the cause is something in that situation. Before we can use Mill's methods, we have to break the situation down into individual factors. Nature won't do this for us. The factors don't come already divided, packaged, and labeled as *a*, *b*, *c*, etc. We have to analyze the circumstances and isolate the factors ourselves. This is essentially a problem of classification; we try to organize the situation in terms of concepts we possess. But we have seen that there is usually more than one way to classify the same set of things, and this can affect our use of inductive methods. An obvious example is the borderline case. A sociologist studying the effects of economic status on the divorce rate will have to draw a line somewhere between the lower and middle classes. Within limits, that line can be drawn at many different places, so that a family might be treated as lower class in one study, middle class in another. This will obviously affect the results of the studies.

Let's look at a more radical case. Suppose you found that the courses you enjoy don't seem to have anything in common. They don't all have good discussions, the teachers don't give the same sorts of lectures, and so on. It may be that you need to rethink your analysis of the factors. Perhaps the real cause is something that cuts across the factors you've been looking at. Suppose the real source of your enjoyment is that, regardless of how the class is organized in terms of lectures and discussions, the teacher makes the learning process a kind of game. If so, you won't discover that fact until you step back from your original way of analyzing the situation and try to classify factors in a different way. We should also notice that the issue of conceptualization applies to the *effect* as well as to the *factors*. In biology and psychology, for example, there is a vast literature on the causes of aggression. But some people argue that aggression per se is too broad a category to study effectively; the different species of aggression should be studied separately because they may have different causes.

Direction of causality. When the methods of agreement and difference reveal a causal relation between *a* and *E*, we have been assuming that it is clear which is the cause, which is the effect. But this is not always so clear. Night follows day with perfect regularity, but day does not cause night; they are joint effects of an underlying cause, the rotation of the earth. It might even turn out that E is the cause and a the effect. To use our old example one more time, suppose that the courses you enjoyed *did* all have lively class discussions. The liveliness of the discussions might be a consequence, rather than a cause, of the fact that you (and the other students) are enjoying the course. So we cannot use the methods of induction mechanically. We have to interpret the results. There is evidence that criminals have an abnormally high rate of unemployment. Does this mean that unemployment drives people to crime? Or do criminal tendencies—perhaps the result of personality or other factors—lead some people to avoid regular work? Or are crime and unemployment joint effects of some underlying cause? To answer these questions, we would have to make judgments about plausibility, appeal to broader theories of human nature, and look for additional inductive evidence.

The problems we have just examined do not discredit induction. We can deal with them by using Mill's methods of agreement and difference. But the problems show that we have to be careful if we want to avoid hasty judgments. And these problems are interesting in a theoretical sense because they reveal once again the contextual nature of induction, the fact that inductive reasoning is affected by the context of other knowledge we possess.

SOLVE Agreement and Difference

To evaluate an inductive argument that uses the methods of agreement or difference:

1. Identify the effect and the factor that the conclusion claims is the cause.

2. If the method used in the argument is:

   a. Agreement, then check whether the factor is the only one present in each case;

   b. Difference, then check that the factor is present when the effect occurs and absent when it doesn't, and that all other factors are the same.

3. Consider whether:

   a. The argument includes all the factors potentially relevant to the effect;

   b. The factors are at an appropriate level of causation;

   c. The factors and effect have been conceptualized in a reasonable way;

   d. The direction of causality could be the opposite of what the argument claims (could the effect actually be the cause of the factor?), or both the factor and the effect could be joint results of an underlying cause.

EXERCISE 11.3

Analyze each of the inductive arguments below. First identify the conclusion: Is it positive or negative? Which factor is being said to be (or not to be) the cause of which effect? Then identify the method used to support the conclusion: agreement, difference, or the joint method. Use the standard schema to represent the cases. Finally, look for problems in the use of the methods.

✳1. ScourClean Cleansing Powder cleans best! We'll scrub half of this dirty sink with a leading cleanser, the other half with ScourClean. Look at the difference!

2. The bull markets of the 2000s and 2010s occurred throughout different phases of the business cycle. In some years unemployment was high; in others it was low. In some cases business profits were high; in other cases they were not. But during these periods interest rates were low or falling. So interest rates clearly affect stock prices.

3. We've all noticed that Monday through Wednesday, when Don is in the office, everyone works well together and a lot gets done. The rest of the week, when he is gone, the same people are not as productive. Don must be the cause of the difference in productivity.

✳4. I planted zinnias in a flower bed with uniform soil, and I watered them all the same, but half the bed got full sun, and the zinnias grew taller there than in the other half, which was partly shaded. So the amount of sunlight makes a difference.

5. Poverty is not the cause of crime, as there are many poor people who are not criminals.

6. Focused attention to the subject is the key to learning. Students who attend carefully improve their knowledge, regardless of differences in ability. Students who are otherwise similar in ability, but do not attend to the subject, make little or no progress.

✳7. If product safety regulations discouraged the introduction of new products, then innovation in the widget industry should have declined after the Widget Control Act was passed. But innovation continued at the same pace.

8. Self-esteem appears to be at least a necessary condition for happiness. All the happy people I've known, whatever their other differences in personality and goals, seem to have basic self-esteem, whereas people who don't have that trait never seem to be happy.

9. In a controlled study, three cars of different types, of different ages, and from different manufacturers were tested for gas mileage before and after a tune-up. In every case, mileage improved after the tune-up, which shows that a well-tuned engine affects fuel efficiency.

✳10. In the past few days I have had four email messages bounce back as undeliverable. They were sent to different people. One was a new contact, one was a reply to someone who emailed me, and the other two were people I email frequently. Of those two, one message had an attachment; none of the others did. They all had gmail addresses, though. Gmail must be blocking my messages.

II. [Integrative Exercise] For each of the following statements, decide whether you think it is true (a) by finding a deductive argument for or against it; and (b) by evaluating the inductive evidence for it.

∗1. All narrative literature (plays, novels, epic poems) involves conflict.

2. Familiarity breeds contempt.

3. People who fear confrontation are eager to forgive those who wrong them.

∗4. Racial or sexual harassment of any kind results in the loss of self-esteem for the victim.

5. Any stable society has a large middle class.

III. [Integrative Exercise] Each of the following passages presents evidence for or against a causal connection. Identify the effect (*E*), the proposed cause (*a*), and decide whether the author is supporting or rejecting the claim that *a* causes *E*. Then identify the method being used.

∗1. In the Clinton section of Manhattan, pigeons were roosting on many apartment buildings. Residents in three buildings put plastic replicas of great horned owls on the rooftops. Result: no pigeons on those buildings.

"'The owls work,' said Sarah Weinberg. . . . 'A month ago we could not stand outside the door because of all this gook falling from the sky.'" [*New York Times*]

2. When salmon are old enough to spawn, they return from the ocean to the stream in which they were born. How do they tell which stream to return to? Researchers have found that they navigate chiefly by olfactory clues. The chemical composition of each stream is distinctive, and young salmon imprint on that odor during a narrow window in their development. Fish who are caught and moved to a hatchery just before this narrow window will return to the hatchery, not their natal stream, when they are ready to spawn. Researchers have also shown that juvenile salmon exposed to synthetic chemicals, such as morpholine or beta-phenylethyl alcohol (PEA), at the time of imprinting will be attracted, when they return to spawn, into an unfamiliar stream scented with one of these chemicals.

3. ". . . decoration is not given to hide horrible things: but to decorate things already adorable. A mother does not give her child a blue bow because he is so ugly without it. A

lover does not give a girl a necklace to hide her neck." [G. K. Chesterton, *Orthodoxy*]

∗4. "While we typically associate economic growth with technological development, organizational innovation has played an equal if not more important role since the beginning of the industrial revolution. . . .

"The development of transoceanic commerce in the fifteenth century depended on the invention of the carrack, which could sail beyond coastal waters. But it also depended on the creation of the joint-stock company, by which individuals could pool their resources and share risks entailed in funding great voyages. The extension of the railroads across the continental United States in the mid-nineteenth century required large, hierarchically organized companies with geographically dispersed managers." [Francis Fukuyama, *Trust*]

5. "As far as causing mental states is concerned, the crucial step is the one that goes on inside the head, not the external or peripheral stimulus. And the argument for this is simple. If the events outside the central nervous system occurred, but nothing happened in the brain, there would be no mental events. But if the right things happened in the brain, the mental events would occur even if there was no outside stimulus. (And that, by the way, is the principle on which surgical anaesthesia works: the outside stimulus is pre-

vented from having the relevant effects on the central nervous system.)" [John Searle, *Minds, Brains and Science*]

6. People who commit violent crimes have a higher incidence of brain damage than other people—including seizures, head injuries, and other neurological deficits—and some theorists have claimed that such damage is the cause of their violent behavior. But as neurologist Richard M. Restak points out, "most people thus afflicted do not go on to commit violent crimes. For every Robert Harris [a convicted murderer] who may display signs of brain damage, there are many more people with similar histories who have never even thrown a punch." [Richard M. Restak, "See No Evil," *The Sciences*]

∗7. Snowshoe hares like to eat green alder shrubs. Both the stems and the flower buds are nutritious for the hares, but they eat only the stems. Scientists found that the flower buds contain a chemical, pinosylvin methyl ether (PME), which they suspected might be a repellent. So they prepared oatmeal, which hares like, and infused the chemical in some batches. The hares would not eat those batches. [Adapted from John P. Bryant et al., "Pinosylvin Methyl Ether Deters Snowshoe Hare Feeding on Green Alder," *Science*]

8. In 1896, the French scientist Henri Becquerel discovered the phenomenon of radioactivity. He had placed uranium on a photographic plate that was carefully wrapped to block light from reaching it, and then exposed the uranium to sunlight. When he developed the photographic plate, he found a silhouette of the uranium. He assumed that the sunlight had excited the uranium to emit radiation. Later, though, he left a similarly wrapped plate and some uranium in a dark place. Once again, when he developed the plate, he found an image of the uranium. The uranium itself, therefore, was spontaneously emitting radiation that caused the image.

9. During the 2006 conflict between Israel and Hezbullah in southern Lebanon, many claimed that Israel's military action increased the prestige of Hezbullah, at least within the Arab world. "Well, sure," wrote Jonathan Chait. "But Hezbullah's prestige was also boosted by Israel's 2000 withdrawal from Lebanon. If aggressive Israeli actions boost Hezbullah, and conciliatory Israeli actions boost Hezbullah, then maybe Israel's actions aren't really the prime mover here." [Jonathan Chait, " 'Back Off, Israel' Doesn't Cut It," *Los Angeles Times*]

∗10. "The very first point to note is that the freedom at issue (as indeed the very name 'Free Will Problem' indicates) pertains primarily not to overt acts but to inner acts. . . . We do not consider the acts of a robot to be morally responsible acts; nor do we consider the acts of man to be so save in so far as they are distinguishable from those of a robot by reflecting an inner life of choice. Similarly, from the other side, if we are satisfied . . . that a person has definitely elected to follow a course which he believes to be wrong, but has been prevented by external circumstances from translating his inner choice into an overt act, we still regard him as morally blameworthy." [C. A. Campbell, "Has the Self Free Will?"]

11. "Backers of the Common Core [national educational standards] argue that it will improve U.S. performance on international tests. And while it is true that students in countries with national standards, such as South Korea and Japan, regularly do better than American students, so do many in countries without national standards, such as Canada. It is also true that a U.S. without national standards has outperformed plenty of countries that have them." [Jason L. Riley, "Common Core Has a Central Problem," *Wall Street Journal*]

12. When you're out in the sun, your skin reacts with various protections against ultraviolet radiation, which can harm skin, including DNA damage. One of these protective mechanisms is melanin, which darkens the skin; it's what causes a tan. But how quickly does

this work? To find out, Carmit Levy of Tel Aviv University and her colleagues shone UV-B light on mice every 24 and 48 hours for 60 days. The result: "Mice exposed to UV-B radiation on the 48-hour schedule developed darker skin and had less DNA damage than mice in the other group." [Tina Hesman Saey, "To Get a Deeper Tan, Don't Sunbathe Every Day," *Science News*]

*13. "Aristotle had argued that plants derive their sustenance from the soil. . . . To knock Aristotle from his pedestal and bolster his own theory, van Helmont performed a now famous experiment. He planted a five-pound willow sapling in 200 pounds of soil, which he had carefully dried in a furnace, weighed, and then placed in a large pot. . . . After five years, he again weighed both the tree and the soil. The willow tree now weighed 169 pounds, while the soil weighed only 2 ounces less than the starting 200 pounds." Van Helmont concluded that the tree's weight gain was not just from the soil. [Allan J. Tobin and Jennie Dusheck, *Asking About Life*, 3rd edition]

14. "In the winter of 1890–91, while crossing tomatoes, two stigmas [the part of a flower that receives pollen] in the same cluster of flowers were given different amounts of pollen. The first was given a very small amount—10 to 20 grains—on one side of the stigma; the other was given an excess of pollen, the stigma being well smeared. The effect on the form and size of the fruit was very marked. The fruit receiving the large amount of pollen was of normal size and nearly symmetrical form, while the other was small and deformed." [*Annual Report of the Maine Agricultural Experiment Station*, University of Maine]

15. "Interestingly, there is at least one life form that appears to possess a constant mortality hazard rate. The lowly hydra (*Hydra vulgaris*) seems to have exactly this property; that is, regardless of how long a hydra has lived, its probability of dying in the next instant remains unchanged. . . . Hydras, like all other living organisms, are subject to wear from various types of body damage, including nonfatal accidents and illnesses. Therefore, if the hydra's death rate is constant, then there must be some other factor—some other force—that counters the effect of wear." [Michael R. Powers, *Acts of God and Man: Ruminations on Risk and Insurance*]

IV. [Integrative Exercise] Use what have you learned about inductive reasoning to evaluate the claims made in the following chain letter. What conclusions can you draw from the information contained in the letter? What additional information would you need to have?

KISS SOMEONE YOU LOVE WHEN YOU RECEIVE THIS LETTER AND MAKE MAGIC.

This paper has been sent to you for good luck. The original copy is in New England. It has been around the world 9 times. The luck has now been sent to you. You will receive good luck within 4 days of receiving this letter.

Send copies to people you think need good luck. Don't send money, as fate has no price. Do not keep this letter. It must leave your hands within 96 hours. An Air Force officer received $70,000. Joe Elliot received $42,000, and lost it because he broke the chain. While in the Philippines, Gene Welch lost his wife 6 days after receiving this letter. He failed to circulate the letter. However, before her death she had won $50,000 in a lottery. The money was transferred to him 4 days after he decided to mail out the letter.

Please send 20 copies of this letter and see what happens in 4 days. The chain comes from Venezuela and was written by Saul Anthony dé Croix, a missionary from South America. Since the copy must make a tour of the world, you must make 20 copies and send them out to your friends and associates. After a few days you will get a surprise. This is true even if you are not superstitious.

Do note the following: Constantine Dias received the chain in 1953. He asked his secretary to make 20 copies and send them out. A few days later he won a lottery of 2 million dollars. Andy Daddit, an office employee, received the letter and forgot it had to leave his hands within 96 hours. He lost his job. Later, after finding the letter again, he mailed out 20 copies. A few days later he got a better job. Dalen Fairchild received this letter and not believing threw it away. Nine days later he died.

PLEASE SEND NO MONEY. PLEASE DON'T IGNORE THIS. IT WORKS!!!!!

12 Analogical, Legal and Moral Reasoning

LEARNING OBJECTIVES

On successful completion of the chapter, you will be able to:

✓ Distinguish analogical arguments from other uses of analogy. (12.1)

✓ Analyze and evaluate analogical arguments. (12.2)

✓ Understand the role that argument by analogy plays in ethical and legal reasoning. (12.3)

Analogies are comparisons between things to bring out a point of similarity, often among things that are otherwise not similar. The analogy of a pump, for example, is often used to describe the function of the heart. A common idea of God is that He is like a father who cares for His children, punishes them for disobedience, etc. These analogies are explanatory or descriptive. We are not saying that the heart literally is a pump, nor that the conception of God as father is exact.

But analogies can also be used to argue for a conclusion. Arguments by analogy are inductive, for reasons we will see in due course. This chapter explains how to analyze and evaluate such arguments. We will also review the special importance this mode of argument plays in reasoning about ethics and law.

12.1 Analogy and Similarity

Suppose several candidates are running for class president and you are trying to decide whom to vote for. You think that Jasmine, the former president, was a great leader. Since Ava has a lot in common with Jasmine, you decide to vote for her. In this case, you are using the similarity between Ava and Jasmine as a premise in an argument.

In the same way, we have used an analogy in this book to support the conclusion that learning to reason well takes a lot of practice:

> The art of reasoning is a skill, like knowing how to play tennis. And you can't learn to play tennis just by reading a book. No matter how much you know about the theory of the game, you can't acquire the skill without actually playing. So you need to practice.

You can distinguish an argumentative analogy from a descriptive or explanatory analogy by the same techniques we learned in Chapter 2 for identifying arguments of any kind: Look for indicator words like "therefore," ask whether the speaker is trying to convince you of some conclusion, etc.

What is the logical structure of these arguments? As a first step in analysis, we can formulate the structure as follows:

1. Jasmine and Ava are similar.	1. Tennis and reasoning are similar.
2. Jasmine is a good leader.	2. Skill in tennis requires practice.
3. Ava will be a good leader.	3. Skill in reasoning requires practice.

The arguments clearly have a common structure, which we can represent abstractly:

1. *A* and *B* are similar.
2. *A* has property *P*.
3. *B* has property *P*.

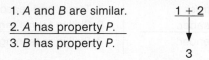

Here *A* and *B* are the two things being compared: Jasmine and Ava, tennis and reasoning. These are the **analogues**. *A* is the **source analogue** and *B* is the **target**. In the argument on the left, Jasmine is the source of the comparison; her leadership ability is the premise you argue from. Ava is the target; her leadership ability is the conclusion you aim to support. In the other argument, tennis is the source and reasoning is the target analogue. In both cases, the conclusion is that *B* has a certain property *P*: Ava will be a good leader, skill in reasoning must be acquired by practice. And the argument is that *B* has this property because it is similar to *A*, which has the property. So far, so good. But notice that the relationship between the source *A* and the target *B* is not like any of the logical relations we have studied so far. *A* is not a wider class that includes *B*, as in a categorical syllogism. Nor is *A* an instance or subclass of *B*, as in an inductive generalization. Jasmine and Ava are two separate, individual people. Tennis is not a species of logic, nor is logic a species of tennis. So how can a premise about one yield a conclusion about the other?

The answer obviously lies in premise 1: *A* and *B* are similar. The similarity may not be stated explicitly, but it is a crucial assumption. If there is no similarity between Jasmine and Ava, then the fact that Jasmine is a good leader has no bearing on Ava; the argument would have no strength whatsoever. The same is true of the analogy between tennis and reasoning. But similarity per se is not enough, because with a little ingenuity we can find some similarity between any two things, and thus we could prove anything this way. We could prove that you should take your bicycle to the dentist for a regular checkup, because the gear sprockets are shaped like teeth. That's ridiculous. So we need to look more carefully at the role of similarity.

If two things are similar, they must be similar in some particular respect—in shape, color, function, or whatever. To put it differently, two things are similar because they share some property or properties. So the first task in analyzing an argument by analogy is to identify the properties that the analogues have in common. There may be more than one such property, but there must be at least one. In the argument about tennis and logic, the property was stated explicitly: They are both skills. The argument about Jasmine and Ava as leaders did not state how they were similar. Perhaps the property they share is charisma, or competence, or vision, or the trust they inspire, or all of those traits. But there must be some shared quality to sustain the analogy.

We'll use the letters S_1, S_2, S_3, etc., to stand for properties that the analogues have in common, the properties that make them similar. We can then reformulate the structure of arguments by analogy as follows:

1. *A* and *B* have properties $S_1, S_2, S_3, \ldots$
2. *A* has property *P*.
_____
3. *B* has property *P*.

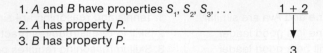

1. Jasmine and Ava have charisma, competence, vision, and/or the capacity to inspire trust.
2. Jasmine is a good leader.
_____
3. Ava will be a good leader.

1. Tennis and reasoning are skills.
2. Skill in tennis requires practice.
_____
3. Skill in reasoning requires practice.

We can now go on to ask the next—and crucial—question. What is the relationship between the properties S_1, S_2, S_3, etc., and *P*? If there is no connection between the properties, then the conclusion does not follow. That is the problem with the argument about bicycles. The property that gear sprockets and human teeth have in common is shape, but it is not because of their shape that human teeth require dental care. The source and target analogues may have many properties in common, but unless there is some link between one or more of these properties and the further property *P*, the analogy will not work.

So the strength of the argument depends on the likelihood of a connection between the properties involved, and our goal in evaluating an argument by analogy is to estimate this likelihood. We will see how to do this in the next section.

REVIEW **Analogy and Similarity**

An argument by analogy has four elements:

1. A source analogue (*A*)
2. A target analogue (*B*), about which the argument draws a conclusion
3. The properties that we know are shared by the analogues (S_1, S_2, S_3, etc.)
4. The further property (*P*) of the source that we infer is a property of the target as well

---

EXERCISE 12.1

Each of the paragraphs below contains an analogy. First decide whether the analogy is used to make an argument or merely to describe or explain something. If it is an argument, identify the elements in the structure of the argument: the source (*A*) and target (*B*) analogues, the property attributed to the target in the conclusion (*P*), and the property or properties (*S*) that make the analogues similar. If the latter property is not stated explicitly, try to find a plausible candidate.

＊1. Murray's mind is a cave: deep, dark, and full of bats.

2. The writing of history is like the telling of a story in that it relates events

connected in time, so it must have a narrative structure.

3. Writing is a medium of communication, as air is a medium of vision; and good writing is as crisp and clear as the autumn air in Vermont.

✳4. Just as decorations can beautify our homes, jewelry can beautify our bodies. But an excessively decorated home looks cluttered, not beautiful, and so we should not wear excessive jewelry.

5. The internet is our information superhighway. And just as our highways would be unbearably dangerous without laws and regulations, so too would the internet.

6. A concept is like a file folder in which we store information about a category of objects.

✳7. Since concepts are like file folders storing information about categories of objects, they must be kept in a hierarchical system comparable to file drawers.

8. The layers in a crystal are spaced at regular intervals, like the floors of a building, and connected by chemical bonds, like girders; so a substance with a crystalline structure is solid and rigid.

9. Kidneys are like the air filters in our homes. Air filters promote health by removing pollutants from the air we breathe. And similarly, kidneys promote health by purifying our blood.

✳10. A person who keeps his emotions bottled up has pressure building up inside, like a boiler with too much steam; eventually, as with the boiler, the person is going to break down.

11. Moving away from a community where you have lived for a long time can be like the end of a romantic relationship. You have shared time together, made memories together, and each left your imprint on the other. And as your time together comes to an end, it can feel like you are losing a piece of yourself.

12. For someone who has created a work of art, a book, a new discovery or idea, the creation is like a child. So it is not surprising that creators feel intensely protective about their creations.

✳13. Fatalism sees the world as moving in a certain inevitable direction, toward a predetermined future. But the future is an unwritten book, with every page blank, and each of us as an author. We may write whatever story we wish!

14. Our desires provide the motive power for our actions, in the way a car's engine provides power to the wheels. But free will acts like a clutch: We can choose whether to act on a given desire, just as we can suspend power to the car's wheels by disengaging the clutch.

15. Our planet is like a ship sailing on the vast ocean of space; hence the nations of the earth, like the members of a ship's crew, can survive only if they learn to live together.

12.2 Evaluating Analogical Arguments

We have seen that an argument by analogy has the structure:

1. *A* and *B* have properties S_1, S_2, S_3, . . .
2. *A* has property *P*.
   _____
3. *B* has property *P*.

These arguments are inductive. Premises 1 and 2 provide support for the conclusion but do not guarantee that the conclusion is true; as with other types of inductive arguments, support comes in degrees of strength. To evaluate the strength of a given argument, we will apply a set of four standards.

The fundamental basis for these standards is the issue of relevance. As we noted in the previous section, there must be some connection between the properties shared by the source and target analogues (S_1, S_2, S_3, . . .) and the property *P* in the conclusion. That is, the similarities between the analogues must be *relevant* to the further property we ascribe to the target. In the analogy between Jasmine and Ava, for example, the charisma they have in common must be relevant to leadership ability. The fact that tennis and reasoning are both skills must be relevant to the need for practice. The similarity in shape between teeth and gear sprockets, by contrast, is not relevant to dental care. With the concept of relevance in mind, we can evaluate analogical arguments by the following standards:

1. The number of relevant properties
2. The number and variety of source analogues
3. The number of relevant differences
4. The number and variety of negative source analogues

1. The number of relevant properties.

In many cases, the property that the analogues have in common will not be mentioned explicitly, as in the argument about Ava and Jasmine. So we have to think of properties that might be relevant. On the other hand, there is usually more than one common property that could be relevant. When we try to decide how we feel about another person, for example, we often compare that person to others we've known in the past, and our decision usually turns on more than one personality or character trait. When we use historical analogies, we are comparing two very complex situations that have many similarities (and many differences). And in the law, as we will see in the next section, the use of precedents is a kind of analogical reasoning: A lawyer will argue that the present case is like one that was decided in the past and will try to find as many similarities as possible. The first standard for evaluating analogical arguments, then, is that the more relevant similarities there are between the source and target analogues, the stronger the argument.

2. The number and variety of source analogues.

In the previous chapter we discussed the standards for evaluating an inductive generalization—an inference that supports a general proposition of the form "All *S* are *P*" with a sample of *S*s that are *P*. The first rule for generalizing is that the sample should be sufficiently numerous and various. In an argument by analogy, the conclusion is not a generalization; the conclusion is that the target analogue is P, and the target is an individual thing, like the source analogue. Nevertheless, the argument depends on a generalization because there must be some general connection between the properties shared by source and target (S_1, S_2, S_3, etc.) and the property P. In that sense, the argument involves an implicit generalization. The argument about skill in tennis and in reasoning, for example, rests on the generalization that all skills must be acquired through practice.

In that argument, tennis is the only skill used to support the generalization. That's typical of analogical arguments. We are supporting a claim about the target B on the basis of its similarity to the source A, so A is the only instance available to support the generalization. But we can look for other instances to broaden the sample. In the argument about Jasmine and Ava, are there other good leaders who have charisma? Can we find other leaders who have the other relevant properties, such as competence, vision, and the capacity to inspire trust? The more confirming cases we find, the stronger the argument.

Variety in the source analogues is also important. If Jasmine is a psychology major, then we should look for leaders with other majors. If good leaders differ in other ways, we have stronger evidence that charisma, competence, etc., really are relevant factors in leadership. In the same way, the argument that reasoning requires practice would be strengthened by considering other skills. Tennis is a physical skill, but the implicit generalization is about *all* skills: physical, mental, social, etc. So we need to consider whether or not examples from the other categories would confirm the generalization. Are the differences between, say, physical and mental skills relevant to the question of

APPLY Analogy Tests

Many standardized tests include a section on analogies, including the Scholastic Aptitude Test (SAT), Graduate Record Exam (GRE), Miller Analogies Test, and many others. Most of the tests ask you to identify the relationship between pairs of terms and choose among other pairs that have the same relationship. For example:

EVAPORATE : VAPOR ::

- (A) petrify : stone
- (B) centrifuge : liquid
- (C) saturate : fluid
- (D) corrode : acid
- (E) incinerate : fire

Evaporation is a process that changes a liquid into a vapor. The same relationship holds in (A), petrify and stone, whereas choice B involves a tool for separating liquids and C–E are effects of substances on other things.

These test questions do not involve arguments. But understanding analogous relationships is important for evaluating analogical arguments. In many such arguments, the shared properties of the analogs are relationships—as in our example of the practice needed for logic and tennis.

To develop further your ability to deal with analogical arguments—and to prepare for these tests if you plan to take any of them—you can consult the many test-prep sites online.

whether they must be acquired by practice? (In this case, we would say that the differences are not relevant, so the argument is a fairly strong one.)

3. The number of relevant differences.

When we evaluate an inductive generalization, the second rule is to look for disconfirming instances. An *S* that is not *P* disconfirms the generalization that all *S*s are *P*. This rule is also relevant to analogical arguments. In any argument by analogy, there will be differences between the analogues as well as similarities. If the differences are relevant, they decrease the strength of the argument. Relevant differences are called **disanalogies**, and they weaken the argument in accordance with standard 3.

4. The number and variety of negative source analogues.

We can establish the relevance of the differences by finding analogues that disconfirm the link between the shared properties and the property *P*. These disconfirming cases may have the shared properties S_1, S_2, S_3, etc., but not *P*; or they may have *P* but lack the shared properties. Disconfirming examples are called **counter-analogies**, and they weaken the argument in accordance with standard 4.

Suppose someone argues that war is like arm wrestling, so victory usually goes to the strongest party. How would we evaluate the argument by our standards?

1. The point of similarity between war and arm wrestling is that both are contests. Strength is obviously relevant to victory in arm wrestling, and it is also a relevant factor in war, in the sense that the larger army with more powerful weapons has an advantage.
2. Are there additional source analogues to support the link between strength and victory? Business competition might be an example, if we interpret the strength of a company in terms of its financial resources, market share, and other assets.
3. But there are also many relevant differences. Arm wrestling is a contest between two individuals; war is a conflict between nations, whose armies have many soldiers in a complex organization. Victory in war depends not only on strength but on strategy, speed, and teamwork, which have little relevance in arm wrestling.
4. We can establish the relevance of the differences with counter-analogies. Chess matches, for example, are usually won by the player with better strategy; basketball games by the side with better speed, precision, and teamwork. So you might reply to the original argument by saying, "Yes, but war is also like a chess game, so victory will go to the side with the best strategy"; or, "Yes, but war is also like basketball, so the side with the most speed and teamwork will win." Counter-analogies like these are one of the most effective ways of rebutting such arguments.

In light of these standards, the argument is very weak.

Let's consider one final argument by analogy. Some thinkers hold that the brain is like the hardware of a computer and that the mind is like the software, the programs that run on the machine. The basis of the analogy is the fact that both computers and minds process information. A computer can perform many of the tasks that a human mind can, such as do arithmetic calculations, store information, and solve problems. The computer is used to support the generalization that any information-processing device must have a hardware and a software component. The conclusion is that the

SOLVE Tables of Similarity and Difference

To analyze and evaluate analogical arguments, it is often useful to construct a table of similarities and differences. We list the relevant similarities, then the differences, then the conclusion. For the analogy about war, the table would look like this:

	Arm wrestling	**War**
Similarities	Contest	Contest
	Strength	Strength
Differences	Strategy not important	Strategy important
	Speed, precision, teamwork not important	Speed, precision, teamwork important
Conclusion	Victory	Victory

The last row is the conclusion that victory in war goes to the strongest side, and we indicate that it *is* the conclusion by placing an inference line above it in the column for war. (We do *not* put an inference line above Victory in the other column; that the strongest person wins in arm wrestling is a premise, not a conclusion.)

In general, the table for analyzing analogical arguments would be:

	Source (A)	**Target (B)**
Similarities	S_1	S_1
	S_2	S_2
	S_3	S_3
Differences	D_1	D_1
	D_2	D_2
Conclusion	P	P

thought processes of the mind consist in programs running on the neural "hardware" of the brain. But critics of this view claim there are significant disanalogies. Computers are technological devices invented by people; minds and brains are natural, biological systems. Software programs would not exist unless there is a programmer—which there isn't in the case of the mind. And minds involve conscious awareness, emotions, and desires, which computers don't seem to have. Whichever side you take in this dispute, the techniques we have discussed will help you understand this argument by analogy— and *any* such argument.

REVIEW Evaluating Analogical Arguments

Use the following standards to evaluate the strength of an argument by analogy.

Factors that increase the strength of the argument:

1. The number of relevant similarities between the source and target analogues, i.e., the number of properties they share that are relevant to the conclusion.

2. The number of source analogues that confirm the relevance of the similarities to the conclusion.

Factors that decrease the strength of the argument:

3. The number of differences (disanalogies) between the source and target analogues that are relevant to the conclusion.

4. The number of source analogues (counter-analogies) that confirm the relevance of the differences.

EXERCISE 12.2

Integrative Exercise Analyze and evaluate each of the following analogical arguments.

∗1. Jim is an intellectual, like Fred, and Fred doesn't like sports. So Jim probably doesn't like them either.

2. This bread machine was made by the same company that made my coffee-maker. I've had the coffeemaker for 3 years and it works great, so the bread machine should work fine.

3. I believe in reincarnation because it doesn't make sense that God would give us only one chance in life. A batter gets more chances than that in baseball.

∗4. "Do you like parsnips?"
"Parsnips? What are they?"
"They're a root vegetable, like carrots, only sweeter."
"Oh, like sweet potatoes? I like them."
"Sort of, but not as soft. Sweet potatoes are more like pastry, parsnips are harder, like candy."
"I like candy better, so I'm sure I'll like parsnips."

5. Psychotherapies that promise instant happiness are comparable to "get rich quick" schemes in the economic realm and therefore cannot be expected to work.

6. An experiment is a question put to nature, and like a lawyer cross-examining a witness, the scientist needs to know what answer he expects.

∗7. A family must bind itself together, like a bundle of sticks. Individually, the sticks might be easy to break, but when they are fastened together, they are strong.

8. One way paleontologists determine the diet of a long-extinct animal is through examination of its teeth. From fossils, we know that the saber-toothed cat had sharp, pointy teeth, like a lion or shark. And so it probably shared their carnivorous diet.

9. Television is for the mind what junk food is for the body. And excessive consumption, while enjoyable, can eventually result in ill health.

∗10. Golf balls are dimpled because, in the middle of the 19th century, it was discovered that slightly damaged balls with nicks in them flew further. Likewise, a person who is a bit damaged can go further in life than those whose lives have been easy.

11. A college course catalog is like a menu of delicious foods. And just as the person who always orders the same thing from a menu is a boring person, so is the person who only takes one sort of course.

12. A photon of light is like a billiard ball in having a definite velocity, position, and mass. A photon is therefore a particle.

∗13. A photon of light is like an air vibration in having a definite frequency and wavelength. Light is therefore a wave phenomenon.

14. Efforts by the major European powers to achieve arms control, at the turn of the 20th century and again in the 1920s and 1930s, were not successful. So arms control negotiations between the United States and other countries today are not likely to succeed either.

15. Fasting is common across many religious traditions. And perhaps this is because of its value as a tool for developing self-control. Someone who practices at the gym can lift greater weight, so someone who practices restraining animal appetites should have greater strength to control them when the need arises.

12.3 Analogies in Moral and Legal Reasoning

In this section, we discuss the use of argument by analogy in ethics and in law, two fields in which analogies play an especially important role. Examining this role will deepen our understanding of analogical arguments.

12.3A Analogies in Ethics

Consider the difference between two kinds of statements:

It is **wrong** to cheat on an exam.	Ahmed cheated on the exam.
You **should** drive within the speed limit.	The speed limit is 40 miles per hour.
My boss is a **good** man.	My boss is married.
Francesca is an **honest** person.	Francesca is very outgoing.
X is **evil**.	I don't approve of X.
Teaching is a **worthy** profession.	Teachers earn less than doctors.
Self-respect is an important **value** in life.	Self-respect is not the same as conceit.

Statements in the first column are moral or ethical statements (we will use these terms as equivalent). They are *normative* judgments, involving concepts like the ones in bold that indicate a moral evaluation of something as right or wrong, good or bad. By contrast, statements in the second column are *descriptive*: they simply describe a fact or event. That Ahmed cheated is a matter of fact; it is a description of what he did. That cheating is wrong is a *moral* judgment about cheating. Francesca's honesty is a moral virtue; that she is outgoing is a personality trait, attractive perhaps but not something we expect of everyone. To say that X is evil (whatever X might be) is a moral condemnation; to say that I don't approve of X is a psychological statement about my attitude. And so on for the other cases.

Ethical issues pertain to our actions—what we should or should not do; to our goals—what is valuable, what is worthy or unworthy to pursue; and to moral character—what traits are virtues to cultivate or vices to correct. Ethics is a branch of philosophy that deals with such questions systematically. Most religions include a moral code, such as the Ten Commandments. And apart from these comprehensive approaches, we all deal with moral issues in our lives as we make choices about how to act, choose the values we pursue in life, and pass judgment on actions and character—our own and those of others.

Reasoning about moral issues can involve all forms of deductive and inductive inference. If we argue that Ahmed did something wrong because he cheated on the exam, we are making a deductive inference, applying a general principle, "Cheating is wrong," to a particular action. As for induction, consider the adage that honesty is the best policy. Those who support the claim appeal to cases in which dishonesty led to bad consequences, such as loss of trust, and to cases of positive results from honesty. That argument is an inductive generalization. Indeed, previous chapters on these argument forms have included many examples of moral issues.

But argument by analogy plays a special role in moral reasoning because of the complexity of the situations we reason about. Those situations may involve people with various motives, rights, and obligations; various facts, past and present, that are relevant; and more than one moral principle that may apply. That complexity makes analogical reasoning especially useful. An argument by analogy is based on the similarity between two analogues, a source and a target. As we have seen, the analogues may be similar in multiple ways, with more than one property in common. In addition, we may have an intuitive sense that the analogues are similar without being sure exactly how to break that similarity down into distinct properties. Indeed, we tend to use arguments by analogy precisely when two things are similar in ways that are hard to analyze. For example, a piece of music may sound quite similar to another one you are familiar with, leading you to infer that the first comes from the same historical period as the second; but if you don't know much about musical theory, you may be unable to say specifically what they have in common. In the same way, a complicated situation you need to evaluate may remind you of other situations you have encountered, even before you can say what common features make them similar. Of course, you must break the similarity down before you can construct an argument. But the analogy can be useful in orienting the search for relevant facts and principles.

Let's take a relatively simple example. You are my classmate in a course and you ask me to give comments on your term paper before you turn it in. Would that be helping you cheat, which is wrong? Or helping you learn, which is good? The term paper is graded work, and the instructor wants to grade you on *your* work, not someone else's.

That's what is wrong with cheating on an exam. You are passing off someone else's answers as your own, in order to get a better grade. That is deceptive. So let's create a table of similarities and differences for the analogy with cheating:

	Cheating	Helping with paper
S_1	Graded work	Graded work
S_2	Grade is to be based on the student's own work	Grade is to be based on the student's own work
S_3	Goal: Better grade	Goal: Better paper
D_1	Deceptive	Deceptive?
P	Wrong	Wrong?

The source and target analogues have the first three properties in common. The possible difference is whether getting help with the paper is deceptive. And that is the decisive moral issue. There's nothing wrong with wanting a better grade or aiming to improve your term paper. And there's nothing wrong in principle with helping another person. The only moral issue is deception. And that's an easy issue to resolve. Ask the instructor, or at least acknowledge in the paper that you had help with this or that point.

　　Here's another example. When you bargain over the price of a new car, the dealer has a lowest price he will accept (the "reservation price"). If you offer a price that is low but still above that price, and the dealer says he can't do it, is he being dishonest? We might argue that it is dishonest by analogy with fraud. It would be fraud if the dealer sets the odometer mileage back from 20,000 miles to 2,000 miles, or fails to tell you about a defect in the transmission. Is it equally fraudulent not to tell you the lowest offer he would accept? Once again, let's note the similarities:

	Fraud	Negotiation offer
S_1	The dealer does not reveal a relevant fact.	The dealer does not reveal a relevant fact.
S_2	The dealer's goal is monetary gain.	The dealer's goal is monetary gain.
S_3	The dealer has a one-sided advantage in bargaining.	The dealer has a one-sided advantage in bargaining.
P	Wrong	Wrong

　　But let's take a closer look at the third point. What is the dealer's advantage? In a clear case of fraud, the dealer knows things about the car that you are not in a position to know, like the number of miles driven or a defect that is not apparent. The dealer knows that the mileage or defect would affect your decision, or at least the price you would pay, and he is deceiving you for monetary gain. But the price seems different. The dealer knows more than you do about the pricing of cars. But you are in a position to know what you're willing to pay, and you could easily find price information about that model of car. You don't have to rely on the dealer for that information. And the dealer has no obvious obligation to tell you the price he or she will accept. So we should add these differences to our table:

	Fraud	Negotiation offer
S_1	The dealer does not reveal a relevant fact.	The dealer does not reveal a relevant fact.
S_2	The dealer's goal is monetary gain.	The dealer's goal is monetary gain.
S_3	The dealer has a one-sided advantage.	The dealer has a one-sided advantage.
D_1	The dealer has an obligation to provide information about the car.	The dealer does not have an obligation to provide information about his price.
D_2	You rely on the dealer for information about the car.	You do not rely on the dealer for price information.
P	Wrong	Wrong?

The differences we have added to the table raise a significant question about the conclusion of the analogical argument. And we might offer a counter-analogy: that bargaining over the price of a car is more like a game of poker, where your opponent is not obliged to tell you what cards he has, and bluffing is a legitimate element in the game.

Analogical arguments about moral issues may be more complex than in other areas. As these examples show, however, they have the same basic form and can be analyzed and evaluated by the same methods—identifying the relevant properties the analogues have in common, noting their differences (disanalogies), and creating counter-analogies.

The examples so far involved analogies between new or problematic ethical issues and actual situations—fraud, cheating on exams—whose moral status is clear-cut. Another form of analogical argument involves thought experiments about hypothetical cases, cases designed to bring out a relevant principle. An example is a thought experiment that philosopher Peter Singer used in a classic article about the moral responsibility of people in developed countries to relieve suffering in other countries. Here is Singer's argument, in essence:

1. Suffering and death from lack of food, shelter, and medical care are bad.
2. If it is in our power to prevent something bad from happening, without thereby sacrificing anything of moral importance, then we ought, morally, to do it.
3. Consumer luxuries and other components of an affluent lifestyle are not of moral importance. ("When we buy new clothes not to keep ourselves warm but to look 'well-dressed' we are not providing for any important need.")
4. Therefore, we are morally obligated to contribute to famine relief any money we don't need for mere sustenance.
   [Peter Singer, "Famine, Affluence and Morality," *Philosophy & Public Affairs*, Vol. 1, No. 3 (Spring, 1972), pp. 229-243]

To support premises 2 and 3, Singer offers a thought experiment:

If I am walking past a shallow pond and see a child drowning in it, I ought to wade in and pull the child out. This will mean getting my clothes muddy, but this is insignificant, while the death of the child would presumably be a very bad thing.

This is an argument by analogy. The analogy is intended to bring out three points of similarity between rescuing the child and providing aid to people suffering and dying "from lack of food, shelter, and medical care."

	Drowning child	People suffering in other countries
S_1	The child's death would be bad.	Suffering and death from lack of food, shelter, and medical care are bad.
S_2	The passerby can save the child.	Contributing to aid can save some lives.
S_3	The cost of the rescue (ruined clothes) is of no moral importance.	The cost of contributing (forgoing all discretionary spending) is of no moral importance.
P	We would have an obligation to save the child.	We have an obligation to contribute to famine relief any money we don't need for mere sustenance.

Singer's argument has been widely discussed in philosophical ethics, and many objections have been raised, not all of them related to the thought experiment. But philosophers have raised objections to the analogy itself, in the form of disanalogies. To mention a few: (1) In the source analogue, the passerby is in a unique position to save the child; in the target analogue, the contributor to famine relief is one of many who can contribute. (2) The passerby can save the child by direct action; the contributor must act indirectly through aid agencies which may be more or less effective. (3) Ruining his clothes is a minimal, one-time cost for the passerby; contributing a large portion of one's income is a large and ongoing commitment with major effects on one's life. To evaluate Singer's argument, we would need to take account of these differences in his analogy as well as the similarities.

As you can see from the examples, argument by analogy is an important method of reasoning in ethics. In light of the complexities of the situations in which we need to make moral judgments or decisions, analogies can be very helpful in orienting us to relevant issues. They are useful in dealing with new or uncertain cases by comparing them with well-established cases, and by constructing thought experiments to highlight relevant moral principles.

12.3B Legal Reasoning

Law is another field in which analogical reasoning plays a major role. To understand that role, we first need to understand something about the nature of law. When a legal case comes to court, the court needs to rule on how the governing law applies to the case. That depends partly on the type of law involved. We usually think of laws as rules that are issued by a government and written down in codes of law. That is true of statutes passed by a legislature. The Constitution of the United States is also written law, as are the regulations adopted by agencies such as the U.S. Food and Drug Administration. In Anglo-American law, however, many cases are adjudicated under common law, the body of past decisions about what is fair, especially in matters of property, contract, and injury. In common law, judges do not rule solely on the basis of a written statute or regulation; instead, they rely on precedent. How did courts rule in previous cases similar to the case at hand? The use of precedents is a form of argument by analogy.

The common-law system is used in the United States, the United Kingdom, Australia, and India, among other countries. Litigants couch their arguments in terms of the "fit" between the case at hand and the particulars of prior cases. The fact that a current case is analogous with the circumstances of past cases strongly binds judges to rule in ways that are consistent with that body of case law. This is known as the rule of stare decisis, a Latin phrase roughly translated as "let the decision stand." The goal of stare decisis is to achieve consistency in the law, so that people have a measure of predictability about how laws are interpreted and enforced. Thus, the degree to which a given case is relevantly similar to previously decided cases largely determines the outcome. The arguments between litigants are framed in terms of which cases achieve the best, or most relevantly analogous, fit with the particulars of the case at hand. (There are circumstances under which judges may depart from and even overturn precedent, but these are exceptional.)

In contrast, the civil code or "Continental" model, common in Europe, Latin America, and much of Asia, rarely cites precedent as a source of authority. This model of law attempts to codify, in advance, a set of rules intended to govern any potential dispute. Though prior case law may be instructive, legal arguments usually hinge mostly on the fit to whatever the written codes may already say about the situation. Written decisions are brief, compared with their counterparts in common-law jurisdictions, so they would rarely have the opportunity to engage in discussions and comparisons of past cases.

To illustrate the role of precedent in common law, consider a hypothetical example about inheritance. Rosa Mendoza is an elderly woman, in the hospital with a terminal illness. The day before she dies, she amends her will to exclude her ex-husband and leave her estate to her children. The ex-husband sues, claiming that the last-minute change in the will is not legally valid. His attorney argues that a similar last-minute amendment was rejected in the prior case of Herbert Wycliff, in which there was evidence that the amendment to his will had been coerced by an interested party. The attorney for the children cites a different precedent, in which Georgia Brown altered her will shortly before her death and the altered will was upheld. The argument would then largely turn on whether Ms. Mendoza's case more closely resemble that of Brown, where there was no allegation of coercion, or of Wycliff, where there was.

The question of coercion, then, would be the element serving to distinguish the two cases, and thereby suggest which case ought to govern here. A long line of precedents (as well as laws in most U.S. states) established the rule that a will is not legally valid if it has been the result of coercion. But what counts as coercion? The attorneys will argue back and forth, citing relevant precedents, about various criteria of coercion, such as:

- Was the person in a state of emotional duress immediately prior to or after the amendment?
- Was a family member lying to the person, inflating circumstances of need, or otherwise exerting undue pressure?
- Was anyone threatening to withhold care if the person didn't make the amendment?

Suppose that all three factors were present in Wycliff's case, none of them in Brown's case, and only the first in Ms. Mendoza's case. The attorneys will look for other precedents involving those criteria; in particular, they will look for prior cases in which a court ruled on the significance of emotional duress for the validity of wills. And then the court in this case will have to decide whether Mendoza's situation is more similar to that of Wycliff or to that of Brown. Either way, the principle of stare decisis will compel the court to rule on the basis of the closest analogy. And its decision will itself become a precedent for future disputes about inheritance.

Let's consider now an actual case that will illustrate more of the complexities of legal reasoning: the dispute over labor unions for graduate students. Graduate students often work as teaching assistants (TAs) for undergraduate courses or as research assistants (RAs) on faculty projects. There is a long-running legal issue, going back to the 1960s, about whether that makes them a kind of employee. If they are "employees" in the eyes of the law, then under the 1935 Labor Relations Act, they are entitled to form legally recognized labor unions; and universities, as their "employers," are required to negotiate with them in good faith over salary, benefits, and other terms of their employment. They would have the right to strike and would be entitled to bring grievances to the U.S. Department of Labor for adjudication.

The first graduate student unions were recognized in Wisconsin in 1966, and later in Illinois, California, New York, and other states. But those unions were at public universities and organized under state labor laws, which explicitly provide unionization rights to graduate students. These unions function like government employee unions, with the state governments as "management." The primary dispute is over graduate students at private universities, which are governed by federal law, which does not explicitly settle the question. The National Labor Relations Act of 1935 (also known as the Wagner Act) is of course written law, but it does not include any specific criteria for "employees," so litigation over this question is primarily a common-law issue about whether and to what extent TAs and RAs are analogous to clear cases of employees covered by the act, such as hourly workers in a factory.

The courts have gone back and forth on this question several times. In 1974, the Department of Labor's internal court, the National Labor Relations Board, ruled in a case involving Stanford University that graduate students were not employees under the terms of the Labor Relations Act. In 2000, the NLRB reversed itself somewhat in a case involving New York University, but only under specific circumstances unique to NYU. Emboldened by this ruling, the United Auto Workers attempted to unionize graduate students at other private universities, including Brown. They failed: In 2004, the NLRB reversed its 2000 ruling, finding that the 1974 *Stanford* decision was correct all along: grad students are not employees. This didn't end the controversy, as the UAW returned in 2016, and a more labor-friendly NLRB reversed the 2004 *Brown* ruling in a case at Columbia University, holding that graduate students were indeed employees, and thus entitled to unionization rights. Nevertheless, as of early 2020, the NLRB is considering an explicit rule change, defining graduate students as nonemployees, thereby reversing the 2016 decision by regulatory fiat.

The issue here is not whether graduate student unions are a good idea. There are reasonable arguments on both sides of that issue. In the absence of any legal requirement, universities could choose one way or the other. But there is a law, and the question is to interpret what it means. TAs and RAs legally qualify for collective bargaining only if they can be classified as employees under the law, and that depends on the strength of the analogy between graduate student work and employee labor. Thus the question is not the desirability of collective bargaining for graduate students, but the narrower question of legal classification.

Consider first the ways in which the relationship between graduate students and their universities resembles that of employee and employer. The *Columbia* decision in

2016 held that the term "employment," under the Labor Relations Act as well as common law, ought to be construed widely. Two major points of similarity are that TAs and RAs work under the direction of a faculty member, and that they are paid a stipend for their work. The court applied what it describes as the "doctrine of the conventional master-servant relationship," a relationship that exists "when a servant performs services for another, under the other's control or right of control, and in return for payment." One might object that a "stipend" isn't quite the same as a wage or salary. For tax purposes, however, the IRS treats stipends the same as fully taxable wages or salary. So far, then, the positive analogy is:

	Employee	Graduate student TA, RA
S_1	Paid a salary or wage for labor	Paid a stipend for labor
S_2	Income is taxable	Stipend is taxable as wage/salary
S_3	Works under the direction of an employer	Works under the direction of the university faculty
P	Employees have the legal right to form unions to negotiate wages and benefits	TAs and RAs have the legal right to form unions to negotiate wages and benefits

Earlier decisions, however, noted relevant differences that should be accounted for as well. The 2004 *Brown* decision emphasized the difference between the *economic* relation that employees have with their employers and the *academic* relation between graduate students and their universities. Employees are hired and evaluated for doing work that serves the purpose of the employer—profit in the case of commercial firms, other kinds of impact for noncommercial organizations. But graduate student work is intended primarily as training, to develop the teaching or research skills students will need in order to earn a graduate degree. Students are given the positions for reasons that have less to do with their qualifications for those "jobs" than with their academic progress toward the degree. That distinction, the court said, includes a number of specific differences:

- Employees are paid for their time and effort. Graduate stipends for work are one form of aid, which also includes tuition waivers and other support that is not contingent on work.
- Most jobs have an open application process: anyone can apply, and employers try to select the best qualified individual. In contrast, there is no open application for TA or RA work. The only individuals considered for such positions are those who have already been accepted as graduate students within their respective departments; and they are accepted primarily for their scholarly potential, not for the skills they bring to the tasks of teaching or research.
- U.S. labor law assumes that the employee–employer relationship is adversarial. The two sides have opposing economic interests; employees want higher wages and benefits, employers want to pay less. That's the basic rationale for labor laws that try to foster equal bargaining strength by enabling labor unions. But the relation of graduate students to their department faculty is cooperative, with the shared goal of developing new scholars in the discipline.
- An employee who does a good job can expect to keep the job indefinitely, as long as the position is needed, and may advance to higher positions. But graduate

assistantships are temporary positions, and rarely enable the student to be promoted to the faculty at his or her university.

Let's add these disanalogies to our table of similarities and differences:

	Employee	Graduate student
S_1	Paid a salary or wage for labor	Paid a stipend for labor
S_2	Income is taxable	Stipend is taxable as wage/salary
S_3	Works under the direction of an employer	Works under the direction of the university faculty
D_1	Position based on work qualifications	Position based on scholarly potential
D_2	Open application process for the job	Jobs given only to students accepted by the department
D_3	Paid for time and effort	Paid as one form of aid
D_4	Employees and employer have adversarial economic interests	Graduate students and faculty have mutual academic interests
D_5	Employment can be ongoing	Positions are temporary
P	Employees have the legal right to form unions to negotiate wages and benefits	TAs and RAs have the legal right to form unions to negotiate wages and benefits?

The differences we have added to the table raise a question about whether the analogy between graduate assistants and employees is strong enough to support a ruling that the students should have the right to unionize. The differences also suggest a counter-analogy: Graduate assistantships might be more analogous to undergraduate work/study programs and internships, which similarly are conditioned on being an enrolled student making satisfactory progress toward a particular degree, are intended as a kind of financial aid to defray tuition, and are temporary.

On the other hand, graduate students at a number of universities have argued that the 2016 *Columbia* decision was correct and should not be reversed by the NLRB. They can be both employees *and* students, they argue, with an economic as well as an academic relationship to their schools. They can spend as much as 40 hours a week on preparing and teaching classes, grading papers, and meeting with students. They may teach required undergraduate courses with large enrollments. If graduate students were not doing this work, the university would have to hire additional faculty, at additional expense. These considerations would strengthen the analogy with employees.

Our purpose in reviewing this case is not to take sides, but to illustrate the central role of analogical reasoning in law. A major function of courts is to decide how a general rule should be applied to new cases. The rule may be established by common-law precedents, or it may be a written law or regulation. Either way, the task is to examine the similarities between the new case and prior cases. And no matter how complex the issues are, the same techniques for analyzing and evaluating analogical arguments can be applied: Identify relevant similarities between the source and target analogues, take note of relevant differences (disanalogies), and consider plausible counter-analogies.

The judges here found in favor of the defendants, on the basis that no line of causality could be established over such a long period of time for that home's lead-based

pigments, and that lead-based pigments are not fungible (interchangeable), varying wildly in the degree of toxicity and risk they pose.

CHAPTER REVIEW

Summary

- Analogies between two things can be used to argue for a conclusion as well as to describe or to explain.
- When used in an argument, an analogy purports to show that one thing, the target analogue, has a certain property P because the source analogue has that property and because the analogues are similar in various respects. To analyze such an argument, we must identify the relevant dimensions of similarity between the analogues—the properties S_1, S_2, S_3, etc., they share.

- To evaluate the argument, we consider the number of shared properties and the number and variety of source analogues—factors that strengthen the argument. We must also consider relevant differences (disanalogies) between the analogues, as well as counter-analogies with other analogues.
- Analogical arguments are used extensively in moral and legal reasoning.

Key Terms

analogue (p. 545)

source analogue (p. 545)

target analogue (p. 545)

disanalogy (p. 550)

counter-analogy (p. 550)

Putting It All Together

I.   **Integrative Exercise**   Find an argument by analogy to support each of the following conclusions. Even if you don't agree with the conclusion, try to find the most plausible analogy.

✶1. Friend to potential car buyer: "That Porsche is going to cost more to insure."

  2. Doctors should be allowed to advertise their services and prices.

3. The United States should not set up trade barriers against imported goods.

✶4. Playing the stock market is risky.

5. Children should not be overly protected against the vicissitudes of life.

II. **Integrative Exercise** Each of the passages that follows contains an analogy. First decide whether the analogy is being used as an argument. Then if it is, analyze and evaluate it.

*1. "Prayer is like a rocking chair. It'll give you something to do, but it won't get you anywhere." [Gypsie Rose Lee]

2. Some doctors recommend that people over the age of 40 should get a physical exam every year. As one physician argued, "People take their car in for servicing every few months without complaint. Why shouldn't they take similar care of their bodies?" [*U.S. News & World Report*]

3. "Absence diminishes small loves and increases great ones, as the wind blows out the candle and blows up the bonfire." [La Rochefoucauld, *Maxims*]

*4. "Vigorous writing is concise. A sentence should contain no unnecessary words, a paragraph no unnecessary sentences, for the same reason that a drawing should have no unnecessary lines and a machine no unnecessary parts." [William B. Strunk, Jr., and E. B. White, *The Elements of Style*]

5. "The mode of taxation is, in fact, quite as important as the amount. As a small burden badly placed may distress a horse that could carry with ease a much larger one properly adjusted, so a people may be impoverished and their power of producing wealth destroyed by taxation, which, if levied another way, could be borne with ease." [Henry George, *Progress and Poverty*]

6. Life's but a walking shadow, a poor player,
   That struts and frets his hour upon the stage,
   And then is heard no more. It is a tale
   Told by an idiot, full of sound and fury,
   Signifying nothing.
   [Shakespeare, *Macbeth*]

*7. "Society is like a stew. If you don't stir it up every once in a while then a layer of scum floats to the top." [Edward Abbey]

8. "Taxation of earnings from labor is on a par with forced labor. Some persons find this claim obviously true: taking the earnings of *n* hours labor is like taking *n* hours from the person; it is like forcing the person to work *n* hours for another's purpose." [Robert Nozick, *Anarchy, State, and Utopia*] (You may assume from the character of the analogy that Nozick's conclusion is: Taxation of earnings from labor is *wrong*.)

9. "One day, Bill Klann, a Ford employee . . . , took a trip to a Chicago slaughterhouse. There, he saw a model of industrial butchering efficiency: animal carcasses moved by on overhead trolleys, while a series of butchers performed specialized tasks in sequence as the carcasses advanced. As Klann watched this bloody symphony of movement, he had an analogical epiphany: dismantling something (a carcass) was fundamentally similar to building something (an engine); therefore, adopting a moving assembly line at Ford would increase productivity and reduce costs, he felt." [David Zax, "How Steve Jobs's Mastery of Analogies Sent Apple Skyrocketing," fastcompany.com]

*10. "We can follow the path taken by physics and biology by turning directly to the relation between behavior and the environment and neglecting supposed mediating states of mind. Physics did not advance by looking more closely at the jubilance of a falling body, or biology by looking at the nature of vital spirits, and we do not need to try to discover what personalities, states of mind, feelings, traits of character, plans, purposes, intentions, or the other perquisites of autonomous man really are in order to get on with a scientific analysis of behavior." [B. F. Skinner, *Beyond Freedom and Dignity*]

11. "If 'good' and 'better' are terms deriving their sole meaning from the ideology of each people, then of course ideologies themselves cannot be better or worse than one another. Unless the measuring rod is independent of the things measured, we can do no measuring." [C. S. Lewis, *Christian Reflections*]

12. Opponents of "guaranteed issue"—the mandate that insurance companies must insure people with preexisting conditions—argue that it will raise premiums for other policyholders. It is like selling fire insurance on a burning building.

*13. Proponents of guaranteed issue argue that, since workers with company health insurance lose their insurance if they are fired, it is unfair if those who developed health problems during their employment now cannot get affordable insurance. It is like a college that cancels all your course credits if you take a year off from school, even for a health emergency, quite possibly leaving you unable to afford starting college again from scratch.

14. In a talk at the 2020 World Economic Forum in Davos, Israeli historian and author Yural Noah Harari said that nationalism and globalism are compatible. "Nationalism isn't about hating foreigners. It's about loving your compatriots." He used the example of the FIFA [soccer] World Cup to show how global cooperation coexists with passionate national loyalty. "Countries can't play unless they agree to the same rules. If you like the World Cup, you are already a globalist." [Jug Suraiya, "How to Be a Referee in the Match between Nationalism and Globalism," *The Times of India*]

15. In developing his theory of evolution by natural selection, Charles Darwin relied partly on an analogy with the practice of "artificial selection." To produce the traits they wanted in dogs, pigeons, or other animals, breeders allowed just the ones with desirable traits to reproduce. Species in nature do not have a breeder selecting traits, but members of the species with traits that increase their chances of survival are likely to have more offspring than members without those traits.

*16. "Thus it is observable that the buildings which a single architect has planned and executed, are generally more elegant and commodious than those which several have attempted to improve. . . . In the same way

I thought that the sciences contained in books . . . composed as they are of the opinions of many different individuals massed together, are farther removed from truth than the simple inferences which a man of good sense using his natural and unprejudiced judgment draws respecting the matters of his experience." [René Descartes, *Discourse on Method*]

17. The Syrian Civil War spurred the largest refugee crisis of recent memory, with millions of Syrians seeking refuge in other countries. Some people opposed the policy of accepting them as refugees, even in proscribed limited numbers, because they may include some terrorists. On September 19, 2016, Donald Trump, Jr., the son of the then-candidate, tweeted an image of Skittles candies, with the text: "If I had a bowl of Skittles and I told you three would kill you, would you take a handful? That's our Syrian refugee problem." [National Public Radio, "Taste the Outrage: Donald Trump Jr.'s Tweet Compares Refugees to Skittles."]

18. A band from Texas called the Judy's had their heyday on college campuses in the 1980s, but by 2000 their independently released music was no longer commercially available, and the band itself had long since broken up and abandoned the music industry. One fan, Michael Wilson, established a website for the band, and created MP3 files for download. But he then had second thoughts and took the files down. "No matter how you look at it, distribution of MP3 files without the permission of the copyright owner is just plain illegal." Many fans complained that if the Judy's are not going to rerelease their music, MP3 trading should be acceptable. Wilson disagreed, observing that if he had a car in his garage that had gone unused for years, it would not entitle random strangers to take it out for joyrides without his permission.

*19. Isn't socialism a better kind of society than capitalism? Imagine a camping trip among friends. Everyone wants everyone to have a great time; they share the equipment and food they bring; they take turns doing the work. The campers are living by socialist principles: Everyone is equal; they share everything; there is no hierarchy; everyone does his or her part. Now imagine the camping trip if the campers began to act like people in real-life capitalism. One person demands better food because he is good at fishing. Another charges everyone else for apples from a tree she found. The person who brought the tents allows the others to use them only if they pay him rent. Who would want to go on *that* trip? Socialism is clearly a better way to organize society. [Adapted from G. A. Cohen, *Why Not Socialism?*]

20. In 1972, Dr. Ananda Mohan Chakrabarty, a genetic engineer, modified the genes of a bacterium to make it capable of consuming oil, to assist in cleaning oil spills. The U.S. Patent and Trademark Office (PTO) rejected his application to patent his new bacterium on the basis that life-forms could not be patented, only nonliving inventions. The U.S. Supreme Court overruled the PTO, citing the Patent Act, which allows patents for "any new and useful process, machine, manufacture, or composition of matter, or any new or useful improvement [thereof]." The court contrasted Chakrabarty's genetically modified bacterium with another case in which someone had mixed previously existing bacteria to make a soil culture that inoculated seeds of legumes. In that case, the court had ruled that the person had discovered "only some of the handiwork of nature," since the bacteria there had all performed exactly according to their known nature. Chakrabarty, in contrast, offered a "nonnaturally occurring manufacture or composition of matter—a product of human ingenuity— 'having a distinctive name, character [and] use.'" [*Diamond v. Chakrabarty*, 447 U.S. 303 (1980)]

III. **Integrative Exercise** The arguments below are classic arguments by analogy, which indicate how deeply analogies are woven into some of our fundamental conceptions. For each one, find a counter-analogy.

∗1. Anger is like steam under pressure, so you shouldn't keep it bottled up.

2. In defense of equality of opportunity: Life is a race; victory should go to the swiftest but the runners should start at the same place.

3. Human knowledge is like a building, and it must therefore rest on foundations.

∗4. Society is like a family, and the more productive members should provide for the needs of the less productive.

IV. **Integrative Exercise** Perhaps the most famous argument by analogy is the "argument from design," used to defend the belief in the existence of God. The passages below are from a work by the 18th-century philosopher David Hume. The first one is a statement of the argument itself; the second is a counter-analogy to the argument. Create a table of similarities and differences for each argument.

a. "Look round the world: Contemplate the whole and every part of it: You will find it to be nothing but one great machine, subdivided into an infinite number of lesser machines, which again admit of subdivisions to a degree beyond what human senses and faculties can trace and explain. All these various machines, and even their most minute parts, are adjusted to each other with an accuracy which ravishes into admiration all men who have ever contemplated them. The curious adapting of means to ends, throughout all nature, resembles exactly, though it much exceeds, the productions of human contrivance—of human design, thought, wisdom, and intelligence. Since therefore the effects resemble each other, we are led to infer, by all the rules of analogy, that the causes also resemble, and that the Author of Nature is somewhat similar to the mind of man, though possessed of much larger faculties, proportioned to the grandeur of the work which he has executed."

b. "Now, if we survey the universe, so far as it falls under our knowledge, it bears a great resemblance to an animal or organized body, and seems actuated with a like principle of life and motion. A continual circulation of matter in it produces no disorder; a continual waste in every part is incessantly repaired; the closest sympathy is perceived throughout the entire system; and each part or member, in performing its proper offices, operates both to its own preservation and to that of the whole. The world, therefore, I infer, is an animal; and the Deity is the *soul* of the world, actuating it, and actuated by it." [David Hume, *Dialogues Concerning Natural Religion*]

V. **Integrative Exercise** Many people who oppose abortion do so on the grounds that the fetus is a person from the time of conception; and since people have the right to life, the fetus may not be killed by abortion. Some would argue that this is the case even if the pregnancy resulted from rape: The fetus in this case is not responsible for the rape; it is still a person with the right to life. Against this view, philosopher Judith Jarvis Thomson offered the following thought experiment:

You wake up in the hospital one morning and find yourself with a tube attached to a famous violinist who has a fatal kidney ailment. The Society of Music Lovers has kidnapped you, and last night they plugged the violinist's circulatory system into yours, so that your kidneys can be used to extract poisons from his blood as well as your own. If he is unplugged from you now, he will die; but in nine months he will have recovered from his ailment, and can safely be unplugged from you. "Is it morally incumbent on you to accede to this situation?" Thomson asks. She considers it obvious that you do *not* have any such obligation. Though the violinist has a right to life, he does not have the right to use your body to preserve his life. And so, by analogy, a woman pregnant by rape is within her rights to abort the fetus. [Paraphrased from Judith Jarvis Thomson, "A Defense of Abortion," *Philosophy & Public Affairs*, Vol. 1, no. 1 (Fall 1971)]

Analyze and evaluate this argument. Consider similarities between the violinist case and a pregnancy by rape: their involuntary character, the rights of the people involved, etc. Consider the differences between the violinist and the fetus. And try to find a possible counter-analogy.

Statistical Reasoning | 13

Consider the following statements:

> The population of South Carolina is about 5.1 million people.
>
> The annual homicide rate in the United States is 5.0 per 100,000.
>
> Ninety-seven percent of people who eat chocolate bunnies start with the ears.
>
> In France before the Revolution of 1789, the median age of death was lower than the median age of marriage.
>
> Other things being equal, someone who smokes tobacco is more likely to get lung cancer than is someone who does not.

Each of these statements is a *statistical* proposition. It attributes a quantitative, numerical property to some class of things: the population of South Carolina, people who eat chocolate bunnies, smokers, etc. We have not dealt systematically with this sort of proposition in our study of reasoning so far. Logic deals primarily with qualitative reasoning, while mathematics deals with quantitative. And a full treatment of statistical reasoning would require a separate book going over the relevant mathematical techniques. But the subject is too important to ignore.

LEARNING OBJECTIVES

On successful completion of the chapter, you will be able to:

✓ Understand the relation between variables and values in statistics. (13.1)

✓ Identify different types of statistical propositions: totals, ratios, frequencies, distributions, averages, and medians. (13.2)

✓ Understand how statistical generalizations are inferred from random samples, within a margin of error. (13.3)

✓ Understand how statistical correlations can provide evidence for causal connections. (13.4)

13.1 Logic and Statistics

For one thing, statistical arguments are often used in connection with the kinds of topics we have been dealing with: political issues, personal decisions, generalizations about human nature. It is not unusual for a given conclusion to be supported by statistical as well as nonstatistical arguments. A proposed change in the tax laws, for example, might be supported by the claim that it will spur the economy as well as by the claim that it will be fairer. The first argument would probably involve statistical data, the second probably not. The daily news offers plenty of other examples. So you need to know how to evaluate *both* kinds of argument in order to weigh all the evidence for the conclusion.

For another thing, statistical evidence is indispensable for conclusions about causality in complex systems—such as the health of a human body or a trend in the economy—where no single factor by itself is either necessary or sufficient. In this respect, some understanding of statistics is necessary to complete our study of Mill's methods.

It's important at the outset to avoid two opposite mistakes about statistics. One mistake is a misplaced worship of numbers. Statements involving numbers have a hard, clean, precise air about them; they give the impression of objectivity and expertise. For that reason, political advocates seem to think that no argument is complete without a statistic to back it up. But we should remember that a statistic is no better than the reasoning process by which it was derived. When the reasoning is fallacious, or arbitrary, or flawed in some other way, the statistic may bear no relation to reality. If someone complains that Americans represent only about 4% of the world's population, but have 23% of the world's fun, you would be right to wonder how the second statistic was derived. Or if someone defends a change in the tax code on the ground that it will create 34,578 new jobs, we should be skeptical. It's extremely doubtful whether anyone could predict, with that kind of precision, the effects of legislation on something as complex as an economy. Indeed, the first and fundamental rule for evaluating a statistical claim is to step back and ask whether the phenomenon can be counted or measured at all (how could anyone measure the amount of fun in the world?), and if so, with what kind of accuracy.

The opposite mistake is to mistrust statistics entirely, an attitude expressed in the statement that "you can prove anything with statistics." This is not true. It *is* true that you can often create the *appearance* of proof by manipulating statistical information, just as fallacious reasoning can give the appearance of a strong argument. But the proper response is to learn how to identify and avoid the fallacies, not to throw the baby out with the bath water. In this chapter, we are going to cover some of the more common fallacies involving statistics. To spot them when they occur, it's a good idea to adopt a healthy skepticism about statistics in general. But you should balance that skepticism with an awareness of the value statistics can have. We rely on them in our daily lives when we make decisions about our health or our jobs, about where to live and where not to, about where to travel and how to get there. Statistical information is often relevant to political arguments. And statisticians have given us some amazingly powerful instruments for discovering patterns in nature and in human affairs that are not visible to the naked eye.

A statistic takes a mass of quantitative information about a group of objects and reduces it to a single number (or set of numbers). In the next section, we're going to look at three basic kinds of statistical information: totals and ratios, frequencies and frequency distributions, and averages. Virtually all the statistics you will encounter in everyday discussion and in the media fall into one of these basic categories or involve some combination of them. Our goal is to understand how the numbers are derived, what they stand for, and the dangers to watch out for when we use these numbers in arguments.

Before we look at the different kinds of statistical information, however, a few general points are in order. Statistics deal with *classes* of things, and for the sake of continuity with previous chapters we will use the letter *S* to stand for a class (and *T*, *U*, etc., if there is more than one class). Statistics also deal with the *properties* that members of a class possess, especially the measurable properties. And properties, like classes of objects, have different levels of abstractness that we can arrange in a hierarchy. Color, for example, is a more abstract, generic quality in relation to specific colors such as red or green. In statistics, a generic quality is called a **variable**, and the specific qualities are called *values* of that variable. So red and green are values of the variable *color*; A, B, AB, and O are values of the variable *blood type*; Republican and Democrat are values of the variable *political party affiliation*.

The concept of a variable is a key link between logic and mathematics, To see why, consider two variables that we might use to classify people:

The first diagram is our familiar classification scheme, with the generic quality or variable above, and the specific qualities or values below. The same is true of the second diagram. The only difference is that hair color is a *qualitative* variable (its values differ from one another qualitatively and could have been listed in any order), whereas age is a *quantitative* variable (a specific age can be measured by number of years, and thus the values are arranged in a specific order along the numerical scale). But in either case, the variable could serve as a principle of classification, and we would group together people who have the same value. Statistics make use of both kinds of variable, but as we will see, certain kinds of statistics apply only to quantitative variables.

EXERCISE 13.1

I. For each of the following variables that apply to human beings, list three or more values of that variable.

＊1. Eye color

2. Income

3. Ethnicity

＊4. Occupation

5. Intelligence

II. For each of the following sets of values, name the variable.

＊1. Liberal, conservative, libertarian, socialist, progressive

2. Infant, child, adolescent, adult, elderly person

3. Married, single

＊4. Christian, Jew, Muslim

5. Employed, unemployed but looking for work, unemployed but not looking for work

13.2 Using Statistics in Argument

Let's turn now to the various types of statistical information and the questions to consider when we use this information in reasoning.

13.2A Totals and Ratios

The simplest operation in arithmetic is addition, and the simplest statistic, which we'll call a **total**, is the result of adding up a set of units. Examples would include:

Total population of the United States.
Total number of new jobs created in the past decade.
Total number of movies that Fred Astaire and Ginger Rogers made together.
Total number of traffic fatalities in 2015.
Total calories consumed in Boston on Thanksgiving Day, 2018.
Total money spent in political campaigns in the 2016 elections.

In the first four examples, the total is the number of members in some class—residents of the United States, new jobs, etc.—and we can find the total simply by counting. In the last two examples, we are also concerned with classes—meals in Boston, political campaigns in 2016—but we are not given the number of members. We are given the sum of their values on some variable: calories and expenditures, respectively.

Totals are probably the kind of statistic we encounter most often in the media. But a simple total by itself is usually not very illuminating. In 2005, there were 15,495 murders in the United States. That's a large and frightening number. But to draw any conclusions from it, we need a standard of comparison. It would help to know, for example, whether the number has been rising or falling. So we could look up the statistics for earlier years and arrange the information in a table:

Year	Number of Murders in the United States	Homicide Rate per 100,000
1990	23,438	9.4
1995	21,606	8.2
2000	15,517	5.5
2005	15,495	5.9
2010	13,941	4.9
2015	14,856	5.0

By comparing equivalent totals (in the middle column), we can identify the trend: Murders declined during 1990s and 2000s, then rose slightly by 2015.

An even more meaningful statistic is the **ratio** of murders to population, shown in the right-hand column. The ratio allows us to compensate for changes in population from year to year, so that we can see whether the chances of being victimized are rising or falling. You can see from the table that the murder rate has fallen even more than the total number. Such ratios also allow us to compare crime rates in different countries. Suppose you wanted to know, for example, whether the United States is a more violent country than Italy. Comparing the total number of murders, or any other crime, would be misleading because the population of the United States is much larger. But if there is a difference in the murder rate per 100,000 residents, then we have evidence that one country is more violent than the other. In general, then, a ratio is a total expressed in relative terms. It is a statistic specifying the number of items in a class or the sum of their values on a variable per unit of some other class.

When we use totals or ratios, finally, it is important to make sure that we are comparing apples to apples. People who gather statistics may use somewhat different definitions for the categories they are measuring. In some places, for example, manslaughter is included in the definition of murder, in other places it is not. You need equivalent definitions before you can draw any meaningful comparison.

EXERCISE 13.2A

For each of the following totals, give an example of (a) a related comparison and (b) a ratio.

*1. Total visitors to the Jefferson Memorial in 2016

2. Fat calories you consumed yesterday

3. Hours you spent watching television last month

*4. Total salmon catch in Alaska last year

5. Budget deficit of the U.S. government in 2019

6. Number of traffic fatalities in Canada in 2018

*7. Number of privately owned automobiles in China

8. Number of calories in a pint of Häagen-Dazs ice cream

9. Number of shots made by Kobe Bryant in 2013

*10. Number of advertising pages in *Vanity Fair* magazine last year

---

13.2B Frequency and Distribution

A **frequency** statement says how many things in a class *S* have the property *P*; it tells us the frequency with which *P* occurs in that class. An *absolute frequency* statement gives the actual number of *S*s that are *P*—for example, 2,149 students at Tiptop College are humanities majors. A *relative frequency* statement gives the *proportion* of *S*s that are *P*—for example, 36% of the students at Tiptop College are humanities majors. As you can see, an absolute frequency is a special sort of total, and a relative frequency is a special sort of ratio. Some of the most commonly reported statistics are frequencies, such as the unemployment rate (percentage of the workforce that is unemployed), the illiteracy rate (percentage of adults who can't read), the poverty rate (percentage of the populace living below the poverty line), or a baseball player's batting average (which is not an average at all, but the proportion of times at bat on which the player gets a hit).

A frequency statement divides the *S*s into two subclasses, those that are *P* and those that are not *P*: humanities majors versus nonhumanities majors, employed people versus unemployed people, and so on. But we can also do a more thorough classification, dividing the Ss into those that are P, Q, R, etc., indicating the proportion that fall into each subclass. The result is called a frequency **distribution**. From a logical standpoint, a distribution is simply a classification with numbers attached and could be represented by a classification diagram. For example, the distribution of students by major might look like this:

It is more common, however, to see this information expressed by either a bar graph or a pie chart:

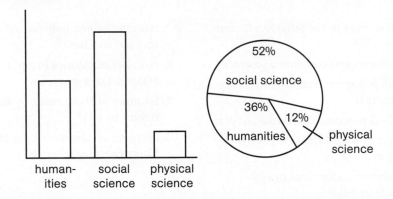

You have probably seen charts of this kind used to represent distributions such as the market share of each company in an industry, the ethnic or racial makeup of a country's population, or the proportion of government spending for military, Social Security, welfare, and other categories.

To have a meaningful distribution, we should use a single principle or a consistent set of principles—that is, a single variable or set of variables. The variable could be a qualitative one such as a student's major, or it could be a quantitative one such as age, IQ, income, height, or corporate revenues. The subgroups into which the Ss are distributed are defined by specific values of the variable. With a quantitative variable, we would usually pick certain intervals on the scale—such as ages 0 to 5, 6 to 10, 11 to 15, etc. In any case, the subgroups should be mutually exclusive, so that we don't count individual things twice. If they are not mutually exclusive, the frequencies could add up to more than 100%. The subgroups should also be jointly exhaustive, so that all the Ss can be assigned to one subclass (value) or another. If they are not jointly exhaustive, the frequencies could add up to less than 100%.

Statements about frequencies and distributions also require that we define our terms carefully. If we are going to measure the proportion of Ss that are P or the distribution of Ss into subgroups P, Q, and R, we need definitions of all these groups. And unlike a definition used in ordinary reasoning, a definition used for statistical purposes can't have fuzzy borders; it must give us a clear criterion for deciding whether to include or to exclude any given thing. This usually involves an element of stipulation, and different researchers will make different decisions. One implication is that you cannot always compare statistics compiled by different researchers, even when they deal with the same subject. For example, the U.S. Bureau of Labor Statistics estimates the unemployment rate in two different ways. The figure most often reported is based on a survey of households, asking individuals whether they are currently employed. But the bureau also does a separate survey of business payrolls. Among other differences, the household survey counts people on strike as employed, while the payroll survey counts them as unemployed; so the two numbers are not comparable.

Let's consider a final and very important role of frequency information. As we will see in Chapter 14, we can use frequency information to make probability judgments. In the 2019 baseball season, for example, Christian Yelich had a batting average of .329, the best in the league. So on every trip to the plate, other things being equal, he had a 32.9% chance of a hit. Similarly, if an insurance company wants to know the probability that a 35-year-old woman will die during the term of her 20-year life insurance policy, it consults a mortality table that says what proportion of 35-year-old women die before they reach 55. In general, we estimate the probability of something from its frequency in the class it belongs to, which in this context is called a reference group. (See Chapter 14 for further discussion of probability.)

EXERCISE 13.2B

Evaluate each of the following distribution statements by determining whether it uses a consistent variable and whether the subclasses are mutually exclusive and jointly exhaustive. Note any questions you have about the definitions of subclasses.

*1. Book sales: adult fiction, 30%; adult nonfiction, 41%; young adult fiction, 23%; young adult nonfiction, 6%.

2. Land use in the United States, in millions of acres: rural, 1,374; developed, 111; forest, 538.6; federal, 644.

3. Nutrients in Oreo cookies (serving size: 3 cookies): fat, 7 grams; carbohydrate, 25 grams; protein, 1 gram; calories, 160.

*4. 2017 expenditures by a nonprofit organization: programs, 87%; administration, 8%; fundraising, 5%.

5. Matter in Earth's crust: rock, 50%; water, 10%; solids, 60%; gases, 10%.

13.2C Average and Median

We are all familiar with averages: grade point averages, average prices of new homes, average SAT scores for this year's freshman class, average yards gained by the Green Bay Packers on third-down plays. An **average** gives us information about some class of things, S; what it tells us is the central value of Ss on some quantitative variable. It is an especially useful way of reducing a mass of quantitative information to a single number.

An average is the sum of the values of each S divided by the number of Ss. Thus, if a class of five students had the following scores on a test:

Student	Score
Joan	97
Elijah	89
Harry	85
Zahra	82
Tom	80

the class average would be:

$$\frac{97 + 89 + 85 + 82 + 80}{5} = \frac{433}{5} = 86.6$$

Another common measure of the central value on a quantitative variable is the **median**: the value that lies in the middle of the range, dividing the Ss into an upper and a lower half. In our example, the median score is Harry's 85. There are two scores above his and two below. (If there had been a sixth member of the class who scored below Tom, then the median would have been halfway between Harry's and Zahra's scores—with an even number of values, the median lies halfway between the two values closest to the middle.) Notice that the average score and the median score are not the same. There was one extreme value—Joan's score—and the average is sensitive to extreme values in a way the median is not. If Joan had received a 90, the average would change to 85.2, but the median would be the same.

Even with a much larger group, an extreme value can pull the average in its direction, just as a child at the end of a seesaw can balance an adult sitting near the middle. Consider a group of 1,000 people with an average income of $35,000 a year. If we now add a single wealthy individual earning $5 million, the group average increases to nearly $40,000, whereas there would be little if any change in the median income. The reason is that income cannot get any lower than $0, but the upper end of the scale is effectively unlimited. So the figure you will often see in the newspapers is the median income, not the average.

Both the average and the median are useful measures of the central tendency in a set of values. Which one is the better measure depends on the situation. The average is the more commonly used measure, but the median is usually better if there are extreme values only in one direction, as in the case of income. Sometimes it isn't clear whether the average or the median is the better measure, and an argument may hang in the balance. For example, doctors carry malpractice insurance; if someone sues for malpractice and wins, the insurance pays the award. Manufacturers carry similar insurance against product liability suits. When the cost of such insurance increases rapidly, people argue about the causes. Some hold the courts responsible, citing the increase in the average amount of damages awarded by juries against doctors and manufacturers. Others reject this explanation on the ground that the average is pulled upward by a few "million-dollar" verdicts, whereas the median award is still quite small. Which number do you think better represents the situation (given that our goal is to understand the rise in insurance premiums)?

We have now covered the main types of statistical information that we use in every-day discussion and encounter in the media. If you understand the differences among these numbers and the dangers to watch out for in using each type of information, you should be able to understand most of the statistics you encounter in everyday contexts and to use them intelligently in arguing for conclusions. The fundamental point to remember is that the numbers depend on the process by which they were derived and are informative only to the extent that the process is logical.

REVIEW Kinds of Statistics

Total: The number of items in a class S or the sum of their values on a variable P.

Ratio: The number of Ss or the sum of their values on a variable P per unit of some other class T; a ratio is a total expressed in relative terms.

Frequency: The number or proportion of Ss that have some particular value on a variable P.

Distribution: The number or proportion of Ss that have each of the values (P, Q, R, etc.) on some variable.

Average: The sum of the values that the Ss have on a quantitative variable P, divided by the number of Ss.

Median: The middle value of the Ss on a quantitative variable P.

EXERCISE 13.2C

Integrative Exercise Identify the type of statistic contained in each of the following statements. Then evaluate how well it supports the conclusion in brackets.

*1. The population of the United States is 327 million. [The United States is a large country.]

2. Between 1990 and 2008, the rate of marriage declined from 9.8 to 5.4 per 1,000 people in the United States. [Fewer people got married in 2008 than in 1990.]

3. For first marriages, the median age of the grooms was 28.9. [Grooms are getting older.]

*4. Among the foreign-born population of the United States in 2009, 53% of Asians had a college degree or more, while 12% of those from Latin America had that much education.

[Asians place more value on education than do Latin Americans.]

5. South Korea and the United States reported their first positive cases of COVID-19 in January 2020. By March 1, South Korea's reported total constituted 4.25% of cumulative global cases while the United States reported .07% of total cases. [Between January and March, the United States was more successful than South Korea in containing the spread of COVID-19.]

6. Population density in the United States is about 93 people per square mile. [It's crowded here.]

*7. Measured in constant 2005 dollars, spending by the federal government increased from $1,832 billion in 1990 to $2,041 billion in 2000 to $3,315 billion in 2010. [Government spending increased less rapidly in the 1990s than in the following decade.]

8. The median starting salary for law school graduates in 2017 was $72,500. [Lawyers are highly paid.]

9. Completion rates within 10 years for those entering graduate school:

Humanities	49%
Mathematics and physical sciences	55%
Social sciences	56%
Life sciences	63%
Engineering	64%

[Engineering students are smarter, on average, than humanities students.]

*10. In 2011, the average salary of players for the New York Mets baseball team was $4,916,741, but the median was $2,112,500. [A few players had much larger salaries than the others.]

13.3 Statistical Generalization

As we saw in the last section, a statistic gives us numerical information about some class of things. In statistics, that class is called a *population* (regardless of whether or not it's a class of people). The different types of statistics—totals, frequencies, averages—tell us about certain quantitative properties of the class. And we know from our study of the basic nature of induction that there are two ways to support a statement about a class. We can examine each and every member—the method of complete enumeration—or we can study a sample of the class and then generalize our findings to the class as a whole. Statisticians use both methods. Many statistics on health, such as the frequency of various diseases or the proportion of people who die from various causes, reflect a complete tabulation of data from local public health officials around the country. And the U.S. Census Bureau issues a number of statistics based on surveys of the entire population. In contrast, opinion polls, the unemployment rate, and many other statistics are based on samples.

Samples can be used to estimate a ratio, a frequency, a frequency distribution, or an average value in a population. The unemployment rate (the *frequency* of unemployment in the workforce) is based on a monthly survey of about 100,000 people. An opinion poll tries to discover the *distribution* of voter preferences for rival candidates by interviewing a random sample of voters. *Average* values for physical and psychological variables—blood pressure, pulse rate, IQ, and the like—are inferred from samples; obviously we can't survey the entire human race. These *statistical generalizations* have much in common with the universal generalizations that we studied earlier (e.g., All S are P). In both cases, we infer that what is true of a sample is true of the entire population. And in both cases, the inference is strong only to the extent that the sample is *representative* of the population. But there are important differences in the way we try to ensure that the sample *is* representative.

For a universal generalization, as we have seen, we want a sample that reflects the qualitative diversity in the class of Ss. We should actively seek out instances that vary in every respect (other than being *S*) that might be relevant to *P*. We should also look actively for negative instances, because even a single *S* that is not *P* would refute the generalization. But this approach would not make sense for a statistical generalization. Suppose we want to know the proportion of *S*s that are *P*—a question of frequency (similar arguments would apply to distributions and averages). There is no point in looking for negative instances. Presumably we already know that some *S*s are not *P*; the question is not whether such instances exist, but rather how frequent they are. For the same reason, the *qualitative* variety of the sample is not necessarily relevant. We are interested in a *quantitative* property of the population: the proportion of *S*s that are *P*. What we need is a method of choosing our sample so that the proportion of *P*s in the sample will reflect the proportion of *P*s in the population.

The method statisticians have devised is the use of *random* samples. The reason is that if we choose our sample randomly, then every member of the population has an equal chance of being included in the sample. Suppose that in the population at large, 17% are *P*. This would mean that every time we choose an *S* to be included in the sample, we have a 17% chance of getting one that is *P*. So in the long run, we would expect to get a *P* about 17% of the time—if our sample is large enough, it should reflect the proportion of *P*s in the population. Thus, instead of actively designing our sample by looking for certain kinds of instances, as we do for a universal generalization, we sit back and let a random process select the sample blindly.

The use of random samples has certain implications that we should be aware of. First, there is always a specific margin of error attached to the conclusion we draw about the population. Suppose you're in charge of quality control for a grain silo. You take a random sample of the grain and find that 3.2% is spoiled. Should you infer that *exactly* 3.2% of grain in the silo is spoiled? No. Your conclusion should be that spoilage in the silo is in the neighborhood of 3.2%. A sample is an instrument for measuring a quantity, and like other measuring instruments it has a specific margin of error. Second, the margin of error depends on the size of the sample. The larger the sample, the smaller the margin of error, and vice versa. For instance, when the Gallup poll reports the preferences of U.S. voters in an upcoming national election, it uses a sample of about 1,000 voters, and the margin of error is about 4%. So if 56% in the sample favors candidate A, we can infer that somewhere between 52% and 60% of the entire pool of voters favors candidate A. If the sample had included only 100 people, the margin of error would have been larger—around 10%.

Finally, we should be aware that even when we take the margin of error into account, we are still only dealing with probabilities. Because the sample was randomly chosen, there is some chance, however small, that it radically misrepresents the population. In our example above, suppose that in fact only 1% of the electorate favors candidate A. That's a tiny minority, but it's still more than a million voters, and it is possible that 560 of them were included in the sample (560/1,000 = 56%). In generalizing from a sample, therefore, we have to be satisfied with some degree of probability. Most people who use statistics settle for 95%. The 4% margin of error in the Gallup poll, for example, actually means that there's a 95% probability that the proportion of the voters favoring candidate A is within three percentage points of the reported figure.

There are precise mathematical techniques for computing a margin of error, given the size of the sample and the degree of probability we want. We'll leave all that to the experts. The techniques are not controversial, at least not for the types of statistics we are likely to encounter, and we can assume that if a statistic comes from a reputable source, the computations were done correctly. It is important to emphasize, however, that the margin of error refers only to the statistical relationship between the sample and the population. It does not include errors that arise in choosing and testing the sample itself. In particular, the techniques for calculating the margin of error assume that the sample was randomly chosen. This assumption is rarely true in the strict sense. A true random sample would be one chosen randomly from a complete list of the population. For a population the size of the U.S. electorate, however, it is rarely possible to find a complete list, and it is usually too expensive to choose and test a completely random sample. So researchers typically use methods that they think will approximate randomness. But the approximation is never perfect, and there is plenty of room for biases to creep in. Let's look at some examples.

You want to know the average test score of the students in a class you're taking, so you ask the first 10 students who arrive at class one day—but that sample may overrepresent the more conscientious students, who may tend to score higher. An opinion poll uses a questionnaire distributed in airports—but people who travel by air are not a random cross section of the populace, and besides, people who fill out and return questionnaires are not a random cross section of those who receive them. A study of criminals relies on a sample of prison inmates—but criminals who are caught, convicted, and imprisoned may not be representative of criminals as a whole. All these samples are *biased* in one way or another and therefore won't tell us what we want to know about the relevant populations. Problems can also arise in testing the sample once it is chosen. A telephone interview, for example, would be a poor way to estimate the proportion of parents who abuse their children: Even if the sample was randomly chosen, you could hardly count on abusers to tell you the truth.

Another source of bias in opinion polls is the exact wording of the question. A classic example comes from the General Social Survey, which asks people whether they think the government is spending too much, too little, or the right amount on a variety of programs. Respondents were asked about government spending on "welfare" and spending on "assistance to the poor." These two descriptions refer to essentially the same programs, but the results always differ. Here is the data from the year 2018:

Is Government Spending . . .	Welfare	Assistance to the Poor
Too little	23.6%	73.2%
About right	37.6%	19.7%
Too much	38.9%	7.2%

Source: General Social Survey, National Opinion Research Center.

It seems clear that people are responding to connotations of the terms. "Welfare" has acquired a negative connotation of dependence, whereas "assistance to the poor" has a more positive invocation of a helping hand.

An opinion poll is an especially complicated case of generalizing from a sample, because opinions are such intangible and slippery things. It's likely that some respondents make up their minds on the spot, under the influence of subtle factors like the exact wording of the question or the structure of the alternatives they're given. But opinion polls are also the kind of statistical generalization we encounter most often in the media, and they illustrate very well the kinds of biases to watch for.

Despite the problems that can arise in generalizing from a sample, this method can be a reliable way of supporting statistical claims about a population. An example is the crime rate: the number of burglaries (or other crimes) per thousand people. The FBI computes this figure by complete enumeration; it tabulates all the burglaries reported to all the police departments in the country. The National Crime Victimization Survey, however, uses a sample; it interviews about 49,000 households to see how many were victims of burglary in the previous 6 months. The NCVS runs the risks associated with any use of samples. But the FBI figures have their own flaw: Many burglaries are not reported to the police (a fact we know from the survey of victims). So the two approaches must be used to supplement each other.

As you can see, investigating the statistical properties of large populations in the real world takes a blend of common sense and specialized technique. If you need to use statistics in your studies or your work, you will need a separate course of training in the proper methods. This section is intended for the non-expert—the consumer of statistical information, not the producer. As consumers, we must rely to some extent on the authority of experts. But as in any other case of relying on authorities, we can—and should—use our own common sense to evaluate their credibility.

SOLVE   Generalizing from a Sample

A statistical generalization is a claim about ratio, frequency, distribution, average, or median value in a population, based on information about a random sample. To assess the strength of the generalization, consider the following questions:

1. Was the margin of error reported? If so, how large is it?

2. How was the sample selected? Was the selection procedure random? Was there anything about the selection process to suggest that the sample might not be representative of the population?

3. How was information about the sample acquired? Was there anything to suggest that the process of testing the sample was unreliable? In the case of opinion polls, for example, consider whether the question used slanted language or forced respondents to choose among too small a range of alternatives.

EXERCISE 13.3

Identify potential biases and other problems in each of the following generalizations.

✳1. A conservative organization reports that 71% of the populace is opposed to national health insurance, based on a questionnaire sent to its mailing list.

2. To find the average salary of doctors, a reporter interviews a random sample of doctors attending a convention of the American Medical Association.

3. *Road and Track* magazine polls its readers to find out what percentage of the population favors increased speed limits on interstate highways.

∗4. To find the average age of Taylor Swift fans, researchers survey people at a Taylor Swift concert.

5. A poll is conducted by telephone to find the percentage of men who cannot swim.

6. Researchers telephone a random sample of households in the evening to find what percentages of families eat dinner together.

∗7. To assess how engaged parents are in their children's education, researchers send a questionnaire to the email list of the Parent Teacher Association.

8. Two percent of apples are estimated to have pesticide residues above allowable levels, based on a sample drawn from supermarkets across the country.

9. An environmental organization uses the following question in a mail survey: "Do you believe Americans have an ethical obligation to preserve unique riverine natural systems for future generations?"

∗10. An opinion survey asks respondents: Which of the following best represents your position on government funding of the arts? a. Museums, symphonies, and other arts organizations should be funded by tax dollars. b. Such organizations should rely on ticket sales to people patronizing the organizations.

13.4 Statistical Evidence of Causality

We have seen that a statistic gives us numerical information about a class, such as the total number of its members or their average values on a variable. Statistics can also tell us about *correlations* among these numerical properties. A correlation can take many forms, depending on the type of statistic involved. For example, *average* income correlates with the *total* years of education people have. The *frequency* of lung cancer is higher among smokers than among nonsmokers. A high *ratio* of high- to low-density cholesterol is correlated with a low risk (*frequency*) of heart attack. What these examples have in common, what makes them examples of correlation, is a systematic, nonrandom relationship between two variables: income and education, smoking and lung cancer, cholesterol levels and heart attacks.

13.4A Correlation and Causality

Correlations are important because they can give us evidence of causality. Medical researchers use statistical evidence to trace the causes of health and disease—the link between smoking and cancer is the best known example, but there are many others. Economists look for correlations that will explain inflation, unemployment, productivity, etc. In these and other cases, the use of correlations is required by the nature of the subject. In a complex system like the human body or the economy, a given effect is often the result of a great many factors—none of which by itself is either necessary or sufficient. Smoking, for example, is not a necessary condition for lung cancer: Some nonsmokers get the disease. Nor is it sufficient: Some smokers don't. But smoking *is* a partial or *contributing* factor, something that increases the likelihood of lung cancer, something that weighs in the balance—and can tip the balance if the right combination of other factors is also present.

To identify a contributing factor, we have to look at a large number of cases. For example, a drop in interest rates tends to cause an increase in purchases of homes. That's because individuals take the cost of a mortgage into account in deciding whether to buy. Of course, some people are going to buy a home no matter what, and others are simply not in the market. But for some individuals, a drop in mortgage costs will tip the balance. An economist, however, has no way of knowing who those particular individuals are; he can only examine the class of home buyers as a whole and see whether the class gets bigger when interest rates fall. In general, a contributing factor usually can't be identified by looking at individual cases, but it will reveal itself in the existence of a correlation among variables in the relevant class.

The existence of a correlation, however, does not prove causality—not by itself. A correlation may occur by chance, or it may reflect a causal relationship quite different from the one it suggests. For example:

> During a 19-year stretch, the stock market went up almost every year when a team from the NFC won the Super Bowl and down when the AFC team won.

> Before the introduction of polio vaccine, investigators found a strong correlation between soft drink sales and new polio cases reported.

> In certain areas of Europe, there is a correlation between births and the number of stork nests.

> Arizona has one of the highest death rates in the country from bronchitis, emphysema, asthma, and other lung diseases.

It should not be surprising that some correlations, as in the first example, occur by chance. Think of all the variables you could measure—from the average number of Oakland A's home runs during double-headers, to the fertility rate of zebras in Tanzania. If you look long enough, you're bound to find some bizarre correlations. In other cases, variables are correlated because both reflect a third factor. Before the vaccine was developed, polio epidemics tended to occur in the summer, when soft drink sales were also high. Storks do not in fact bring babies, but they do tend to nest in buildings, and the number of buildings increases with population. Arizona's death rate from lung disease does not mean that clean air kills; it means that many people with these diseases move there to prolong their lives.

Thus inferring that variable *a* causally affects variable *E* merely because *a* and *E* are correlated is analogous to the *post hoc* fallacy. If one event causes another, the first must precede the second, but the converse does not hold; the fact that *a* came first does not imply that it caused *E*. To establish causality, as we saw in Chapter 11, we must use Mill's methods to show that there is a connection between *a* and *E*. In the same way, a contributing factor should give rise to a correlation among variables, but not every correlation reveals a causal relation. We need a method for separating the statistical wheat from the chaff.

APPLY Regression to the Mean

We have noted that correlation does not necessarily imply causation. The same is true in reverse: The lack of an expected correlation may not have a causal explanation either. That's because of what statisticians call *regression to the mean* ("mean" is another name for average). One form of this pattern occurs for results on repeated tasks, such as exams in a college course or athletic performance, among many others. We expect the results to reflect the ability of the person, and that's largely true. But there is variation among the results on repeated tasks, due to "chance"—external factors outside the person's control. When a student has an unusually high test score, for example, it may well be partly the result of good "luck," and there's a good chance that the next score will be lower, closer to the student's average. In the same way, an unusually low score may reflect bad luck, and the next score will probably be higher.

Regression to the mean is a purely statistical pattern, due to variation that is unrelated to ability or other relevant causal factors. Yet we have a cognitive bias, like the ones we discussed in Chapter 4, to seek a causal explanation. Psychologist Daniel Kahneman gives the example of treating depressed children with an energy drink. It's likely that they would improve on tests for depression, and it's natural to assume that the treatment caused the improvement. But:

> It is also the case that depressed children who spend some time standing on their head or hug a cat for twenty minutes a day will also show improvement. Depressed children are an extreme group, they are more depressed than most other children—and extreme groups regress to the mean over time. The correlation between depression scores on successive occasions of testing is less than perfect, so there will be regression to the mean: depressed children will get somewhat better over time even if they hug no cats and drink no Red Bull.

In the four examples before, you could rely on common sense to avoid drawing the wrong conclusion. But many other cases are less obvious. Does lowering a tax rate cause an increase in tax revenues? How much of a person's intelligence is due to heredity? Does caffeine cause bladder cancer? Is a murderer more likely to get the death penalty for killing a white person than for killing a Black person? There is correlational evidence on all these questions, but it is not immediately obvious how to interpret the evidence, and these issues are extremely controversial. Let's take a look at some rules we should follow.

13.4B Evaluating Correlations

The rules for evaluating statistical evidence of causality rest on the same basic principle as Mill's methods, just as drawing a statistical generalization from a sample is governed by the same basic principle as universal generalizations. But there are also some important differences. Let's start by looking at an idealized case in the abstract. Then we'll look at some of the problems and issues that come up in practice.

Suppose we want to know whether some variable E is causally affected by another variable a. The ideal test would be an experiment in which we can control a and watch for corresponding changes in E; in this context, a is called the *independent* variable and E the *dependent* variable. One way to design the experiment could be diagrammed as follows:

Group 1: $a, b, c, \ldots$
Group 2: $-, b, c, \ldots$

We have two groups that are identical except that one (the *experimental* group) has the property we're testing, while the other (the *control* group) does not. You can see that this is the same basic pattern as Mill's method of difference. Alternatively, if a is a quantitative variable, we could give different experimental groups different levels of a, using the same pattern as Mill's method of concomitant variation:

Group 1: $a-, \quad b, \quad c, \ldots$
Group 2: $a, \quad b, \quad c, \ldots$
Group 3: $a+, \quad b, \quad c, \ldots$

Notice, however, that we are comparing two or more *groups* instead of comparing two or more *individual* cases, as we did when we studied Mill's methods earlier. We have to use groups when a is only a contributing factor, for the reason explained above. And we will also have to make an adjustment in the way we measure the dependent variable, the effect. The question is not whether the effect occurs, or in what degree, in a particular case; we are not comparing particular cases directly. We are comparing groups. So the question is whether a makes a *statistical* difference in the effect. If E is a qualitative variable, we would typically measure a frequency—for example, the frequency of tumors in mice fed a diet high in saccharin.

Group 1: saccharin, $b, \quad c, \ldots$ $\longrightarrow$ higher frequency
Group 2: no saccharin, $b, \quad c, \ldots$ $\longrightarrow$ lower frequency

If E is a quantitative variable, we would typically look at average values for experimental and control groups—for example, average SAT scores for students taking test-preparation classes.

Group 1: test prep class, $b, \quad c, \ldots$ $\longrightarrow$ higher average SAT
Group 2: no test prep, $b, \quad c, \ldots$ $\longrightarrow$ lower average SAT

But those are fairly minor adjustments to make in our use of Mill's methods. The major adjustment has to do with the other variables—b, c, etc. As we have seen, it's essential to the methods of difference and concomitant variations that we hold these factors constant. That is what allows us to infer that a is responsible for any differences in E. When we use statistical evidence, we have to meet this requirement in a somewhat different way. We want to know whether a certain test-preparation course can raise people's SAT scores. We would have an experimental group take the course and a control group not take it, holding all other factors constant. But how are we going to do that? Individual students differ on an enormous number of variables that might affect their SAT scores: IQ, verbal ability, memory, ability to concentrate, ambition, response to stress, test-taking savvy, and so on. It would be extraordinarily difficult to find two individuals who are identical with regard to all these variables. Finding two *groups* whose members are all identical is out of the question. Fortunately, that isn't necessary. Since we are dealing with groups, what matters is that they have the same *distribution* on those variables—the same distribution by verbal ability, memory, etc. In that case, the experimental and control groups will be statistically identical except for the variable we are testing (taking the course vs. not taking it), and a statistical difference in the effect can then be attributed to that variable.

Setting things up this way is easier said than done. It takes a great deal of scientific knowledge and skill to make sure that the groups are statistically similar on these variables. In some cases, researchers try to match the groups by deliberately pairing off individuals. But this is quite difficult, especially if there are more than a few variables to keep track of. And with really complex phenomena, we simply don't know what all the relevant variables are. So it is more common to use random procedures for selecting the two groups, and the rationale is the same as in the case of generalizing from a sample. Suppose that in our pool of volunteers for the SAT experiment, 10% have IQs in the 140+ range. If we assign volunteers to groups by a random process, then every time we select someone for either group, there's a 10% chance we'll select someone in the 140+ range. So if the groups are large enough, there's a good chance that each one will have about 10% in that range. And the same would be true for values on the other variables.

Suppose, then, that we have assigned our volunteers to their groups by a random process; our experimental group has taken the cram course, and its average SAT score is higher than the average for our control group. Does this prove that the course affected the scores? It depends. Remember that we are using a random process, so we have to apply what we learned in the last section about random sampling. First, we would not expect the averages to be *exactly* the same even if the cram course had no effect whatever. The difference in averages must be of a certain size before we have evidence of causality. Second, the size of that difference depends on the size of our groups, just as the margin of error in an opinion poll depends on the size of the sample. As we increase the size of our experimental and control groups, it becomes more likely that traits such as intelligence will be distributed evenly between them, so it becomes less likely that a large difference in average scores could occur merely by chance. In general, the larger the group, the smaller the correlation has to be to count as causally significant. But third, and finally, we are still only dealing with probabilities. Even with a large sample, there is some chance, however tiny, that our random process assigned all the geniuses to the experimental group. So if the difference in average scores is x points, then to be precise we should state our result as follows: There is only a y percent probability that an x point difference could occur by chance, given the size of our groups. Most researchers consider a result *statistically significant* if y is less than 5%.

There are mathematical techniques for determining whether a correlation is statistically significant. Once again, as with generalizing from a sample, we'll leave these calculations to the experts. But once again, it's important to emphasize the limitations of these techniques. Just as the margin of error in a poll does not take account of errors in choosing the sample, a correlation that is statistically significant may not be significant in the usual sense of being important. With a large enough sample, it is possible to identify factors that play a very small causal role in contributing to an effect. This is true, for example, of many substances that have been found to "cause" cancer in laboratory animals. Or suppose a researcher found a statistically significant difference in traffic fatality rates between states with different drinking ages. That wouldn't necessarily provide an argument for raising the drinking age. Perhaps the difference was minor, and it would be more effective to impose stiffer penalties on drunk driving.

In the previous section, moreover, we saw that the techniques for computing a margin of error rest on the assumption that the sample was randomly selected—an assumption that is rarely true in the strict sense. An analogous point can be made about correlations. A statistically significant correlation is evidence of causality on the assumption that we have taken into account all the other variables that might affect our result. The idealized experiment described earlier is an attempt to meet that standard. In practice, however, problems invariably arise that call the assumption into question. After we pause for a bit of practice, we will look at a few of these problems.

EXERCISE 13.4B

Integrative Exercise

Analyze the statistical inferences below as instances of Mill's methods. First identify the independent and dependent variables and the type of statistic (frequency or average) used to measure the effect; then determine whether the method of difference or the method of concomitant variations is being used.

∗1. In a sample of pea plants grown under ultraviolet light, 80% of the seeds sprouted within a week, as against 60% of a control group, grown in normal conditions. Thus ultraviolet light fosters growth.

2. A large statistical study of doctors shows that exercise affects the risk of heart disease. Those who exercised three times a week had half the rate of heart attacks as those who exercised irregularly and a quarter as many heart attacks as those who never exercised.

3. The effects of a new gasoline additive were tested on a group of 30 automobiles of different makes, models, and model years. Each car used the same brand of gasoline for a month, measuring the miles driven on each tankful; then the same gasoline with the additive was used for a month.

Average mileage for these 30 cars was 5% higher with the additive than without.

∗4. Twenty students who used planners to track their assignments and plan their study time each week were matched for intelligence, field of study, and year of graduation with 20 students who did not. The average grade point average for the first group was 3.1, versus 2.8 for the second group, a result that shows the value of using planners.

5. In a large study of the effects of advertising, 300 consumer-product companies were divided into four groups, depending on the size of their advertising budgets as a percentage of total expenditures. It was discovered that as the size of the advertising budget increased, average profit margins increased also.

13.4C Experiments Versus Observational Studies

Suppose we want to know whether there's a significant difference in the way men and women react to stress. We can't randomly assign our volunteers to the two groups, male and female—nature has already made that decision. For a true experiment, the experimenter must be able to control the independent variable. But many variables can't be controlled: Meteorologists can't control the properties of storm systems, economists can't manipulate the economy to see what causes depressions, geologists can't decide when to have an earthquake. There are other variables that can't be manipulated for ethical reasons. You can't ask someone to smoke for 20 years for the sake of cancer research. You can't abuse an experimental group of children to see whether abuse breeds violent behavior. In all these cases, we are limited to *observational* studies. We have to observe the variables as they occur naturally, outside our control, and try to find the relevant correlations.

In the right circumstances, an observational study *can* provide evidence of causality. But it has two major drawbacks in relation to an experiment. First, it does not involve random assignment to experimental and control groups. So there's a danger that any correlation we find between two variables may be due to some third variable that is not evenly distributed among the groups. For example, it is plausible to think that a person who was abused as a child is more likely than other people to have certain problems later in life: to abuse his or her own children, engage in criminal activity, etc. And there is correlational evidence to support this hypothesis. But is the abuse actually the cause of these later problems? Parents who abuse their children are not a random sample from the population. They tend to have other traits in common: They tend to be emotionally distant and neglectful of their children, for example, and subject to economic stresses such as unemployment or poverty. Perhaps it is these traits, rather than the physical abuse per se, that contribute to the child's later problems. We can't tell from the correlation itself. In the language of statistics, the correlation we observe between two variables may be *confounded* by some other variable.

Second, an experiment allows us to control one variable and look for changes in another. If we find them, there is no question which is the cause, which the effect. But this question does arise in observational studies. Cities have higher crime rates than rural areas. Is that because urban life breeds criminals or because criminals migrate to cities to find victims? People with higher levels of education have higher average incomes. Does that mean you can boost your income by getting a college degree? Perhaps. Or perhaps the correlation is a by-product of an underlying factor—people with more intelligence or ambition may tend to do better both in school and in the job market, but for different reasons.

As a general rule, therefore, it is more difficult to draw causal conclusions from an observational study than from an experiment. But this is merely a general rule. For one thing, experiments are not immune from problems of confounding variables. Suppose you want to study the effects of political advertising on voter preferences. So you show an ad for candidate A to your experimental group and find that the proportion who say they'd vote for candidate A goes up. That may indicate that the ad had a real effect. Or it may simply mean that your subjects figured out what you were up to and were simply telling you what they knew you wanted to hear.

Careful researchers can structure experiments to avoid these problems. An observational study can also take steps to screen out confounding variables. For example, the death rate from lung cancer is higher for smokers than for nonsmokers. That fact alone would not prove that smoking plays a causal role. The age distribution among smokers and nonsmokers may not be the same. Or perhaps the class of smokers includes a higher proportion who live in cities and are exposed to more air pollution. But cancer researchers control for such factors by comparing people of the same age, who live in the same area, and so on for many other variables—and the death rate for smokers is still higher. Among the class of smokers, moreover, the death rate varies concomitantly with the number of cigarettes a person smokes per day, the number of years that person has smoked, and the degree of inhalation. And among ex-smokers, the death rate goes down in correlation with the number of years since a person quit. When you put all this together, there is little doubt that a causal relationship does exist.

13.4D External Validity

The issues we have considered so far pertain to what is sometimes called the *internal* validity of a study or experiment. They pertain to the conclusions we can draw about cause and effect in regard to the class of things actually observed or included in an experiment. But of course we normally want to generalize from that class to a wider population. We want to know whether smoking causes cancer for people in general, not just for those who happened to be included in a particular study. And this raises questions of *external* validity, questions you should ask when a researcher claims that his findings apply to a population as a whole.

A great deal of psychological research is conducted at colleges and universities using undergraduate students as subjects. If an experiment is done properly and finds a significant correlation, we can infer that the independent variable was causally affecting the dependent variable—for the particular subjects involved. But how far can we generalize the result? To all people of college age? Perhaps—if we assume that the differences between those who go to college and those who don't are irrelevant to the outcome. Can we generalize to people of all ages? Perhaps—if we assume that age makes no difference. These assumptions may or may not be reasonable in a given case. The point to remember is that they are not supported by the experiment itself.

To evaluate external validity, finally, we should remember the special importance of definitions in statistical reasoning. To establish a correlation between two variables, we must define the variables in such a way that they can be counted or measured. In some cases this is fairly easy; in others it is difficult if not impossible. Cancer researchers do not face any major difficulty in defining the category of people who smoke. Economists don't need specialized definitions of men and women to study sex differences in income. By their very nature, however, psychological traits such as intelligence, values, attitudes, or feelings cannot be observed directly. Nor is statistical information readily available for many economic and sociological categories—such as undocumented residents, entrepreneurs, fundamentalists.

To test a hypothesis involving one of these variables, therefore, a researcher must find some other variable to stand in for it, a *proxy variable* to serve as a measuring rod.

Suppose you wanted to see whether some classroom exercise had any effect on racial prejudice in college students. The dependent variable you are interested in is *prejudice*. But you cannot observe what is going on in a student's mind directly, so for the purposes of the experiment you would have to measure prejudice indirectly—say, by the student's willingness to contribute to a civil rights organization. That is where the problem of external validity arises. Suppose you found a strong correlation between the classroom exercise and the willingness to contribute, a correlation strong enough to convince you that a causal relationship is involved. Does that prove the exercise affects prejudice? Only if we assume that the willingness to contribute is a good barometer of prejudice—an assumption that may or may not be true. In addition to prejudice, the willingness to contribute to a particular organization may reflect a person's level of generosity, his awareness of political issues, his agreement with the specific political goals of the organization, or simply his desire for popularity. And it may be that the exercise affected one of these other variables, not prejudice per se. In general, then, when someone claims to have established a causal relationship, and one or more of the variables involved strike you as things that can't be measured or counted directly, make sure to ask what variables were actually being correlated in the study or experiment, and consider whether those stand-in variables really do reflect the variable they purport to measure.

This completes our discussion of statistical evidence of causality. Once again, we have approached this as consumers of information, not producers. If you are going to conduct experiments or observational studies yourself, you will need more training in the subject matter and relevant statistical techniques. As consumers, we must rely to some extent on the authority of those who have that expertise. But once again, we should be intelligent consumers, using the considerations we've discussed here, along with our common sense, to ask critical questions about the research results we encounter in the media and elsewhere.

SOLVE Internal and External Validity

When statistical methods are used to support a causal generalization that factor *a* affects *E*, the chief questions to ask about the *internal* validity of the inference are:

1. Confounding variables: Were there any variables, other than the ones being tested, that may have been responsible for *E*?

2. Direction of causality: Is it clear whether *a* is affecting *E* or *E* affecting *a*?

The chief questions to ask about *external* validity are:

1. Extrapolation: Is the claim that *a* affects *E* being extended beyond the class of *a*'s or *E*s or extrapolated beyond the range of the variables that were tested?

2. Proxy variables: When a causal factor or an effect cannot be studied directly, and other variables are studied as their proxies, how reasonable is it to assume a connection between the observed variable and the variation of interest?

*EXERCISE 13.4D

| Integrative Exercise | The paragraph below is a fictional report of research purporting to prove a causal relationship. Using what you've learned in this section, evaluate the causal inference. |

Scientists at Flywheel Polytechnic have established that backseat driving can be hazardous to your health. Prior to this research, which was funded by the U.S. Department of Transportation, there had been speculation that nagging advice from passengers on how to drive might cause stress for some exasperated drivers and increase the likelihood of accidents. The Flywheel team, reasoning that spouses and other family members are the commonest source of such advice, compared traffic near Disney World, at the height of the vacation season, with commuter traffic outside New York City, consisting largely of drivers alone in their cars. Average speeds were the same in the two cases, as were driving conditions, but the accident rate in vacation traffic was 34.5% higher, a difference found to be statistically significant.

CHAPTER REVIEW

Summary

- Statistics give us numerical information about a class or population of things; the information normally concerns their values on one or more variables.
  - A total is the number of things in a class S or the sum of their values on a variable. A ratio is a total stated in relationship to another class T.
  - A frequency is the number or proportion of Ss that have some property P; a distribution is the proportion of Ss that have each of the values $(\underline{P}, Q, R, \ldots)$ on some variable. Frequencies and distributions are often used to estimate probability.
  - Averages and medians are central values of Ss on a quantitative variable.
- A statistical statement about a population can be supported either by complete enumeration or by generalization from a sample.

  - A randomly chosen sample allows us to conclude that the relevant value of the population is the same as the value of the sample, within a certain margin of error, to a certain degree of probability.
  - Perfectly random samples are rarely used, however, and the techniques used to approximate randomness may introduce biases.
- Statistical correlations among variables provide an important source of evidence for causal connections. A correlation per se, however, is not proof of causality; we must control for other variables according to the pattern of Mill's methods of difference or concomitant variations.
  - This may be done through an experiment in which subjects are randomly assigned to control and experimental groups or through an observational study.

- In either case, we should watch for problems of internal validity: Are there any confounding variables? Is it clear which variable is the cause and which the effect?

- And we should watch for problems of external validity: Is it reasonable to generalize from the sample actually studied to a larger population? Are the variables actually measured good stand-ins for the variables of interest?

Key Terms

variable (p. 571)

total (p. 572)

ratio (p. 572)

frequency (p. 573)

distribution (p. 574)

average (p. 575)

median (p. 576)

Putting It All Together

I.   Integrative Exercise   For each pair of statements, determine whether the statements are compatible or contradictory.

✳1. (a) Thirty-six percent of seniors at Tiptop College are international students. (b) Eighty-four percent of students at Tiptop College are American citizens.

2. (a) The number of people employed in the U.S. economy increased 1.1% to 109.7 million. (b) The unemployment rate increased to 7.1% last month, from 7.0% the previous month.

3. (a) Among those who reported incomes below the poverty line in 2011, only 9% worked full-time, year-round. (b) In 2011, only 2.6% of people who worked full-time, year-round, reported incomes below the poverty level.

✳4. (a) The human brain contains about 10 billion nerve cells. (b) The human brain contains about 100 billion nerve cells.

5. (a) Sixty-three percent of American voters think that taxes should be cut. (b) Twenty-seven percent of American voters think that government spending on social programs should be cut.

6. (a) Accidental Petroleum's profits this year were up 91% over last year. (b) Accidental Petroleum's profits this year were 4% of revenues.

✳7. (a) In eight courses this year, Chris's grade distribution was four As, three Bs, and one C. (b) Chris's grade point average this year was 2.2.

8. (a) Fifty percent of individuals with incomes of $75,000 or more have individual retirement accounts (IRAs), while only 25% of individuals earning less than $75,000 have IRAs. (b) Ninety percent of IRA contributions are made by people earning less than $50,000 per year.

II. `Integrative Exercise` Match names of statistic types to definitions.

❋1. frequency _____

2. average _____

3. total _____

❋4. distribution _____

5. ratio _____

6. median _____

a. a statistic specifying the number of items in a class or the sum of their values on a variable.

b. A statistic specifying the number or proportion of items in a class that have each of the values (P, Q, R, etc.) on some variable.

c. A statistic specifying the middle value of the items in a class on a quantitative variable P.

d. A statistic specifying the sum of the values that the items in a class have on a quantitative variable P, divided by the number of items.

e. A statistic specifying the number or proportion of items in a class that have a given property.

f. A statistic specifying the number of items in a class or the sum of their values on a variable per unit of some other class.

III. `Integrative Exercise` Each question below is followed by references to various statistics. Which statistic would be most helpful in answering the question?

❋1. Has it become more expensive in the past 10 years to purchase a house?
   a. The median price of houses on the market, now versus then
   b. The average price of houses on the market, now versus then
   c. The median price, adjusted for inflation
   d. The median price as a multiple of the median family's income, now versus then

2. Has divorce become more common in the past 10 years?
   a. Total number of divorces, now versus then
   b. The ratio of divorces to marriages, now versus then
   c. The number of divorces as a percentage of all married couples, now versus then
   d. The divorce rate (per unit of population), now versus then

3. Is it safer to travel by plane or by car?
   a. Fatalities per vehicle mile for planes and cars
   b. Fatalities per passenger mile for planes and cars

❋4. Has my investment in the Random Walk Fund given me a satisfactory return over the past year?
   a. Dollar amount of increase in value of investment
   b. Amount of increase as percent of amount invested
   c. Percent of increase as compared to interest rate
   d. Percent of increase as compared to increase in Standard and Poor's stock index

5. Is private education cheaper than public education? (Choose one figure from each column.)

Private Schools	Public Schools
(a) Average tuition	(d) Average expenditure per pupil
(b) Median tuition	(e) Average fee charged to pupils from outside the district
(c) Median tuition at nonreligious schools	

IV. A common poll question is, "What do you think is the most important problem facing the country today?" Developed by the Gallup organization, it lists a range of issues that respondents can choose as most important—and environmental issues get relatively few "votes." Researchers at Stanford asked whether a change in wording would affect the results. They used four versions of the question with different groups:

1. What do you think is the most important problem facing the country today?

2. What do you think is the most important problem facing the world today?

3. What do you think will be the most important problem facing the world in the future?

4. What do you think will be the most serious problem facing the world in the future if nothing is done to stop it?

The table shows response totals on some of the issues. Explain why the different questions might have had different results.

Problem	1	2	3	4
"The economy" / unemployment	49%	32%	21%	10%
Global warming / the environment	1%	7%	14%	25%
Health care	11%	6%	6%	5%
Debt / government spending	6%	2%	1%	2%

Source: D. S. Yeager et al., *Public Opinion Quarterly.*

V. Using everything you have learned in this chapter, evaluate each of the following arguments for its use of statistic claims.

*1. A pharmaceutical company advertises skin rash cream to relieve the symptoms of poison ivy. For 70% of the people using the cream, it says, the rash and itching disappear within 1 week.

2. Shakespeare scholar Bernard Beckerman studied the records of Shakespeare's theater company (the Lord Admiral's Men) to determine how important new plays were for a company's bottom line, as opposed to revival of plays from previous seasons. For the 1595–1596 season, "the company gave one hundred and fifty performances of thirty differ-ent plays. Eighty-seven performances, or 58 per cent of the total, were of the fourteen new plays produced that season. Five performances, 3.3 per cent, were of one play, *The Jew of Malta*, revived that season. Forty-six performances, or 30.7 per cent, were given of the eight plays from the previous season, which were less than a year old. . . . Only twelve performances, 8 per cent, were of the seven plays which were more than a year old. This distribution, which is similar for all the seasons covered by Henslowe's records, emphasizes how dependent the company was

on the continuous addition of new plays to its stock in order to maintain itself in London." [Bernard Beckerman, *Shakespeare at the Globe*]

3. An organization supporting research on Alzheimer's disease urges more government spending to find causes and possible treatments for the disease. After all, it argues, government-sponsored research for the millions of people with Alzheimer's comes to only $50 per victim, whereas spending on AIDS is over $10,000 per victim.

*4. "Researchers at a university reported that younger wives appear to be a basis for a longer life span in men between 50 and 80 years old. The death rate for older men married to women 1 to 24 years younger was 13% lower than average for their age group. Men with older wives seemed to have a death rate 20% higher than average." [*Wall Street Journal*]

5. In defending farm programs that increase the price of products like sugar, a U.S. congressman from the Midwest asserted, "The way to determine whether or not prices of food that are from price-supported commodities are high is to go to the grocery store and compare them with those products that are not processed from price-supported products." To clinch the argument, he held up a five-pound bag of sugar costing $1.79 and a two-pound package of cat food costing $2.83. [James Brovard, "How to Think Like a Congressman," *Wall Street Journal*]

6. Psychologists Leif D. Nelson and Joseph P. Simmons conducted research purporting to show that because people like their names, they are unconsciously drawn to negative outcomes that they would consciously avoid if those outcomes reminded them of their names. In one study, they compiled the strikeout records of major-league baseball players. "For scoring clarity, strikeouts have always been recorded using the letter K. . . . Accordingly, we predicted that players whose first or last names begin with K would show an increased tendency to strike out." They ana-

lyzed the records of 6,397 players from 1913 (the first year for which there are complete data) through 2006. "Across more than 90 years of professional baseball, batters whose names began with K struck out at a higher rate (in 18.8% of their plate appearances) than the remaining batters (17.2%)," a statistically significant difference. ["Moniker Maladies: When Names Sabotage Success," *Psychological Science*, vol. 18, no. 12]

*7. The Police Executive Research Forum, a research and policy organization for law enforcement agencies, argues that police departments in the United States are facing workforce shortages, citing data from research by the U.S. Department of Justice.

From 1997 to 2016, the number of full-time sworn officers in general-purpose law enforcement agencies increased by about 52,500 (up 8%). During the same period, the total U.S. population increased by about 56 million (up 21%). As a result, the number of full-time sworn officers per 1,000 residents decreased, from 2.42 in 1997 to 2.17 in 2016 (down 11%). [U.S. Department of Justice, Bureau of Justice Statistics, Full-Time Employees in Law Enforcement Agencies]

8. A 1998 article on NASA notes that funding for scientific research by the federal government "has declined from a peak of 1.6 percent of total federal outlays in 1965 to about 1 percent in 1995. In other words, research funds fell while nearly every other category of government spending climbed to its highest peak in U.S. history." [Richard Miniter, "Why NASA Must Go," *The American Enterprise*]

9. Since the school shooting at Columbine High in 1999, around 200 students have been fatally shot in schools, generating fear among parents, teachers, and children themselves. Harvard instructor David Ropeik argues that the actual risk is lower than most people think.

The Education Department reports that roughly 50 million children attend public schools for roughly 180 days per year. . . . That means the statistical likelihood of any given public school student being killed by a gun, in school, on any given day since 1999 was roughly 1 in 614,000,000.

The chance of a child being shot and killed in a public school is extraordinarily low, . . . far lower than almost any other mortality risk a kid faces, including traveling to and from school, catching a potentially deadly disease while in school or suffering a life-threatening injury playing interscholastic sports. [David Ropeik, "School Shootings Are Extraordinarily Rare. Why Is Fear of Them Driving Policy?" *Washington Post*]

[Assume that the conclusion is: We should be more concerned about and take more precautions against the other risks.]

✳10. DNA evidence is commonly used in criminal law. If a sample from a crime scene exactly matches a person's DNA, the odds of an exact match with any other person are one in 1 billion. But that assumes the DNA analysis was done rigorously by the forensic team. And that is not always the case. In a rape case, a man was convicted by DNA evidence; forensic analysts said that the defendant could not be excluded as the source of sperm found in the victim. Later, two scientists, Itiel Dror and Greg Hampikian,

gave the DNA evidence to 17 lab technicians for examination, withholding context about the case to ensure unbiased results. All of the techs were experienced, with an average of nine years in the field. Dror and Hampikian asked them to determine whether the mixture included DNA from the defendant.

. . . Only one of the 17 lab technicians concurred that the defendant could not be excluded as a contributor. Twelve told Dror and Hampikian that the DNA was exclusionary, and four said that it was inconclusive. [Matthew Shaer, "The False Promise of DNA Testing," *The Atlantic*]

DNA evidence should therefore not be relied on exclusively in trials.

Probability 14

Much of logic is concerned with methods of determining whether a statement is true on the basis of premises stating the evidence for it. But we also make judgments about probabilities:

> There's a 60% chance of rain this evening.
>
> The probability of getting two 6's on a roll of the dice is 1/36.
>
> Lumberjacks have a higher probability of dying on the job than do accountants.
>
> I'd say my chance of getting into a top-20 law school is 40%.

Estimates of probability are used pervasively in planning our personal lives, in business decisions, and in government policy, among many other areas. Probability plays a major role in science, especially the social sciences, and it is a basis for statistical reasoning, which we examined in Chapter 13. This chapter reviews the methods of supporting judgments about probability.

These methods fall into two classes. (1) There are *direct* methods for assigning a probability to an event, by looking at the nature of the event and its circumstances, as well as the amount of evidence about whether the event will occur. (2) There are rules that give us an *indirect* method: If we have probabilities for two or more events, we can compute the probability of combinations of those events. And, if we can break a complex event down into its simpler components, and if we know the probability of each component, then we can calculate the probability of the whole. These rules are known as the probability calculus. The probability calculus allows us to compute the probability of complex or multiple outcomes when we know the individual components. One particular rule in the calculus, known as Bayes' theorem, is important for estimating probabilities in medicine, science, and other fields, as we discuss in Section 14.3.

CHAPTER OUTLINE

14.1 Probability Measures

14.2 The Probability Calculus

14.3 Conditional Probability and Bayes' Theorem

LEARNING OBJECTIVES

On successful completion of the chapter, you will be able to:

- Use three methods of identifying the probabilities of events. (14.1)
- Use the rules for conjunction, disjunction, and negation to calculate complex probabilities. (14.2)
- Use Bayes' theorem to interpret conditional probabilities, including the results of diagnostic tests in medicine and scientific experiments. (14.3)

14.1 Probability Measures

A probability judgment attributes a degree of probability to an event (e.g., that it will rain tomorrow), to an effect (e.g., that a roll of the dice will get two 6's), or to a thing's having some property (e.g., that a patient has the flu). It is customary to use the term "event" in all these cases: Probability judgements are propositions about what might happen or turn out to be true. We are not actually asserting the proposition in question, but we are not simply confessing ignorance or abstaining from judgment altogether. Instead, we are judging *how likely* the event is. This is a quantitative judgment, a matter of degree—we are locating the event on a quantitative scale or dimension. And so we use numbers to measure the likelihood.

A probability can be expressed as an ordinary fraction (1/2), a decimal fraction (0.5), or a percentage (50%). These are mathematically equivalent, and we can use whichever form is most convenient. But whichever form we use, a probability must lie between 0 and 1 (or 100%). An event that cannot occur has a probability of 0, while an event that must occur has a probability of 1; all other probabilities lie between these extremes. If $p(A)$ stands for the probability of a certain event A, we can put this point mathematically as follows:

$$0 \leq p(A) \leq 1$$

Finding the probability of an outcome, therefore, means locating $p(A)$ at the right point in the interval between 0 and 1—finding the right fraction or percentage.

There are two basic ways of establishing probabilities. The first is familiar from games of chance. A coin has two sides, and when you flip a coin it is equally likely to land on either one, so there's a 50% chance of getting a head on a single flip of a coin. When you are dealt a card from a full deck, the chance that it will be the ace of hearts (or any other particular card) is 1/52 because there are 52 cards in the deck. If a number from 1 to 10 is randomly selected, the chance that it is 4 (or any other number in the interval) is 1/10. The general rule can be stated as follows. To find the probability of a given event A, we count the number of possible outcomes. If that number is n, then the probability of A (or any other particular outcome) is $1/n$. This method of assigning probabilities can be called the **method of equal alternatives** because we have to consider all alternative outcomes that are possible in the situation.

The method also applies when an event A can occur in more than one way. There are four aces in a deck of cards, for example, so if A is the event of drawing an ace, there are four ways it could happen, and $p(A)$ is 4/52. The probability of an even number on a roll of a single die is 3/6. For the sake of clarity, we will use the following terms to describe probabilities:

- An **outcome** is a single possible result, such as drawing a particular card from the deck.
- An **event** is an outcome or a set of outcomes for which we want to know the probability, such as drawing an ace.
- A **favorable outcome** is an outcome included in the event, such as drawing the ace of hearts, the ace of clubs, etc.

The term "favorable" can be a bit misleading. It does not necessarily mean that the outcome is something we would favor. If you bet $10 that the next roll of the die will be an even number, and we want to know the probability of *losing* your money, the "favorable" outcomes are 1, 3, and 5. Be that as it may, it is customary to use the term in the sense defined above.

The general rule for the method of equal alternatives is therefore:

$p(A) = f/n$, where f is the number of favorable outcomes and n is the number of all possible outcomes

When an event includes only a single outcome, like drawing the ace of hearts, the formula reduces to $1/n$.

An alternative way to formulate the probability of A is in terms of the odds of A versus *not-A*. The odds of getting 6 on a single roll of a die, for example, is 1:5—one favorable outcome versus five unfavorable ones. In speaking of odds, we are relating favorable outcomes not to the total set of possible outcomes but to the subset of unfavorable ones. If you bet $1 on rolling a 6, the other person should put up $5 for a bet on the remaining numbers, and the winner goes home with $6. The general rule of determining odds is:

Odds(A) = f:u, where f is the number of favorable outcomes and u is the number of unfavorable ones

There's a simple relationship between the probability of A and the odds for it. The total number n of possible outcomes is the sum of the favorable and the unfavorable ones:

Probability of A	Odds of A
$\dfrac{f}{n} = \dfrac{f}{f+u}$	f:u

(In some contexts, such as betting, odds are stated in the reverse order, with the unfavorable odds stated first. For example, "The odds that the Green Bay Packers will win their league championship is 7 to 1" means that the odds are 1 in favor of the Packers and 7 against. In what follows, we will use the convention that favorable odds are stated first and unfavorable second.)

The method of equal alternatives works only when certain conditions are satisfied. First, there must be a definite number of alternatives. If there isn't, then we have no n to divide by. Second, the alternative outcomes must be equally probable. Given that the coin is a fair one, or the deck of cards well-shuffled and the dealer honest, any outcome is just as likely as any other. But if one outcome were more likely than the others, we could not simply divide by n; the probability of that outcome would be higher than $1/n$, and the probability of the other outcomes would be lower.

These two conditions are satisfied in games of chance, but not often in other contexts. Suppose you want to know the probability that the next car to pass you on the street will be white. The alternative is that it will be some other color, but how many alternatives are there? Is red a single alternative, or do we separate red from orange and purple? Do we treat gray as an alternative in addition to white and black? These different ways of classifying color will give us different numbers for n, so the first condition is not satisfied. Nor is the second condition. Regardless of how we classify colors, we can't assume that the next car has an equal chance of being each of the colors.

In a case like this, it is more appropriate to use what is called the **method of frequency**. To assign a probability by this method, we find the frequency with which a given outcome has occurred in a reference group of similar cases. Thus the chance that the next car that passes will be white would be estimated by finding out how many cars in your area are white as opposed to any other color. By this method, it doesn't matter how we classify the other colors or how probable it is that a given car has one of those other colors. We are comparing our outcome (a white car) not to alternative outcomes (cars with other colors) but to the class of all cars in the area. So the formula for estimating probability by the method of frequency is:

$p(A) = f/y$, where f is the number of favorable outcomes and y is the total number in the reference class

To determine the chance the next car is white, we divide the number of white cars in the area, f, by the number of all cars in the area, y.

The method of frequencies is widely used in business and finance, medicine, social science, and many other areas. Here are some of the more common uses:

- *Prediction*: In situations that are complex, there are often too many factors at work for us to predict the exact outcome with any certainty. Instead, we estimate outcomes by the frequency with which they occurred in similar cases in the past. Thus, a weather forecast might predict a 60% chance of rain because it has rained 60% of the time in the past when weather conditions were similar to the current ones. If an insurance company wants to know the likelihood that a 35-year-old woman will die during the term of her life insurance policy, say, 20 years, it consults a mortality table that says what proportion of 35-year-old women die before they reach 55.

- *Risk assessment*: Estimating risks is a special type of prediction that deserves special mention because numerical data are often available. Public health officials keep records based on the frequency of specific injuries and diseases among the population. Banks set interest rates, in part, by estimating the risk that people will renege on loans. Engineers have ways of calculating the risk that a mechanical system, such as a nuclear reactor, will fail. The concept of probability is implicit in these cases because a risk is the probability that some event will occur.

- *Diagnosis*: Prediction is concerned with future outcomes, but we also use the frequency method to make probability judgments about the present. A patient comes to a doctor with certain symptoms. In most cases, more than one illness can cause the same symptoms, and the doctor makes a judgment about which illness is the most likely cause. The doctor may order a diagnostic test such as a biopsy. But diagnostic tests are rarely if ever 100% accurate. In a small percentage of cases there are "false positives" (the test is positive but the patient does *not* have the illness) or "false negatives" (the test is negative but the patient *does* have the illness). So even with the tests, we can only say there is a certain probability that the patient has that illness. (In Section 14.3, we will discuss diagnostic tests in more detail.)

To use the method of frequency, we obviously need information about the frequency of a given outcome in the relevant class of cases. If we do not already have that information, we have to acquire it by an inductive procedure of tracking the number of times the outcome occurs in that class. This is another difference between the two methods. When you flip a coin, you know that, by the nature of the coin, there are two equally likely outcomes, so the method of equal alternatives tells you that the probability of heads is 1/2. You can make that judgment before you actually flip the coin. (Because the probability is known in advance, this method is sometimes called the *a priori* method.) To use the method of frequency, by contrast, you would flip the coin many times in succession and note the proportion of heads. The result will approximate 1/2 (though it isn't likely to be exactly 1/2, and the expected deviation from 1/2 is affected by the number of trials).

As we have seen, the advantage of the method of frequency is that we need not classify all the possible outcomes or assume that they are equally probable. But the method does have dangers and limitations of its own. For one thing, it has its own kind of classification problem. Before we can measure the frequency with which an outcome has occurred in similar cases in the past, we have to select the group of similar cases: We have to choose a reference group. There is usually more than one such group that could reasonably be chosen, and different groups will give us different frequencies.

Suppose we want to know the probability that a certain student will graduate from college. What is the appropriate reference group? The whole population of college students? That's awfully broad; it doesn't take account of factors that affect this particular student's chances of graduating. So perhaps we should consider the frequency of graduation in a narrower class of students. But which one? Students at the particular college? Students with the same SAT scores? The same family, ethnic, or religious backgrounds? The same personality traits? The same degree of intelligence and ambition? You can see that if we tried to find a reference group that takes account of every factor that might be relevant, we would end up with a group containing only one member—the student himself. And then there would be no frequency to measure. So between the broadest and the narrowest extremes, we have to find a reference group that takes account of the obviously relevant factors but is still broad enough to give us a reliable measure of frequency. There is no mechanical, cut-and-dried method of making this choice.

Once we have chosen a reference class, how do we determine frequency? In some cases, we can examine each and every member of the class; this would be like the method of generalization by complete enumeration. Around April 15 of each year, for example, newspapers report the probability of having your tax return audited by the Internal Revenue Service; the frequency of audits can be calculated from IRS records on the total number of returns filed and the number it has audited in each income category. Similarly, information on mortality that insurance companies use is based on all deaths reported to local health authorities. In other cases, we can't survey the entire reference class, so we have to extrapolate or generalize from a sample of the class. Most frequency statistics are of this kind, and they require the methods of statistical generalization discussed in Chapter 13. Suffice it to say for now that the basic rules for generalizing apply here. The larger and more varied the sample, the more reliable it is: the more confidence we can have that the frequency of an event in the sample is close to its frequency in the class as a whole.

In addition to the two methods we have discussed, we also make **intuitive judgments** about probabilities, especially in regard to particular outcomes to which the methods of frequency and equal alternatives cannot be applied easily, if at all. For example:

You turn in a paper and think you have a good chance, maybe 60%, of getting an A.

A corporate executive approves a new product line based on a judgment that it has a better than even chance of being profitable.

A gambler bets on the Baltimore Ravens to win the Super Bowl, at 2:3 odds, judging that the probability of a Ravens win is at least 40%.

Probability judgments of this kind are often described as subjective because they reflect a person's individual judgment about the probability of a given outcome—his or her best guess—and two people may well assign different probabilities to the same outcome. But these judgments need not be subjective in the sense of being arbitrary or indifferent to evidence. In the first example, your judgment presumably reflects knowledge about the course material, the instructor's standards and expectations, and the work you put into the paper. In the same way, the executive takes account of a large amount of information about the product line, market research, the competition, etc. And people who bet on sports events, as in the third example, typically know a lot about the teams. In these and similar cases, the judgment reflects the integration of relevant information to produce a kind of gestalt, a single intuitive judgment that some outcome has a certain probability, all things considered. We may not be able to spell out all the considerations in the form of explicit inferences, so this is not exactly a *method* for determining probabilities. But such intuitive judgments are common in personal and professional life and deserve recognition as a way of assigning probabilities.

Precisely because these judgments are intuitive, however, we should also recognize that they are liable to biases. Suppose I was cheated once by a used car dealer. A single incident of cheating affects the frequency of cheating by the same amount (and it's a very small amount) regardless of who the victim was. But I am more likely to remember it than if it happened to someone else, and so I may have an inflated judgment about the probability of getting cheated the next time. (This is an example of the availability bias that we discussed in Chapter 4.) To guard against biases, we should try to examine the bases of our judgments and weed out the nonobjective factors as best we can.

The three ways of assigning probabilities to outcomes are often described as different theories of probability, or as different meanings of the term "probability." That's because it isn't clear that we are talking about the same thing in all three cases. In flipping a coin or rolling a die, it is natural to think of probability as a property of the object. The method of frequency is also concerned with objective properties: We classify

---

REVIEW Probability Measures

The probability of an event is between 0 and 1: $0 \leq p(A) \leq 1$. Probabilities can be assigned to events in three ways:

1. Equal alternatives: If there is a definite number, n, of equally likely outcomes, the probability of a given outcome or set of outcomes is f/n, where f is the number of favorable outcomes. The odds of a given outcome or set of outcomes is $f{:}u$, where u is the number of unfavorable outcomes.

2. Frequency: If an event belongs to a reference class, y, of related events, the probability of a given outcome or set of outcomes is f/y, where f is the number of favorable outcomes and y is the total number in the reference class.

3. Intuitive judgment: The probability of an event can be assigned by an intuitive judgment based on integrating relevant evidence.

an outcome in a reference class on the basis the properties of the objects and actions involved. But we also have some options in choosing a reference class, and the frequency percentage is affected by the amount of inductive data we have. With intuitive judgments, finally, probability seems to be a matter of an individual's particular context of knowledge.

Probability is indeed a complex idea, and experts have put forward a range of very different theories about it. For our purposes, however, it is enough to know the different methods we use in making probability judgments. And no matter which method we use in assigning probabilities to outcomes, we use the same principles in calculating combinations of outcomes. We turn to those principles—the probability calculus—in the next section.

EXERCISE 14.1

I. Use the method of equal alternatives to determine the probability of each of the following events.

✳1. What is the probability of getting a 4 on a single roll of a die?

2. What are the odds of drawing the queen of spades from a full deck of cards?

3. A number between 1 and 20 (inclusive) is randomly selected. What is the probability that the number will be even?

✳4. A box contains 7 blue marbles, 4 white marbles, and 10 yellow marbles. What is the probability that a marble drawn at random will be blue?

5. A poll is asking students on your campus how they would vote in an election for governor of your state. Three candidates are running in the election, there are 9,500 students on campus, and the poll will survey a sample of 250. What is the probability that you will be in the sample?

II. Using the method of frequency, what reference class and frequency would you use to estimate the following probabilities?

✳1. The chance that it will rain today.

2. The probability that the next time the phone rings it will be someone trying to sell you something.

3. The probability that the next car you see will have New Jersey license plates.

✳4. The probability that a baby will be a girl.

5. The risk of being struck by lightning.

6. The probability that a baby born to an HIV-positive mother will test positive for HIV.

III. Determine the probability of each of the following events. Name the method involved (equal alternatives, frequency, or intuitive judgment).

✳1. What is the probability that on a single role of a die, you will get a number above 4?

2. You are attending your 10-year high school reunion. You somewhat enjoyed high school. Four or five of

your old friends will be there, people you still like. There is an open bar, but bad music. What are the chances that you will enjoy yourself?

3. Of 4,675 Ballista sedans sampled off the production line, 187 were found to have defective transmissions. What is the probability that a randomly selected Ballista sedan has a defective transmission?

✳4. What are the odds of drawing a spade from a standard deck of playing cards?

5. In 11,003 at-bats, baseball player Dave Winfield got 3,110 hits. What is the probability that, at an arbitrary at-bat, Dave Winfield would get a hit? Represent your answer as a decimal fraction to the nearest thousandths place.

6. If a random square is selected on a tic-tac-toe board, what is the probability that the square is one of the corners?

✳7. Of 6,200 patients tested, 155 were found to have a particular recessive gene. What is the probability that Adam lacks this gene?

8. In a random sampling of 980 books at the local library, your class found that 71 books were over a hundred years old. What is the probability that a random book pulled from the shelves will be over a hundred years old?

9. While hiking in the forest, you see a frog. The frog has noticed you too, and it is approximately 3 feet away from a stream. The frog appears to be in good health. What is the probability that it will jump into the stream in the next 10 seconds?

✳10. You take city bus #70 to campus, one of four that serves your local bus stop. Your Next Bus app says that #70 will be there in four minutes, bus #66 in three minutes. What is the probability that the 70 will arrive before the 66?

14.2 The Probability Calculus

Suppose we want to know the probability that the first card dealt from a full deck is *either* a heart *or* a spade. This is a complex event, which we can analyze into its components: drawing a heart, drawing a spade. If we can assign probabilities to the component events, as we can in this case, then it is possible to compute the probability of the complex event. In fact, mathematicians have developed a set of procedures, known as the **probability calculus**, for doing just this. This section reviews three elementary rules of the probability calculus:

Conjunction: the probability that two events will *both* occur. $p(A \text{ and } B)$

Disjunction: the probability that one or the other of two events will occur. $p(A \text{ or } B)$

Negation: the probability that an event will not occur. $p(-A)$

14.2A Conjunction

If you roll a pair of dice, what is the probability of getting "snake-eyes" (two 1's)? Since there are two dice, let's take them one at a time. By the method of alternatives, the chance of getting a 1 on the first die is 1/6, so we know that the chance of snake-eyes cannot be any greater than 1/6. But in fact it must be less, because even if the first die comes up 1, there is only a 1/6 chance that the second die will do likewise. The probability of snake-eyes, then, is 1/6 × 1/6 = 1/36. (You can confirm this by directly listing all the possible outcomes of rolling a pair of dice; you'll find that there are 36.) In the same way, we would use multiplication to find the probability that two unrelated people will both get the flu in the next 12 months. If person A has a 10% chance of flu and some randomly chosen person, B, has a 15% chance, then the probability that both will get the flu is 10% × 15% = 1.5%. The rule for determining the conjunctive probability that two events will both occur is:

$$p(A \text{ and } B) = p(A) \times p(B)$$

But there's an important qualification, which we can see by considering other cases. What is the chance of drawing two aces in a row from a deck of cards? The chance of drawing the first ace is 4/52, since there are 4 aces and 52 cards altogether. But once you've drawn the first ace, only 51 cards remain in the deck, and only 3 aces. So the probability of drawing a second ace is 3/51, and the probability of the complex event is 4/52 × 3/51, about 1/221. The difference from the previous cases is simple but important. In a roll of the dice, the components are **independent events**: The outcome on the first die does not affect the outcome on the other. So we can treat the probability of each component in isolation from the other. In drawing the cards, however, the first event *does* affect the second. They are **dependent events**, and we cannot consider them in isolation. Instead, we have to consider the probability that the second event will occur *given that* the first one has already occurred. Similarly, suppose we want to know the probability of flu, not for two unrelated people but for two college roommates. Flu being contagious, B's getting the flu is not an independent event; if A gets the flu, there's a higher probability that B will also get it. If the probability that B gets the flu *given that* A did is 50%, then the probability that both get the flu is 10% × 50% = 5%.

In the standard notation, the probability of B *given* A is written $p(B \mid A)$, where the vertical stroke, $\mid$, means "given that." The general rule for conjunction is therefore:

$$p(A \text{ and } B) = p(A) \times p(B \mid A)$$

If two events are independent, like the dice, then A makes no difference to B. The probability of B given A is simply the probability of B considered by itself, and so this general rule reduces to the restricted rule that applies to independent events.

The formula $p(B \mid A)$ expresses the concept of **conditional probability**: the probability that one event will occur on condition that another event occurs. It is an important concept in many fields of knowledge and many types of planning. For example, suppose you are thinking about a career in law and want to know the probability of getting a job in a top law firm. Such firms hire chiefly from the top law schools, so you would first try to estimate your chance of getting into one of those schools by looking at their admission rates, the average GPAs and LSAT scores of those admitted, etc. The next question is the chance of a job in a top law firm given that you graduate from a top law school. You might estimate that conditional probability from the school's placement records. So the probability of getting into a top school and a job at a top firm is:

$$p(\text{top school and top firm}) = p(\text{top school}) \times p(\text{top firm} \mid \text{top school})$$

To summarize: The probability that two events will both occur is given by the general conjunction rule:

$$p(A \text{ and } B) = p(A) \times p(B \mid A)$$

In the special case where A and B are independent, $p(B \mid A) = p(B)$, and we can use the special or restricted conjunction rule:

$$p(A \text{ and } B) = p(A) \times p(B)$$

APPLY The Conjunction Fallacy

An implication of the conjunction rule (in both the general and the restricted forms) is that the probability of A and B cannot be greater than the probabilities of either A or B by itself. Numerical probabilities range from 0 to 1 (0 to 100%); they are usually fractions in between, and the result of multiplying fractions is a lower fraction. So:

$$p(A \text{ and } B) = p(A) \times p(B \mid A) \leq p(A), \text{ and}$$
$$p(A \text{ and } B) = p(A) \times p(B \mid A) \leq p(B)$$

But we sometimes make probability estimates that are inconsistent with those facts, in what is known as the *conjunction fallacy*.

In a famous experiment, psychologists Amos Tversky and Daniel Kahneman gave this description of "Linda" to the experimental subjects:

Linda is 31 years old, single, outspoken, and very bright. She majored in philosophy. As a student, she was deeply concerned with issues of discrimination and social justice, and also participated in anti-nuclear demonstrations.

The subjects were then asked which is more probable—

Linda is a bank teller.

Linda is a bank teller and is active in the feminist movement.

—and the majority chose the second statement, which cannot be correct. Regardless of how likely it may be that Linda is a feminist, given her profile, the probability that she is both feminist and a bank teller cannot be greater than the probability that she is a teller.

Tversky and Kahneman argued that the error occurred because Linda fits the stereotype of a feminist more closely than the stereotype of a bank teller. This is an example of the representativeness bias we discussed in Chapter 4. Linda seems more "representative" of a feminist—or even a feminist bank teller—than of bank tellers in general.

In any case, we should be alert to the potential for conjunction fallacies and check our probability estimates to make sure they comply with the multiplication rule for conjunction.

[A. Tversky and D. Kahneman, "Extensional versus Intuitive Reasoning: The Conjunction Fallacy in Probability Judgment," *Psychological Review* 90 (1983): 293–315.]

14.2B Disjunction

A disjunctive event has the structure *A or B*. To find the probability of such an event, there is once again a restricted rule and a more general rule. And, once again, let's start with the restricted rule because it is simpler.

Suppose we wanted to know the probability that a randomly chosen student at College X is either a junior or a senior. Let's say 20% of the students are seniors and 23% are juniors. Then the probability that the student is in one or the other of these two classes is:

$p(\text{senior or junior}) = p(\text{senior}) + p(\text{junior}) = 20\% + 23\% = 43\%$

Instead of multiplying the probabilities of the components, as we did for conjunction, we add them. We followed this rule implicitly in Section 14.1 when we assigned a probability of 3/6 to the event of rolling an even number because it can happen in three different ways: $p(\text{even number}) = p(2) + p(4) + p(6)$. Just as 2, 4, and 6 are favorable outcomes for that event, picking any of the individual juniors and seniors is a favorable outcome for the event of picking someone from either class. In abstract form:

$p(A \text{ or } B) = p(A) + p(B)$

This is the restricted rule for disjunction, as it can be used only when outcomes are **mutually exclusive**. The die cannot come up both 2 and 4. A student cannot be both a junior and a senior. But what if we are dealing with **compatible** events—events that are *not* mutually exclusive? Suppose we wanted to know the probability that a randomly chosen student is either a junior or a philosophy major. If juniors are 23% of the student body and philosophy majors are 5%, we cannot simply add the two percentages. There is obviously a subgroup that will be counted twice: junior philosophy majors. If they represent 1% of the student body, then we have to subtract 1% to correct for counting them twice:

$$p(\text{junior or philo major}) = p(\text{junior}) + p(\text{philo major}) - p(\text{junior and philo major})$$
$$= 23\% + 5\% - 1\%$$
$$= 27\%$$

The general rule for disjunctive events is therefore:

$p(A \text{ or } B) = p(A) + p(B) - p(A \text{ and } B)$

In the special case where *A* and *B* are mutually exclusive, we don't need to worry about any overlap between them or double-counting. If the two events cannot both occur, then $p(A \text{ and } B) = 0$. It drops out of the equation, and the general rule reduces to the restricted rule:

$p(A \text{ or } B) = p(A) + p(B)$

This last point raises an issue that many people find confusing at first. For conjunctive events, *A and B*, we have to ask whether the components are independent or dependent. For disjunctive events, *A or B*, we ask whether they are mutually exclusive (incompatible) or compatible. These distinctions are *not* the same.

Two events are *mutually exclusive* if and only if they cannot both occur; otherwise they are compatible.

Two events are *independent* if and only if the occurrence of one does not affect the probability of the other; otherwise they are dependent.

In a strict sense, mutually exclusive events are necessarily dependent. The occurrence of one does affect the probability of the other—by reducing it to zero. But for our purposes in reasoning about probability, it is more natural to think of it this way: The question of whether two events are dependent or independent arises in a substantive way only if they are compatible. If they are mutually exclusive—if they cannot both occur—then it is really beside the point to ask whether one affects the other. Many people are familiar with the gambler's fallacy. If you flip a coin three times and it comes up heads on all three, is tails is more likely on the next toss? No. That's the gambler's fallacy. Coin tosses are independent events; the chance of tails is 50% on every toss regardless of previous outcomes. But the fallacy can be seductive if we confuse the probability for the next toss with the antecedent probability of a series. By the conjunction rule, the antecedent probability of H H H H is $0.5 \times 0.5 \times 0.5 \times 0.5 = 0.0625$, which may suggest that it's time for a T. But the sequence H H H T has exactly the same antecedent probability (as does *any* sequence). To put the point another way, when you get to the fourth toss, the first three heads are no longer probabilities. They are facts, and they have no effect on the next toss.

14.2C Negation

For any event A, there is an opposite event, $-A$: the nonoccurrence of A. And if we know the probability of one, we can compute the probability of the other. On a single roll of a die, the probability of getting 1 is 1/6. That leaves five ways of not getting a 1, so that probability is 5/6. In the same way, there are 51 ways of not drawing the ace of hearts, so the probability is 51/52. No matter what event we are talking about, A and $-A$ are mutually exclusive. By the restricted rule of disjunction, therefore, the probability that one or the other will occur is the sum of their individual probabilities: $p(A) + p(-A)$. In addition, they exhaust the possibilities: No matter what event we are talking about, it must either occur or not occur. The probability of its occurrence and the probability of its nonoccurrence must add up to 1, or 100%:

$p(A) + p(-A) = 1$

So if we know the probability of A, we can subtract it from 1 to find the probability of $-A$, and vice versa. In mathematical terms:

$p(-A) = 1 - p(A)$ and $p(A) = 1 - p(-A)$

This rule is a useful one to keep in mind because—as we will see shortly—it is sometimes easiest to figure out the probability of an event by first establishing the probability that it will not occur.

REVIEW **The Probability Calculus**

The three elementary rules for calculating the probabilities of complex events are as follows.

Event	General Rule	Restricted Rule
Conjunction	$p(A \text{ and } B) = p(A) \times p(B \mid A)$	$p(A \text{ and } B) = p(A) \times p(B)$ Restriction: A and B are independent events, so that $p(B \mid A) = p(B)$.
Disjunction	$p(A \text{ or } B) = p(A) + p(B) - p(A \text{ and } B)$	$p(A \text{ or } B) = p(A) + p(B)$ Restriction: A and B are mutually exclusive events, so that $p(A \text{ and } B) = 0$.
Negation	$p(-A) = 1 - p(A)$	

14.2D Extending the Rules

We formulated the conjunction and disjunction rules for the case of two events. But we may want to know the probability for a combination of three or more events. The rules can be extended to such cases, but there are a few complications.

Let's start with conjunction. What is the probability of getting three 6's on three rolls of the die? These are independent events, and the restricted conjunction rule can be extended in a straightforward way to give us the probability:

$$p(6 \text{ and } 6 \text{ and } 6) = p(6) \times p(6) \times p(6) = 1/6 \times 1/6 \times 1/6 = 1/216$$

With dependent events, we have to take account of conditional probabilities. Consider the chance of drawing three face cards (jack, queen, or king) in a row from a full deck of cards. Let's call these events FC1, FC2, and FC3. There are 12 face cards, so the probability on the first draw, FC1, is 12/52, about 23%. For the second draw, the probability is FC2|FC1 (the conditional probability of a face card given that we drew a face card on the first draw), which is 11/51. For the third draw, the probability of yet another face card is conditional upon *both* of the first two draws: FC3|(FC1 and FC2), or 10/50. The conjunctive probability is then:

$$
\begin{aligned}
p(\text{FC1 and FC2 and FC3}) &= p(\text{FC1}) \times p(\text{FC2} \mid \text{FC1}) \times p[\text{FC3} \mid (\text{FC1 and FC2})] \\
&= 12/52 \times 11/51 \times 10/50 \\
&= 1{,}320/132{,}600 \\
&= \text{about } 1\%
\end{aligned}
$$

You can see that the formula for three dependent events gets complicated by the need to make the probability of the third event conditional on both of the first two. With every additional event we add to the sequence, the complications increase further because we must make it conditional on all the previous events in the series. Notice also that when we multiply probabilities, the resulting probability can decrease rapidly—from 23% for a face card on the first draw to 1% for three in a row.

The rule for disjunction can also be extended to three or more events. If the events are mutually exclusive, we use the restricted rule for disjunction, and the extension is straightforward. We simply add the probability of the third event to the sum for the first two. Indeed, we already used this procedure implicitly in the previous example of drawing face cards. For the first draw, the probability of drawing a face card is the probability of drawing either a jack, a queen, or a king:

$$p(\text{jack or queen or king}) = p(\text{jack}) + p(\text{queen}) + p(\text{king}) = 4/52 + 4/52 + 4/52$$
$$= 12/52$$

If the events are not mutually exclusive, however, the issue is more complicated. For example, suppose you are going to toss a coin three times and want to know the probability of getting at least one head. On each toss your chance of getting a head is 1/2. By the rule for disjunction, the probability so far is $1/2 + 1/2 + 1/2 = 3/2$. That's greater than 1—an indication that we are not dealing with mutually exclusive events. By the general rule for disjunction, we now have to subtract the probabilities of getting two heads (on the first and second toss, the first and third, and the second and third), as well as the probability of getting heads on all three tosses. That adds up to quite a bit of calculation. We can get to the correct answer much more quickly if we realize that there's only one way *not* to get at least one head—the outcome in which we get three tails—and then use the negation rule. Getting three tails is a conjunctive event, for which we can multiply the probabilities: $1/2 \times 1/2 \times 1/2 = 1/8$. So the chance of getting at least one head is $1 - 1/8 = 7/8$. With three or more events that are not mutually exclusive, it is almost always better to use the negation rule in this way.

Let's apply these insights to another example, this one from the criminal justice system. When a crime is committed, there is a sequence of steps from reporting the crime to the police to the arrest, conviction, and sentencing of the perpetrator, with each event having some degree of conditional probability. In the case of burglary, suppose that these probabilities are as follows:

Probability that a burglary is reported	75%
Probability of arrest, given that the burglary is reported	25%
Probability of conviction, given an arrest	80%
Probability of a prison sentence, given conviction	70%

Though the probability of arrest is low, the other probabilities are much higher. It may seem that a would-be burglar faces a good chance of ending up in prison. By the general rule for conjunction, however, we have to multiply all these probabilities to find the overall probability that the sequence will run its course:

$p(\text{report and arrest and conviction and prison})$
$\quad = p(\text{report}) \times p(\text{arrest | report}) \times p(\text{conviction | arrest}) \times p(\text{prison | conviction})$
$\quad = 0.75 \times 0.25 \times 0.8 \times 0.7$
$\quad = 0.105$

Our would-be burglar has only a 10% chance of prison and a 90% chance of going free. Here we see again how multiplying fractions quickly leads to much lower numbers.

Before we conclude that crime pays, however, let's consider what happens with repeated burglaries. What is the probability of getting caught and going to prison after committing 5, or 10, or 20 burglaries? That would be the disjunctive probability of going to prison the first time or the second time or the third time, etc. As with the example of getting at least one head on multiple coin-flips, however, we also have to subtract the probability of going to prison multiple times: the first and third, the second and eighth, and so on, for every possible combination. So we will use the negation rule again to find the probability of *not* going to prison for *any* burglary, and then subtract that fraction from 1 to find the probability of going to prison in *some* cases (one or more). For a single burglary, the probability of going free is 0.9. The probability for getting away with two burglaries is 0.9 × 0.9 = 0.81, so the chance of going to prison has increased: 1 − 0.81 = 0.19. For three burglaries, the chance is 1 − (0.9 × 0.9 × 0.9) = 1 − 0.73 = 0.27. Here is what happens as the number of burglaries keeps increasing:

Number of Burglaries	Probability of Not Going to Prison for Any Burglary	Probability of Going to Prison for One or More Burglaries
1	0.90	0.10
5	0.59	0.41
10	0.35	0.65
15	0.21	0.79
20	0.12	0.88

With 10 burglaries, the chance of prison is well over half; with 20 it is highly probable. (In the real world, each arrest will increase the probability of conviction and prison for repeat offenses, but we will ignore that point for the sake of simplicity.)

The example illustrates the difference between the conjunctive probability that *every* event in a set of events will occur and the disjunctive probability that one or more of the events will occur, and the difference has a bearing on the positive, noncriminal goals we pursue. When a goal requires a series of steps, each with only a probability of success, the probability of achieving the goal by that route declines rapidly due to the multiplication rule for conjunction and conditional probability. Perhaps that's the meaning of the old saying, "There's many a slip between the cup and the lip." The good news is that there are often multiple routes to a goal, and in that case the addition rule for disjunction *increases* the likelihood of success.

EXERCISE 14.2

I. For each of the following pairs of events, determine whether the events are compatible or mutually exclusive.

✱1. Drawing either a spade or a queen from a deck of cards.

2. Drawing either an ace or a queen from a deck of cards.

3. Winning first place or winning second place in the 200-meter dash.

＊4. Being the class valedictorian or winning second place in the 200-meter dash.

5. Pitching three balls or pitching three strikes (to a single batter).

II. For each of the following pairs of events, determine whether the outcomes are dependent or independent.

＊1. Winning an Oscar for Best Original Song and winning an Oscar for Best Picture.

2. Bench-pressing 100 pounds or being able to do a cartwheel.

3. The Stevens Point track team winning the regional competition for track & field and its swimming team winning the state competition for swimming.

＊4. The Stevens Point track team winning the regional competition for track & field and winning the state competition for track & field.

5. Alexis Mohanty becoming her party's nominee for governor and Mohanty being elected as governor.

III. **Integrative Exercise** Use the probability calculus to answer the following questions.

＊1. What is the probability that a single roll of a fair die does not result in a 3?

2. What is the probability that a queen or king is drawn from a standard deck of playing cards?

3. Dan has applied to three law schools: Jale, Smerkeley, and SafeLaw. He estimates that his chances of being accepted are 60% at SafeLaw, 30% at Jale, and 50% at Smerkeley.
   a. What is the probability that he will be accepted at all three schools?
   b. What is the probability that he will be accepted at SafeLaw or Smerkeley?

＊4. An urn contains three black balls, five red balls, and seven yellow balls.
   a. If two balls are drawn sequentially, replacing the first ball before drawing the second, what is the probability that both drawn balls are black?
   b. If the balls are drawn without replacing the first ball, what is the probability that both drawn balls are black?

5. For graduation day, assume there's a 50% chance of rain and also a 5% chance that the invited commencement speaker will have to cancel at the last minute and the dean will speak instead.
   a. What is the probability that it will rain or that the invited speaker will cancel?
   b. What is the probability that the dean will speak in the rain?

6. The CEO of Wholesome Foods plans to acquire the Very Berry fruit drink company. If he acquires Very Berry he has a 70% chance of increasing his revenue by $1 million. His investment bankers give him an 85% chance of acquiring the company. What is the probability that he will both acquire Very Berry and increase his revenue by $1 million?

＊7. John Q. Ball is trying to win a game of pool, and it is his turn to shoot. He estimates that he has a 90% chance of sinking the 3 ball in one corner pocket and a 70% chance of sinking the 6 ball in the other corner. If he sinks the 3, he will then have a 60% chance of sinking the 6; if he sinks the 6 first, he will have a 90% chance of sinking the 3. Which initial shot gives him the highest probability of making both shots?

8. Latisha and Mason are informed by their doctor that if they have a child, the probability that it has a recessive trait is 0.22. Latisha and Mason plan on having two children.
   a. What is the probability that both children have the recessive trait?
   b. What is the probability that at least one child has the recessive trait?

9. On a small family farm, there are 15 cows, 3 horses, 22 chickens, and 10 pigs. If we randomly select 2 of these animals, what is the probability that both will be pigs?

✳10. The new hit movie, *How the Probability Calculus Changed My Life*, with Tom Hanks and Lin Manuel Miranda, has been nominated for two Academy Awards: Hollywood insiders estimate that Tom Hanks has a 20% chance of winning Best Supporting Actor for his role as the young Robert Frost, and Lin Manuel Miranda has a 30% chance of winning Best Original Song for "Odds Are I'm Shakin' the Road Not Taken." What is the probability that the movie will win at least one of the awards?

11. Two coins are flipped at the same time. Then they are flipped at the same time again.
    a. What is the probability that both coins will be heads on the first flip and both coins will be tails on the second flip?
    b. What is the probability that this will not happen?

12. There is a 75% chance that you will have enough money saved up to go on a two week trip to Asia next summer. There is a 15% chance that the restaurant next to your house will go out of business next year. What is the probability that neither event will happen?

✳13. Students at University X received scholarships on the basis of scores on a placement test.

Percentile	Percentage in That Percentile	Scholarship
25th to 50th	15	None
50th to 75th	30	Partial tuition
50th to 75th	40	Full tuition
90th to 99th	15	Full tuition, room, and board

   a. What is the probability that a randomly selected student has a scholarship of any kind?
   b. If a student has a scholarship of any kind, what is the probability that he is in the 75th to 90th percentile?
   c. What is the probability that a student receives full tuition?

14. Each person has a specific blood type, with either a positive or negative Rh factor. The frequency of these types in the United States is given in the table.
    a. What is the probability that a person chosen at random has blood type A+ or B−?
    b. Blood type B+ is compatible with types B+, B−, O+, and O−.

Mary, who is type B+, has had an accident and needs a blood transfusion. What is the probability that a person chosen at random will not be a compatible donor for Mary?

Type	Rh	Frequency
O	+	37.40%
O	−	6.60%
A	+	35.70%
A	−	6.30%
B	+	8.50%
B	−	1.50%
AB	+	3.40%
AB	−	0.60%
		100.00%

15. At a school fundraiser, raffle tickets are sold for $1 each. To increase his chances of winning, Mario buys 200 tickets. In the end, a total of 1426 raffle tickets are sold. The first winning ticket is randomly selected and then discarded. Then the second winning ticket is randomly selected.
    a. What is the probability that Mario will win both prizes?
    b. What is the probability that Mario will not win both prizes?

14.3 Conditional Probability and Bayes' Theorem

14.3A Conditional Probability

English clergyman Thomas Bayes devised a theorem in the probability calculus for conditional probability that allows us to update probabilities as new information is added. Bayes' theorem has been influential in a wide range of fields including medicine, computer science, and law. In this section, you'll see how it's used to analyze diagnostic tests in medicine and how it helps scientists adjust their probability estimates in light of new information. Perhaps even more importantly, you'll see that Bayes' theorem is immune to information that fails as genuine evidence. But first, let's see how this powerful theorem developed out of conditional probability.

We've already used the notion of conditional probability in our discussion of the general rule for conjunction. That rule states the conditional probability of event B, given that event A occurs, is $p(B \mid A)$. This is important because some events are interdependent, and thus more or less likely to occur in the presence of another event. For example, estimate how likely you are to pass this class. Okay, now this one: How likely are you to pass this class (B) given that you skip the exam (A)? Did your estimate change? If so, you'll see the importance of conditional probability.

The general conjunction rule is $p(A \text{ and } B) = p(A) \times p(B \mid A)$. We use this formula to calculate the probability of A and B when we know the probability of B given that A. But suppose we know the probability of the conjunction and want to figure out the conditional probability? All we need is a simple algebraic reordering of the terms of the general conjunction rule. To determine the conditional probability of an event, B, given our knowledge of event A, we use the formula on the right:

Conjunction Rule	Conditional Probability Rule
$p(A \text{ and } B) = p(A) \times p(B \mid A)$	$p(B \mid A) = \dfrac{p(A \text{ and } B)}{p(A)}$

We know A occurred. So what we're really trying to figure out is the probability of B and A happening among all occurrences of A. A diagram may help:

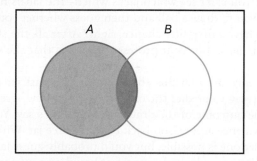

If we consider all occurrences of A, we see that they include some cases in which both A and B occur. And the ratio between that intersection—the darker-shaded area—and all occurrences of B is what we're now interested in. In other words, assuming A occurs, how frequently does B occur also?

Let's look at an example. Imagine your professor shows you two jars, Jar 1 and Jar 2, containing red and green balls. She tells you that Jar 1 has 5 green balls and 20 red balls while Jar 2 has 15 green balls and 10 red balls. The chance of drawing a green ball if you're allowed to draw from either jar at random is 20/50 or 2/5.

	Green	Red	Totals
Jar 1	5	20	25
Jar 2	15	10	25
Totals	20	30	50

Your professor asks you to calculate the probability of drawing a green ball given that you draw from Jar 1. You could answer directly by the method of equal alternatives:

There are 5 green balls in a total of 25 balls, so the probability is 5/25 = 1/5. But let's see how the rule for conditional probability applies to this simple problem.

$$p(\text{green ball} \mid \text{Jar 1}) \quad = \quad \frac{p(\text{green ball and Jar 1})}{p(\text{Jar 1})} \quad = \quad \frac{1/10}{1/2} \quad = \quad \frac{1}{5}$$

You know that only five of the 50 balls are both green and in Jar 1. That gives us a numerator of 5/50 or 1/10. Since there are still just two jars to choose from, our denominator is 1/2. This means that the probability of drawing a green ball given that you must draw from Jar 1 is 1/5, or 20%.

14.3B Bayes' Theorem

Your professor asks if you would like to play again, this time for a prize. She brings out the same jars and asks you to draw from one of them. You remember that Jar 1 contains 5 green balls and 20 red balls and that Jar 2 contains 10 red balls and 15 green balls, but here's the catch: You can't see which jar is which—the labels have been concealed. Your professor asks you to draw a ball and then guess whether you drew from Jar 1 or Jar 2. You figure you have a fifty–fifty chance, right? After all, the jar you choose is just as likely to be Jar 1 as Jar 2. But your professor explains that she wants you to justify your answer.

Notice the difference between this challenge and her last jar game. In the earlier example, you were trying to predict the outcome of the draw—green ball or red? This time, you'll know the outcome of the draw, a red ball, let's say. You want to use that knowledge as new evidence and reason back to the source jar. Which jar do you think you drew from? Either one is possible, but you'd probably guess Jar 1, right, because it has more red balls? You've readjusted your guess based on new evidence. We all do this as a matter of routine; it's part of reasoning well about the world around us.

The power and utility of **Bayes' theorem** is that it helps us refine that inference using reverse conditional probabilities. The theorem is:

$$p(A \mid B) = \frac{p(B \mid A) \times p(A)}{p(B)}$$

To understand the theorem, it may help to see how it is derived. The rule for conditional probability is $p(B \mid A) = p(A \text{ and } B) / p(A)$, a simple transformation of the rule for conjunction: $p(A \text{ and } B) = p(B \mid A) \times p(A)$. But the probability of A and B is the same as the probability of B and A. So the corresponding conditional probability rules are equivalent, too:

$$p(B \mid A) \times p(A) = p(A \mid B) \times p(B)$$

and so,

$$p(B \mid A) = \frac{p(A \mid B) \times p(B)}{p(A)}$$

which is Bayes' theorem.

Let's return to our balls and jars and use the information from our table to fill in the values in the theorem.

	Green	Red	Totals
Jar 1	5	20	25
Jar 2	15	10	25
Totals	20	30	50

The probability of drawing a red ball from Jar 1 is 20/25 or 4/5 and the initial probability of drawing one from Jar 1 is 50% or 1/2. The probability of drawing a red ball (regardless of jar) is 30/50 or 3/5. This gives us:

$$p(\text{Jar 1} \mid \text{red ball}) = \frac{p(\text{red ball} \mid \text{Jar 1}) \times p(\text{Jar 1})}{p(\text{red ball})}$$
$$= \frac{4/5 \times 1/2}{3/5}$$
$$= 2/3$$

Your guess was right; you probably drew from Jar 1. But the probability is 2/3, not 1/2.

DIAGNOSTIC TESTS Bayes' theorem is often used in medicine to interpret the results of diagnostic tests for conditions such as cancer. Such tests are valuable, but they are not 100% accurate, which means they can produce two kind of errors:

- *False positives* are positive test results indicating that someone who does *not* have the condition *does* have it.
- *False negatives* are negative test results indicating that someone who *does* have the condition does *not* have it.

Because of these errors, we cannot assume that a person who tests positive has the condition, nor that a person who tests negative does not have it. Instead, we need to take account of the base rate in the relevant population. And that's where Bayes' theorem comes into play.

Consider a made-up example. There's an outbreak of a disease called studiosis, which affects concentration, affecting 20% of the students at Random College. The college infirmary has a test that detects 80% of cases, but gives false positives for 15% of students without the disease. Juan tests positive. What is the probability that he has the disease? Here's what we know, where S means has studiosis, –S means does not have studiosis, and T+ means a positive test.

$p(S)$: the probability that a given student has studiosis = 20%

$p(T+ \mid S)$: the probability of a positive test, given that a given student has studiosis = 80%

$p(T+ \mid -S)$: the probability of a positive test, given that a given student does not have studiosis = 15%

What we want to know is the probability that Juan has the condition: $p(S \mid T+)$. According to Bayes' theorem:

$$p(S \mid T+) = \frac{p(T+ \mid S) \times p(S)}{p(T+)}$$

We know that $p(T+|S)$ is 80%, or 0.8, and we know that $p(S)$ is 20%, or 0.2. So the numerator is $0.8 \times 0.2 = 0.16$. But what is the denominator? We are not given that probability, but we can calculate it from what we are given. A student who tests positive either has studiosis or doesn't. These are mutually exclusive alternatives, so we can apply the restricted rule for disjunction: $p(A \text{ or } B) = p(A) + p(B)$. In other words, the probability of a positive test is simply the sum of true positives and false positives within the student body:

$$
\begin{aligned}
p(T+) &= \text{true positive test} & + & \quad \text{false positive} \\
&= [p(T+|S) \times p(S)] & + & \quad [p(T+|-S) \times p(-S)] \\
&= (0.8 \times 0.2) & + & \quad (0.15 \times 0.8) \\
&= 0.16 & + & \quad 0.12 = 0.28
\end{aligned}
$$

The result is:

$$
p(S \mid T+) = \frac{0.8 \times 0.2}{0.28} = 0.57
$$

In other words, when Juan gets a positive result on the diagnostic test, he may think he has an 80% chance of having studiosis, since the test is positive for 80% of the actual cases. But the test also has false positives among the larger number of students who don't have the disease. The number of students who have the disease, as a fraction of all students, is the base rate for the disease. As we discussed in Chapter 4, neglecting base rates is a common mistake. Juan's actual chance is only 57%, less than what he might assume from the test results in isolation. (For a real example, see the Apply box.)

HYPOTHESIS AND EVIDENCE The sensitivity of Bayes' theorem to new evidence makes it particularly useful for the empirical sciences, allowing researchers to update the probability of hypotheses as they discover new evidence. Consider the following formulation in which H represents the hypothesis and E represents the new evidence:

$$
p(H \mid E) = \frac{p(E \mid H) \times p(H)}{p(E)}
$$

The probability of the hypothesis, $p(H)$, is called the prior probability, or *prior*. It's the initial probability we assign before we acquire the evidence E. If the probability of the hypothesis given the evidence is higher than the prior probability, $p(H|E) > p(H)$, the new evidence confirms (or partially confirms) the hypothesis. If subsequent evidence is obtained, the result of the previous application of Bayes' theorem becomes the new prior probability of the hypothesis $[p(H)]$.

Let's see how repeated applications of Bayes' theorem can help us update the probability of hypotheses in light of evidence. Imagine that you live in a small community that gets its water from a local reservoir. In the last year, three unrelated members of your community were diagnosed with leukemia. You know that three cases in a population of less than a hundred people is unusual, and you worry that this is more than a coincidence: Is something in your community causing these cancers? You've been learning the scientific method at school. One of your professors always stresses that a good scientist is like a detective building a case based on evidence. The communities' water

APPLY Positive Mammogram? Don't Panic

Mammograms are very effective at discovering breast cancer. So positive tests should always be taken seriously and followed up. But did you know that, even with a single positive test, the odds are in your favor? Bayes' theorem will show why.

Suppose someone you know tests positive for breast cancer. What are the chances she actually has it? We'll need some information to start. Let's assume that the following information garnered from the internet is more or less accurate. The most common age to be diagnosed with breast cancer is 40–50, so that's our sample population. The percentage of women in that population who actually have breast cancer is 1% or 0.01. The likelihood that a woman with breast cancer will test positive is 90% or 0.90, which means that 10% of women who have breast cancer will get a negative test result, a false negative. And the likelihood that a woman without breast cancer will have a false positive is about 8%. We can use a table to organize this information:

	Cancer	No Cancer
Positive test	0.90	0.08
Negative test	0.10	0.92

Looking at this chart would panic most people. Doesn't it show that with a positive mammogram a woman has less than a 10% chance of being cancer free? It looks that way, but we've forgotten to factor in information about the base rate, the prevalence of breast cancer in our sample population. Using Bayes' theorem can help correct this problem. Let's try it. Let A = a woman has cancer and B = she tests positive.

$$p(A \mid B) = \frac{p(B \mid A) \times p(A)}{p(B)} \qquad p(\text{cancer} \mid \text{test+}) = \frac{p(\text{test+} \mid \text{cancer}) \times p(\text{cancer})}{p(\text{test+})}$$

The values in the numerator represent the probability that she tests positive given that she actually has cancer multiplied by the prevalence of cancer in the sample population. Our denominator is the probability of any positive test. That probability, as we saw in discussing diagnostic tests, is the sum of a true positive, $p(\text{test+}|\text{cancer}) \times p(\text{cancer})$, and a false positive, $p(\text{test+}|-\text{cancer}) \times p(-\text{cancer})$. Now we can fill in values. Remember, if 1% of the sample population has breast cancer, then 99% does not.

$$p(\text{cancer} \mid \text{test+}) = \frac{0.90 \times 0.01}{(0.9 \times 0.01) + (0.10 \times 0.99)}$$

$$= \frac{0.009}{0.009 + 0.099}$$

$$= \frac{0.009}{0.108}$$

$$= 9/108 = 8.3\%$$

In other words, even if a woman's mammogram is positive, there is only about an 8% chance she actually has breast cancer. However, each subsequent positive test increases the chance that she really does have cancer. That's why her doctor will want to repeat the test. Bottom line: A positive test is a cause for concern, not panic.

all comes from a single source, your local reservoir. You form the hypothesis that your neighbors' leukemia is caused by impurities in the water supply and apply Bayes' theorem. Here's your initial setup:

$$p(\text{impurities} \mid \text{leukemia}) = \frac{p(\text{leukemia} \mid \text{impurities}) \times p(\text{impurities})}{p(\text{leukemia})}$$

You need information to fill in the elements of the equation. You do some research and learn that the probability of being diagnosed with leukemia sometime during a person's lifetime is about 1.6% or 0.016. What percentage of those patients were exposed to water impurities? You do a little more investigation and, much to your surprise, discover that all water contains impurities. This means that the probability of exposure to impurities in the drinking water is 100% or 1. Thus, the probability of being diagnosed with leukemia given that a person was exposed to water impurities is simply equal to the probability of getting leukemia under all circumstances. Let's plug our values into the formula:

$$p(\text{impurities} \mid \text{leukemia}) = \frac{p(\text{leukemia} \mid \text{impurities}) \times p(\text{impurities})}{p(\text{leukemia})}$$

$$= \frac{0.016 \times 1}{0.016}$$

$$= 1$$

This shows that the probability you have impurities in your water given the leukemia cases is 100%. But wait! You learned that the prior probability of impure water was also 100%. In other words, you've learned that the neighborhood cancer rate is not evidence of impurities in the water. This is important because, in order to be effective, Bayes' theorem must update the probability of the hypothesis in response to genuine evidence but leave the probability untouched in response to false or irrelevant evidence. Increased incidence of leukemia is not evidence of water impurities.

You now know that the leukemias were not caused by impurities in the reservoir water. But you're still worried. Could the reservoir have caused the leukemia in some other way? A friend provides a clue. He suggests that it might be a contaminant rather than impurities. You learn that a common industrial chemical, mataxene, has been linked to leukemia. You wonder, "What are the chances the reservoir is contaminated with mataxene given the increased incidence of leukemia in our community?" You try Bayes' theorem again. This time we're looking for:

$$p(\text{mataxene} \mid \text{leukemia}) = \frac{p(\text{leukemia} \mid \text{mataxene}) \times p(\text{mataxene})}{p(\text{leukemia})}$$

After searching PubMed, you find out that 30% of exposures to mataxene eventually result in leukemia and that nearly 1% of the world's water supply is estimated to be contaminated. Applying these probabilities, we get:

$$p(\text{mataxene} \mid \text{leukemia}) = \frac{p(\text{leukemia} \mid \text{mataxene}) \times p(\text{mataxene})}{p(\text{leukemia})}$$

$$= \frac{0.30 \times 0.01}{0.016}$$

$$= 0.1875, \text{ or about } 19\%$$

A 19% chance that your drinking water is contaminated with a carcinogen is more than enough reason for concern. But you've noticed something even more frightening. You see that 95% of all water polluted with mataxene displays a violet fluorescence in the moonlight. You've noticed a violet glow at the reservoir! There are other reasons for this phenomenon, but you discover that less than one-half of 1% of the world's water fluoresces violet. Bayes' theorem can help us update the probability of your hypothesis.

This time, we want to use 0.19, the results of our previous calculation, as the prior probability of the hypothesis that the reservoir has been contaminated by mataxene. This gives us:

$$p(\text{mataxene} \mid \text{violet}) = \frac{p(\text{violet} \mid \text{mataxene}) \times p(\text{mataxene})}{p(\text{violet})}$$

$$= \frac{0.95 \times 0.19}{0.005}$$

$$= \text{about } 36\%$$

It's time to call in the experts and show them your evidence. Good luck!

In our previous example, we had accurate, albeit fictional, figures to work with. That's not always the case for real scientists. So where do they get their prior probabilities? That's a complex and sometimes controversial matter. Some philosophers of science merge Bayesian thought with the intuitive judgment measure view of probability we discussed in Section 14.1. In this view, probabilities are understood as initial estimates, and Bayes' theorem is thought of as a powerful way to determine how much a new piece of evidence affects our confidence in the hypothesis. Thus, the original probability of the hypothesis may amount to little more than the scientist's rough estimate. That's okay; even rough estimates can help. In our example, you wanted to know if your concerns were plausible enough for experts to get involved. Likewise, scientists sometimes just need to know whether a hypothesis warrants further investigation and resources. Initial probabilities can be rough; over time, as evidence is gathered, the results should become more and more accurate. Think again about our reservoir example.

Bayes' theorem can also help us choose between two hypotheses. Scientific investigation usually produces multiple hypotheses. Hence scientists frequently concentrate on narrowing their research by choosing among competing hypotheses as they collect evidence. All that really matters for this process is which hypothesis is more likely to be correct. Bottom line: However the initial "prior probability" is determined, a scientist using Bayesian probability will be more concerned with whether the calculations are moving closer to zero (impossibility) or 1 (certainty) than with getting the percentages exactly right. Bayes' theorem is one way that the logic provides a decision-making tool for the sciences. In the next chapter, we'll examine scientific reasoning more broadly.

REVIEW Conditional Probability and Bayes' Theorem

Conditional probability: The general conjunction rule is $p(A$ and $B) = p(A) \times p(B \mid A)$. If we divide both sides of that equation by $p(A)$, we have the rule for calculating conditional probability:

$$p(B \mid A) = \frac{p(A \text{ and } B)}{p(A)}$$

Bayes theorem: The theorem is a further derivation from conditional probability, based on the fact that $p(A$ and $B) = p(B$ and $A)$. The theorem is:

$$p(B \mid A) = \frac{p(A \mid B) \times p(B)}{p(A)}$$

Diagnostic tests: The theorem can be used to interpret diagnostic tests for diseases. Since tests are not 100% accurate, we need to determine the probability that a person has a disease given a positive test:

$$p(\text{has the disease} \mid \text{positive test}) = \frac{p(\text{positive test} \mid \text{has the disease}) \times p(\text{has the disease})}{p(\text{positive test})}$$

The denominator $p(\text{positive test})$ is the sum of true positives and false positives:

$p(\text{positive test} \mid \text{has the disease}) \times p(\text{has the disease}) +$
  $p(\text{positive test} \mid \text{does not have the disease}) \times p(\text{does not have the disease})$

Scientific evidence: Bayes theorem can also be used to interpret evidence for scientific hypotheses. If hypothesis H has some prior probability of being true, evidence E can increase that probability in accordance with the theorem:

$$p(H \mid E) = \frac{p(E \mid H) \times p(H)}{p(E)}$$

EXERCISE 14.3

Integrative Exercise   Calculate the conditional probabilities for each of the following. For the first five, use the simple conditional probability formula; for the remainder use Bayes' theorem.

⁎1. You have a jar containing five white, five green, and five red balls. Suppose you are asked to remove one ball at a time and place it in a box. You first draw a red ball. What is the probability that the next ball will also be red?

2. A survey of 100 Amazon customers showed that 40% had purchased an ebook in the past year, 30% had streamed a video, and 20% had done both. If you selected a customer at random, what is the probability that the customer streamed a video given

that he or she had purchased an ebook?

3. Your roommate invites you to come with him to visit his friends, a couple. You want to take small gifts for each of their young children. You know they have at least one daughter but you forgot to ask about the other. What are the chances they have two girls given that at least one child is a girl?

∗4. Women with fibromyalgia account for 2%, or 0.02, of the U.S. population. What is the probability that you have fibromyalgia given that you are a woman? (Assume that women are 50% of the population.)

5. Mr. and Mrs. Hayashizaki have two children. What is the probability that they have two boys given that their oldest child is a boy?

6. Excel College is evaluating its Degree Pathways program. Currently the program is voluntary with about 50% of the student body participating. Graduation records show that 80% of students who participate in the Pathways program graduate in 4 years, and that 60% of all students at Excel complete their degrees in 4 years. What is the probability that Rivka participated in the Pathways program given that she earned her Excel B.A. in 4 years?

∗7. Katie plans on giving each of her twenty friends a book for Christmas. Of the books, 55% are fiction and the rest are nonfiction. Five of the eight hardcover books are nonfiction, three are fiction. She gives her friend Ken a paperback. What is the probability that it's fiction?

8. Every year, Americans file their income tax returns. Some get a refund; some get a bill. Many worry about getting an audit. The chances are slim, as only about 0.1% of returns get audited each year. While the odds are in your favor, there are many factors that increase your chance of being audited. Income is a factor. Taxpayers reporting an income of over $10 million have a 6.66% chance of being audited; those who report they had no income have a 2.04% chance. Location matters as well. International filers account for only about 0.24% of all filers but have a 4.8% chance of being audited. Darrell has received notice from the IRS that he is being audited. What is the probability that he is an international filer?

9. You are a high school math teacher who gives a quiz every week. You have a student, Peter, who is bright but unmotivated. Every time he completes the homework, he makes an A on the quiz. When he doesn't do the homework, he gets an A about 25% of the time. Peter does the assigned homework about half the time. Peter aces the quiz; what's the probability he did the homework this week?

∗10. You've learned that Bayes' theorem can be used to update hypotheses in light of new evidence. In question 4 earlier, you calculated the probability that you have fibromyalgia given that you are a woman, and received an answer of about 4%. A friend points out that you have chronic fatigue and suggests that it may be a symptom. You investigate and discover that while chronic fatigue is common—about 30% of the population complains of it—95% of people diagnosed with fibromyalgia experience chronic fatigue. Use 0.04 as your prior probability of having fibromyalgia and recalculate the probability that you have it given that you have chronic fatigue. (Hint: You may find the Apply box on breast cancer helpful.)

CHAPTER REVIEW

Summary

- A probability judgment attributes a degree of probability to an event on a scale from 0 (the event definitely will not occur) to 1 (it definitely will occur). Such judgments can be made in three ways:
  - The method of equal alternatives: If there is a definite number of equally likely outcomes, the probability of a given event equals the number of ways it can occur (the favorable outcomes) divided by the total number of possible outcomes.
  - The method of frequency: When an event belongs to a reference class of related events, the probability of the event is determined by the frequency of similar events in that reference class.
  - The probability of an event can be assigned by an intuitive judgment, based on integrating relevant evidence.

- The probability calculus is a set of rules for determining the probability of combinations of events. The calculus includes rules for
  - Conjunction: the probability that two events, A and B, will both occur, $p(A$ and $B)$.
  - Disjunction: the probability that either A or B occurs, $p(A$ or $B)$
  - Negation: the probability that an event will not occur: $p(-A)$
- These rules can be extended to three or more events.
- Conditional probability is the probably that an event B will occur *given that* an event A has occurred. Bayes' theorem is a rule in the probability calculus for calculating conditional probabilities.

Key Terms

method of equal alternatives (p. 598)

outcome (p. 598)

event (p. 598)

favorable outcome (p. 598)

method of frequency (p. 599)

intuitive judgment (p. 601)

probability calculus (p. 604)

independent events (p. 605)

dependent events (p. 605)

conditional probability (p. 605)

mutually exclusive (p. 607)

compatible (p. 607)

Bayes' theorem (p. 616)

Putting It All Together

I.   **Integrative Exercise**   Based on what you have learned in this chapter, answer the following questions.

⁎1. In eight coins-flips, which of the following sequences are most probable? (H, heads; T, tails.)
   a. H H T H T T H T
   b. H H H H T T T T
   c. T T T T T T T T
   d. They are equally probable.

2. You are dealt two cards from a full deck.
   a. What is the probability that the second card is a jack?
   b. You turn over the first card and it is a 7. What is the probability that the second card is jack?

3. Can mutually exclusive events be independent?

4. Create an example of a disjunctive probability with two compatible events.

5. Create an example of a conjunctive probability of two events, with the second event dependent on the outcome of the first.

II.   **Integrative Exercise**   Determine the probabilities specified in each of the following.

⁎1. If two dice are rolled:
   a. What is the probability the numbers add to 4?
   b. What is the probability they add to 7?

2. An urn contains 5 red marbles, 7 blue marbles, and 4 green marbles. Three marbles are randomly selected from the urn without replacement. What is the probability that all three are the same color?

3. A fault in a color copier puts a red smudge on 3% of all copies and a green smudge on 7% of all copies.
   a. If a copy has a red smudge on it, what is the probability that it also has a green smudge?
   b. What is the probability that a randomly selected copy has both a red and a green smudge?
   c. What is the probability that a randomly selected copy has a red or green smudge?
   d. What is the probability that a copy has neither a red nor a green smudge?

⁎4. At the end of the regular season, the odds that the Giants will make it to the Super Bowl are 1:9, and the odds that the Patriots make it are 1:4. Also, over the past five years, the Giants and the Patriots have played each other six times. Of those games, the Giants won four.

What is the probability that the Giants will beat the Patriots in the Super Bowl?

5. A blackjack dealer deals you two cards. Face cards are worth 10, and an ace is worth either 1 or 11, your choice. What is the probability that you are dealt blackjack; i.e., two cards whose value adds to 21?

6. Abby is a sales representative for a company making high-end, high-priced software. For the next month, Abby plans to pitch three prospects: IQue, a current customer, for an upgrade worth $75,000; Xenophilia, a new customer, for the complete package, worth $200,000; and DoubleDown, for a streamlined version, worth $125,000. Based on her knowledge of the prospect companies and her general sales experience, she estimates the probabilities of each sale as IQue, 0.9; Xenophilia, 0.6; DoubleDown, 0.7.
   a. What is the probability that Abby will make at least one of the sales?
   b. Abby has a quota of $200,000 in sales for the month. Which prospect or combination of prospects give her the highest probability of meeting the quota?

*7. In 2018, the distribution of Americans by age and sex was as follows:

	Male	Female
Age 0 to 19	41.88	40.10
Age 20 to 39	45.20	43.92
Age 40 to 59	41.01	42.28
Age 60 or over	33.03	39.72

(All figures are in millions of people.)

a. What is the probability that a randomly chosen female American is between 20 and 39 years old?
b. What is the probability that a randomly chosen American who is at least 60 years old is male?
c. What is the probability that a randomly chosen American is a female who is at least 40 years old?

8. The Internal Revenue Service audits a certain number of tax returns each year. For returns filed in 2011, the frequency of audits by major categories of income were as follows:

Income	Number of Returns	Number Audited
Under $200,000	95,000,000	487,000
$200,000 to $999,999	4,500,000	138,000
$1,000,000 and above	337,000	41,000
Totals	99,837,000	666,000

a. Determine the probability of an audit for people in each income category.
b. What is the probability that someone's income is $1 million or more, given that he or she has been audited?

III. **Integrative Exercise**   Imagine you are an electrical engineer. You receive an email from a service technician who is working on a new heart monitor with an electrical problem. He needs help deciding whether to look for an opened circuit or a short. You notice that he reports that one of the internal lead wires appears slightly melted. This indicates heat. You know that electrical problems in similar devices are accompanied by heat about 50% of the time. About half of electrical shorts are accompanied by heat. But electrical shorts have been found in only 1% of this model. An opened circuit, on the other hand, has been found in about 5% of these monitors, but opened circuits are accompanied by heat only 0.25% of the time. Consider two hypotheses:

H1: The malfunction is caused by an opened circuit
H2: The malfunction is caused by a short

Using the information you have, along with Bayes' theorem, (a) determine the probability of each hypothesis, (b) decide which hypothesis is more likely, and (c) write a memo to the technician explaining the likelihood of each of these suggested hypotheses and recommending whether to pursue H1, H2, or to continue troubleshooting the monitor.

Explanation and Science

15

Compare these two statements:

> Joan will be successful because she is bright and ambitious.

> Joan is sad because her cat just died.

Both of these statements make a claim about Joan, and both of them offer a reason, indicated by the word "because." But there's a difference: The first is an argument, and the second is an explanation. My claim that Joan will be successful is a conclusion I am trying to convince you to accept on the basis of the premise that she is bright and ambitious. In the other statement, I am not trying to convince you that Joan is sad. We can both see that she's sad—I'm taking that fact for granted. Instead, I am trying to *explain* that fact by pointing out that her cat just died.

In this chapter, we will learn how to analyze explanations using some of the same methods we have used for analyzing arguments. We will then review the standards for evaluating explanations. Finally, we will learn how those standards allow us to identify pseudo-explanations: unsubstantiated claims, superstitions, and crackpot theories that masquerade as genuine explanations. We will discuss some of the more common forms of pseudo-explanation in history and the sciences.

CHAPTER OUTLINE

15.1 Explanation and Argument
15.2 Adequacy of Hypotheses
15.3 The Truth of Hypotheses
15.4 Pseudo-Explanations

LEARNING OBJECTIVES

On successful completion of the chapter, you will be able to:

- Understand the differences and similarities between explanations and arguments, and learn how to diagram explanations. (15.1)
- Use logical standards for evaluating the adequacy of explanations and the truth of explanatory hypotheses. (15.2–15.3)
- Identify pseudo-explanations in history and science. (15.4)

15.1 Explanation and Argument

The theoretical relationship between arguments and explanations is complex and controversial. But it seems clear that there is at least a difference in emphasis. The primary goal of an argument is to show *that* some proposition is true, while the primary goal of an explanation is to show *why* it is true. In an argument, we reason forward from the premises to the conclusion; in an explanation, we reason backward from a fact to the cause or reason for that fact. Why does ice float in water? How do salmon find their way back to the streams they were spawned in? Why did the Industrial Revolution occur when it did? Why do human beings so often make war on each other? In all these cases, we know that a certain proposition is true: Ice floats, salmon find their way, etc. This proposition is the **explanandum** (plural: *explananda*)—a Latin word meaning "that which is

627

to be explained." What we want to know is the cause or the reason for the *explanandum*. We're looking for a **hypothesis** that will make the *explanandum* intelligible to us by explaining why it is true. Ordinarily, the word "hypothesis" suggests something tentative, an idea that hasn't been proven yet. But we're going to use the term in a broader sense, to mean any explanatory idea, no matter how well confirmed. In this sense, for example, Newton's law of gravitation is a hypothesis when it is used to explain the motion of physical objects.

Any explanation involves a hypothesis and an *explanandum*, just as any argument involves premises and a conclusion. When a doctor diagnoses a disease, the patient's symptoms are the *explananda*, and the diagnosis is the hypothesis. In a criminal trial, the prosecution tries to show that the guilt of the defendant is the only hypothesis that would explain all the evidence, and the defense tries to create doubt in the minds of the jury by arguing that some other hypothesis is possible. If you are given the assignment of interpreting a poem, the *explanandum* is the poem itself—the words, the rhythms, the images. Your assignment is to find a hypothesis about what the poet was trying to convey. The theories of philosophers and religious thinkers can often be regarded as hypotheses to explain fundamental features of the world and human experience. And of course a central goal of science is to find hypotheses that will explain observable phenomena.

Despite the difference between argument and explanation, there is also a fundamental similarity. Let's go back to our original examples.

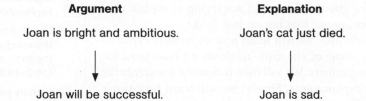

Argument	**Explanation**
Joan is bright and ambitious.	Joan's cat just died.
↓	↓
Joan will be successful.	Joan is sad.

In the argument on the left, we take the premise as a given and use it to establish the conclusion. In the explanation on the right, the *explanandum* is the given, and we are trying to establish the hypothesis. Nevertheless, the arrow means the same thing in both cases. The hypothesis is related to the *explanandum* in such a way that if the hypothesis is true, the *explanandum* is likely to be true as well. Of course, we already know it's true; we know that Joan is sad. But the point is that her sadness is just what we would expect if her cat died. Had we learned about her cat before we saw her, we might have predicted that she would be sad, just as we predict her success from the premise about her character traits. An explanation, then, has the same inner structure as an argument, and we can analyze that structure with the same diagramming techniques we have used for analyzing arguments. Let's review these techniques briefly, and see how they apply to explanations. (For a fuller introduction to the diagramming techniques, see Chapter 2.)

It is rarely, if ever, possible for a single proposition to serve as a complete and adequate explanation of anything. In history, literature, the sciences, or any other discipline, an explanation can involve a highly complex set of propositions. Even in the earlier example, there is more than one. The death of Joan's cat is the only part of the hypothesis mentioned explicitly. But we're also assuming that Joan was attached to her cat; otherwise its death would not have meant anything to her. So the explanation includes two points that are combined additively, like dependent premises in an argument:

Joan's cat died.   +   Joan was attached to her cat.

Joan is sad.

An argument can also have independent premises, which we would diagram with convergent arrows. For example:

The plot of the movie is incoherent.   The acting is terrible.

The movie will not win any awards.

An explanation can have the same structure. Suppose a detective trying to solve a murder suspects the victim's son. The detective has to find a motive to explain why the son would do it, and as with many human actions, there may be more than one motive. Perhaps father and son had just had a violent argument, and the son also stood to inherit a lot of money. Then the hypothesis would be diagrammed:

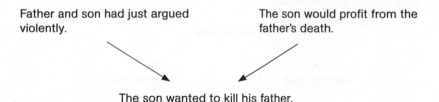

Father and son had just argued violently.   The son would profit from the father's death.

The son wanted to kill his father.

The convergent arrows indicate that the two parts of the hypothesis function independently. Even if one turned out to be false, the other could still (partly) explain the son's motive.

We have also seen that an argument can have more than one step; in fact, most of them do. The same is true of explanations. We explain something by appealing to a hypothesis, and then we can go on to ask why that hypothesis is true, and come up with another hypothesis to explain the first one. As we do so, we increase the *depth* of our explanation, and the deeper the explanation, the more fully we understand the original *explanandum*. In the early 1600s, for example, the German astronomer Johannes Kepler explained the observed motions of the planets on the hypothesis that they follow elliptical orbits around the sun, obeying certain laws that he formulated mathematically. Later in the century, Isaac Newton showed that this hypothesis is itself explained by his law of gravitational attraction. Schematically, then, we have an explanation in two steps.

Finally, a single hypothesis can support more than one *explanandum*, a situation we diagram with divergent arrows:

This structure is extremely important for explanations. One mark of a good explanation is that it unifies a range of phenomena: A single hypothesis explains a number of different *explananda*. A good explanation, in other words, has *breadth* as well as depth. Indeed, these two virtues are related. As we push deeper in the effort to explain something, we typically come up with hypotheses that explain a wider and wider range of things. Thus Newton's theory did more than explain the motions of the planets. It also explained the laws Galileo discovered concerning the motion of falling objects and projectiles. That is, Newton gave a unified explanation for the motion of terrestrial as well as heavenly bodies. Schematically:

Explanations and arguments, then, have the same internal structure. The difference between them lies in their goals: An argument tries to show that something is true; an explanation tries to show why it is true. What about the standards of *evaluation*? Once again, there are similarities as well as differences. To evaluate an argument, we have to ask two questions: Do the premises support the conclusion, and are the premises true? In the same way, there are two basic questions to ask about an explanation.

First, is it *adequate*—would the hypothesis, if true, provide a genuine explanation of the *explanandum*? Does it provide a possible cause or reason or in some way fit the *explanandum* into a wider context that makes it intelligible? In a broad sense, adequacy is to explanation what logical strength is to argument. It pertains to the relation between the hypothesis and the *explanandum*. Indeed, it includes strength as one component. A good explanation is one in which the *explanandum* follows from the hypothesis: The relation between them is such that if the hypothesis is true, the *explanandum* has to be true as well—or at least highly likely. But strength is not the only component. To serve the purposes of explanation, as we'll see, an explanation must satisfy other criteria as well. Second, is the hypothesis *true*? False premises do not prove anything, and false hypotheses do not explain anything. To tell whether a hypothesis is true or false, we would normally use a method that is inductive in the broad sense, but different from the forms of inductive reasoning we've studied so far.

To evaluate explanations, therefore, we need to use what we've already learned about logical relationships, but we also need some additional standards that pertain specifically to explanation. In the next section, we'll look at standards for evaluating adequacy—the relation between hypothesis and *explanandum*. In Section 15.3, we'll consider methods for determining the truth of hypotheses.

EXERCISE 15.1

For each statement, decide whether it is an argument or an explanation. If it is an explanation, identify the *explanandum* and the hypothesis, and diagram the relation between them.

＊1. The stock market went up yesterday because the Federal Reserve lowered interest rates.

2. The stock market will probably rise over the next 6 months because the economy is expanding.

3. The nervous system evolved because animals, which are capable of locomotion, needed a fast and flexible means of guiding their motion.

＊4. Despite her aggressive manner, Natalie is a person with very little self-confidence. That's why she is so boastful. It also explains why she rarely takes on any challenges in her work.

5. One reason for the rise of philosophical inquiry in Athens in the fifth century BCE was that the Athenians were engaged in trade throughout the Mediterranean. Their travels brought them into contact with people of widely different beliefs and customs, which led them to pose philosophical questions about the bases of their own beliefs and customs.

6. The electrical system in a house should be grounded in order to avoid shocks and to prevent fires.

＊7. Babies begin to learn language at about 1 year of age, regardless of what language their parents speak and regardless of other differences among societies and cultures. The timetable of early language acquisition is presumably to be explained by some process of physical maturation in the brain.

8. Suki said that she was going to go shopping yesterday so that she could come over and cook here this evening. But given that she has a history of not following through on her plans, and that she had to work late yesterday, she probably won't be coming by to cook.

9. In Michael Ondaatje's novel *The English Patient*, the narrative is

layered and fragmented: He tells part of one story, involving one set of characters; then switches to another story, involving other characters; then comes back to the first story, providing more background and more of the events. The reason for this is partly to convey how the stories of the different characters intertwine, and partly to illustrate the disjointed nature of human memory.

*10. The continents of the earth are located on different tectonic plates in the earth's crust. The motions of these plates in relation to each other explain the formation of new mountain ranges, the occurrence of earthquakes, and the location of zones of volcanic activity.

11. Had the prisoner maintained her pattern of cooperative behavior, she would have been eligible for early release. But because she participated in a riot and got into a fist-fight with one of the guards, she will have to serve out her entire sentence and also spend a few days in solitary confinement.

12. In her classic work *The Life and Death of Great American Cities*, Jane Jacobs posed the question: Why are some urban areas so much safer and more vibrant than others? Her answer was that the safest areas in a city tend to be those characterized by a mixture of uses—stores, apartments, businesses, restaurants. Such a mixture guarantees that people will be on the streets at all hours, and that in turn is the best deterrent against crime. The presence of people also gives these areas a vibrant feel, attracting new stores and residents.

15.2 Adequacy of Hypotheses

A hypothesis can be true without providing an adequate explanation. Suppose you notice water dripping from your ceiling, and someone ventures the hypothesis that water runs downhill. This would not be very satisfying to you. The statement is true enough, but it doesn't explain what the water is doing up there. In this section, we'll assume that the hypotheses we discuss are all true. The question is: How do we decide whether they are adequate? Every branch of knowledge has its own specific guidelines for evaluating the adequacy of explanations in that area, but there are also some general standards that apply across the board:

1. The inference from hypothesis to *explanandum* should have a high degree of logical *strength*.
2. The explanation should be *complete*: It should explain all significant aspects of the *explanandum*.
3. The explanation should be *informative*: The hypothesis should state the fundamental cause or reason for the *explanandum*.

Let's go over each of these in turn.

15.2A Strength

Explanations and arguments have different goals, but they have the same logical structure, and the *explanandum* should follow from the hypothesis in the same way that a conclusion should follow from the premises. A good explanation will show us that the *explanandum* is not mysterious, but is something we might have expected all along, something we might have predicted or inferred from the facts mentioned in the hypothesis if we had known about them.

The best way to measure strength, in this context, is a general-purpose method. We try to estimate the size of the gap between hypothesis and *explanandum*, the amount of "free play" or slippage between them. And we do this by finding the implicit assumption that would be necessary to close the gap. We explained Joan's sadness by the hypothesis that her cat died, and that she had been attached to it. The implicit assumption is that people who are attached to their pets grieve at their loss. Doubtless there are exceptions to this generalization—it's conceivable that someone would react to loss in a different way. So there is a certain gap here, but it's a small one, and the explanation seems fairly adequate. By contrast, suppose someone said he failed a course because the classroom is on the fifth floor, and he is afraid of heights. There's a sizable gap here between hypothesis and *explanandum*: To connect fear of heights with performance in a course, we would have to tell an elaborate and fairly implausible story. So this explanation is much weaker.

Let's see how this standard applies to a real example. In their effort to control government spending, legislators have found it extremely difficult to eliminate programs that give subsidies to special interests—businesses, labor unions, victims of a certain disease, schoolteachers, farmers, etc. A common explanation runs as follows. The benefits of the programs go to a small class of people, who each have a large stake in the programs and therefore lobby actively to keep them. But the costs are dispersed among all the taxpayers, who have less at stake individually. A \$2 billion program, for example, would cost about \$21 per taxpayer, which is not much of an incentive to organize and lobby against the subsidies. The political pressures on Congress therefore tend to favor the programs. We could diagram the explanation as follows:

1. Those who benefit from subsidies have a lot at stake individually.
2. Those who benefit lobby actively to retain the programs.
3. Those who pay for subsidies do not have a lot at stake individually.
4. Those who pay do not lobby actively against the programs.
5. The political pressures on Congress favor the programs.
6. It is difficult for Congress to eliminate the programs.

This is certainly a plausible explanation. But let's take a closer look, starting at the bottom and checking the strength of each step. The *explanandum* is that it is difficult for Congress to eliminate the programs. Does this follow from proposition 5—that the political pressures favor the programs? The implicit assumption is that the actions of Congress reflect the sum of pressures acting on it. This does not seem like a very large gap. We are not assuming that individual legislators *never* vote independently, on the basis of their own judgment and conscience. We're only assuming that a majority, on most issues, will act in response to pressure. What about the previous step, from 2 and 4 to 5? Notice that 2 and 4 tell us about the *economic* interests at stake in these programs. This implies something about the *political* pressures on Congress only if we assume that lobbying based on economic interest is the only—or at least the primary—source of political pressure. This is a more substantial assumption to make and creates a larger gap in the explanation. One might argue that in some areas, such as civil rights or abortion, Congress acts under tremendous political pressure that is rooted in *moral* rather than economic interests. Perhaps economic interests determine political pressure only by default, in cases where no one raises a moral issue. If so, we would have to amend the explanation to include the point that the press and the voters do not view the question of subsidies in moral terms.

In any case, you can see that checking for strength is an important element in evaluating an explanation. It helps us to identify hidden assumptions that should be made explicit and examined carefully.

15.2B Completeness

We can illustrate our second standard of adequacy with another example concerning money and politics. Increasing amounts of money are being spent in political campaigns. One common explanation is that campaigning has become more expensive. Candidates have to spend huge sums on advertising, media consultants, computerized voter lists, and other high-tech political tools. A common criticism of this hypothesis is that it explains only part of the phenomenon. It explains why candidates need to raise larger sums of money from contributors, but it does not explain why the contributions are forthcoming. People do not part with their money without good reason. So another element in the explanation may be that as government has grown in size and importance, people are willing to invest more money to influence the political process.

1. Campaign spending on elections has increased.
2. Candidates must spend more money to afford advertising and other campaign tools.
3. Candidates must raise more money for their campaigns.
4. Government has grown in size and importance.
5. People have a greater interest in influencing the political process.
6. People are willing to give candidates more money.

To explain the increase in campaign spending, in other words, we must explain the two major components of that *explanandum*. The left side of the diagram is our explanation for the increase in politicians' *demand* for campaign funds. On the right side of the diagram, the shaded portion is our explanation for the increase in donors' willingness to *supply* the funds. If we tried to explain 1 solely in terms of 3, our explanation would be incomplete.

This example illustrates an important point. An *explanandum* is normally complex. Whether it is a single event, a long-term trend, a fact of nature, or whatever, it will have a number of different aspects that a complete explanation must account for. In a criminal trial, the prosecution has to show that the defendant had the opportunity, the motive, and the inclination for the crime. To explain a biological trait like warm-bloodedness, we would want to know what function it serves in the animal's survival, how it arose in the course of evolution, and how it works in biochemical terms. A historical account of an event like the Civil War should explain not only why it occurred, but also why it occurred at that particular time and not 5 years sooner or later.

In applying the rule of completeness, however, there are several qualifications to consider. First, we cannot demand that a hypothesis account for absolutely every-thing; some points are trivial or irrelevant. The prosecution normally would not have to explain why the burglar used a red Ford instead of some other model as a getaway car. Second, we cannot fault a theory for failing to explain something it never set out to explain. Darwin's theory of evolution, for example, explains why a process of natural selection would result in traits that are favorable to survival and reproduction becoming more prevalent in a population. It is not intended to explain how the traits arose in the first place; for that we must turn to genetics and the biochemistry of DNA.

In other words, the rule of completeness is not that a *single* hypothesis must account for *every* aspect of the *explanandum*. The rule is that a *complete* explanation, which may include several hypotheses of different types, must account for every *significant* aspect. To evaluate an explanation in this respect, we should formulate each significant aspect as a separate proposition. When we draw up a diagram, we can then see whether each proposition follows from some element of the explanation as a whole. If not, then we should recognize that fact and not attribute to the hypothesis more explanatory power than it actually has.

15.2C Informativeness

An explanation should be informative. Its purpose, after all, is to make the *explanandum* intelligible, to enlarge our understanding of it. At a minimum, this means it should not be circular, as in the following "explanation":

> "Why are you angry?"
>
> "Because that's the way I feel."

Beyond that minimum standard, however, this rule becomes harder to apply because there are different patterns of explanation that are informative in different ways. In the physical sciences, we explain things in terms of the underlying properties of objects—mass, electrical charge, atomic structure—and the sum of the external forces acting on them. In this context, the more informative explanation is the one that takes us deeper into the inner structure of matter and energy. Biologists explain the traits of living organisms partly in terms of underlying mechanisms (the biochemical processes involved) and partly in terms of the function they serve in helping the organism to survive and reproduce. We explain a human action in terms of its purpose: What was the person's goal? Why did he believe this action would achieve the goal? In history, we explain an event in terms of the prior events that led up to it, within the context of the cultural, political, economic, and other conditions of the society at that time.

We could go on adding to this list—there are many different patterns of explanation. It would take a separate book to describe them all and to review the different standards they give us for telling how informative an explanation is. But there is a common element in these standards. An explanation should get to the bottom of things. No matter what pattern we use, an explanation is informative to the extent that it identifies the *fundamental* cause or reason for the *explanandum*. Newton's theory was more informative than Kepler's or Galileo's and represented an advance in human knowledge because it went deeper; it identified the laws underlying the phenomena that Kepler and Galileo discovered. Darwin's theory of natural selection was a profound insight and another major advance in knowledge because it described a basic mechanism by which organisms come to have traits that promote their survival and reproductive success. We understand a person best when we can trace his actions to fundamental goals and beliefs—the ones that are central to his character, personality, and outlook on the world. In general, the rule that an explanation should be informative is analogous to the rule that a classification or definition should use essential attributes. In both cases we are looking for fundamentality.

This is an open-ended standard. We can hardly fault Kepler or Galileo for failing to discover Newton's laws or Newton for failing to anticipate the discoveries of Albert Einstein. The fact that later theories are more informative does not imply that earlier ones are totally uninformative. But it *is* uninformative, and thus inadequate, to try to explain the *more* fundamental phenomenon by the *less* fundamental. The cause explains the effect, the essential attribute explains the superficial one, the end explains the means. In every case, an explanation that inverts the proper order is uninformative. Suppose we tried to interpret Shakespeare's *Julius Caesar* along the following lines:

> The main character is Cassius, and the basic theme of the play is that you can't trust thin people. "Let me have men about me that are fat," says Caesar. "Yond Cassius

has a lean and hungry look. He thinks too much; such men are dangerous." Everything else in the play—the murder of Caesar, Marc Antony's speech, the campaign against Brutus and his suicide—are all subplots designed to emphasize just how dangerous thin people can be.

This is a ridiculous reading of the play. Cassius is not the main character, his figure is not his essential trait, and Caesar's remark does not express the central theme. These are all tangential elements in the play that would themselves have to be explained in terms of something more basic.

It is not always obvious which of two things is the more fundamental, and there are many controversies on this score. In the early part of the 19th century, biologists debated whether structure or function was primary in evolution. One school said that structure changes first, leading a species to adopt a new way of functioning to take advantage of the new structure. Their opponents (who eventually won) said that a change in function comes first, creating evolutionary pressure for new structures that better serve that function. In the social sciences, some theorists hold that political and economic factors underlie and explain a society's intellectual–cultural life—its dominant ideology, artistic values, religious beliefs, etc. Others take the opposite view, that ideas are the fundamental factor: A society's basic values and view of the world determine the kind of political and economic institutions it will have. Debates like these indicate how difficult it can be to apply the principle of fundamentality. But they also indicate how important the principle is.

15.2D Combining the Standards

An adequate explanation should be strong, complete, and informative. To see how these standards relate to each other, let's look at one final example, a famous hypothesis whose adequacy has been questioned on all three counts. In *The Protestant Ethic and the Spirit of Capitalism*, the German sociologist Max Weber proposed that the rise of capitalism was largely the result of the Protestant Reformation in general and the doctrines of John Calvin and the Puritans in particular. Weber noted that Calvin regarded productive work as a religious virtue: One's trade or profession is a "calling," a way of serving God, and worldly success is a sign of heavenly grace. The Protestant emphasis on asceticism, moreover, discouraged consumption and thereby encouraged thrift; this in turn allowed for the savings and investment that are essential to a capitalist economy.

Some historians have argued that Weber's theory is *incomplete*. It may explain the rise of capitalism in the Protestant countries of northern Europe and North America. And the demand for religious freedom that arose out of the Reformation may have furthered the principle of individual rights (including property rights and economic freedom) that was necessary for the full development of capitalism. But many of the early centers of commerce, such as Venice or Lisbon, were in Catholic countries, and many of the leading merchants and financiers were Catholic or Jewish. So the thesis cannot account for everything.

A different objection to Weber's theory is raised by Marxists. Weber was trying to explain an economic development in terms of religious ideas. But this, they argue, inverts the true relationship. Ideas are consequences, not causes, of underlying economic forces. The Protestant ethic in particular was a by-product of class interest, a rationalization offered by the rising capitalists to sanctify their quest for control over material production. Thus, in the Marxists' view, Weber was trying to explain the fundamental phenomenon by something that was less fundamental. His explanation is *uninformative*, and ultimately circular, because to explain the Protestant ethic itself we would be led back to the very economic trends he was trying to explain.

A third criticism is that, while Weber was right to look for the historical roots of capitalism in the realm of ideas, he picked the wrong ideas. Capitalism required a secular philosophy, emphasizing happiness and prosperity in this life, the pursuit of self-interest, and the virtue of rationality. These ideas were on the rise throughout the Renaissance and the Enlightenment, but they were opposed by the early Protestant thinkers, who were otherworldly in outlook, viewed egoism as a sin, and emphasized revelation and mysticism over reason. Indeed, they went further in each respect than the Catholic Church, which they criticized for being too secular. The *explanandum*, then, simply doesn't follow from the hypothesis: The explanation is *weak*. Anyone observing the Reformation, and unaware of the other forces at work, would have expected a movement away from capitalism.

Of course, this description of Weber's thesis, and the objections to it, is vastly oversimplified. But it serves to illustrate the differences among the standards of adequacy and the way they are applied in practice.

REVIEW   Adequacy of Hypotheses

An adequate explanation should be:

1. *Strong*: The inference from hypothesis to *explanandum* should have a high degree of logical strength.

2. *Complete*: The hypothesis or hypotheses should explain all significant aspects of the *explanandum*.

3. *Informative*: The hypothesis should state the fundamental cause or reason for the *explanandum*.

EXERCISE 15.2

Each of the explanations below can be faulted as inadequate. Identify the standard (or standards) that it violates.

*1. Why did the chicken cross the road? To get to the other side.

2. My term paper was late because I had to go to the dentist for a checkup the day before it was due.

3. Deja needs to buy a new orange toothbrush and some dental floss on her next shopping trip, since her old toothbrush is over six months old, and starting to look worn down.

✳4. At the next exit, I'm going to stop at a fast-food restaurant and buy two hamburgers, an order of fries, and a large drink, because I'm very hungry.

5. The city council voted to change the intersection of Mulberry Street and Oak Avenue from a two-way stop to a four-way stop. This was because, until now, traffic moving north or south through the intersection had to stop, whereas traffic moving east or west did not. But with the new change, traffic moving through the intersection in any direction will have to stop.

6. Wolves travel in packs because they are social animals.

✳7. Prosecutor: "Ladies and gentlemen of the jury, you must convict Imelda Moore of murdering her ex-boyfriend Peter Vassili. She was furious after he broke up with her and thus had a strong motive for wanting him dead."

8. Though no one has yet been able to decipher the inscriptions on the Tagara stones, we know that the stones were intended for use in religious rituals, since they are arranged on the landscape in geometric patterns, and since the inscriptions are all on the tops of the stones, rather than on the sides.

9. I haven't had any contact with my brother for five years, since I haven't called him and he hasn't called me.

✳10. The Pythagorean theorem asserts that the square of the hypotenuse of a right triangle is equal to the sum of the squares of the other two sides. How was this fact discovered? The Greek geometers of antiquity learned it from the Egyptians.

11. In Western societies, people customarily wear wedding bands on the fourth finger of the left hand. That's probably because the Romans believed a vein ran from the fourth finger directly to the heart.

12. Why was George Washington admired so much, with a kind of reverence and awe, in an age filled with other great men? It was largely his height: He towered over most other men.

✳13. The collapse of the Soviet Union and its control over Eastern Europe in the late 1980s occurred because a socialist economic system is incapable of producing goods as abundantly as a capitalist system.

14. If the quality of education has declined, and it certainly has, the main reason is that teachers no longer enjoy the public respect and esteem once accorded their profession and are thus too demoralized to do a good job.

15. Why has art been such a pervasive feature of human life, found in every society? One theory holds that since art has no survival value, it must have evolved instead as a form of sexual display to attract mates, like the peacock's tail. An artistic achievement such as making a realistic drawing or reciting a long epic narrative requires enormous intelligence, persistence, and skill. If someone has these survival-enhancing attributes in such abundance that he can afford to waste them on creating art, that person is more attractive to potential mates.

15.3 The Truth of Hypotheses

The adequacy of an explanation does not guarantee that the hypothesis is true. A theory may be strong, complete, informative—and false. Innocent people have been convicted in cases where their guilt would have explained all the evidence. Scientists have often seen a beautiful theory murdered by the facts. How is this possible? There's a simple logical reason. The adequacy of an explanation tells us that if the hypothesis is true, the *explanandum* is likely to be true as well. It tells us, in other words, that we may accept the hypothetical proposition: if H, then E. And we know that E is true. But to infer from these two propositions that H is true would be to affirm the consequent—and that's a fallacy. There might well be some alternative hypothesis H' that would explain E with equal adequacy.

This point cannot be emphasized too strongly. Affirming the consequent in the manner just described is the most common error in reasoning about explanations—and indeed in all inductive reasoning. We all want things to make sense, and it's all too easy to accept the first plausible explanation we find. We hear that a medical student is going to specialize in brain surgery, and we assume it must be for the money, without considering any other possible motive. The economy falls into a recession, and we blame the president's policies without considering other factors that might have played a role. We adopt a religion or a philosophy because it offers *an* explanation of human nature and experience, without asking whether it offers the *only* or the best explanation. You can see the same thing happening in the spread of a rumor. A couple breaks up, a friend makes a guess about the reason, and by the time the gossip is repeated once or twice, speculation has become "fact."

To combat this tendency, it is crucial to consider alternatives before we accept a given hypothesis. Courts of law use the adversary system, despite its many faults, partly to ensure that the jury will hear an alternative to the prosecution's account of the crime. The canons of scientific research require that a theory not be accepted until it has proven its superiority to rival theories. In everyday life, when someone asks rhetorically, "What other explanation could there be?" the question should serve as a red flag: There almost always is some other explanation worth considering.

15.3A Testing Hypotheses

Assuming, then, that we have several hypotheses on the table, how do we decide which one is true? In some cases, we can use the methods we are already familiar with. If you think the drip in your ceiling might be caused by rain coming in through a hole in the roof, you can check this out by observation: You can look for the hole. Or suppose you want to know why the lilac bush in your garden develops mildew around midsummer. If you consult a gardening book, you will find that this happens to all lilacs. And this generalization can be confirmed by using Mill's methods.

But we can't always test a hypothesis by the standard methods of observation and induction. When you want to explain why someone is acting a certain way, you cannot manipulate the person's mind to see which factors cause the behavior. Scientists did not establish the atomic theory by generalizing from a sample—they didn't discover first that chairs are made of atoms, then that tables are, and carrots, and so on until there were enough instances to support the claim that all physical objects are so constituted. When we are trying to explain a unique individual event or when the possible causes involve things we can't observe directly, the methods of induction we have learned so far will not do the job by themselves.

Instead, we use an indirect approach. If the hypothesis is adequate to begin with, then the *explanandum* follows from it. The indirect method is to ask what *other* consequences would follow. Having first reasoned backward from *explanandum* to hypothesis, we now reason forward, drawing further conclusions from the hypothesis and checking to see whether the conclusions are true. The process could be diagrammed schematically as follows:

If we find that consequences $C_1, C_2, C_3, \ldots$, are not true, we reject the hypothesis. But if they *are* true, they confirm it and become *explananda* that are themselves explained by the hypothesis.

This method of testing hypotheses should not be news; you have almost certainly used it yourself. The toaster isn't working—is the problem in the toaster itself or in the wall outlet? If the latter were the case, then the toaster should work if you plug it into a different outlet. So you try that and find that it does work, confirming the hypothesis. A friend hasn't shown up for a dinner date—did he have to work late at the office? But then he would have called, and he hasn't, so it must be something else. To a large extent, the confirmation of a scientific theory is simply a more elaborate and more refined application of the same method. Newton's theory, for example, was put to an important test when Edmund Halley used the theory to predict the next appearance of the comet named for him. Though the theory already had a good deal of evidence going for it, it gained further confirmation when the comet appeared on schedule.

If one or more of the consequences we derive from a hypothesis turn out to be *false*, then the hypothesis itself can be rejected, in accordance with the hypothetical syllogism:

If *H*, then *C*

Not-*C*
———————
Not-*H*

You can see that this inference is valid even if a single consequence turns out to be false. On the positive side, however, the fact that a single consequence turns out to be *true* does not prove the hypothesis true. The inference:

If *H*, then *C*

C
———————
H

affirms the consequent and is thus fallacious. For confirmation, what counts is the number of consequences we test and their relation to the various alternative hypotheses we've considered.

We assume from the outset, moreover, that there *is* some explanation, that some hypothesis will account for the *explanandum*. The question is: which one? At the outset, there may be many alternatives, but as we test more and more consequences, we narrow down the possibilities, ideally to the point where only one hypothesis is consistent with all the evidence. Indeed, we should actively look for cases in which rival hypotheses have different implications: H implies C_x, H' implies not-C_x. Testing to see whether C_x is true or false will then rule out one of the hypotheses.

Notice that this is an inductive process. The consequences may follow deductively from the hypothesis, as may the *explanandum*. But the evidence for the truth of the hypothesis is inductive. The strength of the evidence is a matter of degree: It can always be increased by testing additional consequences. And when we accept a hypothesis because we have eliminated alternative explanations, our reasoning rests on the presupposition that we have considered all the relevant alternatives—just as Mill's methods rest on the presupposition that we have varied all the relevant factors. As we acquire more information, new alternatives may occur to us. Establishing a hypothesis is an open-ended process that depends on the context of our knowledge at a given time, and we must allow for the possibility that an explanation will have to be modified—or in extreme cases rejected—as we acquire new knowledge.

Let's consider a classic example of the process. The English scientist Isaac Newton is famous for his laws of motion and theory of gravity, which we mentioned earlier. He was also interested in the nature of light, and conducted experiments involving the color spectrum that are a model of scientific reasoning. People had known since antiquity that glass prisms can produce a spectrum of colors, which we also see in rainbows. A common theory in Newton's day was that the prism was the source of the colors, "contaminating" the pure white light. Newton wondered whether the prism did not create the colors but instead *separated* colors that are already in the light.

The *explanandum* is that light shone through a prism produces a color spectrum, illustrated in the diagram below. Newton darkened his room on a sunny day and cut a small hole in his shade to allow through a narrow beam of white light, which he then passed through a prism, with the light projected to a screen.

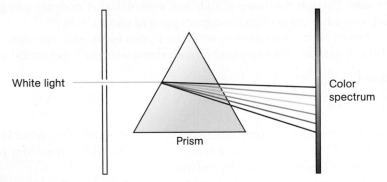

The rival hypotheses, both of which would explain the effects of the prism, are:

H1: The prism converts the pure white light into colors.

H2: The prism separates the colors, which are already in the white light.

To test his hypothesis (H2), Newton reasoned that if the colors are in the light, then isolating one of the colored beams from the first prism and sending it through a second prism should have no further effect, which was indeed the case (top figure on the next page). He also reasoned that if a lens were used to reverse the dispersion of colors from the prism, the colors would be recombined into white light (bottom figure)—indicating, again, that the prism was not creating the colors but only revealing colors in the light itself.

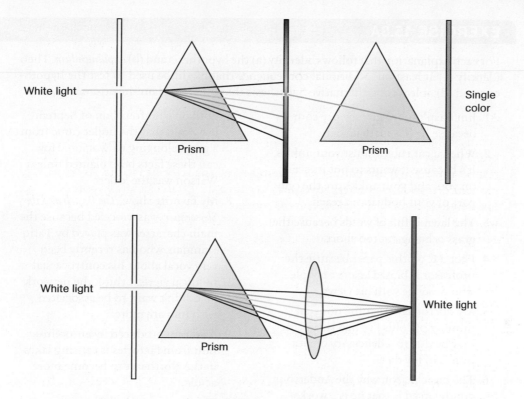

The results of Newton's experiments are well known to us now, and much has been discovered about the nature of light since his time. But his experimental method of testing his hypothesis remains a model of scientific investigation.

SOLVE　Explanation and Bayes' Theorem

Since the evidence for a hypothesis is acquired in an open-ended process that depends on the context of our knowledge, there is no standard way to measure how far along we are in establishing its truth. But some theorists hold that we can use probability theory—Bayes' theorem in particular—as a guide. In the previous chapter, we discussed how the theorem can be used to assess the initial probability of a hypothesis and the increase in probability from specific evidence, when we have statistical information about possible causal factors. We used a fictional example to show how the theorem might

be used to investigate why a certain region has a high rate of leukemia.

If you are interested in pursuing the subject, you might review the example (in Section 14.3) from the standpoint of the logical structure of explanations we have provided in this chapter.

- What are the *explanandum* and hypothesis in the example? Diagram the explanation.
- How would you test the hypothesis, taking account of the quantitative information given?
- How would you use Bayes' theorem to decide whether to investigate other hypotheses?

EXERCISE 15.3A

For each explanation that follows, identify (a) the hypothesis and (b) *explanandum*. Then identify (c) at least one additional consequence that might be used to test the hypothesis and (d) at least one alternative hypothesis that might explain the *explanandum*.

*1. Jim hasn't taken any science courses because he has math anxiety.

2. When a cat rubs against your ankles, it's because it wants to put its scent on you, and your ankles are the only part of your body it can reach.

3. The lawn is full of weeds because the grass is being cut too short.

*4. I got a C on this paper because the professor is biased against people who disagree with his views.

5. My doctor says that the unusual number of colds I've had this winter may be due to a deficiency of vitamin C in my diet.

6. The basic reason why the Andersons got divorced is that he is a workaholic; she felt neglected because he was not spending much time at home.

*7. Police investigating the murder established that the victim died from a gunshot wound in the head as he walked down Fifth Avenue in New York on the afternoon of September 7 and that the bullet came from a gun belonging to Watson. How can these facts be explained unless Watson was the killer?

8. My favorite show, *The Ranch and the Skyscraper*, was canceled because the main character was played by Tariq Hamdan, who has recently been very vocal about his controversial political views. I think the network just didn't want to be associated with him anymore.

9. Acid rain produced by air pollution from factories is causing lakes in the Northeast to become more acidic.

*10. The American Civil War was caused primarily by a conflict over tariffs: The Northern states wanted tariffs to protect their manufacturing industries, while the more agricultural South wanted to be able to import manufactured goods from Europe without having to pay tariffs.

15.3B Plausibility

As in the other forms of inductive reasoning, testing a hypothesis requires that we make various judgments of plausibility along the way. To see why, we have to add a few complications to our picture of confirmation. For one thing, we could not hope to test every conceivable hypothesis. We have to exercise our judgment in deciding which ones are plausible enough to be worth testing, just as we have to decide, in using Mill's methods, which factors should be varied and which ones can be ignored. If we wanted to understand why a usually thrifty person suddenly splurged on a cruise in the Bahamas, there would be various hypotheses to consider, depending on what we know about the person's character and circumstances. But there are countless other hypotheses we would ignore: that cosmic rays had altered his consciousness, that he is a foreign agent living a double life, etc.

A further complication is that we can usually derive a consequence from a hypothesis only in conjunction with some additional, *auxiliary assumptions*. We need to modify our standard diagram to include this point:

Suppose we perform the test and find that *C* is false. This will not necessarily refute the hypothesis. It may be that one of the auxiliary assumptions $A_1, A_2, \ldots$, was false instead. In other words, when a hypothesis fails a test, the logical structure diagrammed above allows us to save the hypothesis by blaming an auxiliary assumption. Whether it is reasonable to do so depends on a judgment of plausibility.

For example, the law of gravity implies that if I release a ball in midair, it will fall. But this consequence follows only on the auxiliary assumption that no other force is acting on the ball to counteract gravity. Suppose I release the ball and it remains motionless, floating in midair. I am certainly not going to abandon the law of gravity; it is much more reasonable to reject the auxiliary assumption and assume that some other force is at work. However, people sometimes cling to a theory in the face of overwhelming evidence against it by inventing reasons to reject auxiliary assumptions rather than the theory itself. If there were any doubt that Earth is not flat, for example, one might think the pictures taken from space would have clinched the matter. But the pictures are decisive only on the assumption that they were indeed taken from space, and some flat-Earthers argued that it was all an elaborate hoax.

What standards should we use in deciding what's plausible? The decision is not always as obvious or clear-cut as in the examples above. How do we decide whether a hypothesis is plausible enough to be considered and tested? If a hypothesis fails a test, how do we decide whether it is more reasonable to reject the hypothesis or one of the auxiliary assumptions? As in other areas of inductive logic, these judgments depend partly on one's knowledge and experience in the specific field. But there are also two general standards that apply across the board. Other things being equal, one hypothesis is more plausible than another if it is more *consistent* with the rest of our knowledge and if it is *simpler*. Let's look at these standards in more detail.

CONSISTENCY Consider two theories that might both be said to assert the existence of a "sixth sense": (1) Certain animals such as migratory birds can perceive the earth's magnetic field; (2) certain human beings are capable of extrasensory perception (ESP). The first is a routine scientific hypothesis; most scientists would regard it as a plausible explanation for the ability of migratory birds to navigate as well as they do. By contrast, the ESP hypothesis has much less initial plausibility and would have to meet a much higher standard of evidence than the first one before it would be taken seriously. Why?

One reason is that the idea of a magnetic sense is entirely consistent with everything we know about sense perception. Perception involves a physical organ containing receptor cells that respond to various forms of energy (light waves, sound waves, etc.) and are capable of detecting various features of the environment (colors, sounds, etc.) with some reliability. A magnetic sense would fit this pattern; we need only accept the possibility of a new type of receptor that responds to a known form of energy. But ESP, as its name implies, is extrasensory. It does not involve identifiable sense organs or receptors; it is not alleged to be a response to any known form of energy; and it does not produce reliable knowledge of the environment: At best, the experiments show that certain people score slightly above chance in various guessing games. So ESP is not consistent with the rest of our knowledge about perception. To accept it as a viable hypothesis, we would have to abandon some fundamental principles derived from the study of vision, hearing, touch, taste, and smell.

We should remember that when we introduce a hypothesis to explain something, we are not operating in a vacuum. We have a vast context of background knowledge—beliefs, principles, and theories for which we have accumulated a great deal of evidence. A new hypothesis therefore starts out with a certain degree of initial plausibility that depends on how consistent it is, how well it fits, with that background knowledge. A hypothesis that conflicts with established principles and theories must meet a higher standard of evidence than a hypothesis that does not conflict. Accepting the first sort of hypothesis, after all, means giving up beliefs for which we have good evidence, so the new evidence must be strong enough and extensive enough to outweigh the old. This does not mean we should be traditionalists and reject every radically new idea just because it conflicts with the established wisdom. It does mean we should know what we're doing and be prepared to back it up.

In science, revolutions can occur when scientists discover phenomena that can't be explained by prevailing theories. But a new theory must do more than explain these anomalies; it must also explain the phenomena that the old theory explained, and it must give some coherent account of the evidence for the older view. Einstein's theory of relativity had to explain why Newton's laws describe the behavior of physical objects as well as they do. As that example suggests, the standard of consistency applies with special force in the physical sciences, where we have a vast edifice of highly integrated and well-confirmed theories. It applies with somewhat less force in the social sciences, which are younger and less highly developed, and with less force still in the humanities. In these branches of knowledge, established views do not have the same degree of evidence as in the physical sciences, and new ideas therefore do not have as large an obstacle to overcome. But they must still take account of whatever genuine evidence there is for the older views.

The rule of consistency is especially important in evaluating claims on the fringes of science: claims about ESP and other alleged psychic powers, alien spacecraft, astrology, the Bermuda Triangle, alien astronauts who visited Earth during ancient times, etc. All of these purport to explain "the unexplained," to solve mysteries that established scientific theories cannot account for. And, as we saw in the case of ESP, the explanations conflict with, and would require us to abandon, principles or theories for which we have a great deal of evidence. Before we accept any such explanation, we should recognize that it is not, as the proponents normally claim, the only possible one. Invariably there are alternative hypotheses that might explain the phenomenon and be more consistent with our background knowledge.

One alternative hypothesis is simply that the *explanandum* isn't true, the event never occurred, and there is nothing to explain. The witnesses who claim to have seen alien spacecraft may have misidentified what they saw; the ancient texts that describe miraculous events may be mistaken; the subjects who seem to have powers of telepathy may instead be using the techniques of magicians and con artists. A second alternative hypothesis applies to amazing coincidences: the man who has a sudden feeling of dread and calls home to find his wife has had a terrible accident; the person who dreams of winning the lottery and does so the next day. These are often taken as signs of higher powers at work, but they may be just coincidences. The laws of probability make it very likely that among all the premonitions, dreams, and sudden dreads that we experience, most of which come to nothing and are quickly forgotten, a few will turn out to be accurate.

These alternative hypotheses may turn out to be false. But because they are fully consistent with our background knowledge, they must be considered and tested before we can accept any explanation that is not consistent.

SIMPLICITY Suppose someone on trial for burglary tries to explain away the evidence as follows:

Prosecutor: Three witnesses said they saw you in the neighborhood the day before the crime. You don't live near there. Weren't you casing the joint?

Defendant: No, I was just taking a walk.

Prosecutor: Why were you loitering around the victim's building and staring at the fire escape?

Defendant: Well, it's an old building, and the fire escape has some ornamental features that are interesting from an architectural point of view. I'm very interested in architecture.

Prosecutor: Where were you on the night of the crime?

Defendant: In Clancey's Bar.

Prosecutor: Why doesn't anyone remember seeing you there that night?

Defendant: I guess they were all drunk.

Prosecutor: Why were the stolen goods found in your car?

Defendant: The thief must have put them there.

A jury listening to this exchange has two hypotheses to consider. The prosecutor would explain all the evidence with a single claim: The defendant committed the crime. The defendant's explanation, by contrast, involves a string of unrelated claims. It's conceivable, of course, that they are all true. The truth is not always simple. But the jury would be justified in considering the defendant's story less plausible than the prosecutor's and in need of more evidence to back it up.

This example illustrates the principle of simplicity or parsimony. The rule is that, other things being equal, one hypothesis is more plausible than another if it involves fewer new assumptions. We have seen that an explanation rarely involves a single proposition.

A full explanation usually requires a complex hypothesis, involving a number of separate propositions. If these separate propositions are new and cannot be derived from knowledge we already possess, then the fewer the better. The reason is appropriately simple. Just as an adequate explanation must account for every significant aspect of the *explanandum*, the evidence for the truth of a hypothesis must cover each positive claim it makes. The fewer the claims, the less evidence will be required. Conversely, the farther out on a limb we go, the stronger the limb must be. This is not to say that the rule is always easy to apply. It can happen that theory *A* is simpler in one respect, theory *B* in another. But if one hypothesis is obviously simpler, it is more plausible.

The standard of simplicity is particularly important in deciding what to do when we test a hypothesis and get a negative result. If the hypothesis has survived a series of tests and provides a single coherent explanation for a number of consequences that have been derived from it, it may be simpler to assume that failure on some further test is due to an auxiliary assumption. If we keep getting negative results, however, and can save the hypothesis only by a series of unrelated, *ad hoc* attempts to blame the auxiliary assumptions, the balance tips against the hypothesis.

The standard of simplicity can also be used in evaluating conspiracy theories. Conspiracies certainly do occur, and sometimes we have direct evidence for them, as when one of the conspirators confesses. But the evidence is often indirect, and in such cases the standard cuts both ways. On the one hand, the hypothesis that a conspiracy is at work may provide a single, unified explanation for a series of events that would otherwise have to be given separate explanations. As the villain in an Ian Fleming novel says, after he has encountered James Bond for the third time and infers that Bond is trying to foil him, "Mr. Bond, they have a saying in Chicago: 'Once is happenstance. Twice is coincidence. The third time it's enemy action.'"

But conspiracy theories do not always simplify. The notion that the U.S. economy and political system are governed by a secret cabal of international bankers, for example,

---

APPLY Write an Essay, Give a Speech

We want the knowledge and skills you've gained from this book to help you in your other courses, your future career, your life. That's why we have tried to show how logic is used in a variety of fields and offered a few suggestions about its possible applications in your life. Here's another suggestion: Many students take an English composition or public speaking class. In your English class, you will probably be asked to write one or more expository essays. In contrast with an argumentative essay, the expository essay seeks to explain rather than to convince. Expository essays may involve a sum-

mary of a topic, but they often involve explanations of cause and effect. Likewise, your speech teacher may assign an explanatory speech.

Let us help! Figure out your *explanandum* and hypothesis, then diagram your explanation the way we've taught you. Write your essay or speech, following your professor's guidelines. As a final check, try to evaluate your explanation according to the standards you've learned from us. Is your explanation adequate? Is your hypothesis true? If so, you're probably on your way to a good grade!

gives only the illusion of simplicity. In fact, it raises more questions than it answers. How did this group gain so much power? Why this particular group and not some other? To control a nation of more than 300 million people, these bankers must give marching orders to hundreds of thousands of political and business leaders. How do they manage to keep all these people in line? How do they manage to keep their own role a secret? To answer these questions, the conspiracy theory would have to be spun out into an elaborate web of arbitrary claims.

As in other types of induction, testing a hypothesis—whether it is a conspiracy theory or a theory about a friend's behavior—requires that we exercise our judgment and allow for the possibility that reasonable people may disagree. That goes with the territory. But the methods and standards discussed earlier will help organize the process of inquiry and direct our attention to the relevant issues.

SOLVE   Testing a Hypothesis

1. Derive consequences from the hypothesis and then see whether the consequences are true.

2. If one or more of the consequences are false, reject the hypothesis unless it would be simpler or more consistent with other knowledge to reject an auxiliary hypothesis.

3. If a number of consequences are true, the hypothesis is confirmed unless an alternative hypothesis is equally consistent with the same evidence and is as simple.

EXERCISE 15.3B

For each *explanandum*, determine which of the hypotheses is more plausible using the standards of consistency and simplicity.

✳1. I get a lot of wrong-number calls at night for Shakey's Pizza.
   a. My telephone number is similar to Shakey's.
   b. Someone is trying to harass me by waking me up during the night.

2. My dog is barking at the door.
   a. The dog was bitten by a raccoon and has rabies, which is making him delirious.
   b. There is a stranger at the door.

3. Samantha's parrot says "Hello, come in" when a guest arrives.
   a. The parrot has learned the cultural norms of politeness in our society.
   b. The parrot is imitating Samantha's greeting to guests.

✳4. I hear the sound of a telephone ringing.
   a. There is a telephone nearby that is ringing.

b. I am in the Matrix and the Machines are stimulating my brain to have the experience as of a telephone ringing.

5. The grocery store is out of onions.
   a. Many other customers bought up all of the onions over the course of the day.
   b. My neighbor knew I would want to buy onions today, so he got to the store before I did and bought them all.

6. The radio in my car is not picking up any stations today.
   a. Someone is jamming the signals.
   b. Something is wrong with my car's radio.

*7. We didn't catch any fish on last Saturday's trip to Lake Eerie.
   a. There were no more fish in the lake.
   b. We weren't using the right sort of bait.

8. On September 11, 2001, two commercial airliners crashed into the World Trade Center and destroyed the towers.
   a. It was a deliberate attack planned by al Qaida terrorists in a plot to harm the United States.
   b. It was an accident.
   c. It was a deliberate attack planned by the U.S. government in order to justify war in the Middle East.

9. The Gospels of the Christian Bible (Matthew, Mark, Luke, and John) describe a man named Jesus who lived in Palestine 2,000 years ago and attracted a religious following.
   a. Religious fanatics later wrote Gospels to create the myth of a founder of their religion.
   b. There was a man named Jesus who lived in Palestine 2,000 years ago and attracted a religious following.

*10. NASA has not yet reported finding any signs of life on Mars.
   a. NASA is hiding its knowledge of life on Mars.
   b. The Martians have concealed themselves from NASA.
   c. There is no life on Mars.

15.4 Pseudo-Explanations

History and science are fields in which methods for evaluating explanations have been highly developed, and we have discussed a number of examples in previous sections. If you are a college student you may well be taking courses in these fields. They are valuable not only for the content you learn about human history and discoveries in the natural and social sciences, but also for the logical methods they employ. In this final section, we will see how understanding those methods will also help you identify imposters. The very success of these fields has led to imitation by people attempting to gain acceptance for **pseudo-explanations**: purported explanations that mimic genuine explanatory theories but violate the standards of explanation. Pseudo-explanations include unsubstantiated claims, superstitions, and crackpot theories that masquerade as genuine explanations. We will discuss some of the more common forms of pseudo-explanation in history and the sciences. In both fields, to be sure, there are borderline cases where there is room for debate about how to classify them. But we will focus on

---

REVIEW **Explanatory Standards**

Adequacy

- Strength: The inference from hypothesis to explanandum should have a high degree of logical strength.
- Completeness: The hypothesis or hypotheses should explain all significant aspects of the explanandum.
- Informativeness: The hypothesis should state the fundamental cause or reason for the *explanandum*.

Truth

- Confirmation: A hypothesis is tested for truth by deriving consequences. If those consequences are true, the hypothesis is confirmed; if not, it is disconfirmed.
- Consistency: A hypothesis is plausible to the extent that it is consistent with established knowledge.
- Simplicity: A hypothesis is plausible to the extent that it is simpler than rival hypotheses.

---

the clear cases of pseudo-explanations in order to see how they differ from the genuine article.

What marks a theory as pseudo is that it violates the standards for a good explanation. As we have seen, those standards pertain to adequacy and truth, summarized in the Review box.

15.4A Pseudohistory

Historical explanations are supported largely on the basis of preserved documents, artifacts, and testimonies. These sources suggest explanatory hypotheses and provide the evidence to test them. History is more subject to interpretation than science, but it is governed by the general standards of explanation as well as specialized methods of research. Most historians try to adhere to these professional standards just as rigorously as scientists adhere to the scientific method. That's why we respect both fields as reliable sources of knowledge. The very respect we accord history, however, has motivated people to engage in pseudohistory.

In this section, we'll see two ways distorted history can give us faulty explanations: denialism and alternative history.

DENIALISM Denialism is a form of what is sometimes called "revisionist history," a term often used to criticize claims or theories that differ from common beliefs about historical events. But the term is misleading because it does not distinguish between legitimate and illegitimate revisions. Revision in history is often legitimate, well justified by explanatory standards. The past doesn't change, but our knowledge and understanding of the past are constantly evolving. The recovery of new and relevant evidence sometimes leads to necessary and proper revision. New documents are discovered that correct our previous misconceptions and fill in historical gaps. New evidence becomes available as governments release classified information. Many such documents released after the end of the Cold War, for example, have given historians more complete information about the former Soviet Union and its conflict with Western countries. History may also be revised in light of scientific advances. The development of X-ray analysis methods has provided information about burial habits. Carbon dating and more recent technologies enable archeologists to explain the distant past with more precision.

Legitimate revision can also be the result of following up on new questions. The modern women's movement, for example, led historians to devote more attention to the role of women in American history. New questions led to new research and new explanations, especially in social history. In the end, these answers provided a fuller, more robust view of many developments in American history. In this case, history was revised not due to previously lost or suppressed documents but in response to documents that had previously been ignored.

But historical revision is not legitimate when it distorts or denies evidence in order to defend a theory at odds with well-established history. An obvious case is Holocaust denial, the claim that death camps in Nazi Germany didn't exist or that the number of deaths has been grossly exaggerated. These claims violate the consistency standard: They are inconsistent with a huge body of evidence, including the physical evidence of camps such as Auschwitz, official documents from the Nazi regime, and the eyewitness testimonies of survivors. In addition, Holocaust deniers must invent conspiracy theories purporting to explain how and why all this evidence was invented—that it was all propaganda by the Allies in World War II to justify the war against the Nazis, for example, or a Jewish conspiracy to justify the state of Israel. Like other conspiracy theories, as we noted in the previous section, such "explanations" fail on the grounds of simplicity by making many arbitrary *ad hoc* assumptions.

A more complex case of revisionism is the academic issue known as the Shakespeare Authorship Question. Was the man known to history as William Shakespeare of Stratford (1564–1616) the actual author of the plays attributed to him? The question is a hardy perennial in literary studies, with many claims that Shakespeare could not have written the plays and with many hypotheses about other people who might have been the real playwrights. Most scholars reject these claims. Your authors are not experts in the field, so we take no position. But let us at least outline the issue as an example of historical explanation—and a possible case of denialism.

William Shakespeare was recognized as a talented playwright and celebrity even in his own day, and is regarded as the author by most biographers and most literary scholars since then. What reason is there to doubt that he really was the author? The doubters raise various questions, most of them based on the evidence of the plays themselves and the features that make them among the greatest works in English literature. These features are the *explanandum*. A short list would include:

- The poetry of their language and their power as drama, which have engaged audiences for centuries
- Their use of Greek and Roman myths and history
- Their use of English history and contemporary life among English aristocrats and the monarch's court
- The large vocabulary and familiarity with many trades
- Their evident familiarity with Italian culture of the time (many of the comedies are set in Italy)

The chief argument among doubters is that Shakespeare did not have the education required to produce these features. He was the son of an illiterate glove-maker, with only a grammar school education. The hypothesis that Shakespeare is the author, argue the doubters, provides at best a logically weak and incomplete explanation of such complex and sophisticated plays. Where would he have acquired knowledge of Italy, or of aristocratic life in England? Most of the other candidate-authors—Edward de Vere (Earl of Oxford), Sir Francis Bacon, and William Stanley (Sixth Earl of Derby)— were highly educated and highly born. This argument is not without plausibility. To assess its plausibility, however, we would also need to ask whether formal education and social position are the only ways to acquire the relevant knowledge. Is it beyond the realm of plausibility that a literary genius and man of the world could have parlayed a basic education (which would have included Greek and Roman mythology) into a much wider familiarity with history and current events?

We can leave that question to the literary historians. But two dimensions of the authorship question suggest that the doubters are engaged in pseudohistory. The first is the number of other candidates proposed as the real authors. On many issues in history, to be sure, there can be rival hypotheses. In this case, however, when the history of the period is so well known and the scholarship so extensive, we would expect a single candidate to have emerged. The reason that that hasn't happened is at least partly because each hypothesis about a candidate-author raises its own unique questions of plausibility. Francis Bacon, for example, was a philosopher highly informed about the New Science being taught in Europe's universities, yet there is no evidence of such knowledge in the plays. The second reason is that each rival hypothesis about authorship depends on an additional hypothesis—in effect, a conspiracy theory—about why the true author was not known.

ALTERNATIVE HISTORY While denialist theories reject our best historical explanations, some theories construct entirely new, alternative accounts in history. Have you ever heard that medieval art depicts flying saucers? Or that the Great Pyramid of Giza was designed by alien astronauts? If so, you or someone you know has probably been watching the History Channel's series *Ancient Aliens*, or a similar program. Reinterpreting world history as evidence of visitors from space is one of the most persistent examples of alternative history. Denialism, even when it is not supported by the evidence, at least invokes known causal factors. Alternative history, by contrast, invents causes beyond the range known to history (or science, for that matter).

The claim that extraterrestrial visitors came to Earth and shaped human civilization can be traced back to early science fiction, but the popularization of this claim as pseudohistorical scholarship is generally attributed to Erich von Däniken's book *Chariots of the Gods?* According to the ancient astronaut hypothesis, extraterrestrial visitors provide the best explanation of various historical facts, including art and artifacts.

In the case of art, consider two examples:

Von Däniken and others have claimed that some paintings and statues have enlarged rounded heads that resemble space helmets used by human astronauts today; so these must be representations of ancient astronauts.

Elongated heads in other works of art should also be regarded as evidence: Don't they resemble extraterrestrials?

These claims violate the standard of informativeness at the most fundamental level, since they involve circular reasoning. How do we know what aliens would actually look like, or what sort of equipment like helmets they would have, without assuming prior knowledge of them?

As for artifacts, most alien-astronaut theorists seem to regard ancient constructions such as the pyramids of Egypt as their strongest evidence. The Great Pyramid of Giza, completed around 2450 BCE, is 481 feet high, built of some two million stone blocks each weighing 2.5 tons. The theory claims that structures such as these would have been beyond ancient human capabilities; only the superior technology of our alien benefactors can explain their existence. But the theory clearly violates several of our standards:

- *Simplicity*: The theory is not the only hypothesis that could explain the building of the pyramid. Scholars and engineers have shown how the Egyptians could have used ramps to place the stones. With rollers under the blocks, and/or water to decrease friction, humans could have moved the blocks into place. This hypothesis is much simpler than the hypothesis of alien astronauts.
- *Confirmation*: The theory implies that the Egyptians had no knowledge of how to build, but this implication is not true. Scholars have found written documents detailing plans for construction. In 2017, for example, a group of Egyptian and French scholars discovered a first-hand account of the Great Pyramid's construction written by Merer, an Egyptian official of the day.
- *Completeness*: The theory fails to account for many significant points. Why did the alien visitors want the pyramids built in the first place? How did they learn to speak Egyptian? And the pyramids, while impressive, display very little in the way of technological sophistication. How do we explain the fact that a species intelligent and technologically advanced enough to journey through space did not exhibit that sophistication in their architecture?

Finally, there is a larger issue of simplicity: The hypothesis of alien astronauts requires a huge number of assumptions: the existence of intelligent beings elsewhere in the universe; a history of technological development by the aliens, including means of space travel more advanced than anything we know of; and some means of knowing about Earth and humans. There is no evidence whatever to support any of these assumptions.

15.4B Pseudoscience

Pseudoscience trades on the respectability of genuine science, as pseudohistory does with genuine history. Pseudoscientific theories mimic the scientific method, presenting a veneer of legitimacy by adopting scientific language and pretending to engage in scientific research and experimentation. But they violate the standards of explanation and the scientific method. Such theories avoid truly open-ended inquiry by cherry-picking data, misrepresenting evidence, appealing to unqualified authorities, even falsifying results.

The demarcation between science and pseudoscience has a vast literature within the philosophy of science. It is difficult to draw a sharp line between them; as with history, there are borderline cases. There are valid scientific disagreements and genuinely competing theories. But there are also many clear examples of pseudoscience. We will consider two that fall into categories parallel to those in pseudohistory: opposition to vaccines, an example of denialism; and the alternative science represented by the flat-Earth theory.

VACCINES Vaccinations have saved millions of lives worldwide and have even eradicated a few diseases. Ask your parents or grandparents if you can see their "vaccination scars." They'll probably know what you mean. Up until 1971, receiving the smallpox vaccine was a rite of passage for most American schoolchildren. By contrast, unless you served in the military or lived abroad, you've probably never had the vaccine. Smallpox was a virulent disease, claiming an estimated 500 million lives. As a result of worldwide immunization efforts, the last confirmed case was in 1977.

Despite the success of vaccines against many diseases, a significant number of parents are refusing medical vaccinations for their children. Do they want their children to get sick? Of course not, quite the opposite. They have been convinced by the anti-vaccination movement that immunization endangers their children. The anti-vaccination, or anti-vac, movement is based on pseudoscientific claims that vaccines are either unsafe or ineffective.

The most common claim about safety is that vaccines, in particular the MMR vaccine (for measles, mumps, and rubella), cause autism. The claim can be traced to a 1998 article published by Dr. Andrew Wakefield in the medical journal *Lancet*. Other researchers were unable to reproduce his results. Eventually, it was discovered that some of his research was fraudulent and that he had a financial conflict of interest. *Lancet* retracted the findings and the article was discredited within the scientific community. But Wakefield's findings continued to be quoted, making many parents afraid.

The incidence of autism has increased since 2000. While the increase may be largely due to changes in diagnostic criteria, it would of course be valuable to understand its causes. But the MMR hypothesis has no strength as an explanation and is inconsistent with well-designed scientific studies. For example, anti-vaxxers point out that an overwhelming majority of children diagnosed with autism had received the MMR vaccine. That's true, but so had the overwhelming majority of children *not* diagnosed with autism. Since most children in the United States are vaccinated, this is meaningless. It's like saying, "The overwhelming majority of children diagnosed with autism like eating cookies, therefore cookie-eating must cause autism." Repeated controlled scientific studies have failed to uncover any connection, causal or otherwise, between the MMR vaccine and autism.

Opponents of vaccines have also claimed that vaccines are ineffective. As evidence, they have cited a 2014 report from the Council on Foreign Relations that cases of infectious disease had increased in countries requiring childhood immunization—the European Union, the United States, Canada, Australia, and Japan. But that is most likely the result of the anti-vaccine movement itself, which has helped lower the number of children getting vaccinated. In any case, vaccine opponents have also claimed that these countries had the greatest number of deaths from infectious disease. This claim is simply false. Of the countries listed, only the United States made the top ten. Most of those deaths were due to HIV/AIDS, an outbreak of the West Nile virus, and a diarrheal infection, caused by *Clostridium* bacteria. What these diseases had in common is that there was no preventative vaccine available. The 2014 statistics for mumps, measles, and rubella are the relevant ones, and there were no deaths from these diseases. Zero. To be sure, the most common causes of infectious disease death in the United States were deaths from pneumonia and flu, both with vaccines available. Vaccines don't always

APPLY   Be Careful...

Imagine you are a physician examining a patient who claims to be blind. She has neurological damage; she can still see colors and textures but can't recognize objects, faces, or shapes. At first, the examination goes as expected. Your patient is unable to read an eye chart or recognize the number of fingers you're holding up. You hold up a pencil and ask her to identify the object; she says she can't. But this time she asks to hold the object and reaches unerringly for the pencil. Astounded, you devise another test. You show her a mail slot. "Is it vertically or horizontally aligned?" She says she can't see it, but you give her an envelope and she turns it vertically and easily slides it into the vertically aligned slot.

Coincidence? A lucky guess? The odds seem heavily against it. The most plausible explanation, it might seem, is that she's not really blind, that she's faking it for some reason, perhaps scamming for attention, or disability benefits. On the other hand, she seems sincere in saying she's blind. Is her ability a form of extrasensory perception? Which is more plausible: a blind woman who can perform these tasks through ESP or someone trying to game the system? The answer is that neither pseudoscience nor fraud is the explanation.

This case—a real one, described by Dr. V.S. Ramachandran, one of the world's leading neurologists—is an example of the phenomenon called blindsight. It is now known that neural signals from the eyes are dispersed to various areas in the brain. The main area is the visual cortex, which gives rise to conscious visual experience. But when that area is damaged, other areas may continue to allow some visual functioning—even if patients are not aware of it.

Consistency and simplicity are the best criteria to judge the plausibility of hypotheses. But blindsight is an example of why we should not jump to conclusions in our plausibility judgments. New evidence can justify an explanation that sounds far-fetched at first glance—and the evidence should be the ultimate guide.

work, but most of these deaths were attributed to deaths among the elderly, people with chronic diseases, and those who didn't get vaccinated.

FLAT EARTH Finally, we will consider the flat-Earth theory, a good example of alternative science. We have known since ancient times that the Earth is a sphere. Ancient Greek thinkers such as Aristotle provided early reasons for this view; the Greek astronomer Eratosthenes (276–194 BC) made a nearly accurate calculation of the Earth's circumference by observing the shadows cast by a pole at different latitudes. The view has been confirmed and elaborated in ever-greater detail by scientists for the last 500 years; and space travel over the last 50 years has produced countless photos of our spherical planet. One might have expected that the flat-Earth theory would have long since disappeared into the mists of ancient myth. Yet there has been a resurgence of interest in the theory—and, apparently, in the number of adherents—on internet sites, especially YouTube. The most common of the recent versions claim that the Earth is shaped like a flat pancake, with the Arctic in the middle, the continents arrayed around it, and Antarctica at the perimeter, typically portrayed as having a high wall of ice to prevent anyone from going beyond.

The theory is an extreme case of pseudoscience. As an extreme case, it provides an especially clear example of how the standards of explanation are violated.

Most adherents seem drawn primarily by the evidence of their senses. If the Earth is a sphere, why does the ground around me look flat? Why don't I see any curvature in the horizon? Why does the road ahead of me seem flat, even on a long drive, if I'm moving along a curve? The answer to these and related questions is simply that the Earth is very large. The diameter of Earth is nearly 8,000 miles. Standing on the ground we can see perhaps 3 miles; even on a mountaintop you would be lucky to see 100 miles. From the heights we easily attain, we are simply not in a position to detect curvature. In addition, the surface of the Earth is not perfectly smooth. Variations in the local geography, even small hills and dips, loom larger—visually and when we travel—than the global curvature.

The flat-Earth hypothesis, in other words, fails the standards of adequacy. The link between the hypothesis and the facts we observe is logically very weak; it fails to provide the best explanation of the facts, much less the only one. But the theory also fails the standards of consistency and simplicity—in spectacular ways. To take consistency first, consider what you would have to explain away to believe in the theory:

- Centuries of accumulated, well-tested theories in astronomy, physics, geology, and other fields, including theories of gravitation, the orbits of the planets, and plate tectonics, to mention a few—based on research by thousands of scientists.
- Technology for GPS navigation, based on satellites orbiting the Earth; navigation systems for international flights; and rockets taking astronauts to the International Space Station and beyond.

As for simplicity, the flat-Earth hypothesis requires the assumption of a vast—and vastly implausible—conspiracy promoting the idea that the Earth is spherical. The conspiracy would have to include many if not all of the scientists in the fields above; space agencies such as NASA and the astronauts who flew missions in space; Photoshop experts who falsified photos of the Earth from space; and conspiratorial agreements among governments that can't agree on anything else—the list goes on. The levels of conspiracy necessary to maintain such a vast international scheme would necessarily involve not only world leaders and scientists but also cartographers, sailors, pilots, and all the millions of actors, secretaries, and office clerks needed to keep it going. These problems of consistency and simplicity put the flat-Earth hypothesis on the far edge of pseudoscience, on the borderline with fantasy fiction.

The problems we have pointed out highlight a larger issue about pseudo-explanations. The standards we presented in this chapter are fundamental logical standards. As such, you can and should apply them in your thinking as an individual. But history and science, like many other fields of research, also have a social, cooperative dimension. Because of the large body of well-tested knowledge they have produced, research in these fields now involves specialization and a division of labor among researchers. The consequence is the need for social practices such as peer review to ensure the accuracy of new work, its consistency with other work, and its logical strength. To be sure, these practices sometimes reject innovators pursuing new ideas. But the innovations that advanced our knowledge have survived such resistance because the innovators had a deep understanding of what others before them had discovered. The thinkers who have made those advances, from Isaac Newton to our own day, have taken responsibility for explaining how their new theories can account for the evidence supporting earlier theories. For those of us who do *not* have expert knowledge, the moral is to be open to new ideas wherever we find them, but not to embrace them uncritically or on superficial grounds of plausibility, without doing our homework in the relevant field.

There is a larger issue still, with which we want to conclude this chapter and the book as a whole. Objectivity has been one of our major themes throughout all the chapters. Objectivity means that the world is what it is, that facts are facts, but that discovering and verifying those facts requires specific methods—methods of explanation, of inductive reasoning in general, of deduction, and conceptual analysis. But the methods are only as good as the spirit in which they are used. Clever people can make logical arguments to rationalize preconceived conclusions. We hope that, in addition to helping you master the methods of inquiry and argument, we have also conveyed the overarching value of objectivity.

EXERCISE 15.4

| Integrative Exercise | What questions would you ask someone who gave the following explanations? Give three questions in each case. |

*1. If you visit Boston, be sure to notice the statues of animals scattered throughout the city. These statues were built by alien astronauts who traveled north from Peru. Notice that both the Peruvian sand formations and the New England statues feature birds, turtles, and rabbits.

2. "The most extreme delusion I've ever heard of is one described by Oliver Sacks, about a man who kept falling out of bed at night. Each time he crashed to the floor, the ward staff would hoist him back up, only to hear a resounding thud a few moments later. After this happened several times, Dr. Sacks asked the man why he kept toppling out of bed. He looked frightened. 'Doctor,' he said, 'these medical students have been putting a cadaver's arm in my bed and I've been trying to get rid of it all night!'" [V.S. Ramachandran and Sandra Blakeslee, *Phantoms in the Brain*]

3. President Trump's border wall is merely part of a centuries old worldwide conspiracy to conceal the fact that the Earth is flat. Flat-Earth scientists have proved that there is a wall of ice around Antarctica that conceals the edge of the Earth. The Great Wall of China, the Berlin Wall, the Wall of Jericho, Hadrian's Wall, and now the border wall are meant to desensitize us to walls so that we won't pay any attention to the Antarctica wall and ask what it hides.

*4. Cats may look like ordinary, harmless companion animals but don't be fooled. They are cunning, invasive extraterrestrials. Predators by nature, they have inveigled their way into an ever-increasing number of American homes. First, they weaken our critical reasoning powers by feigning affection and looking adorable. But soon, their human victims are giving up their chairs and providing treats on demand. Once a cat has sufficiently weakened your will, it will enter your body and assume your place in society. There is evidence that they have already obtained positions of power; look for leaders who seem exceptionally well-groomed. Don't ignore the scientific evidence that proves our theory. If you study the medical literature, you'll see human biology has already been corrupted. Both cats and humans get AIDS, leukemia, diabetes, and Covid-19. We fear that it may already be too late to stop this feline infestation. Genetic testing has revealed that humans already share 90% of their DNA with cats!

5. "Dowsing is commonly used to locate underground water sources, buried metals or ores, gemstones, oil, gravesites, petroleum deposits, . . ., without the use of . . . electronic equipment. There is no accepted scientific rationale behind dowsing, and there is no measurable scientific evidence that it is effective. There is a reason for this. No scientific apparatus today is capable of measuring the energy fields associated with dowsing." [paranormalactivity research.com]

6. From time to time, the exsanguinated bodies of goats and other livestock are found along the southern U.S. border. These deaths are the work of the Chupacabra. The Chupacabra is an animal about the size of a small bear that looks like a cross between a coyote and a large lizard. While many people have reported Chupacabra sightings, both U.S. and Mexican wildlife officials continue to pretend it is nothing more than an urban legend. In reality, data exist that prove that the Chupacabra is real. This proof includes both personal accounts from witnesses and experimentation. For example, in 2019, the South Texas Chupacabra Foundation placed freshly killed goats, chickens, and pigs along a known Chupacabra migration trail. The next day, all of the animal remains had been drained of blood.

*7. The woman was found dead on the parlor floor with a badly burned torso. Her extremities were untouched by the fire. The room showed no signs of a fire, nor was there any evidence that the body had been moved from a previous location. There were no matches or other incendiary devices found nearby. Friends reported that she had been enraged at a letter when they left her alone that evening. The coroner concluded that it was a case of spontaneous human combustion.

CHAPTER REVIEW

Summary

- The goal of an explanation is to show why something is true, to state the cause or reason for the *explanandum*, or to fit it into a wider context that makes it intelligible.
  - The logical relation between hypothesis and *explanandum* is the same as that between premises and conclusion.
  - We can use the same diagramming techniques to analyze explanations.
- To evaluate a proposed explanation, we consider two basic issues: its adequacy and the truth of the hypothesis. An adequate explanation must be
  - Logically strong (the *explanandum* follows from the hypothesis),
  - Complete (the hypothesis explains all significant aspects of the *explanandum*), and
  - Informative (the hypothesis gives a fundamental cause or reason for the *explanandum*).

- To ascertain the truth of a hypothesis, we should consider alternative hypotheses that would also provide adequate explanations.
  - We decide among rival hypotheses by deriving further consequences from them and then checking to see whether those consequences are true.
  - To decide which hypotheses to consider and to decide whether to save a hypothesis in the face of a negative test by rejecting an auxiliary assumption, we rely on the standards of consistency and simplicity.
- Pseudo-explanations are faulty explanations that purport to follow the standards of legitimate explanations, either by rejecting established conclusions (denialism) or inventing new ones (alternative history or pseudoscience).

Key Terms

explanandum (p. 627)
hypothesis (p. 628)

pseudo-explanation (p. 650)

Putting It All Together

I.   Integrative Exercise   Answer each of the following multiple-choice questions.

*1. Which of the following statements best explains the difference between arguments and explanations?
   a. In an explanation, we reason forward from the premises to the conclusion; in an argument, we reason backward from a fact to the cause or reason for that fact.
   b. The primary goal of an explanation is to show that some proposition is true, while the primary goal of an argument is to show why it is true.

   c. The primary goal of an argument is to show that some proposition is true, while the primary goal of an explanation is to show why it is true.
   d. There is no difference between arguments and explanations.
2. In any explanation, the proposition we seek to explain is called the
   a. *explanandum*
   b. hypothesis

c. antecedent

d. *explanans*

3. A good explanation must
   a. be adequate
   b. be interesting
   c. have a true hypothesis
   d. both a and c

✳4. A theory that is falsely presented as based on the scientific method is called
   a. pseudoscience
   b. nonscience
   c. pseudohistory
   d. antiscience

5. An adequate hypothesis should be
   a. strong, valid, and probable
   b. informative, true, and possible
   c. strong, complete, and informative
   d. none of the above

6. Holocaust denialism is an example of
   a. illicit conversion
   b. pseudohistory
   c. invalidity
   d. pseudoscience

✳7. We can test hypotheses by
   a. observation
   b. testing for other consequences that should follow from the same hypothesis
   c. considering rival hypotheses
   d. all of the above

8. In order to determine the plausibility of a hypothesis, we should consider its
   a. sistency and simplicity
   b. simplicity and sensitivity to diversity

c. existential import and validity

d. consistency and inclusivity

9. An explanation offers a _____ that makes the *explanandum* intelligible.
   a. theory
   b. hypothesis
   c. conclusion
   d. none of the above

✳10. Each of the following statements is true except for
   a. The *explanandum* should follow from the hypothesis.
   b. A good explanation has both breadth and depth.
   c. A true hypothesis should make its *explanandum* probable.
   d. A single hypothesis can explain no more than one *explanandum*.

11. Pseudoscience
   a. may deny an established scientific theory by claiming it is the result of a conspiracy
   b. may claim that scientific experimentation and observation support their views
   c. sometimes present their theories as "alternative science"
   d. all of the above

12. Pseudoscience and pseudohistory
   a. offer legitimate ways of understanding the world
   b. have been virtually eliminated by the internet
   c. have experienced a resurgence in recent years
   d. none of the above

II. **Integrative Exercise** A. Identify the *explanandum* and the hypothesis in each of the following explanatory passages, and diagram the explanation.

✳1. Many people today decry the use of the colloquial spelling "Xmas," assuming that it's an attempt by atheists to "take the Christ out of Christmas." But, according to author David Feldman, "Xmas" is as Christian as Christian can be. He writes, "The X in Xmas is actually the descendant of the Greek equivalent of Ch, as in 'Christos,' which means 'Christ.'

The letter X has stood for Christ . . . since at least A.D. 1100. . . ." [David Feldman, *Why Do Clocks Run Clockwise? and Other Imponderables*]

2. Sick and injured cats may purr in order to heal themselves. Purring typically has a frequency between 25 and 150 hertz, exactly the frequency at which feline bones and muscles are most able to grow and repair themselves.

3. Soap prevents disease even though it doesn't kill germs. Soap combined with water becomes slippery, pulling dirt and germs into the rinse water.

∗4. "Here we can glimpse the mechanism of Mendelian inheritance: A zygote [fertilized egg] obtains exactly half its genes from its male parent because it receives exactly half its chromosomes from the male parent and the chromosomes bear the genes." [Philip Kitcher, *Abusing Science: The Case Against Creationism*]

5. Canning preserves food for long-term storage, using either of two methods. Highly acidic foods may be preserved at home using the water bath method. The food is placed in clean jars, then boiled for the specified time. The boiling process sterilizes the food and seals the jar, thus preventing new bacteria from attacking the sterilized food.

6. "Many free-swimming animals, mammals, birds, amphibians and fishes, are silvery white below in order to be invisible to enemies swimming in the depths. Seen from below, the shining white belly blends perfectly with the reflecting surface film of the water." [Konrad Z. Lorenz, "The Taming of the Shrew," in *King Solomon's Ring*]

∗7. "Through this flat and marshy country [the southern coast of the Baltic Sea], four historic rivers make their way to the sea: the Neva, the Dvina, the Vistula, and the Oder, all pouring freshwater into the sea, so that the prevailing current is out of the Baltic. For this reason, it is difficult for saltwater to enter the Baltic, and there are no tides at Riga, Stockholm, or the mouth of the Neva." [Robert K. Massie, *Peter the Great*]

8. "It is of interest that some eastern American azaleas are more closely allied to some east-ern Chinese azaleas than they are to other eastern American azaleas. . . .

"The fact that counterpart species [similar species of plants in widely separated areas of the world] exist has been explained . . . by the existence of a flora (called 'Tertiary flora') which once encircled the Northern Hemisphere before the great cycle of glaciation. . . . In regions like the United States and China, where the mountain ranges run north and south, the vegetation simply retreated south also, only to recolonize much of its former habitat when the ice withdrew." [William H. Frederick, Jr., *100 Great Garden Plants*]

9. "Before printing, there had been no elaborate system of censorship and control over scribes. There did not have to be. The scribes were scattered, working on single manuscripts in monasteries. Moreover, single manuscripts rarely caused a general scandal or major controversy. There was little motive for central control, and control would have been impractical." [Ithiel de Sola Pool, *Technologies of Freedom*]

∗10. "Mexico City . . . is built on a mixture of sand and water. Such soils settle when heavy buildings are erected, squeezing the water out of the sand. The National Theater in the center of Mexico City, originally built at grade level with a heavy cladding of stone, in a few years sank as much as ten feet. Downward stairs had to be built to its entrance. People were amazed when later on the theater began to rise again, requiring the construction of an upward staircase. This strange phenomenon can be explained by the large number of high-rise buildings which had been erected nearby. The water squeezed out from under them by their weight pushed the theater up." [Mario Salvadori, *Why Buildings Stand Up*]

III. [Integrative Exercise] Find an explanation for each of the following facts. Make sure your explanation is adequate, and indicate how you would tell whether the hypothesis is true.

✳1. The subject I had the most trouble with in school was_____. [fill in the blank]

2. When we spend a lot of time looking forward to something, and expect to enjoy it, we're often disappointed.

3. In midterm elections (those held midway through a president's term), the president's party usually loses seats in Congress.

✳4. The number of people working at home instead of at an office or a factory has been rising, both in absolute terms and as a percentage of the workforce. Some are self-employed, running their own businesses; others are employees of companies, doing such work as sewing garments or word processing.

✳**IV.** [Integrative Exercise] The headlines below are from a tabloid newspaper. Relying mainly on the standard of consistency, rank them in order of initial plausibility. Does the claim conflict with established principles and theories? If so, to what extent? How radical a change would we have to make in established principles and theories to accept each story as true?

1. Baby Born on Roller Coaster

2. Snake Tattoo Crawls Up Man's Arm and Chokes Him

3. Pregnancy Makes Women Able to Predict Future

4. Amazing Vitamin Keeps Skin Wrinkle-Free

5. Friendly Bigfoot Saves Dying Girl

6. Woman Adopts Own Child But Doesn't Know It

7. Woman Describes How . . . Sparks from UFO Nearly Blinded Me

8. Bat Attacks Couple Watching *Dracula* on TV

9. Britain's Fattest Woman Ate Fridge and Died

10. Gadget Ends Back Pain Forever

V. [Integrative Exercise] You believe you have discovered a conspiracy. Scientists and political leaders have conspired to convince the public that the moon orbits the Earth. In fact, the opposite is true. You want to reach out to others in the know. Write content for a web page explaining the conspiracy and the "alternative science" that supports your theory.

Answers to
Selected Exercises

CHAPTER 1

Exercise 1.1

I.

1. Genus: animal
   Species: man
   Other examples of species: cat, dog, mouse, etc.

4. Genus: sport
   Species: baseball
   Other species: hockey, football, etc.

7. Genus: countries
   Species: European
   Other species: Asian, African, etc.

10. Genus: tortilla dishes
    Species: burrito
    Other species: taco, enchilada, etc.

13. Genus: states of material substance
    Species: solid
    Other species: liquid, gas

16. Genus: burial place
    Species: mausoleum
    Other species: grave, catacomb, etc.

19. Genus: rectangular
    Species: square
    Other species: oblong

II.

1. Lady Gaga, singer, performer

4. Steel, alloy, metal, mineral

7. iPhone, mobile telephone, telephone, communication device

10. Brother, sibling, family member, kin

13. Cardigan, sweater, top, garment

Exercise 1.2

1. Not mutually exclusive (hardbacks, first editions); not jointly exhaustive (e-books); not a consistent principle.

4. Not mutually exclusive (foreign, pornographic) or jointly exhaustive (horror, drama); not a consistent principle.

7. Not mutually exclusive (individual, aquatic); no consistent principle.

10. Not mutually exclusive (leather dress shoes) or jointly exhaustive (non-leather casual shoes); no consistent principle.

13. Not mutually exclusive (clerical jobs in a service industry); no consistent principle.

Exercise 1.3

I.

1. First genus: aircraft
   Higher-level genus: vehicle

4. First genus: government agency
   Higher-level genus: institutions

II.

1.

III.

1.

4.

7.

10.

IV.

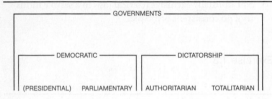

Exercise 1.5A

1. Genus: precipitation
   Differentia: consisting of flakes or clumps of ice crystals

4. Genus: opportunity
   Differentia: to buy something at an unusually low price

7. Genus: none
   Differentia: completing a run or pass across the other team's goal line

10. Genus: feeling
    Differentia: of wrongful detachment from certain people or things

Exercise 1.5B

1. No genus. Too narrow: light snow in a strong wind. Nonessential

4. Too broad: notebook

7. Too broad: radio

10. Too narrow: antidotes can counteract other toxins

13. Too narrow: calculators can be used for purposes other than those for which slide rules were used. Too broad: a computer is also an electronic instrument that could replace a slide rule. Nonessential: the definition doesn't say what calculators are for.

Exercise 1.5C

I.

1. Too narrow
   Genus: jewel
   Differentia: worn on a pendant around the neck

4. Metaphor, too broad (other rodents with fur)
   Genus: rat
   Differentia: wearing a fur coat

7. Vague, too broad
   Genus: trait of a person
   Differentia: playing by the rules

10. Negative. Too broad: someone who is medicated is not sober.
    Genus: person
    Differentia: not sober

13. Negative. No genus. Could also be too broad and too narrow.
    Genus: none
    Differentia: not getting what you want

16. Nonessential, too narrow
    Genus: exercise
    Differentia: obscuring the weakness in one's own position by browbeating one's opponent

19. Too broad: cape, sweater
    Genus: outer garment
    Differentia: designed to protect the wearer from cold, wind, and rain

II.

1. Negative

4. Vague, metaphorical

7. Vague

10. No genus, negative

Exercise 1.6

I.

1. Published on unbound paper / information on current events of interest to the general public

II.

FURNITURE: movable man-made objects designed to support and/or store other objects.

TABLE: an article of furniture designed with the primary purpose of supporting other objects on a flat and rigid top surface.

BED: an article of furniture with a horizontal surface designed to support a sleeper.

CHAIR: an article of furniture designed to support a sitting or reclining person on a horizontal surface, with a vertical surface to support the back.

DESK: a table designed for work by a seated person, with a flat surface to support working materials and drawers or pigeonholes to store them.

Exercise 1.7A

1. Same

4. Different

7. Same

10. Same

13. Different

Exercise 1.7B

I.

1. The teacher's announcement was startling.

4. The budget that the president submitted to Congress has no chance of being passed.

7. The article oversimplified or changed the information about the controversy.

10. Roger was such a good salesman; he was so persuasive that he could convince people to do things against their best interests.

II.

1. Positive—public servant, negative—bureaucrat

4. Positive—eating to excess, negative—pigging out

7. Positive—delirious with joy, negative—giddy

10. Positive—cognitively challenged, negative—a few bricks shy of a full load

Exercise 1.8A

I.

1. Same

4. Same

II.

1. i. She arrived in time.
   ii. She arrived out of breath.

4. i. Beavers build dams.
   ii. Beavers are a type of rodent.
   iii. The dams can flood a whole valley.

III.

1. Unasserted

4. Asserted

Exercise 1.8B

1. Connective: "but"
   (a) His mind was racing.
   (a) His body was in the lead.

4. Connective: "after"
   (a) The ice storm was over.
   (a) The trees glittered in the sun.

7. Connective: "if"
   (u) Sparky hears the car in the driveway.
   (u) He runs to the back door.

10. Connectives: "if," "and"
    (u) Vladimir Putin wants to generate domestic support in Russia.
    (u) He needs to expand control over neighboring countries.
    (u) He needs to portray the United States as an enemy.

Exercise 1.8C

1. who live in glass houses—restrictive

4. that are waged in self-defense—restrictive

7. who was last seen wearing a Cleveland Indians baseball cap—restrictive

10. which is really hard—nonrestrictive

Exercise 1.8D

1. (u) Animals can talk.
   (a) The little girl thinks that animals can talk.

4. (u) Two plus two equals four.
   (a) He is convinced that two plus two equals four.

7. (u) Zack was planning a surprise birthday party for Samantha.
   (a) Samantha suspected that Zack was planning a surprise birthday party for her.

10. (a) If you buy two pairs of jeans, the third pair is free.
    (a) If your purchase is over $50, you get 30% off.
    (u) You buy two pairs of jeans.

(u) The third pair of jeans is free.
(u) Your purchase is over $50.
(u) You get 30% off.
(a) If you buy two pairs of jeans, the third pair is free; and if your purchase is over $50, you get 30% off.

13. (a) David was driving well above the speed limit.
(a) David knew better.
(a) David was driving well above the speed limit and he knew better.

16. (a) Professional baseball players make a lot of money.
(u) The season is too long.
(a) Professional baseball players should not complain that the season is too long.
(a) Professional baseball players make a lot of money and they should not complain that the season is too long.

19. (a) The city planner called the zone developer.
(a) The city planner wanted to find out whether the area had been marked.
(a) The city planner wanted to find out whether the architect had been chosen.
(a) The city planner wanted to find out whether the area had been marked and the architect had been chosen.
(u) The area had been marked.
(u) The architect had been chosen.
(a) The city planner called the zone developer because she wanted to find out whether the area had been marked and the architect had been chosen.

22. (a) Man is a living organism.
(a) Man is mortal.
(a) Man is mortal because he is a living organism.
(a) Man is rational.
(a) Man is aware of his mortality.
(a) Man is aware of his mortality because he is rational.
(a) Because he is a living organism, man is mortal; [and] because he is rational, he is aware of his mortality.

25. (a) We found our seats at the racetrack.
(a) We could hear the announcer.
(a) When we found our seats at the racetrack we could hear the announcer.
(a) The announcer was reporting that Pardon My Dust was already ahead of Try Me.
(a) The announcer thought Try Me still had a chance at winning the handicap.
(a) Pardon My Dust was already ahead of Try Me.
(u) Try Me still had a chance at winning the handicap.
(a) When we found our seats at the racetrack, we could hear the announcer saying that Pardon My Dust was already ahead of Try Me, but he thought Try Me still had a chance at winning the handicap.

Putting It All Together

I.

1. Sauntered, strode, etc.

4. Country, domain (notice the different assumptions behind these terms); quadruped, animal

7. Institution

10. Countless, a huge number, 57, etc.

II.

1. Newspaper, book, pamphlet, etc.

4. Diseases, homicide, suicide, casualties in war, . . .

III.

1.

```
┌──────── HUMAN BEINGS ────────┐
│                              │
│                              │
BORROWERS                   LENDERS
```

4.

7.

IV.

1. Too narrow; nonessential
   An army is the branch of a country's military whose primary function is to fight on land.

4. Circular
   A genus is the broader class to which the referents of a given concept belong.

7. Nonessential, too broad if taken literally (some tasks will be easy for anyone)
   A craftsman is a person who is skilled at creating a specific type of product. (One might argue that craftsmanship should not be limited to specific products,

but should apply to any skill or talent; I consider that a metaphorical extension, but the point is certainly debatable.)

10. Too broad (all the social sciences would be included), too narrow (animal studies would be excluded) Psychology is the science that studies the functioning of the mind. (Theorists of many different schools could accept this definition by interpreting "functioning" and "mind" in different ways, but the definition is still somewhat tendentious. I don't know of a perfectly neutral one.)

13. Too narrow (a person can reform) To reform is to improve a person or organization by changing the principles on which the person or organization acts. (The term "principles" must be taken broadly here to include character, personality, and beliefs in the case of persons; and laws, policies, and structure in the case of organizations.)

V.

1. Too narrow: history is concerned with past ideas, works of art, and other things besides events; and with the explaining as well as discovering and describing.

4. A good definition of crimes in the legal sense, as opposed to metaphorical extensions of the term, such as "crimes against nature (or nature's law)," "crimes against humanity"

7. Metaphorical

10. Metaphorical

13. Good definition

16. Too narrow: payroll taxes (e.g., Social Security) are intended for later benefits to the taxpayer. In addition, "payment" would be a better genus than "contribution," which suggests something voluntary.

19. Obscure. Possibly too broad: some mechanical systems might fit this description.

VI.

1. (b) is clearly a metaphorical extension, deriving from "headshrinker."

4. (b) and (c) seem to involve the same concept: an external force that threatens a thing's internal structure or functioning. [If force is regarded as something inherently physical, then (b) would be a metaphorical extension of (c).] In (a) "stress" is a synonym for "emphasize," at best a metaphorical extension of the concept.

VII.

1. BACHELOR: an unmarried adult human male.

4. COMPUTER: a device for processing information according to an alterable set of instructions.

7. NOVICE: a person who is relatively unskilled in a given activity.

10. FAMILY: a group of people related by birth or marriage.

VIII.

1. Both are types of recreation but reflect subdivisions of the genus by different principles of classification: games are distinguished by rules from less structured activities; sports are distinguished by their physical character from less strenuous activities.

4. All three terms indicate a person's tendency—more or less deliberate and more or less habitual—to make his overt actions reflect his inner beliefs and feelings. "Sincere" is normally used for nonverbal actions and displays of feeling, "honest" for verbal ones, with frankness perhaps best seen as a species of honesty distinguished by the bluntness of the expression or the unpleasantness of what is expressed.

7. Two possibilities: (1) To adorn is to make a person more visually pleasing, to decorate is to make a nonhuman object more pleasing, with "garnish" either a synonym or a subcategory restricted to food. (2) To adorn is to add to the visual attraction of something that is already pleasing in itself; to decorate is to make pleasing something that in itself is plain or unattractive, with "garnish" as in (1).

10. Three different types of personal written communication, distinguished by length and format.

IX.

1. Joanne met Bob for lunch.

4. It is pouring.

7. The mail will not be delivered on Wednesday because it is a holiday.

10. I don't believe that people are innately evil, as John Calvin said.

X.

1. (a) A pedestrian hit me.
   (a) A pedestrian went under my car.
   (a) A pedestrian hit me and went under my car.

4. (a) The pedestrian had no idea which direction to go.
   (a) I ran over the pedestrian.
   (a) The pedestrian had no idea which direction to go, so I ran over him.

7. (a) A car came out of nowhere.
   (a) The car was invisible.
   (a) The car struck my vehicle.
   (a) The car vanished.
   (a) An invisible car came out of nowhere, struck my vehicle, and vanished.

10. (a) The accident happened.
    (a) The right front door of a car came around the corner.
    (a) The right front door of the car did not give a signal.
    (a) The right front door of a car came around the corner and did not give a signal.
    (a) The accident happened when the right front door of a car came around the corner without giving a signal.

XI.

1. John has been practicing for the marathon, and did not find his 7-mile run yesterday very strenuous.

4. The law generally holds a manufacturer responsible for harm caused by its product, unless it warns a buyer that a product is dangerous or the buyer is harmed through his own negligence.

XII.

1. Hamlet is always thinking about what he should do.
   Hamlet cannot decide what to do.
   Hamlet never acts.

XIII.

1. (a) Man is born free.
   (a) Man is everywhere in chains.
   (a) Man is born free, and everywhere he is in chains.

4. (a) The poor in spirit are blessed.
   (a) The kingdom of heaven belongs to the poor in spirit.
   (a) The poor in spirit are blessed because the kingdom of heaven belongs to them.
   (a) They that mourn are blessed.
   (a) They that mourn shall be comforted.
   (a) They that mourn are blessed because they shall be comforted.
   (a) The meek are blessed.
   (a) The meek shall inherit the earth.
   (a) The meek are blessed because they shall inherit the earth.
   (a) The poor in spirit are blessed because the kingdom of heaven belongs to them; and they that mourn are blessed because they shall be comforted; and the meek are blessed because they shall inherit the earth.

7. (a) The bourgeoisie has fashioned the weapons that bring death to itself.
   (a) The bourgeoisie has called into existence the men who are to wield those weapons.
   (a) The men who are to wield those weapons are the modern working class.
   (a) The modern working class are the proletarians.
   (a) The men who are to wield those weapons are the proletarians.
   (a) The bourgeoisie has fashioned the weapons that bring death to itself, and has called into existence the men who are to wield those weapons, and those men are the modern working class, who are the proletarians.

10. (a) All men are created equal.
    (a) All men are endowed with certain inalienable rights.
    (a) They are so endowed by their creator.
    (a) All men have a right to life.
    (a) All men have a right to liberty.
    (a) All men have a right to the pursuit of happiness.
    (a) These truths (all previous assertions in the list so far) are self-evident.
    (a) Governments are instituted to secure these rights.
    (a) Governments derive their powers from the consent of the governed.
    (a) We hold these truths to be self-evident, that all men are created equal, that they are endowed by their creator with certain unalienable rights, that among these are life, liberty, and the pursuit of happiness, [and that] to secure these rights, governments are instituted among men, deriving their just powers from the consent of the governed.

XIV.

Y misrepresented existing fact.
Y intended that X rely on the misrepresentation.
X did rely on the misrepresentation.
X was justified in relying on it.
X was harmed by relying on it.

CHAPTER 2

Exercise 2.1

1. Not an argument. Narrative.

4. Not an argument. Description.

7. Argument. Premise: A new animal is a complex organism, with its material elements organized into complex forms, with a specific arrangement of organs, limbs, and other parts. Conclusion: We can't explain the birth of an animal, including a human being, solely in terms of the material elements of procreation.

10. Argument. Premises: 1. He curtailed freedom of speech. 2. He increased his power over the legislature. 3. He lim-

ited the role of the independent judiciary. 4. He imposed financial costs on organizations that opposed his policies. Conclusion: In 2018, Hungary's prime minister, Victor Orban, was becoming increasingly autocratic.

13. Argument. Premises: 1. Insults, slurs, and other verbal attacks can be an assault on people, causing pain and loss of dignity. 2. Insults, slurs, and other verbal attacks do not contribute anything to education. Conclusion: There have to be campus rules governing speech.

16. Argument. Premise: Treating depression with medication is the same as treating any illness with medication. Conclusion: Therefore, the patient should not stop taking the medication just because his symptoms have gone.

Exercise 2.2

I.

1.

4.

II.

1. 3 is the conclusion, dependent

4. 1 is the conclusion, dependent

7. 3 is the conclusion, dependent

10. 3 is the conclusion, independent

III.

1.

4.

7.

10.

Exercise 2.3

1. b

4. b

7. b

10. a

Exercise 2.4

1. Deductive—valid

4. Inductive

7. Inductive

10. Inductive

13. Inductive

16. Deductive—valid

19. Deductive—invalid

Exercise 2.5

1. Successful salesmen are outgoing people.

4. All copper has the same melting point.

7. (a) It is desirable for a recording to reproduce the spatial features of music.

    (b) Most mp3 recordings do not reproduce the spatial features of music.

10. Placebos isolate physical effects from psychosomatic effects.

13. All non-express trains would stop at this platform.

Exercise 2.6

1. (1) Within the past year you have been in fear of some personal attack.
   (2) You have a stick.
   (3) The stick is inscribed with a date of a year ago.
   (4) You have not had the stick more than a year.

(5) You have filled the stick with lead.
(6) You have made the stick a formidable weapon.
(7) You would not have made the stick a formidable weapon unless you feared some danger.

Putting It All Together

I.

1. (1) If you want to see deer in the woods, you have to be quiet.
(2) Deer tend to run when they hear noise.

4. (1) You shouldn't ask a friend to keep a secret from a spouse.
(2) Marriage is a more intimate relationship than friendship.
(3) One shouldn't ask someone to compromise a more intimate relationship for the sake of a less intimate one.

7. (1) Without welfare, some people would have no means of support.
(2) We must not eliminate welfare.
(3) The government has a duty to provide everyone with the essentials of life.

10. (1) People are allowed to vote when they are 18.
(2) Males have to register for the draft at 18.
(3) Eighteen-year-olds are considered old enough to have these responsibilities.
(4) Eighteen-year-olds are old enough to decide whether to drink.

(5) The drinking age should not be 21.

II.

1. Fairly strong

4. Strength depends on implicit premise that keeping a secret compromises a relationship

7. Very strong

10. Moderately strong at best. The inference from 3 to 4 assumes: (a) that deciding about alcohol does not require a higher degree of responsibility than voting or registering for the draft; and (b) that 18-year-olds are responsible enough to vote and register—note that intermediate conclusion 3 says only that they are considered to be responsible, not that they actually are.

III.

1. (1) Viruses are a form of naked gene.
(2) The best way to find out what a gene is and how it duplicates is to study the properties of viruses.

4. (1) Judging people by their skin color is repugnant.
(2) It is wrong to punish or reward people for something over which they have no control.
(*a*) People have no control over their skin color.
(3) Race is almost never relevant to a person's suitability for anything.
(4) We should treat people as individuals rather than as members of a group.
(*b*) Judging people by skin color is treating them as members of a group.

7. (1) The methane released by the oil spill disappeared from the surrounding water.
(2) Methanotrophs consumed the methane.
(3) The surrounding water was depleted of oxygen.
(4) Methanotrophs use oxygen when they consume methane.

1 + 3 + 4
↓
2

10. Not an argument

13. Not an argument

16. (1) A tree develops vertically only at the top.
(2) The points where the branches spring from the trunk stay at the same level.
(3) A wire fence nailed to the trunk does not rise as the tree grows.
(4) A wire fence nailed to the trunk stays at the same level as the fence nailed to posts.

4
↓
3
↙ ↘
1   2

19. (1) Every organism produces [at least] several offspring during its natural life span.
(2) If every organism lived out its natural life span, the number of organisms would increase geometrically.
(3) If the number of organisms increased geometrically, the earth could not support them.
(4) Not every organism can live out its natural life span.
(5) There must be a struggle for existence (among individuals within a species, among individuals of different species, and/or between an individual and the physical conditions of life).

1
↓
2 + 3
↓
4
↓
5

IV.

1. Deductive—invalid

4. Deductive—valid

7. Deductive —valid

10. Deductive—valid

13. Inductive—This argument is fairly weak since the analogy between the two animals is based on nothing more than appearance. (The conclusion also happens to be false.)

VI.

1. If robbery had been the motive, something would have been taken.

4. A judge should not have an interest that biases his judgment.

7. A worldview is a religion.

CHAPTER 3
Exercise 3.1

1. Appeal to majority

4. *Ad hominem*

7. Appeal to majority

10. Appeal to force

13. Subjectivism

16. Appeal to emotion

19. *Ad hominem*

22. *Ad hominem*

25. Appeal to majority

Exercise 3.2

1. Hasty generalization

4. Accident

7. Composition

10. Hasty generalization

13. False dichotomy

16. Composition

19. False dichotomy

22. *Post hoc*

25. False dichotomy

28. Division

Exercise 3.3

1. Appeal to ignorance

4. Appeal to ignorance

7. Equivocation

10. Begging the question

13. Begging the question

16. Appeal to ignorance

19. Equivocation

22. Appeal to ignorance

25. Begging the question

Putting It All Together

I.

1. Appeal to majority

4. False dichotomy

7. Slippery slope

10. Appeal to majority

13. Begging the question or *ad hominem*

16. Accident

19. Appeal to authority or appeal to force, depending on intent

22. Accident

25. Equivocation

28. Accident

31. Diversion, complex question

34. Division

II.

1. Either ghosts exist or Mary lied . . .

4. The popularity of entrepreneurs implies . . .

7. Capitalism squeezes out all the creative energy of workers into products sold for obscene profits, returning only a trickle to the workers . . .

10. Because logic has a lot of value and deserves your attention . . .

III.

1. *Post hoc*

4. *Post hoc*

7. *Ad hominem*

10. Equivocation, *ad hominem*

13. Diversion

16. *Post hoc*

19. Begging the question

22. Subjectivism, possibly appeal to majority

25. Appeal to emotion

IV.

1. (1) An individual is created at conception.

   (2) Everyone was once a zygote.

   (3) No one was ever an unfertilized ovum or sperm.

Begging the question

4. (1) If the task of the painter were to copy for men what they see, the critic could make only a single judgment: that the copy is right or wrong.

   (2) The critic is not limited to a single judgment.

   (3) The task of the painter is not to copy for men what they see.

Appeal to majority or appeal to authority

CHAPTER 4

Exercise 4.1A

I.

Possible answers include these: successive even numbers; any sequence of even numbers; any two numbers and their sum; any number and its double and triple; etc.

II.

1. Your answer might be: drink water only when you're thirsty and monitor your health; and/or search online for the "eight glasses a day rule."

4. Look for examples of ineffective border walls; search for critical research on the effectiveness of border walls; . . . .

7. Check research cited by food companies using high fructose corn syrup, farm organizations for corn growers; . . . .

10. Compare statistics on changes in obesity rates over time; look for challenges to standard definitions of "obesity" and "epidemic"; . . . .

Exercise 4.1B

I.

1. Fact
4. Opinion
7. Fact
10. Opinion
13. Opinion

II.

1. Reliable: b, c; not reliable: d, a
4. Reliable: a; not reliable: b, c; choice d depends on what kind of ranking is meant: professional medical data or patient reviews
7. Reliable: a, c; not reliable: b, d
10. Reliable: a; not reliable: b, c, d

Exercise 4.2

I.

1. Valid
4. Weak
7. Invalid
10. Invalid
13. Invalid
16. Strong

III.

1. Hindsight bias
4. Hindsight bias
7. Confirmation bias

Exercise 4.3

I.

1. Availability
4. Representativeness
7. Availability
10. Anchoring

II.

1. c
4. d

Exercise 4.4

I.

1. d
4. Both a and c

II.

1. Cognitive dissonance
4. Attribution bias, fundamental attribution error

Putting It All Together

I.

1. d
4. g
7. h

II.

1. Hindsight bias
4. Belief bias
7. Hindsight bias
10. Cognitive dissonance

III.

Street	Information You Have	Information Needed?
Elm	Normal accidents	Y
Oak	Bike lane	Y
Main	No bike lane	
First	Bike lane	Y
Second	Higher accidents	
Third	Higher accidents	
Ocean	No bike lane	
Maple	Normal accidents	Y

IV.

1. Princeton University graduate lists, bio of Grande in reputable publications, . . .
4. Sites on federal and state laws regarding flags, . . .

CHAPTER 5
Exercise 5.1A

I.

	Subject	Copula	Predicate	Quantity and quality; form
1	Some movie stars	are	good actors	Particular affirmative; I
4	All graduate students	are	broke people	Universal affirmative; A
7	No phones	[no . . .] are	laptops	Universal negative; E
10	No one who laughs at my teddy bear	[no . . .] is	a friend of mine	Universal negative; E
13	Some arguments in the works of great philosophers	are	fallacies	Particular affirmative; I

II.

1. Some students who skip class are people who lack motivation.

4. No dogs are animals that enjoy swimming.

III.

1. No convicted felons are deranged individuals.

4. All students who have been convicted of drug-related crimes are students eligible for financial aid.

IV.

1. Some fish are not animals with gills.

4. No businessmen are people who owe their success to a novel idea.

V.

1. All students with an average of B or higher are students on the dean's list.

4. Some classic movies are comedies.

7. All bats are animals with wings.

10. Some finalists are applicants with more than ten years' experience.

Exercise 5.1B

I.

1. All students who do not complete the appropriate course withdrawal form are students at risk of receiving an F for the course.

4. Some conference speakers are people who are eloquent.

II.

	Quantifier	Subject	Copula	Predicate	Quantity and quality; form
1	All	human beings	are	rational beings	Universal affirmative; A
4	Some	people	are not	people who achieve greatness	Paticular negative; O
7	All	men who seek fame for its own sake	are	foolish people	Universal affirmative; A
10	Some	greatest authors in literature	are not	people who attended college	Particular negative; O
13	Some	houses in the area	are not	things affected by the storm	Particular negative; O
16		John F. Kennedy	is not	a politician who succeeded in his domestic policy	Singular negative; E
	or				
	No	person who is John F. Kennedy	is	a politician who succeeded in his domestic policy	Universal negative; E
19	Some	pieces of furniture	are not	things that are on sale	Particular negative; O

Exercise 5.2

I.

1. No *S* is *P*.
4. No *S* is *P*.
7. Some *S* are not *P*.
10. Some *S* are not *P*.

II.

1. True
4. Undetermined
7. Undetermined
10. False

Exercise 5.3

1. Undetermined
4. Undetermined
7. False
10. Undetermined

Exercise 5.4

I.

1. Some cats are friendly things.

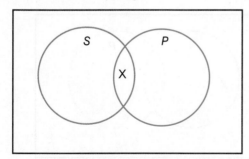

4. All police officers are people who do their best to protect us from criminals.

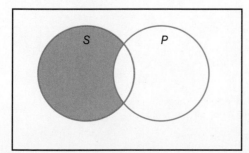

7. All clocks are things that tell time.

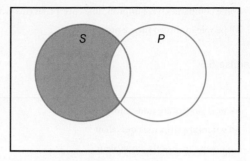

10. Some actors are people who don't know how to act.

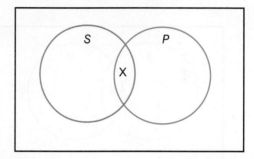

II.

1. Inconsistent
4. Consistent

III.

1. All animals are mammals.
   Some animals are not mammals. Inconsistent
4. Some books are not movies.
   No books are novels. Consistent

Exercise 5.5A

1. Some leaf-shedding plants are trees. Equivalent
4. All things that contain beta-carotene are green vegetables. Not equivalent
7. No adherents of Zoroastrianism were candidates for the legislature this year. Equivalent
10. Some violent things are not video games. Not equivalent
13. Some safe areas are not poor neighborhoods. Not equivalent

Exercise 5.5B

1. All of the athletes are uninjured people.
4. None of Alister's friends is a nonstudent.

7. Some policies are not unwise things.

10. Some companies were unprofitable enterprises this year.

13. All people in this room are nonsuspects.

Exercise 5.5C

I.

1. All non-singers are non-tenors. Equivalent

4. All voters are citizens. Equivalent

7. No poems are novels. Equivalent

II.

1. Some non-*P* are non-*S*. Not equivalent

4. Some *S* are non-*P*. Equivalent

7. Some non-*P* are non-*S*. Not equivalent

10. Some *P* are non-*S*. Equivalent

13. No *P* is *S*. Not equivalent

16. Some *P* are not *S*. Equivalent

19. No *P* is non-*S*. Not equivalent

III.

1.

Not equivalent

4.

Equivalent

7.

Equivalent

10.

Equivalent

13.

Not equivalent

16.

Equivalent

19.

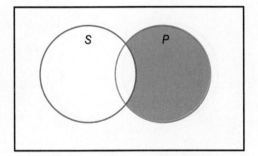

Not equivalent

Putting It All Together

I.

1. O. Some large corporations paid no income tax last year.

4. I. Some statistics that indicate economic growth can be misleading.

7. O. Some proponents of radical economic change have not carefully considered the consequences of their ideas.

10. E. My family never ate meat on Friday.

II.

1. All sonnets are poems that have fourteen lines. A. (No sonnet is a poem that has fourteen lines.)

4. Some fish are not carnivores. O. (Some fish are noncarnivores.)

7. No big girl is a person who cries. E. (All big girls are people who cry.)

10. You are a sweet thing. A. (You are not an unsweet thing.)

13. No real man is a person who eats quiche. E. (No person who eats quiche is a real man.)

16. All countries with the word "Democratic" in their official names are dictatorships. A. (All countries that are not dictatorships are countries that do not have the word "Democratic" in their official names.)

19. No law that forces a person to act against his judgment is a just law. E. (No unjust law is a law that does not force a person to act against his judgment.)

III.

1. All S are P.

4. Some S are not P.

7. All non-S are P; all non-P are S.

IV.

1. Subalternate. Not equivalent. Follows on traditional but not modern interpretation.

4. Subcontrary. Not equivalent.

7. Contrapositive. Not equivalent.

10. Subalternate of converse. Not equivalent. Follows on traditional but not modern interpretation.

V.

1.

Not equivalent

4.

Not equivalent

7.

Not equivalent

10.

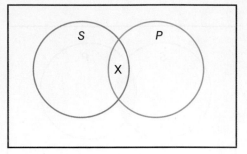

Not equivalent

VI.

1. All bad events are things that have some good aspect.

4. No great work is a thing that is accomplished quickly.

7. All persons with advance warning of a threat are people who can prepare for it.

10. All suggestions or requests backed by financial inducements are things that have a good chance of succeeding.

VII.

1. Premise: All great men are people who have been persecuted and derided.
   Conclusion: All people who have been persecuted and derided are great men.
   Illicit conversion. Conversion is not legitimate for A propositions.

4. Premise: No state that is not well armed is a state with good laws.
   Conclusion: All states that are well armed are states with good laws.
   Does not follow.

VIII.

Legitimate
A. All *S* are *P*.
Obverse: No *S* is non-*P*.
Converse: No non-*P* is *S*.
Obverse: All non-*P* are non-*S*.

O. Some *S* are not *P*.
Obverse: Some *S* are non-*P*.
Converse: Some non-*P* are *S*.
Obverse: Some non-*P* are not non-*S*.

Not legitimate
E. No *S* are *P*.
Obverse: All *S* are non-*P*.
Converse: All non-*P* are *S* [invalid step].
Obverse: No non-*P* is non-*S*.

I. Some *S* are *P*.
Obverse: Some *S* are not non-*P*.
Converse: Some non-*P* are not *S* [invalid step].
Obverse: Some non-*P* are non-*S*.

CHAPTER 6

Exercise 6.1

I.

1. Major term: students with consistently high grades; minor term: student athletes; middle term: honor students

4. Major term: rodents; minor term: deer mice; middle term: mice

II.

1. All ambitious people are people who can learn logic.
   All people reading this book are ambitious people.
   All people who are reading this book are people who can learn logic.
   AAA-1

4. No *Twilight* book is a work of great literature.
   All *Twilight* books are books about vampires.
   Some books about vampires are not works of great literature.
   EAO-3

7. No mineral is an organic substance.
   Some minerals are essential nutrients.
   Some essential nutrients are not organic substances.
   EIO-3

10. Some good poems are works that are difficult to interpret.
    All good poems are things worth reading.
    Some things worth reading are works that are difficult to interpret.
    IAI-3

III.

1. All *M* are *P*
   Some *S* are *M*
   Some *S* are *P*

4. No *M* is *P*
   All *S* are *M*
   No *S* is *P*

7. Some *P* are *M*
   Some *M* are not *S*
   Some *S* are not *P*

10. All *P* are *M*
    No *S* is *M*
    Some *S* are not *P*

Exercise 6.2

1. Valid

4. Invalid

7. Invalid

10. Invalid

Exercise 6.3

I.

1. All cats are irrational by nature.
   (Boots is a cat.)
   Boots is irrational by nature.

4. (No humanities majors will be high earners.)
   Some college students are humanities majors.
   Some college students will not be high earners.

II.

1. All poodles are dogs.
   No dogs are cats.
   (No cats are poodles.)
   Some mammals are cats.
   Some mammals are not poodles.

4. Only salty things cause thirst.
   Nothing that is sweet is salty.
   (Nothing that is sweet causes thirst.)
   Nuts are sweet.
   (No nuts cause thirst.)
   All peanuts are nuts.
   Peanuts do not cause thirst.

III.

1. All food that generates stomach acid is bad for an ulcer patient.
   All fried foods generate stomach acid.
   (All fried foods are bad for an ulcer patient.)
   AAA-1

4. No one who trades stocks on the basis of proprietary information is an honest person.
   (Some investment bankers trade stocks on the basis of proprietary information.)
   Some investment bankers are not honest people.
   EIO-1

   or

   No one who trades stocks on the basis of proprietary information is an honest businessman.
   (Some people who trade stocks on the basis of proprietary information are investment bankers.)
   Some investment bankers are not honest businessmen.
   EIO-3

7. No moral movie is a violent film.
   (Some violent films are entertaining movies.)
   Some entertaining movies are not moral movies.
   EIO-4

   or

   No moral movie is a violent film.
   (Some entertaining movies are violent films.)
   Some entertaining movies are not moral movies.
   EIO-2

10. (No democracy is an unstable nation.)
    Some self-determined nations are unstable nations.
    Some self-determined nations are not democracies.
    EIO-2

    or

    (No unstable nation is a democracy.)
    Some self-determined nations are unstable nations.
    Some self-determined nations are not democracies.
    EIO-1

Exercise 6.4A

I.

1. All (machines—D) are (manufactured objects—U).

4. Some (trees—U) are (deciduous plants—U).

7. Some (cars—U) are (lemons—U).

10. No (person with manners—D) is (a person who would clean his teeth at the dinner table—D).

II.

1. E, universal, negative, subject term distributed, predicate term distributed

4. I, particular, affirmative, subject term undistributed, predicate term undistributed

7. E, universal, negative, subject term distributed, predicate term distributed

10. A, universal, affirmative, subject term distributed, predicate term undistributed

Exercise 6.4B

I.

1. Distribution: undistributed middle term

4. Quantity: existential fallacy (modern view only)

7. Distribution: undistributed middle term

II.

1. Valid

4. Invalid: two negative premises

7. Invalid: affirmative premises, negative conclusion; and undistributed middle

10. Invalid: undistributed middle term

III.

1. All people with things to hide are people who plead the Fifth.
   Tom is a person who pled the Fifth.
   Tom is a person with something to hide.
       AAA-2. Invalid: undistributed middle term

4. No paperback book is expensive.
   Some paperback books are well made.
   Some well made things are not expensive.
       EIO-3. Valid

7. Some countries that can afford AIDS medication are capitalist countries.
   No developing nation is a country that can afford AIDS medication.
   Some developing nations are not capitalist countries.
       IEO-1. Invalid: illicit major term

10. Some inspired ideas are not reasonable ideas.
    All the proposals before this committee are reasonable ideas.
    Some of the proposals before this committee are not inspired ideas.
        IAO-2. Invalid: illicit major

13. Some countries that can participate in the global market are countries that flout drug patent laws.
    All countries that can participate in the global market are countries that can get the imports they need.
    Some countries that get the imports they need are countries that flout drug patent laws.
        IAI-3. Valid

Exercise 6.4C

1. (All plants are things that need water.)
   All trees are plants.
   All trees are things that need water.

4. All things containing coliform bacteria are things that are unsafe to drink.
   (Some water is a thing that contains coliform bacteria.)
   Some water is a thing that is unsafe to drink.

   or

   All things containing coliform bacteria are things that are unsafe to drink.
   (Some things that contain coliform bacteria are water.)
   Some water is a thing that is unsafe to drink.

7. No creature whose actions are wholly determined by heredity and environment is a moral agent.
   (All non-human animals are creatures whose actions are wholly determined by heredity and environment.)
   No non-human animal is a moral agent.

Exercise 6.5A

I.

   1.

Premises combined	Conclusion

Invalid

4.

Premises combined

Conclusion

Invalid

7.

Premises combined

Conclusion

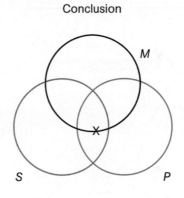

Valid

10.

Premises combined

Conclusion

Valid

13.

Premises combined

Conclusion

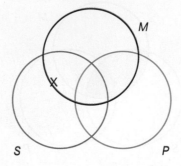

Valid

II.

1. No *M* is *P*
   <u>Some *M* are not *S*</u>
   Some *S* are *P*
   Invalid: two negative premises; negative premises, affirmative conclusion

4. Some *P* are *M*
   <u>No *M* is *S*</u>
   Some *S* are not *P*
   Invalid: illicit major

7. Some *M* are *P*
   <u>All *M* are *S*</u>
   Some *S* are *P*
   Valid

10. All *M* are *P*
    <u>All *S* are *M*</u>
    All *S* are *P*
    Valid

13. No *M* is *P*
    <u>Some *S* are *M*</u>
    Some *S* are not *P*
    Valid

Exercise 6.5B

1. All *M* are *P*

4. All *M* are *P*

7. No *P* is *M* or No *M* is *P*

10. Some *S* are *M* or Some *M* are *S*

Exercise 6.5C

1.

Premises combined

Conclusion

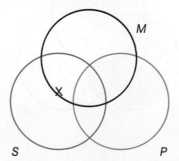

Modern—invalid. Traditional—valid.

4.

Premises combined

Conclusion

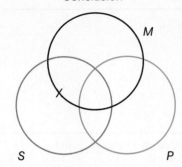

Modern—invalid. Traditional—valid.

7.

Premises combined

Conclusion

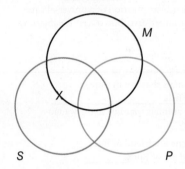

Modern—invalid. Traditional—invalid.

10.

Premises combined

Conclusion

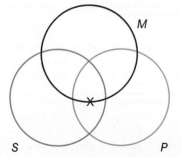

Modern—invalid. Traditional—invalid.

Putting It All Together

I.

1. Valid
4. Invalid
7. Valid
10. Invalid
13. Valid

II.

1. Some children are people who broke the dishes. Subject: U; predicate: U

4. Some of the president's nominees are not people who were confirmed. Subject: U; predicate: D

7. No question is a stupid thing. Subject: D; predicate: D

10. All terms in the subject position of a universal categorical proposition are distributed terms. Subject: D; predicate: U

III.

1. (All fish are animals that live in water.)
   All walleyes are fish.
   All walleyes are animals that live in the water.
   Valid

4. No friend of mine is a friend of Bill's.
   Mary is not a friend of Bill's.
   Mary is a friend of mine.
   Invalid

7. All countries that ignore human rights are tyrannies.
   Some democracies are countries that ignore human rights.
   Some democracies are tyrannies.
   Valid

10. No nonprofit organization is an enterprise that sells stock.
   Some hospital organizations are enterprises that sell stock.
   Some hospital organizations are not nonprofit organizations.
   Valid

13. All dishonest means of gaining wealth are actions that are immoral.
   Some dishonest means of gaining wealth are actions that are expedient in the short term.
   Some actions that are expedient in the short term are actions that are immoral.
   Valid

16. Some international conflicts are conflicts that arise from just motives.
   No aggressive war is a conflict that arises from just motives.
   Some aggressive wars are not international conflicts.
   Invalid

19. There are two possible answers. First possible answer:
   All music is an orderly progression of sounds.
   No noise is an orderly progression of sounds.
   No noise is music.
   Valid

   or

   All noise is a disorderly progression of sound.
   No music is a disorderly progression of sounds.
   No music is noise.
   Valid

IV.

1. No Civil War picture is a movie that made a nickel.
   Gone with the Wind is a Civil War picture.
   Gone with the Wind is not a movie that made a nickel.

4. Anything that is undeservedly forgotten is a good topic for a doctoral thesis.
   Some books are undeservedly forgotten.
   Some books are good topics for doctoral theses.

   and

   All books that are remembered deserve to be remembered.
   McGuffey's Readers are books that are remembered.
   McGuffey's Readers deserve to be remembered.

V.

1. All M are P
   All S are M
   All S are P

4. No M is P
   All S are M
   No S is P

VI.

1. Standard form: Some bonds are things that yield tax-free interest.
   Subject: bonds; predicate: things that yield tax-free interest
   Example syllogism:
   All municipal bonds are things that yield tax-free interest.
   Some bonds are municipal bonds.
   Some bonds are things that yield tax-free interest.

4. Standard form: Some blue-collar workers are highly paid people.
   Subject: blue-collar workers; predicate: highly paid people
   Example syllogism:
   All highly skilled people are highly paid people.
   Some blue-collar workers are highly skilled people.
   Some blue-collar workers are highly paid people.

7. Standard form: Some relationships are things that last a lifetime.
   Subject: relationships; predicate: things that last a lifetime
   Example syllogism:
   All biologically based relationships are things that last a lifetime.
   Some relationships are biologically based relationships.
   Some relationships are things that last a lifetime.

VII.

1. All price controls are harmful things.
   All minimum wage regulations are price controls.
   All minimum wage regulations are harmful things.
      AAA-1. Valid

4. (All people who answer every question put to them are tremendously ignorant people.)
   That man is a person who answers every question put to him.
   That man is a tremendously ignorant person.
      AAA-1. Valid

7. (No one who rejoices at the expense of other men is a person who can expect to thrive in the world of men.)
   All who rejoice loudly of their victories are people who rejoice at the expense of other men.
   No one who rejoices loudly of his victories is a person who can expect to thrive in the world of men.
      EAE-1. Valid

10. (All people who do not revert to normalcy after a violent episode are people who are insane.)
    Some individuals who suffer organic abnormalities or psychoses that produce rage attacks are people who do not revert to normalcy after a violent episode.
    Some individuals who suffer organic abnormalities or psychoses that produce rage attacks are people who are insane.
       AII-1. Valid

13. All animals are mobile.
    All observers are animals.
    All observers are mobile.
       AAA-1. Valid

IX.

1. The middle term in this figure is in the predicate of both premises. It will not be distributed, therefore, unless one premise is negative, in which case the conclusion must be negative.

4. If both premises are particular, then:
   In the first, second, and fourth figures, the only way for the middle term to be distributed is for a premise to be negative, which means the conclusion must be negative, which means that the major term is distributed. But it cannot be distributed in the major premise because of the following:
       In the first figure, that premise would have to be negative, but it must be positive.
       In the second and fourth figures, that premise would need to be universal.
       In the third figure, where the middle term is the subject of both premises, it cannot be distributed if both premises are particular.

CHAPTER 7

Exercise 7.1

1. [I'm hearing things] or [someone is out in the hall singing "Jingle Bells".]
   I'm not hearing things.
   Someone is out in the hall singing "Jingle Bells."
      Valid; denying a disjunct

4. [We send in the troops] or [we negotiate].
   We will not negotiate.
   We will send in the troops.
      Valid; denying a disjunct

7. [Marriage is sacrosanct] or [gay people can get married].
   Gay people can get married.
   Marriage is not sacrosanct.
      Invalid; affirming a disjunct

10. [Paul wins the case] or [he is not promoted to partner].
    Paul is not promoted to partner.
    Paul lost the case.
       Invalid; affirming a disjunct

13. [Kids have access to guns] or [kids play violent video games].
    Kids cannot have access to guns.
    Kids can play violent video games.
       Valid; denying a disjunct

16. [I work hard] or [I fail this course].
    I am working hard.
    I will not fail this course.
       Invalid; affirming a disjunct

Exercise 7.2A

1. Antecedent: You miss your first serve in tennis. Consequent: You get a second try. Already in standard form.

4. Antecedent: A married couple filing a joint return itemize their deductions. Consequent: They may deduct certain child-care expenses. Standard form: If a married couple filing a joint return itemize their deductions, they may deduct certain child-care expenses.

7. Antecedent: Antibodies do not exist in the patient. Consequent: Doctors cannot detect a virus. Standard form: If antibodies do not exist in the patient, then doctors cannot detect a virus.

10. Antecedent: A car does not have a cooling mechanism. Consequent: The car's engine will rapidly overheat. Standard form: If a car does not have a cooling mechanism, then its engine will rapidly overheat.

13. Antecedent: We do not have an understanding of deductive validity. Consequent: We will probably commit fallacies in our reasoning. Standard form: If we do not have an understanding of deductive validity, then we will probably commit fallacies in our reasoning.

16. Two possible standard forms:
    i. If I go out with you tonight, then you have promised not to wear your Nehru jacket. Antecedent: I go out with you tonight. Consequent: You have promised not to wear your Nehru jacket.
    ii. If you do not promise not to wear your Nehru jacket, then I won't go out with you tonight. Antecedent: You don't promise not to wear your Nehru jacket. Consequent: I won't go out with you tonight.

19. Antecedent: The product is not safe. Consequent: People will not buy it. Standard form: If the product is not safe, then people will not buy it.

Exercise 7.2B

I.

1. Mixed hypothetical syllogism; valid, by denying the consequent (*modus tollens*)

4. Mixed hypothetical syllogism; invalid, affirming the consequent

II.

1. If [he had mentioned her name], then [I would have hit him].
   He did not mention her name.
   _____
   I did not hit him.
       Mixed hypothetical syllogism; invalid, denying the antecedent

4. If you want milk, then it is in the refrigerator.
   You don't want milk.
   _____
   It is not in the refrigerator.
       Mixed hypothetical syllogism; invalid, denying the antecedent

7. If [salmon reliably return from the ocean to the streams in which they were spawned], then [they must have some means of detecting subtle differences in the chemical composition of the water of those streams at the point where they flow into the ocean.]
   Salmon reliably return from the ocean to the streams in which they were spawned.
   _____
   [Salmon have some means of detecting subtle differences in the chemical composition of the water of those streams at the point where they flow into the ocean.]
       Mixed hypothetical syllogism; valid, affirming the antecedent (*modus ponens*)

10. If [you install an electrical outlet with a grounding wire], then [you reduce the risk of shorting the circuit].
    If [you install an electrical outlet with a grounding wire], then [you comply with the building code].
    _____
    If [you comply with the building code], then [you reduce the risk of shorting the circuit].
        Invalid form of pure hypothetical syllogism

13. If [men were angels], then [anarchy would be a fine and beautiful system for society to adopt].
    Men are not angels.
    _____
    (Anarchy would not be a fine and beautiful system for society to adopt.)
        Mixed hypothetical syllogism; invalid, denying the antecedent

16. If [our visual system did not have a capacity to detect edges], then [we would not perceive objects].
    (We do perceive objects.)
    _____
    Our visual system does have a capacity to detect edges.
        Mixed hypothetical syllogism; valid, denying the consequent (*modus tollens*)

19. If [the errors and distortions in television news were not the result of political bias], then [they would be randomly distributed across the political spectrum].
    They are not randomly distributed across the political spectrum.
    _____
    The errors and distortions in television news are the result of political bias.
        Mixed hypothetical syllogism; valid, denying the consequent (*modus tollens*)

Exercise 7.3

1. All computers that can run Microsoft Windows 10 are computers with at least 1 gigabyte of memory.
   My computer is not a computer with at least 1 gigabyte of memory.
   My computer is not a computer that can run Microsoft Windows 10.
   Valid

4. If a mechanism of natural selection did not exist, then new species of organisms would not arise.
   New species of organisms do arise.
   There is a mechanism of natural selection.
   Valid, denying the consequent (*modus tollens*)

7. All people who can strike a log with an ax in just the right place are people with a good eye.
   All people who can strike a log with an ax in just the right place are people who can split it with one blow.
   All people who can split logs in a single blow are people with a good eye.
   Invalid, illicit minor

10. If [I am willing to take statistics], then [it is offered in the morning].
    It is not offered in the morning.
    I am not willing to take it.
    Valid, denying the consequent (*modus tollens*)

13. If [a new factory emits a given quantity of pollutants into the air], then [the new factory purchased the right to emit that quantity from some other factory].
    If [the new factory purchased the right to emit that quantity from some other factory], then [the other factory is willing to reduce its emissions by the same amount].
    If [a new factory emits a given level of pollutants into the air], then [another factory was willing to reduce its emissions by the same amount].
    Valid, pure hypothetical syllogism

Exercise 7.4

1. (All criminals who leave fingerprints all over the place are sloppy.)
   The killer left fingerprints all over the place.
   (The killer was sloppy.)

   If the killer were a professional, he would not have been sloppy.
   (The killer was sloppy.)
   The killer was not a professional.
   Valid

4. All metals that can oxidize at normal temperatures will rust.
   (No metal containing chromium is a metal that oxidizes at normal temperatures.)
   (No metal containing chromium is a metal that rusts.)

   (No metal containing chromium is a metal that rusts.)
   Some steel is metal containing chromium.
   Some steel is not metal that rusts.
   Invalid, first step has illicit major

7. (All propositions supported by overwhelming evidence are true [are likely to be true, should be regarded as true].)
   Some laws of economics are propositions supported by overwhelming evidence.
   Some laws of economics are true.

   If every law in economics were false, price controls would work.
   Some laws of economics are true.
   Price controls will not work.
   Invalid, second step denies the antecedent

10. All people with licenses are people who have passed the test.
    All who can drive in this state are people with licenses.
    All who can drive in this state are people who have passed the test.

    All who can drive in this state are people who have passed the test.
    No illiterate person is a person who has passed the test.
    No illiterate person is a person who can drive in this state.
    Valid

Putting It All Together

I.

1. Invalid
4. Valid
7. Invalid
10. Invalid

III.

1. If the Moral Law was one of our instincts, then we ought to be able to point to a particular impulse that is always good.
   We cannot point to a particular impulse that is always good.
   The Moral Law is not one of our instincts.
   Valid, *modus tollens*

4. If imitation is an important factor in language development, then it would be easy to find evidence of its importance.

It is not easy to find evidence of the importance of imitation.

Imitation is not an important factor in language development.

Valid, *modus tollens*

7. If we cannot be sure of the independent existence of objects, then we cannot be sure of the independent existence of people's bodies.

If we cannot be sure of the independent existence of people's bodies, then we cannot be sure of the independent existence of other people's minds.

If we cannot be sure of the independent existence of objects, then we cannot be sure of the independent existence of other people's minds.

Valid, pure hypothetical syllogism

V.

1. All occasions on which one feels pride are occasions followed by destruction.

4. All vigorous minds are curious minds.

7. If one does not know what happened before one was born, then one remains a child.

10. All occasions on which the people give up their liberties are occasions on which they are acting under some delusion.

VII.

1. (If the gun had been fired from a distance of four yards or less, then there would have been powder-blackening on the clothes.)

There was not powder-blackening on the clothes.

The gun was fired from a distance of over four yards.

Valid, *modus tollens*

4. (Either the whole race of mankind is united into one society, or it divides into many societies.)

The whole race cannot unite into one society.

The whole race divides into many societies.

Valid

7. (All opinions about things that do not interest one are absolutely valueless opinions.)

All unbiased opinions are opinions about things that do not interest one.

All unbiased opinions are absolutely valueless opinions.

Valid

10. All things necessary for one who commands are things pertaining to war.

(All things that a prince studies should be things necessary for one who commands.)

All things that a prince studies should be things pertaining to war.

Valid

13. All clowns are people who stand before a crowd and gesture wildly to get their attention.

All politicians are people who stand before a crowd and gesture wildly to get their attention.

(All politicians are clowns.)

Invalid, undistributed middle term

IX.

1. If appellant's conduct is a nuisance, then it is unreasonably noisy.

If appellant's conduct is unreasonably noisy, then it produces noise out of keeping with the character of the neighborhood.

If appellant's conduct is a nuisance, then it produces noise out of keeping with the character of the neighborhood.

If appellant's conduct is a nuisance, then it produces noise out of keeping with the character of the neighborhood.

Appellant's conduct does not produce noise out of keeping with the character of the neighborhood.

Appellant's conduct is not a nuisance.

Valid

4. If thou never wast at court, then thou never saw'st good manners.

If thou never saw'st good manners, then thy manners are wicked.

If thou never wast at court, then thy manners are wicked.

If thou never wast at court, then they manners are wicked.

If thy manners are wicked, then thou art sinful.

If thou never wast at court, then thou art sinful.

If thou never wast at court, then thou art damned.

If thou art sinful, then thou art damned.

If thou never wast at court, then thou art damned.

If thou never wast at court, then thou art sinful.

Thou never wast at court.

Thou art damned.

Valid

7. Some of you are my personal enemies.
   None of you is dead.
   Some of my personal enemies are not dead.

   (All people I considered enemies of the state are dead.)
   Some of my personal enemies are not dead.
   Some of my personal enemies are not people I considered enemies of the state.
   Valid

10. All things that are mixed with one's labor are mixed with a thing that one owns.
    All things that are altered from their natural state through one's labor are things mixed with one's labor.
    All things that are altered from their natural state through one's labor are mixed with a thing one owns.

    All things that are mixed with a thing that one owns are things that one owns.
    All things that are altered from their natural state through one's labor are things mixed with a thing one owns.

    All things that are altered from their natural state through one's labor are things one owns.
    Valid

CHAPTER 8

Exercise 8.1A

1. R: Roses are red; V: Violets are blue; conjunction; R • V

4. R: I can pay the rent; G: I can buy groceries; disjunction; R ∨ G

7. W: Jerry will win the race; S: Jerry will take second place; disjunction; W ∨ S

10. C: The Cucumber County seed-spitting contest is a world-class event; negation; ~C

13. B: The guest of honor wore brown; M: The guest of honor fell in the mud on the way to the party; disjunction; B ∨ M

16. C: Gracie is a cat; H: Gracie eats hummus; conjunction; (C • H)

19. P: All poems are sonnets; negation; ~P

Exercise 8.1B

1. S: These shoes go on sale; B: I'll buy two pairs; conditional; S ⊃ B

4. I: I will scratch your back; Y: You will scratch my back; biconditional; I ≡ Y

7. I: I am ready; Y: You are ready; conditional; Y ⊃ I

10. W: We will launch the new website next month; S: The shopping cart function passes the security test; biconditional; W ≡ S

13. L: The litmus paper in the beaker will turn red; A: The liquid is acidic; biconditional; L ≡ A

16. P: The plant will die; W: You water the plant; conditional; ~W ⊃ P or ~P ⊃ W

19. S: I'll go swimming; W: I can wear my water wings; conditional; S ⊃ W

22. O: Oxygen is present; R: Iron rusts; conditional; R ⊃ O

25. J: Jane will go to the zoo; D: Dan will go to the zoo; conditional; D ⊃ J

Exercise 8.1C

1. H: Holly will take your call; D: Dexter will take your call; disjunction; H ∨ D

4. B: Brazil was settled by aliens; W: Water runs uphill; conditional; B ⊃ W

7. J: Jackson will work on Saturday; P: Jackson is paid overtime; biconditional; J ≡ P

10. I: I love Karen; K: Karen loves Abdul; conjunction; I • K

13. W: Water freezes at 50°F; C: Canada is in North America; disjunction; W ∨ C

16. B: A bank will lend you money; R: You're able to repay it; conditional; B ⊃ R

19. S: Swallows are nesting in the barn; C: Congress is in session; biconditional; S ≡ C

22. A: I'll ask his advice; S: I consider him to be a worthy sage; biconditional; A ≡ S

25. H: Water is heated to 212°F; B: Water boils; biconditional; H ≡ B

28. C: You come to a fork in the road; T: You should take the fork in the road; conditional; C ⊃ T

Exercise 8.2

I.

1. (H • R) ≡ T, biconditional

4. ~(B ⊃ C), negation

7. [(C • W) ⊃ I] • Q, conjuction with Q

10. ~{[(J ⊃ K) ≡ (R ∨ B)] ⊃ (R • K)}, negation

II.

1. D ⊃ A

4. (M • C) ⊃ S

7. B ⊃ (C ∨ M)

10. (Y • I) ⊃ T

13. C ⊃ (P ∨ N)

16. (B • E) ∨ (H • D)
19. W ∨ ~B
22. (P ∨ B) • ~S
25. ~G ⊃ (R ∨ ~C)
28. (Y ⊃ I) • (F ⊃ T)
31. (G • E) ⊃ (~T ⊃ A)
34. ~(R ∨ P) ⊃ (V ⊃ J)   or   ~(V ⊃ J) ⊃ (R ∨ P)
37. (O ⊃ W) • (~M ⊃ ~W)
40. W ≡ [(C ⊃ F) • (H ⊃ B)]
43. (N ⊃ ~R) • (E ⊃ ~S)
46. {O ⊃ [(P • F) ⊃ T]} • (~O ⊃ N)
49. [S ⊃ ~(D ∨ A)] ⊃ (L ⊃ J)

Exercise 8.3

1. Disjunction

A	∨	(B	∨	A)
T	T	T	T	T
T	T	F	T	T
F	T	T	T	F
F	F	F	F	F

4. Conjunction

G	•	~	G
T	F	F	T
F	F	T	F

7. Biconditional

(M	∨	N)	≡	O)
T	T	T	T	T
T	T	T	F	F
T	T	F	T	T
T	T	F	F	F
F	T	T	T	T
F	T	T	F	F
F	F	F	F	T
F	F	F	T	F

10. Biconditional

[(U	⊃	V)	•	(~	V	∨	W)]	≡	(U	⊃	W)
T	T	T	T	F	T	T	T	T	T	T	T
T	T	T	F	F	T	F	F	T	T	F	F
T	F	F	F	T	F	T	T	F	T	T	T
T	F	F	F	T	F	T	F	T	T	F	F
F	T	T	T	F	T	T	T	T	F	T	T
F	T	T	F	F	T	F	F	F	F	T	F
F	T	F	T	T	F	T	T	T	F	T	T
F	T	F	T	T	F	T	F	T	F	T	F

13. Negation

~	[K	V	(L	⊃	~	M)]
F	T	T	T	F	F	T
F	T	T	T	T	T	F
F	T	T	F	T	F	T
F	T	T	F	T	T	F
T	F	F	T	F	F	T
F	F	T	T	T	T	F
F	F	T	F	T	F	T
F	F	T	F	T	T	F

Exercise 8.4A

1. Contingency

(A	•	B)	V	A
T	T	T	T	T
T	F	F	T	T
F	F	T	F	F
F	F	F	F	F

4. Tautology

~	A	⊃	(B	⊃	~	A)
F	T	T	T	F	F	T
F	T	T	F	T	F	T
T	F	T	T	T	T	F
T	F	T	F	T	T	F

7. Self-contradiction

(A	⊃	B)	•	(A	•	~	B)
T	T	T	F	T	F	F	T
T	F	F	F	T	T	T	F
F	T	T	F	F	F	F	T
F	T	F	F	F	F	T	F

10. Tautology

(~	A	V	B)	V	(~	B	•	A)
F	T	T	T	T	F	T	F	T
F	T	F	F	T	T	F	T	T
T	F	T	T	T	F	T	F	F
T	F	T	F	T	T	F	F	F

13. Contingency

~	(P	⊃	Q)	≡	(~	P	⊃	~	Q)
F	T	T	T	F	F	T	T	F	T
T	T	F	F	T	F	T	T	T	F
F	F	T	T	T	T	F	F	F	T
F	F	T	F	F	T	F	T	T	F

16. Contingency

[(A	≡	B)	•	(C	⊃	A)]	•	(C	⊃	~	B)
T	T	T	T	T	T	T	F	T	F	F	T
T	T	T	T	F	T	T	T	F	T	F	T
T	F	F	F	T	T	T	F	T	T	T	F
T	F	F	F	F	T	T	F	F	T	T	F
F	F	T	F	T	F	F	F	T	F	F	T
F	F	T	F	F	T	F	F	F	T	F	T
F	T	F	F	T	F	F	F	T	T	T	F
F	T	F	T	F	T	F	T	F	T	T	F

Exercise 8.4B

1. Equivalent

~	(A	•	B)	~	A	V	~	B
F	T	T	T	F	T	F	F	T
T	T	F	F	F	T	T	T	F
T	F	F	T	T	F	T	F	T
T	F	F	F	T	F	T	T	F

4. Contradictory

~	(A	V	B)	~	(~	A	•	~	B)
F	T	T	T	T	F	T	F	F	T
F	T	T	F	T	F	T	F	T	F
F	F	T	T	T	T	F	F	F	T
T	F	F	F	F	T	F	T	T	F

7. Consistent

C	⊃	D	C	V	~	D
T	T	T	T	T	F	T
T	F	F	T	T	T	F
F	T	T	F	F	F	T
F	T	F	F	T	T	F

10. Equivalent

Y	⊃	(Z	•	W)	~	(Z	•	W)	⊃	~	Y
T	T	T	T	T	F	T	T	T	T	F	T
T	F	T	F	F	T	T	F	F	F	F	T
T	F	F	F	T	T	F	F	T	F	F	T
T	F	F	F	F	T	F	F	F	F	F	T
F	T	T	T	T	F	T	T	T	T	T	F
F	T	T	F	F	T	T	F	F	T	T	F
F	T	F	F	T	T	F	F	T	T	T	F
F	T	F	F	F	T	F	F	F	T	T	F

13. Equivalent

E	•	(F	∨	G)	(E	•	F)	∨	(E	•	G)
T	T	T	T	T	T	T	T	T	T	T	T
T	T	T	T	F	T	T	T	T	T	F	F
T	T	F	T	T	T	F	F	T	T	T	T
T	F	F	F	F	T	F	F	F	T	F	F
F	F	T	T	T	F	F	T	F	F	F	T
F	F	T	T	F	F	F	T	F	F	F	F
F	F	F	T	T	F	F	F	F	F	F	T
F	F	F	F	F	F	F	F	F	F	F	F

16. Equivalent

(J	⊃	K)	•	(K	⊃	J)	(J	•	K)	∨	(~	J	•	~	K)
T	T	T	T	T	T	T	T	T	T	T	F	T	F	F	T
T	F	F	F	F	T	T	T	F	F	F	F	T	F	T	F
F	T	T	F	T	F	F	F	F	T	F	T	F	F	F	T
F	T	F	T	F	T	F	F	F	F	T	T	F	T	T	F

19. Contradictory

(A	⊃	B)	∨	(C	•	A)		~	(A	⊃	B)	•	~	(C	•	A)
T	T	T	**T**	T	T	T		F	T	T	T	**F**	F	T	T	T
T	T	T	**T**	F	F	T		F	T	T	T	**F**	T	F	F	T
T	F	F	**T**	T	T	T		T	T	F	F	**F**	F	T	T	T
T	F	F	**F**	F	F	T		T	T	F	F	**T**	T	F	F	T
F	T	T	**T**	T	F	F		F	F	T	T	**F**	F	T	T	F
F	T	T	**T**	F	F	F		F	F	T	T	**F**	T	F	F	F
F	T	F	**T**	T	F	F		F	F	T	F	**F**	F	T	T	F
F	T	F	**T**	F	F	F		F	F	T	F	**F**	T	F	F	F

22. Consistent

(A	•	B)	⊃	C		B	•	~	C		A	≡	C
T	T	T	**T**	T		T	**F**	F	T		T	**T**	T
T	T	T	**F**	F		T	**T**	T	F		T	**F**	F
T	F	F	**T**	T		F	**F**	F	T		T	**T**	T
T	F	F	**T**	F		F	**F**	T	F		T	**F**	F
F	F	T	**T**	T		T	**F**	F	T		F	**F**	T
F	F	T	**T**	F		T	**T**	T	F		F	**T**	F
F	F	F	**T**	T		F	**F**	F	T		F	**F**	T
F	F	F	**T**	F		F	**F**	T	F		F	**T**	F

Exercise 8.5

1. Invalid, row 3

A	⊃	B		B	/	A
T	**T**	**T**		**T**		**T**
T	**F**	**F**		**F**		**T**
F	**T**	**T**		**T**		**F**
F	**T**	**F**		**F**		**F**

4. Valid

F	≡	G		F	∨	G	/	F	•	G
T	T	T		T	T	T		T	T	T
T	F	F		T	T	F		T	F	F
F	F	T		F	T	T		F	F	T
F	T	F		F	F	F		F	F	F

7. Valid

G	⊃	H	/	G	⊃	(G	•	H)
T	T	T		T	T	T	T	T
T	F	F		T	F	T	F	F
F	T	T		F	T	F	F	T
F	T	F		F	T	F	F	F

10. Valid

~	(M	∨	N)	/	~	N
F	T	T	T		F	T
F	T	T	F		T	F
F	F	T	T		F	T
T	F	F	F		T	F

13. Valid

S	⊃	(T	•	V)	~	V	/	~	S
T	T	T	T	T	F	T		F	T
T	F	T	F	F	T	F		F	T
T	F	F	F	T	F	T		F	T
T	F	F	F	F	T	F		F	T
F	T	T	T	T	F	T		T	F
F	T	T	F	F	T	F		T	F
F	T	F	F	T	F	T		T	F
F	T	F	F	F	T	F		T	F

16. Valid

(M	∨	N)	⊃	S	~	S	∨	O	~	O	/	~	M	•	~	N
T	T	T	T	T	F	T	T	T	F	T		F	T	F	F	T
T	T	T	T	T	F	T	F	F	T	F		F	T	F	F	T
T	T	T	F	F	T	F	T	T	F	T		F	T	F	F	T
T	T	T	F	F	T	F	T	F	T	F		F	T	F	F	T
T	T	F	T	T	F	T	T	T	F	T		F	T	F	T	F
T	T	F	T	T	F	T	F	F	T	F		F	T	F	T	F
T	T	F	F	F	T	F	T	T	F	T		F	T	F	T	F
T	T	F	F	F	T	F	T	F	T	F		F	T	F	T	F
F	T	T	T	T	F	T	T	T	F	T		T	F	F	F	T
F	T	T	T	T	F	T	F	F	T	F		T	F	F	F	T
F	T	T	F	F	T	F	T	T	F	T		T	F	F	F	T
F	T	T	F	F	T	F	T	F	T	F		T	F	F	F	T
F	F	F	T	T	F	T	T	T	F	T		T	F	T	T	F
F	F	F	T	T	F	T	F	F	T	F		T	F	T	T	F
F	F	F	T	F	T	F	T	T	F	T		T	F	T	T	F
F	F	F	T	F	T	F	T	F	T	F		T	F	T	T	F

19. Valid

P	⊃	R		X	⊃	~	M		R	⊃	M		M	⊃	X	/	P	⊃	~	M
T	T	T		T	F	F	T		T	T	T		T	T	T		T	F	F	T
T	T	T		T	T	T	F		T	F	F		F	T	T		T	T	T	F
T	T	T		F	T	F	T		T	T	T		T	F	F		T	F	F	T
T	T	T		F	T	T	F		T	F	F		F	T	F		T	T	T	F
T	F	F		T	F	F	T		F	T	T		T	T	T		T	F	F	T
T	F	F		T	T	T	F		F	T	F		F	T	T		T	T	T	F
T	F	F		F	T	F	T		F	T	T		T	F	F		T	F	F	T
T	F	F		F	T	T	F		F	T	F		F	T	F		T	T	T	F
F	T	T		T	F	F	T		T	T	T		T	T	T		F	T	F	T
F	T	T		T	T	T	F		T	F	F		F	T	T		F	T	T	F
F	T	T		F	T	F	T		T	T	T		T	F	F		F	T	F	T
F	T	T		F	T	T	F		T	F	F		F	T	F		F	T	T	F
F	T	F		T	F	F	T		F	T	T		T	T	T		F	T	F	T
F	T	F		T	T	T	F		F	T	F		F	T	T		F	T	T	F
F	T	F		F	T	F	T		F	T	T		T	F	F		F	T	F	T
F	T	F		F	T	T	F		F	T	F		F	T	F		F	T	T	F

Exercise 8.6A

1. Invalid

A	•	B		C	∨	B	/	~	C
T	T	T		T	T	T		F	T

4. Valid

J	⊃	K		K	⊃	L		~	L	/	~	J
T		F		F	T	F		T	F		F	T

7. Valid

W	⊃	Y		(W	⊃	Z)	∨	(Y	⊃	Z)		~	Z	/	~	(W	•	Y)
T	T	T		T	T	T	T	T	T	T			T		F	T	T	T

10. Valid

(A	•	C)	∨	(B	⊃	C)		~	C	∨	B	/	~	B	∨	C
T/F	F	F		T	F	F		T	F	T	T		F	T	F	F

13. Invalid

(E	⊃	F)	∨	[E	⊃	(G	•	H)]		H	⊃	(F	∨	G)	/	E	⊃	H
T	T	T	T	T	F	T/F	F	F		F	T	T	T	T/F		T	F	F

16. Invalid

~	[A	∨	~	(B	∨	~	C)]		D	⊃	(A	⊃	C)	/	~	A	≡	~	B
T	F	F	F	T	T		T/F		T/F	T	F	T	T/F		T	F	F	F	T

19. Invalid

N	∨	O		P	∨	Q		~	Q	∨	N		P	⊃	(N	∨	R)	/	O
T	T	F		T/F	T	T/F		T/F	T	T		T/F	T	T	T	T/F			F

Exercise 8.6B

1. Consistent

A	⊃	B		A	•	B		~	A	∨	B
T	T	T		T	T	T		F	T	T	T

4. Inconsistent

D	⊃	G		(D	•	F)	∨	G		~	G	•	~	F
F	T	F		F	F	F		F		T	F	T	T	F

7. Consistent

	F	⊃	G		G	∨	~	F		F	≡	G
1	T	T	T		T	T	F	T		T	T	T
2										F	T	F

10. Inconsistent

(P	∨	Q)	•	R		(R	•	P)	∨	(R	•	Q)		~	R	•	D		D	⊃	R
T/F		T/F		F		F	F	T/F		F	F	T/F		T	F	T	T		T		F

13. Consistent

R	⊃	P		T	⊃	P		Q	⊃	P		~	P	•	(~	Q	•	~	T)		~	P	∨	(S	•	~	R)		~	Q	∨	(A	•	B)
F	T	F		F	T	F		F	T	F		T	F	T	T	F	T	T	F		T	F	T	T/F		T	F		T	F	T	T/F		T/F

Putting It All Together

I.

1. $q \supset p$

4. $p \bullet (q \vee r)$

7. $\sim(p \vee q)$

10. $(p \vee q) \equiv r$

13. $(p \supset q) \equiv (r \supset s)$

II.

1. Either Jill is not home or I dialed the wrong number.

4. Jack fell down and either broke his crown or bruised it.

7. If Jack is at work, then either he is out of his office or he is not answering his phone.

10. Jack is at the store or he is at work, and Jill is out running or she is out riding a bicycle.

13. If the price of eggs remains constant, then it is not the case that demand has increased and supply has fallen.

III.

1. $\sim(P \supset W) \supset A$ or $\sim A \supset (P \supset W)$

4. $\{(M \supset \sim F) \bullet [\sim M \supset (F \bullet P)]\} \bullet [(M \vee \sim M) \supset (A \bullet D)]$

IV.

1. Conjunction

~	A	•	B
F	T	F	T
F	T	F	F
T	F	T	T
T	F	F	F

4. Conjunction

(C	∨	D)	•	~	E
T	T	T	F	F	T
T	T	T	T	T	F
T	T	F	F	F	T
T	T	F	T	T	F
F	T	T	F	F	T
F	T	T	T	T	F
F	F	F	F	F	T
F	F	F	F	T	F

7. Conditional

(M	•	N)	⊃	O
T	T	T	T	T
T	T	T	F	F
T	F	F	T	T
T	F	F	T	F
F	F	T	T	T
F	F	T	T	F
F	F	F	T	T
F	F	F	T	F

10. Conjunction

(V	∨	W)	•	~	(V	•	W)
T	T	T	F	F	T	T	T
T	T	F	T	T	T	F	F
F	T	T	T	T	F	F	T
F	F	F	F	T	F	F	F

V.

1. Consistent

B	≡	C	(B	≡	C)	⊃	~	A	~	A	•	~	D
T	T	T	T	T	T	F	F	T	F	T	F	F	T
T	T	T	T	T	T	F	F	T	F	T	F	T	F
T	T	T	T	T	T	T	T	F	T	F	F	F	T
T	T	T	T	T	T	T	T	F	T	F	T	T	F
T	F	F	T	F	F	T	F	T	F	T	F	F	T
T	F	F	T	F	F	T	F	T	F	T	F	T	F
T	F	F	T	F	F	T	T	F	T	F	F	F	T
T	F	F	T	F	F	T	T	F	T	F	T	T	F
F	F	T	F	F	T	T	F	T	F	T	F	F	T
F	F	T	F	F	T	T	F	T	F	T	F	T	F
F	F	T	F	F	T	T	T	F	T	F	F	F	T
F	F	T	F	F	T	T	T	F	T	F	T	T	F
F	T	F	F	T	F	F	F	T	F	T	F	F	T
F	T	F	F	T	F	F	F	T	F	T	F	T	F
F	T	F	F	T	F	T	T	F	T	F	F	F	T
F	T	F	F	T	F	T	T	F	T	F	T	T	F

B	≡	C	(B	≡	C)	⊃	~	A	~	A	•	~	D
T	T	T	T	T	T	T	T	F	T	F	T	T	F

4. Inconsistent

(D	⊃	E)	⊃	(D	⊃	C)	~	D	•	~	F	D	∨	F	C	∨	~	D
T	T	T	T	T	T	T	F	T	F	F	T	T	T	T	T	T	F	T
T	T	T	T	T	T	T	F	T	F	T	F	T	T	F	T	T	F	T
T	T	T	F	T	F	F	F	T	F	F	T	T	T	T	F	F	F	T
T	T	T	F	T	F	F	F	T	F	T	F	T	T	F	F	F	F	T
T	F	F	T	T	T	T	F	T	F	F	T	T	T	T	T	T	F	T
T	F	F	T	T	T	T	F	T	F	T	F	T	T	F	T	T	F	T
T	F	F	T	T	F	F	F	T	F	F	T	T	T	T	F	F	F	T
T	F	F	T	T	F	F	F	T	F	T	F	T	T	F	F	F	F	T
F	T	T	T	F	T	T	T	F	F	F	T	F	T	T	T	T	T	F
F	T	T	T	F	T	T	T	F	T	T	F	F	F	F	T	T	T	F
F	T	T	T	F	T	F	T	F	F	F	T	F	T	T	F	T	T	F
F	T	T	T	F	T	F	T	F	T	T	F	F	F	F	F	T	T	F
F	T	F	T	F	T	T	T	F	F	F	T	F	T	T	T	T	T	F
F	T	F	T	F	T	T	T	F	T	T	F	F	F	F	T	T	T	F
F	T	F	T	F	T	F	T	F	F	F	T	F	T	T	F	T	T	F
F	T	F	T	F	T	F	T	F	T	T	F	F	F	F	F	T	T	F

(D	⊃	E)	⊃	(D	⊃	C)	~	D	•	~	F	D	∨	F	C	∨	~	D
F	T	T/F	T	F	T	T/F	T	F	T	T	F	F	∨	F	T/F	T	T	F

7. Inconsistent

~	(R	≡	T)	R	⊃	T	~	T	⊃	R	R	•	T
F	T	T	T	T	T	T	F	T	T	T	T	T	T
T	T	F	F	T	F	F	T	F	T	T	T	F	F
T	F	F	T	F	T	T	F	T	T	F	F	F	T
F	F	T	F	F	T	F	T	F	F	F	F	F	F

~	(R	≡	T)	R	⊃	T	~	T	⊃	R	R	•	T
~	T	T	T	T	T	T	F	T	T	T	T	T	T

10. Consistent

(P	•	Q)	⊃	(S	•	T)	S	⊃	(T	⊃	V)	P	∨	S	Q	∨	T	S	•	~	Q
T	T	T	T	T	T	T	T	T	T	T	T	T	T	T	T	T	T	T	F	F	T
T	T	T	T	T	T	T	T	F	T	F	F	T	T	T	T	T	T	T	F	F	T
T	T	T	F	T	F	F	T	T	F	T	T	T	T	T	T	T	F	T	F	F	T
T	T	T	F	T	F	F	T	T	F	T	F	T	T	T	T	T	F	T	F	F	T
T	T	T	F	F	F	T	F	T	T	T	T	T	T	F	T	T	T	F	F	F	T
T	T	T	F	F	F	T	F	T	T	F	F	T	T	F	T	T	T	F	F	F	T
T	T	T	F	F	F	F	F	T	F	T	T	T	T	F	T	T	F	F	F	F	T
T	T	T	T	F	F	F	F	T	F	T	F	T	T	F	T	T	F	F	F	F	T
T	F	F	T	T	T	T	T	T	T	T	T	T	T	T	F	T	T	T	T	T	F
T	F	F	T	T	T	T	T	F	T	F	F	T	T	T	F	T	T	T	T	T	F
T	F	F	T	T	T	F	T	T	F	T	T	T	T	T	F	F	F	T	T	T	F
T	F	F	T	T	F	F	T	T	F	T	F	T	T	T	F	F	F	T	T	T	F
T	F	F	T	F	F	T	F	T	T	T	T	T	T	F	F	T	T	F	F	T	F
T	F	F	T	F	F	T	F	T	T	F	F	T	T	F	F	T	T	F	F	T	F
T	F	F	T	F	F	F	F	T	F	T	T	T	T	F	F	F	F	F	F	T	F
T	F	F	T	F	F	F	F	T	F	T	F	T	T	F	F	F	F	F	F	T	F
F	F	T	T	T	T	T	T	T	T	T	T	F	T	T	T	T	T	T	F	F	T
F	F	T	T	T	T	T	T	F	T	F	F	F	T	T	T	T	T	T	F	F	T
F	F	T	T	T	F	F	T	T	F	T	T	F	T	T	T	T	F	T	F	F	T
F	F	T	T	T	F	F	T	T	F	T	F	F	T	T	T	T	F	T	F	F	T
F	F	T	T	F	F	T	F	T	T	T	T	F	F	F	T	T	T	F	F	F	T
F	F	T	T	F	F	T	F	T	T	F	F	F	F	F	T	T	T	F	F	F	T
F	F	T	T	F	F	F	F	T	F	T	T	F	F	F	T	T	F	F	F	F	T
F	F	T	T	F	F	F	F	T	F	T	F	F	F	F	T	T	F	F	F	F	T
F	F	F	T	T	T	T	T	T	T	T	T	F	T	T	F	T	T	T	T	T	F
F	F	F	T	T	T	T	T	F	T	F	F	F	T	T	F	F	F	T	T	T	Q
F	F	F	T	T	T	F	T	T	F	T	T	F	T	T	F	F	F	T	T	T	F
F	F	F	T	T	T	F	T	T	F	T	F	F	T	T	F	F	F	T	T	T	F
F	F	F	T	F	F	T	F	T	T	T	T	F	F	F	F	T	T	F	F	T	F
F	F	F	T	F	F	T	F	T	T	F	F	F	F	F	F	T	T	F	F	T	F
F	F	F	T	F	F	F	F	T	F	T	F	F	F	F	F	F	F	F	F	T	F

(P	•	Q)	⊃	(S	•	T)	S	⊃	(T	⊃	V)	P	∨	S	Q	∨	T	S	•	~	Q
T/F	F	F	T	T	T	T	T	T	T	T	T	T	T/F	T	T	F	T	T	T	T	T	F

VI.

1. Valid

A	⊃	B	~	B	∨	C	/	~	A	∨	C
T	T	T	F	T	(∨)	F		F	T	F	F

4. Valid

(M	•	N)	∨	(M	•	O)	N	≡	O	/	M
F	F	T/F	(∨)	F	F	T/F	T/F	T	T/F		F

7. Invalid

(K	⊃	L)	⊃	(M	⊃	N)	/	(K	⊃	M)	⊃	(L	⊃	N)
F	T	T	**T**	F	T	F		F	T	F	**F**	T	F	F

10. Valid

E	⊃	(F	•	G)	H	⊃	(I	∨	J)	F	⊃	(~	I	•	~	J)	/	~	(E	•	H)
T	T	T	T	T	T	(⊃)	F	F	F	T	T	T	F	T	T	F		F	T	T	T

13. Invalid

[A	∨	(B	•	C)]	⊃	D	~	(D	•	E)	A	⊃	E	/	B	•	C
F	F	F	F	T/F	**T**	F	**T**	F	F	T	F	**T**	T		F	**F**	T/F

or

[A	∨	(B	•	C)]	⊃	D	~	(D	•	E)	A	⊃	E	/	B	•	C
F	F	T/F	F	F	**T**	T	**T**	T	F	F	F	**T**	F		T/F	**F**	F

VII.

1. Invalid

S	∨	F	S	/	~	F
T	T	T	T		F	T
T	T	F	T		T	F
F	T	T	F		F	T
F	F	F	F		T	F

S	∨	F	S	/	~	F
T	T	T	T		F	T

4. Valid

W	∨	M	W	⊃	G	M	⊃	P	/	G	∨	P
T	T	T	T	T	T	T	T	T		T	T	T
T	T	T	T	T	T	T	F	F		T	T	F
T	T	T	T	F	F	T	T	T		F	T	T
T	T	T	T	F	F	T	F	F		F	F	F
T	T	F	T	T	T	F	T	T		T	T	T
T	T	F	T	T	T	F	T	F		T	T	F
T	T	F	T	F	F	F	T	T		F	T	T
T	T	F	T	F	F	F	T	F		F	F	F
F	T	T	F	T	T	T	T	T		T	T	T
F	T	T	F	T	T	T	F	F		T	T	F
F	T	T	F	T	F	T	T	T		F	T	T
F	T	T	F	T	F	T	F	F		F	F	F
F	F	F	F	T	T	F	T	T		T	T	T
F	F	F	F	T	T	F	T	F		T	T	F
F	F	F	F	T	F	F	T	T		F	T	T
F	F	F	F	T	F	F	T	F		F	F	F

W	∨	M	W	⊃	G	M	⊃	P	/	G	∨	P
F	F	F	F	T	F	F	T	F		F	F	F

CHAPTER 9

Exercise 9.1B

I.

1. DS

4. HS

7. MP

10. MT

13. MT

16. HS

19. MP

II.

1.
  a. The consequent of line 2
  b. MP
  c. ~A, no, yes, premise 1
  d. MT
  e. ~B, yes, on line 3

4.
  a. Yes, the consequent of premise 3
  b. MP
  c. ~E, no, yes, from premise 1
  d. MT
  e. ~D, yes, premise 2

III.

1.

4. ~A	1,3 MT
5. C	2,4 MP

4.

4. ~E	1,2 MT
5. C	3,4 MP

7.

4. ~A	1,2 MP
5. D	3,4 DS

10.

4. A ⊃ D	1,2 DS
5. B ⊃ D	3,4 HS
6. ~B	1,5 MT

or

4. A ⊃ D	1,2 DS
5. ~A	1,4 MT
6. ~B	3,5 MT

13.

4. I ⊃ H	1,3 HS
5. ~I	2,4 MT

or

4. ~G	1,2 MT
5. ~I	3,4 MT

16.

6. ~(A ∨ B)	2,5 MT
7. B ⊃ C	1,6 DS
8. B ⊃ ~D	3,7 HS
9. G ⊃ ~D	4,8 HS

or

6. ~(A ∨ B)	2,5 MT
7. B ⊃ C	1,6 DS
8. G ⊃ C	4,7 HS
9. G ⊃ ~D	3,8 HS

Exercise 9.1C

I.

1. Simp
4. Conj
7. DD
10. CD
13. CD
16. Conj
19. Add

II.

1.
a. No, yes, B and C
b. Add
c. A ∨ B
d. Add

4.
a. No, yes, as the consequents of the two conditionals
b. CD
c. A ∨ C, no, yes, premise 1
d. Add

III.

1.

1. A	/ (A ∨ B) ∨ C	Premise / Conclusion
2. A ∨ B		1 Add
3. (A ∨ B) ∨ C		2 Add

4.

1. A		Premise
2. (A ⊃ B) • (C ⊃ D)	/ B ∨ D	Premise / Conclusion
3. A ∨ C		1 Add
4. B ∨ D		2,3 CD

7.

1. (A ⊃ C) • (B ⊃ D)		Premise
2. ~C	/ ~A ∨ ~B	Premise / Conclusion
3. ~C ∨ ~D		2 Add
4. ~A ∨ ~B		1,3 DD

10.

1. (D ⊃ E)		Premise
2. (F ⊃ G)		Premise
3. D ∨ F	/ E ∨ G	Premise / Conclusion
4. (D ⊃ E) • (F ⊃ G)		1,2 Conj
5. E ∨ G		3,4 CD

13.

1. B • C		Premise
2. ~A • D	/ ~A • B	Premise / Conclusion
3. ~A		2 Simp
4. B		1 Simp
5. ~A • B		3,4 Conj

16.

1. A ⊃ D		Premise
2. B ⊃ C		Premise
3. B ∨ A	/ C ∨ D	Premise / Conclusion
4. (B ⊃ C) • (A ⊃ D)		1,2 Conj
5. C ∨ D		3,4 CD

19.

1. (A ⊃ C) • (B ⊃ D)		Premise
2. ~C ∨ ~D		Premise
3. [(~A ∨ ~B) ⊃ E] • (~E ⊃ F)	/ E ∨ F	Premise / Conclusion
4. ~A ∨ ~B		1,2 DD
5. (~A ∨ ~B) ∨ ~E		4 Add
6. E ∨ F		3,5 CD

22.

1. (D ∨ A) ⊃ ~C		Premise
2. (D • B) ⊃ A		Premise
3. D • ~B	/ ~C ∨ A	Premise / Conclusion
4. [(D ∨ A) ⊃ ~C] • [(D • B) ⊃ A]		1,2 Conj
5. D		3 Simp
6. D ∨ A		5 Add
7. (D ∨ A) ∨ (D • B)		6 Add
8. ~C ∨ A		4,7 CD

IV.

1.
1,3 MT
2,4 MP

4.
3 Simp
2 Simp
4,5 Conj
1,6 MP

V.

1.

1. A		Premise
2. A ⊃ ~B		Premise
3. B ∨ C	/ C	Premise / Conclusion
4. ~B		1,2 MP
5. C		3,4 DS

4.

1. D ⊃ E		Premise
2. D ∨ A		Premise
3. ~E	/ A	Premise / Conclusion
4. ~D		1,3 MT
5. A		2,4 DS

7.

1. (A ∨ B) ⊃ C		Premise
2. E ⊃ (A ∨ B)		Premise
3. C ⊃ D	/ E ⊃ D	Premise / Conclusion
4. E ⊃ C		1,2 HS
5. E ⊃ D		3,4 HS

10.

1. A ⊃ B		Premise
2. C ⊃ D		Premise
3. ~B	/ ~A ∨ ~C	Premise / Conclusion
4. ~A		1,3 MT
5. ~A ∨ ~C		4 Add

13.

1. B ⊃ C		Premise
2. B ∨ (A • E)		Premise
3. ~C	/ A • E	Premise / Conclusion
4. ~B		1,3 MT
5. A • E		2,4 DS

16.

1. ~(A ⊃ B)		Premise
2. (A ⊃ B) ∨ C		Premise
3. G ⊃ (A ⊃ B)	/ ~G • C	Premise / Conclusion
4. ~G		1,3 MT
5. C		1,2 DS
6. ~G • C		4,5 Conj

19.

1. E ⊃ B		Premise
2. B ⊃ C		Premise
3. A ⊃ E		Premise
4. C ⊃ G	/ A ⊃ G	Premise / Conclusion
5. A ⊃ B		1,3 HS
6. A ⊃ C		2,5 HS
7. A ⊃ G		4,6 HS

22.

1. ~C		Premise
2. B ⊃ C		Premise
3. B ∨ A		Premise
4. A ⊃ E	/ E	Premise / Conclusion
5. ~B		1,2 MT
6. A		3,5 DS
7. E		4,6 MP

25.

1. (A ≡ B) ⊃ (E ∨ C)		Premise
2. (B ⊃ D) ⊃ (A ≡ B)		Premise
3. (E ∨ C) ⊃ ~G		Premise
4. ~G ⊃ A	/ (B ⊃ D) ⊃ A	Premise / Conclusion
5. (E ∨ C) ⊃ A		3,4 HS
6. (A ≡ B) ⊃ A		1,5 HS
7. (B ⊃ D) ⊃ A		2,6 HS

28.

1. E ⊃ A		Premise
2. B ⊃ E		Premise
3. A ⊃ ~C		Premise
4. B	/ ~C	Premise / Conclusion
5. B ⊃ A		1,2 HS
6. B ⊃ ~C		3,5 HS
7. ~C		4,6 MP

31.

1. A ∨ B	Premise
2. C ⊃ D	Premise
3. ~A • ~D / B • ~C	Premise / Conclusion
4. ~A	3 Simp
5. B	1,4 DS
6. ~D	3 Simp
7. ~C	2,6 MT
8. B • ~C	5,7 Conj

34.

1. (B • A) ⊃ (C • D)	Premise
2. E ≡ F	Premise
3. (~C ⊃ ~G) ⊃ [F ⊃ (D ⊃ H)]	Premise
4. [F ⊃ (D ⊃ H)] ⊃ [(E ≡ F) ⊃ (B • A)]	Premise
5. ~C ⊃ ~G / C • D	Premise / Conclusion
6. (~C ⊃ ~G) ⊃ [(E ≡ F) ⊃ (B • A)]	3,4 HS
7. (E ≡ F) ⊃ (B • A)	5,6 MP
8. B • A	2,7 MP
9. C • D	1,8 MP

37.

1. D ⊃ B	Premise
2. C ⊃ A	Premise
3. E ⊃ D	Premise
4. B ⊃ C	Premise
5. E ∨ B / (B ∨ A) • (D ∨ C)	Premise / Conclusion
6. (E ⊃ D) • (B ⊃ C)	3,4 Conj
7. D ∨ C	5,6 CD
8. (D ⊃ B) • (C ⊃ A)	1,2 Conj
9. B ∨ A	7,8 CD
10. (B ∨ A) • (D ∨ C)	7,9 Conj

40.

1. (A ∨ D) ⊃ [(B ⊃ G) • (C ⊃ E)]	Premise
2. A • ~G	Premise
3. ~C ⊃ D	Premise
4. B ∨ E / E	Premise / Conclusion
5. A	3 Simp
6. A ∨ D	6 Add
7. (B ⊃ G) • (C ⊃ E)	1,7 MP
8. B ⊃ G	8 Simp
9. ~G	3 Simp
10. ~B	9,10 MT
11. E	5,11 DS

Exercise 9.2A

I.

1. B • (D • F)
4. ~(E ∨ N)
7. (A • K) ∨ (A • M)
10. ~(A ≡ B) ∨ ~O

II.

1. Com
4. DN
7. Com
10. Dist
13. DM
16. Com
19. DM

III.

1.

1. (A • A) ∨ ~~B	/ A ∨ B	Premise / Conclusion
2. ~~B ∨ (A • A)		1 Com
3. (~~B ∨ A) • (~~B ∨ A)		2 Dist
4. ~~B ∨ A		3 Simp
5. A ∨ ~~B		4 Com
6. A ∨ B		5 DN

4.

1. ~(D ∨ E)	/ ~D	Premise / Conclusion
2. ~D • ~E		1 DM
3. ~D		2 Simp

7.

1. A • (B ∨ C)		Premise
2. ~(A • B)	/ A • C	Premise / Conclusion
3. (A • B) ∨ (A • C)		1 Dist
4. A • C		2,3 DS

10.

1. C ∨ ~D	/ ~(~C •D)	Premise / Conclusion
2. ~~C ∨ ~D		1 DN
3. ~(~C • D)		2 DM

13.

1. (B ∨ C) ∨ D		Premise
2. ~B	/ C ∨ D	Premise / Conclusion
3. B ∨ (C ∨ D)		1 Assoc
4. C ∨ D		2,3 DS

16.

1. A • G		Premise
2. ~G ∨ B	/ B ∨ F	Premise / Conclusion
3. G		1 Simp
4. ~~G		3 DN
5. B		2,4 DS
6. B ∨ F		5 Add

19.

1. E ∨ F		Premise
2. ~G ∨ H		Premise
3. ~(E ∨ H)	/ F • ~G	Premise / Conclusion
4. ~E • ~H		3 DM
5. ~E		4 Simp
6. F		1,5 DS
7. ~H		4 Simp
8. ~G		2,7 DS
9. F • ~G		6,8 Conj

EXERCISE 9.2B

I.

1. ~B ⊃ ~A

4. ~F ∨ ~G

7. [F ⊃ (G ≡ H)] • [(G ≡ H) ⊃ F]

   or

   [F • (G ≡ H)] ∨ [~F • ~(G ≡ H)]

10. ~~(F ⊃ H) ∨ (M ∨ ~N)

II.

1. Taut

4. Equiv

7. Imp

10. Imp

13. Taut

16. Imp

III.

1.

1. (A • A) ∨ ~~B / A ∨ B	Premise / Conclusion
2. A ∨ ~~B	1 Taut
3. A ∨ B	2 DN

4.

1. ~A ∨ (B ⊃ C) / (A • B) ⊃ C	Premise / Conclusion
2. A ⊃ (B ⊃ C)	1 Imp
3. (A • B) ⊃ C	2 Exp

7.

1. A • G	Premise
2. ~G ∨ B / B ∨ F	Premise / Conclusion
3. G	1 Simp
4. ~~G	3 DN
5. B	2,4 DS
6. B ∨ F	5 Add

10.

1. C ≡ D / (C • D) ∨ ~(C ∨ D)	Premise / Conclusion
2. (C • D) ∨ (~C • ~D)	1 Equiv
3. (C • D) ∨ ~(C ∨ D)	2 DM

13.

1. E ⊃ (F ⊃ G) / F ⊃ (E ⊃ G)	Premise / Conclusion
2. (E • F) ⊃ G	1 Exp
3. (F • E) ⊃ G	2 Com
4. F ⊃ (E ⊃ G)	3 Exp

16.

1. ~(G ≡ M) / (G ∨ M) • ~(G • M)	Premise / Conclusion
2. ~[(G • M) ∨ (~G • ~M)]	1 Equiv
3. ~(G • M) • ~(~G • ~M)	2 DM
4. ~(G • M) • ~~(G ∨ M)	3 DM
5. ~(G • M) • (G ∨ M)	4 DN
6. (G ∨ M) • ~(G • M)	5 Com

19.

1. (E ⊃ K) • (K ⊃ O)	Premise
2. O ⊃ E / O ≡ E	Premise / Conclusion
3. K ⊃ O	1 Simp
4. E ⊃ K	1 Simp
5. E ⊃ O	3,4 HS
6. (O ⊃ E) • (E ⊃ O)	2,5 Conj
7. O ≡ E	6 Equiv

22.

1. D	Premise
2. ~D ∨ (E ≡ F) / ~E ⊃ ~F	Premise / Conclusion
3. ~~D	1 DN
4. E ≡ F	2,3 DS
5. (E ⊃ F) • (F ⊃ E)	4 Equiv
6. F ⊃ E	5 Simp
7. ~E ⊃ ~F	6 Trans

25.

1. A ⊃ (H ∨ J)		Premise
2. J ≡ H		Premise
3. ~J	/ ~A	Premise / Conclusion
4. (J ⊃ H) • (H ⊃ J)		2 Equiv
5. H ⊃ J		4 Simp
6. ~H		3,5 MT
7. ~H • ~J		3,6 Conj
8. ~(H ∨ J)		7 DM
9. ~A		1,8 MT

28.

1. (I ∨ J) ⊃ K		Premise
2. (L ∨ M) ⊃ ~K		Premise
3. M	/ ~J	Premise / Conclusion
4. ~(I ∨ J) ∨ K		1 Imp
5. (~I • ~J) ∨ K		4 DM
6. M ∨ L		3 Add
7. L ∨ M		6 Com
8. ~K		2,7 MP
9. ~I • ~J		5,8 DS
10. ~J		9 Simp

31.

1. (A ∨ B) ⊃ (C ∨ D)		Premise
2. E • [E ⊃ (C ⊃ G)]		Premise
3. (B ∨ A) ⊃ (D ⊃ H)		Premise
4. (F ∨ E) ⊃ (A ∨ B)	/ G ∨ H	Premise / Conclusion
5. E ⊃ (C ⊃ G)		2 Simp
6. E		2 Simp
7. C ⊃ G		5,6 MP
8. F ∨ E		6 Add
9. A ∨ B		4,8 MP
10. C ∨ D		1,9 MP
11. (A ∨ B) ⊃ (D ⊃ H)		3 Com
12. D ⊃ H		9,11 MP
13. (C ⊃ G) • (D ⊃ H)		7,12 Conj
14. G ∨ H		10,13 CD

Exercise 9.3A

1.

1. H ⊃ (I • G)	/ H ⊃ I	Premise / Conclusion
2. H		Assumption
3. I • G		1,2 MP
4. I		3 Simp
5. H ⊃ I		2–4 CP

4.

1. D ⊃ (E ⊃ F)		Premise
2. D ⊃ (F ⊃ G)	/ D ⊃ (E ⊃ G)	Premise / Conclusion
3. D		Assumption
4. E ⊃ F		1,3 MP
5. F ⊃ G		2,3 MP
6. E ⊃ G		4,5 HS
7. D ⊃ (E ⊃ G)		3–6 CP

7.

1. A ⊃ B	Premise
2. (B • A) ⊃ D	Premise
3. [(B • A) • D] ⊃ E / A ⊃ E	Premise / Conclusion
4. A	Assumption
5. B	1,4 MP
6. B • A	4,5 Conj
7. D	2,6 MP
8. (B • A) • D	6,7 Conj
9. E	3,8 MP
10. A ⊃ E	4–9 CP

13.

1. (E ⊃ F) • (G ⊃ H)	Premise
2. E ∨ (I ⊃ G) / I ⊃ (F ∨ H)	Premise / Conclusion
3. E ∨ (~I ∨ G)	2 Imp
4. (~I ∨ G) ∨ E	3 Com
5. ~I ∨ (G ∨ E)	4 Assoc
6. I	Assumption
7. ~~I	6 DN
8. G ∨ E	5,7 DS
9. E ∨ G	8 Com
10. F ∨ H	1,9 CD
11. I ⊃ (F ∨ H)	6–10 CP

10.

1. ~(N • P)	Premise
2. T ∨ P	Premise
3. (T • ~P) ⊃ O	Premise
4. ~N ⊃ (M • S)	Premise
5. O ⊃ ~M / N ≡ O	Premise / Conclusion
6. N	Assumption
7. ~N ∨ ~P	1 DM
8. ~~N	6 DN
9. ~P	7,8 DS
10. T	2,9 DS
11. T • ~P	9,10 Conj
12. O	3,11 MP
13. N ⊃ O	6–12 CP
14. O	Assumption
15. ~M	5,14 MP
16. ~M ∨ ~S	15 Add
17. ~(M • S)	16 DM
18. ~~N	4,17 MT
19. N	18 DN
20. O ⊃ N	14–19 CP
21. (N ⊃ O) • (O ⊃ N)	13,20 Conj
22. N ≡ O	21 Equiv

16.

1. (~A ⊃ ~B) ⊃ (C • D)	Premise
2. D ⊃ (C • E) / ~(A • ~E)	Premise / Conclusion
3. (B ⊃ A) ⊃ (C • D)	1 Trans
4. A	Assumption
5. A ∨ ~B	4 Add
6. ~B ∨ A	5 Com
7. B ⊃ A	6 Imp
8. C • D	3,7 MP
9. D	8 Simp
10. C • E	2,9 MP
11. E	10 Simp
12. A ⊃ E	4–11 CP
13. ~A ∨ E	12 Imp
14. ~A ∨ ~~E	13 DN
15. ~(A • ~E)	14 DM

19.

1. (A ⊃ B) ⊃ ~C / ~(C • B)	Premise / Conclusion
2. C	Assumption
3. ~~C	2 DN
4. ~(A ⊃ B)	1,3 MT
5. ~(~A ∨ B)	4 Imp
6. ~~A • ~B	5 DM
7. ~B	6 Simp
8. C ⊃ ~B	2–7 CP
9. ~C ∨ ~B	8 Imp
10. ~(C • B)	9 DM

4.

1. (N ⊃ O) ⊃ P	Premise
2. (N • ~O) ⊃ P / P	Premise / Conclusion
3. ~P	Assumption
4. ~(N ⊃ O)	1,3 MT
5. ~(~N ∨ O)	4 Imp
6. ~~N • ~O	5 DM
7. N • ~O	6 DN
8. P	2,7 MP
9. P • ~P	3,8 Conj
10. P	3–9 IP

22.

1. T • ~W / S ⊃ [S ⊃ (R ⊃ S)]	Premise / Conclusion
2. S	Assumption
3. S	Assumption
4. ~R ∨ S	3 Add
5. R ⊃ S	4 Imp
6. S ⊃ (R ⊃ S)	3–5 CP
7. S ⊃ [S ⊃ (R ⊃ S)]	2–6 CP

7.

1. ~J ⊃ (K ∨ L)	Premise
2. J ⊃ M	Premise
3. ~K • ~L / M	Premise / Conclusion
4. ~M	Assumption
5. ~J	2,4 MT
6. K ∨ L	1,5 MP
7. ~(K ∨ L)	3 DM
8. (K ∨ L) • ~(K ∨ L)	6,7 Conj
9. M	4–8 IP

Exercise 9.3B

1.

1. A ∨ B	Premise
2. B ⊃ (C • ~C) / A	Premise / Conclusion
3. ~A	Assumption
4. B	1,3 DS
5. C • ~C	2,4 MP
6. A	3–5 IP

10.

1. (R ∨ S) ⊃ T	Premise
2. V ⊃ T	Premise
3. S ∨ V / T	Premise / Conclusion
4. ~T	Assumption
5. ~ (R ∨ S)	1,4 MT
6. ~R • ~S	5 DM
7. ~S	6 Simp
8. ~V	2,4 MT
9. V	3,7 DS
10. ~V • V	8,9 Conj
11. T	4–10 IP

13.

1. ~(R • ~R)	Assumption
2. T • ~T	Assumption
3. (T • ~T) ∨ (T • ~T)	2 Taut
4. T • ~T	3 Taut
5. ~(T • ~T)	2–4 IP
6. ~(R • ~R) ⊃ ~(T • ~T)	1–5 CP
7. ~(T • ~T)	Assumption
8. R • ~R	Assumption
9. (R • ~R) ∨ (R • ~R)	8 Taut
10. R • ~R	9 Taut
11. ~(R • ~R)	8–10 IP
12. ~(T • ~T) ⊃ ~(R • ~R)	7–11 CP
13. [~(R • ~R) ⊃ ~(T • ~T)] • [~(T • ~T) ⊃ ~(R • ~R)]	6,12 Conj
14. ~(R • ~R) ≡ ~(T • ~T)	13 Equiv

16.

1. (A ⊃ B) ⊃ (C • D)	Premise
2. B ⊃ E	Premise
3. C ⊃ ~ E / ~B	Premise / Conclusion
4. B	Assumption
5. E	2,4 MP
6. ~~E	5 DN
7. ~C	3,6 MT
8. ~A ∨ B	4 Add
9. A ⊃ B	8 Imp
10. C • D	1,9 MT
11. C	10 Simp
12. C • ~C	7,11 Conj
13. ~B	4–12 IP

19.

1. (A ⊃ B) ⊃ C	Premise
2. (A ⊃ D) • (~B ⊃ ~D) / E ∨ C	Premise / Conclusion
3. ~(E ∨ C)	Assumption
4. ~E • ~C	3 DM
5. ~C	4 Simp
6. ~(A ⊃ B)	1,5 MT
7. ~(~A ∨ B)	6 Imp
8. ~~A • ~B	7 DM
9. A ⊃ D	2 Simp
10. ~B ⊃ ~D	2 Simp
11. ~B	8 Simp
12. ~D	10,11 MP
13. ~A	9,12 MT
14. ~~A	8 Simp
15. ~A • ~~A	13,14 Conj
16. E ∨ C	3–15 IP

22.

1. (R ∨ M) ⊃ N	Premise
2. (T • N) ⊃ ~(B ⊃ B) / R ⊃ ~T	Premise / Conclusion
3. R	Assumption
4. T	Assumption
5. R ∨ M	3 Add
6. N	1,5 MP
7. T • N	4,6 Conj
8. ~(B ⊃ B)	2,7 MP
9. ~(~B ∨ B)	8 Imp
10. ~~B • ~B	9 DM
11. B • ~B	10 DN
12. ~T	4–11 IP
13. R ⊃ ~T	3–12 CP

PUTTING IT ALL TOGETHER

I.

1. Simp
4. Conj
7. MP
10. Conj
13. HS

II.

1. DN
4. Imp
7. Taut
10. Exp
13. Com

III.

1.

1 Imp
3 Com
4 Assoc
2,5 DS
6 DN
7 DM

4.

3 Simp
2,4 MT
5 Imp
6 DM
7 Simp
1,8 MT
9 DM
3 Simp
11 DN
10,12 DS

IV.

1. S: The earth's crust is divided into separate tectonic plates; E: Earthquakes occur; M: The plates are moving; L: It's possible that the continents were once joined in a single giant landmass.

S	E	•	(E	⊃	M)	(S	•	M)	⊃	L	/	L
T	T	T	T	T	T	T	T	T		F		F

Valid

1. S	Premise
2. E • (E ⊃ M)	Premise
3. (S • M) ⊃ L / L	Premise / Conclusion
4. E	2 Simp
5. E ⊃ M	2 Simp
6. M	4,5 MP
7. S • M	1,6 Conj
8. L	3,7 MP

4. B: Smith is guilty of burglary; T: Smith took the goods from Jones's residence; C: Jones consented.

B	≡	(T	•	~	C)	(T	•	C)	/	~	B
T		T	F	F	T	T	T	T		F	T

Valid

1. B ≡ (T • ~C)	Premise
2. T • C / ~B	Premise
3. [B ⊃ (T • ~C)] • [(T • ~C) ⊃ B]	1 Equiv
4. B ⊃ (T • ~C)	3 Simp
5. C	2 Simp
6. ~T ∨ C	5 Add
7. ~T ∨ ~~C	6 DN
8. ~(T • ~C)	7 DM
9. ~B	4,8 MT

7. D: Human choices are determined; F: Human choices are free; A: We can act differently than we do; M: We are morally responsible for our actions.

D	∨	F	D	⊃	~	A	~	A	⊃	~	M	M	/	F
F		F	F	T	F	T	F	T	T	F	T	T		F

Valid

1. D ∨ F	Premise
2. D ⊃ ~A	Premise
3. ~A ⊃ ~M	Premise
4. M / F	Premise / Conclusion
5. D ⊃ ~M	2,3 HS
6. ~~M	4 DN
7. ~D	5,6 MT
8. F	1,7 DS

10. G: Giscan is guilty of the murder of Alice Lovelace; M: Giscan had a motive; W: Giscan possessed the murder weapon; A: Giscan was with Sally Alibi; E: Lovelace ended her relationship with Giscan; T: Alibi is telling the truth; J: Alibi is jealous.

G	≡	[M	•	(W	•	~	A)]	E	A	⊃	T	J	⊃	~	T
F	T	T	F	T	F	F	T	T	T	T	T	F	T	F	T

E	⊃	(M	•	J)	W	/	G
T	T	T	F	F	T		F

Valid

1. G ≡ [M • (W • ~A)]	Premise
2. E	Premise
3. A ⊃ T	Premise
4. J ⊃ ~T	Premise
5. E ⊃ (M • J)	Premise
6. W / G	Premise / Conclusion
7. M • J	2,5 MP
8. J	7 Simp
9. ~T	4,8 MP
10. ~A	3,9 MT
11. W • ~A	6,10 Conj
12. M	7 Simp
13. M • (W • ~A)	11,12 Conj
14. {G ⊃ [M • (W • ~A)]} • {[M • (W • ~A)] ⊃ G}	1 Equiv
15. [M • (W • ~A)] ⊃ G	14 Simp
16. G	13,15 MP

13. B: A book repeats what is in the Bible; R: You read the book; W: You waste your time; C: A book contradicts the Bible; S: You commit a sin.

B	∨	C		B	⊃	(R	⊃	W)		C	⊃	(R	⊃	S)		~	(W	∨	S)	/	~	R
F		F		F	T	T	F	F		F	T	T	F	F		T	F	F	F		F	T

Valid

1. B ∨ C	Premise
2. B ⊃ (R ⊃ W)	Premise
3. C ⊃ (R ⊃ S)	Premise
4. ~(W ∨ S) / ~R	Premise / Conclusion
5. [B ⊃ (R ⊃ W)] • [C ⊃ (R ⊃ S)]	2,3 Conj
6. (R ⊃ W) ∨ (R ⊃ S)	1,5 CD
7. (~R ∨ W) ∨ (R ⊃ S)	6 Imp
8. (~R ∨ W) ∨ (~R ∨ S)	7 Imp
9. [(~R ∨ W) ∨ ~R] ∨ S	8 Assoc
10. [~R ∨ (W ∨ ~R)] ∨ S	9 Assoc
11. [~R ∨ (~R ∨ W)] ∨ S	10 Com
12. [(~R ∨ ~R) ∨ W] ∨ S	11 Assoc
13. (~R ∨ W) ∨ S	12 Taut
14. ~R ∨ (W ∨ S)	13 Assoc
15. ~R	4,14 DS

V.

1.

1. ~C	/ C ⊃ D	Premise / Conclusion
2. ~C ∨ D		1 Add
3. C ⊃ D		2 Imp

4.

1. B ⊃ D	/ B ⊃ (B ⊃ D)	Premise / Conclusion
2. (B • B) ⊃ D		1 Taut
3. B ⊃ (B ⊃ D)		2 Exp

7.

1. A ⊃ ~F	/ F ⊃ ~A	Premise / Conclusion
2. ~~F ⊃ ~A		1 Trans
3. F ⊃ ~A		2 DN

10.

1. (A ⊃ C) • (B ⊃ C)		Premise
2. A ∨ B	/ C	Premise / Conclusion
3. C ∨ C		1,2 CD
4. C		3 Taut

13.

1. E ⊃ (F ⊃ G)	/ F ⊃ (E ⊃ G)	Premise / Conclusion
2. (E • F) ⊃ G		1 Exp
3. (F • E) ⊃ G		2 Com
4. F ⊃ (E ⊃ G)		3 Exp

16.

1. ~C ∨ ~D		Premise
2. C	/ ~D	Premise / Conclusion
3. ~~C		2 DN
4. ~D		1,3 DS

19.

1. [~(D ≡ E) • (B ≡ C)] ∨ (G ⊃ A)		Premise
2. ~[~(D ≡ E) • (B ≡ C)]		Premise
3. G	/ A	Premise / Conclusion
4. G ⊃ A		1,2 DS
5. A		3,4 MP

22.

1. W ⊃ X		Premise
2. ~Y ⊃ ~X	/ W ⊃ Y	Premise / Conclusion
3. ~X ⊃ ~W		1 Trans
4. ~Y ⊃ ~W		2,3 HS
5. W ⊃ Y		4 Trans

25.

1. A ⊃ B		Premise
2. (C ⊃ D) • (E ≡ G)		Premise
3. A ∨ C	/ B ∨ D	Premise / Conclusion
4. C ⊃ D		2 Simp
5. (A ⊃ B) • (C ⊃ D)		1,4 Conj
6. B ∨ D		3,5 CD

28.

1. A ⊃ (B • C)		Premise
2. ~(A ⊃ D)	/ B	Premise / Conclusion
3. ~(~A ∨ D)		2 Imp
4. ~~A • ~D		3 M
5. A • ~D		4 DN
5. A		5 Simp
6. B • C		1,6 MP
7. B		7 Simp

31.

1. (H • I) ⊃ J		Premise
2. (I ⊃ J) ⊃ (K ∨ L)	/ ~L ⊃ (H ⊃ K)	Premise / Conclusion
3. H ⊃ (I ⊃ J)		1 Exp
4. H ⊃ (K ∨ L)		2,3 HS
5. ~H ∨ (K ∨ L)		4 Imp
6. ~H ∨ (L ∨ K)		5 Com
7. (L ∨ K) ∨ ~H		6 Com
8. L ∨ (K ∨ ~H)		7 Assoc
9. L ∨ (~H ∨ K)		8 Com
10. L ∨ (H ⊃ K)		9 Imp
11. ~~L ∨ (H ⊃ K)		10 DN
12. ~L ⊃ (H ∨ K)		11 Imp

34.

1. (~E • F) ⊃ G		Premise
2. (H • J) ⊃ (E ∨ J)		Premise
3. ~E • (F ∨ ~J)	/ H ⊃ (J ⊃ G)	Premise / Conclusion
4. (~E • F) ∨ (~E • ~J)		3 Dist
5. (~E • F) ∨ ~(E ∨ J)		4 DM
6. ~G ⊃ ~(~E • F)		1 Trans
7. [~G ⊃ ~(~E • F)] • [(H • J) ⊃ (E ∨ J)]		2, 6 Conj
8. ~~(~E • F) ∨ ~(E ∨ J)		5 DN
9. ~~G ∨ ~(H • J)		7,8 DD
10. G ∨ ~(H • J)		9 DN
11. ~(H • J) ∨ G		10 Com
12. (H • J) ⊃ G		11 Imp
13. H ⊃ (J ⊃ G)		12 Exp

40.

1. [(A • B) ∨ C] ⊃ [D ⊃ (E • F)]		Premise
2. B • ~(A ⊃ E)	/ D ⊃ F	Premise / Conclusion
3. ~(A ⊃ E)		2 Simp
4. ~(~A ∨ E)		3 Imp
5. ~~A • ~E		4 DM
6. A • ~E		5 DN
7. A		6 Simp
8. B		2 Simp
9. A • B		7,8 Conj
10. (A • B) ∨ C		9 Add
11. D ⊃ (E • F)		1,10 MP
12. ~E		6 Simp
13. ~E ∨ ~F		12 Add
14. ~(E • F)		13 DM
15. ~D		11,14 MT
16. ~D ∨ F		15 Add
17. D ⊃ F		16 Imp

37.

1. [K ⊃ (L ⊃ K)] ⊃ (~M ⊃ M) / M	Premise / Conclusion
2. [K ⊃ (L ⊃ K)] ⊃ (~~M ∨ M)	1 Imp
3. [K ⊃ (L ⊃ K)] ⊃ (M ∨ M)	2 DN
4. [K ⊃ (L ⊃ K)] ⊃ M	3 Taut
5. ~M	Assumption
6. ~[K ⊃ (L ⊃ K)]	4,5 MT
7. ~[~K ∨ (L ⊃ K)]	6 Imp
8. ~~K • ~(L ⊃ K)	7 DM
9. K • ~(L ⊃ K)	8 DN
10. K	9 Simp
11. ~(L ⊃ K)	9 Simp
12. ~(~L ∨ K)	11 Imp
13. ~~L • K)	12 DM
14. L • ~K	13 DN
15. ~K	14 Simp
16. K • ~K	10,15 Conj
17. M	5–16 IP

43.

1. (A ∨ B) ⊃ [~(C • D) ⊃ E]	Premise
2. B • C	Premise
3. E ⊃ (F ∨ G)	Premise
4. (B ⊃ ~F) • (C ⊃ ~G) / D	Premise / Conclusion
5. B	2 Simp
6. A ∨ B	5 Add
7. ~(C • D) ⊃ E	1,6 MP
8. B ⊃ ~F	4 Simp
9. ~F	5,8 MP
10. C ⊃ ~G	4 Simp
11. C	2 Simp
12. ~G	10,11 MP
13. ~F • ~G	9,12 Conj
14. ~(F ∨ G)	13 DM
15. ~E	3,14 MT
16. ~~(C • D)	7,15 MT
17. C • D	16 DN
18. D	17 Simp

46.

1. H ⊃ {I • [(J • K) ⊃ (L • M)]}	Premise
2. K ⊃ ~(I • L) / J ⊃ ~(H • K)	Premise / Conclusion
3. J	Assumption
4. H • K	Assumption
5. H	4 Simp
6. I • [(J • K) ⊃ (L • M)]	1,5 MP
7. (J • K) ⊃ (L • M)	6 Simp
8. K	4 Simp
9. J • K	3,8 Conj
10. L • M	7,9 MP
11. I	6 Simp
12. L	10 Simp
13. I • L	11,12 Conj
14. ~~(I • L)	13 DN
15. ~K	2,14 MT
16. K • ~K	8,15 Conj
17. ~(H • K)	4–16 IP
18. J ⊃ ~(H • K)	3–17 CP

CHAPTER 10

Exercise 10.1A

1. Bt

4. Fl

7. ~Sr • Sn

10. Cj ∨ Tj

13. Lw • ~Mw

16. Tm • Cm

19. (Ps ∨ Pi) ⊃ Mo

22. (Cs ⊃ Di) • (~Cs ⊃ Ti)

25. (Bb ∨ Gb) ⊃ Jb

Exercise 10.1B

1. $(x)Ix$

4. $(x)Gx$

7. $(\exists x)Cx$

10. $(x)Ax$

13. $(x)Rx$

Exercise 10.2

1. $(x)(Sx \supset Bx)$

4. $(\exists x)(Kx \cdot Ax)$

7. $(\exists x)(Kx \cdot Sx)$

10. $(\exists x)(Px \cdot Hx)$

13. $(\exists x)(Rx \cdot Sx)$

16. $(x)(Cx \supset Sx)$

19. $(x)(Cx \supset \sim Fx)$

Exercise 10.3

I.

1. $(x)(Px \supset Dx)$

4. $(\exists x)(Sx \cdot Px) \cdot (\exists x)(Sx \cdot \sim Px)$

7. $Om \lor Hm$

10. $(x)(Px \supset Cx) \supset (y)(Gy \supset \sim My)$

13. $(x)[(Px \cdot Sx) \supset Cx]$

16. $(x) \sim Ix$ or $\sim(\exists x)Ix$

19. $\sim(\exists x)Lx$ or $(x) \sim Lx$

22. $(x)[(Px \cdot Sx) \supset Bx]$

25. $(\exists x)(Tx \cdot Lx) \supset (y)[(Ty \cdot By) \supset Wy]$

28. $(x)[(Dx \lor Gx) \supset (Lx \cdot Fx)]$

II.

1. $(\exists x)(Dx \cdot Vx)$

4. $\sim(x)(Px \supset Jx)$

7. $La \cdot \sim Lv$

10. $(\exists x)[(Px \cdot (Wx \lor Rx)]$ or $(\exists x)(Px \cdot Wx) \lor$
    $(\exists x)(Py \cdot Ry)$

13. $\sim(x)(Sx \supset Ax)$

16. $\sim(\exists x)Gx$ or $(x)\sim Gx$

19. $(x)(Dx \supset Bx)$

22. $(\exists x)(Dx \cdot Tx) \supset (x)(Dx \supset Tx)$

25. $(x)[(Px \cdot Cx) \supset Fx]$

28. $(x)[(Ox \lor Lx) \supset Cx] \supset \sim(x)(Cx \supset Yx)$

Exercise 10.4A

1.

1. $(x)Hx \supset \sim(\exists y)My$		Premise
2. $(\exists y)My$	/ $\sim(x)(Hx)$	Premise / Conclusion
3. $\sim\sim(\exists y)My$		2 DN
4. $\sim(x)Hx$		1,3 MT

4.

1. $[\sim(x)Bx \lor (x)Cx] \supset \sim(x)Dx$		Premise
2. $\sim(x)Bx$	/ $\sim(x)Dx$	Premise / Conclusion
3. $\sim(x)Bx \lor (x)Cx$		2 Add
4. $\sim(x)Dx$		1,3 MP

7.

1. $Cl \equiv Dt$	/ $(Cl \supset Dt) \cdot (\sim Cl \supset \sim Dt)$	Premise / Conclusion
2. $(Cl \supset Dt) \cdot (Dt \supset Cl)$		1 Equiv
3. $Dt \supset Cl$		2 Simp
4. $\sim Cl \supset \sim Dt$		3 Trans
5. $Cl \supset Dt$		2 Simp
6. $(Cl \supset Dt) \cdot (\sim Cl \supset \sim Dt)$		4,5 Conj

10.

1. $\sim Ga \lor Ha$		Premise
2. $Fa \supset Ha$		Premise
3. $Ga \lor Fa$	/ Ha	Premise / Conclusion
4. $Ga \supset Ha$		1 Imp
5. $(Ga \supset Ha) \cdot (Fa \supset Ha)$		2,4 Conj
6. $Ha \lor Ha$		3,5 CD
7. Ha		6 Taut

Exercise 10.4B

I.

Statements		Answers
1. $(x)(Px \supset Qx)$	$\sim(\exists x) \sim(Px \supset Qx)$	Equivalent
4. $\sim(x) \sim[Px \supset (Qx \bullet Rx)]$	$(\exists x)[Px \supset (Qx \bullet Rx)]$	Equivalent
7. $\sim(x)[Px \supset (Qx \lor Rx)]$	$(\exists x)[Px \supset (Qx \lor Rx)]$	Not equivalent

II.

1.

1. $\sim(\exists x)(Sx \bullet Rx) \supset Pa$		Premise
2. $(x)(Sx \supset \sim Rx)$	/ Pa	Premise / Conclusion
3. $(x)(\sim Sx \lor \sim Rx)$		2 Imp
4. $(x) \sim(Sx \bullet Rx)$		3 DM
5. $\sim(\exists x)(Sx \bullet Rx)$		4 QN
6. Pa		1,5 MP

4.

1. $(x)Hx \supset \sim(\exists y)My$		Premise
2. $(\exists y)My$	/ $(\exists x) \sim Hx$	Premise / Conclusion
3. $\sim\sim(\exists y)My$		2 DN
4. $\sim(x)Hx$		1,3 MT
5. $(\exists x) \sim Hx$		4 QN

7.

1. $[(x)Cx \bullet (x)Dx] \lor \sim[(\exists x) \sim Cx \supset (x)Dx]$	/ $(x)Cx \equiv (x)Dx$	Premise / Conclusion
2. $[(x)Cx \bullet (x)Dx] \lor \sim[\sim(x)Cx \supset (x)Dx]$		1 QN
3. $[(x)Cx \bullet (x)Dx] \lor \sim[\sim\sim(x)Cx \lor (x)Dx]$		2 Imp
4. $[(x)Cx \bullet (x)Dx] \lor \sim[(x)Cx \lor (x)Dx]$		3 DN
5. $[(x)Cx \bullet (x)Dx] \lor [\sim(x)Cx \bullet \sim(x)Dx]$		4 DM
6. $(x)Cx \equiv (x)Dx$		5 Equiv

Exercise 10.4C

I.

1. EI. Valid.
4. EG. Valid.
7. UG. Invalid.
10. EG. Invalid.

II.

1.

1. $(x)Gx$	/ Ga $\bullet$ Gb	Premise / Conclusion
2. Ga		1 UI
3. Gb		1 UI
4. Ga $\bullet$ Gb		2,3 Conj

4.

1. $\sim Ca$		Premise
2. $(x)(\sim Bx \supset Cx)$	/ Ba	Premise / Conclusion
3. $\sim Ba \supset Ca$		2 UI
4. $\sim\sim Ba$		1,3 MT
5. Ba		4 DN

7.

1. $(x)(Hx \supset Mx)$		Premise
2. Hs	/ Hs $\bullet$ Ms	Premise / Conclusion
3. Hs $\supset$ Ms		1 UI
4. Ms		2,3 MP
5. Hs $\bullet$ Ms		2,4 Conj

10.

1. $(\exists x)Bx \bullet (x)(Cx \supset Dx)$		Premise
2. $\sim Da$	/ $\sim Ca$	Premise / Conclusion
3. $(x)(Cx \supset Dx)$		1 Simp
4. Ca $\supset$ Da		3 UI
5. $\sim Ca$		2,4 MT

13.

1. $(x)Fx$	Premise
2. $(\exists y)Fy \supset (x)Gx$ / Ga	Premise / Conclusion
3. Fa	1 UI
4. $(\exists y)Fy$	3 EG
5. $(x)Gx$	2,4 MP
6. Ga	5 UI

16.

1. $(x)Sx$	Premise
2. $(\exists y)Sy \supset (y)Wy$ / Wa	Premise / Conclusion
3. Sa	1 UI
4. $(\exists y)Sy$	3 EG
5. $(y)Wy$	2,4 MP
6. Wa	5 UI

19.

1. $(\exists x)Tx \supset (y)Gy$	Premise
2. $Ig \lor Tg$	Premise
3. $\sim(\exists x)Ix$	Premise
4. $(x)(Gx \supset \sim Rx)$ / $(x) \sim Rx$	Premise / Conclusion
5. $(x) \sim Ix$	3 QN
6. $\sim Ig$	5 UI
7. Tg	2,6 DS
8. $(\exists x)Tx$	7 EG
9. $(y)Gy$	1,8 MP
10. $Gy \supset \sim Ry$	4 UI
11. Gy	9 UI
12. $\sim Ry$	10,11 MP
13. $(x) \sim Rx$	12 UG

Exercise 10.4D

I.

1.

1. $(x)(Bx \supset \sim Cx)$	Premise
2. Ba	Premise
3. $(x)(Cx \lor Dx)$ / Da	Premise / Conclusion
4. $Ba \supset \sim Ca$	1 UI
5. $\sim Ca$	2,4 MP
6. $Ca \lor Da$	3 UI
7. Da	5,6 DS

4.

1. $(x)(Ax \supset Bx)$	Premise
2. $(x)(Cx \supset \sim Bx)$ / $(x)(Cx \supset \sim Ax)$	Premise / Conclusion
3. $Ax \supset Bx$	1 UI
4. $Cx \supset \sim Bx$	2 UI
5. $\sim Bx \supset \sim Ax$	3 Trans
6. $Cx \supset \sim Ax$	4,5 HS
7. $(x)(Cx \supset \sim Ax)$	6 UG

7.

1. $(x) \sim(\sim Fx \supset Gx)$ / $\sim(x)Gx$	Premise / Conclusion
2. $(x) \sim(\sim\sim Fx \lor Gx)$	1 Imp
3. $(x) \sim(Fx \lor Gx)$	2 DN
4. $(x)(\sim Fx \bullet \sim Gx)$	3 DM
5. $\sim Fa \bullet \sim Ga$	4 UI
6. $\sim Ga$	5 Simp
7. $(\exists x) \sim Gx$	6 EG
8. $\sim(x)Gx$	7 QN

10.

1. (∃x)Gx ⊃ (x) ~Bx		Premise
2. Ga	/ (∃x) ~(Bx • Ax)	Premise / Conclusion
3. (∃x)Gx		2 EG
4. (x) ~Bx		1,3 MP
5. ~Bb		4 UI
6. ~Bb ∨ ~Ab		5 Add
7. ~(Bb • Ab)		6 DM
8. (∃x) ~(Bx • Ax)		7 EG

13.

1. (x)(Ax ≡ Bx)		Premise
2. (x)(Bx ≡ Cx)	/ Ag ⊃ Cg	Premise / Conclusion
3. Ag ≡ Bg		1 UI
4. Bg ≡ Cg		2 UI
5. (Ag ⊃ Bg) • (Bg ⊃ Ag)		3 Equiv
6. (Bg ⊃ Cg) • (Cg ⊃ Bg)		4 Equiv
7. Ag ⊃ Bg		5 Simp
8. Bg ⊃ Cg		6 Simp
9. Ag ⊃ Cg		7,8 HS

16.

1. Fa		Premise
2. ~(∃x)(Fx • Gx)	/ (∃x)(Fx • ~Gx)	Premise / Conclusion
3. (x) ~(Fx • Gx)		2 QN
4. ~(Fa • Ga)		3 UI
5. ~Fa ∨ ~Ga		4 DM
6. ~~Fa		1 DN
7. ~Ga		5,6 DS
8. Fa • ~Ga		1,7 Conj
9. (∃x)(Fx • ~Gx)		8 EG

19.

1. ~(y) ~Ty ⊃ (∃x)Sx		Premise
2. (∃x)Sx ⊃ ~(∃z) ~(Rz • Tz)	/ (∃y)Ty ⊃ (z)(Rz • Tz)	Premise / Conclusion
3. ~(y) ~Ty ⊃ ~(∃z) ~(Rz • Tz)		1,2 HS
4. (∃y)Ty ⊃ ~(∃z) ~(Rz • Tz)		3 QN
5. (∃y)Ty ⊃ (z)(Rz • Tz)		4 QN

22.

1. (x)(Bx • Ax)		Premise
2. (y)(Cy ⊃ ~By)	/ (∃x)(Ax • ~Cx)	Premise / Conclusion
3. Ba • Aa		1 UI
4. Ca ⊃ ~Ba		2 UI
5. Ba		3 Simp
6. ~~Ba		5 DN
7. ~Ca		4,6 MT
8. Aa		3 Simp
9. Aa • ~Ca		8,7 Conj
10. (∃x)(Ax • ~Cx)		9 EG

25.

1. Ta ⊃ (y)Gy	Premise
2. Ia ∨ Ta	Premise
3. ~Ia	Premise
4. (x)(Gx ⊃ Hx) / (x)Hx	Premise / Conclusion
5. Ta	2,3 DS
6. (y)Gy	1,5 MP
7. Gx	6 UI
8. Gx ⊃ Hx	4 UI
9. Hx	7,8 MP
10. (x)Hx	9 UG

28.

1. $(x)\{[Bx \bullet (Cx \lor Dx)] \supset Ex\}$	Premise
2. $(\exists x)(Dx \bullet \sim Ex)$ / $(\exists x) \sim Bx$	Premise / Conclusion
3. $Da \bullet \sim Ea$	2 EI
4. $[Ba \bullet (Ca \lor Da)] \supset Ea$	1 UI
5. Da	3 Simp
6. $\sim Ea$	3 Simp
7. $\sim[Ba \bullet (Ca \lor Da)]$	4,6 MT
8. $\sim Ba \lor \sim(Ca \lor Da)$	7 DM
9. $Ca \lor Da$	5 Add
10. $\sim\sim(Ca \lor Da)$	9 DN
11. $\sim Ba$	8,10 DS
12. $(\exists x) \sim Bx$	11 EG

31.

1. $\sim(\exists x)(Rx \bullet Fx)$	Premise
2. $(x)(Tx \supset Rx)$	Premise
3. $(x)(Dx \supset Fx)$ / $(\exists x)(\sim Tx \lor \sim Dx)$	Premise / Conclusion
4. $(x) \sim(Rx \bullet Fx)$	1 QN
5. $(x)(\sim Rx \lor \sim Fx)$	4 DM
6. $Tx \supset Rx$	2 UI
7. $Dx \supset Fx$	3 UI
8. $\sim Rx \lor \sim Fx$	5 UI
9. $(Tx \supset Rx) \bullet (Dx \supset Fx)$	6,7 Conj
10. $\sim Tx \lor \sim Dx$	8,9 DD
11. $(\exists x)(\sim Tx \lor \sim Dx)$	10 EG

34.

1. $(z)(Sz \supset Tz)$	Premise
2. $(z)Sz$ / $Ta \bullet Tb$	Premise / Conclusion
3. $Sa \supset Ta$	1 UI
4. Sa	2 UI
5. Ta	3,4 MP
6. $Sb \supset Tb$	1 UI
7. Sb	2 UI
8. Tb	6,7 MP
9. $Ta \bullet Tb$	5,8 Conj

II.

1. $Tx = x$ is a philosopher; $Px = x$ is a Platonist; $Ax = x$ is an Aristotelian

1. $(x)[Tx \supset (Px \lor Ax)]$	Premise
2. $\sim Pj \bullet Tj$ / Aj	Premise / Conclusion
3. $Tj \supset (Pj \lor Aj)$	1 UI
4. Tj	2 Simp
5. $Pj \lor Aj$	3,4 MP
6. $\sim Pj$	2 Simp
7. Aj	5,6 DS

4. $Ex = x$ is an engineer; $Gx = x$ is good at math; $Ux = x$ understands basic algebra

1. $(x)(Ex \supset Gx)$	Premise
2. $Em \supset Gm$	Premise
3. $(x)(Gx \supset Ux)$	Premise
4. $\sim Um$ / $\sim Em$	Premise / Conclusion
5. $Gm \supset Um$	3 UI
6. $\sim Gm$	4,5 MT
7. $\sim Em$	2,6 MT

Exercise 10.4E

1.

1. $(x)[(Sx \lor Cx) \supset Ex]$ / $(x)(Cx \supset Ex)$	Premise / Conclusion
2. Cx	Assumption
3. $(Sx \lor Cx) \supset Ex$	1 UI
4. $Sx \lor Cx$	2 Add
5. Ex	3,4 MP
6. $Cx \supset Ex$	2–5 CP
7. $(x)(Cx \supset Ex)$	6 UG

4.

1. $(x)(Dx \supset Ex)$	Premise
2. $(x)[(Dx \bullet Ex) \supset Fx]$ / $(x)(Dx \supset Fx)$	Premise / Conclusion
3. $Dx \supset Ex$	1 UI
4. $(Dx \bullet Ex) \supset Fx$	2 UI
5. Dx	Assumption
6. Ex	3,5 MP
7. $Dx \bullet Ex$	5,6 Conj
8. Fx	4,7 MP
9. $Dx \supset Fx$	5–8 CP
10. $(x)(Dx \supset Fx)$	9 UG

7.

1. $(x)[(Ax \lor Bx) \supset Cx]$	Premise
2. $(x)[Cx \supset (\sim Ax \lor Dx)]$ / $(x)(Ax \supset Dx)$	Premise / Conclusion
3. Ax	Assumption
4. $(Ax \lor Bx) \supset Cx$	1 UI
5. $Ax \lor Bx$	3 Add
6. Cx	4,5 MP
7. $Cx \supset (\sim Ax \lor Dx)$	2 UI
8. $\sim Ax \lor Dx$	6,7 MP
9. $\sim\sim Ax$	3 DN
10. Dx	8,9 DS
11. $Ax \supset Dx$	3–10 CP
12. $(x)(Ax \supset Dx)$	11 UG

10.

1. $(x)(Px \equiv Tx)$	Premise
2. $(x)(Tx \equiv Ax)$ / $Pm \supset Am$	Premise / Conclusion
3. Pm	Assumption
4. $Pm \equiv Tm$	1 UI
5. $Tm \equiv Am$	2 UI
6. $(Pm \supset Tm) \bullet (Tm \supset Pm)$	4 Equiv
7. $(Tm \supset Am) \bullet (Am \supset Tm)$	5 Equiv
8. $Pm \supset Tm$	6 Simp
9. $Tm \supset Am$	7 Simp
10. Tm	3,8 MP
11. Am	9,10 MP
12. $Pm \supset Am$	3–11 CP

13.

1. (x)[Bx ⊃ (Cx ∨ Dx)]	Premise
2. (x)(Dx ⊃ ~Ex) / (x)[(Bx • Ex) ⊃ Cx]	Premise / Conclusion
3. Bx ⊃ (Cx ∨ Dx)	1 UI
4. Dx ⊃ ~Ex	2 UI
5. Bx • Ex	Assumption
6. Bx	5 Simp
7. Cx ∨ Dx	3,6 MP
8. Ex	5 Simp
9. ~~Ex	8 DN
10. ~Dx	4,9 MT
11. Cx	7,10 DS
12. (Bx • Ex) ⊃ Cx	5–11 CP
13. (x)[(Bx • Ex) ⊃ Cx]	12 UG

16.

1. (x)[(Bx • ~Cx) ⊃ Dx]	Premise
2. (x)(Dx ⊃ Cx) / (x)(Bx ⊃ Cx)	Premise / Conclusion
3. (Bx • ~Cx) ⊃ Dx	1 UI
4. Dx ⊃ Cx	2 UI
5. Bx	Assumption
6. ~Cx	Assumption
7. Bx • ~Cx	5,6 Conj
8. Dx	3,7 MP
9. Cx	4,8 MP
10. Cx • ~Cx	6,9 Conj
11. Cx	6–10 IP
12. Bx ⊃ Cx	5–11 CP
13. (x)(Bx ⊃ Cx)	12 UG

19.

1. (∃x)(Bx • ~Cx)	Premise
2. (x){[Bx • ~(Dx ∨ Ex)] ⊃ Cx} / (∃x)[Dx ∨ (Ex • Bx)]	Premise / Conclusion
3. Ba • ~Ca	1 EI
4. [Ba • ~(Da ∨ Ea)] ⊃ Ca	2 UI
5. Ba	3 Simp
6. ~Ca	3 Simp
7. ~[Ba • ~(Da ∨ Ea)]	4,6 MT
8. ~Ba ∨ ~~(Da ∨ Ea)	7 DM
9. ~~Ba	5 DN
10. ~~(Da ∨ Ea)	8,9 DS
11. Da ∨ Ea	10 DN
12. ~Da	Assumption
13. Ea	11,12 DS
14. Ea • Ba	5,13 Conj
15. ~Da ⊃ (Ea • Ba)	12–14 CP
16. ~~Da ∨ (Ea • Ba)	15 Imp
17. Da ∨ (Ea • Ba)	16 DN
18. (∃x)[Dx ∨ (Ex • Bx)]	17 EG

Exercise 10.5A

1. Lmc

4. Riad

7. (∃x)(Axg • Cx)

10. Lfj

13. (x)(Px ⊃ ~Six) Px means x is a place

16. (∃x)(Dx • Hix)

19. (∃x)(Px • Bsxt)

22. (∃x)(Dx • Axh)

25. Ams • Asm

28. (∃x)[(Tx • Ax) • Sx]

Exercise 10.5B

1. (∃x)(Px • Lxm)

4. (x)(y)[(Wx • Dy) ⊃ Axy]

7. (x)[Dx ⊃ (∃y)(Ny • Liyx)]

10. $(x)[Px \supset (\exists y)(Py \bullet Fxy)]$

13. $(\exists x)(\exists y)[(Px \bullet By) \bullet Styx]$

16. $\sim(\exists x)(Rx \bullet Ixg)$ or $(x)(Rx \supset \sim Ixg)$

19. $(x)[(Px \bullet Wmx) \supset Wlx]$

22. $(x)[(Rx \lor Hx) \supset (\exists y)(Py \bullet Dxy)]$

25. $(x)(Ax \supset (\exists y)\{Sy \bullet [Ry \supset (z)(Sz \supset Fz)]\})$

28. $(x)(y)[(Mx \bullet Lxy) \supset Kxy]$ [Each man kills everything
                                              he loves]

   or

   $(x)[Mx \supset (\exists y)(Lxy \bullet Kxy)]$ [Each man kills something
                                              he loves]

31. $(x)(y)\{[(Cx \bullet Py) \bullet (Lyg \bullet Hxy)] \supset \sim Jgx\}$

34. $(x)(\exists y)(\exists z)\{[(Px \bullet Py) \bullet Tz] \bullet Lxyz\}$

37. $(x)(\exists y)[(Px \bullet Py) \bullet \sim Lxy]$

40. $(\exists x)(Sx \bullet Fx) \supset (y)(Sy \supset Ry)$

Exercise 10.5C

I.

1.

1. Ca ⊃ (Mp ⊃ Hap)		Premise
2. ~Hap	/ ~Ca ∨ ~Mp	Premise / Conclusion
3. (Ca • Mp) ⊃ Hap		1 Exp
4. ~(Ca • Mp)		2,3 MT
5. ~Ca ∨ ~Mp		4 DM

4.

1. (∃y)(x)Axy	/ (x)(∃y)Axy	Premise / Conclusion
2. (x)Axb		1 EI
3. Axb		2 UI
4. (∃y)Axy		3 EG
5. (x)(∃y)Axy		4 UG

7.

1. Aa / (x)(Ax ⊃ Bx) ⊃ (∃x)(Ax • Bx)	Premise / Conclusion
2. (x)(Ax ⊃ Bx)	Assumption
3. Aa ⊃ Ba	2 UI
4. Ba	1,3 MP
5. Aa • Ba	1,4 Conj
6. (∃x)(Ax • Bx)	5 EG
7. (x)(Ax ⊃ Bx) ⊃ (∃x)(Ax • Bx)	2–6 CP

10.

1. (x)[(~Mxa ∨ Nx) ⊃ Lxx)]		Premise
2. (∃y) ~Lyy	/ (∃x)Mxa	Premise / Conclusion
3. ~Lbb		2 EI
4. (~Mba ∨ Nb) ⊃ Lbb		1 UI
5. ~(~Mba ∨ Nb)		3,4 MT
6. ~~Mba • ~Nb		5 DM
7. Mba • ~Nb		6 DN
8. Mba		7 Simp
9. (∃x)Mxa		8 EG

13.

1. (x)(Exx ∨ Qx)		Premise
2. (y) ~Eyy		Premise
3. (z)(Qz ⊃ Kz)	/ (x)Kx	Premise / Conclusion
4. Exx ∨ Qx		1 UI
5. ~Exx		2 UI
6. Qx ⊃ Kx		3 UI
7. Qx		4,5 DS
8. Kx		6,7 MP
9. (x)Kx		8 UG

16.

1. $(x)[(Hx \cdot Gx) \supset Cx]$	Premise
2. $(y)Gy \cdot \sim(x)Mxa$ / $(x)(Hx \supset Cx)$	Premise / Conclusion
3. Hx	Assumption
4. $(y)Gy$	2 Simp
5. Gx	4 UI
6. $(Hx \cdot Gx) \supset Cx$	1 UI
7. $Hx \cdot Gx$	3,5 Conj
8. Cx	6,7 MP
9. $Hx \supset Cx$	3–8 CP
10. $(x)(Hx \supset Cx)$	9 UG

22.

1. $(x)(Cxx \supset Sx)$	Premise
2. $(y)[(Sy \lor Tyy) \supset Wy]$ / $(x)[(Cxx \cdot \sim Kx) \supset (Wx \cdot \sim Kx)]$	Premise / Conclusion
3. $Cxx \cdot \sim Kx$	Assumption
4. $Cxx \supset Sx$	1 UI
5. Cxx	3 Simp
6. Sx	4,5 MP
7. $(Sx \lor Txx) \supset Wx$	2 UI
8. $Sx \lor Txx$	6 Add
9. Wx	7,8 MP
10. $\sim Kx$	3 Simp
11. $Wx \cdot \sim Kx$	9,10 Conj
12. $(Cxx \cdot \sim Kx) \supset (Wx \cdot \sim Kx)$	3–11 CP
13. $(x)[(Cxx \cdot \sim Kx) \supset (Wx \cdot \sim Kx)]$	12 UG

19.

1. $(z)(y)[(\exists x)Myx \supset Mzy]$	Premise
2. Mba / $(\exists x)(\exists y)Mxy$	Premise / Conclusion
3. $(\exists x)Mbx$	2 EG
4. $(y)[(\exists x)Myx \supset Mzy]$	1 UI
5. $(\exists x)Mbx \supset Mzb$	4 UI
6. Mzb	3,5 MP
7. $(\exists y)Mzy$	6 EG
8. $(\exists x)(\exists y)Mxy$	7 EG

II.

1. $Sx = x$ is a student; $Rx = x$ is in the room; $Oxy = x$ is older than y

1. $(x)[(Sx \cdot Rx) \supset Oxd]$		Premise
2. $Rj \supset Sj$		Premise
3. Rj	/ Ojd	Premise / Conclusion
4. Sj		2,3 MP
5. $(Sj \cdot Rj) \supset Ojd$		1 UI
6. $Sj \cdot Rj$		3,4 Conj
7. Ojd		5,6 MP

4. $Sx = x$ is a smartphone; $Ex = x$ is an electronic gadget; $Oxy = x$ owns y

1. $(x)(Sx \supset Ex)$ $/ (x)(y)[(Oxy \bullet Sy) \supset (Oxy \bullet Ey)]$	Premise / Conclusion
2. $Oxy \bullet Sy$	Assumption
3. $Sy \supset Ey$	1 UI
4. Sy	2 Simp
5. Ey	3,4 MP
6. Oxy	2 Simp
7. $Oxy \bullet Ey$	5,6 Conj
8. $(Oxy \bullet Sy) \supset (Oxy \bullet Ey)$	2–7 CP
9. $(y)[(Oxy \bullet Sy) \supset (Oxy \bullet Ey)]$	8 UG
10. $(x)(y)[(Oxy \bullet Sy) \supset (Oxy \bullet Ey)]$	9 UG

Exercise 10.6A

1. $p = h$

4. $(\exists x)[(Fx \bullet Cx) \bullet Mx]$

7. $(\exists x)[Wxm \bullet (y)(Wym \supset y = x) \bullet Ax]$

10. $(x)(y)(z)[(Mx \bullet Lx \bullet My \bullet Ly \bullet Mz \bullet Lz) \supset$
    $(x = y \vee x = z \vee y = z)]$

13. $p = h \bullet r \neq c$

16. $Pm \bullet Pr \bullet (x)(Px \supset x = m \vee x = r)$

19. $(\exists x)[Dxb \bullet (y)(Dyb \supset y = x) \bullet Fxj]$

22. $(x)(y)(z)[(Px \bullet Tx \bullet Py \bullet Ty \bullet Pz \bullet Tz) \supset$
    $(x = y \vee x = z \vee y = z)]$

25. $Wdw \bullet Wda \bullet \sim Wdo \bullet (x)[(Cx \bullet x \neq o) \supset Wdx]$

Exercise 10.6B

1.

1. $(x)(Rx \supset x = g)$	Premise
2. Rb $/ (\exists x)Rg$	Premise / Conclusion
3. $Rb \supset b = g$	1 UI
4. $b = g$	2,3 MP
5. Rg	2,4 IT

4.

1. $(z)(z = g)$	Premise
2. $(\exists z)Fz$ $/ Fg$	Premise / Conclusion
3. Fa	2 EI
4. $a = g$	UI
5. Fg	3,4 IT

7.

1. $(x)(Tx \vee x \neq p)$ $/ Tp \vee Rn$	Premise / Conclusion
2. $\sim(Tp \vee Rn)$	Assumption
3. $\sim Tp \bullet \sim Rn$	2 DM
4. $Tp \vee p \neq p$	1 UI
5. $\sim Tp$	3 Simp
6. $p \neq p$	4,5 DS
7. $p = p$	IR
8. $(p = p) \bullet (p \neq p)$	6,7 Conj
9. $Tp \vee Rn$	2–8 IP

10.

1. $Ss \bullet (x)(Sx \supset f = x)$	Premise
2. $Rp \bullet (x)(Rx \supset x = s)$ $/ (\exists x)(Rx \bullet Sx)$	Premise / Conclusion
3. Ss	1 Simp
4. Rp	2 Simp
5. $(x)(Sx \supset f = x)$	1 Simp
6. $(x)(Rx \supset x = s)$	2 Simp
7. $Ss \supset f = s$	5 UI
8. $Rp \supset p = s$	6 UI
9. $f = s$	3,7 MP
10. $p = s$	4,8 MP
11. $s = p$	10 IS
12. Sp	3,11 IT
13. $Rp \bullet Sp$	4,12 Conj
14. $(\exists x)(Rx \bullet Sx)$	13 EG

Exercise 10.7

I.

1. All primates are mammals.
   All mammals are animals.
   All animals are primates.

4. All Persians are cats.
   All Siamese are cats.
   Everything is a cat.

7. If roosters exist, then pigs exist.
   All pigs are roosters.

10. All monkeys are primates.
    All monkeys are mammals.
    All mammals are primates.

II.

1. For a universe containing two members, we have

(Ba	•	Fa)	∨	(Bb	•	Fb)	(Ba	⊃	Ga)	•	(Bb	⊃	Gb)	/	Ga	•	Gb
T	T	T	T	F	F	T	T	T	T	T	F	T	F		T	F	F

4. For a universe containing two members, we have

(Pa	⊃	~	Ta)	•	(Pb	⊃	~	Tb)	Ta	∨	Tb	/	~	Pa	•	~	Pb
F	T	F	T	T	T	T	T	F	T	T	F		T	F	F	F	T

7. For a universe containing one member, we have

Pa	⊃	Ma	Ma	⊃	Ra	/	Pa	•	Ra
F	T	T	T	T	T		F	F	T

10. For a universe containing one member, we have

Ma	∨	Ta	Ma	/	~Ta
T	T	F	T		F

7. $(x)[(Px • Hgx) ⊃ Hxx]$

10. $(x)(Gx ⊃ \{Dx ≡ (y)[(Cy • Ay) ⊃ Vy]\})$

13. $(x)[(∃y)Mxy ⊃ (∃z)Dxz] • ~(x)[(∃y)Dxy ⊃ (∃z)Mxz]$

16. $(x)\{Px ⊃ [(∃y)(Myx • Cxy) • (∃z)(Jzx • ~Cxz)]\}$

19. $(∃y)(Ty • (x)(Px ⊃ Fxy)) • (∃x)[Px • (y)(Ty ⊃ Fxy)] • ~(x)[Px ⊃ (y)(Ty ⊃ Fxy)]$

Putting It All Together

I.

1. If Bob is sober, he is coherent.

4. Something is wet and clammy.

7. Either this apartment or the next one is available, but this one is not suitable.

10. There's a student who is either very slow or not interested.

13. Every positively charged particle attracts any negatively charged particle.

II.

1. $~(∃x)(Bx ∨ Wx) • (y)Gy$

4. $(x)(y)[(Px • Ty) ⊃ ~Bxy]$

III.

1. MT

4. Exp

7. Imp

10. DD

IV.

1. Line 3: a cannot be used for EI since it has been used before.

4. Line 3: QN requires a change of quantifier.

V.

1.

1. Tm	Premise
2. (∃y)(Ey • ~Cmy)	Premise
3. (x){Tx ⊃ [Px ⊃ (y)(Ey ⊃ Cxy)]} / ~Pm	Premise / Conclusion
4. Tm ⊃ [Pm ⊃ (y)(Ey ⊃ Cmy)]	3 UI
5. Pm ⊃ (y)(Ey ⊃ Cmy)	1,4 MP
6. ~(y)~(Ey • ~Cmy)	2 QN
7. ~(y)(~Ey ∨ ~~Cmy)	6 DM
8. ~(y)(~Ey ∨ Cmy)	7 DN
9. ~(y)(Ey ⊃ Cmy)	Imp
10. ~Pm	5,9 MT

4.

1. (x){(Px • Mx) ⊃ (y)[(Fy • Uxy) ⊃ Ty]}	Premise
2. (x)(Tx ⊃ Hx)	Premise
3. Pa • Ma / (x)[(Fx • Uax) ⊃ Hx]	Premise / Conclusion
4. (Pa • Ma) ⊃ (y)[(Fy • Uay) ⊃ Ty]	1 UI
5. (y)[(Fy • Uay) ⊃ Ty]	3,4 MP
6. (Fy • Uay) ⊃ Ty	5 UI
7. Ty ⊃ Hy	2 UI
8. (Fy • Uay) ⊃ Hy	6,7 HS
9. (x)[(Fx • Uax) ⊃ Hx]	8 UG

7.

1. (x)[Dx ⊃ (Ax ∨ Wx)]	Premise
2. (x)[(Ax ⊃ Vx) • (Wx ⊃ Bx)]	Premise
3. (x)[(Dx ∨ Bx) ⊃ ~Lix] / (x)(Dx ⊃ ~Lix)	Premise / Conclusion
4. Dx	Assumption
5. (Dx ∨ Bx) ⊃ ~Lix	3 UI
6. Dx ∨ Bx	4 Add
7. ~Lix	5,6 MP
8. Dx ⊃ ~Lix	4–7 CP
9. (x)(Dx ⊃ ~Lix)	8 UG

10.

1. (x)(Dx ⊃ Ex)	Premise
2. (x)[Ex ⊃ (∃y)Cyx]	Premise
3. (x)(y)[Cxy ⊃ (Ex ∨ Ax)] / (x){Dx ⊃ (∃y)[(Ey ∨ Ay) • Cyx]}	Premise / Conclusion
4. Dx	Assumption
5. Dx ⊃ Ex	1 UI
6. Ex ⊃ (∃y)Cyx	2 UI
7. Ex	4,5 MP
8. (∃y)Cyx	6,7 MP
9. Cbx	8 EI
10. (y)[Cby ⊃ (Eb ∨ Ab)]	3 UI
11. Cbx ⊃ (Eb ∨ Ab)	10 UI
12. (Eb ∨ Ab)	9,11 MP
13. (Eb ∨ Ab) • Cbx	9,12 Conj
14. (∃y)[(Ey ∨ Ay) • Cyx]	13 EG
15. Dx ⊃ (∃y)[(Ey ∨ Ay) • Cyx]	4–14 CP
16. (x){Dx ⊃ (∃y)[(Ey ∨ Ay) • Cbx]}	15 UG

13.

1. $(x)[(\exists y)(Cy \bullet Axy) \supset \sim Mx]$	Premise
2. $(x)(Dx \supset Cx)$	Premise /
$\qquad\qquad / (x)(y)[(Mx \bullet Dy) \supset \sim Axy]$	Conclusion
3. $(\exists y)(Cy \bullet Axy) \supset \sim Mx$	1 UI
4. $\sim\sim Mx \supset \sim(\exists y)(Cy \bullet Axy)$	3 Trans
5. $Mx \supset \sim(\exists y)(Cy \bullet Axy)$	4 DN
6. Mx	Assumption
7. $\sim(\exists y)(Cy \bullet Axy)$	5,6 MP
8. $(y) \sim(Cy \bullet Axy)$	7 QN
9. $\sim(Cy \bullet Axy)$	8 UI
10. $\sim Cy \vee \sim Axy$	9 DM
11. $Cy \supset \sim Axy$	10 Imp
12. $Dy \supset Cy$	2 UI
13. $Dy \supset \sim Axy$	11,12 HS
14. $Mx \supset (Dy \supset \sim Axy)$	6–13 CP
15. $(Mx \bullet Dy) \supset \sim Axy$	14 Exp
16. $(y)[(Mx \bullet Dy) \supset \sim Axy]$	15 UG
17. $(x)(y)[(Mx \bullet Dy) \supset \sim Axy]$	16 UG

VI.

1.

1. $(\exists x)Px \supset (y)Qy$ $\qquad / (y)(\exists x)(Px \supset Qy)$	Premise / Conclusion
2. Pa	Assumption
3. $(\exists x)Px$	2 EG
4. $(y)Qy$	1,3 MP
5. Qy	4 UI
6. $Pa \supset Qy$	2–5 CP
7. $(\exists x)(Px \supset Qy)$	6 EG
8. $(y)(\exists x)(Px \supset Qy)$	7 UG

4.

1. $(x)[Px \supset (Qx \vee Rx)]$	Premise
2. $(\exists x)(Px \bullet \sim Rx)$ $\qquad / (\exists x)Qx$	Premise / Conclusion
3. $Pa \bullet \sim Ra$	2 EI
4. Pa	3 Simp
5. $Pa \supset (Qa \vee Ra)$	1 UI
6. $Qa \vee Ra$	4,5 MP
7. $\sim Ra$	3 Simp
8. Qa	6,7 DS
9. $(\exists x)Qx$	8 EG

7.

1. $(x)(Px \equiv Qx)$	Premise
2. $(x)[Px \supset (\exists y)Rxy]$	Premise
3. $(\exists x)Qx$ $\qquad / (\exists x)(\exists y)Rxy$	Premise / Conclusion
4. Qa	3 EI
5. $Pa \equiv Qa$	1 UI
6. $(Pa \supset Qa) \bullet (Qa \supset Pa)$	5 Equiv
7. $Qa \supset Pa$	6 Simp
8. Pa	4,7 MP
9. $Pa \supset (\exists y)Ray$	2 UI
10. $(\exists y)Ray$	8,9 MP
11. $(\exists x)(\exists y)Rxy$	10 EG

10.

1. Tb • (x)(Tx ⊃ x = b)		Premise
2. b ≠ g		Premise
3. Rg • Wg	/ (∃x)(Rx • ~Tx)	Premise / Conclusion
4. (x)(Tx ⊃ x = b)		1 Simp
5. Tg ⊃ g = b		4 UI
6. g ≠ b		2 IS
7. ~Tg		5,6 MT
8. Rg		3 Simp
9. Rg • ~Tg		7,8 Conj
10. (∃x)(Rx • ~Tx)		9 EG

13.

1. (x)(Pxa ⊃ Rx)		Premise
2. (∃x)(Qx • Pxb)		Premise
3. (x)(Qx ⊃ ~Rx)	/ ~(x)(Pxb ⊃ Pxa)	Premise / Conclusion
4. Qc • Pcb		2 EI
5. Qc		4 Simp
6. Qc ⊃ ~Rc		3 UI
7. ~Rc		5,6 MP
8. Pca ⊃ Rc		1 UI
9. ~Pca		7,8 MT
10. Pcb		4 Simp
11. Pcb • ~Pca		9,10 Conj
12. ~~(Pcb • ~Pca)		11 DN
13. ~(~Pcb ∨ ~~Pca)		12 DM
14. ~(Pcb ⊃ ~~Pca)		13 Imp
15. ~(Pcb ⊃ Pca)		14 DN
16. (∃x) ~(Pxb ⊃ Pxa)		15 EG
17. ~(x)(Pxb ⊃ Pxa)		16 QN

16.

1. (∃x)(Px • ~Qx) ⊃ Ra		Premise
2. (∃x)Rx ⊃ (y)(Py ⊃ Qy)	/ (x)(Px ⊃ Qx)	Premise / Conclusion
3. ~(x)(Px ⊃ Qx)		Assumption
4. (∃x) ~(Px ⊃ Qx)		3 QN
5. ~(Pb ⊃ Qb)		4 EI
6. ~(~Pb ∨ Qb)		5 Imp
7. ~~Pb • ~Qb		6 DM
8. Pb • ~Qb		7 DN
9. (∃x)(Px • ~Qx)		8 EG
10. Ra		1,9 MP
11. (∃x)Rx		10 EG
12. (y)(Py ⊃ Qy)		2,11 MP
13. Py ⊃ Qy		12 UI
14. (x)(Px ⊃ Qx)		13 UG
15. (x)(Px ⊃ Qx) • ~(x)(Px ⊃ Qx)		3,14 Conj
16. (x)(Px ⊃ Qx)		3–15 IP

19.

1. $(\exists x)[Qx \bullet (Rx \lor Sx)]$	Premise
2. $(x)[(Qx \lor Sx) \supset Tx]$	Premise
3. $(x) \sim(Px \lor Tx)$	Premise /
$\quad\quad\quad / (\exists x)[(Qx \bullet Rx) \bullet \sim Px]$	Conclusion
4. $Qa \bullet (Ra \lor Sa)$	1 EI
5. $(Qa \lor Sa) \supset Ta$	2 UI
6. $\sim(Pa \lor Ta)$	3 UI
7. $\sim Pa \bullet \sim Ta$	6 DM
8. Qa	4 Simp
9. $\sim Pa$	7 Simp
10. $\sim Ta$	7 Simp
11. $\sim(Qa \lor Sa)$	5,10 MT
12. $\sim Qa \bullet \sim Sa$	11 DM
13. $\sim Sa$	12 Simp
14. $Ra \lor Sa$	4 Simp
15. Ra	13,14 DS
16. $Qa \bullet Ra$	8,15 Conj
17. $(Qa \bullet Ra) \bullet \sim Pa$	9,16 Conj
18. $(\exists x)[(Qx \bullet Rx) \bullet \sim Px]$	17 EG

22.

1. $(x)\{Px \supset (y)[(Qy \bullet Rxy) \supset (\exists z)(Sz \bullet Txyz)]\}$	Premise
2. $(x)(\exists y)(Sx \equiv \sim Sy)$	Premise /
$\quad / (\exists x)(\exists y)[Px \bullet (Qy \bullet Rxy)] \supset \sim(z)Sz$	Conclusion
3. $(\exists x)(\exists y)[Px \bullet (Qy \bullet Rxy)]$	Assumption
4. $(\exists y)[Pa \bullet (Qy \bullet Ray)]$	3 EI
5. $Pa \bullet (Qb \bullet Rab)$	4 EI
6. $Pa \supset (y)[(Qy \bullet Ray) \supset (\exists z)(Sz \bullet Tayz)]$	1 UI
7. Pa	5 Simp
8. $(y)[(Qy \bullet Ray) \supset (\exists z)(Sz \bullet Tayz)]$	6,7 MP
9. $(Qb \bullet Rab) \supset (\exists z)(Sz \bullet Tabz)$	8 UI
10. $Qb \bullet Rab$	5 Simp
11. $(\exists z)(Sz \bullet Tabz)$	9,10 MP
12. $Sc \bullet Tabc$	11 EI
13. $(\exists y)(Sc \equiv \sim Sy)$	2 UI
14. $Sc \equiv \sim Sd$	13 EI
15. $(Sc \supset \sim Sd) \bullet (\sim Sd \supset Sc)$	14 Equiv
16. $Sc \supset \sim Sd$	15 Simp
17. Sc	12 Simp
18. $\sim Sd$	16,17 MP
19. $(\exists z)\sim Sz$	18 EG
20. $\sim(z)Sz$	19 QN
21. $(\exists x)(\exists y)[Px \bullet (Qy \bullet Rxy)] \supset \sim(z)Sz$	3–20 CP

CHAPTER 11

Exercise 11.1

1. This could be true or false, depending on the restaurant. Rule 1: Consider the quality of the different dishes served, the quality of the food at different times of day and on different days of the week, and the quality when the restaurant is crowded as well as when it is not. Rule 2: Visit the restaurant under the most favorable circumstances; ask people who patronize the restaurant regularly. Rule 3: Consider what is the most likely explanation for the quality of the food.

4. To our knowledge, this is false. Rule 1: Consider different breeds; observe their behavior indoors as well as outdoors. Rule 2: Ask dog owners whether they have seen their dogs not lying down in this manner. Rule 3: Is there any evolutionary reason why dogs might have this behavior?

7. This is true of many but not all doctors. Rule 1: Consider doctors in different specialties, regions (rural as well as urban), and institutions (hospitals, clinics, private practice, etc.). Rule 2: Consider doctors working in free clinics for the poor or in programs in poor countries abroad. Rule 3: What does the nature and value of doctors' services suggest about their expected income?

10. This is false. Rule 1: Consider geniuses in a variety of subjects, from a variety of historical periods. Rule 2: Look for geniuses who were normal in personality and mode of life. Rule 3: Is there any reason to think that exceptional mental ability necessarily has the sorts of effects on personality or mode of life that we would describe as eccentric?

13. This is true of most glass, but not all (depending on what standard of fragility one uses). Rule 1: Consider different types of glass—windows, stained glass, car windshields, wine glasses, etc. Rule 2: Bulletproof glass is a disconfirming instance. Rule 3: Glass is a material. Is it plausible that materials of the same type have the same properties?

Exercise 11.3

1. Conclusion: ScourClean use causes a clean sink (positive). Cause: ScourClean. Effect: clean. Method of difference.

Case 1:	ScourClean,	dirty sink	→	clean
Case 2:	leading cleanser,	dirty sink	→	~clean

4. Conclusion: Sunlight causes tall growth (positive). Cause: sunlight. Effect: tall growth. Method of difference.

Case 1:	zinnias,	soil,	water,	sun	→	tall growth
Case 2:	zinnias,	soil,	water,	~sun	→	~tall growth

7. Conclusion: Regulations do not cause decreased innovation (negative). Cause: regulations. Effect: decreased innovation. Negative use of method of difference.

Case 1:	~product safety regulations,	widget industry	→	innovation
Case 2:	product safety regulations,	widget industry	→	innovation

10. Conclusion: gmail caused emails to bounce (positive). Cause: gmail. Effect: emails bounced. Method of agreement.

Case 1:	gmail address,	new contact,	~attachment	→	email bounced
Case 2:	gmail address,	reply to received email,	~attachment	→	email bounced
Case 3:	gmail address,	frequently emailed,	~attachment	→	email bounced
Case 4:	gmail address,	frequently emailed,	attachment	→	email bounced

Exercise 11.4

I.

1. Conclusion: Sleep affects energy level. Cause: sleep. Effect: energy. Method of concomitant variations.

Case 1:	less than 7 hours of sleep	→	less energy
Case 2:	7 hours of sleep	→	normal energy
Case 3:	more than 7 hours of sleep	→	more energy

4. Conclusion: Overhead spotlight caused shadow. Cause: Brightness of overhead spotlight. Effect: shadow on person's face. Concomitant variations.

Case 1:	full brightness	→	dark shadow
Case 2:	half brightness	→	moderately dark shadow
Case 3:	quarter brightness	→	faint shadow

II.

1. Cause: some problem up ahead. Effect: traffic jam. Method of residues.

4. Cause: mosquitoes. Effect: transmission of yellow fever. Joint method:

Method of agreement: Residents of the general Army base and Building 2 both contracted the fever. Exposure to mosquitoes was the only factor they had in common.

Method of difference: Both the Army base and Building 1 had exposure to fever victims, but the Army base residents contracted the fever while Building 1 residents did not.

Living Quarters	Exposure to Fever Victims	Exposure to Mosquitoes		Yellow Fever
Army base	Y	Y	→	contracted
Building 1	Y	N	→	~contracted
Building 2	N	Y	→	contracted

7. Cause: employee recognition awards. Effect: turnover. Joint method:

Method of agreement: Glenville, Aster, and Johnstown had low turnover; having employee recognition awards was the only common factor.

Method of difference: Brookfield and Johnstown were the same except that Johnstown had employee recognition awards and low turnover while Brookfield had no awards and high turnover.

10. Cause: dried leaves in gutters. Effect: house catches fire within 1 minute of exposure to high flames. Method of agreement.

Case	Windows	Landscaping	Siding	Roof	Gutters		Effect
House 1:	Class E,	rose bushes,	vinyl,	composition shingles,	dried leaves	→	catches fire within 1 min
House 2:	Class E,	buckthorn,	stone,	wood shake,	dried leaves	→	catches fire within 1 min
House 3:	Class E1,	dogwood,	vinyl,	metal,	dried leaves	→	catches fire within 1 min

13. Cause: prevalence of agriculture. Effect: visits from Senator Travers. Joint method.

Cheedon:	small,	agriculture	→	visit from Travers
Owensville:	large,	agriculture	→	visit from Travers
Waterton:	large,	~agriculture	→	~visit from Travers
Gojan:	large,	~agriculture	→	~visit from Travers

Putting It All Together

I.

1.

Case 1:	oxygen,	flame,	paper	→	paper burns
Case 2:	no oxygen (e.g., in a vacuum tube),	flame,	paper	→	~paper burns

4.

Case 1a:	colder than air,	glass,	window	→	condensation
Case 1b:	warmer than air,	glass,	window	→	~condensation
Case 2a:	colder than air,	glass,	ice tea pitcher	→	condensation
Case 2b:	warmer than air,	glass,	ice tea pitcher	→	~condensation
Case 3a:	colder than air,	metal,	bicycle	→	condensation
Case 3b:	warmer than air,	metal,	bicycle	→	~condensation

II.

1. Deductive: All narrative literature has a plot, and any plot involves conflict. Inductive: Variety of instances: Consider narrative literature by different authors, from different eras, etc. Disconfirming cases: Look for works that do not involve conflict. Plausibility: The plausibility of this generalization depends a good deal on our definitions and criteria for the key terms, "narrative" and "conflict." For example, would it count as a narrative if an author described a series of events without connecting them in a plot? Again, does it count as a conflict if a story presents a person overcoming challenges but without opposition from other people?

4. Deductive: All racial and sexual harassment is demeaning to the person harassed, and anything demeaning to a person lowers his self-esteem.

Inductive: Joint method: Compare people subjected to harassment—do all of them have a loss of self-esteem afterward? (Comparing people who vary in other respects is the element of agreement; comparing any particular person's level of self-esteem before and after the incident is the element of difference.)

Method of concomitant variations: Compare cases of harassment that differ in degree of severity and look for corresponding differences in degree to which self-esteem is lowered.

III.

1. Effect: no pigeons. Proposed cause: plastic owls. Method: agreement, used to support the causal claim. There is also an implicit use of difference in the final contrast with conditions a month ago.

Building 1:	plastic owls	→	~pigeons
Building 2:	plastic owls	→	~pigeons
Building 3:	plastic owls	→	~pigeons

4. Effect: economic growth. Proposed cause: organization innovation. Method: agreement, used to support a causal claim.

	Cause: Organization Innovation		Effect: Economic Growth
Case 1:	creation of joint-stock companies	→	growth of transoceanic commerce
Case 2:	hierarchically organized companies	→	extension of railroads across the U.S.

7. Effect: hares' aversion to eating buds. Proposed cause: pinosylvin methyl ether (PME). Method: joint, used to support causal claim.

Case	PME	Nutritional Value		Effect
Stems:	~PME	Y	→	eat
Buds:	PME	Y	→	~eat
Oatmeal:	~PME	Y	→	eat
Oatmeal:	PME	Y	→	~eat

10. Effect: attribution of responsibility. Proposed cause: inner choice. Method: joint, used to support causal claim.

Normal case:	inner choice	overt act	→	responsible
Robot:		overt act	→	~responsible
Frustrated intention:	inner choice		→	responsible

13. Effect: mass gain of growing plants. Cause: something other than soil consumption. Method: residues, used to support a causal claim.

CHAPTER 12

Exercise 12.1

1. Not an argument

4. A: decorations; B: jewelry; S: excess; P: not beautiful

7. A: file folders; B: concepts; P: necessity of hierarchical system; S: storing information about categories of objects

10. A: steam boiler; B: person who keeps his emotions bottled up; P: inevitability of breakdown; S: buildup of internal pressure

13. A: unwritten book; B: future [of one's life]; S: not predetermined; P: open to choice

Exercise 12.2

1. Source: Fred. Target: Jim. Shared property: intellectuals. Conclusion property: does not like sports. The example of Fred is very weak inductive evidence for the generalization that no intellectual likes sports. Athletic and intellectual interests are not incompatible, and the many intellectuals who like sports are counter-analogies.

4. Source: candy and pastry. Target: parsnips and sweet potatoes. Shared properties: sweetness, hardness. Conclusion property: liking, preference. The analogy rests on a somewhat distant similarity between the candy/pastry difference and the parsnip/sweet potato difference. All the items are food, but of very different types. The strength of the analogy depends partly on one's personal taste in food.

7. Source: bundle of sticks. Target: family. Shared property: strength of group over separate members. Conclusion property: should bind together. A counter-analogy is that some things do not strengthen—and may actually weaken—when they are joined together. For example, a group of runners bound together could run no faster than the slowest runner. And, as the old adage says, "Too many cooks spoil the broth." Not a strong argument.

10. Source: golf balls. Target: damaged people. Shared property: things that are slightly damaged. Conclusion property: go further. This is an extremely weak argument. The golf ball is unusual in being improved by damage. And even in the case of the golf ball, not every sort of

damage would improve it. Only certain fortuitous, or today intentional, reshaping aids the ball.

13. Source: air vibration. Target: photon. Shared properties: definite frequency and wavelength. Conclusion property: wave. The analogy seems strong since frequency and wavelength are essential properties of macroscopic waves. But any analogy between macroscopic and microscopic phenomena can be misleading.

Exercise 12.3

1. a. Strengthens, b. strengthens, c. weakens, d. weakens, e. weakens

4. a. Strengthens, b. strengthens, c. weakens

Putting It All Together

I.

1. Analogy with Jaguar, Corvette, etc., cars that are known to be expensive to insure.

4. The usual analogy is with gambling, but there are many significant differences (there's more to investing than money changing hands in a zero-sum game). Another analogy would be starting a business.

II.

1. Not an argument

4. Sources: drawing, machine. Target: writing. Shared property: created to serve a purpose. Conclusion property: no unnecessary parts. Since the shared property was not stated, we have supplied one. Though an effort of persuasion is clearly being made here, the basis of the analogy may be too vague to count as an argument. No matter how florid, rococo, or redundant a sentence is, couldn't an author claim that everything in it served some purpose?

7. Source: stew. Target: society. Shared property: composed of many elements. Conclusion property: must occasionally be disrupted to prevent degeneration. The conclusion is not well-established, since it is supported only by the example of stew, which is unusual in its need to be stirred. Most things composed of many elements (such as buildings, human bodies, and paintings) are actually damaged by disruption.

10. Source: physics and biology. Target: psychology. Shared property: personifying the objects of study. Conclusion property: benefit of avoiding mediating states in object. The obvious disanalogy to consider is the nature of the objects: Personifying persons may be appropriate even if personifying inanimate things or plants is not.

13. Source: college canceling course credits for person (involuntarily) taking a year off from school. Target: workers losing health insurance when they are fired. Shared property: loss of an earned benefit through no fault. Conclusion property: unfair. The thought experiment in the analogy provides reasonable support for the moral conclusion.

16. Source: buildings. Target: knowledge. Shared property: things that require design. Conclusion property: better designed by one person than by many. The link between design and a single designer is supported only by the single example of buildings. A counter-analogy would be anything that is better designed by several people working together than by a single person. We could also question whether acquisition of knowledge always requires design. Isn't knowledge sometimes acquired fortuitously?

19. Source: camping trip. Target: society—specifically the economic-political system. Shared properties: care for others, sharing, equality. Conclusion property: more desirable than the alternative. The strength of this argument depends on minimizing the differences between a small group who know each other and a society with millions of (mostly) strangers, between the relative simplicity of a camping trip and the complexities of production and exchange in an economy, and so on.

III.

1. Anger is like a Danger sign, a high-voltage wire, etc.— anything that is not hydraulic.

4. Society is like a party, a convention, a marketplace, etc.— anything that involves interaction but not necessarily shared interests.

IV.

a.

	Machine	World
S_1	Composed of parts (at many levels of organization)	Composed of parts (at many levels of organization)
S_2	Parts are adjusted to each other with great accuracy	Parts are adjusted to each other with great accuracy
S_3	Means are adapted to serve ends	Means are adapted to serve ends
D_1	Man-made	Not man-made
P	Created by intelligent designer	Created by intelligent designer

b.

	Living organism	World
S_1	Continual circulation of matter	Continual circulation of matter
S_2	Constant repair of "waste" (damage)	Constant repair of "waste" (damage)
S_3	Parts act to preserve themselves as well as the whole	Parts act to preserve themselves as well as the whole
D_1	Mortal	Immortal or unknown
P	Intrinsically actuated with "life and motion" (not designed)	Intrinsically actuated with "life and motion" (not designed)

CHAPTER 13

Exercise 13.1

I.

1. Brown to black, blue, green, etc.

4. Lawyer, banker, construction worker, etc.

II.

1. Political position

4. Religious affiliation

Exercise 13.2A

1. (a) Total visitors to the Jefferson Memorial in other years; (b) visitors per day, ratio of Jefferson Memorial visitors to visitors at other sites, etc.

4. (a) Total salmon catch in Alaska in other years, total catch in other fisheries, etc.; (b) ratio of salmon catch in Alaska to harvest of other fish, etc.

7. (a) Number of privately owned automobiles in other countries; (b) ratio of automobiles to population in China.

10. (a) Number of advertising pages in *Vanity Fair* magazine in other years or advertising pages in other magazines; (b) ratio of advertising pages to total pages, etc.

Exercise 13.2B

1. Consistent variables, mutually exclusive and jointly exhaustive

4. Consistent variables, mutually exclusive and jointly exhaustive

Exercise 13.2C

1. Total. The premise does not give much if any support to the conclusion. "Large" is a relative term, and the premise tells us nothing about the size of the United States in relation to other countries.

4. Distribution. The premise provides little support for the conclusion. A country's share of cases worldwide does not take account of differences in population. And the percentage of reported cases may not reflect real cases, which depends on factors such as number of tests performed per population and the difficulties in measuring asymptomatic spread.

7. Totals. The premise provides strong support for the conclusion.

10. Average, median. This is a good inference. (In fact, the top six of the 27 players had salaries from $11 to $21 million.)

Exercise 13.3

1. The mailing list overrepresents conservatives, who are more likely than those of other persuasions to oppose national health insurance.

4. People with the time and money to attend a concert are not necessarily representative of all fans. For example, the concert goers might well tend to be older than Taylor Swift fans overall.

7. Parents who sign up for the PTA's list may be more engaged than other parents.

10. The question allows only two alternatives; it does not allow people to express the view that arts organizations can or should be funded by private philanthropy.

Exercise 13.4B

1. Independent variable: ultraviolet light. Dependent variable: frequency of sprouting in the population of pea plants.

| Group 1 | UV light | pea plants | → | 80% sprouted within week |
| Group 2 | no UV light | pea plants | → | 60% sprouted within week |

Method of difference.

4. Independent variable: use of planners. Dependent variable: average grade point average.

| Group 1 | used planners, students | → | 3.1 GPA |
| Group 2 | did not use planners, students | → | 2.8 GPA |

Method of difference.

Exercise 13.4D

Problems of internal validity: This is an observational study, subject to various possibly confounding factors. Vacationers may be more impatient to get to their destination than are those commuting to work or they may be less familiar with the road or with their route. And despite what the report says, it is unlikely that driving conditions were exactly the same in all respects, including the number of police on the road, the number of lanes, the width of shoulders, the outside temperature, etc.

Problems of external validity: Neither New York City commuters nor Disney World patrons are likely to be representative samples of drivers in general. And the presence or absence of family members is not a good variable to use for estimating the presence or absence of backseat driving. The presence of the family may distract the driver in other ways: children playing, marital squabbles, etc.

Putting It All Together

I.

1. Incompatible

4. Whether (a) or (b) are compatible depends on how much imprecision is allowed by the word "about."

7. Incompatible (assuming the 4-point system)

II.

1. e

4. b

III.

1. The best choice would be (c). An adjustment for inflation is clearly required, but there is no reason to adjust for changes in median income.

4. Everything here depends on what kind of satisfaction one is looking for. (c) is probably the most reasonable measure for the nonprofessional investor, since everyone has the option of putting money into an interest-yielding instrument; (d) ignores the element of risk.

V.

1. The 70% improvement rate provides no evidence for the skin cream's effectiveness since we are not told how many poison-ivy victims who do *not* use any treatment also recover within a week.

4. The potential for confounding variables here is enormous: differences in health, wealth, vitality, etc., might explain both the lower death rate of men with younger wives and their attraction to younger women. And if there is a direct causal connection, it's conceivable that

it runs in the opposite direction: younger women may be more attracted to older men whom they expect to live longer.

7. The argument has some strength since it cites the ratio of officers to the population rather than just the total number of officers. The question is whether the decline in the ratio from 2.42 to 2.17 has important consequences, for example, on the crime level.

10. The conclusion says that DNA should not be the *only* evidence in a trial, not that it should be excluded altogether, so the argument provides some support. But we should get more empirical evidence on the reliability of DNA testing to tell whether these results are anomalous.

CHAPTER 14

Exercise 14.1

I.

1. 1/6
4. $7/21 = 1/3$

II.

1. Reference class: Past days when meteorological conditions were similar. Frequency: Percentage of those days when rain occurred.

4. Reference class: Babies born in the same region and time period. Frequency: Percentage of girls in that class.

III.

1. 2/6, equal alternatives
4. 1:4, equal alternatives
7. 0.975, or 97.5%, frequency
10. Answers may vary, but the probability seems less than 50%; intuitive judgment

Exercise 14.2

I.

1. Compatible
4. Compatible

II.

1. Independent
4. Dependent

III.

1. 5/6
4. a. $3/15 \cdot 3/15 = 1/5 \cdot 1/5 = 1/25$
   b. $3/15 \cdot 2/14 = 1/5 \cdot 1/7 = 1/35$
7. 6, then 3: $0.7 \cdot 0.9 = 0.63$
   3, then 6: $0.9 \cdot 0.6 = 0.54$
10. $0.3 + 0.2 - (0.3 \cdot 0.2) = 0.44$, or 44%
13. a. $85/100 = 0.85$, or 85%
    b. $40/85 = 0.47$, or 47%
    c. $55/100 = 0.55$, or 55%

Exercise 14.3

1. $p(red_2 | red_1) = \dfrac{p(red_1 \text{ and } red_2)}{p(red_1)}$

   $= \dfrac{5/15 \times 4/14}{5/15} = 4/14$

4. $p(fibro | woman) = \dfrac{p(fibro \text{ and } woman)}{p(woman)}$

   $= 0.02/0.5 \text{ or } 0.04$

7. $p(fiction | paper) = \dfrac{p(paper | fiction) \times p(fiction)}{p(paper)}$

   $= \dfrac{8/11 \times 11/20}{3/5}$

   $= 2/5 \ / \ 3/5$

   $= 2/3$

10. $p(fibro | fatigue) = \dfrac{p(fatigue | fibro) \times p(fibro)}{p(fatigue)}$

    $= \dfrac{0.95 \times 0.04}{0.30}$

    $= 12.7\%$

Putting It All Together

I.

1. d

II.

1. a. 1/12
   b. 1/6

4. p(Giants make Super Bowl): $1/10 = 0.1$

p(Patriots make Super Bowl): $1/5 = 0.2$

p(both teams make Super Bowl): $0.1 \cdot 0.2 = 0.02$

p(Giants beat Patriots in any game they play): $4/6 = 0.667$

p(Giants beat Patriots in Super Bowl | both teams make Super Bowl): $0.667 \cdot 0.02 = 0.01334$, or $1/75$

7. a. $43.92/166.02 = 0.265$

b. $33.03/72.75 = 0.454$

c. $(42.28 + 39.72)/327.14 = 0.251$

CHAPTER 15
Exercise 15.1

1. Explanation
   1. The stock market went up yesterday. [*Explanandum*]
   2. The Federal Reserve lowered interest rates. [Hypothesis]

4. Explanation
   1. Natalie has very little self-confidence. [Hypothesis]
   2. Natalie is very boastful. [*Explanandum*]
   3. Natalie rarely takes on challenges in her work. [*Explanandum*]

7. Explanation
   1. Babies begin to learn language at about 1 year of age, regardless of language, society, or culture. [*Explanandum*]
   2. A physical process of maturation in the brain governs language acquisition. [Hypothesis]

10. Explanation
    1. The continents are located on tectonic plates. [Hypothesis]
    2. The tectonic plates move in relation to each other. [Hypothesis]
    3. New mountain ranges are formed. [*Explanandum*]
    4. Earthquakes occur. [*Explanandum*]

5. Volcanic activity occurs in specific zones. [*Explanandum*]

Exercise 15.2

1. Extremely uninformative. The hypothesis tells us that the chicken had some motive for crossing the road but doesn't tell us what it was. (That is presumably the point of this ancient joke.)

4. Incomplete. The hypothesis tells us why food will be needed soon, but not why the food must come from a fast-food restaurant, why it must consist of these specific foods, or why it must be purchased at the next exit (though perhaps this follows from the degree of hunger).

7. Logically weak. The prosecutor's hypothesis is based solely on alleged motive, but very few angry ex-lovers commit murder. Also incomplete. There is no explanation of how Imelda had the means, the intent, or the opportunity.

10. Incomplete. The hypothesis may explain how the Greek geometers learned the Pythagorean theorem but tells us nothing about how it was discovered in the first place. For that reason, it may also be considered uninformative.

13. Incomplete. If the hypothesis is true, it was presumably true prior to the 1980s. It does not explain why the Soviet empire collapsed when it did.

Exercise 15.3A

1. (a) *Explanandum*: Jim hasn't taken any science courses; (b) hypothesis: Jim has math anxiety; (c) additional consequences: Jim hasn't taken any math courses; (d) alternative hypothesis: Jim doesn't like science or knows a lot of science already.

4. (a) *Explanandum*: I got a C on this paper; (b) hypotheses: (i) I disagreed with the professor's view, and (ii) he is biased against people who disagree with him; (c) additional consequences: other students who agreed with the professor got higher grades, I will get a higher grade if I write a paper agreeing with him; (d) alternative explanation: the paper deserved a C because it was poorly written, uninsightful, etc.

7. (a) *Explananda*: (i) the victim died of gunshot wounds, (ii) on Fifth Avenue on the afternoon of September 7, (iii) from a bullet from Watson's gun; (b) hypothesis:

Watson shot the victim; (c) additional consequences: someone saw Watson shoot the victim, Watson's fingerprints are on the gun; (d) alternative hypothesis: someone else stole the gun and committed the murder.

10. (a) *Explanandum*: the occurrence of the American Civil War; (b) hypothesis: the war was caused primarily by a conflict over tariffs; (c) additional consequences: Southern states would have emphasized tariffs in making their case for secession from the Union; (d) alternative hypothesis: the war was caused by the conflict over slavery.

Exercise 15.3B

1. Hypothesis *a* is more plausible. It is simpler than *b*, which posits a person deliberately pretending to make a deceptive call and having a malicious purpose.

4. Hypothesis *a* is obviously simpler and—skeptical arguments aside—is more consistent with our body of knowledge.

7. Hypothesis *b* is more plausible. Hypothesis *a* is inconsistent with our knowledge of large lakes, which are not suddenly and surprisingly depleted of fish.

10. Hypothesis *c* is most plausible. It is far simpler than hypotheses *a* and *b*. And hypothesis *a* is inconsistent with our knowledge of NASA as an institution that seeks to disseminate information, rather than conceal it.

EXERCISE 15.4

1. Possible questions:
Birds, turtles, and rabbits are native to the Boston area. Why couldn't the statues have been made by local people?
Why would alien astronauts build the statues?
Did they build the statues just in Boston, or other places as well?
Why would they do the sand carvings in Peru but statues in Boston?

4. How does a cat enter your body?
Why do cats want to take over our bodies?
Are cats the only other species that get AIDS, etc.?
When did cat extraterrestrials arrive on Earth? How did they get here?
Don't all mammals share a large percentage of DNA?

7. How does combustion happen spontaneously in a person?
Are human organs flammable?
Are there other known cases?
How much can anger raise body temperature?

Putting It All Together

I.

1. c
4. a
7. d
10. d

II.

1.

Explanandum:	1. "Xmas" is a Christian term.
Hypotheses:	2. The *X* is from χ, the Greek letter chi, or Ch.
	3. Ch was an abbreviation for *Christos*.

4.

Explanandum:	1. A zygote obtains half its genes from its male parent.
Hypotheses:	2. A zygote receives half its chromosomes from its male parent.
	3. The chromosomes bear the genes.

7.

Explananda:	1. It is difficult for saltwater to enter the Baltic.
	2. There are no tides at Riga, Stockholm, or the mouth of the Neva.
Hypotheses:	3. Four rivers flow into the Baltic along its southern coast.
	4. The rivers pour freshwater into the Baltic.
	5. The prevailing current is out of the Baltic.

10.

Explananda:
1. The National Theater sank ten feet after it was erected.
2. The National Theater rose (more than ten feet) when high-rise buildings were erected nearby.

Hypotheses:
3. Mexico City is built on a mixture of sand and water.
4. Such soils settle when heavy buildings are erected.
5. When heavy buildings are erected, their weight squeezes the water out of the mixture, decreasing its volume.

III.

1. Hypothesis: The teachers were not good at explaining the subject. Adequacy: Logically strong, partially complete, informative. Truth: Test hypothesis by taking a course in that subject with a good teacher.

4. Hypothesis: Working at home allows working parents to care for their children during the day. Adequacy: Logically strong and informative but not complete; the hypothesis applies only to people with children and does not explain why employers accept the arrangement. Truth: Test the hypothesis by surveying parents working at home to see how much time they spend with their children, how many send their children to school or day care, etc.

IV.

Rank, from most to least consistent with current knowledge, by type:

a. Coincidences that do not involve any physical improbability: 6, 8.
b. Events that are physically unlikely but can be explained by existing knowledge: 1.
c. Events that cannot be explained by existing knowledge, but might be explained by new principles that do not conflict with existing knowledge: 4, 10, 5, 7.
d. Events whose occurrence would conflict with existing knowledge: 2, 3, 9.

Glossary

abusive *ad hominem* a form of *ad hominem* that uses a pejorative claim about a speaker to dismiss his statement or argument **(Ch. 3)**

accident the fallacy of applying a generalization to a special case in disregard of qualities or circumstances that make it an exception to the generalization **(Ch. 3)**

ad hominem the fallacy of using a negative trait of a speaker as evidence that the speaker's statement is false or the argument weak **(Ch. 3)**

addition (Add) a rule of implication in propositional logic permitting inferences of the following forms:

$$\frac{p}{p \vee q} \quad \text{or} \quad \frac{p}{q \vee p} \quad \textbf{(Ch. 9)}$$

affirming the antecedent (*modus ponens*) a valid mixed hypothetical syllogism in which the categorical premise affirms the antecedent of the hypothetical premise and the conclusion affirms the consequent **(Ch. 7)**

affirming the consequent an invalid mixed hypothetical syllogism in which the categorical premise affirms the consequent of the hypothetical premise and the conclusion affirms the antecedent **(Ch. 7)**

analogue something that is similar to something else **(Ch. 12)**

anchoring the tendency to estimate a quantity by starting with a reference point (the anchor) and moving away from the anchor insufficiently **(Ch. 4)**

antecedent the "if" component in a hypothetical proposition **(Ch. 7)**

appeal to authority (*argumentum ad verecundiam*) the fallacy of using what an authority says as evidence for the truth of a proposition when the conditions for credibility are not satisfied **(Ch. 3)**

appeal to emotion the fallacy of trying to get someone to accept a proposition on the basis of an emotion one induces **(Ch. 3)**

appeal to force (*argumentum ad baculum*) the fallacy of trying to get someone to accept a proposition on the basis of a threat **(Ch. 3)**

appeal to ignorance (*argumentum ad ignorantiam*) the fallacy of using the absence of proof for a proposition as evidence for the truth of the opposing proposition **(Ch. 3)**

appeal to majority the fallacy of using the fact that large numbers of people believe a proposition to be true as evidence of its truth **(Ch. 3)**

argument a unit of reasoning in which one or more propositions (the premises) purport to provide evidence for the truth of another proposition (the conclusion) **(Ch. 2)**

association (Assoc) a rule of replacement in propositional logic permitting the following substitutions:

$$[p \bullet (q \bullet r)] \ :: \ [(p \bullet q) \bullet r]$$
$$[p \vee (q \vee r)] \ :: \ [(p \vee q) \vee r] \quad \textbf{(Ch. 9)}$$

atomic statement in symbolic logic, a statement with no internal connectives **(Ch. 8)**

attribution bias the tendency to make errors in explaining the cause of a person's action by overestimating the role of either internal traits of the person or the external circumstances of the action to others and to oneself **(Ch. 4)**

availability the tendency to estimate the frequency or likelihood of an event on the basis of how quickly instances or associations come to mind **(Ch. 4)**

average a statistic specifying the sum of the values that the items in a class have on a quantitative variable P, divided by the number of items **(Ch. 13)**

Bayes' theorem A theory in the probability calculus for calculating conditional probabilities **(Ch. 14)**

begging the question (circular argument) the fallacy of trying to support a proposition with an argument in which that proposition is a premise **(Ch. 3)**

belief bias the tendency for agreement or disagreement with a conclusion to affect one's evaluation of the validity or strength of the argument for that conclusion **(Ch. 4)**

biconditional a compound proposition asserting that one component proposition is true if and only if the other component is true **(Ch. 8)**

bound variable   in predicate logic, a variable that falls within the scope of a quantifier for that variable **(Ch. 10)**

categorical proposition   a proposition containing a subject and a predicate term and asserting that some or all of the referents of the subject term are included in or excluded from the class designated by the predicate term **(Ch. 5)**

categorical syllogism   a deductive argument containing two categorical premises, a categorical conclusion, and three terms—major, minor, and middle—with each term occurring in two propositions **(Ch. 6)**

classify   to group things into species and genuses according to their similarities and differences **(Ch. 1)**

closed sentence   in predicate logic, a sentence in which all variables are bound **(Ch. 10)**

cogent   the property of an inductive argument that is strong and whose premises are true **(Ch. 2)**

cognitive biases   systematic psychological tendencies to make errors in seeking and interpreting information **(Ch. 4)**

cognitive dissonance   the tendency to experience discomfort at the inconsistency between one's actions and one's standards, and to reduce or remove the dissonance by nonrational means **(Ch. 4)**

commutation (Com)   a rule of replacement in propositional logic permitting the following substitutions:

$(p \cdot q)$ :: $(q \cdot p)$
$(p \vee q)$ :: $(q \vee p)$ **(Ch. 9)**

compatible   in probability theory, two events are compatible if they could both occur **(Ch. 14)**

complement   a term designating the class of all things excluded by another term **(Ch. 5)**

complex question   the fallacy of trying to get someone to support a proposition by asking a question that presupposes that proposition **(Ch. 3)**

composition   the fallacy of inferring that a whole has a property merely because its parts have that property **(Ch. 3)**

conclusion   a proposition whose truth an argument seeks to establish **(Ch. 2)**

conditional   a compound proposition containing two component propositions (the antecedent and the consequent) and asserting that the truth of one component would be sufficient for the truth of the other **(Ch. 8)**

conditional probability   the probability that one event will occur on condition that another event occurs **(Ch. 14)**

conditional proof (CP)   a method of proving that a hypothetical (or conditional) proposition follows from a set of premises; one assumes the antecedent and then derives the consequent from the antecedent together with the premises **(Ch. 9)**

confirmation bias   the tendency to look for and take account of evidence supporting a conclusion, assumption, or hypothesis; while ignoring, downplaying, or failing to seek evidence against it **(Ch. 4)**

conjunction   a compound proposition asserting that two or more component propositions (the conjuncts) are all true **(Ch. 8)**

conjunction (Conj)   a rule of implication in propositional logic permitting inferences of the following forms:

p or p
q q
$p \cdot q$ $q \cdot p$ **(Ch. 9)**

connective   a word or symbol that creates a compound proposition from component propositions **(Ch. 1)**

consequent   the "then" component in a hypothetical proposition **(Ch. 7)**

consistent   a relation between two or more statements that are both true on at least one assignment of truth values to their atomic components **(Ch. 8)**

constructive dilemma (CD)   a rule of implication in propositional logic permitting an inference of the following form:

$(p \supset q) \cdot (r \supset s)$
$p \vee r$
$q \vee s$ **(Ch. 9)**

contingent statement   a compound statement that is true for some assignments of truth values to its atomic components and false for other assignments **(Ch. 8)**

contradiction   a relation between two statements that have opposite truth values for every assignment of truth values to their atomic components **(Ch. 8)**

contradictories   in the traditional and modern squares of opposition, a pair of categorical propositions that, in virtue of their logical form, could neither both be true nor both be false (i.e., A and O, E and I) **(Ch. 5)**

contrapositive   the proposition that results from replacing the subject term in a categorical proposition with the complement of the predicate and the predicate with the complement of the subject **(Ch. 5)**

contraries   in the traditional square of opposition, a pair of categorical propositions that, in virtue of their logical form, could not both be true but could both be false (i.e., A and E) **(Ch. 5)**

converse   the proposition that results from switching the subject and predicate terms in a categorical proposition **(Ch. 5)**

copula   a verb of being ("is," "are," "is not," etc.) that links the subject and the predicate in a categorical proposition **(Ch. 5)**

counter-analogy   an additional or alternative source analogue that weakens an argument by analogy **(Ch. 12)**

counterexample   a particular instance that proves a definition wrong **(Ch. 1)**

De Morgan's law (DM)   a rule of replacement in propositional logic permitting the following substitutions:

$\sim(p \bullet q)$ :: $(\sim p \vee \sim q)$
$\sim(p \vee q)$ :: $(\sim p \bullet \sim q)$ **(Ch. 9)**

deductive argument   an argument that attempts to show that its conclusion follows necessarily from the premises **(Ch. 2)**

definite description   an identifying phrase unique to a particular individual **(Ch. 10)**

definition   a statement that identifies the referents of a concept by specifying the genus they belong to and the differentia (the set of essential characteristics) that distinguishes those referents from other species in the genus **(Ch. 1)**

denying the antecedent   an invalid mixed hypothetical syllogism in which the categorical premise denies the antecedent of the hypothetical premise and the conclusion denies the consequent **(Ch. 7)**

denying the consequent (*modus tollens*)   a valid mixed hypothetical syllogism in which the categorical premise denies the consequent of the hypothetical premise and the conclusion denies the antecedent **(Ch. 7)**

dependent events   two events are dependent if the occurrence of one affects the probability of the other **(Ch. 14)**

destructive dilemma (DD)   a rule of implication in propositional logic permitting an inference of the following form:

$(p \supset q) \bullet (r \supset s)$
$\underline{\sim q \vee \sim s}$
$\sim p \vee \sim r$ **(Ch. 9)**

differentia   the element in a definition that specifies the attribute(s) distinguishing a species from other species of the same genus **(Ch. 1)**

disanalogy   a relevant difference between a source and target analogue that weakens an argument by analogy **(Ch. 12)**

disjunct   a component of a disjunctive proposition **(Ch. 7)**

disjunction   a compound proposition containing two or more component propositions (the disjuncts) and asserting that at least one of them is true **(Ch. 8)**

disjunctive proposition   a compound proposition that uses the connective "or" **(Ch. 7)**

disjunctive syllogism   a deductive argument with a disjunctive premise, other premises denying all but one of the disjuncts, and a conclusion affirming the remaining disjunct **(Ch. 7)**

disjunctive syllogism (DS)   a rule of implication in propositional logic permitting inferences of the following forms:

$p \vee q$ $p \vee q$
$\underline{\sim p}$ or $\underline{\sim q}$
q p **(Ch. 9)**

distribution   a property of a term in a categorical proposition; the term is distributed if and only if the proposition makes an assertion about all members of the class designated by the term **(Ch. 6)**; a statistic specifying the number or proportion of items in a class that have each of the values (P, Q, R, etc.) on some variable **(Ch. 13)**

distribution (Dist)   a rule of replacement in propositional logic permitting the following substitutions:

$[p \bullet (q \vee r)]$ :: $[(p \bullet q) \vee (p \bullet r)]$
$[p \vee (q \bullet r)]$ :: $[(p \vee q) \bullet (p \vee r)]$ **(Ch. 9)**

diversion   the fallacy of trying to support one proposition by diverting attention to another proposition or issue **(Ch. 3)**

division   the fallacy of inferring that a part has a property merely because the whole has that property **(Ch. 3)**

double negation (DN)   a rule of replacement in propositional logic permitting the following substitution:

p :: $\sim\sim p$ **(Ch. 9)**

enthymeme   a categorical syllogism with an unstated premise or conclusion **(Ch. 6)**

equivalence   a relation between two or more statements that have the same truth value for every assignment of truth values to their atomic components **(Ch. 8)**

equivalence (Equiv)   a rule of replacement in propositional logic permitting the following substitutions:

$(p \equiv q)$ :: $[(p \supset q) \bullet (q \supset p)]$
$(p \equiv q)$ :: $[(p \bullet q) \vee (\sim p \bullet \sim q)]$ **(Ch. 9)**

equivocation   the fallacy of using a word in two different meanings in the premises and/or conclusion of an argument **(Ch. 3)**

event   an outcome or set of outcomes for which we want to know the probability, such as drawing an ace from a deck of cards **(Ch. 14)**

existential generalization (EG)   an implication rule in predicate logic that allows us to (existentially) generalize over a statement **(Ch. 10)**

existential import   a property of categorical propositions: A proposition has existential import if its truth depends on the existence of things of the kinds specified by terms in the proposition **(Ch. 5)**

existential instantiation (EI)   an implication rule in predicate logic that allows us to take an instance of an existential statement, thus removing the existential quantifier **(Ch. 10)**

existential quantifier   the quantifier that specifies that a statement applies to some of the things a variable can represent **(Ch. 10)**

explanandum   the proposition whose truth one is attempting to explain (plural *explananda*) **(Ch. 15)**

exportation (Exp)   a rule of replacement in propositional logic permitting the following substitution:

$[(p \bullet q) \supset r]$ :: $[p \supset (q \supset r)]$ **(Ch. 9)**

fallacy   an argument in which the premises appear to support the conclusion but actually provide little or no support **(Ch. 3)**

false dichotomy   the fallacy of excluding relevant possibilities without justification **(Ch. 3)**

favorable outcome   in probability theory, an outcome included in an event **(Ch. 14)**

figure   the position of the middle term in the premises of a categorical syllogism **(Ch. 6)**

free variable   a variable that does not fall within the scope of a quantifier **(Ch. 10)**

frequency   a statistic specifying the number or proportion of items in a class that have a given property **(Ch. 13)**

genus   a class of things regarded as having various subcategories (its species) **(Ch. 1)**

hasty generalization   the fallacy of inferring a general proposition from an inadequate sample of positive instances **(Ch. 3)**

hindsight bias   the tendency for knowledge of the outcome of an event to affect one's judgment about the antecedent likelihood of that outcome and one's memory of one's prior estimate of its likelihood **(Ch. 4)**

hypothesis   the proposition (or propositions) in an explanation that purport to show why another proposition (the explanandum) is true **(Ch. 15)**

hypothetical proposition   another term for a conditional (if . . . then) proposition **(Ch. 7)**

hypothetical syllogism (HS)   a rule of implication in propositional logic permitting an inference of the following form:

$p \supset q$
$q \supset r$
$p \supset r$ **(Ch. 9)**

identity reflexivity (IR)   a rule of inference in predicate logic that states a constant is equal to itself **(Ch. 10)**

identity symmetry (IS)   a replacement rule in predicate logic that allows us to switch the order of statements on each side of the identity operator (=) **(Ch. 10)**

identity transitivity (IT)   an implication rule in predicate logic: if two names represent the same individual, anything that may be predicated of one may also be predicated of the other **(Ch. 10)**

illicit conversion   in traditional logic, an invalid immediate inference of taking the converse of an A proposition **(Ch. 5)**

implication (Imp)   a rule of replacement in propositional logic permitting the following substitution:

$(p \supset q)$ :: $(\sim p \vee q)$ **(Ch. 9)**

implicit premise   a premise that is assumed by an argument but is not stated **(Ch. 2)**

independent events   two events are independent if and only if the occurrence of one does not affect the probability of the other **(Ch. 14)**

indirect proof (IP)   a method of proving that a proposition follows from a set of premises by deriving a contradiction from the denial of that proposition together with the premises **(Ch. 9)**

inductive argument   an argument that attempts to show that its conclusion is supported by the premises even though the conclusion amplifies—it goes beyond—what the premises state **(Ch. 2)**

intuitive judgment   a judgment about the probability of an event based on integrating relevant evidence **(Ch. 14)**

joint method   a method of identifying a cause of an effect by using Mill's methods of agreement and difference in combination **(Ch. 11)**

jointly exhaustive   in a classification, the property that the species taken together cover all the objects in the genus **(Ch. 1)**

major premise   in a categorical syllogism, the premise in which the major term appears **(Ch. 6)**

major term   in a categorical syllogism, the term that occurs in the predicate of the conclusion **(Ch. 6)**

median   a statistic specifying the middle value of the items in a class on a quantitative variable P **(Ch. 13)**

method of agreement   a method of identifying a cause of an effect by isolating a factor common to a variety of cases in which the effect occurs **(Ch. 11)**

method of concomitant variations   Mill's method of identifying a cause of an effect by isolating a factor whose variations are correlated with variations in the effect, all other factors remaining constant **(Ch. 11)**

method of difference   Mill's method of identifying a cause of an effect by isolating a factor in whose presence the effect occurs and in whose absence the effect does not occur, all other factors remaining constant **(Ch. 11)**

method of equal alternatives   Mill's method of determining the probability of an event by finding the ratio of favorable outcomes to the total number of possible outcomes **(Ch. 14)**

method of frequency   a method of determining the probability of an event by the frequency of similar events in a reference class **(Ch. 14)**

method of residues   Mill's method of identifying a cause of an effect by isolating that portion of the effect not explained by known causal relationships **(Ch. 11)**

middle term   in a categorical syllogism, the term that appears in both premises and links together the major and minor terms **(Ch. 6)**

minor premise   in a categorical syllogism, the premise in which the minor term appears **(Ch. 6)**

minor term   in a categorical syllogism, the term that occurs in the subject of the conclusion **(Ch. 6)**

missing the point   the fallacy of arguing for a conclusion that is different from the conclusion in question **(Ch. 3)**

mixed hypothetical syllogism   a syllogism with a hypothetical premise and a premise which either affirms or denies a component of the hypothetical proposition **(Ch. 7)**

modus ponens **(MP)**   a rule of implication in propositional logic permitting an inference of the following form (*see also* affirming the antecedent):

$$p \supset q$$
$$\underline{p}$$
$$q \qquad \textbf{(Ch. 9)}$$

modus tollens **(MT)**   a rule of implication in propositional logic permitting an inference of the following form (*see also* denying the consequent):

$$p \supset q$$
$$\underline{\sim q}$$
$$\sim p \qquad \textbf{(Ch. 9)}$$

mood   the order of the standard forms (A, E, I, O) that make up the premises and conclusion of a categorical syllogism **(Ch. 6)**

mutually exclusive   in a classification, the property that each species excludes the members of every other species **(Ch. 1)**; in probability theory, two events are mutually exclusive if and only if they cannot both occur **(Ch. 14)**

negation   a compound statement whose truth value is the opposite truth of its component statement **(Ch. 8)**

negative instance   an item that belongs to a given class and does not possess the trait attributed to the class by a given generalization **(Ch. 11)**

obverse   the proposition that results from changing the quality of a categorical proposition and replacing the predicate term with its complement **(Ch. 5)**

open sentence   a sentence with a variable not bound by a quantifier for that variable **(Ch. 10)**

outcome   in probability theory, a single possible result, such as drawing a particular card from a deck of cards **(Ch. 14)**

particular proposition   a categorical proposition that makes an assertion about at least one but not all members of the class designated by its subject term (I and O are particular propositions) **(Ch. 5)**

poisoning the well   a form of ad hominem that tries to refute a proposition or argument by claiming that the speaker has a nonrational motive for it **(Ch. 3)**

positive instance   an item that belongs to a given class and possesses the trait attributed to the class by a given generalization **(Ch. 11)**

post hoc   the fallacy of using the fact that one event preceded another as sufficient evidence for the conclusion that the first caused the second **(Ch. 3)**

premise   a proposition used in an argument to provide evidence for another proposition (the conclusion) **(Ch. 2)**

probability calculus   a set of rules for determining the probability of compound events **(Ch. 14)**

proposition   the meaning or content of a statement **(Ch. 1)**

pseudo-explanation   a purported explanation that mimics genuine explanatory theories but violates the standards of explanation **(Ch. 15)**

pure hypothetical syllogism   a syllogism in which the conclusion and both of the premises are hypothetical propositions **(Ch. 7)**

quality   the affirmative or negative character of a categorical proposition **(Ch. 5)**

quantifier   in traditional logic, the element in a statement's logical form that indicates whether the predicate term is asserted of all or some of the referents of the subject term **(Ch. 5)**; in symbolic logic, a function that specifies whether a statement applies to all or some of the things a variable represents **(Ch. 10)**

quantifier negation (QN)   a replacement rule in predicate logic that allows us to move a negation over a quantifier and change that quantifier into its opposite **(Ch. 10)**

quantity   the particular or universal character of a categorical proposition **(Ch. 5)**

ratio   a statistic specifying the number of items in a class or the sum of their values on a variable per unit of some other class; a ratio is a total expressed in relative terms **(Ch. 13)**

red herring   a form of diversion that involves diverting attention from the issue by introducing irrelevant points **(Ch. 3)**

referent   a member of the class of things for which a concept stands **(Ch. 1)**

representativeness   the tendency to estimate the probability that a thing or event belongs to a class

primarily by the similarity of the thing or event to the stereotype of the class **(Ch. 4)**

scope   the portion of a sentence to which a given quantifier applies **(Ch. 10)**

self-contradiction   a compound statement that is false for every assignment of truth values to its atomic components **(Ch. 8)**

simplification (Simp)   a rule of implication in propositional logic permitting inferences of the following forms:

$$\frac{p \bullet q}{p} \qquad \text{or} \qquad \frac{p \bullet q}{q} \qquad \textbf{(Ch. 9)}$$

singular proposition   in traditional logic, a categorical proposition whose subject term designates a specific thing rather than a class **(Ch. 5)**

singular statement   in predicate logic, a subject–predicate statement whose subject is a name **(Ch. 10)**

slippery slope   the fallacy of arguing against a proposed action or policy by claiming, with insufficient evidence, that it will lead to a series of increasingly bad consequences **(Ch. 3)**

sorites   a chain of categorical syllogisms with one or more omitted intermediate conclusions **(Ch. 6)**

sound   the property of a deductive argument that is valid and whose premises are true **(Ch. 2)**

source analogue   in an argument by analogy, the analogue whose properties serve as premises **(Ch. 12)**

species   a class of things regarded as a subcategory of a wider class (a genus) **(Ch. 1)**

statement form   an expression using statement variables and connectives to state the logical form of an actual or possible statement **(Ch. 8)**

statement variables   symbols (p, q, r, etc.) used to represent any actual or possible statement **(Ch. 8)**

stipulative definition   a definition that introduces a new concept (or a new meaning for an existing concept) by specifying the criteria for inclusion in the concept **(Ch. 1)**

straw man   trying to refute a speaker's position by arguing against a distorted version of that position **(Ch. 3)**

strength   the degree to which the premises of an inductive argument support the conclusion **(Ch. 2)**

subalternates   in the traditional square of opposition, the relationships between a universal and a particular proposition of the same quality (i.e., A and I, E and O): if the universal is true, the particular must be true, and if the particular is false, the universal must be false **(Ch. 5)**

subcontraries   in the traditional square of opposition, a pair of propositions that, in virtue of their logical form, could both be true but could not both be false (i.e., I and O) **(Ch. 5)**

subjectivism   using the fact that one believes or wants a proposition to be true as evidence of its truth **(Ch. 3)**

substitution instance   any argument resulting from replacing the statement variables in an inference rule with atomic or compound propositions. **(Ch 13)**

syllogism   a deductive argument with two premises and a conclusion **(Ch. 6)**

target analogue   in an argument by analogy, the analogue we attribute a property to in the conclusion **(Ch. 12)**

tautology   a compound statement that is true for every assignment of truth values to its atomic components **(Ch. 8)**

tautology (Taut)   a rule of replacement in propositional logic permitting the following substitutions:

$p \quad :: \quad (p \bullet p)$

$p \quad :: \quad (p \vee p) \qquad$ **(Ch. 9)**

total   a statistic specifying the number of items in a class or the sum of their values on a variable **(Ch. 13)**

transposition (Trans)   a rule of replacement in propositional logic permitting the following substitution:

$(p \supset q) \quad :: \quad (\sim q \supset \sim p) \qquad$ **(Ch. 9)**

truth table   a diagram displaying the truth or falsity of a compound statement as a function of the truth or falsity of its atomic statements and connectives **(Ch. 8)**

truth value   the truth or falsity of a proposition **(Ch. 8)**

tu quoque   a form of *ad hominem* that argues against a person's statement by claiming it is inconsistent with the person's behavior or prior statements **(Ch. 3)**

universal generalization (UG)   an implication rule in predicate logic that allows us to (universally) generalize over a statement **(Ch. 10)**

universal instantiation (UI)   an implication rule in predicate logic that allows us to take an instance of a universal statement, thus removing the universal quantifier **(Ch. 10)**

universal proposition   a categorical proposition that makes an assertion about all members of the class designated by its subject term (A and E are universal propositions) **(Ch. 5)**

universal quantifier   the quantifier that specifies that a statement applies to all the things a variable can represent **(Ch. 10)**

validity   the property of a deductive argument in which, in virtue of the logical form of the argument, it is impossible for the premises to be true and the conclusion false **(Ch. 2)**

variable   in symbolic logic, a symbol that stands for any individual thing without standing for a particular individual thing **(Ch. 10)**; in statistics, a property regarded as a generic attribute that can exist in different forms or degrees **(Ch. 13)**

Index

Propositional Logic

Implication Rules

MODUS PONENS (MP)

$p \supset q$
p
───
q

MODUS TOLLENS (MT)

$p \supset q$
$\sim q$
───
$\sim p$

HYPOTHETICAL SYLLOGISM (HS)

$p \supset q$
$q \supset r$
───
$p \supset r$

DISJUNCTIVE SYLLOGISM (DS)

$p \vee q$ or $p \vee q$
$\sim p$ $\sim q$
───   ───
q p

SIMPLIFICATION (SIMP)

$p \bullet q$ or $p \bullet q$
───   ───
p q

CONJUNCTION (CONJ)

p or p
q q
───   ───
$p \bullet q$ $q \bullet p$

ADDITION (ADD)

p or p
───   ───
$p \vee q$ $q \vee p$

CONSTRUCTIVE DILEMMA (CD)

$(p \supset q) \bullet (r \supset s)$
$p \vee r$
───
$q \vee s$

DESTRUCTIVE DILEMMA (DD)

$(p \supset q) \bullet (r \supset s)$
$\sim q \vee \sim s$
───
$\sim p \vee \sim r$

Replacement Rules

COMMUTATION (COM)

$(p \bullet q) \; :: \; (q \bullet p)$
$(p \vee q) \; :: \; (q \vee p)$

ASSOCIATION (ASSOC)

$[p \bullet (q \bullet r)] \; :: \; [(p \bullet q) \bullet r]$
$[p \vee (q \vee r)] \; :: \; [(p \vee q) \vee r]$

DOUBLE NEGATION (DN)

$p \; :: \; \sim \sim p$

DISTRIBUTION (DIST)

$[p \bullet (q \vee r)] \; :: \; [(p \bullet q) \vee (p \bullet r)]$
$[p \vee (q \bullet r)] \; :: \; [(p \vee q) \bullet (p \vee r)]$

DE MORGAN'S LAW (DM)

$\sim(p \bullet q) \; :: \; (\sim p \vee \sim q)$
$\sim(p \vee q) \; :: \; (\sim p \bullet \sim q)$

TRANSPOSITION (TRANS)

$(p \supset q) \; :: \; (\sim q \supset \sim p)$

IMPLICATION (IMP)

$(p \supset q) \; :: \; (\sim p \vee q)$

EQUIVALENCE (EQUIV)

$(p \equiv q) \; :: \; [(p \supset q) \bullet (q \supset p)]$
$(p \equiv q) \; :: \; [(p \bullet q) \vee (\sim p \bullet \sim q)]$

TAUTOLOGY (TAUT)

$p \; :: \; (p \bullet p)$
$p \; :: \; (p \vee p)$

EXPORTATION (EXP)

$[(p \bullet q) \supset r] \; :: \; [p \supset (q \supset r)]$